lonely planet

GREAT BRITAIN'S
BEST TRIPS

36 AMAZING ROAD TRIPS

This edition written and researched by
Belinda Dixon,
Oliver Berry, Marc Di Duca, Peter Dragicevich,
Catherine Le Nevez, Hugh McNaughtan, Isabella Noble,
Andy Symington, Neil Wilson

SYMBOLS IN THIS BOOK

✓ Top Tips	📖 History & Culture	📷 Essential Photo
🆂 Link Your Trips	👪 Family	🏃 Walking Tour
◐ Tips from Locals	🍷 Food & Drink	🍴 Eating
↱ Trip Detour	🌳 Outdoors	🛏 Sleeping

☎ Telephone Number	@ Internet Access	⊖ Tube
☺ Opening Hours	📶 Wi-Fi Access	🅳 English-Language Menu
P Parking	✍ Vegetarian Selection	Family-Friendly
⊖ Nonsmoking	☰ Swimming Pool	Pet-Friendly
✳ Air-Conditioning		

MAP LEGEND

Routes
- Trip Route
- Trip Detour
- Linked Trip
- Walk Route
- Tollway
- Freeway
- Primary
- Secondary
- Tertiary
- Lane
- Unsealed Road
- Plaza/Mall
- Steps
- Tunnel
- Pedestrian Overpass
- Walk Track/Path

Boundaries
- International
- State/Province
- Cliff

Hydrography
- River/Creek
- Intermittent River
- Swamp/Mangrove
- Canal
- Water
- Dry/Salt/ Intermittent Lake
- Glacier

Highway Markers
- M1 Motorway
- A44 Highway

Trips
- 1 Trip Numbers
- 9 Trip Stop
- 🚶 Walking tour
- ↱ Trip Detour

Population
- ✪ Capital (National)
- ◉ Capital (State/Province)
- ● City/Large Town
- ● Town/Village

Areas
- Beach
- Cemetery (Christian)
- Cemetery (Other)
- Park
- Forest Reservation
- Urban Area
- Sportsground

Transport
- ✈ Airport
- Cable Car/ Funicular
- ⊖ London Tube station
- Ⓜ Metro station
- P Parking
- Train/Railway
- Tram

Note: Not all symbols displayed above appear on the maps in this book

PLAN YOUR TRIP

Welcome to Great Britain 7

Great Britain Highlights 8

If You Like... 20

Need to Know 22

City Guide 24

Great Britain by Region 30

Great Britain's Classic Trips 32

ON THE ROAD

1 The Best of Britain .... 21 Days   35

2 Britain's Wild Side .... 21 Days   49

3 The Historic South .... 9–11 Days   63

4 Urban & Art Odyssey .... 13–15 Days   75

SOUTHERN & EASTERN ENGLAND 87

5 Seaside Saunter .... 8 Days   91

6 History, Art, Hops & Grapes .... 4 Days   101

7 Magic, Royalty & Dons .... 5–6 Days   109

CONTENTS

8 Around
the Cam ....6–7 Days   117

9 Suffolk-Norfolk
Shore........................8 Days   125

SOUTHWEST ENGLAND 137

10 Winchester, Glastonbury
& Bath .... 12–14 Days   141

11 North Devon & Exmoor
National Park ...... 5–6 Days   153

12 Jurassic
Coast.......................... 7 Days   161

13 South
Devon ....4 Days   169

14 Epic
Cornwall.................. 10 Days   177

CENTRAL ENGLAND 191

15 Shakespeare &
Rolling Hills......... 7–8 Days   195

16 Industrial
Powerhouse.............. 4 Days   205

17 Peak
District ....5 Days   213

18 Battlefields, Castles &
Stately Homes...........5 Days   227

Scotland
p347

Lake District &
Northern England
p239

Central
England
p191

Wales
p293

Southern &
Eastern England
p87

Southwest
England
p137

Contents cont.

LAKE DISTRICT & NORTHERN ENGLAND 239

19 Classic Lakes .... 5 Days 243

20 Yorkshire Dales .... 3–4 Days 257

21 North York Moors & Coast .... 4–5 Days 265

22 Hadrian's Wall .... 3–4 Days 273

23 Northumbria .... 3–4 Days 281

WALES 293

24 West Wales: Swansea to St Davids .... 4 Days 297

25 Snowdonia National Park .... 4 Days 309

26 Landscapes & Literature .... 3 Days 319

27 Wilderness Wales .... 4 Days 329

28 Northwest Wales .... 4 Days 337

SCOTLAND 347

29 The Borders .... 2–3 Days 351

30 Stirling & Fife Coast .... 2–3 Days 359

31 Lower West Coast .... 4–6 Days 367

32 Upper West Coast .... 3–5 Days 379

33 Royal Highlands & Cairngorms .... 4–5 Days 391

34 Great Glen .... 2–3 Days 401

35 Whisky Trails .... 2–3 Days 409

36 Ferry Hopping .... 6–8 Days 417

ROAD TRIP ESSENTIALS

Great Britain Driving Guide 427

Great Britain Travel Guide 432

Index 441

The Lizard, Cornwall Fishing boats at Cadgwith village

MATT MUNRO / LONELY PLANET ©

Peak District National Park Winnats Pass

WELCOME TO
GREAT BRITAIN

Great Britain overflows with unforgettable experiences and spectacular sights. There's the grandeur of Scotland's mountains; England's quaint villages and country lanes; and the haunting beauty of Welsh and West Country coasts. You'll also find wild northern moors, the exquisite university colleges of Oxford and Cambridge, and a string of vibrant cities boasting everything from Georgian architecture to 21st-century art.

Our 36 drives reveal it all, leading you from gem to gem – prepare to encounter royal palaces, stone circles, gourmet hot-spots, castles, stately homes, historic ships and enough literary locations to fill a book. From the world-famous to the well-hidden, our trips will help you discover all the elements that make Britain truly great.

History, cities, food, scenery, the arts – we've unearthed the best experiences and crafted them into superb drives. And if you've only got time for one trip, make it one of our 10 Classic Trips, which take you to the very best of Great Britain. Turn the page for more.

→

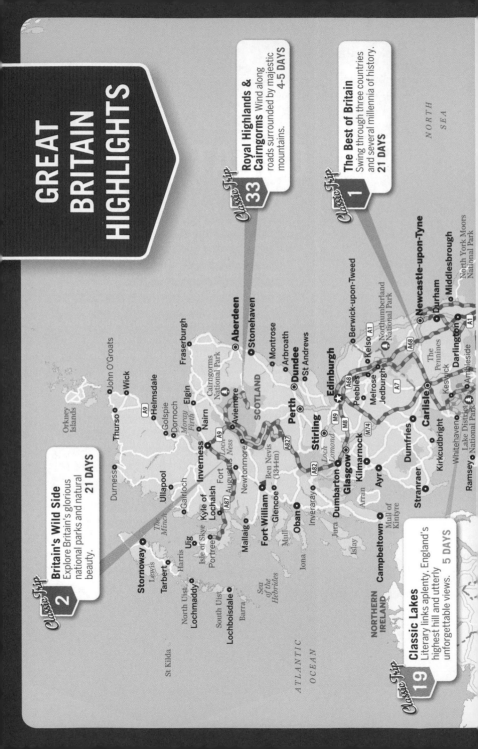

GREAT BRITAIN HIGHLIGHTS

Classic Trip 33 Royal Highlands & Cairngorms Wind along roads surrounded by majestic mountains. 4-5 DAYS

Classic Trip 1 The Best of Britain Swing through three countries and several millennia of history. 21 DAYS

Classic Trip 2 Britain's Wild Side Explore Britain's glorious national parks and natural beauty. 21 DAYS

Classic Trip 19 Classic Lakes Literary links aplenty, England's highest hill and utterly unforgettable views. 5 DAYS

NORTH SEA

SCOTLAND

NORTHERN IRELAND

ATLANTIC OCEAN

Orkney Islands

Durness
John O'Groats
Thurso
Wick
Helmsdale
Ullapool
Golspie
Dornoch
Elgin
Fraserburgh
Gairloch
Nairn
Aberdeen
Stornoway
Lewis
Uig
Inverness
Loch Ness
Aviemore
Stonehaven
Harris
Isle of Skye
Kyle of Lochalsh
Portree
Fort Augustus
Newtonmore
Cairngorms National Park
Montrose
Arbroath
Tarbert
The Minch
Mallaig
Ben Nevis (1344m)
Fort William
Glencoe
Dundee
St Andrews
North Uist
Lochmaddy
Perth
South Uist
Oban
Inveraray
Stirling
Edinburgh
Berwick-upon-Tweed
Lochboisdale
Barra
Sea of the Hebrides
Mull
Loch Lomond
Glasgow
Dumbarton
Kilmarnock
Peebles
Kelso
Northumberland National Park
Iona
Jura
Ayr
Melrose
Jedburgh
Islay
Arran
Dumfries
The Pennines
St Kilda
Mull of Kintyre
Campbeltown
Stranraer
Kirkcudbright
Carlisle
Keswick
Newcastle-upon-Tyne
Durham
Middlesbrough
Whitehaven
Lake District National Park
Ambleside
Darlington
North York Moors National Park
Ramsey

A9
A87
A82
A827
A9
M9
M8
M74
A68
A7
A1
A68
A1

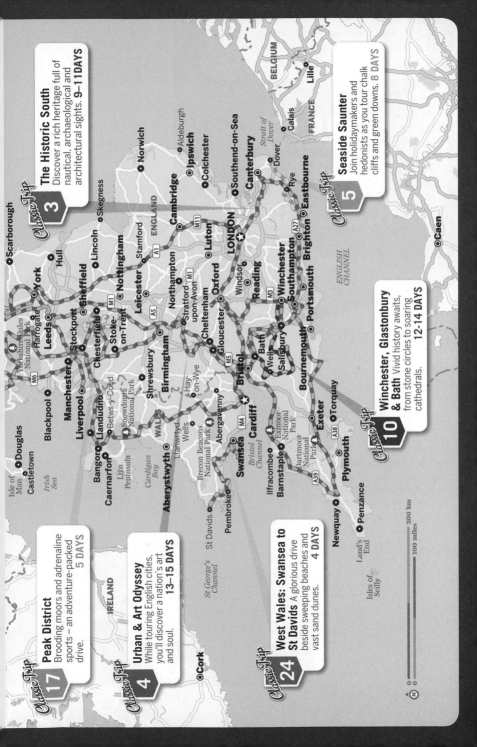

Classic Trip 3 — The Historic South
Discover a rich heritage full of nautical, archaeological and architectural sights. **9–11 DAYS**

Classic Trip 5 — Seaside Saunter
Join holidaymakers and hedonists as you tour chalk cliffs and green downs. **8 DAYS**

Classic Trip 10 — Winchester, Glastonbury & Bath
Vivid history awaits, from stone circles to soaring cathedrals. **12–14 DAYS**

Classic Trip 17 — Peak District
Brooding moors and adrenaline sports – an adventure-packed drive. **5 DAYS**

Classic Trip 4 — Urban & Art Odyssey
While touring English cities, you'll discover a nation's art and soul. **13–15 DAYS**

Classic Trip 24 — West Wales: Swansea to St Davids
A glorious drive beside sweeping beaches and vast sand dunes. **4 DAYS**

Scarborough
York
Hull
Sheffield
Lincoln
Skegness
Scunthorpe
Norwich
Cambridge
Aldeburgh
Ipswich
Colchester
Southend-on-Sea
Canterbury
Dover
Strait of Dover
Rye
Eastbourne
Brighton
Eastbourne
LONDON
Luton
Reading
Windsor
Oxford
Stamford
Leicester
Nottingham
Stoke-on-Trent
Chesterfield
Stockport
Leeds
Harrogate
Manchester
Blackpool
Liverpool
Bangor
Caernarfon
Llandudno
Douglas
Castletown
Isle of Man
Irish Sea
Yorkshire Dales National Park
Northampton
Stratford-upon-Avon
Cheltenham
Gloucester
Birmingham
Shrewsbury
Hay-on-Wye
Betws-y-Coed
Snowdonia National Park
Llŷn Peninsula
Aberystwyth
Cardigan Bay
WALES
Brecon Beacons National Park
Llanwrtyd Wells
Abergavenny
Cardiff
Swansea
Pembroke
St Davids
St George's Channel
Isles of Scilly
Land's End
Penzance
Newquay
Plymouth
Exeter
Torquay
Dartmoor National Park
Exmoor National Park
Barnstaple
Ilfracombe
Bristol Channel
Bournemouth
Portsmouth
Southampton
Winchester
Salisbury
Wells
Bath
Bristol
ENGLAND
ENGLISH CHANNEL
FRANCE
BELGIUM
Lille
Calais
Caen
IRELAND
Cork

M6
M1
A1
M11
M3
A27
A38
A39
M4
M5
A5

100 miles
200 km

N

Great Britain's best sights and experiences, and the road trips that will take you there.

GREAT BRITAIN
HIGHLIGHTS

Scottish Lochs & Mountains

Scotland's wild places abound in breathtaking views: spray-dashed coasts; glinting lochs; imposing mountains. The scenery here is truly awe-inspiring. Drive right into the views on **Trip 33: Royal Highlands & Cairngorms**, which delivers castles, peaks and wildlife galore – and the chance to explore the Royal family's summer holiday haunts.

Trips

Loch Awe Kilchurn Castle

11

Bath Roman Baths

Edinburgh

Famous for festivals, and especially lively in the summer, Edinburgh is a city of many moods. Glimpse them in a daffodil-framed castle silhouetted against a blue spring sky or on a chill December morning when the fog snags the spires of the Old Town. Discover your own version of the city on **Trip 1: The Best of Britain**, which sweeps the length of the country, from blockbuster sight to blockbuster sight.

Trip

The West Country

Britain's wild western corner is well worth the trip to the very end of England. Here tawny moors roll to jagged cliffs, ancient fishing ports tuck into spectacular cliffs and sandy beaches stretch for miles. Find your favourite south west spot on **Trip 14: Epic Cornwall**, which loops through Arthurian ruins, surfer bays and foodie ports.

Trips 11 12 13 14

Bath

Britain boasts many great cities, but Bath is the belle of the ball. The natural hot springs that bubble to the surface prompted the Romans to build a health resort here, while the Georgians turned the city into a fashionable watering hole. Soaking up Bath's sumptuous architecture is a highlight of **Trip 10: Winchester, Glastonbury & Bath**, a route also rich in cathedrals, ancient sites and myth.

Trips  1 3 10 15

Cornwall Fish and chips at The Ship Inn, Mousehole

BEST ROADS FOR DRIVING

A939 Scottish Highlands Drive beside ski slopes at rollercoaster Lecht Pass. **Trip** 33

A379 South Devon Beaches, first-gear bends and a straight-as-an-arrow coast road. **Trip** 13

A4086 Snowdonia Climb past the scree-scattered slopes of Pen-y-Pass. **Trip** 25

Off A896 Bealach na Ba Gradients of 25% and dramatic Isle of Skye views. **Trip** 32

B3157 Portland Glorious driving beside a fossil rich shore. **Trip** 12

The Cotswolds

The most wonderful thing about the Cotswolds is that no matter where you go or how lost you get, you'll still end up in a village of honey-coloured stone complete with rose-clad cottages, an ancient pub and a view of the lush green hills. Find your very own slice of medieval England on **Trip 15: Shakespeare & Rolling Hills**, a tour of impossibly picturesque villages, with prestigious literary locations thrown in.

Trip 15

13

Wiltshire Stonehenge

Stonehenge

Mysterious and compelling, Stonehenge is Britain's most iconic ancient site. People have been drawn to this myth-laden ring of bluestones for the last 5000 years, and we still don't know quite why it was built. Come up with your own theories while gazing at the 50-ton megaliths on **Trip 3: The Historic South**, a voyage which charts a centuries-long timeline through Britain's compelling past.

Trips

BEST CASTLES & STATELY HOMES

Windsor Castle Nosey round the Queen's favourite home. **Trip** 15

Castle Howard Stunning, baroque setting for Brideshead Revisited. **Trips** 4 21

Beaumaris Castle A 13th century masterpiece. **Trip** 28

Chatsworth House The exquisite 'palace of the Peak District'. **Trip** 17

Dover Castle 12th-century defences meet secret WWII tunnels. **Trip** 5

Wales Snowdonia National Park

Oxford Radcliffe Camera

Welsh Mountains

Rugged Wales has rocky mountain peaks, glacier-hewn valleys, sinuous shores, sparkling lakes, and charm-infused villages. The high point (literally) is Snowdonia, a remote enclave offering hikes to lofty summits, adrenaline sports and off-the-beaten-track explorations. Tap into the wilderness vibe on **Trip 25: Snowdonia National Park**.

Trips

Cambridge

Abounding with exquisite architecture and steeped in tradition, Cambridge is a university town extraordinaire. The tightly packed core of ancient colleges, the picturesque riverside 'Backs' (college gardens) and the surrounding green meadows linger in your mind. Prepare to fall more than a little in love on **Trip 8: Around the Cam**, which also explores the city's beguiling surrounds.

Trip 8

Oxford

For centuries, the brilliant minds and august institutions of Oxford University have made Oxford famous across the globe. Glimpse this revered world as you stroll hushed college quads and cobbled lanes roamed by cycling students. Touch base with your inner academic on **Trip 7: Magic, Royalty & Dons**, as it takes in prestigious southern sights.

Trips

17

Northern Wildernesses

Poets and painters have long championed Britain's remote northern landscapes, which still hold a haunting appeal. Here you'll find wind-blasted moors, soaring mountains, whaleback fells, Roman ruins and glistening lakes. Motor through this craggy corner of England, and take in its literary links, on **Trip 19: Classic Lakes**.

Trips **2** **19** **20** **21** **22**

Stratford-upon-Avon

The pretty English Midlands town of Stratford-upon-Avon is famed around the world as the birthplace of the nation's best-known dramatist, William Shakespeare. Today, the town's tight knot of Tudor streets forms a living map of Shakespeare's life and times. Visit his historic houses on a voyage around the pick of the country's top sights with **Trip 1: The Best of Britain**.

Trips **1** **4** **15**

(left) **Northumberland** Hadrian's Wall

(below) **Falmouth** Fresh crabs being delivered to a restaurant

Blenheim Palace

One of Britain's grandest stately homes, this early-18th century baroque confection is overpoweringly ornate. Objects d'art, ostentatious oil paintings and decadent decor fill grand rooms overlooking lavish grounds. Imagine living there when you drop by on **Trip 3: The Historic South**.

Trip

BEST SEAFOOD STOPS

Wheeler's Oyster Bar Famously fabulous molluscs. **Trip** `6`

Robson & Sons The kippers produced here are good enough for royalty. **Trip** `23`

Crab House Cafe Super-fresh crustaceans and fish. **Trip** `12`

Anstruther A busy fishing port is the idea place to enjoy fish and chips. **Trip** `30`

Sportsman Pub For food so good it's been awarded a Michelin star. **Trip** `6`

19

IF YOU LIKE

JUSTIN FOULKES / LONELY PLANET ©

Glen Coe Whisky at Clachaig Inn

History

In Great Britain the past is ever present. Everywhere lies evidence of an enthralling heritage stretching back thousands of years – from vast stone circles to elaborate palaces, via cathedrals, castles and stately homes. This history is a seam stitched through the entire country – it's one our trips help you explore.

3 The Historic South Stonehenge, UNESCO-city Bath, sublime cathedrals and Napoleonic ships.

18 Battlefields, Castles & Stately Homes Indulge your inner Royalty enthusiast and medieval knight.

22 Hadrian's Wall Haunting landscapes and Britain's blockbuster Roman site.

10 Winchester, Glastonbury & Bath Expect prehistoric monuments, cathedrals and Arthurian myths.

Mountains & Moors

Awe-inspiring mountains, wind-whipped moors. Great Britain can claim superb landscapes linked by ribboning roads – these are truly unforgettable drives. From Scotland's soaring Highlands and bewitching lochs to the more intimate peaks of Wales. In between you'll encounter the often-eerie beauty of the northern lakes and moors.

33 Royal Highlands & Cairngorms Spectacular scenery encircling the Queen's summer home.

19 Classic Lakes A feast of mountains, valleys and views.

25 Snowdonia National Park Adventure sports await all around the highest summit in Wales.

17 Peak District Ancient stone villages shelter among hills, valleys and lakes.

Coasts

This island nation is blessed by beautiful shores. Surfer-hangouts, expansive sand dunes, fossil-filled cliffs, golden beaches, geology-rich bays, remote islands, seafood havens and genteel resorts flanked by promenades and piers – they're all here. What's more, they all link up into routes making for epic drives, where the sea is always by your side.

12 Jurassic Coast A photogenic cruise past age-old, sea-sculpted cliffs, stacks and bays.

9 Suffolk-Norfolk Shore Salt marshes, bewitching ports, seafood a-plenty and shingle shores.

24 West Wales Discover surf breaks, sand dunes and tranquil farms.

36 Ferry Hopping Encounter beautiful beaches and laid-back island life in Scotland's Hebrides.

20

Cambridge Bridge of Sighs

Urban Adventures

Britain's cities are among its most appealing assets – thriving urban areas rich in history, architecture, warmth and wit. It's often in these centres of contemporary culture that the country's diverse nature emerges; the experiences you have here may well prove some of the most memorable of your trip.

4 **Urban & Art Odyssey**
Revelling in dynamic cities; a metropolitan dream.

1 **Best of Britain**
London, Bath, Cardiff, Oxford, Edinburgh – hard to beat.

5 **Seaside Saunter**
Exploring coastal urban zones; from quaint Rye to hedonistic Brighton.

7 **Magic, Royalty & Dons** Chic Windsor, Henley and Oxford (and Harry Potter, too).

Art & Architecture

Britain's centuries-long love affair with the arts has left a lasting legacy. You'll encounter it everywhere: from Shakespeare's birthplace to the Beatles' home town, via guerilla artists, futuristic galleries and the set of *Dr Who*. Architectural masterpieces pepper villages, land- and city-scapes.

15 **Shakespeare & Rolling Hills** Touring beautiful Bath, Cotswold villages and literary Stratford-upon-Avon.

8 **Around the Cam**
Enchanting explorations of university-city Cambridge and it's gorgeous surrounds.

3 **Historic South** Three spectacular cathedrals, plus London and Bath's architectural delights.

4 **Urban & Art Odyssey**
The pick of modern Britain's modern art.

Food & Drink

These days Britain boasts some seriously good food. Everywhere you'll see an emphasis on local and seasonal – and often organic too. Regional treats include net-fresh seafood, succulent lamb and tangy cheese. And, once you've parked the car for the night, there's craft beer, fine wines and whisky.

6 **History, Art, Hops & Grapes** Fine dining, oysters and breweries in England's rural south east.

13 **South Devon** Discover vineyards, the freshest seafood and a Michelin-starred eatery.

14 **Epic Cornwall** A county still in the vanguard of Britain's culinary renaissance – plus great pasties too.

35 **Whisky Trails**
Spectacular Scottish scenery and scores of distilleries.

NEED ^{TO} KNOW

CURRENCY
Pound sterling (£)

LANGUAGE
English; also Scottish Gaelic and Welsh

VISAS
Generally not needed for stays of up to six months. Not a member of the Schengen Zone.

FUEL
Urban petrol (gas) stations are plentiful; service stations are regularly-spaced on motorways. Fill up before heading into rural areas, where they're scarcer. Expect to pay around £1.10 per litre.

RENTAL CARS
Avis (www.avis.co.uk)

Budget (www.budget.co.uk)

Europcar (www.europcar.co.uk)

Thrifty (www.thrifty.co.uk)

IMPORTANT NUMBERS
Emergency (🖉112 or 🖉999) Police, fire, ambulance, mountain rescue, coastguard

AA (🖉0800 88 77 66) Roadside assistance

RAC (🖉800 197 7815) Roadside assistance

Climate

Warm to hot summers, mild winters

Edinburgh
GO May–Sep

Manchester
GO Any time

Cardiff
GO May–Sep

Bath
GO Apr–Oct

London
GO Any time

When to Go

High Season (Jun–Aug)
» Weather at its best.

» Accommodation rates peak.

» Busy roads, especially in seaside areas, national parks and big-draw cities.

Shoulder (Mar–May & Sep & Oct)
» Crowds reduce.

» Prices drop.

» Weather often good.

Low Season (Nov–Feb)
» Wet and cold.

» Snow falls in mountain areas.

» Outside London, opening hours often reduced.

Your Daily Budget

Budget: Less than £55
» Dorm beds: £15–30
» Cheap cafe and pub meals: £7–11

Midrange: £55–120
» Double hotel or B&B room: £65–130 (London £100–200)
» Restaurant main meal: £10–20

Top End: More than £120
» Four-star hotel room: from £130 (London from £200)
» Three-course meal in a good restaurant: around £40
» Car rental per day: from £35

Eating

Restaurants From cheap-and-cheerful to Michelin-starred, covering all cuisines.

Pubs Serve reasonably-priced meals, some are top notch.

Cafes Good daytime option for casual breakfasts, lunch or afternoon tea.

Vegetarian Find meat-free restaurants in towns and cities. But rural menus may contain just one 'choice'.

Sleeping

Hotels From small townhouses to grand mansions; from budget via corporate offerings to boutique.

B&Bs Range from a room in someone's house (with shared bathroom) to luxury spoils.

Inns Rooms above rural pubs; can be a cosy choice

Hostels Bare-bones, often dorm-style accommodation.

Arriving in Great Britain

Heathrow airport Trains, London Underground (tube) and buses to central London from 5am to around midnight (night buses run later) and cost £5.70 to £21.50. Taxis to central London cost £45 to £85.

Gatwick airport Trains to central London from 4.30am to 1.35am £10–20; 24hr buses (hourly) to central London from £5. Taxis to central London £100.

Eurostar trains from Paris or Brussels Arrive at London St Pancras International station.

Buses from Europe Arrive at London Victoria Coach Station.

Mobile Phones

The UK uses the GSM 900/1800 network, which covers Europe, Australia and New Zealand, but isn't compatible with the North American GSM 1900, although most modern mobiles can function on both networks.

Internet Access

» 3G and 4G mobile broadband coverage is good in urban centres, but limited in rural areas.

» Many accommodation providers and eateries have wi-fi access (fees: nothing–£6 per hour).

» Internet cafes (from £1 per hour) are rare away from tourist spots.

Money

ATMs ('cash machines') are common in cities and towns. Visa and MasterCard are widely accepted although some B&Bs take cash or cheque only.

Tipping

Restaurants Around 10-15% in eateries with table service.

Pubs & Bars If you order and pay at the bar, tips are not expected. If you order at the table, your meal is brought to you, and you pay afterwards, then 10% is usual.

Taxis Roughly 10%.

Useful Websites

BBC (www.bbc.co.uk) National broadcaster.

Lonely Planet (www.lonelyplanet.com/great-britain) Destination info, hotel bookings, traveller forum and more.

Visit Britain (www.visitbritain.com) Comprehensive tourist info.

Opening Hours

In rural areas opening hours may be shorter between October and April; some places close completely.

Banks 9.30am to 4pm or 5pm Monday to Friday; some open 9.30am to 1pm Saturday.

Pubs & Bars 11am to 11pm Monday to Thursday, 11am to 1am Friday and Saturday, 12.30pm to 11pm Sunday.

Shops 9am to 5.30pm or 6pm Monday to Saturday, and often 11am to 5pm Sunday. Cities have 24/7 convenience stores.

Restaurants Lunch is noon to 3pm, dinner 6pm to 9pm/10pm (later in cities).

For more, see Road Trip Essentials (p426).

CITY GUIDE

LONDON

Britain's capital of cool is an endlessly fascinating metropolis. Its multicultural streets and unique sights yield a rich harvest of history, popular culture, architecture and art. Add a world's worth of languages and cuisines and you get a truly great city that's easy to love and hard to leave.

Notting Hill Shopping on Portobello Road

Getting Around

London has a congestion charge to reduce central traffic. For details of affected areas and charges, see www.tfl.gov.uk/roadusers/congestioncharging.

Alternatively, use TFL's frequent London Underground ('tube') and bus networks; see www.tfl.gov.uk.

Parking

Street parking is scarce and costly; wheel clampers are diligent. Few central hotels offer parking; if they do it comes at a premium. **Q-Park** (www.q-park.co.uk) and the **NCP** (www.ncp.co.uk) run numerous car parks.

Where to Eat

London is an undisputed dining destination. Top-notch restaurants abound, but it's the diversity that's head-spinning. Sample it in the West End, South Bank, Hammersmith and Islington.

Where to Stay

Accommodation in London is expensive, but you might snag pre-booked deals in the central West End, edge-of-centre South Bank, traveller-friendly Earl's Court and still-cool Notting Hill.

Useful Websites

Lonely Planet (www.lonelyplanet.com/london) Bookings, traveller forum and more.

Visit London (www.visitlondon.com) The official visitor guide.

BBC London (www.bbc.co.uk/london) All the city's news.

Trips Through London: 1 3

007 / SHUTTERSTOCK ©

TOP EXPERIENCES

➡ **Go Royal Roaming**
From Buckingham Palace to the Royal Mews, via the Changing of the Guard – exploring London's regal landmarks is a unique treat.

➡ **Experience Parklife**
London's green oases are a joy; perfect places for strolling, picnicking and people-watching. Highlights include Regent's Park and Hyde Park.

➡ **Visit Theatreland**
The world capital of theatre, London excels at both mammoth musicals and highbrow dramas. Top venues include the National, Royal Court, Donmar Warehouse and the Almeida.

➡ **Go Shopping**
They may be posh – Harrods and Harvey Nichols. Or street stalls – Portobello Road, Spitafields and Bourough Market. Either way they're great places to splash the cash.

➡ **Get Cultural**
London's museums and galleries are simply superb. A long list of must-sees includes the National Portrait Gallery and the Tate Modern, and the Victoria & Albert, Science and British museums

➡ **Get Eating**
From serious gastronomy to superb street food, London has it all. Great grazing grounds include the West End, East End, Fitzrovia and Notting Hill.

➡ **Go Bar Hopping**
In London the pub is the hub of local social life – dip into it in sophisticated Soho, boho Hoxton, grungy Camden and neighbourhood-feel Notting Hill.

LENSECALLEA PHOTOGRAPHY / SHUTTERSTOCK ©

Cardiff The Arab Room at Cardiff Castle

CARDIFF

Newly confident Cardiff delights in being one of Britain's leading urban centres. Stretching from ancient Cardiff Castle to the ultramodern architecture at Cardiff Bay, this city's aura of loving life is infectious – tap into it at a rugby match or in any of the thriving live-music venues, pubs and bars.

Getting Around

Cardiff doesn't pose many difficulties for drivers, although most of the central city streets between Westgate St, Castle St and St David's are closed to traffic. Local bus services are extensive.

Parking

Car parks dot the city centre; it's also often possible to find free street parking in the suburbs. Pontcanna's Cathedral Rd has unrestricted parking, but gets busy during working hours.

Where To Eat

Appealing eateries cluster in the streets just south of Cardiff Castle. The chic Pontcanna district is another good foodie focus point, boasting bistros, gastropubs and modern Indian cuisine.

Where To Stay

Revelers love the plentiful budget and upmarket accommodation of Central Cardiff. Light sleepers should head for Pontcanna and the Victorian townhouse B&Bs of leafy Cathedral Rd; just 20 minutes' walk from the city centre.

Useful Websites

Visit Cardiff (www.visitcardiff. com) is the city's official tourism website.

Cardiff Bus (www.cardiffbus. com) details the city's bus links.

Trips Through Cardiff:

1 4

Manchester Imperial War Museum North (IWMN), designed by Daniel Libeskind

MANCHESTER

The uncrowned capital of the north overflows with history and culture. World-class venues include the Imperial War Museum North, Manchester Art Gallery and the People's History Museum. But what makes Manchester really fun is the swirl of hedonism that lets you dine, drink and dance yourself into happy oblivion.

Getting Around

Central Manchester is relatively easy to navigate by car, but excellent public transport systems might prompt you to get out from behind the wheel. Three free bus routes loop around the centre, while frequent Metrolink trams shuttle to outlying areas.

Parking

Manchester has reasonable city centre car-park and on-street parking provision, although demand can be high and charges can mount up. The city's on-street parking bays are usually free to use between 8pm and 8am; many of the bigger hotels have on-site parking too, although there can be an extra charge.

Where To Eat

Manchester's choice of restaurants is second only to London. Spinningfields, just off Deansgate, has some interesting spots while the Northern Quarter is great for off-beat cafes and organic eats. They city's Indian and Middle Eastern restaurants are legendary, while the outlying suburb of Didsbury is where in-the-know Mancunians like to dine.

Where To Stay

Numerous hotels aimed at business travellers and sports fans dot the city centre, placing you firmly in the heart of the action. More discerning visitors have a choice of designer digs and boutique lodgings. Beds are in short supply on home match days during the football season (August to May)

Useful Websites

Visit Manchster (www.visitmanchester.com) Official tourism website.

BBC Manchester (www.bbc.co.uk/manchester) News, weather and travel updates.

Restaurants of Manchester (www.restaurantsofmanchester.com) Reliable guide to the city's eateries.

Trips Through Manchester: 4 16

EDINBURGH

Exquisite Edinburgh's quirky, come-hither nooks tempt you to explore. Draped across rocky hills, its cultured soul has seen it dubbed the Athens of the North. But this famously down-to-earth city also mocks artistic pretensions. Come here to delight in crowded pubs, decadent restaurants, beer-fuelled poets, foul-mouthed comedians and lofty ideals.

Getting Around

A car in central Edinburgh is more of a liability than a convenience. There's restricted access on Princes St, George St and Charlotte Sq, and many streets are one-way. Fortunately, as well as a handy tram line, the city has an extensive bus network.

Parking

Finding a parking place in the city centre is like striking gold. There's also no parking on main roads into the city from 7.30am to 6.30pm Monday to Saturday. Large long-stay car parks include those at the St James Centre, Greenside Pl, New St, Castle Tce and Morrison St.

Edinburgh Iconic Royal Mile

TOP EXPERIENCES

➡ Stroll the Royal Mile
This mile-long street leads from Edinburgh Castle to the Palace of Holyroodhouse, via St Giles Cathedral and the Scottish Parliament, taking in scores of restaurants, street performers and bars.

➡ Climb Arthur's Seat
Scaling the summit of Edinburgh's 251m-high miniature mountains involves a hike through a former royal hunting ground.

➡ Go On A Pub Crawl
Edinburgh's 19th- and early-20th-century pubs have often preserved their original decor and serve a staggering selection of malt whiskies.

➡ Get Cultural
In this arts-aware city you're spoilt for choice, from live-music to theatre and comedy. Even if a festival isn't underway, there's always something going on.

Where To Eat
Fabulous-for-foodies Edinburgh has more restaurants per head of population than any other UK city. Top choices cluster around the High St (Royal Mile); good-value eats concentrate in Bruntsfield and Newington; and for fine dining head for New Town and Leith.

Where To Stay
Edinburgh's sleep spots include boutique hotels and gorgeous B&Bs set in Victorian and Georgian townhouses. Old Town accommodation is superbly central but tends to be either very budget or fairly pricey. New Town choices can be cheaper and are still in the heart of things.

Useful Websites
This is Edinburgh (www.thisisedinburgh.com) The city's official tourism website.

Edinburgh Festivals (www.wow247.co.uk/edinburgh-festivals) Information on the city's big events.

Trips Through Edinburgh: 1

GREAT BRITAIN
BY REGION

Cloud-snagged mountains, wilderness moors, winding country lanes – Great Britain offers irresistible drives. Our guide to each region and its road trips will help you choose the very best routes and experiences.

Wales (p293)

Rugged, hauntingly beautiful and remote, Wales is a place to live Cardiff's high-life or get away from the crowds on sweeping sand-dunes or dramatic peaks.

Scale some mountains on Trip 25

Go barefoot beachcombing on Trip 24

Southwest England (p137)

The wild West Country makes for breathtaking drives: sea-carved shores, stag-dotted moors, seafood ports and a lush landscape laced with myth.

Discover a powerful past on Trip 10

Enjoy awesome food and epic views on Trip 14

Scotland (p347)

Driving in Scotland is simply spectacular. Here mountains encircle glinting lochs, fairy-tale castles vie to be photographed, cities greet you with a whisky and islands tempt you off shore.

Go ferry hopping on Trip 36

Drink in fit-for-royalty Highland views on Trip 33

Lake District & Northern England (p239)

In this slice of northern England the scenery notches up a gear. From the so-scenic Lakes to dramatic, wind-blasted moors. And then there's the ribboning Roman remnant that is Hadrian's Wall.

Discover Lake-land literary connections on Trip 19

Motor across moorland on Trip 21

Central England (p191)

Rolling hills and a rich heritage define the drives at Britain's core. Quaint villages usher in imposing castles and grand stately homes. The spectacular city of Bath waits in the wings.

Explore a glorious Georgian cityscape on Trip 15

Encounter a Royal past on Trip 18

Southern & Eastern England (p87)

England's southern, eastern corner is full of charm. Here you can motor from cool-again resorts to exquisite university cities via a trail of castles, ancient villages and foodie pit stops.

Explore retro resorts on Trip 6

Get an English history fix on Trip 8

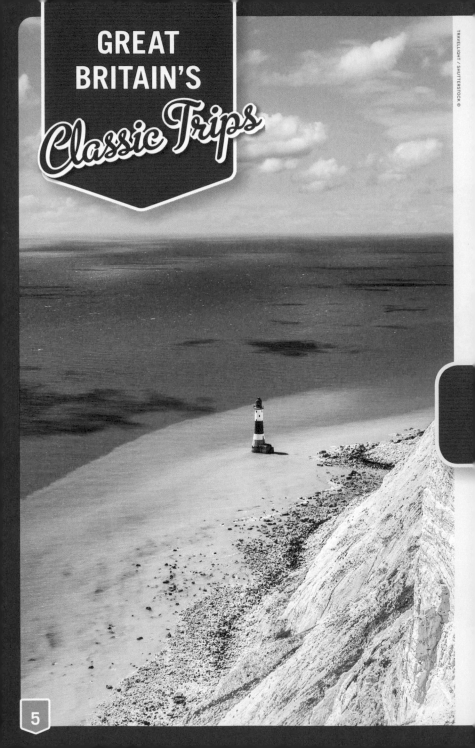

GREAT BRITAIN'S
Classic Trips

URBANCOW / GETTY IMAGES ©

2

What is a Classic Trip?

All the trips in this book show you the best of Great Britain, but we've chosen 10 as our all-time favourites. These are our Classic Trips – the ones that lead you to the best of the iconic sights, the top activities and the unique British experiences. Turn the page to see our cross-regional Classic Trips, and look for more Classic Trips on the following pages:

1 The Best of Britain ....21 Days   35

2 Britain's Wild Side ....21 Days   49

3 The Historic South ....9–11 Days   63

4 Urban & Art Odyssey..... 13–15 Days   75

5 Seaside Saunter ....8 Days   91

10 Winchester, Glastonbury & Bath .... 12–14 Days   141

17 Peak District ....5 Days   213

19 Classic Lakes.....................5 Days   243

24 West Wales: Swansea to St Davids.............4 Days   297

33 Royal Highlands & Cairngorms...... 4–5 Days   391

Above: Dartmoor National Park
Left: Beachy Head

The Best of Britain

1

Swing through three countries and several millennia of history as you take in a greatest hits parade of Britain's chart-topping sights.

TRIP HIGHLIGHTS

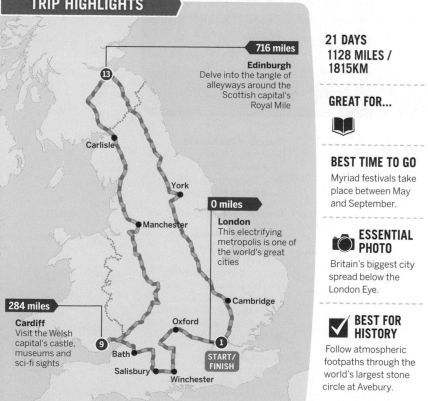

716 miles

Edinburgh
Delve into the tangle of alleyways around the Scottish capital's Royal Mile

13

Carlisle

York

Manchester

0 miles

London
This electrifying metropolis is one of the world's great cities

Cambridge

284 miles

Cardiff
Visit the Welsh capital's castle, museums and sci-fi sights

9

Oxford

Bath

Salisbury

Winchester

1

START/
FINISH

**21 DAYS
1128 MILES /
1815KM**

GREAT FOR...

BEST TIME TO GO
Myriad festivals take place between May and September.

ESSENTIAL PHOTO
Britain's biggest city spread below the London Eye.

BEST FOR HISTORY
Follow atmospheric footpaths through the world's largest stone circle at Avebury.

Edinburgh View of the city from Calton Hill

35

Classic Trip

1 The Best of Britain

London's bright lights and blockbuster attractions bookend this epic expedition around the British mainland. In between, you'll encounter ancient sights, learn about fabled figures from King Arthur to Shakespeare, and visit masterpiece-filled museums and galleries and celebrated football stadiums – interleaved by quaint villages, patchworked farmland and glorious rolling green open countryside, along with the best of British drinking, dining and nightlife.

TRIP HIGHLIGHT

❶ London

Gear up for your trip with at least a couple of days in Britain's most exhilarating city. Traversed by the serpentine River Thames, London is awash with instantly recognisable landmarks and open spaces, from **Trafalgar Square** (⊖Charing Cross) to the **London Eye** (☏0871 781 3000; www.londoneye. com; adult/child £21.20/16.10; ⊙10am-8pm, to 9.30pm in summer; ⊖Waterloo). Other unmissable sights incude:

Houses of Parliament (www.parliament.uk; Parliament Sq, SW1; ⊖Westminster), topped by the **Big Ben** clock tower.

Tower Bridge (⊖Tower Hill)

Westminster Abbey (☏020-7222 5152; www. westminster-abbey.org; 20 Dean's Yard, SW1; adult/child £20/9, verger tours £5, cloister & gardens free; ⊙9.30am-4.30pm Mon, Tue, Thu & Fri, to 7pm Wed, to 2.30pm Sat; ⊖Westminster)

St James's Park (www. royalparks.org.uk; The Mall, SW1; deckchairs per hr/day £1.50/7; ⊙5am-midnight,

deckchairs daylight hours
Mar-Oct; St James's Park
or Green Park) and **Palace**
(www.royal.gov.uk; Cleveland
Row, SW1; Green Park)

Buckingham Palace
(📞020-7766 7300; www.
royalcollection.org.uk;
Buckingham Palace Rd,
SW1; adult/child/under-5
£21.50/12.30/free; ⏰9.30am-
7.30pm late Jul–Aug, to 6.30pm
Sep; St James's Park,
Victoria or Green Park)

Hyde Park (www.royalparks.
org.uk/parks/hyde-park;
⏰5am-midnight; Marble
Arch, Hyde Park Corner or
Queensway)

Kensington Gardens
(www.royalparks.org.uk/
parks/kensington-gardens;
⏰6am-dusk; Queensway
or Lancaster Gate) and
Palace (www.hrp.org.uk/
kensingtonpalace; Kensington
Gardens, W8; adult/child
£16.30/free; ⏰10am-6pm
Mar-Oct, to 5pm Nov-Feb;
High St Kensington)

🔗 LINK YOUR TRIP

15 **Shakespeare &
Rolling Hills**

From Bath, you can set
out for a spin through the
picturesque Cotswolds.

21 **North York Moors
& Coast**

York is the starting point for
a glorious drive through wild
moorland and charming
coastal villages.

World-leading, often-free museums and art galleries include the **Tate Modern** (www.tate.org.uk; Queen's Walk, SE1; ⊙10am-6pm Sun-Thu, to 10pm Fri & Sat; 🚻; 🚇Blackfriars, Southwark or London Bridge) and the **British Museum** (📞020-7323 8299; www.british museum.org; Great Russell St, WC1; ⊙10am-5.30pm Sat-Thu, to 8.30pm Fri; 🚇Russell Sq or Tottenham Court Rd).

London's drinking, dining and nightlife options are limitless (Soho and Shoreditch make great starting points), as are its entertainment venues, not least grand theatre stages such as **Shakespeare's Globe** (📞020-7401 9919; www.shakespearesglobe. com; 21 New Globe Walk, SE1; seats £10-43, standing £5; 🚇Blackfriars or London Bridge).

🛏 p47

The Drive » Take the M40 northwest through High Wycombe and the Chilterns AONB (Area of Outstanding Natural Beauty) to Oxford (59 miles in total).

- - - - - - - - - - - -

❷ Oxford

Oxford's elegant honey-toned buildings of the university's colleges, scattered throughout the city, wrap around tranquil courtyards and along narrow cobbled lanes. The oldest colleges date back to the 13th century and little has changed inside since, although there's a busy, lively world beyond the college walls. **Christ Church** (📞01865-276492; www.chch. ox.ac.uk; St Aldate's; adult/child £8/7; ⊙10am-4.15pm Mon-Sat, 2-4.15pm Sun) is the largest of all of Oxford's colleges, with the grandest quad. From the quad, you access 12th-century **Christ Church Cathedral** (📞01865-276150; www.chch. ox.ac.uk/cathedral; St Aldate's; admission free; ⊙10am-4.15pm Mon-Sat, 2-4.15pm Sun), originally the abbey

church and then the college chapel, before it was declared a cathedral by Henry VIII.

Other highlights include Oxford's **Bodleian Library** (📞01865-287400; www.bodleian.ox.ac.uk/bodley; Catte St; tours £6-14; ⊙9am-5pm Mon-Sat, 11am-5pm Sun), one of the oldest public libraries in the world, and Britain's oldest public museum, the 1683-established **Ashmolean Museum** (📞01865-278000; www.ashmolean.org; Beaumont St; ⊙10am-5pm Tue-Sun), second in repute only to London's British Museum.

🍴 🛏 p115

The Drive » Head southwest on the A420 to Pusey and continue southwest on the B4508. You'll reach the car park for the White Horse 2.3 miles southwest of Uffington off the B4507, a 24-mile journey altogether.

- - - - - - - - - - - -

❸ Uffington White Horse

Just below Oxfordshire's highest point, the highly stylised **Uffington White Horse** (NT; www.national trust.org.uk; White Horse Hill; ⊙dawn-dusk) image is the oldest chalk figure in Britain, dating from the Bronze Age. It was created around 3000 years ago by cutting trenches out of the hill and filling them with blocks of chalk; local inhabitants have maintained the figure for centuries. Perhaps

TOP TIP: LONDON'S CONGESTION CHARGE

Central London levies a congestion charge (www. tfl.gov.uk/roadusers/congestioncharging) from 7am to 6pm Monday to Friday (excluding public holidays). Entering the 'C'-marked zone costs £11.50 (in advance or on the day) or £14 (by midnight on the first charging day after travel). You can pay online, at petrol stations or some shops.

it was planned for the gods: it's best seen from the air above. It's a half-mile walk east through fields from the hillside car park.

The Drive » It's a 49-mile trip to Winchester: return to the B4507 and drive southeast to Ashbury and take the B4000 southeast to join the southbound A34.

- - - - - - - - - - - - - - -

❹ Winchester

Set in a river valley, this ancient cathedral city was the capital of Saxon kings and a power base of bishops, and evokes two of England's mightiest myth-makers: famous son Alfred the Great (commemorated by a **statue**) and King Arthur (a 700-year-old copy of the round table resides in Winchester's cavernous **Great Hall** (☎01962-846476; www. hants.gov.uk/greathall; Castle Ave; suggested donation £3; ☺10am-5pm), the only part of 11th-century Winchester Castle that Oliver Cromwell spared from destruction).

Winchester's architecture is exquisite, from the handsome Elizabethan and Regency buildings in the narrow streets to the wondrous **Winchester Cathedral** (☎01962-857225; www. winchester-cathedral.org.uk; The Close; adult/child incl cathedral body & crypt tours £8/ free; ☺9.30am-5pm Mon-Sat, 12.30-3pm Sun) at its core. One of southern England's most awe-inspiring

buildings, the 11th-century cathedral has a fine Gothic facade, one of the longest medieval naves in Europe (164m), and highlights including intricately carved medieval choir stalls, Jane Austen's grave (near the entrance, in the northern aisle) and one of the UK's finest illuminated manuscripts, the dazzling, four-volume Winchester Bible dating from the 12th century. Book ahead for excellent tours of the ground floor, crypt and tower.

🛏 p151

The Drive » From Winchester, hop on the B3049 then the A30 for the 26-mile drive west to Salisbury.

- - - - - - - - - - - - - - -

❺ Salisbury

Salisbury has been an important provincial city for more than a thousand years, and its streets form an architectural timeline ranging from medieval walls and half-timbered Tudor town houses to Georgian mansions and Victorian villas. Its centrepiece is the majestic 13th-century **Salisbury Cathedral** (☎01722-555120; www.salisburycathedral.org. uk; Cathedral Close; requested donation adult/child £7.50/ none; ☺9am-5pm Mon-Sat, noon-4pm Sun). This early English Gothic–style structure has an elaborate exterior decorated with pointed arches and flying buttresses, and is topped by Britain's tallest spire at

123m, which was added in the mid-14th century. Beyond the cathedral's highly decorative West Front, a small passageway leads into the 70m-long nave. In the north aisle look out for a fascinating medieval clock dating from 1386, probably the oldest working timepiece in the world. Don't miss the cathedral's original, 13th-century copy of the **Magna Carta** (www. salisburycathedral.org.uk; Cathedral Close; ☺9.30am-4.30pm Mon-Sat, noon-3.45pm Sun) in the chapter house, or a 90-minute tower tour (adult/child £12.50/8; pre-booking essential), which sees you climbing 332 vertigo-inducing steps to the base of the spire for jaw-dropping views across the city and the surrounding countryside.

🛏 p151

The Drive » It's just 9.6 miles northwest from Salisbury via the A360 to otherworldly Stonehenge.

- - - - - - - - - - - - - - -

❻ Stonehenge

Despite countless theories about this site's purpose, ranging from a sacrificial centre to a celestial timepiece, no one knows for sure what drove prehistoric Britons to expend so much time and effort constructing **Stonehenge** (EH; ☎0370 333 1181; www.english-heritage. org.uk; adult/child on-the-day tickets £18/11, advance booking £15.50/9.30; ☺9am-8pm Jun-Aug, 9.30am-7pm Apr, May

Top: Tower Bridge

Classic Trip

WHY THIS IS A CLASSIC TRIP
CATHERINE
LE NEVEZ, WRITER

A trip titled Best of Britain is bound to be a classic, but what seals it for me is its incredible sweep of history. From neolithic-era stone circles to a Bronze Age chalk figure, Roman baths, medieval walls and mighty cathedrals, wonky black-and-white Tudor towns, multilayered cityscapes and futuristic developments, every era of British endeavour is represented along this journey.

Top: Tower Bridge
Left: Stone circle, Avebury
Right: St James's Park, London

ANDRAS POLONYI / EYEEM / GETTY IMAGES ©

VALERY EGOROV / SHUTTERSTOCK ©

& Sep, 9.30am-5pm Oct-Mar; [P]); it is one of Britain's great archaeological mysteries. The first phase of building started around 3000 BC, when the outer circular bank and ditch were erected. A thousand years later, an inner circle of granite stones, known as bluestones, was added.

An ultramodern makeover has brought an impressive visitor centre and the closure of an intrusive road (now restored to grassland). The result is a far stronger sense of historical context; dignity and mystery returned to an archaeological gem. A pathway frames the ring of massive stones. Although you can't walk in the circle, unless on a recommended **Stone Circle Access Visit** ([✆]0370 333 0605; www.english-heritage.org.uk; adult/child £32/19), you can get close-up views. Admission is through timed tickets – secure a place well in advance.

The Drive » Drive east to Durrington and take the A345 north, climbing over the grassy Pewsey Downs National Nature Reserve (home to another chalk figure, the Alton Barnes White Horse, dating from 1812), to reach Avebury (24 miles in total).

- - - - - - - - - - - - -

7 Avebury

With a diameter of 348m, **Avebury** (NT; [✆]01672-539250; www.nationaltrust.org.uk; [🕐]24hr; [P]) is the largest stone circle in the world, and is also one of

Classic Trip

the oldest, dating from 2500 to 2200 BC. Though it lacks the dramatic trilithons of its sister site Stonehenge, the massive stone circle is at least as rewarding to visit. Today, more than 30 stones are in place (pillars show where missing stones would have been) and a large section of the village is actually inside the stones – footpaths wind around them, allowing you to really soak up the extraordinary atmosphere. National Trust–run guided walks (£3) take place most days.

🛏 p47

The Drive » It's a 27-mile drive along the A4 past patchwork fields, country pubs and a smattering of villages to the Georgian streetscapes of Bath.

- - - - - - - - - - - -

❽ Bath

World Heritage–listed Bath was founded on top of natural hot springs and has been a tourist draw for some 2000 years. Its 18th-century heyday saw the construction of magnificent Georgian architecture from the 18th century. The best way to explore the city's Roman Baths complex and beautiful neoclassical buildings is on foot (p188).

Bath is known to many as a location in Jane Austen's novels, including *Persuasion* and *Northanger Abbey*. Although Austen lived in Bath for only five years, from 1801 to 1806, she remained a regular visitor and a keen student of the city's social scene. At the **Jane Austen Centre** (☏01225-443000; www.janeausten.co.uk; 40 Gay St; adult/child £11/5.50; ⏱9.45am-5.30pm Apr-Oct, 10am-4pm Nov-Mar), guides in Regency costumes regale you with Austen-esque tales as you tour memorabilia relating to the writer's life in Bath.

🛏 p151, p203

The Drive » It's 56.5 miles from Bath to the Welsh capital. Take the A46 north and join the westbound M4 over the Severn Estuary on the six-lane, cable-stayed Second Severn Crossing bridge (westbound bridge traffic incurs a £6.60 toll, payable by cash, debit card or credit card).

- - - - - - - - - - - -

TRIP HIGHLIGHT

❾ Cardiff

Set between an ancient fort and ultramodern waterfront, Cardiff has been the capital of Wales since only 1955, but has embraced the role with vigour and is now one of Britain's leading urban centres, as you can see on a stroll (p344) through its compact streets.

The huge success of the reinvented classic TV series *Doctor Who* has brought Cardiff to the attention of sci-fi fans worldwide. You can find

yourself sucked through a crack in time and thrown into the role of the Doctor's companion at the interactive, highly entertaining **Doctor Who Experience** (☏0844 801 2279; www.doctorwhoexperience.com; Porth Teigr; adult/child £15/11; ⏱10am-5pm Jul & Aug, Tue-Sun Mar-Jun, Sep & Oct, Wed-Sun Nov-Feb, last admission 3.30pm daily) exhibition, located next to the BBC studios where the series is filmed (look for the TARDIS outside).

If you time it right, you can catch a fired-up rugby test at Cardiff's **Principality Stadium** (Millennium Stadium; ☏029-2082 2432; www.principalitystadium.wales; Westgate St; tours adult/child £13/9).

🛏 p47

The Drive » Take the A48 northeast for 32 miles, bypassing Newport, to riverside Chepstow.

- - - - - - - - - - - -

❿ Chepstow

Nestled in an S-bend in the River Wye, Chepstow (Welsh: Cas-gwent) was first developed as a base for the Norman conquest of southeast Wales, later prospering as a port for the timber and wine trades. As river-borne commerce gave way to the railways, Chepstow's importance diminished to reflect its name, which means 'market place' in Old English.

One of Britain's oldest castles, imposing **Chepstow Castle** (Cadw;

www.cadw.gov.wales; Bridge St; adult/child £4.50/3.40; ⊙9.30am-5pm Mar-Oct, 10am-4pm Nov-Feb) perches atop a limestone cliff overhanging the river, guarding the main river crossing from England into South Wales. Building commenced in 1067, less than a year after William the Conqueror invaded England, and it was extended over the centuries. Today there are plenty of towers, battlements and wall walks to explore. A cave in the cliff below the castle is one of many places where legend says King Arthur and his knights are napping until the day they're needed to save Britain.

🛏 p327

The Drive » Farmland makes up most of this 68-mile drive. Head northeast on the A48 along the River Severn to Gloucester then continue northeast on the A46 to Stratford-upon-Avon.

- - - - - - - - - - - - - - -

⓫ Stratford-upon-Avon

Experiences linked to the life of Stratford's fêted son William Shakespeare range from the touristy – medieval re-creations and Bard-themed tearooms – to the humbling, such as Shakespeare's modest grave in **Holy Trinity Church** (✆01789-266316; www.stratford-upon-avon.org; Old Town; Shakespeare's grave adult/child £2/1; ⊙8.30am-6pm Mon-Sat, 12.30-5pm Sun Apr-Sep, shorter hours

Oct-Mar). There's also a sublime play by the **Royal Shakespeare Company** (RSC; ✆box office 01789-403493; www.rsc.org.uk; Waterside; tours adult £6.50-8.50, child £3-4.50, tower adult/child £2.50/1.25; ⊙tour times vary, tower 10am-6.15pm Sun-Fri 10am-12.15pm & 2-6.15pm Sat Apr-Sep, 10am-4.30pm Sun-Fri, 10am-12.15pm & 2-4.30pm Sat Oct-Mar).

One of the best ways to get a feel for the area's Tudor streets and willow-lined riverbanks is on foot (p236).

Combination tickets are available for the three houses associated with Shakespeare in town – Shakespeare's Birthplace, Shakespeare's New Place and Hall's Croft. If you also visit the childhood home of Shakespeare's

wife, **Anne Hathaway's Cottage** (✆01789-204016; www.shakespeare.org.uk; Cottage Lane, Shottery; adult/child £10.25/6.50; ⊙9am-5pm mid-Mar–Oct, closed Nov–mid-Mar), and his mother's farm, **Mary Arden's Farm** (✆01789-204016; www.shakespeare.org.uk; Station Rd, Wilmcote; adult/child £13.25/8.50; ⊙10am-5pm mid-Mar–Oct, closed Nov–mid-Mar), you can buy a combination ticket covering all five properties.

Don't miss a pint with the locals at Stratford's oldest and most atmospheric pub, the 1470-built **Old Thatch Tavern** (www.oldthatchtavernstratford.co.uk; Greenhill St; ⊙11.30am-11pm Mon-Sat, noon-6pm Sun; 🛜).

🛏 p203

BRITAIN'S BEST FESTIVALS

In London, see stunning blooms at the Royal Horticultural Society's **Chelsea Flower Show** (www.rhs.org.uk/chelsea; Royal Hospital Chelsea; admission from £23; ⊙May), military bands and bear-skinned grenadiers during the martial pageant **Trooping the Colour** (⊙Jun), or steel drums, dancers and outrageous costumes at the famous multicultural Caribbean-style street festival, **Notting Hill Carnival** (www.thenottinghillcarnival.com; ⊙Aug).

Wales' **National Eisteddfod** (✆08454-090900; www.eisteddfod.cymru; ⊙Aug) is descended from ancient Bardic tournaments. It's conducted in Welsh, but welcomes all entrants and visitors. It moves about each year, attracting some 150,000 visitors.

Edinburgh's most famous happenings are the **International Festival** (✆0131-473 2000; www.eif.co.uk) and **Fringe** (✆0131-226 0026; www.edfringe.com), but August also has an event for anything you care to name – books, art, theatre, music, comedy, marching bands... (www.edinburghfestivals.co.uk).

The Drive » The fastest route from Stratford-upon-Avon to Manchester is to head northwest on Birmingham Rd and pick up the northbound M42, which becomes the M6. You'll see the hilly Peak District National Park to your east. It's a 116-mile journey; this stretch incurs road tolls totalling £3.

12 Manchester

A rich blend of history and culture is on show in this Northern Powerhouse's museums, galleries and innovative, multigenre art centres such as **HOME** (📞0161-200 1500; http://homemcr.org; 2 Tony Wilson Pl, First St; tickets £5-20; ⏰ box office noon-8pm; bar 10am-11pm Mon-Thu & Sun, to midnight Fri & Sat).

The **Manchester Art Gallery** (📞0161-235 8888; http://manchesterartgallery. org; Mosley St; tours 20min/ 1hr free/£80; ⏰10am-5pm Mon-Wed & Fri-Sun, to 9pm Thu) has a superb collection of British art and a hefty number of European masters. The older wing has an impressive selection that includes 37 Turner watercolours, as well as the country's best assemblage of Pre-Raphaelite art, while the newer gallery is home to 20th-century British art starring Lucien Freud,

Francis Bacon, Stanley Spencer, Henry Moore and David Hockney. A wonderful collection of British watercolours are displayed at Manchester's **Whitworth Art Gallery** (📞0161-275 7450; www. whitworth.manchester.ac.uk; Oxford Rd, University of Manchester; ⏰10am-5pm, to 9pm Thu; ♿), which also has an exceptional collection of historic textiles.

Manchester is famed for its rival football teams **Manchester United** (📞0161-868 8000; www. manutd.com; Sir Matt Busby Way; tours adult/child £18/12; ⏰ museum 9.30am-5pm, tours every 10min 9.40am-4.30pm except match days) and **Manchester City** (www. mcfc.co.uk; Etihad Campus), and its **National Football Museum** (📞0161-605 8200; www.nationalfootballmuseum. com; Corporation St; Urbis, Cathedral Gardens; admission free; ⏰10am-5pm) charts the evolution of British football.

The city is also world renowned for its live-music scene, with gigs in all genres most nights of the week.

✕ 🛏 p47, p85, p211

The Drive » This trip's longest drive, at 216 miles, takes you northwest via the M61 and M6, passing between the Yorkshire Dales National Park to the east and the Lake District National Park to the west. Once you cross into Scotland the road becomes the A74 and climbs into the Southern Uplands, then becomes the A702 as it leads into Edinburgh.

MAREMAGNUM / GETTY IMAGES ©

TRIP HIGHLIGHT

13 Edinburgh

The Scottish capital is intimately entwined with its landscape, with buildings and monuments perched atop crags and overshadowed by cliffs. From the Old Town's picturesque jumble of medieval tenements piled high along the Royal Mile, its turreted skyline

Cardiff Principality Stadium

strung between the black, bull-nosed Castle Rock and the russet palisade of Salisbury Crags, to the New Town's neat neoclassical grid, the city offers a constantly changing perspective.

Along with a walk through the Old Town (p424), unmissable experiences here include visiting **Edinburgh Castle** (www.edinburghcastle.gov.uk; Castle Esplanade; adult/child £16.50/9.90, audioguide additional £3.50; ☺9.30am-6pm Apr-Sep, to 5pm Oct-Mar, last admission 1hr before closing; 🚌23, 27, 41, 42), which has played a pivotal role in Scottish history, both as a royal residence – King Malcolm Canmore (r 1058–93) and Queen Margaret first made their home here in the 11th century – and as a military stronghold; and climbing to the hilltop **Arthur's Seat** (Holyrood Park; 🚌6, 35) for city panoramas.

Edinburgh has 700-plus pubs, more per square mile than any other UK city. Sample a dram of Scottish whisky at icons like **Malt Shovel** (📞0131-225 6843; www.taylor-walker.co.uk; 11-15 Cockburn St; ☺11am-11pm Sun-Thu, to

Classic Trip

1am Fri & Sat; 📶 ♿; 🚌36, 41), with over 100 single malts behind the bar.

🛏 p47

The Drive » Drive southeast on the A68, passing through the Scottish Borders, and enter Northumberland National Park at the English border. Join the southbound A1 at Darlington, then take the eastbound A59 to York (191 miles altogether).

⑭ York

A magnificent ring of 13th-century walls encloses York's medieval narrow streets. At its heart lies the immense, awe-inspiring **York Minster** (www.yorkminster. org; Deangate; adult/child £10/ free, incl tower £15/5; 🕘9am-5.30pm Mon-Sat, 12.45-5pm Sun, last admission 30min before closing). Built mainly between 1220 and 1480, it encompasses all the major stages of Gothic architectural development.

The transepts (1220–55) were built in Early English style; the octagonal chapter house (1260–90) and nave (1291–1340) in the Decorated style; and the west towers, west front and central (or lantern) tower (1470–72) in Perpendicular style.

Don't miss a walk on York's City Walls, which follow the line of the original Roman walls and give a new perspective on the city. Cover the highlights (p290) or allow 1½ to two hours for the full circuit of 4.5 miles.

York is considered England's most haunted city, from the ghosts of Roman soldiers marching through the **Treasurer's House** (NT; www. nationaltrust.org.uk; Chapter House St; adult/child £8/4; 🕘11am-4.30pm Apr-Oct) to manifestations in pubs including the **Old White Swan** (www.nicholsonspubs. co.uk; 80 Goodramgate; 🕘10am-midnight Sun-Thu, to 1am Fri & Sat); even shops like the **Antiques Centre** (www.theantiquescentreyork.

co.uk; 41 Stonegate; 🕘9am-5.30pm Mon-Sat, to 4pm Sun) are said to be haunted.

🛏 p47, p271

The Drive » From York, it's 156 miles to Cambridge. Take the A64 southwest to join onto the A1 heading southeast.

- - - - - - - - - - - -

⑮ Cambridge

Surrounded by meadows, Cambridge is a university town extraordinaire, with a tightly packed core of ancient colleges and riverside 'Backs' (college gardens), which you can stroll around (p134).

The colossal neoclassical pile containing the **Fitzwilliam Museum** (www.fitzmuseum.cam.ac.uk; Trumpington St; donation requested; 🕘10am-5pm Tue-Sat, noon-5pm Sun) was built to house the fabulous treasures that the seventh Viscount Fitzwilliam bequeathed to his old university. Standout exhibits include Roman and Egyptian grave goods, artworks by many of the great masters and some quirkier collections such as banknotes and literary autographs.

For the full Cambridge experience, rent a river boat from operators such as **Scudamore's Punting** (☎01223-359750; www. scudamores.com; Granta Place; chauffeured punt per 45 min per person £16-19, 6-person self-punt per hr £22-28; 🕘9am-dusk).

🛏 p47, p123

LOCAL KNOWLEDGE: SCOTLAND'S CRAFT GIN

Scotland is famed around the world for its whisky, but Scottish craft gin (http://ginclubscotland.com) is also fast gaining ground. Over 70% of UK gin is produced in Scotland – there are more than a dozen gin distilleries in the country, and no fewer than five in the Edinburgh area. Bars all over the capital are offering cocktails based on brands such as NB, Pickering's, Crossbill and Strathearn.

Eating & Sleeping

London ①

🛏 Hoxton Hotel   Hotel £

(📞020-7550 1000; www.hoxtonhotels.com; 81 Great Eastern St, EC2; r from £49; ❄ @ 🛜; Ⓔ Old St) In the heart of hip Shoreditch, this sleek hotel takes the easyJet approach to selling its rooms – book long enough ahead and you might pay just £49. The 210 renovated rooms are small but stylish, with flatscreen TVs, a desk, fridge with complimentary bottled water and milk, and breakfast (orange juice, granola, yoghurt, banana) in a bag delivered to your door.

Avebury ⑦

🛏 Manor Farm   B&B ££

(📞01672-539294; www.manorfarmavebury. com; High St; s £70-80, d £90-100; P 🛜) A rare chance to sleep in style inside a stone circle – this red-brick farmhouse snuggles just inside Avebury henge. The elegant, comfy rooms blend old woods with bright furnishings, while the windows provide spine-tingling views of those 4000-year-old standing stones.

Cardiff ⑨

🛏 Lincoln House   Hotel ££

(📞029-2039 5558; www.lincolnhotel.co.uk; 118 Cathedral Rd, Pontcanna; r £90-150; P 🛜) Walking a middle line between a large B&B and a small hotel, Lincoln House is a generously proportioned Victorian property with heraldic emblems in the stained-glass windows of its sitting room, and a separate bar. For added romance, book a four-poster room.

Manchester ⑫

🛏 King Street Townhouse   Boutique Hotel £££

(📞0161-667 0707; www.eclectichotels. co.uk; 10 Booth St; r from £210, ste from £350; ❄ @ 🛜 ⊠) Arguably the city centre's finest lodgings is in this beautiful 1872 Italian renaissance-style former bank, now an exquisite boutique hotel with 40 bedrooms ranging from snug to suite. Furnishings are the perfect combination of period elegance and contemporary style. On the top floor is a small spa with an infinity pool overlooking the town hall; downstairs is a nice bar and restaurant.

Edinburgh ⑬

🛏 Southside Guest House   B&B ££

(📞0131-668 4422; www.southsideguesthouse. co.uk; 8 Newington Rd; s/d from £80/105; 🛜; 🖵 all Newington buses) Though set in a typical Victorian terrace, the Southside transcends the traditional guest-house category and feels more like a modern boutique hotel. Its eight stylish rooms ooze interior design, standing out from other Newington B&Bs through the clever use of bold colours and modern furniture. Breakfast is an event, with Bucks fizz (cava mixed with orange juice) on offer to ease the hangover!

York ⑭

🛏 Hedley House Hotel   Hotel ££

(📞01904-637404; www.hedleyhouse.com; 3 Bootham Tce; d/f from £105/115; P 🛜 ♿) This redbrick terrace-house hotel sports a variety of smartly refurbished, family-friendly accommodation, including rooms that sleep up to five, and some self-catering apartments – plus it has a sauna and spa bath on the outdoor terrace at the back, and is barely five minutes' walk from the city centre through the Museum Gardens.

Cambridge ⑮

🛏 Worth House   B&B ££

(📞01223-316074; www.worth-house.co.uk; 152 Chesterton Rd; s £75-85, d £95-145; P 🛜) The welcome is wonderfully warm, the great-value rooms utterly delightful. Soft grey and cream meets candy-stripe reds, fancy bathrooms boast claw-foot baths and tea trays are full of treats. There's also a three-person, self-catering apartment (per week £550) two doors down.

Classic Trip

Britain's Wild Side

2

Take a drive on the wild side on this tri-country trip through Britain's glorious national parks and protected Areas of Outstanding Natural Beauty.

TRIP HIGHLIGHTS

1290 miles
Cairngorms National Park
Explore Britain's biggest – and loftiest – national park

1007 miles
Kielder Water & Forest Park
Stargaze at state-of-the-art Kielder Observatory

432 miles
Brecon Beacons National Park
Discover the four completely different facets of the Brecon Beacons

21 DAYS
1435 MILES / 2310KM

GREAT FOR...

BEST TIME TO GO
June to September offers the best conditions for outdoor activities.

ESSENTIAL PHOTO
Cornwall's Bedruthan Steps at sunset.

BEST FOR WILDLIFE
Spot wild red deer, especially in autumn, at Exmoor National Park.

Cairngorms National Park River Spey, Aviemore

Classic Trip

2 Britain's Wild Side

Leave the city lights behind on this adventure into Britain's natural heartland. On this intrepid trip you'll get up close to soaring mountain peaks, desolate moorland, sea-sprayed beaches, scalloped bays, lush hills, green dales, high, barren fells, and glassy lakes, all teeming with wildlife. Along the way, opportunities abound to get out and explore the breathtaking countryside on foot, bicycle, horseback and kayak.

❶ New Forest

With typical, accidental, English irony the New Forest is anything but new – it was first proclaimed a royal hunting preserve in 1079. It's also not much of a forest, being mostly heathland ('forest' is from the Old French for 'hunting ground'). For an overview of New Forest, which was designated a national park in 2005, stop by the **New Forest Museum** (www.newforestcentre.org.uk; main car park, Lyndhurst; ⊙10am-5pm Apr-Oct, to 4pm Nov-Mar). Wild ponies mooch around pretty scrubland, deer flicker in the distance and rare birds flit among the foliage. Genteel villages dot the landscape, connected by a web of walking and cycling trails. **Lyndhurst tourist office** (📞02380-282269; www.thenewforest.co.uk; main car park, Lyndhurst; ⊙10am-5pm Easter-Oct, to 4pm Nov-Easter) stocks maps and guides; they're also available from its website. New Forest is also a popular spot for horse riding; **Burley Villa**

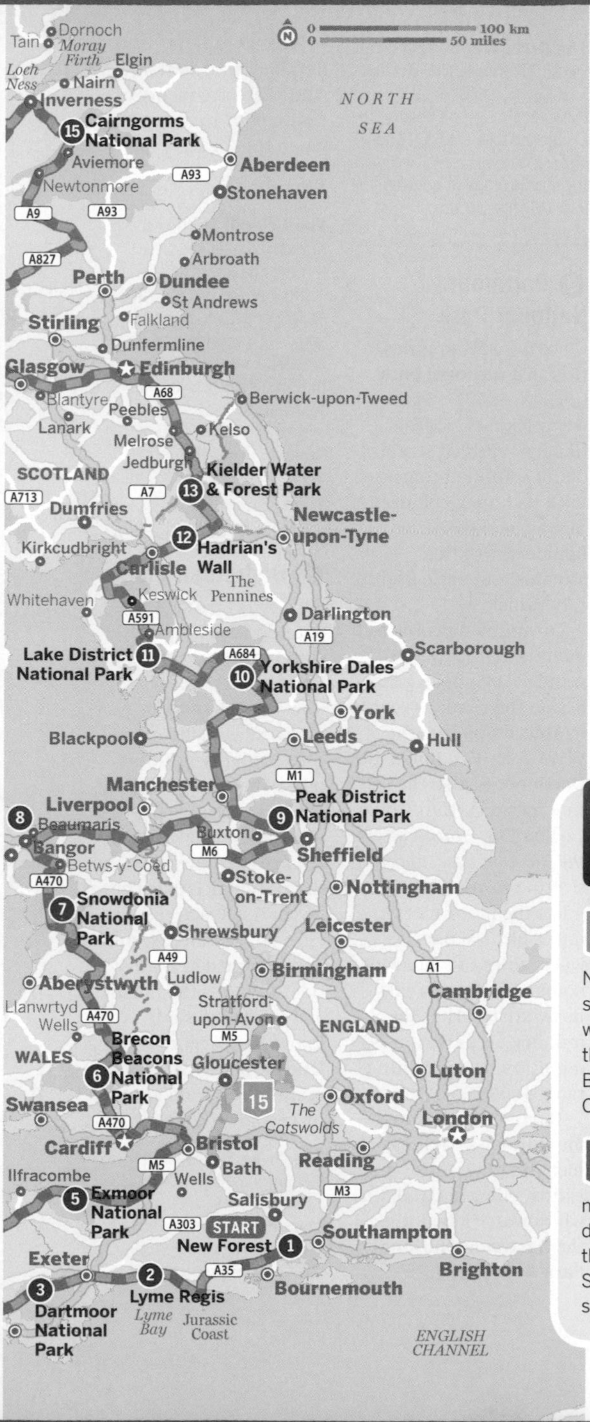

(Western Riding; ☎01425-610278; www.burleyvilla.co.uk; near New Milton; per hr from £35) organises rides using traditional English and also Western saddle styles (per 90 minutes £48).

🛏 p61

The Drive >> Take the A31 southwest to Weymouth and Chesil Beach. Follow the Jurassic Coast northwest along the B3157 to Lyme Regis (81 miles in total).

- - - - - - - - - - - - -

❷ Lyme Regis

Fossils regularly emerge from the unstable cliffs surrounding Lyme Regis, exposed by the landslides of a retreating shoreline, making this a key stop along the Unesco-listed Jurassic Coast.

§ **LINK YOUR TRIP**

15 Shakespeare & Rolling Hills

New Forest is 48 miles southeast of Bath, from where you can travel through more picturesque British countryside in the Cotswolds.

32 Upper West Coast

The Isle of Skye's main town, Portree, is the departure point for a voyage through jaw-dropping Scottish highland and island scenery.

51

Classic Trip

For an overview, **Dinosaurland** (📞01297-443541; www.dinosaurland.co.uk; Coombe St; adult/child £5/4; ⏰10am-5pm mid-Feb–mid-Oct) overflows with fossilised remains; look out for belemnites, a plesiosaurus and an impressive locally found ichthyosaur. Kids love the lifelike dinosaur models, rock-hard tyrannosaur eggs and 73kg dinosaur dung.

Three miles east of Lyme, the **Charmouth Heritage Coast Centre** (📞01297-560772; www.charmouth.org; Lower Sea Lane, Charmouth; ⏰10.30am-4.30pm daily Easter-Oct, Thu-Sun Nov-Easter) runs one to seven fossil-hunting trips a week (adult/child £7.50/3). In Lyme itself, **Lyme Regis Museum** (📞01297-443370; www.lymeregismuseum.co.uk; Bridge St; adult/child £4/free; ⏰10am-5pm Easter-Oct, 11am-4pm Wed-Sun Nov-Easter) organises three to seven walks a week (adult/child £11/6); local expert **Brandon Lennon** (📞07854 377519; www.lymeregisfossil walks.com; adult/child £8/6; ⏰Sat-Mon) also leads expeditions. Book walks in advance.

🛏 p167

The Drive » Drive west on the A3052 through the dazzling East Devon AONB (Area of Outstanding Natural Beauty) to Exeter and take the B3212 up into Postbridge, a small village in the middle of Dartmoor National Park (52 miles all up).

- - - - - - - - - - -

❸ Dartmoor National Park

Covering 368 sq miles, this vast **national park** (📞01626-834684; www.visitdartmoor.co.uk) feels like it's tumbled straight out of a Tolkien tome, with its honey-coloured heaths, moss-covered boulders, tinkling streams and eerie granite tors (hills).

On sunny days Dartmoor is idyllic: ponies wander and sheep graze beside the road, as seen in Steven Spielberg's WWI epic *War Horse*. But Dartmoor is also the setting for Sir Arthur Conan Doyle's *The Hound of the Baskervilles*, and in sleeting rain and swirling mists the moor morphs into a bleak wilderness where tales of a phantom hound seem very real. Be aware too that the military uses live ammunition in its training ranges (p53).

Dartmoor is a haven for outdoor activities, including hiking, cycling, riding, climbing and white-water kayaking; the **Dartmoor National Park Authority** (DNPA;

www.dartmoor.gov.uk) has detailed information. And there are plenty of rustic pubs to cosy up in when the fog rolls in.

🛏 p61

The Drive » Head west through Tavistock to pass through the Tamar Valley, another AONB, on the A390. At Dobwalls, pick up the A38 and drive west along the forested River Fowey to join the southwest-bound A30. Take the Victoria turn-off and travel northwest past Newquay Cornwall Airport to the Bedruthan Steps (62 miles altogether).

- - - - - - - - - - -

❹ Bedruthan Steps

On Cornwall's surf-pounded coast loom the stately rock stacks of **Bedruthan** (Carnewas; NT; www.nationaltrust.org.uk/carnewas-and-bedruthan-steps). These mighty granite pillars have been carved out by thousands of years of wind and waves, and the area is now owned by the National Trust. The beach itself is accessed via a steep staircase and is submerged at high tide. Towards the north end is a rocky shelf known as Diggory's Island, which separates the main beach from another little-known cove.

The Drive » Drive east to join the northeast-bound A39, which runs parallel to the Cornish coast, to the town of Lynmouth in Exmoor National Park (94 miles in total).

5 Exmoor National Park

In the middle of Exmoor National Park is the higher moor, an empty, expansive, other-worldly landscape of tawny grasses and huge skies.

Exmoor supports one of England's largest wild red deer populations, best experienced in autumn when the annual 'rutting' season sees stags bellowing, charging at each other and clashing horns in an attempt to impress prospective mates. The Exmoor National Park Authority (ENPA; www. exmoor-nationalpark.gov. uk) runs regular wildlife-themed guided walks (free), which include evening deer-spotting hikes. Or head out on an organised jeep safari.

The open moors and a profusion of marked bridleways offer excellent hiking. Cycling is also popular here; **Exmoor Adventures** (☎07976-208279; www.exmoor adventures.co.uk) runs a five-hour mountain-biking skills course (£50) and also hires bikes (per day £25).

The Drive ›› From Lynmouth to Libanus in the Brecon Beacons National Park it's 143 miles. Take the A39 east along the coast to join the M5 at Bridgwater. Take the Second Severn Crossing bridge (westbound bridge traffic incurs a £6.60 toll, payable by cash, debit card or credit card) and head west towards Cardiff to join the northwest-bound A470.

TRIP HIGHLIGHT

6 Brecon Beacons National Park

Brecon Beacons National Park (Parc Cenedlaethol Bannau Brycheiniog) ripples for 45 miles from the English border to near Llandeilo in the west. High mountain plateaus of grass and heather, their northern rims scalloped with glacier-scoured hollows, rise above wooded, waterfall-splashed valleys and green, rural landscapes.

Within the park there are four distinct regions: the wild, lonely **Black Mountain** (Mynydd Du) in the west, with its high moors and glacial lakes; **Fforest Fawr** (Great Forest), whose rushing streams and spectacular waterfalls form the headwaters of the Rivers Tawe and Neath; the **Brecon Beacons** (Bannau Brycheiniog) proper, a group of very distinctive, flat-topped hills that includes Pen-y-Fan (886m), the park's highest peak; and the rolling heathland ridges of the **Black Mountains** (Y Mynyddoedd Duon) – not to be confused with the Black Mountain (singular) in the west. The park's main **visitor centre** (☎01874-623366; www.breconbeacons. org; Libanus; ☺9.30am-5pm Easter-Sep) has details of walks, hiking and biking trails, outdoor activities, wildlife and geology (call first to check it's open).

🛏 p61

The Drive ›› Drive north along the A470 to reach the southern boundary of Snowdonia National Park at Mallwyd (79 miles altogether).

7 Snowdonia National Park

Wales' best-known and most-visited slice of nature, Snowdonia National Park (Parc Cenedlaethol Eryri) became the country's first national park in 1951. Every year

---

**TOP TIP:
WARNING: DARTMOOR MILITARY RANGES**

Live ammunition is used on Dartmoor's training ranges. Check locations with the **Firing Information Service** (☎0800 458 4868; www.mod.uk/access) or tourist offices. Red flags fly at the edges of in-use ranges by day; red flares burn at night. Beware unidentified metal objects lying in the grass. Don't touch anything; report finds to the **Commandant** (☎01837-650010).

ELGOL / GETTY IMAGES ©

DUNCAN SHAW / GETTY IMAGES ©

WHY THIS IS A CLASSIC TRIP
CATHERINE LE NEVEZ, WRITER

For a relatively small island, Britain's landscapes have an astonishing diversity and this classic trip offers a taste, from wooded forests to windswept moors, and coastal cliffs to tranquil lakes, with opportunities all along the route for more in-depth exploration. Bring rain gear at any time of year as getting out into Britain's great outdoors invariably means encountering classic British weather.

Top: Sea kayaker, Isle of Skye
Left: Reindeer, Cairngorms National Park
Right: Isle of Anglesey

more than 350,000 people walk, climb or take the rack-and-pinion **railway** (☎01286-870223; www.snowdonrailway.co.uk; Llanberis; adult/child return diesel £29/20, steam £37/27; ☺9am-5pm mid-Mar–Nov) to the 1085m summit of Snowdon. The park's 823 sq miles embrace stunning coastline, forests, valleys, rivers, bird-filled estuaries and Wales' biggest natural lake. The **Snowdonia National Park Information Centre** (☎01690-710426; www. eryri-npa.gov.uk; Royal Oak Stables; ☺9.30am-5.30pm Easter-Oct, to 4pm rest of year) is an invaluable source of information about walking trails, mountain conditions and more.

The Drive » Continue north on the A470 and take the A5 northwest to Bangor. Cross Robert Stephenson's 1850-built Britannia Bridge over the Menai Strait and take the A545 northwest to Beaumaris (a 72-mile trip).

- - - - - - - - - - - -

❽ Isle of Anglesey

The 276-sq-mile Isle of Anglesey (Ynys Môn) offers miles of inspiring coastline, hidden beaches and the country's greatest concentration of ancient sites.

Almost all of the Anglesey coast has been designated as an AONB (Area of Outstanding Natural Beauty). Beyond the handsome Georgian town of Beaumaris (Biwmares), there are

Classic Trip

GREAT BRITAIN'S BEST TRIPS **2** BRITAIN'S WILD SIDE

hidden gems scattered all over the island. It's very much a living centre of Welsh culture, too, as you can see for yourself at **Oriel Ynys Môn** (☎01248-724444; www.orielynysmon.info; Rhosmeirch, Llangefni; ⏱10.30am-5pm; **P**). A great, introductory day walk from Beaumaris takes in the ancient monastic site of **Penmon Priory** (Cadw; www.cadw.wales.gov.uk; Penmon; parking £2.50; ⏱10am-4pm; **P**), Penmon Point with views across to Puffin Island, and Blue Flag beach Llanddona.

🛏 p61

The Drive ›› Return to the mainland and take the A55 northeast, crossing the border into England where the road becomes the M56. Continue northeast towards Manchester before turning off on the southeast-bound M6. At Sandbach turn east on the A534 and follow the signs to Leek,

then take the A53 northeast before turning east towards Longnor then Bakewell (138 miles all-up).

- - - - - - - - - - - - - -

❾ Peak District National Park

Founded in 1951, the Peak District was England's first national park and is Europe's busiest. But even at peak times, there are 555 sq miles of open countryside in which to soak up the scenery. Caving and climbing, cycling and, above all, walking (including numerous short walks) are the most popular activities. The **Peak District National Park Authority** (☎01629-816200; www.peakdistrict.gov.uk; bicycle hire per half-day/day adult £14/17, child £10/12) has reams of information about the park and also operates several cycle-hire centres. The charming town of Bakewell also has a helpful **tourist office** (☎01629-816558; www.visitpeakdistrict.com; Bridge St; ⏱9.30am-5pm Apr-Oct, 10.30am-4.30pm Nov-Mar).

🛏 p61

The Drive ›› From Bakewell take the A623 northwest towards Manchester and pick up the northbound M66, then at Burnley take the northeast-bound M65 to Skipton. Enter the Yorkshire Dales National Park on the B6265 to Grassington and head northwest on the B6160 to Aysgarth. Then take the A684 along the River Ure to Hawes (a total of 118 miles).

- - - - - - - - - - - - - -

❿ Yorkshire Dales National Park

Protected as a national park since the 1950s, the glacial valleys of the Yorkshire Dales (named from the old Norse word *dalr*, meaning 'valleys') are characterised by a distinctive landscape of high heather moorland, stepped skylines and flat-topped hills above valleys patchworked with drystone dykes and little barns. Hawes is home to the **Wensleydale Creamery** (www.wensleydale.co.uk; adult/child £2.50/1.50; ⏱10am-4pm; **P** ♿), producing famous Wensleydale cheese. In the limestone country of the southern Dales you'll encounter extraordinary examples of karst scenery (created by rainwater dissolving the underlying limestone bedrock).

The Drive ›› Head southwest on the B6255 to Ingleton. Take the A65 northwest to Sizergh then the A590 southwest to the Lake District's southern reaches at Newby Bridge. Drive north along Lake Windermere

TOP TIP: WALKING SAFETY TIPS

The British countryside can appear gentle, and often is, but conditions can deteriorate quickly. Year-round on the hills or open moors carry warm waterproof clothing, a map and compass, and high-energy food (eg chocolate) and drinks. If you're really going off the beaten track, leave your route details with someone.

The photographer credit runs vertically along the left edge of the image: IAN WOOLCOCK / SHUTTERSTOCK ©

Cornwall Bedruthan Steps

before veering northwest to Hawkshead (53 miles all up).

- - - - - - - - - - - - - - - -

⑪ Lake District National Park

The Lake District (or Lakeland, as it's commonly known round these parts) is by far the UK's most popular national park. Ever since the Romantic poets arrived in the 19th century, its postcard panorama of craggy hilltops, mountain tarns and glittering lakes has stirred visitors' imaginations. It's awash with outdoor opportunities, from lake cruises to mountain walks.

Many people visit for the region's literary connections: among the many writers who found inspiration here are William Wordsworth, Samuel Taylor Coleridge, Arthur Ransome and, of course, Beatrix Potter, a lifelong lover of the Lakes, whose delightful former farmhouse, **Hill Top** (NT; ☎015394-36269; www.nationaltrust.org.uk/hill-top; adult/child £10/5, admission to garden & shop free; ⏱ house 10am-5.30pm Mon-Thu, 10am-4.30pm Fri-Sun, garden 10am-5.45pm Mon-Thu, 10am-5pm Fri-Sun), inspired many of her tales including *Peter Rabbit*.

🛏 p61

The Drive » Drive northwest on the A591 to join the A595 to Carlisle. Then take the A689 and A69 northeast to Walltown along Hadrian's Wall (72 miles altogether).

- - - - - - - - - - - - - - - -

⑫ Hadrian's Wall

Hadrian's Wall is one of Britain's most revealing and dramatic Roman ruins, its 2000-year-old procession of abandoned forts, garrisons, towers and milecastles marching across the wild and lonely landscape of northern England. This wall was about defence and control, but this

edge-of-empire barrier also symbolised the boundary of civilised order – to the north lay the unruly land of the marauding Celts, while to the south was the Roman world of orderly taxpaying, underfloor heating and bathrooms. There's an excellent visitor centre at **Walltown** (Northumberland National Park Visitor Centre; ☏01697-747151; www.northumberlandnational park.org.uk; Greenhead; ☉10am-6pm Apr-Sep, to 5pm Oct, 10am-4pm Sat & Sun Nov-Mar). The finest sections of the wall run along the southern edge of remote Northumberland National Park.

The Drive » Follow the B6318 northeast along Hadrian's Wall. Turn north on the B6320 to Bellingham. Continue northwest alongside the North Tyne river and Kielder Water lake to the village of Kielder (a 43-mile journey).

⑬ Kielder Water & Forest Park

Adjacent to Northumberland National Park, the Kielder Water & Forest Park is home to the vast artificial lake Kielder Water, holding 200,000 million litres. Surrounding its 27-mile-long shoreline is England's

largest plantation forest, with 150 million spruce and pine trees. Kielder Water is a water-sports playground (and midge magnet; bring insect repellent), and also has walking and cycling as well as great birdwatching. Comprehensive information is available at www.visitkielder.com.

The lack of population here helped the area be awarded dark-sky status by the International Dark Skies Association in 2013 (the largest such designation in Europe), with controls to prevent light pollution. For the best views of the Northumberland International Dark Sky Park, attend a stargazing session at state-of-the-art, 2008-built **Kielder Observatory** (☏0191-265 5510; www.kielderobservatory .org; Black Fell, off Shilling Pot; public observing session adult/child £16.50/15; ☉by reservation). Book ahead and dress warmly as it's chilly here at night.

The Drive » It's a 139-mile drive from Kielder to Balloch on the southern shore of Loch Lomond. Head north into Scotland and join the A68 towards Edinburgh. Take the M8 to Glasgow and then the A82 northwest to Balloch.

⑭ Loch Lomond

Loch Lomond is mainland Britain's largest lake and, after Loch Ness, the most famous of Scotland's lochs. It's part of

the **Loch Lomond & the Trossachs National Park** (www.lochlomond-trossachs.org), which became the heart of Scotland's first national park, created in 2002. The park extends over a huge area, from Balloch north to Tyndrum and Killin, and from Callander west to the forests of Cowal.

From Balloch, **Sweeney's Cruises**

Kielder Water & Forest Park Mountain biking through the forest

(☎01389-752376; www.
sweeneyscruiseco.com;
Balloch Rd) **offers a range
of trips including a
one-hour return cruise
to Inchmurrin (adult/
child £10.20/7, five times
daily April to October,
twice daily November to
March), and a two-hour
cruise (£18/10.20 twice
daily May to September
plus weekends April and
October) around the**
islands. **CanYou
Experience** (☎01389-
756251; www.canyouexperi
ence.com; Loch Lomond
Shores; ☺10am-5.30pm
Easter-Oct) **also arranges
boat trips and water- and
land-based activities
from various bases
around Loch Lomond.**

The Drive » Follow the
A82 along Loch Lomond's
western shoreline and pick
up the northeast-bound A85
at Crianlarich. Then take
the northwest-bound A9 to
Aviemore (a total of 141 miles).

- - - - - - - - - - - -

TRIP HIGHLIGHT

**15 Cairngorms
National Park**
The vast Cairn-
gorms National Park
(www.cairngorms.co.uk)
stretches from Aviemore
in the north – with a
handy **tourist office**

(📞01479-810930; www.
visitaviemore.com; The Mall,
Grampian Rd; 🕙9am-5pm
Mon-Sat, 10am-4pm Sun
year-round, longer hrs Jul &
Aug) – to the Angus Glens
in the south, and from
Dalwhinnie in the west
to Ballater and Royal
Deeside in the east.

The park encompasses
the highest landmass in
Britain – a broad moun-
tain plateau, riven only
by the deep valleys of the
Lairig Ghru and Loch
Avon, with an average al-
titude of over 1000m and
including five of the six
highest summits in the
UK. This wild mountain
landscape of granite and
heather has a sub-Arctic
climate and supports
rare alpine tundra
vegetation and high-
altitude bird species,
such as snow bunting,
ptarmigan and dotterel.
Lower down, scenic glens
are softened by beauti-
ful open forests of native
Scots pine, home to
rare animals and birds
such as pine martens,
wildcats, red squirrels,
ospreys, capercaillies and
crossbills.

🔖 p61

The Drive » Take the A9
northwest to Inverness, then
the southwest-bound A82
along Loch Ness (keeping an
eye out for mythical beasts).
At Invermoriston join the
westbound A887, which
becomes the A87, and continue
to Kyle of Lochalsh where you'll
cross the Skye Bridge to the
Isle of Skye. Continue along the
A87 to reach Portree (a 145-mile
journey all up).

OUTER HEBRIDES

If you're not ready to return to the mainland after
visiting the Isle of Skye, consider a trip to the Outer
Hebrides (aka the Western Isles; Na h-Eileanan an
Iar in Gaelic) – a 130-mile-long string of islands
west of Skye. More than a third of Scotland's
registered crofts are here, and no less than 60%
of the population are Gaelic speakers. With limited
time, head straight for the west coast of Lewis
with its prehistoric sites, preserved blackhouses,
beautiful beaches, and arts and crafts studios – the
Lochmaddy Tourist Office (📞01867-500321; Pier Rd;
🕙10am-5pm Mon-Sat Apr-Oct) can provide a list. Ferries
(car £30, driver and passenger £6.10 each) run once
or twice daily from Uig on Skye to Lochmaddy (1¾
hours) and Tarbert (1½ hours).

🔟 Isle of Skye

The Isle of Skye (an
t-Eilean Sgiathanach in
Gaelic) takes its name
from the old Norse *sky-a*,
meaning 'cloud island', a
Viking reference to the
often-mist-enshrouded
Cuillin Hills. It's a
50-mile-long patchwork
of velvet moors, jagged
mountains, sparkling
lochs and towering sea
cliffs. Lively Portree
(Port Righ) has the
island's only **tourist office** (📞01478-612992; www.
visitscotland.com; Bayfield Rd;
🕙9am-6pm Mon-Sat, 10am-
4pm Sun Jun-Aug, shorter
hours Sep-May; 📶).

Skye offers some of
the finest walking in
Scotland, including some
short, low-level routes.
The sheltered coves and
sea lochs around the
coast of Skye provide
magnificent sea-kayaking
opportunities. **Skyak Adventures** (📞01471-820002;
www.skyakadventures.com; 29
Lower Breakish, Breakish; 1-day
course per person from £100)
runs expeditions and
courses for both begin-
ners and experienced
paddlers to otherwise
inaccessible places.

Skye's stunning scen-
ery is the main attrac-
tion, but when the mist
closes in there are plenty
of castles, crofting museums and cosy pubs and
restaurants, along with
dozens of art galleries
and craft studios.

Eating & Sleeping

New Forest ❶

🛏 The Pig   Boutique Hotel £££
(📞0345 225 9494; www.thepighotel.co.uk;
Beaulieu Rd, Brockenhurst; r £175-265; [P] [🛜])
One of the New Forest's classiest hotels remains
an utter delight: log baskets, croquet mallets
and ranks of guest gumboots give things a
country-house air; espresso machines and
minilarders lend bedrooms a luxury touch. The
effortless elegance makes it feel like you've just
dropped by a friend's (very stylish) rural retreat.

Dartmoor National Park ❸

🛏 Tor Royal Farm   B&B ££
(📞01822-890189; www.torroyal.co.uk; Tor
Royal Lane, near Princetown; s £60, d £80-100;
[P] [🛜]) An easygoing, country cottage–styled
farmhouse packed with lived-in charm. The
rooms are rather old-fashioned – cream-and-
white furniture, puffy bedspreads, easy chairs –
but they're cosy, and the sumptuous afternoon
tea (£14) is reason to stay here alone.

Brecon Beacons National Park ❻

🛏 Peterstone Court   Hotel £££
(📞01874-665387; www.peterstone-court.com;
Llanhamlach; r from £150; [P] [🛜] [🏊]) At this
elegant Georgian manor house, the rooms are
large and comfortable, and the views across the
valley to the Beacons are superb. The boutique
spa centre is a big drawcard, pampering guests
with organic beauty products. It also has an
excellent **restaurant** (breakfast £8-14, lunch
£15-17, dinner £14-21; ⏱7.30-9.30am & noon-
9.30pm). Llanhamlach is 3 miles southeast of
Brecon, just off the A40.

Isle of Anglesey ❽

🛏 Ye Olde Bulls Head
Inn & Townhouse   Hotel ££
(📞01248-810329; www.bullsheadinn.co.uk;
Castle St; d inn/townhouse from £90/110; [🛜])

These sister properties, located just across the
road from each other, provide quite a contrast.
Where the Bulls Head accommodation –
occupying the oldest pub in town – is historic
and elegant, the townhouse is contemporary,
high-tech and design driven. Breakfast for both
is served at the old inn.

Peak District National Park ❾

🛏 Melbourne House &
Easthorpe   B&B ££
(📞01629-815357; www.bakewell-accommo
dation.co.uk; Buxton Rd; d from £70; [P] [🛜])
Occupying a picturesque, creeper-covered
building (Melbourne House) dating back
more than three centuries and a new annex
(Easthorpe), with uncluttered, neutral-toned
rooms, this inviting B&B is handily situated on
the main road leading to Buxton.

Lake District National Park ⓫

🛏 Summer Hill
Country House   Hotel ££
(📞015394-36180; www.summerhillcountry
house.com; Hawkshead Hill; d £102-122;
[P] [@] [🛜]) On Hawkshead Hill, this 1700s house
has a wonderfully out-of-the-way setting, 3
miles from both Coniston and Hawkshead. The
five rooms vary in shape and size, but all feature
posh bath products and net-connected Mac
Minis for getting online or watching DVDs. The
garden boasts sculptures and a summerhouse
that belonged to John Ruskin.

Cairngorms National Park ⓯

🛏 Old Minister's House   B&B £££
(📞01479-812181; www.theoldministershouse.
co.uk; Ski Rd, Inverdruie; s/d £125/140; [P] [🛜])
This former manse dates from 1906 and has
five rooms with a luxurious, country-house
atmosphere. It's in a lovely setting amid Scots
pines on the banks of the River Druie, southeast
of Aviemore.

Classic Trip

The Historic South

3

England's rich heritage runs like a glittering seam through this remarkable road trip. Discovering sights nautical, archaeological and architectural, you'll travel the ages as you clock up the miles.

TRIP HIGHLIGHTS

440 miles

Blenheim Palace
Noseying around the rooms of Winston Churchill's home

14 Oxford **FINISH**

Bath

 START
LONDON ⭐

9

2

Beaulieu

Brighton

Salisbury
Staring upwards at Salisbury Cathedral's soaring spire

262 miles

Leeds Castle
Delighting in the beauty of this moat-framed fortification

39 miles

9–11 DAYS
450 MILES /
720KM

GREAT FOR...
📖 🌳

BEST TIME TO GO
Spring and autumn. Summer if you don't mind more crowds.

📷 **ESSENTIAL PHOTO**
Lounging in a punt with a backdrop of Oxford's divine buildings.

☑ **BEST FOR SURPRISES**
The world's biggest stone circle: Avebury (not Stonehenge).

Salisbury Cathedral A 13th-century building with the tallest spire in England

Classic Trip

3 The Historic South

Stand by to tour some of the world's most beautiful castles and most memorable archaeological sites. Take in three of England's most impressive cathedrals, Georgian cityscapes, Churchill's palace and Oxford's spires. Discover guerilla art and this country's fine tradition of seaside kitsch. Motor to a motor museum, explore unspoiled villages and encounter 14th-century fellow travellers' tales. In short, take a road trip through the very best of Britain's past.

❶ London

Vibrant London is so packed with historic sights, where's best to start? In the capital's touchstone: **St Paul's** (☎020-7246 8350; www.stpauls.co.uk; St Paul's Churchyard, EC4; adult/child £18/8; ⊙8.30am-4.30pm Mon-Sat; ⊖St Paul's). Designed by Sir Christopher Wren in 1675 after the Great Fire, its vast dome is famed for avoiding Luftwaffe raids during the Blitz. Head inside and up 257 steps to the walkway called the Whispering Gallery, then to the Golden Gallery at the top for unforgettable London views. Next explore the city's rich past at the **Museum of London** (www.museumoflondon.org.uk; 150 London Wall, EC2; ⊙10am-6pm; ⊖Barbican). Then head east to elegant Tower Bridge to learn in its **exhibition** (☎020-7403 3761; www.towerbridge.org.uk; Tower Bridge, SE1; adult/child £9/3.90, incl Monument £11/5; ⊙10am-6pm Apr-Sep, 9.30am-5.30pm Oct-Mar, last admission 30min before closing; ⊖Tower Hill) just how they raise the arms – and the road – to let ships through.

🛏 p47

The Drive » London's streets and suburbs meet bursts of the Kent countryside; you're heading for the A20 towards Sidcup, then the M20 towards Dover. Shortly after Maidstone leave the motorway behind, picking up A20 signs for Lenham and then Leeds Castle, some 40 miles from the capital.

TRIP HIGHLIGHT

❷ Leeds Castle

Immense and moat-ringed, for many **Leeds Castle** (www.leeds-castle.com; adult/child £24.50/16.50; ⊙10am-6pm Apr-Sep, to 5pm Oct-Mar) is one of the world's most romantic. The formidable, intricate structure balancing on two islands is known as something of a 'ladies castle'. This stems from the fact that in its more than 1000 years of history, it has been home to a who's who of medieval

LINK YOUR TRIP

6 History, Art, Hops & Grapes

Encounter seashores, seafood and modern art on this Kentish cruise. Start at Margate, 17 miles northeast of Canterbury.

15 Shakespeare & Rolling Hills

Explore the enchanting Cotswold villages, then visit the home of the bard himself. Join the fun at Tetbury, 50 miles west of Oxford.

Classic Trip

GREAT BRITAIN'S BEST TRIPS **3** THE HISTORIC SOUTH

queens, most famously Henry VIII's first wife, Catherine of Aragon.

The Drive » Next up is a 25-mile cruise, high up over the vast chalk ridge of the North Downs. You're headed northeast, largely along the A252/A28 – the Canterbury Rd which echoes the old pilgrim footpath to the cathedral city.

❸ Canterbury

Canterbury tops the charts for English cathedral cities – and no wonder. Here medieval alleyways frame exquisite architecture, with **Canterbury Cathedral** (www.canterbury-cathedral.org; adult/concession £12/10.50, tours £5/4, audioguide £4/3; ⊙9am-5.30pm Mon-Sat, 12.30-2.30pm Sun) the centrepiece. This towering Gothic cathedral features fine stonework, a cavernous crypt and the

site of English history's most famous murder: Archbishop Thomas Becket was killed here in 1170 after 'hints' from King Henry II, drawing thousands of pilgrims for more than 800 years. The **Canterbury Tales** (www.canterburytales.org.uk; St Margaret's St; adult/child £9.75/7.50; ⊙10am-5pm Mar-Oct, to 4.30pm Nov-Feb) exhibition uses animatronics and audio guides to explore Chaucer's stories of these 14th-century travellers. For a taste of even older Canterbury, head to the mosaics of the **Roman Museum** (www.canterburymuseums.co.uk; Butchery Lane; adult/child £8/free; ⊙10am-5pm).

✗ ⊨ p73, p107

The Drive » Now for a 35-mile drive. Head back up and over the North Downs on the A28 towards Ashford. Then plunge down to roll, along the A2070, through the verdant valley of the Weald of Kent. Soon you're edging the flat-lands of Romney Marsh and arriving at Rye.

THE CANTERBURY TALES

The Canterbury Tales is the best-known work of English literature's father figure: Geoffrey Chaucer (1342–1400). Chaucer was the first English writer to introduce characters – rather than 'types' – into fiction. They feature strongly in *The Canterbury Tales*, an unfinished series of 24 vivid stories told by a party of pilgrims travelling between London and Canterbury. The text remains one of the pillars of the literary canon. But more than that, it's a collection of rollicking good yarns of adultery, debauchery, crime and edgy romance, and is filled with Chaucer's witty observations about human nature.

❹ Rye

Welcome to one of England's prettiest towns. Here cobbled lanes, wonky Tudor buildings and tales of smugglers abound. The best place to start stretching your legs is **Mermaid Street**. It bristles with 15th-century timber-framed houses with quirky names such as 'The House with Two Front Doors' and 'The House Opposite'. A short walk away the 13th-century **Ypres Tower** (www.ryemuseum.co.uk; Church Sq; adult/child £4/free; ⊙10.30am-5pm Apr-Oct, to 3.30pm Nov-Mar) affords views of Rye Bay, the marshes and sometimes France. The **Rye Heritage Centre** (☎01797-226696; www.ryeheritage.co.uk; Strand Quay; ⊙10am-5pm Apr-Oct, shorter hours Nov-Mar) offers themed walking tours.

✗ ⊨ p99

The Drive » The next 50-mile leg sees you taking a string of A roads west. They lead past the woods and farms of the High Weald AONB up to another chalk ridge, this time the amphitheatre of hills that is the South Downs. Eventually, it's time to descend to Brighton on the shore.

❺ Brighton

Famously hedonistic, exuberant and home to the UK's biggest gay scene, Brighton rocks. The bright n' breezy seafront boasts the grand, century-old **Brighton Pier** (www.brightonpier.co.uk;

Madeira Dr), complete with fairground rides, amusement arcades and candy floss stalls. Stroll inland to the magnificent **Royal Pavilion** (📞03000-290901; http://brightonmuseums. org.uk/royalpavilion; Royal Pavilion Gardens; adult/child £12.30/6.90; ⏱9.30am-5.45pm Apr-Sep, 10am-5.15pm Oct-Mar), the glittering palace of Prince George (later King George IV). It's one of the most opulent buildings in England, and Europe's finest example of early-19th-century chinoiserie. Take in the Salvador Dalí sofa modelled on Mae West's lips at the **Brighton Museum & Art Gallery** (www.brighton-hove-museums.org.uk; Royal Pavilion Gardens; adult/child £5.20/3; ⏱10am-5pm Tue-Sun), then gear up for a lively night out by shopping amid the boutiques of the tightly packed **Brighton Lanes**.

🍴 🛏 p73, p99

The Drive ⟫ Next is a 50-mile blast due west, largely along A roads, to the historic port of Portsmouth. As the 170m-high Spinnaker Tower gets closer on the horizon, pick up signs for the Historic Dockyard Car Park.

---

❻ Portsmouth

Portsmouth's blockbuster **Historic Dockyard** sees you gazing at the hulk of Henry VIII's flagship, the **Mary Rose** (www.maryrose. org; adult/child £18/13; ⏱10am-5.30pm Apr-Oct, to 5pm Nov-Mar), and jumping aboard **HMS Victory**

DETOUR: BEACHY HEAD

Start: ❹ Rye
An 8-mile detour off your route leads to a truly remarkable view. Around 25 miles west of Rye, peel off the A27 onto the A22 to Eastbourne. Head to the seafront to take the signed route that climbs to **Beachy Head**. Pick a parking spot and follow the footpaths to the cliffs themselves. These 162m-tall sheer chalk faces are the highest point of cliffs that slice across the rugged coastline at the southern end of the South Downs. Far below sits a squat red-and-white-striped lighthouse. Appealing walks include the 1.5 mile hike west to the beach at Birling Gap.

(www.hms-victory.com; adult/child £18/13; ⏱10am-5.30pm Apr-Oct, to 5pm Nov-Mar) – the warship Nelson captained at the Battle of Trafalgar. Then there's the Victorian **HMS Warrior** (www.hmswarrior.org; adult/child £18/13; ⏱10am-5.30pm Apr-Oct, to 5pm Nov-Mar) and a wealth of imaginative, maritime-themed museums, along with waterborne **harbour tours** (📞02392-839766; www.historicdockyard.co.uk; adult/child £7/5; ⏱hours vary). Round it all off with the WWII-era submarine **HMS Alliance** (www. submarine-museum.co.uk; Haslar Rd, Gosport; adult/child £14/10; ⏱10am-5.30pm Apr-Oct, 10am-4.30pm Wed-Sun Nov-Mar) or by strolling around the defences in the historic **Point district** and by climbing the sail-like **Spinnaker Tower** (📞02392-857520; www.spinnakertower.co.uk; Gunwharf Quays; adult/child £10/8; ⏱10am-6pm) for 23-mile views.

The Drive ⟫ Time to head inland; a 30-mile motorway cruise (the M27 then the M3) takes you to Winchester.

---

❼ Winchester
Calm, collegiate Winchester is a mellow must-see. One of southern England's most awe-inspiring buildings, 11th-century **Winchester Cathedral** (📞01962-857225; www.winchester-cathedral.org. uk; The Close; adult/child incl cathedral body & crypt tours £8/free; ⏱9.30am-5pm Mon-Sat, 12.30-3pm Sun) sits at its core. It boasts a fine Gothic facade, one of the longest medieval naves in Europe (164m) and intricately carved medieval choir stalls, sporting everything from mythical beasts to a mischievous green man. Jane Austen's grave is near the entrance, in the northern aisle. The fantastical crumbling remains of **Wolvesey Castle** (EH; 📞0370-333 1181;

Classic Trip

WHY THIS IS A CLASSIC TRIP
BELINDA DIXON, WRITER

For me, Classic Trips need classic sights, and this journey delivers in spades. As well as the big-name attractions, you also get intriguing insights and some surprises: the stone circle preferred by purists; hip, hedonistic Brighton's seaside heritage; and some of this nautical nation's most important ships, the *Mary Rose*, HMS *Victory* and Brunel's pioneering SS *Great Britain*. If only history lessons at school had been this much fun.

Above: Traditional wooden punts, Oxford
Right: Blenheim Palace

www.english-heritage.org.uk; College St; 10am-5pm Apr-Oct) sit nearby, as does one of England's most prestigious private schools: **Winchester College** (01962-621209; www.winchestercollege.org; College St; adult/child £7/free; tours 10.15am, 11.30am, 2.15pm, 3.30pm Mon, Wed, Fri-Sun), which you can visit on a tour.

p73, p151

The Drive » Leave Winchester's ancient streets to take the motorways towards Southampton (initially the M3). After 14 miles turn off onto the A35 towards Lyndhurst. From here it's 9-miles to Beaulieu through the New Forest's increasingly wooded roads.

- - - - - - - - - - -

8 Beaulieu

The vintage car museum and stately home at **Beaulieu** (☎01590-612345; www.beaulieu.co.uk; adult/child £24/12; ◷10am-6pm Apr-Sep, to 5pm Oct-Mar) is centred on a 13th-century Cistercian monastery that fell to the ancestors of the current proprietors, the Montague family, after Henry VIII's 1536 monastic land-grab. Today its **motor museum** includes F1 cars and jet-powered land-speed record-breakers and wheels driven by James Bond and Mr Bean. The **palace** began life as a 14th-century Gothic abbey gatehouse, and received a 19th-century Scottish makeover in the 1860s.

The Drive » The SatNav wants to start this 28-mile leg by routing you onto the A326. Resist! Opt for the A and B roads that wind through the villages of Lyndhurst, Cadnam, Brook and North Charford, revealing the New Forest's enchanting blend of woods and open heath. Eventually join the A338 to Salisbury.

Classic Trip

9 Salisbury

Salisbury's skyline is dominated by the tallest spire in England, which soars from its central, majestic 13th-century **cathedral** (01722-555120; www.salisburycathedral.org.uk; Cathedral Close; requested donation adult/child £7.50/none; 9am-5pm Mon-Sat, noon-4pm Sun). This early English Gothic–style structure's elaborate exterior is decorated with pointed arches and flying buttresses, while its statuary and tombs are outstanding. Don't miss the daily **tower tours** and the cathedral's original, 13th-century copy of the **Magna Carta** (9.30am-4.30pm Mon-Sat, noon-3.45pm Sun). The surrounding **Cathedral Close** has a hushed, other-worldly feel. Nearby, the hugely important finds at **Salisbury Museum** (01722-332151; www.salisburymuseum.org.uk; 65 Cathedral Close; adult/child £8/4; 10am-5pm Mon-Sat year-round, plus noon-5pm Sun Jun-Sep) include Iron Age gold coins, a Bronze Age gold necklace and the **Stonehenge Archer**, the bones of a man found in the ditch surrounding the stone circle.

p73, p151

The Drive » Next: a 10-mile drive taking you back 5000 years. The A345 heads north. Soon after joining the A303, detail a passenger to watch the right windows – the world's most famous stone circle will soon pop into view. The entry to the site is just beyond.

10 Stonehenge

Welcome to Britain's most iconic archaeological site: **Stonehenge** (EH; 0370 333 1181; www.english-heritage.org.uk; adult/child on-the-day tickets £18/11, advance booking £15.50/9.30; 9am-8pm Jun-Aug, 9.30am-7pm Apr, May & Sep, 9.30am-5pm Oct-Mar; P), a compelling ring of monolithic stones that dates, in parts, back to 3000 BC. Head into the **Visitor Centre** to see 300 finds from the site and experience an impressive 360-degree projection of the stone circle through the ages and seasons. Next hop on a trolley bus (or walk; it's 1.5 miles) to the monument. There, as you stroll around it, play 'spot-the-stone': look out for the **bluestone horseshoe** (an inner semi-circle), the **trilithon horseshoe** (sets of two vertical stones topped by a horizontal one) and the **Slaughter Stone** and **Heel Stone** (set apart, on the northeast side). Then try to work out what on earth it all means. Note that entrance is by timed ticket; secure yours well in advance.

The Drive » Now for a 24-mile, A-road meander through rural England. After dodging through Devizes, it's not long before signs point left to Avebury's main car park.

11 Avebury

A two-minute stroll from the car park (£7 per day) leads to a ring of stones that's so big an entire village sits inside. Fringed by a massive bank and ditch and with a diameter of 348m, **Avebury** (NT; 01672-539250; www.nationaltrust.org.uk; 24hr; P) is the largest stone circle in the world. Dating from 2500 to 2200 BC, more than 30 stones are still in place and you can wander between them and clusters of other stones at will. On the fringes, 16th-century **Avebury Manor** (NT; 01672-539250; www.nationaltrust.org.uk; adult/child £6.75/3.35; 11am-5pm Apr-Oct, to 4pm mid-Feb–Mar, 11am-4pm Thu-Sun Nov & Dec) is home to interiors spanning five periods, ranging from Tudor, through Georgian, to the 1930s.

p47

The Drive » Next a cruise due west; as the A4 winds for 30 miles past fields and through villages to the city of Bath.

12 Bath

Sophisticated, stately and ever-so-slightly snooty, Bath is graced with some of Britain's finest Georgian architecture. Wandering around the streets (p188) is a real joy. For an insight into how the city came to have the shape it does, head to the **Museum of Bath Architecture** (☎01225-333895; www.museumofbatharchitecture.org.uk; The Vineyards, The Paragon; adult/child £5.50/2.50; ☺2-5pm Tue-Fri, 10.30am-5pm Sat & Sun mid-Feb–Nov). The **Bath Assembly Rooms** (www.nationaltrust.org.uk; 19 Bennett St; ☺10.30am-5pm Mar-Oct, to 4pm Nov-Feb), where socialites once gathered, gives an insight into the Georgian world. Discover the city's culinary heritage at **Sally Lunn's** (☎01225-461634; www.sallylunns.co.uk; 4 North Pde Passage; mains £6-17; ☺10am-9.30pm Sun-Thu, to 10pm Fri & Sat), which bakes the famous Bath Bun (a brioche-meets-bread treat). For a free glass of the spring water that made the city rich, stop by the **Pump Room** (www.romanbaths.co.uk; Stall St; ☺10am-5pm). Then perhaps soak in it: at **Thermae Bath Spa** (☎01225-331234; www.thermaebathspa.com; Hot Bath St; Mon-Fri £34, Sat & Sun £37; ☺9am-9.30pm, last entry 7pm), steam rooms, waterfall showers and a choice of swimming pools (including a gorgeous rooftop one) will help you relax.

🛏 p73, p151, p203

The Drive >> It's a 13-mile blast from Bath to Bristol along the A36/A4.

- - - - - - - - - -

⑬ Bristol

In Bristol a fascinating seafaring heritage meets an edgy, contemporary vibe. The mighty **SS Great Britain** (☎0117-926 0680; www.ssgreatbritain.org; Great Western Dock, Gas Ferry Rd; adult/child £14/8; ☺10am-5.30pm Apr-Oct, to 4.30pm Nov-Mar) sits on the city's waterfront. Designed in 1843 by engineering genius Isambard Kingdom Brunel, its interior has been impeccably refurbished, including the galley, the surgeon's quarters and a working model of the original steam engine. The whole vessel is contained in an air-tight dry dock, dubbed a 'glass sea'. At the **Bristol Museum & Art Gallery** (☎0117-922 3571; www.bristolmuseums.org.uk; Queen's Rd; ☺10am-5pm Mon-Fri, to 6pm Sat & Sun) take in the *Paint-Pot Angel* by world-famous street artist Banksy. In the suburb of **Clifton** explore Georgian architecture, especially in Cornwallis and Royal York Crescents. The **Clifton Observatory** (☎0117-974 1242; www.cliftonobservatory.com; Litfield Rd, Clifton Down; adult/child £2.50/1.50; ☺10am-5pm Feb-Oct, to 4pm Nov-Jan), meanwhile, features a rare *camera obscura* which offers incredible views of the deep fissure that is the Avon Gorge.

🍴 🛏 p73, p85

The Drive >> Travelling partly on motorways and partly on A-roads, the next 80-mile leg sees you skirting Oxford (for now) and arriving at the tree-lined avenue that leads to one of Britain's finest stately homes.

- - - - - - - - - -

SITES AROUND STONEHENGE

As you drive the roads around Stonehenge it's worth registering that the site forms part of a huge complex of ancient monuments. North of Stonehenge and running roughly east–west is the **Cursus**, an elongated embanked oval; the smaller **Lesser Cursus** is nearby. Two clusters of burial mounds, the **Old Barrow** and the **New Kings Barrow**, sit beside the ceremonial pathway **The Avenue**. This routeway originally linked the site with the River Avon, 2 miles away. Theories abound as to what these sites were used for, ranging from ancient sporting arenas to processional avenues for the dead.

TRIP HIGHLIGHT

⑭ Blenheim Palace

A monumental baroque fantasy designed by Sir John Vanbrugh and Nicholas Hawksmoor, **Blenheim Palace** (☎01993-810530; www.blenheimpalace.com; Woodstock; adult/child £24.90/13.90, park & gardens only £14.90/6.90; ☺palace 10.30am-5.30pm, park & gardens 9am-6pm; P) was built between 1705 and 1722. The house is stuffed with statues,

tapestries, ostentatious furniture, priceless china and giant oil paintings. Highlights include the **Great Hall**, a soaring space topped by a 20m-high ceiling adorned with images of the first duke. Britain's legendary WWII prime minister, Sir Winston Churchill, was born here in 1874 – the **Churchill Exhibition** is dedicated to his life, work, paintings and writings.

The house is encircled by vast, lavish **gardens** and **parklands**, parts of which were landscaped by the great Lancelot 'Capability' Brown. A minitrain (50p) whisks you to the **Pleasure Gardens**, which feature a yew **maze**, adventure playground, lavender garden and butterfly house.

The Drive » From Blenheim's grandeur, it's a 10-mile pootle down the A44/A4144 to Oxford's dreaming spires.

⓯ Oxford

One of the world's most famous university towns,

the centre of Oxford is rich in history and studded with august buildings. The city has 38 colleges – **Christ Church** (☎01865-276492; www.chch. ox.ac.uk; St Aldate's; adult/child £8/7; ⏰10am-4.15pm Mon-Sat, 2-4.15pm Sun) is the largest, with 650 students, and has the grandest quad. Founded in 1524 by Cardinal Thomas Wolsey, alumni include Albert Einstein and 13 British prime ministers. It's also famous as a location for the Harry Potter films. At the **Ashmolean** (☎01865-278000; www.ashmolean.org; Beaumont St; ⏰10am-5pm Tue-Sun), Britain's oldest public museum showcases treasures such as Egyptian mummies, Indian textiles and Islamic art. Beautiful **Magdalen College** (☎01865-276000; www.magd.ox.ac.uk; High St; adult/child £5/4, 45min tours £6; ⏰1-6pm Oct-Jun, noon-7pm Jul-Sep, tours 6pm daily Jul-Sep) is worth a visit for its medieval chapel, 15th-century cloisters and 40-hectare grounds. Nearby, let someone else navigate for a bit: head to **Magdalen Bridge Boathouse** (☎01865-202643; www.oxfordpunting.co.uk; High St; chauffeured 4-person punt per 30min £30, punt rental per hour £24; ⏰9.30am-dusk Feb-Nov) for a ride on a chauffeured punt.

✕ 🛏 p73, p115

DETOUR: LACOCK

Start: ⓫ Avebury (p70)

Around 16 miles into your Avebury-to-Bath cruise, consider a detour south. A drive of just 4 extra miles leads to a real rarity: a medieval village that's been preserved in time. In Lacock, the sweet streets framed by stone cottages, higgledy-piggledy rooftops and mullioned windows are a delight to stroll around. Unsurprisingly, it's a popular movie location – it's popped up in the Harry Potter films, *The Other Boleyn Girl* and a BBC adaptation of *Pride and Prejudice*. The 13th-century former Augustinian nunnery of **Lacock Abbey** (NT; ☎01249-730459; www.nationaltrust. org.uk; Hither Way; adult/child £12/6; ⏰10.30am-5.30pm Mar-Oct, 11am-4pm Nov-Feb) is a must-see: its deeply atmospheric rooms and stunning Gothic entrance hall are lined with bizarre terracotta figures – spot the scapegoat with a lump of sugar on its nose. The **Fox Talbot Museum** (NT; ☎01249-730459; www.nationaltrust. org.uk; Hither Way; adult/child £12/6, includes entry to Lacock Abbey; ⏰10.30am-5.30pm Mar-Oct, 11am-4pm Nov-Feb) features an intriguing display on early photography, while the **George Inn** (www.georgeinnlacock.co.uk; 4 West St; mains £10-16; ⏰food noon-2.30pm & 6-9pm Mon-Sat, 6-8pm Sun) is an atmospheric pub in which to re-fuel.

Eating & Sleeping

Canterbury ❸

🛏 Cathedral Gate Hotel　　Hotel ££

(📞01227-464381; www.cathgate.co.uk; 36 Burgate; s/d £50/112, without bathroom £50/81.50; 📶) Predating the spectacular cathedral gate it adjoins, this quaint 15th-century hotel is a medieval warren of steep staircases and narrow passageways leading to 27 pleasingly old-fashioned rooms with angled floors, low doors and cockeyed walls. Some have cathedral views, while others overlook pretty Buttermarket. There's no lift.

Brighton ❺

🛏 Artist Residence　　Boutique Hotel £££

(📞01273-324 302; www.artistresidence brighton.co.uk; 33 Regency Sq; d £129-260; 📶) Eclectic doesn't quite describe the rooms at this wonderful 23-room townhouse hotel, set amid the splendour of Regency Sq. As befits the name, every bedroom is a work of funky art with bold wall murals, bespoke and vintage furniture, rough wood cladding and in-room roll-top baths. The Set Restaurant downstairs has a glowing reputation. Book direct and breakfast is free.

Winchester ❼

🛏 St John's Croft　　B&B ££

(📞01962-859976; www.st-johns-croft.co.uk; St John's St; s/d/f £55/90/120; 🅿 📶) You may fall in love with this oh-so-casually stylish, rambling Queen Anne townhouse, where rattan carpets are teamed with bulging bookcases, and Indian art with shabby-chic antiques. The rooms are vast, the garden is tranquil and breakfast is served beside the Aga in the country-house kitchen.

Salisbury ❾

🛏 Chapter House　　Inn ££

(📞01722-412028; www.thechapterhouseuk. com; 9 St Johns St; r £100-140) In this 800-year-old boutique beauty, wood panels and wildly wonky stairs sit beside duck-your-head beams. The cheaper bedrooms are swish but the posher ones are stunning, starring slipper baths and the odd heraldic crest. The pick is room 6, where King Charles is reputed to have stayed.

Bath ⓬

🛏 Queensberry Hotel　　Hotel £££

(📞01225-447928; www.thequeensberry. co.uk; 4 Russell St; r £125-185, ste £225-275; 📶) Award-winning, quirky Queensberry is Bath's best boutique spoil. Four Georgian town houses have been combined into one seamlessly stylish whole where heritage roots meet snazzy designs; expect everything from gingham checks and country creams to bright upholstery, original fireplaces and free-standing tubs. Rates exclude breakfast; parking is £7.

Bristol ⓭

🍴 Riverstation　　British ££

(📞0117-914 4434; www.riverstation.co.uk; The Grove; lunch 2/3 courses £14/17, dinner mains £15-18; ⏱ noon-2.30pm & 6-10.30pm) Riverstation is one of Bristol's original dining-out destinations, and still leads the pack. The waterside location is hard to beat, with a view over the Floating Harbour, but it's the food that keeps the punters coming back: classic in style with a strong European flavour, from French fish soup to steak à la béarnaise.

Oxford ⓯

🛏 Burlington House　　B&B ££

(📞01865-513513; www.burlington-hotel-oxford. co.uk; 374 Banbury Rd, Summertown; s/d from £70/96; 🅿 📶) Twelve elegantly contemporary rooms with patterned wallpaper, immaculate bathrooms and luxury touches are available at this beautifully refreshed Victorian merchant's house. Personal service is as sensational as the delicious breakfast, complete with organic eggs and homemade bread. It's 2 miles north of central Oxford, with good public transport links.

Classic Trip

Urban & Art Odyssey

4

England's creative credentials are extraordinary, and this trip ensures you encounter them one by one. Touring cities from the southwest to the northeast, you'll discover a nation: art and soul.

TRIP HIGHLIGHTS

645 miles

Liverpool
Lapping up pop and classical culture in vibrant Liverpool

Leeds

15
FINISH
Manchester

200 miles

Birmingham
Marvelling at the spectacular £189 million Library of Birmingham

6

Stratford-upon-Avon

CARDIFF ★
1
START

0 miles

Bristol
Hunting out guerrilla works by edgy street artist Banksy

13–15 DAYS
645 MILES / 1030KM

GREAT FOR...

BEST TIME TO GO

Autumn avoids the worst of the weather on the northern legs.

ESSENTIAL PHOTO

Standing, arms outstretched, beside the 20m-high Angel of the North.

BEST FOR CAR FANS

The classic lines on show at Great Malvern's Morgan Motor Company.

Gateshead *The Angel of the North*, by sculptor Sir Antony Gormley

4 Urban & Art Odyssey

This exploration of all things English, urban and artistic makes for an exhilarating, creative drive. Legs link visual art ranging from prehistoric chalk figures via Old Masters to sprayed-on street deigns. Discover classical composers and design classics; exquisite bridges and hand-crafted motor cars. Experience film locations, stunning sculpture and pop culture ranging from the Beatles to football. On this tour you'll see England's arts in all their diverse glory.

TRIP HIGHLIGHT

❶ Bristol

The creative, edgy city of Bristol is the perfect place to see works by the anonymous guerilla artist Banksy. The central **Well Hung Lover** (Frogmore St) depicts an angry husband, a two-timing wife, and a naked man dangling from a window. The startling **Paint-Pot Angel** (think pink paint meets funerary monument) resides in the foyer of the **Bristol Museum & Art Gallery** (☎0117-922 3571; www.bristolmuseums.org. uk; Queen's Rd; ◷10am-5pm Mon-Fri, to 6pm Sat & Sun).

Banksy's **Mild Mild West** (80 Stokes Croft) features a Molotov cocktail–wielding teddy bear facing three riot police, while his stencil of the **Grim Reaper** rowing a boat is now on the 1st floor of the city's **M Shed museum** (☎0117-352 6600; www.bristolmuseums.org.uk; Princes Wharf; ◷10am-5pm Tue-Fri, to 6pm Sat & Sun). The city's **tourist office** (☎0906 711 2191; www. visitbristol.co.uk; E-Shed, 1 Canons Rd; ◷10am-4pm

Mon-Sat, 11am-4pm Sun) sells an excellent Banksy info sheet (50p).

 p73, p85

The Drive ›› It's a 45-mile motorway drive to Cardiff, a route enlivened by the cruise along the six-lane, cable-stayed Second Severn Crossing bridge. There's a toll (cars £6.60) for west-bound traffic only; pay by cash or credit or debit card at a relevant booth. In Cardiff, follow signs for City Centre car parks; Greyfriars and Westgate St are ideal.

----

2 Cardiff

The capital of Wales has a vibrant, confident air. And, in the **National Museum Cardiff** (📞0300 111 2 333; www.museumwales. ac.uk; Gorsedd Gardens Rd; ⏱10am-4pm Tue-Sun), one of Britain's best museums. Highlights include a trio of Monet's *Water Lilies*, alongside his scenes of London, Rouen and Venice; Sisley's *The Cliff*

LINK YOUR TRIP

24 **West Wales**
A cracking cruise along a spectacular stretch of surf-dashed coast. Starts 40 miles west of Cardiff.

21 **North York Moors & Coast**
A tour of Yorkshire's gorgeous moors and shores. Starts just 15 miles south of this trip's Castle Howard at York.

at Penarth (the artist was married in Cardiff); Renoir's shimmering *La Parisienne*; a cast of Rodin's *The Kiss*; and Van Gogh's anguished *Rain: Auvers*. At nearby **Cardiff Castle** (☎029-2087 8100; www.cardiffcastle.com; Castle St; adult/child £12/9, incl guided tour £15/11; ☺9am-5pm) the artistic decor includes zodiac symbols in the winter smoking room, mahogany-and-mirrors in the bedrooms, and marble and acres of gold leaf in the Arab room. Cardiff is a great city to explore on foot (p344) – stroll 1 mile south to **Cardiff Bay** to take in the grand modern architecture of the **Wales Millennium Centre** (☎029-2063 6464; www.wmc.org.uk; Bute Pl, Cardiff Bay; tours adult/child £6/free; ☺9am-7pm) and the TV artistry of the **Doctor Who Experience** (☎0844 801 2279; www. doctorwhoexperience.com; Porth Teigr; adult/child £15/11; ☺10am-5pm (last admission 3.30pm) daily Jul & Aug, Tue-Sun Mar-Jun, Sep & Oct, Wed-Sun Nov-Feb) – the sci-fi hit is filmed next door.

🛏 p47

The Drive >> Head back over the Second Severn Crossing (not paying a toll this time) for the 70-mile jaunt up the M4/M5 to Cheltenham.

- - - - - - - - - - - - -

❸ Cheltenham

Gracious, 18th-century spa town Cheltenham offers some fine Regency buildings, including the **Pittville Pump Room** (☎0844 576 2210; www.pitt villepumproom.org.uk; Pittville Park; ☺10am-4pm Wed-Sun). Built in 1830 it was modelled on an ancient Athenian temple and has a pillared exterior and a park with lake, lawns and blue-green gates. Walking south towards the town centre, drop by the **Holst Birthplace Museum** (☎01242-524846; www.holst museum.org.uk; 4 Clarence Rd; adult/child £5/2; ☺10am-5pm Tue-Sat, 1.30-5pm Sun Jun-Sep, 10am-4pm Tue-Sat Feb-May & Oct–mid-Dec) to see how the composer lived; look out for the piano on which his orchestral suite *The Planets* was devised. Nearby, **The Wilson** (☎01242-237431; www. thewilson.org.uk; Clarence St; ☺9.30am-5.15pm) museum features strong displays on William Morris and the Arts and Crafts movement, including a painted pine table designed by Morris himself.

The Drive >> Make for the M5 to glide north for 14 miles before peeling off onto the A38 for the climb to hillside Great Malvern, a further 11 miles away.

- - - - - - - - - - - - -

❹ Great Malvern

The gateway to the towering, 9-mile-long ridge of the Malvern Hills, Great Malvern is a picturesque spa town. The **Great Malvern Priory** (☎01684-561020; www.greatmalvern priory.org.uk; Church St; ☺9am-5pm) showcases designs ranging from Norman pillars via 15th-century tiles to surreal

---

DETOUR: UFFINGTON WHITE HORSE

Start: ❸ **Cheltenham**

A 40-mile detour southeast from Cheltenham leads to the oldest chalk figure in Britain. The **Uffington White Horse** (NT; www.nationaltrust.org. uk; White Horse Hill; ☺dawn-dusk) was created in the Bronze Age, some 3000 years ago, on the crest of Oxfordshire's highest point. A highly stylised horse image, it was crafted by cutting trenches out of the hill and filling them with blocks of chalk; local inhabitants have maintained the figure for centuries. From Cheltenham, head south on A-roads towards Swindon, then join the A420 towards Oxford; the horse is signposted from that road. It's then a 0.5-mile walk east through fields from the National Trust car park to the chalk figure itself.

modernist stained glass. The town's other great attraction is the **Morgan Motor Company** (☎01684-584580; www.morgan-motor. co.uk; Pickersleigh Rd; museum free, tours adult/child £20/10; ☺ museum 8.30am-5pm Mon-Thu, to 3pm Fri, tours 10am, 12.30pm & 2.30pm Mon-Fri), where Britain's most famous sports cars are made. The firm has been handcrafting the vehicles since 1909, and you can see the mechanics at work on two-hour guided tours of the unassuming shed-like buildings comprising the factory (prebooking essential). Then view a fleet of vintage classics next to the museum.

✗ ⊨ p211

The Drive » Time to leave the wooded ridge of the Malvern Hills behind on a 30-mile leg east; it's an A-road meander alongside green fields to Stratford-upon-Avon.

- - - - - - - - - -

❺ Stratford-upon-Avon

Birthplace of the man who wrote some of the most quoted sentences in the English language, for many a trip to Tudor Stratford is akin to a literary pilgrimage, and an opportunity to retrace his steps (p236). **Shakespeare's Birthplace** (☎01789-204016; www. shakespeare.org.uk; Henley St; incl Shakespeare's New Place & Halls Croft adult/child £17.50/11.50; ☺9am-5.30pm Jul & Aug, to 5pm Sep-Jun) has

restored Tudor rooms and live presentations from famous Shakespearean characters. The playwright died in a house on the site of **Shakespeare's New Place** (☎01789-204016; www.shakespeare. org.uk; cnr Chapel St & Chapel Lane; incl Shakespeare's Birthplace & Hall's Croft adult/child £17.50/11.50; ☺9am-5.30pm Jul & Aug, 9am-5pm mid-Mar–Jun, Sep & Oct, 10am-4pm Nov–mid-Mar) in 1616; an attractive Elizabethan knot garden occupies part of the grounds. Next visit **Holy Trinity Church** (☎01789-266316; www. stratford-upon-avon.org; Old Town; Shakespeare's grave adult/child £2/1; ☺8.30am-6pm Mon-Sat, 12.30-5pm Sun Apr-Sep, shorter hours Oct-Mar), Shakespeare's final resting place. Look out for handsome 16th- and 17th-century tombs, some fabulous carved choir stalls and the grave of the Bard, with its ominous epitaph: 'cvrst be he yt moves my bones'.

⊨ p203

The Drive » Make for the M40 to start your 40-mile drive north. This is true motorway territory; you'll navigate the M42 and the M6 before arriving in Birmingham. Head for the central Bull Ring Car Park.

- - - - - - - - - -

TRIP HIGHLIGHT

❻ Birmingham

Birmingham delivers a big-city vibe and culture by the truckload. Britain's second biggest city is (rightly) hugely proud

of its glittering £189 million **Library of Birmingham** (www.libraryofbirmingham.com; Centenary Sq; ☺ground fl 9am-9pm Mon & Tue, 11am-9pm Wed-Fri, 11am-5pm Sat, rest of bldg 11am-7pm Mon & Tue, to 5pm Wed-Sat). Designed by Francine Houben, it features a subterranean amphitheatre, spiralling interior, viewing decks and glass elevator to the 7th-floor 'secret garden' with panoramic city views. Nearby, Victoria Sq features civic architecture of another era in the 1870s-built **Council House**. To the west Centenary Sq is home to the art-deco **Hall of Memory War Memorial**. From there it's a short stroll to the **Birmingham Museum & Art Gallery** (☎0121-348 8038; www. birminghammuseums.org.uk; Chamberlain Sq; ☺10am-5pm Sat-Thu, 10.30am-5pm Fri; 🚻) and its fine collection of Victorian art and major Pre-Raphaelite works by Rossetti and Edward Burne-Jones.

⊨ p85

The Drive » Time for more motorways (M6/M42), initially, on this 45-mile leg. After about 18 miles, though, it's onto the A38 for a rural cruise to Derby.

- - - - - - - - - -

❼ Derby

One of the crucibles of the Industrial Revolution, these days Derby is home to impressive cultural developments and a rejuvenated riverfront.

Classic Trip

WHY THIS IS A CLASSIC TRIP
BELINDA DIXON, WRITER

Classic Trips are about more than top sights and great drives; they also reveal deeper trends. On this exploration of urban, artistic heartlands, you're actually encountering the elements that help shape England today: visual arts, industry, architecture, trade, sculpture, film, TV, sport, music, design. And because this trip reveals how far back these themes stretch, it also suggests they're actually essentials of, not additions to, our daily lives.

Top: Library of Birmingham
Left: *Iron Tree*, by artist Ai Weiwei, at Yorkshire Sculpture Park
Right: National Football Museum, Manchester

CREATIVEONEUK / SHUTTERSTOCK ©

The central **Quad**
(☎01332-290606; www.
derbyquad.co.uk; Market Pl;
gallery free, cinema tickets
£5-17; ◷gallery 11am-6pm
Mon-Sat, noon-6pm Sun,
cinema 11am-9pm), a striking modernist cube on
Market Pl, contains a
futuristic art gallery and
an art-house cinema. A
short walk away, at the
**Derby Museum & Art Gal-
lery** (www.derbymuseums.
org; The Strand; ◷10am-5pm
Tue-Sat, noon-4pm Sun), local
history and industry
displays include fine
ceramics produced by
Royal Crown Derby – get
an even greater insight
into this artistry at the
**Royal Crown Derby
Factory** (☎01332-712800;
www.royalcrownderby.co.uk;
Osmaston Rd; museum & factory tour adult/child £5/2.50,
museum only £2/1; ◷museum
10am-4pm Mon-Sat, factory
tours 1.30pm Tue-Thu, shop
10am-5pm Mon-Sat, tearoom
10am-4pm Tue-Fri), which
still produces some of
the finest bone china in
England. Prebook for the
factory tour.

🛏 p225

The Drive » Next a 60-mile
drive, at first on the A61 and the
A38, but largely via that great
route north: the M1. Around 57
miles in, pick up signs for the
Yorkshire Sculpture Park.

- - - - - - - - - - - - - -

❽ Yorkshire Sculpture Park

One of England's most
impressive collections
of sculpture is housed at
Yorkshire Sculpture Park

Classic Trip

(www.ysp.co.uk; Bretton Park, near Wakefield; parking 2hr/ all day £5/8; ⊙10am-5pm; P 🚻 🐕). It's scattered across the formidable 18th-century estate of Bretton Park, 200-odd hectares of lawns, fields and trees. A bit like the art world's equivalent of a safari park, the Yorkshire Sculpture Park showcases the work of dozens of sculptors both national and international. But the main focus of this out-door gallery is the work of local kids Barbara Hepworth (1903–75), who was born in nearby Wake-field, and Henry Moore (1898–1986).

The Drive » Head due north again, but this time on a much shorter leg: 18 miles, largely up the M1. At Leeds, follow the signs for the city centre.

⑨ Leeds

One of the UK's fastest-growing cities, Leeds is a vision of 21st-century urban chic. The **Leeds Art Gallery** (www.leeds.gov.uk/artgallery; The Headrow; ⊙10am-5pm Mon, Tue & Thu-Sat, noon-5pm Wed, 1-5pm Sun) is packed with British heavyweights – Turner, Constable, Stanley Spencer and Wyndham Lewis. Plus pieces by re-cent arrivals such as Sir Antony Gormley, sculptor

of the *Angel of the North*. Nearby, the **Henry Moore Institute** (www.henry-moore. org/hmi; The Headrow; ⊙11am-5.30pm Tue & Thu-Sun, to 8pm Wed) showcases the work of 20th-century sculptors. For a different culture fix, the **Victoria Quarter** (www.victoria-quarter.co.uk; Vicar Lane) delivers striking architec-ture in the form of mosaic paving and stained-glass-roofed Victorian arcades. There's also cutting-edge fashion boutiques including Louis Vuitton and Vivienne Westwood, plus the flagship Harvey Nichols store.

🛏 p85

The Drive » Continue north, slicing between two national parks: the Yorkshire Dales and the North York Moors. Again, it's largely up the M1/A1 (M). At about 58 miles in, turn off, first onto the A66 towards Brough, then to the town of Barnard Castle (13 miles). From there, signs point to the Bowes Museum.

⑩ Barnard Castle

Tucked in at the edge of the town of Barnard Cas-tle, the **Bowes Museum** (www.thebowesmuseum.org.uk; Newgate; adult/child £10.50/ free; ⊙10am-5pm) is a monumental French-style château. Funded by the 19th-century industrialist John Bowes and opened in 1892, this brainchild of his Parisian actress wife, Josephine, was built by French architect Jules Pellechet. The aim was

to display a collection the Bowes had travelled the world to assemble. The star attraction is the marvellous 18th-century mechanical swan, which performs every day at 2pm. If you miss it, a film shows it in action.

The Drive » Take the A688 through Bishop Auckland and Spennymoor for 23 miles. Then rejoin the A1 (M), towards Newcastle. Some 14 miles later take the A167 towards Gateshead South, and watch the windows for the towering *Angel of the North*. There's a free car park by the base.

⑪ Angel of the North

Nicknamed the Gateshead Flasher, the extraordinary 200-tonne, rust-coloured, winged human-form *Angel of the North* (Durham Rd, Low Eighton) has loomed over the A1 (M) since 1998. Sir Antony Gorm-ley's iconic work (which saw him knighted in 2014) stands 20m high, with a wingspan wider than a Boeing 767.

The Drive » Hop on the A167/ B1318 for the 6-mile cruise into Newcastle city centre. Just after 3 miles in, stand by to drive along one of England's most famous river crossings: the mighty Tyne Bridge. Head for a city centre car park; those at Dean St, Akenside Hill or Painters Heugh are ideal.

⑫ Newcastle-upon-Tyne

Historic, sophisticated and bursting with night-life, Newcastle is one of

England's most appealing cities. Stroll to the Quayside to contemplate its most striking pieces of engineering. The imposing **Tyne Bridge** (1925–28) resembles the Sydney Harbour Bridge – no wonder, both were built by the same firm, Dorman Long of Middlesbrough. The quaint **Swing Bridge** (1876), just to the west, pivots in the middle to let ships through. Next, walk 500m to the east over the gorgeous **Millennium Bridge** (2002). This opens like an eyelid to enable vessels to pass and leads to the **BALTIC – Centre for Contemporary Art** (www.balticmill.com; Gateshead Quays; ⏰10am-6pm). Once a huge mustard-coloured grain store, this art gallery rivals London's Tate Modern. Rotating shows feature the work of some of the art world's biggest show-stoppers. You'll also find artists in residence, a performance space, a cinema, a bar, a spectacular rooftop restaurant (bookings essential) and a 4th-floor outdoor platform with fabulous panoramas of the Tyne.

✕ 🛏 p85, p279, p289

The Drive » After hundreds of miles driving north, it's time to head 84 miles south. Drive back over the Tyne Bridge, making for the A19 towards York. At Thirsk take the A170 towards Helmsley. Peel off right onto the B1257 and follow the brown signs to Castle Howard; a route of rolling fields and woods.

----

⑬ Castle Howard

Grand, theatrical **Castle Howard** (www.castlehoward.co.uk; adult/child house & grounds £17.50/9, grounds only £9.95/7; ⏰house 10.30am-4pm (last admission), grounds 10am-5pm; 🅿) is one of the world's most beautiful buildings, instantly recognisable from its starring role in the 1980s TV series *Brideshead Revisited* and in the 2008 film of the same name. The baroque house, commissioned in 1699, boasts a magnificent central cupola and plentiful treasures – the breathtaking Great Hall with its soaring Corinthian pilasters, Pre-Raphaelite stained glass in the chapel, and corridors lined with classical antiquities. A wander around the peacock-haunted grounds reveals views of the Howardian Hills and architect Sir John Vanbrugh's playful Temple of the Four Winds.

The Drive » Another near 90-mile stretch, this time heading southwest largely along the A64 towards Leeds and then the M62 to Manchester, eventually leaving the motorways to follow city centre signs.

----

⑭ Manchester

Packed with history and culture, Manchester is the uncrowned capital of the north. Here, football – seen by some as a game – is acknowledged as an art form. The **National Football Museum** (📞0161-605 8200; www.nationalfootballmuseum.com; Corporation St, Urbis, Cathedral Gardens; ⏰10am-5pm)

↱ **DETOUR: HAWORTH**

Start: ⑬ **Castle Howard**

As you arrive at Leeds, en route from Castle Howard to Manchester, consider a 20-mile detour west, past Bradford to Haworth. This village set beside the moors of the South Pennines has an impeccable artistic pedigree. It was home to the Brontë sisters – Charlotte, Emily and Anne, responsible for *Jane Eyre*, *Wuthering Heights* and *The Tenant of Wildfell Hall* respectively. The house where they lived from 1820 to 1861 is now the **Bronte Parsonage Museum** (www.bronte.org.uk; Church St; adult/child £7.50/3.75; ⏰10am-5.30pm Apr-Oct, to 5pm Nov-Mar). Rooms are decorated as they were in the Brontë era, including Charlotte's bedroom, her clothes and her writing paraphernalia.

explores the evolution of the beautiful game, while engaging, hands-on displays include Football Plus, a series of interactive stations allowing you to test your skills in simulated conditions. A 500m walk south leads to the **Manchester Art Gallery** (📞0161-235 8888; http://manchesterartgallery.org; Mosley St; tours 20min/1hr free/£80; ⏱10am-5pm Mon-Wed & Fri-Sun, to 9pm Thu) where a superb collection of British and European art includes 37 Turner watercolours, and the country's best assemblage of Pre-Raphaelite art. The 20th-century

galleries include works by Lucien Freud, Francis Bacon, Stanley Spencer, Henry Moore and David Hockney. Next, hop on one of the city's swish trams to **MediaCityUK**, making for the **Lowry** (📞0161-876 2020; www.thelowry.com; Pier 8, Salford Quays; ⏱11am-6pm Sun-Fri, 10am-8pm Sat) to study 300 beautifully humanistic depictions of urban landscapes by LS Lowry (1887–1976), the local artist famous for painting matchstick figures amid the north's mill-dotted urban landscapes.

✖ 🛏 p47, p85, p211

The Drive >> A final, 35-mile, motorway cruise: after the A57 (M), join the M62 to roll towards Liverpool, eventually picking up the brown tourist signs for the car parks at the Albert Dock.

DETOUR: WEDGWOOD VISITOR CENTRE

Start: ⓮ **Manchester (p83)**

A 50-mile detour south from Manchester, largely via the M56/M6, leads to the **Wedgwood Visitor Centre** (📞01782-282986; www.worldofwedgwood.com; Wedgwood Dr, Barlaston; factory tour & museum adult/child £15/7.50, factory tour only £10/5, museum only £7.50/3.75; ⏱10am-5pm Mon-Fri, to 4pm Sat & Sun), 5 miles south of Stoke-on-Trent. The modern production plant for Josiah Wedgwood's porcelain empire, it also offers an insight into this whole area's defining industrial and artistic characteristic: ceramics – the region is still known as the Potteries to this day. Look out for extensive displays of historic pieces, including plenty of Wedgwood's delicate, neoclassical blue-and-white jasperware. The fascinating industrial process is revealed, and there's an interesting film on Josiah's life and work, including his involvement in canal-building and opposition to slavery.

TRIP HIGHLIGHT

⓯ Liverpool

A thriving city famous for music, football and wit, Liverpool also has, at **Albert Dock**, the country's largest collection of protected buildings. This World Heritage site includes the **Tate Liverpool** (📞0151-702 7400; www.tate.org.uk/liverpool; special exhibitions adult/child from £5/4; ⏱10am-5.50pm), with its substantial checklist of 20th-century artists. Just paces away, the **International Slavery Museum** (📞0151-478 4499; www.liverpoolmuseums.org.uk/ism; ⏱10am-5pm) is a clear, uncompromising and profoundly affecting depiction of slavery's unimaginable horrors. The nearby **Beatles Story** (📞0151-709 1963; www.beatlesstory.com; adult/child £14.95/9; ⏱9am-7pm, last admission 5pm) features plenty of genuine fab four memorabilia, a full-size replica Cavern Club (which was actually tiny) and the Abbey Rd studio where the lads recorded their first singles. A short walk north at **Pier Head** discover the trio of Edwardian buildings beloved by locals: the domed **Port of Liverpool Building** (1907), the Italian palazzo-style **Cunard Building** and the 1911 **Royal Liver Building**, crowned by Liverpool's symbol, a 5.5m copper **Liver Bird**.

🛏 p85

Eating & Sleeping

Bristol ❶

🛏 Brooks Guest House   B&B ££

(📞0117-930 0066; www.brooksguest
housebristol.com; Exchange Ave; d £90-130,
trailers £100-105; 🛜) Improbable as it seems,
three vintage Airstream trailers sit on the
AstroTurf of the bijou roof garden at this
central Bristol B&B. They're predictably tiny
but still feature seating areas and pocket-sized
bathrooms. In the guesthouse, bedrooms
are compact but pleasing, with olive colour
schemes and tartan throws.

Birmingham ❻

🛏 Hotel La Tour   Hotel ££

(📞0121-718 8000; http://hotel-latour.co.uk;
Albert St; d from £119; ❄🛜) Sunlight streams
through floor-to-ceiling windows into the public
areas and spacious rooms of this state-of-
the-art independent hotel, purpose-built
in 2012. Tech-savvy room features include
digitally controlled 'do not disturb' signs and
media hubs. There's a 24-hour gym and a
swish Modern British restaurant, **Mr White's
English Chophouse**, run by star chef Marco
Pierre White.

Leeds ❾

🛏 Quebecs   Boutique Hotel £££

(📞0113-244 8989; www.quebecshotel.co.uk;
9 Quebec St; d/ste from £99/179; @🛜)
Victorian grace at its opulent best is the
theme of Quebecs, a conversion of the former
Leeds & County Liberal Club. The elaborate
wood panelling and heraldic stained-glass
windows in the public areas are mirrored in the
contemporary design of the bedrooms. Booking
online can get you a suite for as little as half the
rack rate.

Newcastle-upon-Tyne ⓬

✘ Broad Chare   Gastropub ££

(📞0191-211 2144; www.thebroadchare.co.uk; 25
Broad Chare; mains £10-19.50; ⊗kitchen noon-
2.30pm & 5.30-10pm Mon-Sat, noon-5pm Sun)
Spiffing English classics and splendid cask ales
are served in the dark-wood bar and mezzanine
of this perfect gastropub. Starters such as
crispy pig ears, pork pies and venison terrine
are followed by mains including a divine grilled
pork chop with black pudding and cider sauce
and desserts such as treacle tart with walnut
brittle to finish.

Manchester ⓮

🛏 ABode   Hotel ££

(📞0161-247 7744; www.abodemanchester.
co.uk; 107 Piccadilly St; r from £100; ❄@🛜)
The original fittings at this converted textile
factory have been combined successfully with
61 bedrooms divided into four categories of
ever-increasing luxury: Comfortable, Desirable,
Enviable and Fabulous on Fifth, the latter being
five seriously swanky top-floor suites.

Liverpool ⓯

🛏 Hope Street Hotel   Boutique Hotel ££

(📞0151-709 3000; www.hopestreethotel.co.uk;
40 Hope St; r/ste from £90/120; @🛜) One
of the classiest digs in town is this handsome
boutique hotel on the city's most elegant
street. King-sized beds draped in Egyptian
cotton, oak floors with underfloor heating, LCD
TVs and sleek modern bathrooms are but the
most obvious touches of sophistication at this
supremely cool address. Breakfast (£16.50),
taken in the marvellous London Carriage Works,
is not included.

Southern & Eastern England

TEMPTING TRAILS FAN OUT ALL AROUND LONDON. After revelling in the capital's world-class sights, it's time to take to the road. Within an hour or two you're cruising down country lanes en route to fairy-tale castles and some of England's loveliest historic homes.

In this corner of the country, road trips are peppered with superb heritage sights. Spectacular cathedrals are a short hop from rejuvenated resorts; university cities are just a quick trip from imposing baronial piles.

Whether you're cresting rolling chalk ridges, meandering beside salt marshes or tracing trails down rustic lanes, these are irresistible drives.

Flatford Historic Willy Lott's House
MEL THOMPSON / SHUTTERSTOCK ©

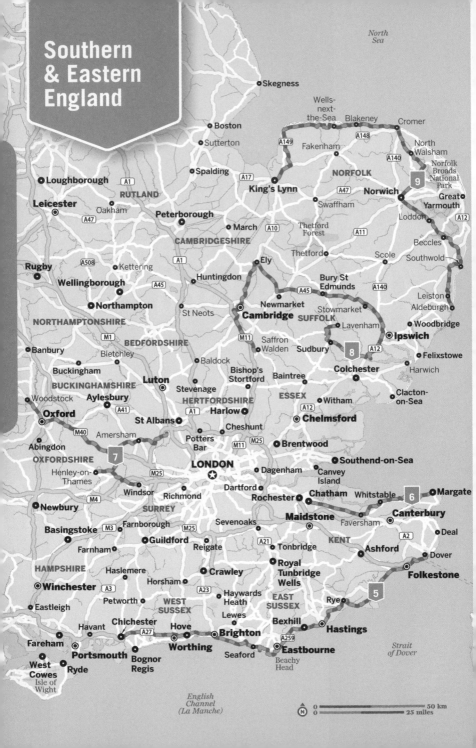

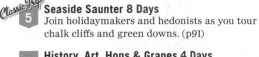

Brighton Century-old Brighton Pier

Seaside Saunter 8 Days
Classic Trip
5 Join holidaymakers and hedonists as you tour chalk cliffs and green downs. (p91)

6 **History, Art, Hops & Grapes 4 Days**
Hip resorts and foodie pit-stops galore on a Garden of England tour. (p101)

7 **Magic, Royalty & Dons 5–6 Days**
Pure class: a Queen's castle, university city and Harry Potter sights. (p109)

8 **Around the Cam 6–7 Days**
From exquisite, collegiate Cambridge to history-rich villages and stately homes. (p117)

9 **Suffolk-Norfolk Shore 8 Days**
Delight in fantastic seafood, bird-packed reserves, quaint creeks and wide, wide views. (p125)

 DON'T MISS

Dover Castle
Hidden deep below Dover's famous medieval defences is a set of secret WWII tunnels on Trip **5**

Christ Church Cathedral
This Oxford college's 12th-century, vaulted cathedral is as glorious as it is serene. See it on Trip **7**

Shepherd Neame Brewery
Many people bypass Faversham, but seeing how these traditional ales are made makes it well worth a detour on Trip **6**

Henry Blogg Museum
It may be bijou but the RNLI's life-saving exhibits on show here are absorbing, and include a full-sized lifeboat on Trip **9**

Willy Lott's House
It's not often you get to visit the site of a world-famous painting: see the setting for Constable's *The Hay Wain* on Trip **8**

89

Classic Trip

Seaside Saunter

5

This string of shingle beaches and chalk cliffs, grand old Victorian resorts and medieval castles covers quintessential ground when it comes to the British seaside experience.

TRIP HIGHLIGHTS

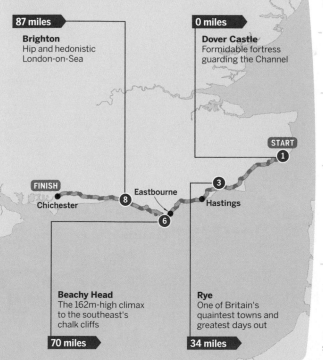

87 miles

Brighton
Hip and hedonistic
London-on-Sea

0 miles

Dover Castle
Formidable fortress
guarding the Channel

START
1

FINISH
8   Eastbourne   3
Chichester   Hastings
6

Beachy Head
The 162m-high climax
to the southeast's
chalk cliffs

70 miles

Rye
One of Britain's
quaintest towns and
greatest days out

34 miles

8 DAYS
117 MILES / 188KM

GREAT FOR...

BEST TIME TO GO
April to October, when
the weather is at its
warmest and driest.

ESSENTIAL
PHOTO
The impressive view
of the Seven Sisters
chalk cliffs from
Cuckmere Haven.

BEST FOR
SHOPPING
Brighton's Lanes and
North Laine spots
have some of the best
shopping in the UK.

Classic Trip

5 Seaside Saunter

This week-long saunter along the coast of Kent and Sussex takes you across undulating chalk cliffs, over the downs and through marshes, calling at some of the most famous names on the south's seaside map in the process. London's riviera bears many reminders of those who have pitched up on this shingle coast, from holidaying Victorians to some famous invaders of yesteryear.

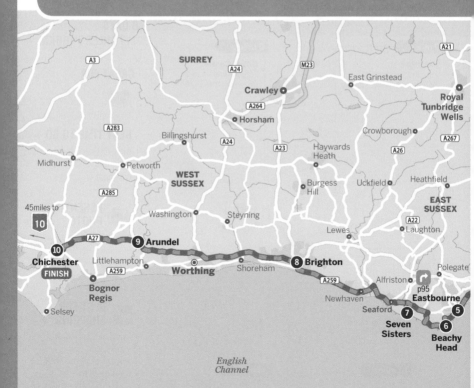

❶ Dover

Dover is hardly a highlight of the south coast, but this port city has a stellar attraction – a huge **castle** (EH; adult/child £18.30/11; ⏰10am-6pm Apr-Jul & Sep, 9.30am-6pm Aug, to 5pm Oct, 10am-4pm Sat & Sun Nov-Mar; ⓟ) that has guarded England's closest point to France since medieval times.

The 12th-century Great Tower, with walls up to 7m thick, is a medieval warren filled with interactive exhibits and light-and-sound shows that take visitors back to the times of Henry II.

However, the biggest draw is the network of secret wartime tunnels, first excavated during the Napoleonic Wars and then expanded to house a command post and hospital in WWII. The highly enjoyable 50-minute guided tour (every 20 minutes, included in the ticket price) tells the story of one of Britain's most famous wartime operations, code-named Dynamo, which was directed from here in 1940 and oversaw the

LINK YOUR TRIP

6 History, Art, Hops & Grapes

The start of this North Kent route begins in Margate, just 22 miles north of Dover.

10 Winchester, Glastonbury & Bath

Chichester is just 42 miles from historic Winchester.

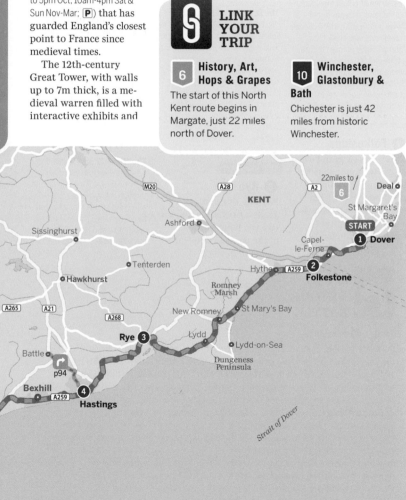

evacuation of thousands from the beaches at Dunkirk.

✖ 🛏 p99

The Drive » Follow the London-bound foreign lorries out of Dover on the M20, which climbs steeply onto the chalk cliffs. After a couple of miles there's a turn-off for Capel-le-Ferne where you'll find the Battle of Britain Monument. The suburbs of Folkestone, your next stop, lie just beyond (9 miles in total).

❷ Folkestone

This formerly grand old resort was once a favourite stomping ground of royal bon viveur King Edward VII but today is a wonderfully forgotten piece of England's

seaside past. Take a stroll through the seafront Leas Coastal Park with its subtropical flora, then halt for fish and chips at the old fish market before ambling up through the Creative Quarter, Folkestone's old town now occupied by artists' studios and craft shops.

The Drive » Sat-navs will send you back to the M20, but instead follow the coastal A259 to Hythe. This is the terminus of the idyllic Romney Hythe & Dymchurch narrow-gauge railway, worth a day off the road itself. At New Romney the road swings inland and crosses the Romney Marsh, a sweep of wetland flats dotted with grazing sheep and wind turbines. Total 25 miles.

TRIP HIGHLIGHT

❸ Rye

Possibly the south of England's quaintest town, Rye is a little nugget of the past, a medieval

settlement that looks like it's been dunked in formaldehyde and left on the shelf for all to admire. Cobbled lanes, mysterious passageways and crooked Tudor buildings echo to the tales of resident smugglers, ghosts and writers.

Wandering and browsing are the way to go here but the town's main sight is the **Church of St Mary the Virgin** (Church Sq; tower adult/child £3.50/1; ⏰9am-5.30pm Apr-Sep, to 4.30pm Nov-Mar), a hotchpotch of medieval and later styles. Climb the tower for pretty views of the town and surroundings.

✖ 🛏 p99

The Drive » Just 12 miles separate Rye from your next stop, Hastings. The route passes through pretty Winchelsea – watch out for the steep hairpin turn below the village. There's another steep climb through the suburbs of Hastings before

➡ DETOUR: BATTLE

Start: ❹ Hastings

If there's one date that's seared itself into every English schoolchild's brain, it's 1066, the year of the most famous battle in the country's history – the Battle of Hastings – which saw invading French duke William of Normandy, aka William the Conqueror, score a decisive victory over local king Harold. This major bend in the road in English history actually took place 6 miles north of Hastings in what is now the town of Battle.

Battle Abbey (EH; adult/child £10.10/6; ⏰10am-6pm Apr-Sep, to 4pm Sat & Sun Oct-Mar) was built on the battlefield, a penance ordered by the pope for the loss of life incurred here. Only the foundations of the original church remain; the altar's position is supposedly the spot King Harold famously took an arrow in his eye. High-tech interactive presentations and a film at the visitor centre, as well as blow-by-blow audio tours, do their utmost to bring the battle to life. The biggest crowds turn up here mid-October to witness the annual re-enactment on the original battlefield.

a quick descent to back to sea level and Hastings seafront.

④ Hastings

Forever associated with the Norman invasion of 1066, Hastings thrived as one of the Cinque Ports and, in its Victorian heyday, was one of the country's most fashionable resorts. After a period of steady decline, the town is enjoying a mini-renaissance.

The beach and new pier are the biggest draws, but Hastings also has several worthwhile museums and lots of independent shops. Away from the old town, the most interesting neighbourhood is the **Stade** (Rock-A-Nore Rd), home to distinctive black clapboard structures known as Net Shops. These were built to store fishing gear back in the 17th century, but some now house fishmongers.

🛏 p99

The Drive » Follow the A259 along the coast as far as Bexhill, where you could stop off to view the art deco De La Warr Pavilion. Stick to the A259 (as opposed to the A27) at Pevensey, site of a castle built by the Romans – this will eventually bring you past Eastbourne's Sovereign Harbour and along Britain's most impressive seafront. Total distance 17 miles.

⑤ Eastbourne

'Britain's sunniest town' welcomes visitors with a grand seafront, white-

DETOUR:
SOUTH DOWNS
NATIONAL PARK

Start: ⑤ Eastbourne

The UK's newest national park, South Downs National Park is more than 600 sq miles of rolling chalk downs that stretches west from Eastbourne to Winchester, a distance of about 100 miles. A long-distance hiking trail called the South Downs Way famously extends its entire length: the ridge hike takes at least 10 days and affords amazing views much of the way. However, many of the route's most interesting and prettiest locations can be found just west of Eastbourne and can be reached on foot in a there-and-back day walk, or by using local buses.

washed late-Victorian hotels and palm trees lining the Channel, the scene given focus by one of the country's finest Victorian piers. Associated primarily with sedate retirement, Eastbourne has had a shot in the arm in recent years with huge Polish and student communities arriving to lower the average age.

The traditional seaside duo of beach and pier are the main draws, but the **Towner Art Gallery** (📞01323-434670; www. townereastbourne.org.uk; Devonshire Park, College Rd; ⏱10am-5pm Tue-Sun) has added significant cultural interest. Another major development is the creation of the South Downs National Park that nudges Eastbourne's western suburbs. The town is the start and end point for a hike along the 100-mile South Downs Way, which passes through the park.

The Drive » To reach Beachy Head (3.5 miles away), drive west along Eastbourne seafront until the road turns inland and begins to climb. A brown tourist sign points the way to the famous cliff along a narrow road. There's ample parking around the area.

TRIP HIGHLIGHT

⑥ Beachy Head

At 162m tall, the cliffs of Beachy Head are the highest point of the chalky rock faces that slice across the rugged coastline at the southern end of the South Downs. It's a spot of thrilling beauty, the brilliant white chalk rising high into the blue Sussex sky. At the foot of the cliffs stands a much-photographed, candy-striped lighthouse.

If you follow the clifftop path, you'll stumble upon the tiny seaside hamlet of **Birling Gap**. The cafe is currently closed due to cliff falls

Classic Trip

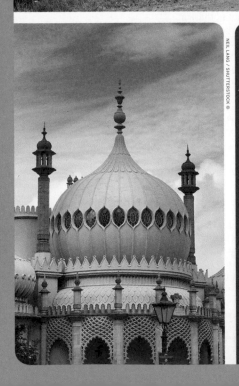

WHY THIS IS A CLASSIC TRIP
MARC DI DUCA, WRITER

As a resident of England's southeast corner for over a decade, I've driven this stretch, or sections of it, many times and never tire of its undulating downland landscapes, quaint flint villages, seaside experiences for every taste and grandly fading Victoriana. This is a pre-motorway route, with A-class roads often passing straight through towns it links, another nostalgic experience this most enjoyable of routes serves up.

Above: Chalk cliffs of the Seven Sisters
Left: Brighton's Royal Pavilion, built in the 1820s
Right: Colton's Gate at Dover Castle, Kent

FULCANELLI / SHUTTERSTOCK ©

but the secluded beach is still a sun-trap popular with locals and walkers taking a breather.

The Drive » Your next stop, the Seven Sisters, is best viewed from Cuckmere Haven, 6 miles away. From the clifftop head to Birling Gap then join the A259 at East Dean. Leave your car at the Cuckmere Inn in Exceat and continue towards the sea on foot, following the slow River Cuckmere.

❼ Seven Sisters

The undulating chalk cliffs of the Seven Sisters create one of the southeast's quintessential views. The best place to admire them is from Cuckmere Haven, the only spot on England's south coast where a river meets the sea with no town to keep it company. The walk from the car park at Exceat down to the shingle beach is a pleasant one, following the crazily meandering River Cuckmere all the way.

The Drive » Some 17 miles divide Cuckmere Haven from Brighton, your next halt. The A259 passes straight through Seaford and Newhaven, the latter home to an obscure cross-Channel ferry service. Nearer to Brighton, Rottingdean was home to Rudyard Kipling from 1897 to 1902. The A259 becomes Brighton seafront just beyond.

TRIP HIGHLIGHT

❽ Brighton

Brighton warrants a couple of days' exploration. This colourful city evokes

many images for the British but one thing is certain: with its bohemian, cosmopolitan and hedonistic vibe, Brighton is where England's seaside experience goes from cold to cool. Outside London it boasts the south's best shopping and nightlife and is the de facto gay capital of the UK.

Away from the beach, top billing goes to the **Royal Pavilion** (☎03000-290901; http://brighton museums.org.uk/royalpavilion; Royal Pavilion Gardens; adult/child £12.30/6.90; ◷9.30am-5.45pm Apr-Sep, 10am-5.15pm Oct-Mar), the eye-popping palace party pad of Prince George, later Prince Regent and then King George IV. It's one of the most opulent buildings in England, packed with weird-and-wonderful interiors and outrageous chinoiserie.

The **i360 Tower** (☎03337-720 360; www. britishairwaysi360.com; Lower King's Rd; adult/child £15/7.50; ◷10am-7.30pm, till 9.30pm Fri & Sat) opened in 2016 at the point the now-defunct West Pier used to make landfall. The world's most slender tower is a brutal, 162m-tall column of reinforced steel and concrete rising rudely from the seafront, Take the huge glass

doughnut 138m above the city for gob-smacking vistas of the coast.

✕ 🛏 p73, p99

The Drive » There are two routes you can take to reach the next port of call at Arundel, 23 miles to the west. The A259 and the A27 run parallel to each other, the latter a much quicker option, the former a more interesting drive through Worthing and Littlehampton.

❾ Arundel

Arguably the prettiest town in West Sussex, Arundel is clustered around a vast fairy-tale **castle** (www.arundelcastle. org; adult/child £18/9; ◷10am-5pm Tue-Sun Easter-Oct), home to the Dukes of Norfolk for centuries.

Arundel's ostentatious 19th-century **cathedral** (www.arundelcathedral.org; London Rd; ◷9am-6pm Apr-Oct, to dusk Nov-Mar) is the other dominating feature of the town's skyline. Commissioned by the 15th duke of Norfolk in 1868, this impressive structure was designed by Joseph Aloysius Hansom (inventor of the Hansom cab) in French Gothic style.

When you're done with the sights, Arundel's hilly streets overflow with antique emporiums, teashops and eateries.

The Drive » A mere 11 miles separate Arundel from your final stop, the cathedral city of Chichester and capital of West Sussex. The only feasible route is to take the fast A27 all the way.

❿ Chichester

Founded by the Romans, this lively Georgian market town is still almost encircled by its medieval town walls that keep watch over the plains between the South Downs and the sea. Away from the sights, Chichester has four pedestrianised shopping streets that meet at the Chichester Cross, the town's epicentre.

Top billing here naturally goes to **Chichester Cathedral** (www.chichester cathedral.org.uk; West St; ◷7.15am-7pm, free tours 11.15am & 2.30pm Mon-Sat), begun in 1075 and largely rebuilt in the 13th century. The spire dates from the 19th century, when its predecessor famously toppled over. Inside, three storeys of beautiful arches sweep upwards and Romanesque carvings are dotted around. Interesting features to track down include a smudgy stained-glass window added by artist Marc Chagall in 1978 and a section of Roman mosaic flooring.

The **Novium** (www. thenovium.org; Tower St; ◷10am-5pm Mon-Sat, to 4pm Sun Apr-Oct, 10am-5pm Mon-Sat Nov-Mar) is Chichester's purpose-built museum, a home for the eclectic collections of the erstwhile District Museum, built around a set of Roman baths (thermae) discovered in the 1970s.

🛏 p99

Eating & Sleeping

Dover ❶

✕ Allotment
British ££

(www.theallotmentdover.com; 9 High St; mains £8.50-16; ⏱8.30am-10pm Tue-Sat) Dover's best dining spot plates up local fish and meat from around Canterbury, seasoned with herbs from the tranquil garden out back, for breakfast, lunch and dinner. Cleanse your palette with a Kentish wine in a relaxed, understated setting as you admire the view of the Maison Dieu (13th-century pilgrims' hospital) directly opposite through the exquisite stained-glass frontage.

🛏 Dover Marina Hotel
Hotel ££

(☎01304-203633; www.dovermarinahotel.co.uk; Waterloo Cres; r £97-164; 🛜) Just a few steps from Dover's beach, this seafront hotel crams 81 rooms of varying dimensions into a gently curving 1870s edifice. The undulating corridors show the building's age, but there's nothing wonky about the rooms with their trendy fabrics and contemporary artwork. Half the rooms have sea views and 10 boast balconies.

Rye ❸

✕ Landgate Bistro
British ££

(www.landgatebistro.co.uk; 5-6 Landgate; mains £14-20; ⏱noon-3.30pm Sat & Sun, 7-11pm Wed-Sat) Escape the medieval excesses of Rye's central eateries to this fresh-feeling bistro, slightly off the tourist trail near the impressive 14th-century Landgate. The focus here is on competently crafted dishes using local lamb and fish. The dining space is understated with tables gathered around an ancient fireplace.

🛏 Jeake's House
Hotel ££

(☎01797-222828; www.jeakeshouse.com; Mermaid St; s/d from £75/95; 🅿🛜) This 17th-century town house once belonged to US poet Conrad Aitken. The 11 rooms are named after writers who stayed here. The decor was probably slightly less bold then, minus the beeswaxed antiques and lavish drapery. Take a pew in the snug book-lined bar and enjoy breakfast in an 18th-century former Quaker chapel.

Hastings ❹

🛏 Swan House
B&B ££

(☎01424-430014; www.swanhousehastings.co.uk; 1 Hill St; s/d from £90/120; @🛜) Inside its 15th-century timbered shell, this place blends contemporary and vintage chic to perfection. The four rooms feature organic toiletries, fresh flowers, hand-painted walls and huge beds. The guest lounge, where painted floorboards and striking modern sculpture rub shoulders with beams and a huge stone fireplace, is a stunner.

Brighton ❽

✕ Terre à Terre
Vegetarian ££

(☎01273-729051; www.terreaterre.co.uk; 71 East St; mains £15; ⏱noon-10.30pm Mon-Fri, 10am-11pm Sat, 10am-10pm Sun; 🍴) Even staunch meat eaters will rave about this legendary vegetarian restaurant. A sublime dining experience, from the vibrant modern space to the entertaining menus and inventive dishes stuffed with excitingly zingy ingredients. There's also plenty for vegans. Desserts are on the steep side.

🛏 Hotel Una
Boutique Hotel £££

(☎01273-820464; www.hotel-una.co.uk; 55-56 Regency Sq; s £55-75, d £115-200, all incl breakfast; ❄🛜) All of the 19 generous rooms here wow guests with their bold-patterned fabrics, supersized leather sofas, in-room free-standing baths and vegan, veggie or carnivorous breakfast in bed. Some, such as the two-level suite with its own mini-cinema, and the under-pavement chambers with their own spa and Jacuzzi, are truly show-stopping and not as expensive as you might expect.

Chichester ❿

🛏 Trents
B&B ££

(☎01243-773714; www.trentschichester.co.uk; 50 South St; d from £75; 🛜) Just about the only place to sleep in the thick of the city centre action, the five snazzy rooms above this trendy bar-cum-restaurant are understandably popular.

History, Art, Hops & Grapes

6

From Margate to Chatham, this eclectic route follows the north Kent coast, a stretch of shingle and shipyards, Roman heritage and seaside fun that's only just being discovered.

TRIP HIGHLIGHTS

0 miles

Margate
See the stellar Turner contemporary gallery

25 miles

Seasalter
Tuck in at East Kent's only Michelin-starred eatery

Chatham
FINISH

Sittingbourne

Herne Bay Birchington

④ ⑤ ⑥

① START

Faversham
Tour the country's oldest brewery

30 miles

Whitstable
Enjoy the south's finest oysters, harvested here since Roman times

21 miles

**4 DAYS
46 MILES / 74KM**

GREAT FOR...

BEST TIME TO GO
April to October sees mild temperatures and the least rainfall.

ESSENTIAL PHOTO
The Reculver Towers rising high above the sea is one of the Kent coast's most memorable images.

BEST FOR FOODIES
The Sportsman Pub has the only Michelin star in this part of the world.

Margate Turner Contemporary art gallery

6 History, Art, Hops & Grapes

From Margate's seafront to the oyster houses of gentrified Whitstable, from the shipping heritage of Chatham to Britain's oldest brewery in Faversham, the theme along Kent's north coast is local tradition. Kent is the 'Garden of England' and produces the tastiest of ingredients – most notably the country's finest hops – but on this trip you'll also discover what a vital role the sea has played in the county's traditional life.

TRIP HIGHLIGHT

❶ Margate

A popular resort for more than two centuries, Margate's late-20th-century slump was long and bleak. But this grand old seaside town, with fine-sand beaches and artistic associations, has bounced off the bottom and there's no greater symbol of this rejuvenation than the spectacular **Turner Contemporary** (www.turnercontemporary.org; Rendezvous; ⊙10am-6pm Tue-Sun) **art gallery, bolted**

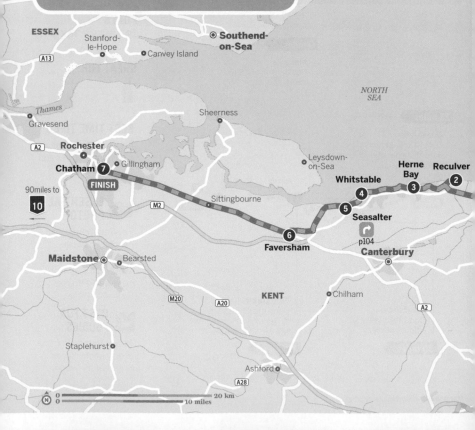

together on the site of the seafront guesthouse where master painter JMW Turner used to stay. Within the impressive building are staged top-notch contemporary installations by high-calibre artists such as Tracey Emin (who grew up in Margate) and Alex Katz.

Another of Margate's vital signs to have re-appeared in recent years is **Dreamland** (www.dream land.co.uk; Marine Terrace; adult/child £18/15; ⏱11am-9pm May-Oct), a once-famous amusement park that had lain derelict for a decade. The main attraction here is the so-called Scenic Railway, a 1920s heritage-listed wooden rollercoaster that was rebuilt after an arson attack in 2008, but there are plenty of other period rides and attractions to keep adults and kiddies thrilled.

✕ ⌂ p107

The Drive » From Margate seafront head east along Canterbury Rd until you come to the roundabout junction with the A299. Follow this until you see the turn-off for Reculver. The journey is around 12 miles long.

- - - - - - - - - - - - - -

➋ Reculver

When the Romans first arrived in Britain they built two fortresses at either end of the strategic Wantsum Channel, a stretch of water that divided the Isle of Thanet from the mainland. The channel silted up in the 16th century but the ruins of the fortresses remain – Richborough near Sandwich and Reculver here on the north Kent coast. The Roman remnants here are not as impressive as the ruins of the 12th-century church whose twin towers can be seen for miles along the coast. This was part of an Anglo-Saxon monastery but today the site, creeping ever closer to the sea, is deserted.

The Drive » Just 4.5 miles divide Reculver and Herne Bay, your next stop. Don't head back to the A299 but take the back roads along the coast through residential areas and with the occasional sea view.

- - - - - - - - - - - - - -

➌ Herne Bay

The seaside town of Herne Bay is light on sights but does have a long shingle beach that extends for miles either side of town. The shingle shelves ever so gradually into the North Sea, making this ideal territory for water sports and hot-weather water fun. The Reculver Country Park lines the coast west of the town, a wild stretch

Westgate-on-Sea
START
➊ **Margate**
Birchington
Broadstairs
Ramsgate
Ash
Sandwich
Eastry
English Channel (La Manche)
Deal
St Margaret's Bay
Dover
5
Strait of Dover

⑧ **LINK YOUR TRIP**

Seaside Saunter
5 It's just 22 miles from Margate to Dover, the start of an epic route along the south coast.

Winchester, Glastonbury & Bath
10 It looks a long way on the map, but it's a mere two hours from Chatham to Winchester.

SOUTHERN & EASTERN ENGLAND 6 HISTORY, ART, HOPS & GRAPES

of rocky shore backed by cliffs, operated by the Kent Wildlife Trust.

The Drive » Herne Bay and Whitstable are almost joined at the hip, but the drive from the centre of one to the centre of the other is still 5 miles. The best routing is to head onto the A299 then turn off at Tankerton, the local main road morphing eventually into Whitstable's high street.

TRIP HIGHLIGHT

❹ Whitstable

Oysters, weatherboard houses, a shingle beach, an old-fashioned high street and an easy-going vibe – these are the factors that attract so many Londoners to Whitstable, just a few miles north of Canterbury. It's most fa-mous for its oysters, best sampled at **Wheeler's Oyster Bar** (☏01227-273311; www.wheelersoysterbar.com; 8 High St; mains £18.50-22.50; ☺10.30am-9pm Mon, Tue & Thu, 10.15am-9.30pm Fri, 10am-10pm Sat, 11.30am-9pm Sun), which has been offering the fabled molluscs since 1856. The town holds an annual oyster festival in

DETOUR: CANTERBURY

Start: ❹ Whitstable

It's an easy 8-mile drive south from Whitstable to Canterbury, which tops the charts for English cathedral cities and is one of southern England's biggest attractions. Many consider the World Heritage–listed cathedral that dominates its centre to be one of Europe's finest, and the town's narrow medieval alleyways, riverside gardens and ancient city walls are a joy to explore. But Canterbury isn't just a showpiece for the past – it's a bustling, busy place with an energetic student population and a wide choice of contemporary bars, restaurants, venues and independent shops.

Canterbury Cathedral (www.canterbury-cathedral.org; adult/concession £12/10.50, tours £5/4, audioguide £4/3; ☺9am-5.30pm Mon-Sat, 12.30-2.30pm Sun) is a rich repository of more than 1400 years of Christian history, and the Church of England's mother ship is a truly extraordinary place. This Gothic cathedral, the highlight of the city's World Heritage sites, is southeast England's top tourist attraction as well as a place of worship. It's also the site of English history's most famous murder: Archbishop Thomas Becket was done in here in 1170. Allow at least two hours to do the cathedral justice.

Of the city's other sites, the **Heritage Museum** (www.canterbury-museums.co.uk; Stour St; adult/child £8/free; ☺11am-5pm daily) is housed in a fine 14th-century building, once the Poor Priests' Hospital. It contains a jumble of exhibits ranging from pre-Roman times to the assassination of Thomas Becket, and from the likes of Joseph Conrad to locally born celebs. The kids' room is excellent, with a memorable glimpse of real medieval poo among other fun activities. Train fans can admire the Invicta locomotive, which ran on the world's third passenger railway, the 'Crab & Winkle' Canterbury–Whitstable line.

For a different perspective of the city's history, take a River Stour cruise with **Canterbury Historic River Tours** (☏07790-534744; www.canterburyrivertours.co.uk; Kings Bridge; adult/child £9/5; ☺10am-5pm Mar-Oct). Knowledgeable guides double up as energetic oarsmen on these fascinating, multi-award-winning trips, which depart from behind the Old Weaver's House.

✕ 🛏 p107

Seasalter Oysters at the Sportsman Pub

late July. The modest local **museum** (www.canter burymuseums.co.uk; 5 Oxford St; adult/concession £3/2; ⊙11am-4.30pm) has glass cases examining Whitstable's oyster industry, the Crab & Winkle Railway, which once ran from Canterbury, and the local fishing fleet, as well as a corner dedicated to actor Peter Cushing, star of several Hammer Horror films and the town's most famous resident, who died in 1994.

✕ ⊨ p107

The Drive ≫ It's 4 miles to the next stop, the Sportsman

Pub. From Whitstable centre follow Joy Lane until it becomes Faversham Rd – this will take you all the way to Seasalter, the village this Michelin-starred tavern calls home.

TRIP HIGHLIGHT

5 Seasalter

The anonymous and oddly named village of Seasalter would hardly receive a trickle of visitors were it not for the **Sportsman Pub** (www. thesportsmanseasalter.co.uk; Faversham Rd; mains around £20; ⊙ restaurant noon-2pm & 7-9pm Tue-Sat, 12.30-2.45pm Sun, bar noon-3pm & 6-11pm Tue-Sat, noon-10pm Sun),

East Kent's only eatery adorned with a Michelin star. Local ingredients from sea, marsh and woods are crafted by Whitstable-born chef Stephen Harris into taste-packed Kentish creations that have food critics drooling at the mouth. Oysters dominate the starter line-up, fish the mains menu. All the butter, salt and cured meats here are made by the chef himself. It's a real treat and proof that Michelin-standard food can be served in an informal bar setting and at a price affordable to most.

The Drive » From the culinary delights of Seasalter take the 5-mile drive east to Faversham for one of Kent's drinking highlights. From the pub take Seasalter Rd south until just after Goodnestone, where you should turn right onto the B2040 – this will take you into Faversham.

TRIP HIGHLIGHT

6 Faversham

The undervisited market town of Faversham is a pleasant old place packed with architecture from medieval times right up to the present day. Light on blockbuster sights, it does have one big draw – the **Shepherd Neame Brewery** (☎01795-542016; www.shepherdneame.co.uk; 10 Court St, Faversham; tours £11.50), Britain's oldest and the pride of Kent when it comes to traditional ales made using the county's unrivalled

hops. There are brewery tours, ale samplers' suppers, beer and food matching evenings, but you'll have to book ahead for all of these as it's very popular. Otherwise Shepherd Neame ale is available across the county, the most famous brand being the aptly named Spitfire.

The Drive » Faversham to Chatham is the longest uninterrupted stretch on this route at 19 miles. Shun the M2 for the 'old' A2, the original Roman road that runs almost arrow-straight from Canterbury to the River Medway.

7 Chatham

On the Medway riverfront, the **Chatham Historic Dockyard** (☎01634-823800; www.thedockyard.co.uk; Dock Rd; adult/child £22/13; ⏰10am-4pm mid-Feb–Mar & Nov, to

6pm Apr-Oct), a candidate for Unesco heritage status, occupies a third of what was once the Royal Navy's main dock facility. It is possibly the most complete 18th-century dock in the world and has been transformed into a maritime museum examining the Age of Sail. Exhibits include well-restored ships, exhibitions on a variety of shipbuilding themes and a working steam railway.

Chatham's other sight of note is **Dickens World** (☎0844-858 6656; www.dickensworld.co.uk; Leviathan Way; admission £5.50; ⏰10am-5.30pm Sat & Sun), a multi-million-pound leisure complex that seeks to re-create the novels of Charles Dickens in theme-park style. Tours leave every hour and must be booked in advance.

Eating & Sleeping

Margate ❶

✕ Mad Hatter   Cafe £
(www.facebook.com/TheMadHatterMargate;
9 Lombard St; snacks & light meals £3.50-11;
🕐11am-5.30pm Sat, other days occasionally
Jul & Aug) This unmissable, completely cuckoo
eatery run by a top-hatted proprietor packs
two rooms of a 1690s house with regalia and
knick-knackery from down the ages. Christmas
decorations stay up all year and the toilets are
original Victorian porcelain. The yummy cakes
and snacks are all homemade. Just a shame it
isn't open more often.

🛏 Reading Rooms   B&B £££
(☎01843-225166; www.thereadingrooms
margate.co.uk; 31 Hawley Sq; r £180; 🛜)
Occupying an unmarked 18th-century Georgian
town house in a tranquil square just five
minutes' walk from the sea, this luxury boutique
B&B is as stylish as they come. Generously cut
rooms with waxed wooden floors and beautiful
French antique reproduction furniture contrast
with the 21st-century bathrooms fragrant with
Ren cosmetics. Breakfast is served in your
room. Bookings essential; no children or pets.

Whitstable ❹

✕ Samphire   Modern British ££
(☎01227-770075; www.samphirewhitstable.
co.uk; 4 High St; mains £10-19; 🕐10am-10pm)
The shabby chic jumble of tables and chairs,
big-print wallpaper and blackboard menus
create the perfect stage for meticulously
crafted mains containing East Kent's most
flavour-packed ingredients. An interesting side

dish is its namesake samphire, an asparagus-
like plant that grows on sea-sprayed rocks and
cliffs, often found on menus in these parts.

🛏 Hotel Continental   Hotel ££
(☎01227-280280; www.hotelcontinental.co.uk;
29 Beach Walk; r from £75; 🛜) The rooms at
this elegant seaside art-deco building have
undergone a complete refit and are now bright
and breezy quarters with light-painted wood
cladding, brilliant white beds and sparkling
bathrooms. There's a decent restaurant and bar
on the premises.

Canterbury: Detour

✕ Tiny Tim's Tearoom   Cafe £
(www.tinytimstearoom.com; 34 St Margaret's
St; mains £6-10.50; 🕐9.30am-5pm Tue-Sat,
10.30am-4pm Sun) It's no mean feat to be
declared 'Kent Tearoom of the Year' but this
swish 1930s cafe was awarded the accolade in
2015. It offers hungry shoppers big breakfasts
bursting with Kentish ingredients, and tiers of
cakes, crumpets, cucumber sandwiches and
scones plastered in clotted cream. On busy
shopping days you are guaranteed to queue for
a table.

🛏 Arthouse B&B   B&B ££
(☎07976-725457; www.arthousebandb.com;
24 London Rd; r from £65; 🅿🛜) A night at
Canterbury's most laid-back digs, housed in a
19th-century fire station, is a bit like sleeping
over at a really cool art student's pad. The
theme is funky and eclectic, with furniture by
local designers and artwork by the instantly
likeable artist owners, who have a house-studio
out back.

Magic, Royalty & Dons

7

West of London's bright lights, venture into a wonderfully rewarding world of timeworn castles, literary legends, glorious gardens, Harry Potter frenzy and architectural wizardry.

TRIP HIGHLIGHTS

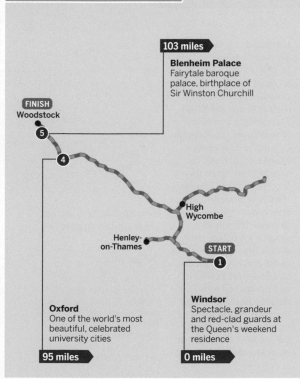

103 miles

Blenheim Palace
Fairytale baroque palace, birthplace of Sir Winston Churchill

FINISH
Woodstock
5

4

High Wycombe

Henley-on-Thames

START
1

Oxford
One of the world's most beautiful, celebrated university cities

95 miles

Windsor
Spectacle, grandeur and red-clad guards at the Queen's weekend residence

0 miles

5–6 DAYS
105 MILES / 169KM

GREAT FOR...

BEST TIME TO GO
Anytime; particularly April to July, for flower-filled gardens and sunny weather.

ESSENTIAL PHOTO
Any of Oxford's stunning, spire-topped colleges, but especially Christ Church.

BEST FOR FAMILIES
Disappearing into Harry Potter's world at Warner Bros Studio Tour.

Windsor The royal residence of Windsor Castle

7 Magic, Royalty & Dons

Zigzagging from whimsical Windsor to scholarly Oxford, this richly varied trip whisks you off to some of south England's most magical destinations. You'll find royal flair and the world's oldest continually occupied fortress in Windsor, one of the country's most magnificent stately homes at Blenheim, and architectural wonders, academic buzz and historical curiosities in Oxford. Then there's Henley-on-Thames' rowing extravaganza, Woodstock's prosperous charm and, for detouring adventurers, landscaped Stowe.

TRIP HIGHLIGHT

1 Windsor

Flaunting royal pomp at every turn, from the ceremonious changing of the guards to the magnificent outdoor marvel that is **Windsor Great Park** (📞01753-860222; www.windsorgreatpark.co.uk; ☺dawn-dusk), Windsor has a rather surreal atmosphere. Crowning the Thames-side town is Windsor Castle – a majestic vision of battlements and towers.

The **castle** (📞0303 123 7304; www.royalcollection. org.uk; Castle Hill; adult/child £20/11.70; ☺9.30am-5.15pm Mar-Oct, 9.45am-4.15pm Nov-Feb; ♿; 🚌702 from London Victoria, 🚆London Waterloo to Windsor & Eton Riverside, 🚆London Paddington to Windsor & Eton Central via Slough) is one of the Queen's principal residences; if she's at home, the Royal Standard flies from the Round Tower. William the Conqueror first established a royal dwelling here in 1080. Since then successive monarchs have rebuilt, remodelled and refurbished the complex to create the massive, sumptuous palace that stands here today, with its lavish State Apartments and beautiful St George's and Albert Memorial chapels. Book tickets online to avoid queues. The triumphant changing of the guards takes place at 11am Monday to Saturday from April to July, and on alternate days August to March.

🍴 🛏 p115

The Drive » This section of the drive involves some inevitable big roads, but they'll speed by! Head west out of Windsor along Arthur Rd (which becomes Maidenhead Rd), taking the A308 5 miles northwest to bypass the M4

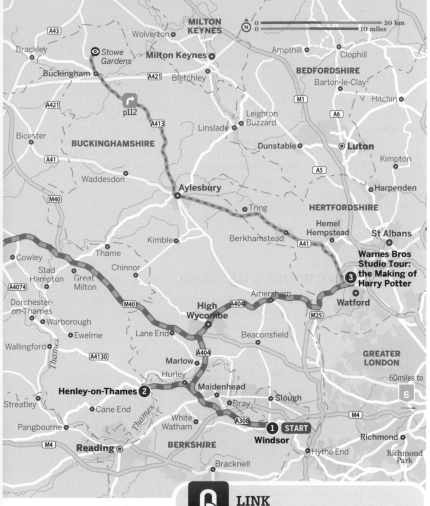

motorway. Follow signs onto
the A404(M), head 3.5 miles
northwest and exit onto the
A4130. It's 6 miles northwest to
Henley-on-Thames.

- - - - - - - - - - - -

❷ Henley-on-Thames

Standing elegantly beside
the Thames, Henley is
an attractive commuter

LINK YOUR TRIP

15 **Shakespeare & Rolling Hills**

Whizz 20 miles west
from Oxford to Burford
to get lost in this
in-depth tour of the
dreamy gold-tinged
Cotswolds.

6 **History, Art, Hops & Grapes**

From Windsor, skirt 60
miles around London's
southern edge to meet
this culture-fuelled jaunt
at Royal Tunbridge Wells.

town of red-brick and half-timbered houses, buzzy pubs, lovely riverside saunters and a long-established rowing tradition. For the full lowdown, drop into the excellent, modern **River & Rowing Museum** (☎01491-415600; www.rrm.co.uk; Mill Meadows; adult/child £11/9; ☺10am-5pm; **P**), where the airy 1st-floor galleries tell the story of rowing as an Olympic sport,

alongside striking boat displays that include the early-19th-century Royal Oak, Britain's oldest racing boat.

If you're lucky enough to be visiting in July, book ahead for the world-famous **Henley Royal Regatta** (www.hrr. co.uk; tickets £27-30; ☺Jul), a high-calibre rowing tournament that doubles up as a major social fixture for the upper classes.

The Drive ≫ Whizz 10.5 miles northeast from Henley to High Wycombe (A4130 and A404). It's mostly major roads into London from here, but, for a prettier, more rural drive, continue 15 miles northeast along the A404, passing Amersham, through the Chilterns Area of Outstanding Natural Beauty (AONB). Join the M25; 5 miles northeast is Warner Bros Studio Tour (signposted), with free parking.

DETOUR: STOWE HOUSE & GARDENS

Start: ❸ Warner Bros Studio Tour: The Making of Harry Potter

From Leavesden and the Harry Potter studios, it's a rewarding 41-mile diversion northwest to Stowe, home to some of England's most spectacularly beautiful gardens. Take the A41 23 miles northwest to Aylesbury, then the A413 16 miles northwest to Buckingham. From here, brown signs lead along fabulous 1.5-mile-long tree-lined Stowe Ave to Stowe.

Covering 160 hectares, Stowe's glorious **gardens** (NT; ☎01280-817156; www. nationaltrust.org.uk; New Inn Farm; adult/child £11.20/5.60; ☺10am-6pm Mar-Oct, to 4pm Nov-Feb; **P**) were shaped in the 18th century by Britain's greatest landscape gardeners. Among them was master landscape architect Lancelot 'Capability' Brown, who kick-started his career at Stowe. The gardens are best known for their many temples and follies, commissioned by the super-wealthy Richard Temple (1st Viscount Cobham), whose family motto was Templa Quam Dilecta (How Lovely are Thy Temples). Paths meander past lakes, bridges, temples, fountains and cascades, and through Capability Brown's Grecian Valley.

Lording over the gardens, neoclassical **Stowe House** (☎01280-818166; www.stowe. co.uk/house; Stowe; adult/child £6.20/free, incl Stowe Gardens £17.40; ☺11am-5pm May-Oct, 12.30-4pm Dec-Apr, closed Nov; **P**) is now an exclusive private school, but mere mortals can visit its eight state rooms by way of 15- to 45-minute guided tours (check the website for times) or, during school holidays, at their own pace. Although rooms are left bare (the house's contents were sold off to rescue the original owners from financial disaster), the sheer scale and ornamentation of the building is highly impressive.

From Stowe, head 32 miles southwest via the A421, A43, M40 and A34 to Oxford to rejoin the main route. This detour totals 72 miles; you'll need at least half a day to explore Stowe properly.

❸ Warner Bros Studio Tour: the Making of Harry Potter

Whether you're a fair-weather fan or a full-on Potterhead, this magical **studio tour** (☏0345 084 0900; www.wbstudiotour.co.uk; Studio Tour Dr, Leavesden, WD25; adult/child £35/27; ⊙10am-8pm, hours vary; P; ⛟Watford Junction, then shuttle bus) is well worth its out-the-way Leavesden location and admittedly hefty admission price. You'll need to pre-book your visit for an allocated time slot, arrive 20 minutes beforehand and allow two to three hours. It starts with a short film before you're ushered through giant doors into the actual set of Hogwarts' Great Hall – just the first of many 'wow' moments.

You're then free to explore the rest of the complex, including a large hangar featuring all the most familiar interior sets (Dumbledore's office, the Gryffindor common room, Hagrid's hut), another starring Platform 9¾ and the Hogwarts Express, and an outdoor section displaying Privet Dr, the purple triple-decker Knight Bus, Sirius Black's motorbike and a shop selling butterbeer (sickly sweet).

Other highlights include a stroll down Di-agon Alley, but the most enchanting treat is saved for last – a shimmering, gasp-inducing 1:24 scale model of Hogwarts.

The Drive » Exit the major M25 5 miles southwest of Leavesden and backtrack along the scenic A404, past Amersham, to High Wycombe. Zip 17 miles northwest on the M40, take the A40 5 miles west and follow Oxford signs. Driving and parking in central Oxford is a nightmare; use one of five Park & Ride car parks (per day £2 to £4).

EXPOSE / SHUTTERSTOCK ©

Oxford Great Hall of Christ Church

TRIP HIGHLIGHT

❹ Oxford

One of the world's most famous university cities, Oxford is a beautiful, privileged place, and deserves at least two days on your itinerary. Loved by literary greats JRR Tolkien, CS Lewis and Oscar Wilde, it's steeped in history and studded with august honey-toned buildings, yet maintains a young, lively studenty feel.

The university's 38 colleges are scattered throughout the city, the oldest dating back to the 13th century. Seek out your own corner of studious calm, but don't miss extraordinary, wealthy **Magdalen College** (☏01865-276000; www.magd.ox.ac.uk; High St; adult/child £5/4, 45min tours £6; ⊙1-6pm Oct-Jun, noon-7pm Jul-Sep, tours 6pm daily Jul-Sep), peaceful and exclusive **All Souls College** (☏01865-279379; www.asc.ox.ac.uk; High St; ⊙2-4pm Mon-Fri, closed Aug), and magnificent, popular **Christ Church** (☏01865-276492; www.chch.ox.ac.uk; St Aldate's; adult/child £8/7; ⊙10am-4.15pm Mon-Sat,

2-4.15pm Sun), with the grandest of quads. Christ Church is Oxford's largest college, famous as a location for the Harry Potter films (check out the Great Hall and staircase) and for its wonderful vaulted **cathedral** (☎01865-276150; www.chch.ox.ac.uk/cathedral; St Aldate's; admission free; ☺10am-4.15pm Mon-Sat, 2-4.15pm Sun).

Explore the fantastic **Ashmolean Museum** (☎01865-278000; www. ashmolean.org; Beaumont St; ☺10am-5pm Tue-Sun) and stroll down exquisite Catte St, flanked by golden colleges, the steeped 1914 **Bridge of Sighs** (Hertford Bridge; New College Lane), the relatively unadorned (but historically important) **University Church of St Mary the Virgin** (☎01865-279111; www.university-church. ox.ac.uk; High St; admission free; ☺9.30am-5pm Mon-Sat, 11.30am-5pm Sun Sep-Jun, 9am-6pm daily Jul & Aug), and the striking, circular, columned **Radcliffe Camera** (www.bodleian. ox.ac.uk; Radcliffe Sq). Also here is Oxford's **Bodleian Library** (☎01865-287400; www.bodleian.ox.ac.uk/bodley; Catte St; tours £6-14; ☺9am-5pm Mon-Sat, 11am-5pm Sun), one of the oldest public libraries in the world and quite possibly the most impressive one you'll ever see; admission is by guided tour.

Outstanding buildings aside, punting is a quintessential, unmiss-able Oxford experience; **Magdalen Bridge Boathouse** (☎01865-202643; www.oxfordpunting.co.uk; High St; chauffeured 4-person punt per 30min £30, punt rental per hour £24; ☺9.30am-dusk Feb-Nov) is the most central location to take to the water. Oxford's many literary-linked pubs, such as the **Turf Tavern** (☎01865-243235; www.turftavern-oxford.co.uk; 4-5 Bath Pl; ☺11am-11pm) or **Eagle & Child** (☎01865-302925; www.nicholsonspubs. co.uk/theeagleandchildoxford; 49 St Giles; ☺noon-11pm), provide the perfect post-punt retreat.

✕ ⊨ p73, p115

The Drive ≫ It's a quick 8-mile trip northwest on the A44 to Blenheim Palace, which has a sprawling free car park.

- - - - - - - - - - - - -

TRIP HIGHLIGHT

❺ Blenheim Palace

Absolutely worth travelling for, **Blenheim Palace** (☎01993-810530; www.blen heimpalace.com; Woodstock; adult/child £24.90/13.90, park & gardens only £14.90/6.90; ☺palace 10.30am-5.30pm, park & gardens 9am-6pm; P), one of Britain's greatest stately homes, is a monumental baroque fantasy designed by Sir John Vanbrugh and Nicholas Hawksmoor, and built between 1705 and 1722. The land and funds to build the house were granted to John Churchill, Duke of Marlborough, by a grateful Queen Anne, after his victory over the French at the 1704 Battle of Blenheim. Sir Winston Churchill was born here in 1874. Now a Unesco World Heritage site, Blenheim (*blen*-num) is home to the 12th duke.

If the palace crowds become too oppressive, escape into the vast, lavish **gardens and parklands**, parts of which were landscaped by the great Lancelot 'Capability' Brown.

The Drive ≫ Leaving Blenheim Palace, you'll emerge on the A4095. Turn left, skirting the splendid palace grounds, and, from the roundabout, signs lead 1 mile northwest into Woodstock.

- - - - - - - - - - - - -

❻ Woodstock

Though the main reason to swing by Woodstock is, of course, to visit nearby Blenheim Palace, the town itself is blessed with a delightful, affluent centre dotted with old pubs, antique stores, fine stone houses and several luxuriously stylish hotels. It's well worth exploring, and makes the perfect final overnight stop to your trip.

If you're craving a stroll, the **Wychwood Way** (www.wychwoodproject. org) is a historic, 37-mile loop route from Woodstock through an ancient royal forest, divided into manageable sections for those who fancy tackling a smaller part.

Eating & Sleeping

Windsor ❶

✕ Two Brewers   Pub Food ££

(📞01753-855426; www.twobrewerswindsor.
co.uk; 34 Park St, Windsor; mains £12.50-17;
🕙11.30am-11pm Mon-Thu, 11.30am-11.30pm
Fri & Sat, noon-10.30pm Sun) Pack into this
atmospheric 18th-century inn perched on
the edge of Windsor Great Park for tasty,
well-prepped pub meals that are a cut above
the usual pub grub. Menus range from soups,
salads and tapas to steaks, fishcakes and
cheese boards. Outdoor sunny benches front
the flower-covered exterior; inside, think low-
beamed ceilings, dim lighting and a roaring
winter fire.

🛏 Alma House   B&B ££

(📞01753-862983; www.almahouse.co.uk;
56 Alma Rd, Windsor; s/d from £65/75; 🛜)
Within this pretty Victorian town house, 0.5
miles southwest of the castle, the four smartly
revamped rooms feature comfy beds, plenty
of light and tasteful cream or purple decor.
Two rooms accommodate families, as does
the equally homey annexe room out the back.
Breakfast is a minimal self-service continental
spread.

🛏 Macdonald Windsor Hotel   Hotel £££

(📞0344 879 9101; www.macdonaldhotels.
co.uk/Windsor; 23 High St, Windsor; r from
£158; P🛜🍽) Looking small and quaint from
the road but magically transforming into 120
elegant rooms beyond its revolving door, the
floral-scented Windsor is the slickest choice in
town. Dark browns, creams, reds and purples
add a plush, rich feel to the resolutely modern
decor and facilities (such as capsule-coffee
kits), and service hits that perfect friendly and
professional note. Some rooms have castle
glimpses.

Oxford ❹

✕ Vaults & Garden   Cafe £

(📞01865-279112; www.thevaultsandgarden.
com; University Church of St Mary the Virgin,

Radcliffe Sq; mains £7-10; 🕙8.30am-6pm;
🛜🍴) Hidden away in the vaulted 14th-century
Old Congregation House of the University
Church, this buzzy local favourite serves
a wholesome seasonal selection of soups,
salads, pastas, curries, sandwiches and cakes,
including plenty of vegetarian and gluten-free
options. It's one of Oxford's most beautiful
lunch venues, with additional tables in a pretty
garden overlooking Radcliffe Sq. Arrive early to
grab a seat.

✕ Door 74   Modern British ££

(📞01865-203374; www.door74.co.uk; 74 Cowley
Rd; mains £10-14; 🕙11am-2.30pm & 5-9.30pm
Tue-Sat, 11am-2.30pm Sun; 🍴) This cosy little
place woos fans with its rich mix of British
and Mediterranean flavours, friendly service
and intimate setting. The menu is limited and
tables are tightly packed, but the cooking is
consistently good (pastas, risottos, burgers)
and weekend brunches (full English, French
toast, salmon with scrambled eggs, etc) are
supremely filling. Book ahead.

🛏 Oxford Coach & Horses   B&B ££

(📞01865-200017; www.oxfordcoachandhorses.
co.uk; 62 St Clement's St; s/d/tr £125/135/165;
P🛜) Once an 18th-century coaching inn,
this fabulous English-Mexican-owned boutique
B&B hides behind a fresh powder-blue exterior,
just a few metres from the Cowley Rd action.
The eight light-filled rooms are cosy, spacious
and individually styled with soothing pastels with
the odd splash of purple, turquoise or exposed
wood. The converted ground floor houses an
airy, attractive breakfast room.

🛏 Old Bank Hotel   Hotel £££

(📞01865-799599; www.oldbank-hotel.co.uk;
91-94 High St; r from £285; P🛜) Slap bang in
the centre of Oxford, this grand hotel strewn
with contemporary art offers 42 elegant,
spacious, pale-hued rooms. Sleek, freshly
refurbished pads feature sensor lighting and
Nespresso machines; others are less flashy
but comfortable and characterful. Front rooms
overlook the University Church and the heart of
Oxford University. For spectacular views, splash
out on glossy junior suite 45.

Around the Cam

8

Settle in for a grand tour though the essence of old England; a trip that meanders through beguiling countryside into ancient villages and takes in a truly spectacular university city.

TRIP HIGHLIGHTS

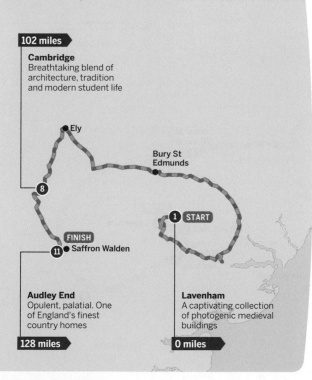

102 miles

Cambridge
Breathtaking blend of architecture, tradition and modern student life

Ely

Bury St Edmunds

8

START **1**

FINISH
11 Saffron Walden

Audley End
Opulent, palatial. One of England's finest country homes

128 miles

Lavenham
A captivating collection of photogenic medieval buildings

0 miles

6–7 DAYS
130 MILES / 210KM

GREAT FOR...

BEST TIME TO GO
Mid-June to September brings fine weather and Cambridge's colleges are open for visitors.

ESSENTIAL PHOTO
Amid the very riverside scene that features in Constable's *The Hay Wain.*

BEST FOR CULTURE
One of the world's most important centres of learning: Cambridge.

Lavenham Medieval streetscape

117

8 Around the Cam

Prepare to fall more than a little in love with your destinations. You'll discover a spectacular cathedral, villages teaming with half-timbered houses, scenery immortalised by famous painters, and sumptuous stately homes. Plus Cambridge: a bewitching university city, where learning, heritage and tradition seem to emanate from the exquisite college buildings and bicycle-crowded streets. This is gentle, take-your-time driving; a truly enchanting ride.

TRIP HIGHLIGHT

❶ Lavenham

One of East Anglia's most beautiful towns, the former wool-trade centre of Lavenham is home to beautifully preserved medieval buildings that lurch and lean to dramatic effect. Take in whitewashed **Lavenham Guildhall** (NT; www.nationaltrust.org.uk; Market Pl; adult/child £6.20/3.10; ⊙11am-5pm daily Mar-Oct, to 4pm Sat & Sun Nov-Feb), a superb early-16th-century example of a close-studded, timber-framed

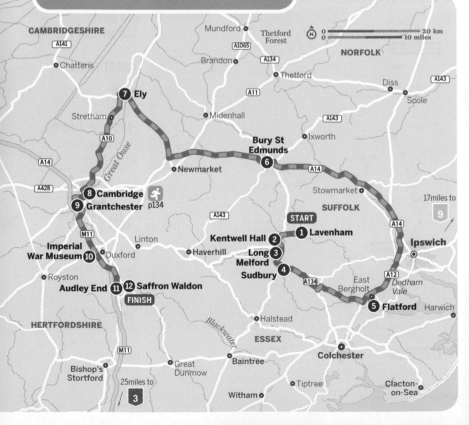

building. Inside displays explain the wool trade and medieval guilds. At nearby caramel-coloured, 14th-century **Little Hall** (www.littlehall.org.uk; Market Pl; adult/child £4/free; ⏱10am-1pm Mon & 1-4pm Tue-Sun Easter-Oct), rooms have been fully restored to period splendour.

A few steps away, the church of **St Peter & St Paul** (www.lavenhamchurch.wordpress.com; Church St; ⏱8.30am-5.30pm) is a late-Perpendicular structure built between 1485 and 1530, with beautifully proportioned windows, soaring flint tower and gargoyle waterspouts.

🛏 p123

The Drive » Your first leg is a 5-mile countryside cruise southwest, initially along the B1071, then Bridge St Rd, to

LINK YOUR TRIP

9 Suffolk-Norfolk Shore

A glorious cruise along a sublime stretch of sandy shore. Starts 45 miles east of Bury St Edmunds at Aldeburgh.

3 The Historic South

A nine-day exploration of the pick of southern England's heritage sights. Starts in London, 60 miles south of Saffron Walden.

Long Melford. Turn right at its High St; seconds later you arrive at Melford Hall.

- - - - - - - - - - - - - -

2 Long Melford

The charming village of Long Melford has an ace up its sleeve: the romantic Elizabethan mansion of **Melford Hall** (NT; www.nationaltrust.org.uk; Hall St; adult/child £7.50/3.75; ⏱noon-5pm Wed-Sun Apr-Oct; **P**). From the outside it seems little changed since it entertained Queen Elizabeth I in 1578. Inside, there's a panelled banqueting hall, masses of Regency and Victorian finery, and a display on Beatrix Potter, who was a cousin of the Hyde Parkers, who owned the house from 1786 to 1960.

The Drive » Turn right out of Melford Hall to glide beside Long Melford's famous village green. Then turn left, up the straight-as-an-arrow road to Kentwell Hall; just over a mile away in all.

- - - - - - - - - - - - - -

3 Kentwell Hall

Gorgeous, turreted **Kentwell Hall** (☎01787-310207; www.kentwell.co.uk; adult/child £12.20/9.20; ⏱hours vary; **P**) dates from the 1500s and is full of Tudor grandeur. Highlights are a rectangular moat, glorious gardens and an irresistible rare-breeds farm. It tends to be open 11am to 5pm during school summer holidays, plus other weekends; call to check.

The Drive » Dart back towards Long Melford, then briefly north, then cut back south onto the A134/131 for the 6-mile stretch to Gainsborough's House in Sudbury.

- - - - - - - - - - - - - -

4 Sudbury

Today a bustling market town, Sudbury is also where, in the 18th century, the painter Thomas Gainsborough was born. His birthplace, **Gainsborough's House** (www.gainsborough.org; 46 Gainsborough St; adult/child £6.50/2; ⏱10am-5pm Mon-Sat, 11am-5pm Sun), is now home to the world's largest collection of his work. The 16th-century house and gardens feature a Georgian facade built by the artist's father. Inside, look out for *Pitminster Boy* in the entrance hall, the exquisite *Portrait of Harriett, Viscountess Tracy*, celebrated for its delicate portrayal of drapery, and the landscapes that were his passion.

The Drive » Time for a bucolic, field-framed, rolling 18-mile drive, initially along the A131/134. After a brief stint on the A12, take the B1070 through East Bergholt, then turn off right for Flatford.

- - - - - - - - - - - - - -

5 Flatford

If this languid landscape feels familiar it'll be down to local lad and artist John Constable, who depicted its country lanes and babbling streams in his paintings. The hamlet of Flatford is home to thatched **Bridge Cottage** (Bridge Cottage, NT; 🖉01206-298260; www. nationaltrust.org.uk; Bridge Cottage, near East Bergholt; parking £4; ⊙10.30am-5.30pm Apr-Oct, to 3.30pm Sat & Sun Nov-Mar; P), which has an exhibition that provides a fine introduction to the artist's life and works. Daily guided tours (£3, noon and 2pm, April to October) take in views of **Flatford Mill** and **Willy Lott's House** (which features in *The Hay Wain*). There are also self-guided routes.

The Drive » Retrace your route back to the A12, then wind onto A-roads (the A14 and A134) to curve round into Bury St Edmonds, 35 miles in all.

----

❻ Bury St Edmonds

History-rich Bury is a delight to explore. At picturesque **Abbey Gardens** (Mustow St; ⊙dawn-dusk) the walls of a once-mighty abbey have crumbled and

eroded into a series of fantastical shapes. Look out too for the decorative **Great Gate** and the diminutive **dovecote**. Next door, largely 16th-century **St Edmundsbury Cathedral** (www.stedscathedral. co.uk; Angel Hill; requested donation adult/child £3/50p; ⊙8.30am-6pm) features a 45m-high tower and lofty interior, with a gorgeous hammerbeam roof. A short walk south leads to the **Greene King Brewery** (🖉01284-714297; www. greeneking.co.uk; Westgate St; visitor centre free, tours £12; ⊙10.30am-4.30pm Mon-Sat) where they've been making beer since 1799. Pop into the visitor centre to learn more about the brewery; or prebook for a tour.

🍴 🛏 p123

The Drive » Pick up the A14 towards Newmarket, turning off 15 miles later to head northwest onto the A142. From here it's a 12-mile cruise through a flat Fenland landscape, with Ely Cathedral's towering spire beckoning you into the city.

❼ Ely

Ely may technically be a city, but it's small enough to be dominated by **Ely Cathedral** (www.elycathe dral.org; The Gallery; adult/child £8/free, entry & tower tour £15/free; ⊙7am-6.30pm), dubbed the 'Ship of the Fens' because it's so visible across the area's vast, flat sweeps of land. The early-12th-century nave dazzles, the 14th-century Octagon is masterly, and towers soar upwards in shimmering colours. A few minutes' walk away, the half-timbered **Oliver Cromwell's House** (www. olivercromwellshouse.co.uk; 29 St Mary's St; adult/child £4.90/3.40; ⊙10am-5pm Apr-Oct, 11am-4pm Nov-Mar) is where England's premier Puritan lived in the mid-1600s. The interior has been restored to feature flickering candles, floppy hats and writing quills.

🍴 p123

The Drive » This one's simple: 16 miles south along the A10, through the flat Fens to Cambridge. Make for the Grand Arcade car park.

TRIP HIGHLIGHT

❽ Cambridge

Abounding with exquisite architecture and oozing tradition, Cambridge is a perfect city to explore on foot (p134). There are more than 30 colleges here; superbly photogenic **St John's College** (www.joh.cam.

FAMOUS CAMBRIDGE STUDENTS

The honour roll of famous Cambridge students and affiliates reads like an international who's who of high achievers: 92 Nobel Prize winners (more than any other institution in the world), 13 British prime ministers, nine archbishops of Canterbury, an immense number of scientists, and a healthy host of poets and authors. This is the town where Newton refined his theory of gravity, Whipple invented the jet engine and Crick and Watson discovered DNA. William Wordsworth, Lord Byron, Vladimir Nabokov, Stephen Hawking and Stephen Fry all studied here too.

Cambridge Punting along the River Cam

ac.uk; St John's St; adult/child £8/5; ⏰10am-5pm Mar-Oct, to 3.30pm Nov-Feb, closed mid-Jun) is one of the biggest. Founded in 1511 by Henry VII's mother, Margaret Beaufort, it sprawls along both river banks, joined by the **Bridge of Sighs**, a masterpiece of stone tracery. A short walk south, diminutive 14th-century **Trinity Hall College** (☎01223-332500; www.trinhall.cam.ac.uk; Trinity Lane; admission by donation; ⏰9.15am-noon & 2pm-dusk, closed early Apr–end-Jun) has one of the most beautiful chapels in Cambridge. Next, head to the fabulous **Fitzwilliam Museum**

(www.fitzmuseum.cam.ac.uk; Trumpington St; donation requested; ⏰10am-5pm Tue-Sat, noon-5pm Sun) to encounter Roman and Egyptian grave goods, artworks by many of the great masters and some more quirky collections: banknotes, literary autographs, watches and armour.

✗ 🛏 p47, p123

The Drive » A 4-mile drive, heading south through Cambridge's streets – you're making for the A603, aka the Fen Causeway. Soon, take the left to Grantchester, via Grantchester Rd, and roll into the Orchard Tea Garden car park.

- - - - - - - - - - -

❾ Grantchester

In the picture postcard village of Grantchester, old thatched cottages sit in flower-filled gardens. The quintessentially English **Orchard Tea Garden** (☎01223-551125; mlsb.org/ orchardteagarden; Mill Way; lunch mains £4-10, cakes £3; ⏰9.30am-7.30pm Jun-Aug, to 5.30pm Mar-May & Sep-Nov, to 4.30pm Dec-Feb) is set just beside the church. Here you'll find deck chairs snuggling beneath leafy apple trees and reassuringly calorific cakes and light lunches. It was the favourite haunt of the Bloomsbury Group who

121

came to camp, picnic, swim and discuss their work.

The Drive » From Grantchester's lanes, snake south via the A1134, onto the M11, southbound. Leave it at junction 10, heading for Duxford, then pick up signs for the Imperial War Museum. It's 7 miles in all.

---

⑩ Imperial War Museum

The **Imperial War Museum** (www.iwm.org.uk; Duxford; adult/child £16.35/8.15; ⏰10am-6pm Easter-Oct, to 4pm Nov-Easter; P 🚻) is Europe's biggest aviation museum, with some 200 lovingly preserved vintage aircraft, housed in several enormous hangars. The vast airfield showcases everything from dive bombers to biplanes, Spitfires and Concordes. The awe-inspiring American Air Museum hangar pays homage to US WWII servicemen, hosting the largest collection of American civil and military aircraft outside the USA. Modern warfare is also covered, including the latest conflicts in Afghanistan and Iraq, with an assortment of tanks and artillery from WWII onwards.

The Drive » Another short drive, this time just under 10 miles and on minor roads: first the A505, then the A1301, before the B1383 leads lazily to Audley End.

TRIP HIGHLIGHT

⑪ Audley End

One of England's grandest country homes is **Audley End** (EH; ☎01799-522842; www.english-heritage.org.uk; off London Rd; adult/child £16.60/10; ⏰house noon-5pm Apr-Sep, to 4pm Oct, gardens 10am-6pm Apr-Sep, to 5pm Oct). Positively palatial in its scale, style and the all-too-apparent ambition of its creator, the first earl of Suffolk, the fabulous early-Jacobean mansion did eventually become a royal palace when it was bought by Charles II in 1668. Lavishly decorated rooms glitter with silverware, priceless furniture and paintings – you can also explore a service wing, restored to feature the sounds and smells of servant life in the 1880s, and a Victoria-era stable yard, complete with horses.

The Drive » This last leg is one of the briefest – a fraction under 2 miles, east via Spring Hill and Audley End Rd, into the picturesque streets of Saffron Walden.

---

⑫ Saffron Walden

The 12th-century market town of Saffron Walden is a delightful knot of half-timbered houses and narrow lanes. Start explorations at the **Saffron Walden Museum** (www.saffronwaldenmuseum.org; Museum St; adult/child £2.50/free; ⏰10am-4.30pm Tue-Sat, 2-4.30pm Sun), where eclectic collections range from geology and 18th-century costumes to Victorian toys. The bramble-covered ruins of **Walden Castle Keep**, built about 1125, lie in the grounds. Nearby sits the church of **St Mary the Virgin** (www.stmarys saffronwalden.org; Church St; ⏰9am-5pm). With sections dating back to 1250, it's one of the largest churches in the county and features impressive Gothic arches and local landowner Lord Audley's tomb. From here it's a few minutes' stroll to the carefully restored Victorian **Bridge End Gardens** (Bridge End; ⏰gardens 24hr, maze & kitchen garden 9am-3pm Mon-Thu, to 1pm Fri, 10am-4pm Sat & Sun). Check to see if the maze and produce-packed kitchen garden are open too.

🍴 p123

Eating & Sleeping

Lavenham ❶

🛏 Swan
Hotel £££

(📞01787-247477; www.theswanatlavenham.
co.uk; High St; s/d/ste £100/140/315; 🅿 📶)
Marvellously medieval and utterly indulgent, the
Swan might just spoil you in terms of other places
to stay. Tasteful furnishings team oatmeal with
olive and gentle reds, latticework of ancient wood
climbs all around. The service is smooth, while
the suites are simply stunning: expect soaring
arched ceilings criss-crossed with beams.

Bury St Edmunds ❻

🍷 Old Cannon
Pub

(📞01284-768769; www.oldcannonbrewery.
co.uk; 86 Cannon St; ⏰11am-11pm) In this
microbrewery gleaming mash tuns sit alongside
the funky bar – try the Rusty Gun (ABV 4%) or
the more feisty St Edmund's Head (5%). A fair
bit of the ale goes into the food (served 8.30am
to 9pm Monday to Saturday, to 3pm Sunday);
perhaps sample some Gunner's Daughter
sausages and bacon cured in stout.

🛏 Chantry
Hotel ££

(📞01284-767427; www.chantryhotel.com;
8 Sparhawk St; s/ste £75/145, d £115-130;
🅿 @ 📶) Pretty much everything feels right
about the Chantry – a family-run town house
that's somewhere between a hotel and a B&B.
Sash windows and cast-iron fireplaces signal
its Georgian origins; French beds and walk-in
showers add contemporary comfort; the convivial
lounge and tiny bar help you feel at home.

Ely ❼

🗡 Peacocks
Cafe £

(www.peacockstearoom.co.uk; 65 Waterside;
snacks from £7; ⏰10.30am-4.30pm Wed-Sun,
plus Tue Jun-Sep) An award-winning cafe serving
a vast selection of teas and cream teas, luscious
homemade soups, salads, cakes and scones.
Eat inside surrounded by fun knick-knacks and
bone china, or in the bijou garden framed by
drooping wisteria.

Cambridge ❽

🗡 Pint Shop
Modern British ££

(📞01223-352293; www.pintshop.co.uk; 10
Peas Hill; mains £12-21; ⏰noon-10pm) Popular
Pint Shop's vision is to embrace eating and
drinking equally. So it's created both a busy bar
specialising in craft beer (10 on keg and six on
draft) and a stylish dining room serving classy
versions of traditional grub (dry-aged steaks,
gin-cured sea trout, charcoal-grilled plaice). All
in all, hard to resist.

🛏 Benson House
B&B ££

(📞01223-311594; www.bensonhouse.co.uk;
24 Huntingdon Rd; s £75-115, d £110-115; 🅿 📶)
Lots of little things lift Benson a cut above –
sleep amongst feather pillows and Egyptian
cotton linen, sip tea from Royal Doulton bone
china, then tuck into award-winning breakfasts
featuring kippers, croissants and fresh fruit.

Saffron Walden ⓬

🗡 Eight Bells
Pub Food ££

(www.8bells-pub.co.uk; 18 Bridge St; mains
£12-18; ⏰noon-9.30pm; 📶) A warm mix of
medieval character and contemporary style,
this 16th-century gastropub serves up the likes
of roast Suffolk lamb, lavender-cured duck and –
fittingly – a vivid pea and courgette risotto, with
saffron for extra spice.

Scrubbed wooden floors, half-timbered
walls, abstract art, deep leather sofas and
roaring fires make it an attractive place to sip
on a pint, too.

Suffolk-Norfolk Shore

9

On this trip you'll chart a shore's changing character. From genteel resorts, arch west to encounter a coast of wistful beauty where creeks frame ancient quays and apparently endless stretches of sand.

TRIP HIGHLIGHTS

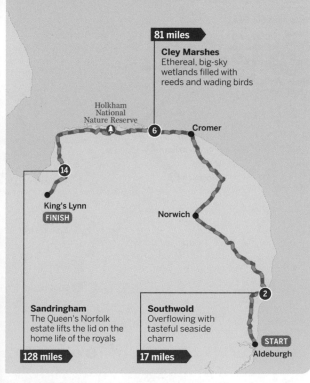

81 miles

Cley Marshes
Ethereal, big-sky wetlands filled with reeds and wading birds

Holkham National Nature Reserve

6 Cromer

14

King's Lynn
FINISH

Norwich

2

Sandringham
The Queen's Norfolk estate lifts the lid on the home life of the royals

128 miles

Southwold
Overflowing with tasteful seaside charm

17 miles

START
Aldeburgh

**8 DAYS
136 MILES / 220KM**

GREAT FOR...

BEST TIME TO GO

Spring though to summer for finer weather. Autumn for fewer crowds.

ESSENTIAL PHOTO

A selfie backed by a shoreline of seals at Blakeney Point.

BEST FOR ROYALTY

Her Majesty the Queen's country estate: Sandringham.

Southwold Bathing huts and sandy beaches at Southwold

Suffolk-Norfolk Shore

Prepare to discover the English seaside at its most appealing, as you motor from Suffolk's piers to North Norfolk's expansive shore. The distances aren't great but the pit stops are: scenic journeys lead you to boats leaning amid sand spits; trails snaking to beaches through scented pine woods; salt marshes thick with wading birds. This is a drive that's enchanting: leisurely and along winding, sea-framed roads. You probably won't want to leave.

1 Aldeburgh

The time-warped coastal town of Aldeburgh (pronounced 'orld-bruh') is one of the region's most charming. Its picturesque streets and sweeping shingle beach are lined with pastel-coloured houses, independent shops, art galleries and ramshackle fresh-fish kiosks. At intricately carved, timber-framed, 16th-century **Moot Hall** (www.aldeburgh museum.org.uk; Market Cross Place; adult/child £2/ free; ⏱ noon-5pm Jun-Aug,

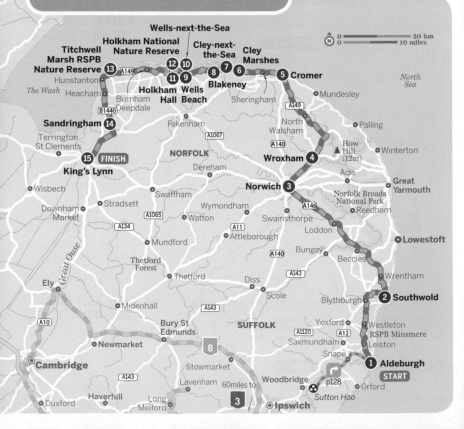

2.30pm-5pm Apr, May, Sep & Oct), displays on fishing, shipbuilding and coastal defences sit beside those on Regency-era tourism. One of Aldeburgh's most famous visitors was 20th-century composer Benjamin Britten. Take a short stroll north along the seafront to reach **Scallop** (near Thorpe Rd car park), a 4m-high sculpture of inscribed scallop-shell-shaped steel by Maggi Hambling, which commemorates Britten's links with the town.

📏 p133

The Drive » For this 18-mile stretch, take the rural B1122/B1125 north. After the broad sweep of the River Blyth, peel off right onto the A1095 to roll beside more fields and into Southwold. Park up near the pier.

LINK YOUR TRIP

8 **Around the Cam**
A history-rich meander through gentle countryside to university city Cambridge. Join it 45 miles west of Aldeburgh at Bury St Edmunds.

3 **The Historic South**
A cross-country blast deep into Britain's past taking in blockbuster heritage sights. Starts in London, 100 miles southwest of Aldeburgh.

TRIP HIGHLIGHT

❷ Southwold

Picturesque Southwold draws well-heeled crowds thanks to its lovely sandy beach, pebble-walled cottages, cannon-dotted clifftop and rows of beach-front bathing huts. The 623ft **Pier** (www.southwold pier.co.uk; ⏱ pier 9am-5pm, to 8pm Fri-Sun) was first built in 1899 but was recently reconstructed. Its **Under the Pier Show** (open 10am to 6pm, to 8pm Friday to Sunday) sports a cooky collection of handmade amusement machines combining daft fun with political satire. In the centre of town is the Victorian **Adnams** (📞01502-727225; www.adnams.co.uk; Adnams Pl; tours £12; ⏱2-4 tours daily Mar-Sep) brewery, which produces some of East Anglia's most popular ales. Book ahead for tours of the high-tech kit, then select a free bottle of beer to take home.

📏 p133

The Drive » Pick up the B1127, then join the A146 for a 30-mile cruise to Norwich. This area's often-straight roads undulate a little like a roller-coaster; the peaks and troughs prompted the authorities to put up the typically East Anglian 'Hidden Dip!' warning signs.

---

❸ Norwich

The affluent and easy-going city of Norwich is a rich tapestry of meandering alleys liberally sprinkled with architectural jewels – spoils of the city's medieval wool boom. The magnificent **Norwich Cathedral** (www.cathedral.org.uk; The Close; donations requested; ⏱7.30am-6pm) has England's second-highest spire, vast cloisters, a mesmerising ceiling and a striking modern Hostry, where high-tech displays explore the cathedral's past. Cutting west, hunt out **Elm Hill**: Norwich's prettiest street features medieval cobblestones, crooked timber beams and tucked-away cafes.

Due south sits the massive, 12th-century **Norwich Castle** (www.museums.norfolk.gov.uk; Castle Hill; adult/child £8.80/7; ⏱10am-4.30pm Mon-Sat, 1pm-4.30pm Sun). Its superb interactive museum crams in lively exhibits on Boudica, the Iceni, the Anglo-Saxons and the Vikings. The atmospheric keep has graphic displays on grisly punishments, while twice-daily guided tours (adult/child £3.50/2.80) run around the battlements and creepy dungeons.

📏 p133

The Drive » Next comes the 8-mile drive northeast to Wroxham along the A1151, a route that slices past fields of terracotta-coloured earth and vivid yellow oilseed rape.

DETOUR:
SUTTON HOO

Start: ❶ Aldeburgh (p126)

From Aldeburgh, it's well worth taking the A1094, B1069 and A1152 15 miles southwest. They lead to the truly remarkable archaeological site of **Sutton Hoo** (NT; ☎01394-389700; www.nationaltrust.org.uk; Sutton Hoo, near Woodbridge; adult/child £8.20/4.10; ⊙10.30am-5pm Easter-Oct, 10.30am-4pm Sat & Sun Nov-Easter; P ⛟). The hull of an enormous Anglo-Saxon ship was discovered here in 1939, buried under a mound of earth. The vessel was the final resting place of Raedwald, King of East Anglia until AD 625, and was stuffed with Saxon riches, reflecting a sophisticated culture that's conveyed beautifully in on-site displays. The massive effort that went into Raedwald's burial gives some idea of just how important a man he was, while the elaborate nature of the treasures transformed perceptions of the era. Many of the original finds and a full-scale reconstruction of his ship and burial chamber can be seen in the **visitor centre**. The finest treasures, including the king's exquisitely crafted helmet, shields, gold ornaments and Byzantine silver, are displayed in London's British Museum, but replicas are on show here, along with an original prince's sword. Paths encircle the 18 burial mounds (which look like bumps in the ground) that make up the 'royal cemetery'. You can only walk onto them as part of one-hour **guided tours** (adult/child £2.50/1.25), which provide a fascinating insight into the site. There's normally at least one tour a day, call ahead to check for times.

❹ Wroxham

Signs in the shape of sail boats signal your arrival at Wroxham, one of the Norfolk Broad's main towns. Head for the central, twin humped-backed bridges. Sink a waterside drink, munch fish 'n' chips or just relax and watch the swans. Then make for **Broads Tours** (☎01603-782207; www.broads.co.uk; Wroxham) to swap the roadway for the waterways on a two-hour cruise (adult/child £10/6).

The Drive » It's hedgerows, fields and leaf-framed lanes for much of the next 20-mile leg (via the A1151 and A149). That plus a scattering of picturesque villages and waterside pubs. After a burst of woodland it's time to join the main road into Cromer.

❺ Cromer

The once-fashionable Victorian watering hole of Cromer is a relaxed mix of old-school English seaside resort and appealing fishing port. Here brightly painted houses line narrow lanes dotted with non-chain shops. In the streets leading back from the shore, track down **Davies** (7 Garden St; crab £3.50-6; ⊙8.30am-5pm Mon-Sat, 10am-4pm Sun Apr-Oct, 8.30am-4pm Tue-Sat Nov-Mar). Less a fish shop, more a local institution, here the sweet-tasting Cromer crab is caught by its own day boat and is boiled, cracked and dressed on-site. Cromer's atmospheric **pier** takes pride of place on the pebble beach; just east is the **Henry Blogg Museum** (Lifeboat Museum; www.rnlicromer.org.uk; The Gangway; ⊙10am-5pm Tue-Sun Apr-Sep, to 4pm Oct-Mar), an excellent Royal National Lifeboat Institution lifeboat museum where hands-on exhibits include Morse code keys and semaphore flags. The town's WWII lifeboat also sits inside.

🛏 p133

The Drive » Next an 11-mile cruise. The A149 peels west along Cromer's seafront; here caravan parks and the occasional windmill sit in front of frequent sea views. At Salthouse the scenery changes – the road sweeps down to flat, marsh-side land, edged to the north by a distant ridge of beach.

TRIP HIGHLIGHT

❻ Cley Marshes

One of England's premier birdwatching sites, **Cley Marshes** (www. norfolkwildlifetrust.org.uk; near Cley-next-the-Sea; adult/ child £5/free; ⏰dawn-dusk; Ⓟ) has more than 300 resident bird species, plentiful migrants and a network of walking trails and bird hides amid its golden reeds. Even if you're not into birding, don't miss the (free) cafe-cum–visitor centre where seats and telescopes line up beside vast picture windows with panoramic reserve views.

The Drive » It's a half-mile, marsh-side hop west along the A149 to Cley-next-the-Sea itself.

❼ Cley-next-the-Sea

As the name suggests, the sleepy village of Cley (pronounced 'cly') huddles beside the shore. Here a cluster of pretty cottages line the main road. Head for the Village Hall car park, then stroll back to explore. Cut down lanes signed towards the postcard-pretty **windmill**, which sits serenely beside reed beds. Next head back to **Cley Smokehouse** (www.cleysmokehouse.com;

High St; ⏰9.30am-4.30pm) to survey the ranks of home-smoked fish and onto **Picnic Fayre** (www. picnic-fayre.co.uk; High St; ⏰9am-5pm Mon-Sat, 10am-4pm Sun). A deli to ditch the diet for, it's crammed full of imaginative versions of English picnic classics – pork pies with chorizo, sweet chilli sauce–smothered sausages, and home-baked lavender bread.

🛏 p133

The Drive » It's a 1½-mile jaunt past hedges and houses to Blakeney. Once in the village, follow signs to Blakeney Quay.

❽ Blakeney

The pretty village of Blakeney was once a busy fishing and trading port before its harbour silted up. These days it offers a steep high street lined with pubs, eateries and gift shops, and a picturesque quay where boats bob in narrow channels between the mudflats. The highlights, though, are the boat trips out to a 500-strong colony of

common and grey seals that live, bask and breed on nearby **Blakeney Point**. **Bishop's Boats** (☎01263-740753; www. bishopsboats.com; Blakeney Quay; adult/child £12/6; ⏰1-4 daily Apr-Oct) run hour-long trips from the quayside.

The Drive » Head west on the A149, which undulates through villages of flint-fronted houses and past salt mashes and fields. Some 8 miles later, in Wells-next-the-Sea, pick up signs for the beach, heading down the mile-long straight road which borders the banked sea defenses to the car park at the end.

❾ Wells Beach

Stroll north out of the car park, taking in views of the sand drifting up to the sea wall lining the beach road and the lifeboat station on the point. Soon the expanse of Wells Beach emerges. Fringed by dense pine forests and undulating dunes, the shore stretches for miles to the west, with jaunty beach huts clustering beside the water and wooden steps leading up into the woods.

THE NORFOLK BROADS

The vast wetlands of the Norfolk Broads were formed when the rivers Wensum, Bure, Waveney and Yare flooded the big gaping inland holes which had been dug by 12th-century crofters looking for peat. They comprise fragile ecosystems and, protected as a national park, are home to some of the UK's rarest plants and birds – the appeal to birdwatchers, naturalists and casual visitors is strong.

The Drive ›› Head back down Beach Rd to the centre of Wells, making either for the Quay car park (£4.50 per day), or the cheaper, short-term one in Staithe St (per hour £1.30).

⑩ Wells-next-the-Sea

In charming Wells-next-the-Sea (abbreviated locally to just Wells), rows of attractive Georgian houses and flint cottages snake down to a boat-lined quay bordered by sandbanks, creeks and smart yachts. It's a top spot to buy an ice cream, then explore the narrow streets behind (often called 'Yards'), which are full of quirky shops. The delightful **Wells & Walsingham Railway** (www.wellswalsinghamrailway. co.uk; Stiffkey Rd; adult/child return £9/7; ⊙ 4-5 trains daily Apr-Oct; P) leaves from Stiffkey Rd. The longest 10.25in narrow-gauge railway in the world, it puffs for 5 picturesque miles (30 minutes) from Wells to the village of Little Walsingham, the site of religious shrines and the ruined but still impressive Walsingham Abbey.

🛏 p133

The Drive ›› Guess what? Yep: it's back onto your old friend the A149 to wind west for 2 miles through a flat, open landscape book-ended by distant lines of trees. Then turn left down the ¼-mile drive to Holkham Hall.

MARTIN CHARLES HATCH / SHUTTERSTOCK ©

⑪ Holkham Hall

The ancestral seat of the original Earl of Leicester, **Holkham Hall** (www.holkham.co.uk; Holkham; adult/child £15/7.50, parking £3; ⊙ noon-4pm Sun, Mon & Thu Apr-Oct; P) still belongs to his descendants. A severe Palladian mansion, it's largely unadorned on the outside but the interior is sumptuous, with a red velvet–lined saloon, copies of Greek and Roman statues, the luxurious Green State Bedroom, and fluted columns in the Marble Hall. It's set in a vast **deer park** (open 9.30am to 5pm daily), which was designed by William Kent. Admission to the hall includes entry to the 6-acre walled

Cley-next-the-Sea Produce for sale at Picnic Fayre

garden and **Field to Fork**, an exhibition charting the life cycle of crop production.

The Drive » Head back up the drive from Holkham Hall. At the crossroads on the A149, go straight ahead for the mile-long, straight-as-an-arrow trip due north to Holkham Beach Car Park – the parking that frames the entrance road to Holkham National Nature Reserve.

⑫ Holkham National Nature Reserve

Stroll to the very end of the car-lined lane – this leads to paths into the stunning **Holkham National Nature Reserve** (www.holkham.co.uk; parking per 2hr/day £3/6.50). Beach, dunes, salt marsh, grazing marsh, pinewoods and scrub – a high num-ber of habitats pack into its 37-sq-km site. From the car park, ribboning pathways lead through forests via bird hides and on to an expansive, pristine sandy shore.

The Drive » This time the A149 is a more winding, undulating route, which passes a picturesque windmill and pops over a narrow bridge. Be wary here of multiple villages featuring the name

131

Burnham – there are seven in these parts. You're heading through Burnham Deepdale and Titchwell village to Titchwell Marsh Nature Reserve – a 10-mile leg in all.

13 Titchwell Marsh

At **Titchwell Marsh** (RSPB; www.rspb.org.uk; Titchwell; parking £5; ☺ dawn-dusk; P) nature reserve, sandbars, marshes and lagoons attract vast numbers of birds. Summer brings avocets, terns, marsh harriers and nesting bearded tits; in winter you'll see more than 20 species of wading birds and countless ducks and geese. It's a perfectly tranquil place to stop.

The Drive » Take the A149 through more flatlands, past the broad sweep of golf course–framed sea at Hunstanton, before peeling off onto the B1440 for the cruise to Sandringham, 15 miles from Titchwell Marsh.

TRIP HIGHLIGHT

14 Sandringham

Both monarchists and those bemused by the English system will have plenty to mull over at **Sandringham** (www.sandringhamestate.co.uk; Sandringham; adult/child £14/7; ☺11am-4.45pm Easter-Sep, to 3.45pm Oct; P), the Queen's country estate. It's set in 25 hectares of beautifully landscaped **gardens**, and wandering around opulent reception rooms regularly used by the royals reveals a wealth of objets d'art and glinting gifts from European and Russian royal families. Sandringham was built in 1870 by the then Prince and Princess of Wales (who later became King Edward VII and Queen Alexandra) and the house's features and furnishings remain much as they were in Edwardian days. The stables, meanwhile, now house a flag-waving museum filled with diverse royal memorabilia. The superb **vintage-car collection** includes the very first royal motor from 1900, and the buggy in which the Queen Mother would bounce around race tracks. There are **guided tours** (£3.50, 11am and 2pm Wednesday and Saturday) of the gardens. The shop stocks organic goodies produced on the vast estate.

The Drive » From Sandringham, it's a 10-mile hop along well-signed A and B roads to King's Lynn.

15 King's Lynn

Once one of England's most important ports, King's Lynn was long known as 'the Warehouse on the Wash'. In its heyday it was said you could cross from one side of the River Great Ouse to the other by simply stepping from boat to boat. Something of the salty port-town tang can still be felt at **True's Yard** (www.truesyard.co.uk; North St; adult/child £3/1.50; ☺10am-4pm Tue-Sat), where two restored fishermen's cottages explore the lives and traditions of the fisherfolk, who were packed like sardines into buildings such as these. At **Stories of Lynn** (www.kingslynntownhall.com; Saturday Market Pl; adult/child £5/3.50; ☺10am-4.30pm) a £2m revamp has seen archive sources converted into multimedia exhibits telling the stories of local seafarers, explorers, mayors and ne'er-do-wells. It's all set in the 15th-century Guildhall and the town's Georgian jail, where you get to roam around the cells.

🛏 p133

Eating & Sleeping

Aldeburgh ❶

🛏 Ocean House   B&B ££

(📞01728-452094; www.oceanhousealdeburgh.
co.uk; 25 Crag Path; s £50, d £100-120, apt per
week £1050) You are just seven paces (count
them) from the beach at Ocean House, and
many of the rustic-chic bedrooms directly
overlook the surging sea. The five-person self-
catering apartment comes with homely kitchen
and pint-sized balcony, while the top-floor
double is a true delight: water views on three
sides and a sitting room with a baby grand.

Southwold ❷

🛏 Swan   Hotel £££

(📞01502-722186; www.adnams.co.uk; Market
Sq; s £115-125, d £185-255; P 🛜 🐾) It's a
boon for beer lovers – an entire hotel owned by
Southwold brewery giant Adnams. A £4-million
refurbishment is bringing this venerable inn
bang up to date. Expect vivid colours and
contemporary bathrooms alongside plenty of
17th-century elegance. In the bar, staff are just
itching to serve you a beer brewed right next door.

Norwich ❸

🛏 Gothic House   B&B ££

(📞01603-631879; www.gothic-house-norwich.
com; King's Head Yard, Magdalen St; s/d £65/95;
P 🛜) Step through the door here and be
whisked straight back to the Regency era.
Original panelling, columns and cornices border
the swirling stairs; fresh fruit and mini-decanters
of sherry sit in elegant bedrooms that are studies
in olive green, lemon yellow and duck-egg blue.

Cromer ❺

🛏 Red Lion   Inn ££

(📞01263-514964; www.redlioncromer.co.uk;
Brook St; s £63-95, d £115-140, ste £150-180;
P 🛜) Coloured floor tiles, wooden banisters
and stained glass signal this seafront inn's 18th-
century heritage; stylish, sea-themed rooms
bring it right up to date. All bedrooms come with
baths, cafetière coffee and fresh milk – the pick
is the suite, where you can see the sea from both
the balcony and the tub. The cosy, flint-walled,
sea-view bar is the ideal spot to down a pint.

Cley-next-the-Sea ❼

🛏 George   Inn £££

(📞01263-740652; www.thegeorgehotelatcley.
co.uk; High St; d £120-345) The George may
be an age-old English inn, but the style is all
contemporary north Norfolk chic. Sure-footed
design sees bare floorboards and feature
fireplaces teamed with upcycled armchairs
and quirky chests of drawers. Opt for a room
overlooking the marshes for mesmerising views
of wind-ruffled reeds.

Wells-next-the-Sea ❿

🛏 Old Customs House   B&B ££

(📞01328-711463; www.eastquay.co.uk,
East Quay; s £80-90, d £100-110; P 🛜) The
stately but comfy feel here comes courtesy of
worn wood panels, alcoves full of books and
gorgeous creek views. Choose from the snug
Captain's Quarters or a grand four-poster room.
Breakfasts see you discussing what you'd
like with the owner – perhaps goats cheese
omelette or smoked haddock.

King's Lynn ⓯

🛏 Bank House   Boutique Hotel ££

(📞01553-660492; www.thebankhouse.co.uk;
King's Staithe Sq; s £85-129, d £115-220; P 🛜)
There's so much to love here: a quayside setting,
gently funky decor and luxury bathrooms all
make this stylish Georgian town house pretty
hard to turn down. The best bedroom (the
expansive Captain's Room) is gorgeous; but
even cheaper, river-view 'Cosy' is still charming.
Downstairs, the hip purple and pink themed
brasserie (dishes £5 to £14; noon to 8.30pm)
serves seriously good Modern British food.

STRETCH YOUR LEGS
CAMBRIDGE

Start/Finish: Grand Arcade

Distance: 3 miles

Duration: Three hours

University city Cambridge is a place in which to walk. This tour takes in a prestigious college, magnificent chapels, an ancient library, a cosy teashop and gardens lining a river filled with punts.

Take this walk on Trips

Grand Arcade

Browse some of the 60 prestigious shops in Cambridge's glitzy Grand Arcade. It's one of the few places you can park centrally, so it's a good place to start.

The Walk » Head for the Lion Yard entrance; exit onto Petty Cury, crossing the square to emerge onto stately King's Parade. Cut left to King's College Chapel.

King's College Chapel

In a city crammed with showstopping buildings, **King's College Chapel** (☎01223-331212; www.kings.cam.ac.uk/chapel; King's Pde; adult/child £9/6; ⏰9.30am-3.15pm Mon-Sat & 1.15-2.30pm Sun term time, 9.30am-4.30pm daily, to 3.30pm Dec, Jan & university holidays) is the scene-stealer. The grandiose structure is one of England's most extraordinary examples of Gothic architecture. Its intricate 80m-long, fan-vaulted ceiling is the world's largest.

The Walk » Stroll north up King's Parade.

Great St Mary's Church

A major expansion of **Great St Mary's** (www.gsm.cam.ac.uk; Senate House Hill; ⏰10am-4pm Mon-Sat, 1-4pm Sun) between 1478 and 1519 resulted in the late–Gothic Perpendicular style you see today. Striking features include the mid-Victorian stained-glass windows, seating galleries and two organs. Climb the **tower** (adult/child £3.90/2.50) for superb vistas.

The Walk » Dodge bicyclists and touting tour guides to marvel at the ornate gates of Gonville & Caius College. Soon Trinity's elaborate Tudor entrance way towers up on the left.

Trinity College

The largest of Cambridge's colleges, elegant **Trinity College** (www.trin.cam.ac.uk; Trinity St; adult/child £3/1; ⏰10am-4.30pm, closed early Apr–mid-Jun) features a sweeping Great Court: the biggest of its kind in the world. It also boasts the renowned **Wren Library** (⏰noon-2pm Mon-Fri, plus 10.30am-12.30pm Sat term time only), containing 55,000 books dated before 1820. Works include those by Shakespeare and Swift.

And an original *Winnie the Pooh*, written by Trinity graduate AA Milne.

The Walk >> Head back through Trinity's entrance and pass the front of gorgeous St John's College.

Round Church

Cambridge's intensely atmospheric **Round Church** (www.christianheritage.org.uk; Bridge St; £2.50; 🕙10am-5pm Mon-Fri, 1.30-5pm Sat, 1.30-4pm Sun) is one of only four such structures in England. It was built by the mysterious Knights Templar in 1130.

The Walk >> Cut right down sweet, narrow Portugal Pl and onto wide Jesus Green. Pass tennis players to stroll the wooden boardwalk beside the river and ranks of punts. After crossing the bridge by Magdalene College, it's not long before you reach the Backs.

The Backs

From here you'll see the stately sweep of **St John's College** amid the trees; Trinity sits next door. Welcome to 'the Backs', a series of riverside parks behind the colleges' grandiose facades and stately courts – picture-postcard snapshots of graceful bridges and student life.

The Walk >> Nip up Garret Hostel Lane for closer college views. Next come the gates of Clare College, then glimpses of the impressive King's College Chapel; the Palladian Fellows' Building is to the right. After curving beside Queens' College, cut left.

Mathematical Bridge

From Silver St's bridge, look left to spy the **Mathematical Bridge**, a flimsy-looking wooden structure built in 1749.

The Walk >> Look out for the fleets of about-to-embark punts on the right as you head up Silver St.

Fitzbillies

Cambridge's oldest bakery, **Fitzbillies** (www.fitzbillies.com; 52 Trumpington St; mains £6-12; 🕙8am-6pm Mon-Fri, 9am-7pm Sat, 10am-6pm Sun) has a soft spot in the hearts of generations of students, thanks to its ultrasticky Chelsea buns.

The Walk >> Stroll up King's Parade, passing now-familiar King's College. Turn right just before Great St Mary's, retracing your steps back to the car.

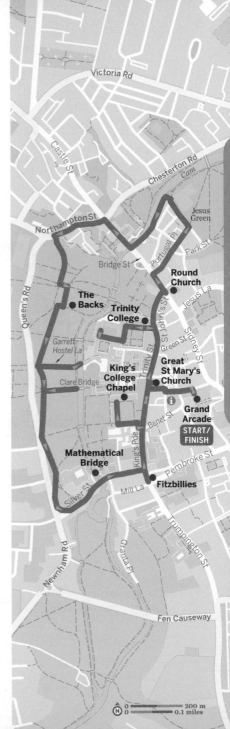

Southwest England

SUNSETS AND ECHOES OF HAPPY HOLIDAYS BECKON YOU TO BRITAIN'S SOUTHWEST. This captivating region has long drawn fleets of road trippers, tempted by rural charm, alternative vibes, sweeping moors and wilderness shores. Famous as holiday hot spots (avoid the bank holiday jams), the routes around Cornwall and south Devon see wind-whipped cliffs linking dreamy beaches, foodie enclaves, grand gardens and salty fishing ports. Dorset's Jurassic Coast offers breathtaking geology and shoreline drives. Exmoor's jagged cliffs and wild moorland deliver memorable cruising. And hipsters, hippies and heritage fans should make a beeline for the routes out of Winchester, heading west.

Jurassic Coast Bat's Head
ALEC OWEN-EVANS / GETTY IMAGES ©

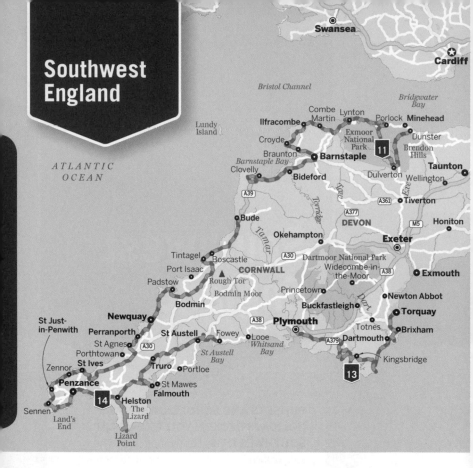

Southwest England

 Classic Trip

10 **Winchester, Glastonbury & Bath 12–14 Days**
Vivid history awaits: monumental stone circles, soaring cathedrals and glorious Roman baths. (p141)

11 **North Devon & Exmoor National Park 5–6 Days**
Steep roads and switchbacks link rugged cliffs and big-sky moors. (p153)

12 **Jurassic Coast 7 Days**
A ribboning road leads west beside fishing ports and a sea-sculpted shore. (p161)

13 **South Devon 4 Days**
Prepare for historic homes, fabulous food and little-visited shores. (p169)

14 **Epic Cornwall 10 Days**
Expect surfer bays, an eco garden, remote headlands and very sandy feet. (p177)

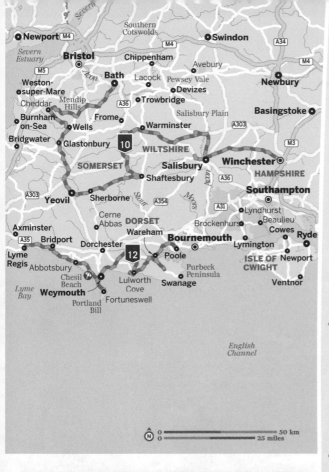

Encounter Cornwall

A kayaking trip on the enchanting River Fowey, passing pastel-coloured fishermen's cottages and thriller writer Daphne du Maurier's home on Trip 14

Coleton Fishacre

A jazz-age gem of a house, complete with theatrical vistas, croquet lawns, a tinkling piano and art deco designs on Trip 13

Tout Quarry

Head here for an extraordinary array of sculptures in-situ – fantastical designs carved into the rock of a limestone quarry on Trip 12

Porlock Hill

A brake-burning descent down a 1:4 gradient – look out for the escape lanes and 'try your brakes' signs on Trip 11

Cerne Giant

One of Britain's rudest sights: a 60m-high, well-endowed chalk figure etched into the Dorset hills on Trip 10

Porlock Weir Yachts moored in the harbour

Classic Trip

Winchester, Glastonbury & Bath

10

Buckle up for a cultural blockbuster of a road trip through England's gentle rural heartland. You'll discover archaeological wonders, imposing castles, stately homes, Georgian streets and Roman baths.

TRIP HIGHLIGHTS

185 miles

Bath
One of Britain's most beautiful cities, a Georgian delight

38 miles

Stonehenge
The unmissable jewel in England's archaeological crown

16 FINISH

● Wells

11

● Shaftesbury

● Sherborne

5

1 START

Glastonbury
Counter-culture focus of legend and myth

120 miles

Winchester
Ancient, enchanting cathedral city

0 miles

12–14 DAYS
185 MILES / 299KM

GREAT FOR...

BEST TIME TO GO
March to June to get better weather and fewer crowds.

ESSENTIAL PHOTO
Standing beside the 5000-year-old, massive monument at Stonehenge.

BEST CITYSCAPES
The exquisite, ancient architecture in Unesco World Heritage city Bath.

Classic Trip

10 Winchester, Glastonbury & Bath

This is a trip for encountering England's most extraordinary constructions. You'll circle the 5000-year-old stones at Stonehenge; prowl the still-stunning Roman baths in Bath and wonder at the soaring cathedrals at Salisbury, Sherborne and Wells. Add a safari park, stalactite-filled caverns and a saucy chalk figure, and it's your chance to explore the essence of old England and experience her best archaeological and architectural sights.

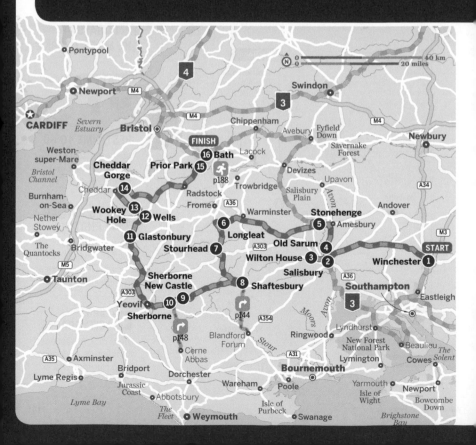

TRIP HIGHLIGHT

❶ Winchester

Calm, collegiate Winchester is a mellow must-see. The past still echoes strongly around the flint-flecked walls of this ancient cathedral city, which has been a capital to Saxon kings and the power base of bishops. Start with an exploration of 11th-century **Winchester Cathedral** (📞01962-857225; www.winchester-cathedral.org.uk; The Close; adult/child incl cathedral body & crypt tours £8/free; ⏰9.30am-5pm Mon-Sat, 12.30-3pm Sun); book ahead if you want a crypt or tower tour. One of southern England's most awe-inspiring buildings, it boasts a fine Gothic facade, one

 LINK YOUR TRIP

4 **Urban & Art Odyssey**

Just 14 miles northwest of Bath, Bristol is the launch pad for an exciting exploration of some of Britain's best cities for culture.

3 **The Historic South**

Even more history awaits on this tour of southern England's big-name heritage sights; it links to the final stop: Bath.

 ✓ **TOP TIP: STONEHENGE TICKETS**

Stonehenge operates by timed tickets, meaning if you want to guarantee entry you have to book in advance – even English Heritage and National Trust members entitled to free admission. If you're planning a peak-season visit, it's best to secure your ticket at least a week in advance.

of the longest medieval naves in Europe (164m), and a fascinating jumble of features from all eras. Highlights include the intricately carved medieval choir stalls, which sport everything from mythical beasts to a mischievous green man, and one of the UK's finest illuminated manuscripts, the dazzling **Winchester Bible**. Next, stroll 10 minutes west to Winchester's 11th-century **Great Hall** (📞01962-846476; www.hants.gov.uk/greathall; Castle Ave; suggested donation £3; ⏰10am-5pm). It holds the **Round Table**, a copy of the mythical piece of furniture that King Arthur and his knights reputedly sat around. It's thought to have been made some 700 years after he died, but is impressive nonetheless.

🛏 p73, p151

The Drive » Pick up the 'Salisbury A30' signs for a 31-mile, often dual carriageway cruise. Eventually Salisbury Cathedral's soaring spire glides into view. Head for one of the central car parks signed from the ring road.

❷ Salisbury

The 790-year-old cathedral that points your way into the city was constructed in the early English Gothic style. **Salisbury Cathedral** (📞01722-555120; www.salisburycathedral.org.uk; Cathedral Close; requested donation adult/child £7.50/none; ⏰9am-5pm Mon-Sat, noon-4pm Sun) has an elaborate exterior boasting pointed arches, flying buttresses and a highly decorative West Front. The 70m-long nave houses a 1386 medieval clock, which is probably the oldest working timepiece in the world. The cathedral's prized **Magna Carta** (www.salisburycathedral.org.uk; Cathedral Close; ⏰9.30am-4.30pm Mon-Sat, noon-3.45pm Sun) is one of only four surviving original copies of the historic agreement made in 1215 between King John and his barons. Outside, the medieval **Cathedral Close** is an atmospheric place for a stroll.

🛏 p73, p151

The Drive » From Salisbury, it's a 3-mile cruise west to gorgeous Wilton House.

③ Wilton House

Stately **Wilton House** (☎01722-746714; www.wilton house.com; Wilton; house & grounds adult/child £15/8; ⏰11.30am-5pm Sun-Thu May-Aug; **P**) provides an insight into the rarefied world of the British aristocracy. One of England's finest stately homes, the earls of Pembroke have lived here since 1542. Highlights are the Single and Double Cube Rooms, designed by the pioneering 17th-century architect Inigo Jones. Look out for magnificent period furniture, frescoed ceilings and elaborate plasterwork; they frame paintings by Van Dyck, Rembrandt and Joshua Reynolds. That will be why *The Madness of King George*, *Sense and Sensibility* and *Pride and Prejudice* were all shot here.

The Drive » Peel back east on the A36 towards Salisbury, before darting north on the A345 to Old Sarum. Total distance? Some 5 miles.

④ Old Sarum

The huge ramparts of **Old Sarum** (EH; ☎01722-335398; www.english-heritage.org.uk; Castle Rd; adult/child £4.50/2.70; ⏰10am-6pm Apr-Sep, to 5pm Oct, to 4pm Nov-Mar; **P**) sit on a grass-covered mound. It began life as a hill fort during the Iron Age, and was later occupied by the Romans, but by the mid-11th century it was an important town, and the first cathedral was built in 1092. Today it's a place to wander grassy defenses, see the original cathedral's stone foundations, and look across the Wiltshire countryside to the spire of the present Salisbury Cathedral.

The Drive » Hop back onto the A345, joining the tour buses for the 10-mile blast (via the A303) to Stonehenge. You'll see the stone circle, suddenly, thrillingly, on the right; carry on to the signed visitor centre, beyond.

TRIP HIGHLIGHT

⑤ Stonehenge

One of England's most recognisable sights, ancient **Stonehenge** (EH; ☎0370 333 1181; www.english-heritage.org.uk; adult/child on-the-day tickets £18/11, advance booking £15.50/9.30; ⏰9am-8pm Jun-Aug, 9.30am-7pm Apr, May & Sep, 9.30am-5pm Oct-Mar; **P**) has had an ultra-modern makeover, bringing an impressive visitor centre, the closure of an intrusive road and a far stronger sense of historical context. A pathway frames the ring of massive stones and although you can't walk in the circle itself, you can get close-up views of a striking sight – the remaining sets of stones, some form-

---

DETOUR: BLANDFORD FORUM

Start: ⑧ **Shaftesbury (p147)**

A 13-mile drive south of Shaftesbury, largely along the B3081/2, leads to the architectural oddity that is Blandford Forum. In 1731 the whole town was consumed in a fire and the subsequent rebuild resulted in a rarity: a town centre that dates from just one period. A short stroll pretty much anywhere here rewards the eye; a good route sees you starting at central **Market Place**, beside the cupola-crowned **Parish Church of St Peter and St Paul**; the imposing **Town Hall** sits nearby. To the west, **Salisbury St** heads up past bow windows and mathematical tiling. The **Plocks** darts off to the right to reveal more grand buildings, before The Close and **Church Walk** lead you back, 30 minutes later, to the start.

Bath Roman baths

ing huge doorways, others towering towards the sky. The **visitor centre** (EH; ☎0370 333 1181; www.english-heritage.org.uk; incl access to Stonehenge, on-the-day tickets adult/child £18/11, advance booking £15.50/9.30; ⏰9am-8pm Jun-Aug, 9.30am-7pm Apr, May & Sep, 9.30am-5pm Oct-Mar) charts the site's 5000-year past; it also sees you standing in the middle of a 360-degree projection of the stone circle through the ages and seasons – complete with midsummer sunrise and swirling starscape. The visitor centre is 1.5 miles from the stones. A fleet of trolley buses makes the 10-minute trip – you can also walk.

The Drive » Next comes a 20-mile drive as the A303/A36 slices through the high chalk plateau of Salisbury Plain. After Warminster, follow the signs for Longleat.

6 Longleat

Half ancestral mansion, half safari park, **Longleat** (☎01985-844400; www.longleat.co.uk; all-inclusive ticket adult/child £34/24, house & grounds £18.50/13.50; ⏰10am-5pm Feb–mid-Oct, to 7pm late Jul & Aug; ℗) was transformed into Britain's first safari park in 1966, turning Capability Brown's landscaped grounds into an amazing drive-through zoo, populated by a menagerie of animals more at home in the African wilderness than the fields of Wiltshire. Longleat's historic house is also packed with fine tapestries, furniture, decorated ceilings and seven libraries containing around 40,000 tomes.

The Drive » Time for a meander off the main roads as the B3092 winds gently past

ploughed fields and through woodland and scattered villages to Stourhead, 10 miles away.

7 Stourhead

Overflowing with vistas, temples and follies, **Stourhead** (NT; ☎01747-841152; www.nationaltrust.org.uk; Mere; adult/child £14.10/7.10; ⏰11am-4.30pm mid-Feb–late Oct, to 3.30pm late Oct–late Dec; ℗) is landscape gardening at its finest. The Palladian house has some fine Chippendale furniture and paintings by Claude and Gaspard Poussin, but it's a sideshow to the magnificent 18th-century **gardens** (⏰9am to 5pm, to 6pm April to October), which spread out across the valley. A picturesque 2-mile stroll in the grounds takes you past the most ornate follies,

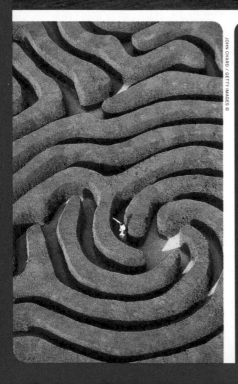

WHY THIS IS A CLASSIC TRIP
BELINDA DIXON, WRITER

For me, this trip qualifies as a classic because it delivers truly memorable moments. Encountering mighty Stonehenge is an experience you never forget; the cathedrals' beauty also lingers in the mind. The drives are special too, taking in high plateaus, ancient villages, stylish cities and chalk plains. It's a trip into the heart of this country's heritage, which also reveals how that history still echoes around England today.

Above: Glastonbury Tor at sunset
Left: Hedge maze, Longleat
Right: Hiking in Cheddar Gorge

DAVID THOMPSON / 500PX ©

JOHN CHARD / GETTY IMAGES ©

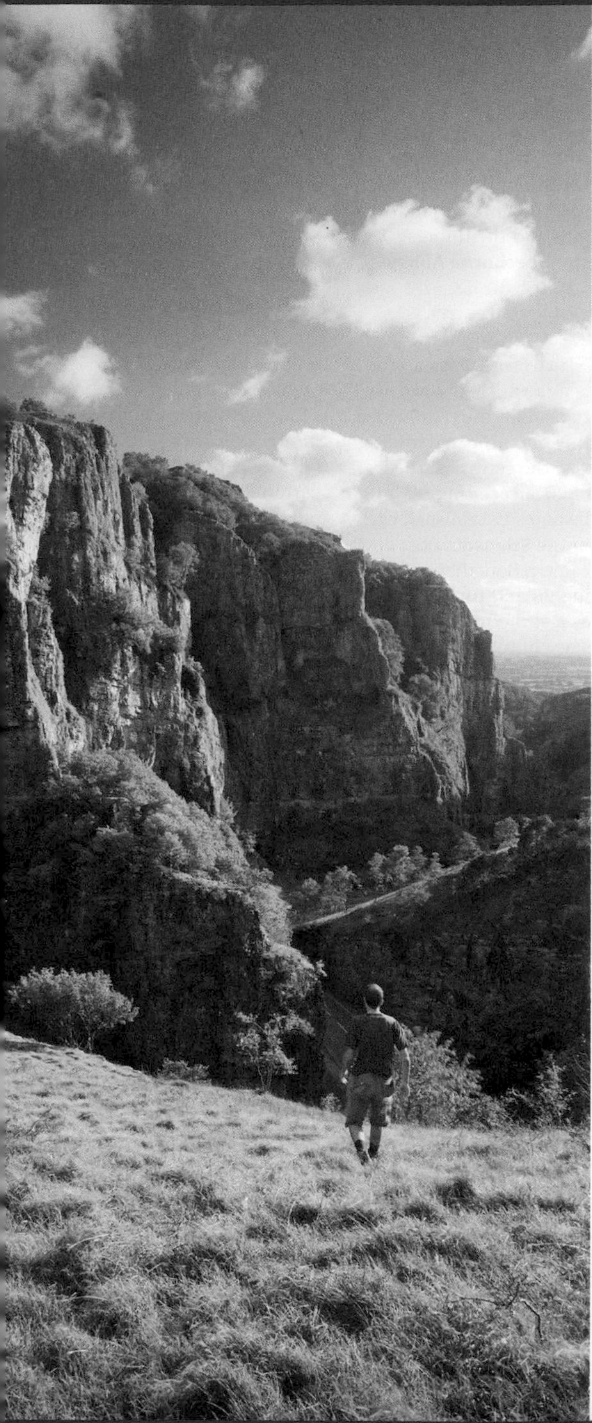

around the lake and to the Temple of Apollo.

The Drive » Keep heading south, as more B-roads snake for 11 miles beside pastoral meadows and hogbacked hills. Then climb the ridge to Shaftesbury.

⑧ Shaftesbury

The appealing market town of Shaftesbury circles around the ruins of **Shaftesbury Abbey** (☎01747-852910; www. shaftesburyabbey.org.uk; Park Walk; adult/child £3/free; ⏱10am-5pm Apr-Oct). Once England's largest and richest nunnery, it was founded in 888 by King Alfred the Great; Alfred's daughter, Aethelgifu, was its first abbess. Most of the buildings were dismantled by Henry VIII, but you can wander its foundations and see statuary and illuminated manuscripts in the museum. A few paces away sits **Gold Hill**, an often-photographed, painfully steep, quaint cobbled slope, lined by chocolate-box cottages.

🛏 p151

The Drive » Join the A30 as it swoops down out of town and undulates besides fields for 17 miles to Sherborne. As you approach, take the turn for Sherborne Castle.

⑨ Sherborne New Castle

Sir Walter Raleigh began building the impressive

Sherborne New Castle
(☎01935-812072; www.
sherbornecastle.com; New Rd;
house & gardens adult/child
£11/free, gardens only £6/free;
⊗11am-5pm Tue-Thu, Sat &
Sun Apr-Oct) in 1594, but
only got as far as the central block before being
imprisoned by James I.
James promptly sold the
castle to Sir John Digby
who added the splendid
wings you see today. In
1753 the grounds received
a mega-makeover at the
hands of landscape-
gardener extraordinaire
Capability Brown, who
added a massive lake and
the 12-hectare waterside
gardens.

The Drive » Pick up the signs
for Sherborne Town Centre; a
few minute's drive.

DETOUR:
CERNE GIANT

Start: ⑩ Sherborne

An 11-mile detour south from Sherborne (along
the B3145 and A352) leads to a truly eye-opening
sight. The **Cerne Giant** (⊗24hr; P) is a 60m-high,
51m-wide depiction of a man, etched into a chalk
hillside. Nude, full frontal and notoriously well
endowed, he's revealed in a stage of excitement that
wouldn't be allowed in most magazines. Once you've
got over his assets, ponder his age: some claim he's
Roman but the first historical reference comes in
1694, when three shillings were set aside for his repair.

⑩ Sherborne

Sherborne gleams with
mellow, orangey-yellow
stone, which has been
used to build a cluster
of 15th-century build-
ings and the impres-
sive **Sherborne Abbey**
(☎01935-812452; www.
sherborneabbey.com; Abbey
Cl; suggested donation £4;
⊗8am-6pm Apr-Sep, to 4pm
Oct-Mar) at their core. At
the height of its influence,
this magnificent building
was the central cathedral
of 26 succeeding Saxon
bishops. Established early
in the 8th century, it became a Benedictine abbey
in 998 and functioned
as a cathedral until 1075.
The church has mesmer-
ising fan vaulting that's
the oldest in the country,
a central tower supported
by Saxon-Norman piers
and an 1180 Norman
porch.

🛏 p151

The Drive » Time to head
north for 20 miles; an A- and
B-road blend which winds past
a patchwork of fields. As you
near Glastonbury, look out for
the iconic hump of Glastonbury
Tor rising out of the pan-flat
landscape.

TRIP HIGHLIGHT

⑪ Glastonbury

Thanks to converging
ley lines and ranks of
legends, Glastonbury
is England's premier
counter-culture town.
It centres around the
scattered ruins of **Glastonbury Abbey** (☎01458-
832267; www.glastonbury
abbey.com; Magdalene
St; adult/child £7.60/4.70;
⊗9am-8pm Jun-Aug, to 6pm
Mar-May & Sep-Oct, to 4pm
Nov-Feb), which was once
one of England's great
seats of ecclesiastical
power. Today's striking
ruins include some of the
nave walls, the remains
of St Mary's chapel,
and crossing arches.
A 20-minute stroll
southeast leads to the
reputedly holy waters of
the **Chalice Well** (☎01458-
835528; www.chalicewell.org.
uk; Chilkwell St; adult/child
£4.20/2.10; ⊗10am-6pm Apr-
Oct, to 4.30pm Nov-Mar), and
then **Glastonbury Tor**
(NT; www.nationaltrust.org.uk),
a vast mound that's the
focal point of Arthurian
legends and is home to a
ruined medieval chapel.
The half-hour hike to the
top reveals wrap-around
views.

🛏 p151

The Drive ›› From Glastonbury, it's a relatively routine 6-mile cruise up the A39 to Wells.

---

⑫ Wells

England's smallest city boasts one of her grandest medieval buildings: **Wells Cathedral** (Cathedral Church of St Andrew; www.wellscathedral.org.uk; Cathedral Green; requested donation adult/child £6/3; ⏱7am-7pm Apr-Sep, to 6pm Oct-Mar), a gargantuan Gothic confection built in stages between 1180 and 1508. Highlights include a **West Front** decorated with more than 300 carved figures, and some fine scissor arches. In the surrounding **Cathedral Close**, hunt out the 14th-century cobbled **Vicar's Close**, then make for the nearby **Bishop's Palace** (www.bishopspalacewells.co.uk; Market Place; adult/child £7/3; ⏱10am-6pm Apr-Oct, to 4pm Nov-Mar), a moat-ringed, 13th-century manor house with state rooms, a ruined great hall and delightful gardens, complete with natural springs.

✕ p151

The Drive ›› Peeling out of town on the A371, it's a mere 3 miles to Wookey Hole.

---

⑬ Wookey Hole

Yes, the **Wookey Hole** (www.wookey.co.uk; adult/child £18.50/14; ⏱10am-5pm Apr-Oct, to 4pm Nov-Mar) limestone caverns are incredibly touristy (the local legend of a witch inhabiting them is played for all it's worth) but the caves themselves are rightly famous for striking stalagmites and stalactites – one of which is the infamous witch herself, purportedly turned to stone by a local priest.

The Drive ›› Continue northwest on the A371 for 8 miles through a string of villages that skirts the Mendip Hills on the right (you'll be up there later). Once in Cheddar, continue through the village, following signs to Cheddar Gorge

---

⑭ Cheddar Gorge

Pick any one of the parking spots in **Cheddar Gorge** (www.cheddargorge.co.uk; Cheddar Gorge; Explorer Ticket adult/child £20/14; ⏱10.30am-5.30pm) then get out and explore. Carved out by glacial meltwater during the last Ice Age, these limestone cliffs form England's deepest natural canyon, in places towering 138m above the twisting B3135. Of the gorge's caves, **Cox's Cave** and **Gough's Cave** are the easiest to reach, and are decorated with impressive stalactites and stalagmites. The 274-step staircase known as **Jacob's Ladder** leads to a spectacular viewpoint over the gorge and a 3-mile clifftop trail. Admission covers parking, Jacob's Ladder and entry to the caves.

The Drive ›› The short drive up the gorge itself is along a twisting, sometimes single-track road that cuts through towering rock formations. At the top, the B3135 becomes a rolling, field-framed route across the roof of the Mendip plateau. Next, a series of A roads cut down from the hills and onto Prior Park, some 24 miles from Cheddar Gorge.

---

⑮ Prior Park

Partly designed by landscape architect Capability Brown, the grounds of the 18th-century **Prior Park** (NT; ☎01225-833977;

TOP TIP: GLASTONBURY TRAFFIC

To many, Glastonbury is synonymous with the **Glastonbury Festival** (www.glastonburyfestivals.co.uk), a majestic and often mud-soaked extravaganza of music and culture that attracts over 150,000 people in mid-June. If you're not festival-bound, avoid the area then as traffic jams can be horrendous; some festival-goers were stuck for 12 hours in 2016.

Classic Trip

www.nationaltrust.org.uk; Ralph Allen Dr; adult/child £6.50/3.40; ⏰10am-5.30pm Feb-Oct daily, to 4pm Sat & Sun Nov-Jan) **estate feature cascading lakes and a graceful Palladian bridge, one of only four such** structures in the world (look out for the period graffiti, some of which dates back to the 1800s). Of the estate's lovely pathways, the pick is the **Bath Skyline**, a 6-mile circular trail offering truly inspirational views.

The Drive ›› From Prior Park, it's a fraction over a mile, via parklands and suburbs, to the city of Bath.

BATH'S HISTORY

Legend has it King Bladud, a Trojan refugee and father of King Lear, founded Bath some 2800 years ago when his pigs were cured of leprosy by a dip in the muddy swamps. The Romans established the town of Aquae Sulis in AD 44 and built the extensive **Roman Baths** complex and a temple to the goddess Sulis-Minerva.

Long after the Romans decamped, the Anglo-Saxons arrived, and in 944 a monastery was founded on the site of the present **Bath Abbey**. Throughout the Middle Ages, Bath was an ecclesiastical centre and a wool-trading town, but it wasn't until the early 18th century that Ralph Allen and the celebrated dandy Richard 'Beau' Nash made Bath the centre of fashionable society. Allen developed the quarries at Coombe Down, constructed **Prior Park** and employed the two John Woods (father and son) to create Bath's signature buildings.

During WWII Bath was hit by the Luftwaffe during the so-called Baedeker raids, which targeted historic cities in an effort to sap British morale. Several houses on the **Royal Crescent** and the **Circus** were badly damaged, and the city's **Assembly Rooms** were gutted by fire, although all have since been restored.

In 1987 Bath became the only city in Britain to be declared a Unesco World Heritage site in its entirety, leading to many subsequent wrangles over construction and development, most recently concerning the design of the redeveloped **Thermae Bath Spa** and **SouthGate** shopping centre.

TRIP HIGHLIGHT

⑯ Bath

Home to some of Britain's grandest Georgian architecture, Bath is also one of the nation's most beautiful cities; a walk (p188) around the streets is richly rewarded. The **Museum of Bath Architecture** (☎01225-333895; www.museumofbath architecture.org.uk; The Vineyards, The Paragon; adult/child £5.50/2.50; ⏰2-5pm Tue-Fri, 10.30am-5pm Sat & Sun mid-Feb–Nov) explores the stories behind the construction of the most striking structures and features antique tools and a 1:500 scale model of the city. Bath is also famously a location featured in Jane Austen's novels including *Persuasion* and *Northanger Abbey*; the writer was a city resident for five years and remained a regular visitor and keen student of the city's social scene. In the **Jane Austen Centre** (☎01225-443000; www.janeausten.co.uk; 40 Gay St; adult/child £11/5.50; ⏰9.45am-5.30pm Apr-Oct, 10am-4pm Nov-Mar) guides in Regency costumes regale you with Austen-esque tales as you tour memorabilia relating to her Bath.

🛏 p73, p151, p203

Eating & Sleeping

Winchester ❶

🛏 Wykeham Arms   Inn £££

(📞01962-853834; www.wykehamarms
winchester.co.uk; 75 Kingsgate St; s/d/ste
£85/150/200; 🅿🛜) At 250-odd years old, the
Wykeham bursts with history – it used to be a
brothel and also put Nelson up for a night (some
say the events coincided). Creaking stairs lead
to plush bedrooms that manage to be both
deeply established but also on-trend; brass
bedsteads meet jazzy throws, oak dressers
sport stylish lights. Simply smashing.

Salisbury ❷

🛏 St Ann's House   B&B ££

(📞01722-335657; www.stannshouse.co.uk;
32 St Ann St; s £64, d £89-110; 🛜) The aromas
wafting from breakfast may well spur you from
your room: powerful coffee; cinnamon-and-
lemon banana bread; chilli and beef sausages;
poached eggs and Parma ham. Utter elegance
reigns upstairs where well-chosen antiques,
warm colours and Turkish linen ensure a
supremely comfortable stay.

Shaftesbury ❽

🛏 Old Chapel   B&B ££

(📞01747-852404; www.theoldchapelbb.co.uk;
9 Breach Lane; s/d £70/100; 🅿🛜) Sleep
spots don't come much more characterful
than this: a converted Victorian chapel with
slender, two-storey windows, light-filled atria
and massive support beams. Smoothly comfy
bedrooms feature fresh flowers and cookie jars;
from the guest lounge you can see all the way to
Salisbury Plain.

Sherborne ❿

🛏 Cumberland House   B&B ££

(📞01935-817554; www.bandbdorset.co.uk;
Green Hill; d £75-80; 🅿🛜) Artistry oozes from
these history-rich rooms – bright scatter rugs

sit on flagstone floors; lemon and oatmeal walls
undulate between wonderfully wonky beams.
Gourmet breakfasts include freshly squeezed
orange juice; arrive around 4pm and expect an
offer of tea, taken in the garden or beside the fire.

Glastonbury ⓫

🛏 Magdalene House   B&B ££

(📞01458-830202; www.magdalenehouse
glastonbury.co.uk; Magdalene St; s £70-
95, d £90-105, f £130-140; 🅿🛜) Artfully
decorated Magdalene used to be a school
run by Glastonbury's nuns, and one room still
overlooks the abbey grounds. Each of the tall,
light rooms is an array of olive, oatmeal and
other soft tones, while tasteful knick-knacks
give it all a homely feel.

Wells ⓬

🍴 Goodfellows Cafe & Seafood
Restaurant   Cafe ££

(📞01749-673866; www.goodfellowswells.co.uk;
5 Sadler St; mains £11-24; 🕚11am-3pm daily,
6-9.30pm Wed-Sat) There's a choice of eating
options in Goodfellows' three vibrant rooms:
the continental cafe menu offers cakes, pastries
and light lunches (opt to pay either £10 or £19
for two courses and a drink). Or book for an
evening fine-dining experience; £29 gets you
three classy courses, while the five-course
seafood tasting menu (£49) is an absolute treat.

Bath ⓰

🛏 Three Abbey Green   B&B ££

(📞01225-428558; www.threeabbeygreen.com;
3 Abbey Green; d £90-200, apt £160; 🛜) Rarely
in Bath do you get somewhere as central as
this Georgian town house with such spacious
rooms. Elegant, 18th-century-style furnishing
are teamed with swish wet room bathrooms,
and the opulent Lord Nelson suite features a
vast four-poster bed. There's also a two-person,
self-catering apartment nearby (two-night
minimum stay).

North Devon & Exmoor National Park

11

Stand by for a rip-roaring roller-coaster of a ride west along a cliff-framed shore. On this drive you'll negotiate precipitous inclines and hairpin bends, and marvel at jaw-dropping sea views.

TRIP HIGHLIGHTS

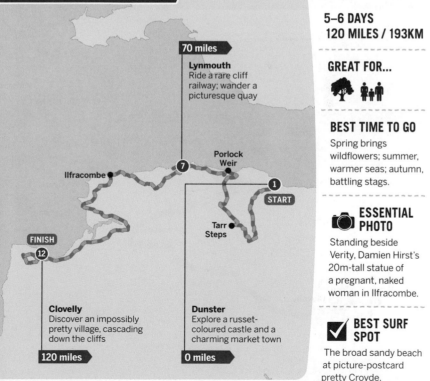

70 miles

Lynmouth
Ride a rare cliff railway; wander a picturesque quay

Porlock Weir

Ilfracombe

7

1

START

Tarr Steps

FINISH

12

Clovelly
Discover an impossibly pretty village, cascading down the cliffs

120 miles

Dunster
Explore a russet-coloured castle and a charming market town

0 miles

5–6 DAYS
120 MILES / 193KM

GREAT FOR...

BEST TIME TO GO
Spring brings wildflowers; summer, warmer seas; autumn, battling stags.

ESSENTIAL PHOTO
Standing beside Verity, Damien Hirst's 20m-tall statue of a pregnant, naked woman in Ilfracombe.

BEST SURF SPOT
The broad sandy beach at picture-postcard pretty Croyde.

Clovelly Boats pulled up on the pebbly shore

153

11

North Devon & Exmoor National Park

It's the kind of road trip cars were made for. From quaint villages you'll climb to open moorland topped by an overarching sky. Here single-track roads wind between free-roaming ponies; you might even spot wild deer. Motor down to picturesque quays, burn your brakes on white-knuckle descents, then bump along toll roads. Coal-black cliffs fill your windscreen en route to surfing beaches and quaint swimming coves. It's an unforgettable drive.

- - - - - - - - - - - -
TRIP HIGHLIGHT

❶ Dunster

The pretty town of Dunster is a tempting tangle of cobbled streets and bubbling brooks. It's presided over by rose-stone **Dunster Castle** (NT; ☎01643-821314; www.nationaltrust.org.uk; Castle Hill; adult/child £10.30/5.15; ⏰11am-5pm Mar-Oct; ℗), whose oldest sections are 13th century. Look out for Tudor furnishings, 17th-century plasterwork and a ridiculously grand staircase. The colourful

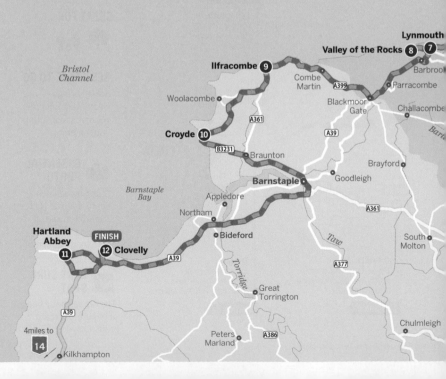

terraced gardens have views across Exmoor's shores and lead to an 18th-century **watermill** (NT; ☎01643-821759; www.nationaltrust.org.uk; Mill Lane; ☺10am-5pm Mar-Oct), where most of the original cogs, wheels and grinding stones still rotate away. A short walk leads to **St George's Church** (St George's St; ☺9am-5pm) with its intricately carved fan-vaulted rood screen; a 16th-century **dovecote** sits just behind.

🛏 p159

The Drive » Motoring 15 miles south along the A396, a steep wooded ridge rises to the west. But on this stretch you're not driving on the higher moor; that comes later. Instead it's a rolling route past moss-covered trees.

----

② Dulverton

Dulverton is a quintessential Exmoor market town. Sitting at the base of the Barle Valley, it's home to a collection of gun-sellers, fishing-tackle stores and gift shops. It's a pleasing place to stock up on local picnic foods at the **Exclusive Cake Co**

(www.exclusivecakecompany.co.uk; 19 High St; snacks from £3; ☺9am-4pm Mon-Fri, to 2pm Sat) and pick up maps and local books at the **tourist office** (☎01398-323841; www.exmoor-national park.gov.uk; 7-9 Fore St; ☺10am-5pm Apr-Oct, limited winter hours).

🛏 p159

The Drive » From the centre of town, take the B3223 north towards Simonsbath. Soon woods clear and you're onto the open, undulating moor. Five miles out of Dulverton pick up signs to Tarr Steps, a mile away down steep, winding lanes. Park at the car park, continuing 500yd on foot.

----

③ Tarr Steps

Exmoor's most famous landmark, **Tarr Steps** (☺24hr) is an ancient stone clapper bridge shaded by gnarled old

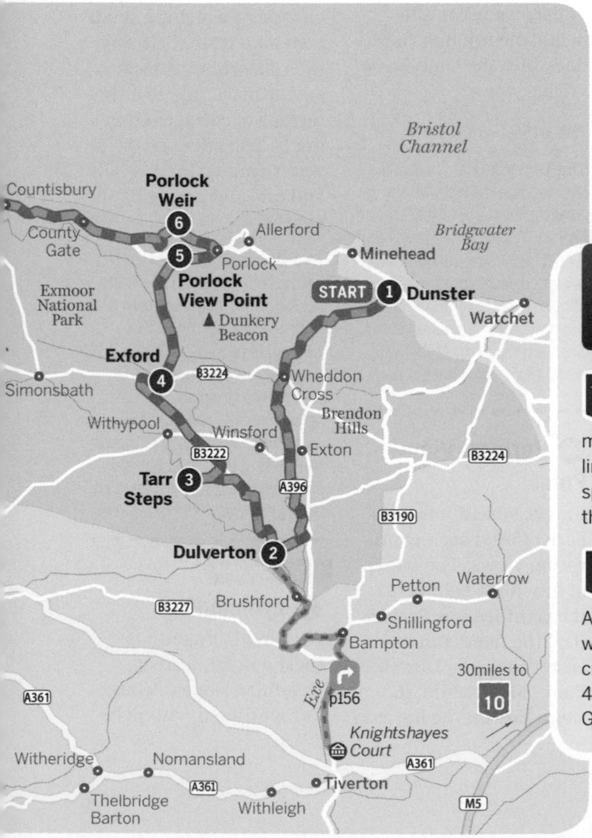

LINK YOUR TRIP

14 Epic Cornwall
From Clovelly, head 17 miles southwest to Bude to link up with a charismatic, spray-dashed drive around the end of England.

10 Winchester, Glastonbury & Bath
A history-rich tour of the west's best big-name cultural sights. Pick it up 40 miles east of Dunster at Glastonbury.

155

DETOUR:
KNIGHTSHAYES COURT

Start: ❷ Dulverton (p155)

An 11-mile detour south from Dulverton (via the B3222 and A396) leads to a glorious example of Victorian architectural excess. **Knightshayes Court** (NT; ☎01884-254665; www.nationaltrust.org.uk; Bolham; adult/child £9.30/4.65; ⊙11am-5pm daily early Feb-Oct; ℗) was designed by the eccentric architect William Burges for the Tiverton MP John Heathcoat Mallory in 1869. Burges' obsession with the Middle Ages resulted in a plethora of stone curlicues, ornate mantles and carved figurines, plus lavish Victorian decoration (the smoking and billiard rooms feel just like a gentlemen's club). Outside is a waterlily pool, topiary, formal terraces and a kitchen garden.

trees. Its huge slabs are propped up on stone columns embedded in the River Barle. Local folklore aside (which declares it was used by the devil for sunbathing), it first pops into the historical record in the 1600s, and had to be rebuilt after 21st-century floods.

The Drive » Back up the hill, for the 7-mile roof-of-the-moor meander to Exford, with swathes of honey-brown bracken and yellow gorse unfolding on either side. Cross the bridge by the Emoor White Horse inn, parking beside the village green.

❹ Exford

There's not much to Exford, but what there is defines quaint. This tiny village clusters around a green: a pleasant muddle of cottages and slate-roofed houses. Time then to stroll beside the rush-

ing river Exe, sip a drink or eat a snack in the neighbouring pubs and duck into the time-warp village stores.

🛏 p159

The Drive » Next, a 6-mile leg. Head up the hill with the village green to your left, signed Porlock. It's another steep climb (you'll feel your ears pop) that's rewarded with a prolonged burst of open moor. Eventually the sea darts into your windscreen. Soon after, you meet the A39; cross it to stop in the car park.

❺ Porlock View Point

Rarely, surely, has a car park offered such captivating views. The sweep of beach far below to the right frames Porlock Bay; the headland at its eastern edge is Hurlstone Point. Meanwhile, the shore line on the horizon,

dotted with cliffs and toy-sized structure, is actually the coast of South Wales.

The Drive » Turn left at the car park mouth, for a second-gear descent down the infamous 1:4 Porlock Hill; expect hairpin bends, escape lanes and 'try your brakes' signs. Once in Porlock village, peel left and down to Porlock Weir. In all, a 4-mile drive.

❻ Porlock Weir

The charismatic breakwater of Porlock Weir has striking coastal views and an arching pebble beach framing the entrance to a pint-sized harbour – watching small boats navigate their way in is absorbing. A lock gate leads across to a tiny terrace of cottages clinging to a slender spit of water-framed land; a pub and gift and art shops sit nearby.

The Drive » Take the lane between the Ship Inn and Cafe Porlock Weir. It cuts sharply right, signed Worthy. At the white gate pay a £2 toll. A bouncing road climbs through woods; sea glimpses emerge below. The A39 rolls along a moorland plateau to spectacular sea views. As the road plunges, signs speak volumes: 'Rockfalls', '12% gradient'. It's 12 miles in all.

TRIP HIGHLIGHT

❼ Lynmouth

Bustling Lynmouth is tucked in amid steep, tree-lined slopes. A busy harbour lined with pubs

Valley of The Rocks Rock formations by the shore

and souvenir shops leads west to a **Cliff Railway** (📞01598-753486; www. cliffrailwaylynton.co.uk; adult single/return £2.70/3.70, child £1.60/2.20; ⏰10am-5pm Feb-Oct, to 7pm Jun-Aug). This extraordinary piece of 1890s water-powered engineering sees two connected cars shuttle up and down the sloping cliff face. All burnished wood and polished brass, it's an unmissable ride. It delivers you in hill town **Lynton** to browse the shops and head to the churchyard of **St Mary the Virgin** (Church Hill) for views of precipitous **Countisbury Hill** (the one

you drove down on the way in). Hop back on the cliff railway and back to your car.

🛏 p159

The Drive ⟩⟩ Now, a 2-mile drive. Take the right fork up the hill into Lynton – another set of 1:4 switchbacks. Ignore the turn for Simonsbath, carrying on to pick up the Valley of the Rocks signs. Soon you're heading into a deep, broad dip, where towering rock formations create a Wild West feel.

- - - - - - - - - -

❽ Valley of the Rocks

Welcome to a perfect pit stop for a dramatic stroll. The awesome

geology in the shore-side **Valley of the Rocks** was described by poet Robert Southey as 'rock reeling upon rock, stone piled upon stone, a huge terrifying reeling mass'. Look out for the formations dubbed the **Devil's Cheesewring** and **Ragged Jack** – and also the feral goats that wander the tracks.

The Drive ⟩⟩ Time for a 20-mile drive. Head back into Lynton to pick up signs to Ilfracombe, initially along a climbing A39. At Blackmoor Gate peel right onto the A399, heading down Combe Martin's long High St, to emerge at Ilfracombe.

157

⑨ Ilfracombe

In Ilfracombe steep headlands plummet down to pint-sized beaches, and paths cling to sheer cliffs. At the harbour mouth Damien Hirst's towering, 20m statue **Verity** (The Pier) depicts a naked pregnant woman holding aloft a huge spear. On the seaward side her skin is peeled back, revealing sinew, fat and foetus. A mile-long stroll west along the waterfront walkway leads to the Victorian **Tunnels-beaches** (📞01271-879882; www.tunnelsbeaches.co.uk; Granville Rd; adult/child £2.50/1.95; ⏰10am-5pm Apr-Oct, to 7pm Jul & Aug), where four tunnels have been hacked out of solid rock. They lead to a strip of beach where you can still plunge into the sea in tidal bathing pools.

🛏 p159

The Drive » Take the A361 south. At Mullacott Roundabout, ignore the SatNav and take the B3343 (signed Woolacombe). Then, amid a web of unclassified lanes, pick up signs for Croyde, to enter the village from the northeast. A 10-mile leg in all.

⑩ Croyde

The cheerful, chilled village of Croyde is Devon's surf central. Here thatched roofs peep out over racks of wetsuits, and cool types in board shorts sip beer in 17th-century inns. **Ralph's** (📞01271-890147; Hobbs Hill, Croyde; surfboard & wetsuit per 4/24hr £12/18, bodyboard & wetsuit £10/15; ⏰9am-dusk mid-Mar–Dec) hires out surf equipment. Lessons are provided by **Surf South West** (📞01271-890400; www.surfsouthwest.com; Croyde Burrows, Croyde; per half-/full day £34/64; ⏰Mar-Nov) and **Surfing Croyde Bay** (📞01271-891200; www.surfingcroydebay.co.uk; 8 Hobbs Hill, Croyde; per half-/full day £35/70). The sandy beach is 10 minutes' walk from the village centre.

🛏 p159

The Drive » Time to cover some miles – 33 to be exact. The B3231 winds west out of the village, revealing remarkable views of the 3-mile sweep of Saunton Sands. After Barnstaple, the A39 (aka the 'Atlantic Hwy') glides southwest. At Higher Clovelly the B3248 branches off to Hartland village; your next stop is 1½ miles further on.

⑪ Hartland Abbey

History seems to flow from the walls of enchanting **Hartland Abbey** (📞01237-441496; www.hartlandabbey.com; adult/child £12/5; ⏰house 2-5pm, grounds 11.30am-5pm Sun-Thu Apr-Sep; 🅿). Built in the 12th century, it was a monastery until Henry VIII grabbed it in the Dissolution; he then gave it to the sergeant of his wine cellar. Today its sumptuous interiors house vivid murals, an ornate Alhambra Passage and a Regency library designed in the Strawberry Hill Gothic style.

The Drive » A 6½-mile leg – largely retracing your route to Higher Clovelly. From there pick up signs to Clovelly village itself.

TRIP HIGHLIGHT

⑫ Clovelly

Picture-postcard pretty **Clovelly** (www.clovelly.co.uk; adult/child £7/4.40; ⏰9am-6.30pm Jun-Sep, 9.30am-5pm Apr-May & Oct, 10am-4pm Nov-Mar; 🅿) is privately owned, so park up beside the hilltop visitor centre and pay your admission. Then stagger down cobbled village streets that are so steep cars can't cope – supplies are still brought in by sledge; you'll see these big bread baskets on runners leaning outside homes. Charles Kingsley, author of the children's classic *The Water Babies*, spent much of his early life in Clovelly – don't miss his former house, or the highly atmospheric fisherman's cottage and the village's twin chapels.

🛏 p159

Eating & Sleeping

Dunster ❶

🛏 Spears Cross   B&B ££

(📞01643-821439; www.spearscross.co.uk; 1 West St; d £97-107; P 🛜) 'We simply like to make breakfasts more fun', says the owner of this 15th-century B&B. That explains tummy-tempting options such as scrambled egg with watercress, tomatoes and Cheddar, and muffins topped with asparagus and poached egg. The just-as-delicious decor sees age-old beams frame wood panels, floral furnishings and raspberry-red walls.

Dulverton ❷

🛏 Town Mills   B&B ££

(📞01398-323124; www.townmillsdulverton.co.uk; High St; s/d £85/95; P 🛜) The top choice if you want to stay in Dulverton itself is a thoroughly contemporary riverside mill with creamy carpets, magnolia walls and bursts of floral art.

Exford ❹

🛏 Exmoor White Horse   Inn £££

(📞01643-831229; www.exmoor-whitehorse.co.uk; Exford; d £180-205; P 🛜) Step through the door here to find everything you want from an Exmoor coaching inn: a friendly bar with a real fire, a local-produce packed restaurant (mains £14 to £22) and smoothly comfy rooms. On summer afternoons the riverside beer terrace is a firm favourite with the locals – an idyllic spot to watch the horse riders trot by. Bar food is served from noon to 9pm, while the restaurant itself serves from 7pm to 9pm.

Lynmouth ❼

🛏 Rock House   B&B ££

(📞01598-753508; www.rock-house.co.uk; Manor Green, Lynmouth; s £45-88, d £110-125) The setting is simply superb: right on Lynmouth's pocket-sized harbour, steep hills sloping up on three sides. Contemporary rooms sport leather headboards, lilac scatter-cushions and mini-armchairs. All have extraordinary views; the best is number four, where the window is right next to the beach.

Ilfracombe ❾

🛏 Westwood   B&B ££

(📞01271-867443; www.west-wood.co.uk; Torrs Park; d £85-125; P 🛜) Modern, minimal and marvellous; this ultra-chic guesthouse is a study of neutral tones and dashes of vivid colour. It's graced by pony-skin chaises longues and stand-alone baths; some rooms have sea glimpses.

Croyde ❿

🛏 Thatch   Inn ££

(📞01271-890349; www.thethatchcroyde.com; 14 Hobbs Hill, Croyde; d £60-110, f £130) A legendary venue among surfers, this cavernous, thatched pub's trendy bedrooms feature subtle creams, stripes and checks; the owners offer extra rooms above another pub and in the cottage opposite. The pick, though, are at their nearby (quieter) Priory, where elegant beams frame exposed stone. Decent pub grub, too (mains £9.95 to £14.95).

Clovelly ⓬

🛏 Donkey Shoe Cottage   B&B £

(📞01237-431601; www.donkeyshoecottage.co.uk; 21 High St; s/d £30/60) A country-style B&B plumb on Clovelly's crazily steep hill, with wooden floors, raspberry-red walls and sea views – the best is from room 3, under the eaves.

Jurassic Coast

On this road trip to remember, the route ribbons along a World Heritage shore. Expect gorgeous bays, iconic castles and a windscreen full of views.

TRIP HIGHLIGHTS

69 miles

Abbotsbury Swannery
Walk amid 600 swans at their lagoon-side nesting-ground

13 miles

Corfe Castle
Fall in love with these romantic, hill top ruins

FINISH
Lyme Regis

11

10

6

3

Poole
START

Lulworth Cove

Chesil Beach
Clamber up an awe-inspiring, 18-mile-long pebble ridge

54 miles

Durdle Door
Swim beside a massive, majestic millennia-old rock arch

28 miles

**7 DAYS
87 MILES / 140KM**

GREAT FOR...

BEST TIME TO GO
Avoid school summer holidays; spring and autumn are ideal.

ESSENTIAL PHOTO
The Durdle Door: a monumental, 150-million-year-old stone arch that rises from the sea.

BEST DISCOVERIES
Fossil-hunting on the beach at history-rich Lyme Regis.

Durdle Door Portland stone arch

12 Jurassic Coast

One of the west's best drives, this route rolls up chalk ridges, through thatched villages and along sea-fringed roads. It takes in vast beaches, unforgettable swim spots, a soaring rock arch and fossils galore. History is everywhere: from fairy-tale castles and an art-packed quarry to the golden cider in your glass. Prepare to see the pick of Dorset's sights, and the sea and the sunset as you keep heading west.

❶ Poole

The attractive historic buildings in the old port of Poole include the Tudor **King Charles pub** on Thames St; the cream **Old Harbour Office** (1820s) next door; and the impressive red-brick **Custom House** (1813) opposite. A few yards away, the **Waterfront Museum** (📞01202-262600; www.boroughofpoole.com/museums; 4 High St; ⏲10am-5pm Mon-Sat, noon-5pm Sun) is a beautifully restored 15th-century warehouse

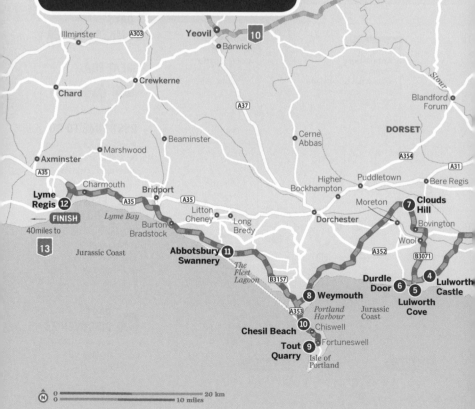

housing a 2300-year-old, 10m-long, 14-tonne Iron Age logboat dredged up from Poole Harbour. From the quay, boats shuttle to the wooded nature reserve of **Brownsea Island** (NT; 01202-707744; www.nationaltrust.org.uk; adult/child £6.30/3.15; ⏱10am-5pm late Mar–Oct), just off shore.

🛏 p167

The Drive » Pick up signs for the A350 to Dorchester/Blandford. Then peel off onto the A351 to Wareham for the 10-mile drive.

❷ Wareham

The Saxons built sturdy Wareham in the 10th century; their legacy lingers in surviving remnants of the market town's defensive walls – explore them on the 45-minute **Walls Walk**. Or make a beeline for one section: the 11th-century **St Martin's on the Walls** (North St, Wareham; ⏱9am-5pm) church at the top of North St. It features a 12th-century fresco and a marble effigy of TE Lawrence (aka Lawrence of Arabia), who lived locally.

The Drive » Continue south on the A351, a tree-lined but unremarkable drive. Unremarkable, that is, until 4 miles on, when the startling, shattered hilltop ruins of mighty Corfe Castle leap into view.

TRIP HIGHLIGHT

❸ Corfe Castle

Make for the National Trust car park, then walk two minutes to **Corfe Castle** (NT; 01929-481294; www.nationaltrust.

org.uk; The Square; adult/child £8.50/4.25; ⏱10am-6pm Apr-Sep, to 4pm Oct-Mar) itself. Once home to Sir John Bankes, Charles I's right-hand man, the castle was besieged by Cromwellian forces in the English Civil War. In 1646 the plucky Lady Bankes directed a six-week defense, and the castle fell only after being betrayed from within. The Roundheads then gunpowdered Corfe Castle apart; turrets and soaring walls still sheer off at precarious angles – the splayed-out gatehouse looks likc it's just been blown up.

🛏 p167

The Drive » Put Corfe Castle in your rear-view mirror: head back up to Wareham then onto the B3070 to East Lulworth, some 6 miles. Rattle over the cattle grid and into Lulworth Castle's grounds.

❹ Lulworth Castle

Pay £3 to park, then delight in creamy, dreamy **Lulworth Castle** (EH; ☎01929-400352;

A354

Moors

Wimborne

Ferndown

A31

Hamworthy

Bournemouth

❶ **Poole**

START

❷ **Wareham**

A351

Norden

❸ **Corfe Castle**

Isle of Purbeck ○ Swanage

English Channel (La Manche)

🔗 LINK YOUR TRIP

10 **Winchester, Glastonbury & Bath**

Stonehenge, soaring cathedrals and the sumptuous city of Bath. Connect with Sherborne, 27 miles north of Weymouth.

13 **South Devon**

Some 50 miles southwest of this trip's end, Torquay leads to a charming tour of historic ports, an eco-town, a vineyard and Agatha Christie's home.

www.lulworth.com; East
Lulworth; adult/child £5/3;
🕐10.30am-5pm Sun-Fri Apr-
Dec). Looking more like
a French chateau than
a traditional English
castle, it was built in
1608 as a hunting lodge,
and has survived extrava-
gant owners, extensive
remodelling and a fire in
1929. It's been extensively
restored; check out the
reconstructed kitchen
and cellars, then climb
the tower for sweeping
coastal views.

The Drive » Turn right for a
2-mile dawdle along rural roads,
past a military tank camp and
through West Lulworth, to the
main Heritage Centre car park
at Lulworth Cove.

- - - - - - - - - -

❺ Lulworth Cove

At the village of Lulworth
Cove a pleasing jumble
of thatched cottages and
fishing gear leads down
to the eponymous bay – a
perfect, narrow-mouthed
crescent of white cliffs.
After admiring the views
and browsing the seafood
at the shack-like **Cove
Fish** (☎01929-400807;
Lulworth Cove; fish from £3,
crab £3-4; 🕐10am-4pm
Tue-Sun Easter-Sep, plus some
winter weekends), pop into
the **Heritage Centre**
(☎01929-400587; www.
lulworth.com; main car park,
Lulworth Cove; 🕐10am-5pm)
to learn how rock types
and erosion have shaped
this remarkable shore.
Then walk two minutes
to see geology in action
at the **Lulworth Crumple**,

where layers of rock form
dramatically zigzagging
folds.

🛏 p167

The Drive » It's back uphill,
turning left with the brown signs
to Durdle Door; a steep 1-mile
climb beside hummocky hills.
Head through the campsite to
the clifftop car park (two/four/
six hours £3/4/5).

- - - - - - - - - -

TRIP HIGHLIGHT
❻ Durdle Door

The 15-minute walk from
the car before you see
the **Durdle Door** is well
worth the effort. This
immense, sea-fringed,
150-million-year-old
Portland stone arch was
created by a combination
of massive geological
movement and erosion.
Today it's framed by
shimmering bays; bring a
swimsuit and head down
the hundreds of steps for
an unforgettable dip.

The Drive » Next, a 12-mile
drive. Head up the B3071 to
Wool then pick up signs to
the Tank Museum. The gorse-
framed route leads past the
museum, through the army
village of Bovington Camp and
onto roadside Clouds Hill.

- - - - - - - - - -

❼ Clouds Hill

Clouds Hill (NT; ☎01929-
405616; www.nationaltrust.
org.uk; near Bovington; adult/
child £6/3; 🕐11am-5pm Mar–
Oct; P) was home to TE
Lawrence (1888–1935),
the British soldier who
became legendary after
working with Arab tribes

against Turkish forces in
WWI. This tiny cottage
provides a compelling
insight into a complex
man; look out for Law-
rence's evocative desert
campaign photos, his
French Crusader castle
sketches and the desk
where he abridged *Seven
Pillars of Wisdom*.

The Drive » Join the B3390/
A353 for the 20-mile cruise
through rolling hills southwest
to Weymouth. There, pass the
reed-filled lagoons of the bird
reserve and ranks of B&Bs
to park up on the seafront or
beside the waterfront Pavilions
theatre.

DAVIDYOUNG / SHUTTERSTOCK ©

Abbotsbury Swannery Annual nesting place for some 600 swans

❽ Weymouth

Historic harbour, 3-mile beach, candy-striped kiosks – welcome to the seaside kitsch-rich resort of Weymouth. The nostalgia-inducing offerings along the fine sandy shore could see you marvelling at highly skilled **sand sculptors**, renting a deckchair or pedalo, or watching a **Punch and Judy** show. A grid of sweet streets leads to an **Old Harbour** packed with fishing boats; the cannon-studded defenses of 19th-century **Nothe Fort** (☏01305-766626; www. nothefort.org.uk; Barrack Rd; adult/child £8/1; ⏰10.30am-5.30pm Apr-Sep) sit nearby.

🛏 p167

The Drive ❯❯ Join the A354 southwest towards Portland. The long straight road onto the Isle is an exhilarating stretch, sweeping between a vast harbour and high-ridged pebble beach. The twisting climb through Chiswell on the Fortuneswell road reveals Portland's unique character: remote, rugged, sometimes bleak, but beautiful. At the hill's crest follow the signs to Tout Quarry Park (around 5 miles in all).

❾ Tout Quarry

Portland's white limestone has been quarried for centuries and features in some of the world's finest buildings, such as the British Museum and St Paul's Cathedral. The disused workings of **Tout Quarry** (near Fortuneswell; ⏰24hr; Ⓟ) now house more than 50 sculptures carved into the rock in situ. It results in a fascinating combination of raw materials, the detritus of the quarrying process and the beauty of chiselled works. Stroll to

TOP TIP: FIRING RANGES

The picturesque Purbeck Hills are also tank live-firing ranges; road signs warn: '! Sudden Gunfire'. Our route avoids restricted areas, but the ranges *are* sometimes accessible. A southerly Corfe Castle to East Lulworth route (offering sea glimpses and tank remnants) is often open holidays and weekend; call ☎01929-404819 to check.

the cliffs at the quarry's edge for 180-degree views sweeping down to the awe-inspiring 18 miles of Chesil Beach.

The Drive » Retrace your route down off the plateau (passengers can drink in the remarkable views) and back along the thin road to the mainland. Near the end, head left into the Chesil Beach car park; in total a mere 2 miles away.

- - - - - - - - - - - -

TRIP HIGHLIGHT

⑩ Chesil Beach

One of the most breathtaking beaches in Britain, Chesil is 18 miles long, 15m high and moving inland at the rate of 5m a century. The stones on this mind-boggling, 100-million-tonne pebble ridge range from pea-sized in the west to hand-sized here in the east. The **Chesil Beach Centre** (Fine Foundation; ☎01305-206191; www.dorsetwildlife trust.org.uk; Ferrybridge; ⊙10am-5pm Easter-Sep, to 4pm Oct-Easter) details its ecosystem. From the car park an energy-sapping hike up sliding pebbles leads to the constant

surge and rattle of waves on stones and dazzling views of the sea, with the thin pebble line and the expanse of the Fleet Lagoon behind.

✗ p167

The Drive » Time to drive the road you saw from Portland: a 9-mile pootle along the B3157, rolling beside undulating fields and hills. In the midst of the thatched-cottage-rich village of Abbotsbury, turn sharp left for the Swannery.

- - - - - - - - - - - -

TRIP HIGHLIGHT

⑪ Abbotsbury Swannery

Every May some 600 free-flying swans choose to nest at **Abbotsbury Swannery** (☎01305-871130; www.abbotsbury-tourism.co.uk; New Barn Rd, Abbotsbury; adult/child £12/9; ⊙10am-5pm late-Mar–Oct), which shelters in the Fleet Lagoon. Wandering the network of trails winding between the swans' nests is an awe-inspiring experience that's punctuated by occasional territorial displays (think snuffling coughs and stand-up

flapping), ensuring that even the liveliest children are stilled.

The Drive » Continue through Abbotsbury for another glorious, second-gear climb, pausing at the lay-bys for cracking views back onto Chesil Beach. Next, a ridge-top roller-coaster of a road, framed by green fields and an improbably wide bay. Some 20 miles later you descend into Lyme Regis.

- - - - - - - - - - - -

⑫ Lyme Regis

Beach-framed and quaint, Lyme Regis is one of Dorset's most delightful towns. It's also fantastically fossiliferous – here rock-hard relics of the past pop out repeatedly from the surrounding cliffs, exposed by the landslides of a retreating shore. Delve into that heritage at **Lyme Regis Museum** (☎01297-443370; www.lymeregismuseum.co.uk; Bridge St; adult/child £4/free; ⊙10am-5pm Easter-Oct, 11am-4pm Wed-Sun Nov-Easter), which also tells the tale of local teenager Mary Anning who famously found the first full ichthyosaur skeleton near here in 1814. To find your own fossils, go on a guided walk with **Brandon Lennon** (☎07854 377519; www.lymeregisfossil walks.com; adult/child £8/6; ⊙Sat-Mon). Beyond the sandy beach stretches the **Cobb** – the town's iconic, curling sea defenses – it's hard to resist wandering their length to the tip.

🛏 p167

Eating & Sleeping

Poole ❶

🛏 Old Townhouse   B&B ££

(📞01202-670950; www.theoldtownhouse.
co.uk; 7 High St; s/d £65/95; 📶) A delightful air
of old England settles cosily over this quayside
B&B. It's largely down to the gleaming wood, big
burnished brass taps and furnishings that aren't
afraid to echo heritage styles. A central setting
and tiny patio add to the appeal.

Corfe Castle ❸

🛏 Olivers   B&B ££

(📞01929-477111; www.oliverscorfecastle.com; 5
West St; s/d/f £80/95/105) Tucked away in the
heart of the old village in a charismatic street,
Olivers combines honey-coloured beams with
country-cottage chic: repro-heritage armchairs,
mock-flock wallpaper and chunky wood
furniture. Stylish, restful, great-value rooms.

Lulworth Cove ❺

🛏 Lulworth Cove   Inn ££

(📞01929-400333; www.lulworth-coveinn.
co.uk; Main Rd, Lulworth Cove; d £110-150; 🅿📶)
What do you get for a £1.4m refurbishment? A
veritable vision of driftwood chic – whitewashed
floorboards, aquamarine panels, painted
wicker chairs and roll-top baths. Add cracking
sea views, a mini roof terrace and top-quality
gastropub grub (food served from noon to 9pm;
mains £9 to £15) and you have an irresistible inn.

🛏 Bishops   Inn £££

(📞01929-400552; www.bishopslulworth.co.uk;
Main Rd, Lulworth Cove; d £160-180; 📶📧) An
idyllic setting, pared-down designs, top-notch
linen and pamper-yourself toiletries combine to
make this a memorable play to stay – especially
if you opt for a room with Lulworth Cove views.

Or just lounge beside the pool, which also
overlooks that circle of bay. Tasty food (served
from noon to 2.30pm and 7pm to 9pm; mains
£15 to £20) spans lobster, risotto and *moules*.

Weymouth ❽

🛏 Roundhouse   B&B ££

(📞01305-761010; www.roundhouse-weymouth.
com; 1 The Esplanade; d £85-145; 📶) The decor
here is as gently eccentric as the owner – vivid
interiors combine sky blue, purple and shocking
pink with fluffy cushions and snazzy modern art.
But the best bit is the views; from all bedrooms
you can see both the beach out front and the
harbour behind.

Chesil Beach ❿

✕ Crab House Cafe   Seafood ££

(📞01305-788867; www.crabhousecafe.co.uk;
Portland Rd, Wyke Regis; mains £11-22; ⊙ noon-
2pm & 6-8.30pm Wed-Sat, noon-3.30pm Sun)
This is where the locals make for on hot summer
days, to sit beside the Fleet Lagoon amid beach-
shack-chic tucking into fresh-as-it-gets seafood.
Fish is enlivened by chilli, curry, lemon and
herbs; crab comes spicy Chinese-style or whole
for you to crack; and the oysters come with
either pesto and Parmesan or bacon and cream.

Lyme Regis ⓬

🛏 Coombe House   B&B ££

(📞01297-443849; www.coombe-house.co.uk;
41 Coombe St; d £64-72, 5-person flats per week
£360-630; 🅿) The airy, easy-going, stylish
bedrooms in this fabulous-value guesthouse
are full of bay windows, wicker and white wood.
Breakfast is delivered to your room on a trolley,
complete with homemade bread and a toaster –
perfect for a lazy lie-in in Lyme.

South Devon

13

Green, gentle and gorgeous, the coastline of south Devon is simply made for a road trip – from salty seaports to classic sandy beaches.

TRIP HIGHLIGHTS

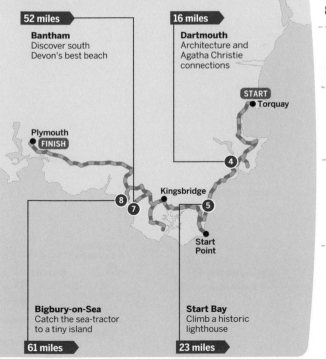

52 miles

Bantham
Discover south
Devon's best beach

16 miles

Dartmouth
Architecture and
Agatha Christie
connections

START
● Torquay

Plymouth
FINISH

④

Kingsbridge

⑧ ⑦ ⑤

**Start
Point**

Bigbury-on-Sea
Catch the sea-tractor
to a tiny island

61 miles

Start Bay
Climb a historic
lighthouse

23 miles

**4 DAYS
88 MILES / 142KM**

GREAT FOR...

BEST TIME TO GO
Bank on the best of
the British summer in
June or July.

**ESSENTIAL
PHOTO**
Standing next to the
Sherman tank at
Slapton Ley.

**BEST FOR
FAMILIES**
Larking about on
Babbacombe or
Bantham Beach.

Bantham Incoming tide at Bantham Beach

13 South Devon

From old seaside villages and thatched cottages to quaint harbours and riverside towns, south Devon sums up something essential about the English countryside. It's a wonderful landscape to drive through, a patchwork of pastoral England: green fields, old farms, pebble beaches, Victorian piers and sudden flashes of the bright blue sea. Take your time here, and pack a picnic.

❶ Torquay

Sometimes dubbed the capital of the English Riviera, this classic seaside resort makes the perfect place to begin a south Devon tour. With its palm trees and russet-red cliffs, there's a dash of elegance to Torquay's seafront, although windbreakers and buckets-and-spades define most of the town's 20-odd beaches. The best thing to do is just embrace it: take a trip on Babbacombe's **funicular railway** (www.centraltram way.co.uk; Marine Pde; per

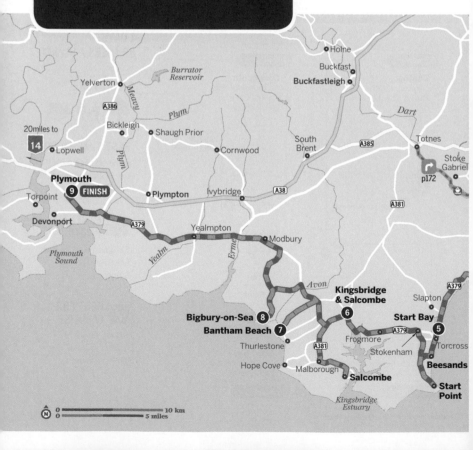

person 90p; ⏰9.30am-5.45pm Feb-Jun, Sep & Oct, to 9.30pm Jul & Aug), soak up the kitsch miniatures of the **Babbacombe Model Village** (📞01803-315315; www.model-village.co.uk; Hampton Ave; adult/child £10.95/8.95; ⏰10am-4pm, until 9pm some summer evenings), and take a sunset stroll along Paignton Pier – candyfloss in hand, of course.

✕ 🏠 p175

The Drive » The easiest route is just to follow the A379 round the bay to Paignton and Brixham; it's a pleasant 9.5-mile drive, although you'll inevitably run into jams in summertime.

35miles to
12

A380
START
① Torquay

Paignton

Tor Bay

② Brixham

A379

Dartmouth

④
③ Coleton Fishacre

River Dart Kingswear

Stoke Fleming

English Channel (La Manche)

✓ TOP TIP: DARTMOUTH-KINGSWEAR FERRIES

There are two ferries that run between Dartmouth and Kingswear. The **Lower Ferry** (www.southhams.gov.uk/DartmouthLowerFerry; car/pedestrian £4.50/1.50; ⏰7.10am-10.55pm) carries you right into Dartmouth's town centre, but if you're driving a big vehicle, the narrow streets will be a real headache to navigate, so you're better off taking the **Higher Ferry** (📞07866 531687; www.dartmouthhigherferry.com; car/pedestrian one way £5.60/60p; ⏰6.30am-10.45pm), which connects the A379 on either side of the River Dart.

- - - - - - - - - - - -

② Brixham

This old harbour is as salty and shipshape as it gets; it still has one of the largest working fishing fleet in the UK. A replica of Francis Drake's globetrotting ship, the **Golden Hind** (📞01803-856223; www.goldenhind.co.uk; The Quay; adult/child £7/5; ⏰10.30am-4pm Mar-Oct), is moored along the horseshoe-shaped harbour, and you can take a guided tour of the **fish market** (📞07973 297620; bfmt2014@gmail.com; The Quay; tours incl breakfast £12.50) before

settling down for some first-class seafood.

The Drive » Head south along Bolton St and Drew St onto the Kingswear Rd, then turn left onto the A379 signed to Dartmouth and Kingswear. Roll south through the green fields on either side of Slappers Hill, and ignore the right turn to Kingswear, following the brown signs to Coleton Fishacre instead.

- - - - - - - - - - - -

③ Coleton Fishacre

Echoes of the Jazz Age still ring through the beautiful art deco house of **Coleton Fishacre** (NT; 📞01803-842382; www.nationaltrust.org.uk;

§ LINK YOUR TRIP

14 Epic Cornwall
From Plymouth, it's just a quick jaunt across the Tamar Bridge into Cornwall: head a little further north to reach Bude.

12 Jurassic Coast
More epic coastal adventures await further to the east – it's 52 miles from Torquay to Lime Regis.

Brownstone Rd, near King-swear; adult/child £10.30/5.10; ⏰10.30am-5pm; 🅿️). Built in the 1920s, the house belonged to a family of theatrical impresarios, the D'Oyly Cartes, and there's a real dash of showmanship on display around their country pad – from the stunning saloon (complete with tinkling piano) and opulent bedrooms through to the oh-so-English croquet lawn.

The Drive » Backtrack along the road and take the first sign to Kingswear along the B3205 (roughly 2 miles).

DETOUR: TOTNES

Start: ❹ Dartmouth

The little town of Totnes has earned a reputation as one of the southwest's most eco-friendly places to live in the UK – it's even issued its own currency (the Totnes Pound) in an attempt to encourage people to spend their cash locally. The town's awash with fine Tudor architecture and interesting shops, but there are two other irresistible reasons to visit – a meal at the **Riverford Field Kitchen** (📞01803-762074; www.riverford.co.uk; Wash Barn; 3-course lunch/dinner £23.50/27; ⏰noon-2.30pm daily, 6-10pm most evenings; 🖉), a local farm which hosts lavish feasts of locally grown produce, and a tasting session at **Sharpham Vineyard** (📞01803-732203; www.sharpham.com; ⏰10am-6pm May-Sep, 10am-5pm Mar-Apr, 10am-3pm Oct-Dec, booking required for some tours; 🅿️), which produces top-class wines and cheeses.

Totnes is about 15 miles' drive from Dartmouth, but it's way more fun to catch a ride upriver with the **Dartmouth Steam Railway and Riverboat Company** (📞01803-555872; www.dartmouthrailriver.co.uk).

🛏️ p175

This will take you down to the Dartmouth-Kingswear Lower Ferry (p171), a quaint float-and-tug which has been running for decades.

TRIP HIGHLIGHT

❹ Dartmouth

South Devon isn't short on photogenic seaports, but Dartmouth still manages to dazzle. With its boat-filled harbour and quaint 17th- and 18th-century architecture, framed by green hills and the bright blue waters of the River Dart, it's a place to explore at leisure – don't miss the half-timbered houses of South Embankment, Fairfax Pl and Duke St, and the punch-drunk buildings of the **Butterwalk**. Once you've explored town, it's time to hop aboard a **river cruise** (📞01803-882811; www.greenwayferry.co.uk; adult/child return £8.50/6.50) for a trip over to **Greenway** (NT; 📞01803-842382; www.nationaltrust.org.uk; Greenway Rd, Galmpton; adult/child £10.30/5.10; ⏰10.30am-5pm), where thriller writer Agatha Christie dreamt up some of her best-loved tales.

🍴 🛏️ p175

The Drive » The next stage of the drive is lovely, along the coastal A379 past shingly beaches, green fields and glorious coast views. It's easy to navigate as far as the Slapton Ley nature reserve (7 miles away) and Torcross, but it's very easy to get lost along the minor roads leading south to Hallsands, Beesands and Start Point. Bring a decent road map.

TRIP HIGHLIGHT

❺ Start Bay

As you head down the coast towards Start Point you'll pass several shingle beaches, but the first essential stop is **Slapton Sands** (despite the name, there's actually precious little sand here – the 3-mile ridge is almost entirely pebbles). Rehearsals for the D-Day Landings

Plymouth The Tinside Lido outdoor pool

were made here in 1944,
but went disastrously
wrong when friendly fire
and a surprise attack
by a school of German
E-Boats resulted in more
than 800 Allied deaths.
A Sherman tank stands
as a memorial next to
the peaceful **Slapton Ley**
nature reserve.

Further south, the
villages of **Beesands** and
South Hallsands make
good stops for lunch or
afternoon tea, but the
best views lie in wait at
Start Point's lonely **lighthouse** (☎01803-771802;
www.trinityhouse.co.uk; Start
Point; adult/child £4/2.50;
⏰tours on the hour 11am-5pm
Sun-Thu Jul & Aug, 11am-4pm

Wed & Sun Apr & May, 11am-
4pm Wed, Thu & Sun Jun & Sep;
P), where you can take a
guided tour up to the top
of the tower for sweeping
360-degree views.

The Drive » Backtrack along
the backroads to the A379, then
turn left towards Kingsbridge
(10 miles from Start Point).
From here it's more pleasant
driving through fields and

EURASIA PRESS / GETTY IMAGES ©

farmland onto the A381 to Salcombe (a further 7 miles).

- - - - - - - - - -

❻ Kingsbridge & Salcombe

Though they're both on the same river estuary, the neighbouring towns of Kingsbridge and Salcombe feel very different in character. Kingsbridge still has the feel of a sleepy country town, with a weekly market and lots of independent shops to browse around. A few miles further south, Salcombe is an altogether more chi-chi affair, a muddle of winding lanes, old cottages and sandy coves, and a favourite for well-heeled holiday-makers (it's one of the UK's priciest places to buy a house).

The Drive ≫ Follow the A381 back the way you came, but don't turn off to Kingsbridge; stay on the A381 (signed to Plymouth/Modbury A379 and Totnes A381), and follow it till you see a roundabout with a left-turn to Bantham Beach (8 miles all up).

- - - - - - - - - -

TRIP HIGHLIGHT

❼ Bantham

It's certainly got stiff competition, but some say the beach at Bantham might just be Devon's best. Backed by dunes, ringed by golden sand and with stunning views across the water to Burgh Island, it's certainly a beauty – and perfect picnic territory. It also happens to have the best surf on the south Devon coast, and thanks to **Bantham Surfing Academy** (www.banthamsurfingacademy. co.uk), it's a perfect place to learn the basics.

The Drive ≫ Return to the roundabout and turn left onto the A379, signed to Aveton Gifford. Follow this road through the countryside until you see the left-run onto the B3392 to Bigbury. It's a gorgeous drive down to the sea from here. It's 9 miles all up.

- - - - - - - - - -

TRIP HIGHLIGHT

❽ Bigbury-on-Sea

While Bantham's charms have largely stayed off the tourist radar, neighbouring Bigbury-on-Sea has been a holiday spot since the heyday of Victorian tourism in the 19th century. Elegant town houses line the hillsides down to the town's sandy beach, but the real reason to visit here is the chance to hop across to **Burgh Island**, a 10-hectare offshore island that's home to a stunning art deco hotel and is encircled by a lovely coast path. At low tide you can walk across to the island, but it's more fun at high tide, when you have to catch the sea-tractor, with its passenger plat-

form perched 6ft above the ocean waves.

The Drive ≫ Return to the A379 and follow signs to Plymouth, about 21 miles' drive through the countryside and into the city's eastern outskirts.

- - - - - - - - - -

❾ Plymouth

Poor old Plymouth gets a bad rap – pummelled by the Luftwaffe during WWII and rebuilt in stark limestone, it's certainly been in need of some TLC. But beyond the bland city centre there are gems, particularly around the **Barbican**, the old harbour area, where the wonky buildings and cobbled lanes provide a glimpse of how the city would once have looked. Look out for the **Mayflower Steps**, which commemorate the departure of the Pilgrim Fathers for the New World. Also worth a wander is the grassy headland known as the **Hoe**, where Francis Drake supposedly spied the Spanish Armada. Don't miss a dip in the **Tinside Lido** (☎01752-261915; www.everyoneactive. com; Hoe Rd; adult/child/family £4/3/11.60; ☺noon-6pm daily Mon-Fri, 10am-6pm Jun-Sep, evening swim 6-7.30pm Wed), a stunning outdoor pool built during the 1930s.

✕ ⸗ p175

Eating & Sleeping

Torquay ❶

✕ Rockfish
Seafood ££

(☎01803-212175; 20 Victoria Pde; mains £11.95-18.95; ☺noon-9.30pm) Mitch Tonks' rapidly expanding mini-chain of seafood restaurants has opened a new branch on the Torquay seafront, and its taste for relaxed catch-of-the-day dining has unsurprisingly proved popular. Whitewashed wood and nautical knick-knacks give it a shipshape ambience, and the food takes in everything from classic fish and chips to a take on Italian *fritto misto* (mixed fried fish).

🛏 Cary Arms
Boutique Hotel £££

(☎01803-327110; www.caryarms.co.uk; Babbacombe Beach; d £195-295, ste £375-450; P 🛜) In a dreamy spot beside Babbacombe's sands, this heritage hotel has more than a hint of a New England beach retreat. Bright, light-filled rooms with candy-stripe throws and white furniture shimmer with style, and the best have sea-view balconies. There's a divine spa, too.

Dartmouth ❹

✕ Alf Resco
Cafe £

(☎01803-835880; www.cafealfresco.co.uk; Lower St; mains from £6; ☺7am-2pm; 🛜) An eclectic crowd hangs out at Alf's – you'll be eating among hipsters, families, tourists and river-boat crews. The same menu spans breakfast through to lunch; expect piled-high fry-ups, irresistible pastries and eye-opening espressos. The gorgeous **B&B rooms** (☎01803-835880; www.cafealfresco.co.uk; Lower St; d from £70-90, apt £100) are pure shabby chic.

🛏 Bayard's Cove
B&B ££

(☎01803-839278; www.bayardscoveinn.co.uk; 27 Lower St; d £125-155, f £185; 🛜) Crammed with character and bursting with beams, Bayard's Cove sees you sleeping amid whitewashed stone walls and huge church candles. The lavish family suites feature grand double beds and kids' cabins, complete with bunk beds and tiny TVs; there are even estuary glimpses from the rooms.

Totnes: Detour

🛏 Dartington Hall
B&B ££

(☎01803-847147; www.dartington.org; Dartington, near Totnes; s/d from £59/99; P 🛜) The wings of this idyllic, ancient manor house have been carefully converted into rooms that range from heritage themed to deluxe modern. Ask for one overlooking the grassy, cobble-fringed courtyard and settle back for a truly tranquil night's sleep. The estate is about 1.5 miles from Totnes.

Plymouth ❾

✕ Rock Salt
Modern British ££

(☎01752-225522; www.rocksaltcafe.co.uk; 31 Stonehouse St; mains lunch £12.95-14.95, dinner £14.95-19.95; ☺noon-3pm & 5-9.30pm; 🛜) Local boy Dave Jenkins has worked wonders at his little brasserie, which has deservedly built up a loyal local following and scooped foodie awards, too. It suits all times of day: tuck into fluffy eggs royale for breakfast, enjoy a light butternut squash risotto for lunch, and savour slow-braised ox cheek for dinner. A local diner par excellence.

🛏 Sea Breezes
B&B ££

(☎01752-667205; www.plymouth-bedandbreakfast.co.uk; 28 Grand Pde; s/d/f £55/85/105; P) 'Luxury to rival the finest 5-star hotels' trumpets the blurb – well let's not get carried away, but this six-roomer is still a good option, with tasteful rooms in whites and sea blues, complete with plush cushions, cast-iron bedsteads, old-fashioned alarm clocks and other thoughtful touches. Sea views abound, and owner Anne Anderson is a fine hostess.

Epic Cornwall

14

Buckle up, roll down the windows and have the camera ready – this round-Cornwall road trip is a photogenic parade of sea, shore, coast, cliff and countryside.

TRIP HIGHLIGHTS

130 miles

St Michael's Mount
Cross the causeway like a modern-day pilgrim

20 miles

Tintagel
Wander the ruins of King Arthur's legendary castle

START • Bude

2

St Agnes •

13 Fowey
FINISH

10

8

Falmouth •

Porthcurno
Catch a play above the Atlantic waves

115 miles

Eden Project
Travel from jungle to desert inside a giant greenhouse

202 miles

10 DAYS
212 MILES / 340KM

GREAT FOR...

BEST TIME TO GO
Summer holidays equal traffic jams; aim for spring or autumn.

ESSENTIAL PHOTO
Standing next to the famous Land's End sign (John O'Groats: 874).

BEST FOR FOODIES
First-rate fish and seafood at Alba, a harbourside bistro.

14 Epic Cornwall

There can be few corners of Britain where scenery packs such an eyes-wide, heart-in-the-mouth, jaw-on-the-floor punch as Cornwall. This unforgettable adventure travels right the way round Britain's most westerly county: top-to-bottom, coast-to-coast. Along the way you'll encounter sparkling beaches, surf bays and seaside ports galore, not to mention curiosities such as a clifftop theatre and a trio of space-age biomes. It's wild and wonderful out west, as you're about to find out.

❶ Bude

This breezy sea town makes a great place to start your cruise around Cornwall – or Kernow, as it's known to locals. It's surrounded by beaches: the family favourite is Summerleaze, smack-bang in the centre of town, and if you don't feel up to tackling the waves, you can take a dip in the bracing sea-waters of the Bude Sea Pool.

For more seclusion, more beaches can be found north and south of town, ranging from tiny coves to impressive sweeps like **Crackington Haven** and **Widemouth Bay**. Many visitors never quite reach it up this far north, so the Bude beaches are often a little quieter than their better-known counterparts along the coast.

🛏 p187

The Drive » Follow the main A39 (sometimes called the Atlantic Hwy on road signs) south, and look for the turn-off to Tintagel. A slightly more scenic alternative is to take the turn-off to Boscastle, a pretty village with an even prettier harbour – the road from here tracks the coast all the way to Tintagel. The distance is roughly the same, around 20 miles.

TRIP HIGHLIGHT

❷ Tintagel

Cornwall's most legend-strewn location is the crumbling clifftop castle

ATLANTIC OCEAN

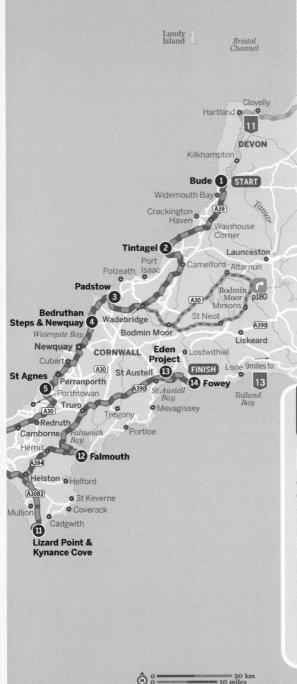

of **Tintagel** (EH; ☎01840-770328; adult/child £7.90/4.70; ⏰10am-6pm Apr-Sep, to 5pm Oct, to 4pm Nov-Mar), rumoured to be the birthplace of England's most heroic of heroes, King Arthur. In truth, there's more fiction than fact here (the castle largely dates from the 1300s), but there's no denying the truly epic setting – a fairy-tale ruined fortress teetering above black cliffs and booming surf. Climb the cliffside staircases and take a blustery wander among the ruins, then head down at low tide to explore the beach and the murky **Merlin's Cave** nearby.

It's also worth walking over to teeny St Materiana Church, which dates back to the 12th century and occupies a dramatic position atop

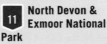

LINK YOUR TRIP

13 **South Devon**
From the stark drama of Cornwall to the gentler countryside of Devon: it's a 38-mile drive from Fowey to Plymouth.

11 **North Devon & Exmoor National Park**
The north coast continued, ending in under-explored Exmoor and its famous starry skies – from Clovelly, it's just an 18-mile hop across the Cornish border to Bude.

SOUTHWEST ENGLAND **14** EPIC CORNWALL

179

DETOUR: BODMIN MOOR

Start: ❷ Tintagel (p178)

Sprawling over an area of 80 sq miles along Cornwall's eastern edge, Bodmin Moor might not be everyone's idea of classic Cornwall, but it has a bleak, magisterial beauty all of its own. Pock-marked with heaths and granite hills, including Cornwall's highest point, Brown Willy (419m), it's a desolate place that works on the imagination; for years there have been reported sightings of the Beast of Bodmin, a large, black cat-like creature, although no one's ever managed to snap a decent picture.

It's a fine place for hiking and biking, and strewn with many beauty spots such as the underground slate chambers of **Carnglaze Caverns** (📞01579-320251; www.carnglaze.com; adult/child £6/4; ⏰10am-5pm) and the tumbling waterfall of **Golitha Falls**. It's also home to the famous Jamaica Inn, made famous by Daphne du Maurier's novel of the same name – although it's been ruthlessly modernised since the author's day.

There are various routes onto the moor; you can join it at several points along the A30 or A39.

Glebe Cliff. Look out for signs from the castle.

The Drive » The most scenic route to Padstow is to explore the backroads via Polzeath and Rock, but it's easy to get lost – better to head south to the main A39 and follow it past Wadebridge, then turn off towards Padstow. It's a drive of 21 miles this way; there's a large car park above town.

---

❸ Padstow

Famous for its foodie culture thanks to celebrity chef Rick Stein, Padstow has to rank as one of north Cornwall's prettiest ports. It's beautifully situated on the Camel Estuary, opposite the treacherous sandbank known as the Doom Bar (after which a popular local beer is named). It's a lovely place for a wander: explore the backstreets,

browse the shops, dangle your toes over the harbour wall, then catch the **Black Tor Ferry** (www.padstow-harbour.co.uk/ phc_ferry.html; adult/child return £4/2, bikes £4, dogs £1) across the estuary to the chi-chi seaside village of **Rock** – a favourite of the poet John Betjeman, who holidayed here as a child, and now one of Cornwall's priciest patches of real estate. Nearby, the sands of **Daymer Bay** are perfect sunbathing territory.

🛏 p187

The Drive » Here's where the driving gets good. Head round the peninsula and follow signs towards Trevone, one of Padstow's 'Seven Bays'. First you'll pass the private headland of Trevose Head, then follow the coast road south past beaches including Harlyn, Constantine Bay and Treyarnon. Shortly after

Porthcothan, you'll climb the hill and see signs to Carnewas & Bedruthan Steps (10 miles).

---

❹ Newquay

The stretch of coast road that runs from Trevose Head down to the surf-central town of Newquay is a real roller-coaster, dipping and swerving past a string of stunning, white-sand beaches, including **Constantine**, **Treyarnon Bay** and **Porthcothan**. A little way south, a line of dramatic rock towers loom out of the surf: known as **Bedruthan Steps** (Carnewas; NT; www.nationaltrust.org.uk/carnewas-and-bedruthan-steps), they make for a great photo op. From here, the coast road rolls on past another impressive beach at **Mawgan Porth** to **Watergate Bay**, where you can learn to surf or stand-up paddleboard at the **Extreme Academy** (✆01637-860840; www.extremeacademy.co.uk; Watergate Bay), then stop for a meal at Jamie Oliver's **Fifteen** (✆01637-861000; www.fifteencornwall.com; Watergate Bay; 2-/3-course lunch menu £26/32, 5-course dinner menu £65; ⊗8.30am-10am, noon-2.30pm & 6.15-9.15pm) restaurant.

Newquay itself is a love-it-or-hate-it affair: brash and busy, it's notorious for its nightlife, but home to several beautiful beaches. Come here to surf, to party, or both: otherwise, steer clear.

The Drive » The best road to take is the A3075, which passes optional turn-offs to Crantock and Holywell Bay. Take the turn-off to Perranporth, then follow the B3285 road out of town past Perranporth airfield and on into St Agnes (12 miles in total).

⑤ St Agnes

Yet more epic stretches of coast await as you head south of Newquay, including the photogenic beaches of **Crantock**, **Holywell Bay** and **Perranporth**. They're all detour-worthy, but we're moving on to the pretty village of St Agnes, once a centre for Cornwall's tin industry, and strewn with reminders of its mighty mining past. At the beautiful beach of **Chapel Porth** (🅿), a trail leads up to the abandoned mine at **Wheal Coates**, towering above heather-covered cliffs and rust-red rock. Hiking trails radiate all around from here, including a path that leads to the panoramic hilltop called the **Beacon**. Alternatively, you can just head back down to the car park for a hot cup of tea and a hedgehog ice cream at the beach cafe.

The Drive » There are some wonderful backroads to explore from here, but they're a maze, so the easiest option is to take the road back to Chiverton Cross and join the main A30, which will zip you all the way past Hayle. From here, follow signs to St Ives. It's 24 miles stop-to-stop.

⑥ St Ives

Few spots in Cornwall have such a wow factor as St Ives. Occupying a graceful curving bay, framed by a jumble of slate rooftops, dazzling blue water and white beaches, it's postcard-perfect – so it's not hard to see why artists find themselves drawn here. Among them was the abstract sculptor Barbara Hepworth, who made her home here in the 1930s: her **house and studio** (✆01736-796226; Barnoon Hill; adult/child £6.60/5.50; ⊗10am-5pm Mar-Oct, to 4pm Nov-Feb) has hardly changed since her death in 1975. There are

LOCAL KNOWLEDGE: THE CAMEL TRAIL

Cornwall still has its fair share of scenic railways (the line from St Erth to St Ives is a particular highlight), but the old route along the Camel River from Bodmin to Padstow was closed in the 1950s. Happily, it's had a second lease of life as the **Camel Trail** (www.cornwall.gov.uk/cameltrail), Cornwall's most popular bike path. The main section starts in Padstow and runs east through Wadebridge (5.75 miles), but the trail runs on all the way to Poley Bridge on Bodmin Moor (18.3 miles).

Bikes can be hired from **Padstow Cycle Hire** (✆01841-533533; www.padstowcyclehire.com; South Quay; per day adult/child £15/7; ⊗9am-5pm, to 9pm summer) or **Trail Bike Hire** (✆01841-532594; www.trailbikehire.co.uk; Unit 6, South Quay; adult £14, child £5-8; ⊗9am-6pm) at the Padstow end, or from **Bridge Bike Hire** (✆01208-813050; www.bridgebikehire.co.uk; adult £12-14, child £6-9; ⊗10am-5pm) at the Wadebridge end.

Most people do the trail from Padstow, but it's much quieter – and much, much easier to park – if you decide to start at the Wadebridge end.

DETOUR: GWITHIAN & GODREVY TOWANS

Start: ❻ St Ives (p181)

Four miles east of St Ives across the Hayle Estuary, the dune-backed flats of Gwithian and Godrevy unfurl in a glimmering golden curve that joins together at low tide to form Hayle's '3 miles of golden sand'. This is one of Cornwall's most glorious beach panoramas, fringed by acres of rock-pools and grassy dunes (known in Cornish as towans) and, at the northern end, the lighthouse that inspired Virginia Woolf's stream-of-consciousness class *To The Lighthouse*. Don't miss it.

The excellent **Godrevy Cafe** (📞01736-757999; www.godrevycafe.com; lunch £6-10; ⊙10am-5pm) is a great place for a post-beach snack, and serves superb coffee, cakes and light lunches.

---

galleries and studios scattered along St Ives' warren of backstreets, but the flagship is the **Tate St Ives** (📞01736-796226; www.tate.org.uk/stives; Porthmeor Beach), which displays key works by St Ives artists and has recently been impressively extended.

After soaking up some art and culture, head for one of the town's lovely beaches to soak up some sunshine. There's **Porthmeor**, opposite the Tate, or little **Porthgwidden** just around the headland, with an excellent beach cafe, but most people favour **Porthminster**, a curl of white sand not far from the train station, home to the sophisticated **Porthminster Beach Café** (📞01736-795352; www.porthminstercafe.co.uk; mains £15-22; ⊙9am-10pm).

✕ 🛏 p187

The Drive » Another epic 18-mile stretch of tarmac lies in store. Take the road up Higher Stennack onto the B3306, signed to Zennor. From here, the wilds of Penwith's moors open up around you: you'll pass ancient fields, rock formations and abandoned mine stacks, including a particularly scenic one at Botallack. Pass through St Just and follow signs down into Sennen.

- - - - - - - - - - - -

❼ Sennen

The skies get bigger and the land gets emptier the further west you head in Penwith. Once a mining and farming heartland, strewn with abandoned wheelhouses and minestacks, this is one of Cornwall's wildest corners – so it's hardly surprising that this was also a regular location used in the BBC's recent barnstorming adaptation of *Poldark*. The

mines at Botallack and Levant are key spots, and you can even experience the miner's life for yourself by heading underground at **Geevor Tin Mine** (📞01736-788662; www.geevor.com; adult/child £12.95/7.50; ⊙9am-5pm Sun-Fri Mar-Oct, to 4pm Nov-Feb).

Many secret beaches await for those intrepid enough to find them, but with its white beach and harbour wall, the pretty village of Sennen is rather easier to find. It's also a great launch-pad for following the coast path all the way round to **Land's End**, where mainland Britain comes to a screeching halt. Though it's now home to an uninspiring theme park, there's still something thrilling about standing on Britain's westernmost point: you'll see cliffs, seagulls and lighthouses, and on a clear day, perhaps, glimpse the silhouettes of the **Isles of Scilly**, 28 miles west.

If you're visiting Land's End by car, you don't have to pay admission to the theme park to access the headland itself. You can just pay to access the car park and then follow the coast path to the cliffs.

The Drive » You'd have to try really hard to get get lost from here: there's only one road from Sennen to Porthcurno, the B3315, for 5 miles. Follow the signs to Porthcurnno and the Minack Theatre.

MATT MUNRO / LONELY PLANET ©

Mousehole Fishing boats at low tide

TRIP HIGHLIGHT

8 Porthcurno

Forget Stratford-upon-Avon or London's West End: if you're looking for Britain's most dramatic place to watch a play, you'll find it above the beach of Porthcurno. Dreamt up by an eccentric theatre-lover called Rowena Cade, and inspired by the amphitheatres of ancient Greece, the **Minack** (☎01736-810181; www.minack. com; tickets from £10) was painstakingly carved out from the granite cliffs during the 1930s and '40s. It now hosts a season of plays throughout the summer: on a clear summer's night it's utterly magical, but experienced theatre-lovers remember to pack a cushion, a picnic and rain gear in case the Cornish weather decides to stage an unscheduled appearance.

The Drive » The prettiest route is to follow the B3315 to Penzance, which passes the lovely village of Mousehole and the busy fishing harbour of Newlyn en route. It's around 12 miles this way.

9 Penzance

The salty seafront town of Penzance is pretty much the end of the line for Cornwall (and the last stop for the railway from Paddington). Established as a fishing and trading port, Penzance has a blustery, lived-in charm, and has resisted the gentrification that's taken over many of Cornwall's other seaside towns. Reminders of its seafaring heyday can be found along lovely Chapel St, lined with grand Georgian mansions and some cracking pubs.

Further down towards the seafront is the town's pride and joy, the **Jubilee Pool** (www.jubileepool.co.uk; Western Promenade Rd; adult/child £4.75/3.80; ⏱10.30am-6pm Wed-Mon, to 8pm Tue late-May-early-Sep), a seawater lido built in 1935, and looking back to its art deco best after its recent £3m renovation following damaging winter storms. There's discounted entry after 3.30pm (adult/child £3.10/2.50).

🛏 p187

CORNISH PASTIES

There's nothing more local to tuck into for lunch than a Cornish pasty. Half-moon shaped, stuffed with steak and vegetables and sealed with a decorative crimp on the side, they've been a staple here since the 13th century, and are said to have been created as a portable lunch for tin-miners: the crust was designed to allow the miners' filthy fingers to hold the pasty by, and could be discarded afterwards. When waves of impoverished Cornish miners emigrated in the mid-1800s, they took their pasty techniques with them, particularly to Australia and the USA; today you can still pop out for a pasty in places as far from Cornwall as Adelaide and Arizona.

Annually, pasty production employs thousands of people, and brings millions of pounds into Cornwall's economy. In 2011 the savoury was finally awarded protected status by the European Commission, meaning only those actually made in Cornwall, according to a traditional recipe, can be called 'Cornish pasties'.

Everyone has their favourite pasty shops: two of our top tips are the **Chough Bakery** (☎01841-533361; www.thechoughbakery.co.uk; 1-3 The Strand, Padstow; pasties £3-5) in Padstow and **Ann's Pasties** (☎01326-290889; www.annspasties.co.uk; pasties £3.10; ⏱9am-3pm Mon-Sat) on the Lizard, both endorsed by Rick Stein, no less.

The Drive » Head out of Penzance on the A30, cross over a couple of roundabouts, and follow signs to Marazion on the A394. It's about an 8-mile drive.

TRIP HIGHLIGHT

10 St Michael's Mount

As you approach Penzance, catching your first sight of **St Michael's Mount** (NT; ☎01736-710507; www.stmichaelsmount.co.uk; house & gardens adult/child £12.50/6; ⏱house 10.30am-5.30pm Sun-Fri Jul-Sep, 10.30am-5pm Mar-Jun & Oct) is an unforgettable experience: it looks like something from the pages of Harry Potter. A cluster of spires and battlements looming up from a rocky island in the middle of Mount's Bay, the fairytale building dates back to the 1100s, and has variously served as an abbey, a fortress, a prison and a trading port; later, it became the ancestral seat of the St Aubyn family, and is now administered by the National Trust. Highlights include the stately great hall and subtropical gardens, but the crossing is almost the best part: at low tide, you can walk across a cobbled causeway from the nearby town of **Marazion**.

The Drive » From Marazion, the A394 runs past the busy beach at Praa Sands all the way to Helston, gateway town to the Lizard. You can take a direct route on the A3083 straight to Lizard Point, passing Kynance

Cornish pasty A lunch staple

Cove en route, but there are countless detours along the way to follow if you have time.

- - - - - - - - - - - - -

⑪ The Lizard

Despite its name, you won't spot too many lizards on this back-of-beyond peninsula (the name is actually thought to derive from the Cornish *lys ardh*, meaning high court or high fortress). What you will spy is mile after mile of cliff, beach, cove and moor: this is another of Cornwall's wildest corners, where sum-mer wildflowers blaze, choughs wheel over the clifftops and countless ships have come to grief on the unforgiving rocks. The coastline is strewn with quaint little fishing villages such as Cadgwith and Coverack, as well as numerous bays and coves – don't miss **Church Cove** near Gunwalloe, used as a ready-made back-drop in *Poldark*, and the wonderful beach of **Kynance Cove**, a pictur-esque concoction of tur-quoise water, white surf and rocky islands. Nearby is the sea-smacked

headland at Lizard Point, where you can take a fas-cinating tour around an 18th-century **lighthouse** (☎01326-290202; www.lizardlighthouse.co.uk; adult/child £3/2; ⊙11am-5pm Sun-Thu Mar-Oct).

The Drive » Backtrack to Helston and continue east on the A394 – not the most exciting 25 miles of road, but the fastest way from here to Falmouth.

- - - - - - - - - - - - -

⑫ Falmouth

Truro might by the county's capital, but Falmouth surely stakes a claim as Cornwall's

185

coolest town. Thanks to its deep-water harbour, this historic port was once a bustling hub for Britain's maritime trade, welcoming clippers and tall ships from all over the globe. It's now home to Cornwall's only university (based at nearby Penryn), meaning it's awash with trendy bars, hip coffee shops and excellent restaurants – as well as the western outpost of the **National Maritime Museum** (☎01326-313388; www.nmmc.co.uk; Discovery Quay; adult/child £12.50/5; ☻10am-5pm), which contains a fascinating collection of boats and other maritime memorabilia.

Out on the headland from town you'll find **Pendennis Castle** (EH; ☎01326-316594; www.english-heritage.org.uk; adult/child £7.90/4.70; ☻10am-6pm Mar-Sep, 10am-5pm Oct, 10am-4pm Sat & Sun Nov-Feb), an imposing Tudor fortress built by Henry VIII to guard the entrance to Falmouth Harbour, in partnership with its sister castle across the bay in St Mawes. It's an atmospheric location, and you can wander round the gundecks and battlements. Don't be too perturbed if you hear a deafening crack at 12pm sharp – it'll just be the noonday gun going off with a bang.

🛏 p187

The Drive » We're taking the most direct route to Eden: the A39 to Truro, then the A390 to St Austell, and another 4 miles further to the Eden Project. It's a pleasant but uneventful drive of 30 miles; count on 50 minutes, longer if there's traffic.

TRIP HIGHLIGHT

⓭ Eden Project

At first glance it looks like something from a sci-fi film set – three gigantic glass biomes, glittering in the sunlight at the bottom of a disused claypit. But you haven't stumbled onto the set of the latest Ridley Scott movie – you've just arrived at the **Eden Project** (☎01726-811911; www.edenproject.com; adult/child/family £25/15/69, joint ticket with Lost Gardens of Heligan £34.65/18/93.50; ☻9.30am-6pm, last admission 4.30pm), a pioneering eco-initiative that aims to re-create habitats from around the globe inside its oversized greenhouses. From tropical jungle to dry desert, soaring palms to spiky cactus, it sometimes feels a bit like wandering through a scene from *Jurassic Park*. Recent additions including a canopy walkway and a zip-wire have added extra thrills and spills.

The Drive » Follow the road back towards St Austell, but once you reach the A390, follow signs to Par, and then the A3082 to Fowey. Once you get past Par, it's a lovely drive through quiet countryside.

⓮ Fowey

The last stop on your Cornish road trip is the riverside town of Fowey. It's another postcard-perfect scene, a jumble of pastel-coloured town houses, fishermen's cottages and winding alleyways, all backed by the wooded banks of the River Fowey. The thriller writer Daphne du Maurier made it her home, and the town hosts a popular arts and literature festival every year. The best way to see it is from the water: **Encounter Cornwall** (☎07976 466123; www.encountercornwall.com; Golant; adult/child £25/15) runs guided kayak trips along the river, and afterwards you can relive your trip over a pint of ale and a plate of fish and chips at the quayside **King of Prussia** (www.kingofprussia.co.uk; Town Quay; ☻11am-11pm). Thank you Cornwall, or *meur ras*, as they say round here – it's been a blast.

🛏 p187

Eating & Sleeping

Bude ❶

🛏 The Beach at Bude   Hotel £££

(📞01288-389800; www.thebeachatbude.
co.uk; Summerleaze Cres; r £135-237.50;
P 🛜) For a proper hotel stay, complete with
all the pampering, this is definitely the choice
in Bude. The main sell is the fine position
behind Summerleaze beach, but the rooms are
attractive too: spacious and smart, with neutral
tones, pine headboards and Lloyd Loom chairs,
conjuring the feel of a New England beach cabin.

Padstow ❸

🛏 Althea Library   B&B ££

(📞01841-532579; www.altheahouse-padstow.
co.uk; 64 Church St, Padstow; d £90-120;
P 🛜) If you want to be in Padstow proper, this
charming ivy-clad house is hard to better. There
are two stylish self-catering suites: Rafters is
accessed via a private staircase, while Driftwood
has a pine four-poster bed. It's luxurious – both
suites have sofas, Nespresso coffee machines,
baths and small studio kitchens. There's also a
nearby cottage for longer stays.

St Ives ❻

✖ Alba   Modern British £££

(📞01736-797222; www.thealbarestaurant.com;
Old Lifeboat House; 2-/3-course dinner menu
£21.95/25.95, mains £16-28.95; ⊙noon-2pm &
6-10pm) Other restaurants have come and gone
in St Ives, but this harbourside bistro next to the
old lifeboat station continues to excel. It's in a
converted boathouse, with a split-level layout:
diner-style downstairs, more formal upstairs
(book well ahead for the prime window tables).
First-class fish and seafood are the mainstays.
The set dinner menu is only available from
5.30pm to 7pm.

🛏 11 Sea View Terrace   B&B ££

(📞01736-798440; www.11stives.co.uk; 11 Sea
View Tce; d £120-140; P 🛜) Occupying one of
the classic Edwardian villas lining the upper part

of St Ives, this three-suite B&B is a chic place to
stay. The two front 'suites' have lovely town and
sea views, while the rear one overlooks a garden
patio; for more space there's a smart holiday flat
(£350 to £975 per week).

Penzance ❾

🛏 Artist Residence Penzance   B&B ££

(📞01736-365664; www.arthotelcornwall.co.uk;
20 Chapel St; d £115-145, 2-bed apt from £255;
🛜) Hands down the most entertaining place
to stay in Penzance, this B&B on Chapel St is
like sleeping inside an art gallery. All rooms are
designed by a local artist, and all are bright,
colourful and brimming with imagination
(we particularly liked the Attic Lofts). There
are apartments for longer stays, and food is
available in the Cornish Barn.

Falmouth ❿

🛏 Highcliffe
Contemporary B&B   B&B ££

(📞01326-314466; www.highcliffefalmouth.
com; 22 Melvill Rd; s £68, d £99-150; 🛜) Vintage
furniture and upcycled design pieces give
each of the rooms here its own individual feel.
The pick of the bunch is the light-filled Attic
Penthouse, with skylight windows overlooking
Falmouth Bay. Room service breakfasts are
served in picnic baskets, or you can tuck into
pancakes and Hog's pudding in the dining room.

Fowey ⓮

🛏 Coriander Cottages   B&B ££

(📞01726-834998; www.foweyaccommodation.
co.uk; Penventinue Lane; r £100-135; P 🛜)
A delightfully rural cottage complex on
the outskirts of Fowey, with eco-friendly
accommodation in a choice of open-plan, self-
catering barns, all with quiet country views. The
stone barns have been beautifully modernised,
and use a combination of solar panels, ground-
source heating and rainwater harvesting to
reduce environmental impact. A lovely retreat.

STRETCH YOUR LEGS BATH

Start/Finish: SouthGate

Distance: 2½ miles

Duration: Three hours

Bath's cityscape is simply sumptuous – so stunning it has World Heritage site status. On this walk you'll encounter architecture ranging from Roman baths via a medieval cathedral to exquisite Georgian designs.

Take this walk on Trips

SouthGate

On cruising into Bath, follow signs to SouthGate car park. It's set beneath a new shopping centre which aims to echo the city's Georgian architecture.

The Walk » Exit into St Lawrence St and head north, to join Stall St, before cutting right down Abbeygate St towards the Roman Baths.

Roman Baths

The Romans built a complex of bath-houses (p150) above three natural hot springs, which emerge at a toasty 46°C (115°F). They form one of the best-preserved ancient Roman spas in the world. A tour reveals the **Great Bath** (a lead-lined pool filled with steaming water), bathing pools, changing rooms and excavated sections revealing the hypocaust heating system.

The Walk » From Bath's baths it's a few steps east to the city's abbey.

Bath Abbey

Towering **Bath Abbey** (p196) was built between 1499 and 1616, making it the last great medieval church raised in England. On the striking west facade angels climb up and down stone ladders, commemorating a dream of the founder, Bishop Oliver King. You can also take tower tours.

The Walk » Cross the square south of Bath Abbey, then wind onto Parade Gardens passing the Empire Hotel (1901) and the rushing weir to Pultney Bridge (1773), a rarity in that it features shops. Then duck up Green St.

Tasting Room

High-class vintages, tapas and piled-high platters of meats and cheese are the modi operandi of the **Tasting Room** (📞01225-483070; www.tastingroom.co.uk; 6 Green St; mains £6-13; 🕙10.30am-11pm Wed-Sat, to 4.30pm Mon & Tue), a slinky cafe-bar set above a wine merchant.

The Walk » Turn into elegant Milsom St, browsing its chic shops as you make your way, via George St, into narrow Bartlett St, a trendy enclave.

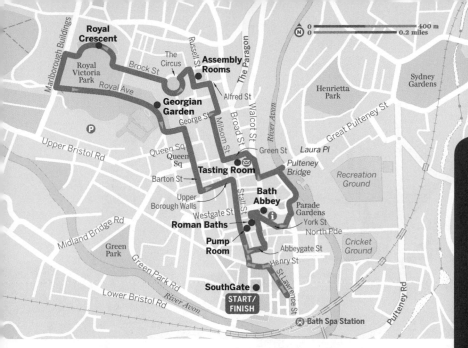

Assembly Rooms

When they opened in 1771, Bath's **Assembly Rooms** (NT; www.nationaltrust.org.uk; 19 Bennett St; ⊘10.30am-5pm Mar-Oct, to 4pm Nov-Feb) were where fashionable socialites gathered to waltz, play cards and listen to the latest chamber music. Tour the card room, tearoom and ballroom.

The Walk ≫ Next it's into The Circus (1768), a gorgeous ring of 33 houses divided into semi-circular terraces. From there gracious Brock St gradually reveals Bath's exquisite Royal Crescent.

Royal Crescent

The imposing, impeccably grand Royal Crescent (p196) curls around private lawns. Designed by John Wood the Younger (1728–82) and built between 1767 and 1775, the houses appear perfectly symmetrical from the outside, but no two houses are quite the same inside.

The Walk ≫ From the Crescent's far end, stroll back along Royal Ave. Opposite the bowling green pavilion, cut left from the main road, up an easy-to-miss path to hunt out the gate in the wall leading into the Georgian Garden.

Georgian Garden

The tiny, walled **Georgian Garden** (off Royal Ave; ⊘9am-5pm) features period plants and gravel walkways. They've been carefully restored, providing an intriguing insight into what would have lain behind the Circus' grand facades.

The Walk ≫ Pass through Queen Sq, the oldest of Bath's Georgian squares to skirt the elaborate Theatre Royal (1805). Upper Borough Walls marks medieval Bath's northern edge; from here it's a short stroll to the Pump Room.

Pump Room

The centre of the grand 19th-century **Pump Room** (www.romanbaths.co.uk; Stall St; ⊘10am-5pm) is filled with restaurant tables, but the interior also shelters an ornate spa fountain from which Bath's famous hot springs flow. Ask staff for a (free) glass; it will be startlingly warm – an impressive 38°C (100°F).

The Walk ≫ Cut down Stall St, back into St Lawrence St and back to your car.

Central England

ROUTES IN THIS REGION REVEAL THE HEART OF BRITAIN, showcasing literature, landscape and history. Drive here and you'll explore the Cotswold Hills, a rolling ridge of quintessentially English villages built out of honey-coloured stone. They lead you to Stratford-upon-Avon, a town with a plethora of Shakespearian links.

History lies at every turn: the sites of battles that dethroned monarchs; the castles that helped keep kings on the throne; some of England's finest stately homes; the industrial heritage that forged a nation. And each just a short drive away. Then there's the Peak District National Park. Here, the motoring is bewitching, winding from limestone dales to wilderness moors.

Stratford-upon-Avon New Place gardens
PHB.CZ (RICHARD SEMIK) / SHUTTERSTOCK ©

Gloucester Gloucester Cathedral

 Shakespeare & Rolling Hills 7–8 Days
The essential England: impossibly pretty villages and the birthplace of the Bard. (p195)

16 **Industrial Powerhouse 4 Days**
History-rich mines, factories and mills; this is where modern England was made. (p205)

Classic Trip
 Peak District 5 Days
Brooding moors, rocky hills and adrenaline sports – an adventure-packed drive. (p213)

18 **Battlefields, Castles & Stately Homes 5 Days**
A drive-through timeline of English history, in all its scheming, bloody, greedy glory. (p227)

✓ **DON'T MISS**

No 1 Royal Crescent
Every tourist goes to Bath's architectural triumph. But by entering this townhouse you'll also glimpse the period lifestyle on Trip **15**

City of Caves Tour
Head deep under Nottingham to discover a WWII air-raid shelter, pub cellars and a Victorian slum on Trip **18**

Morgan Motor Company
England's most elegant sports cars have been handcrafted here since 1909. Watch the mechanics at work on a two-hour tour. Trip **16**

Gloucester Cathedral
A less well-known gem that's among the best examples of English Perpendicular Gothic style (and starring in Harry Potter films) on Trip **15**

Haddon Hall
An enticing example of a medieval manor house, 12th-century Haddon Hall is rich in stone turrets on Trip **17**

Shakespeare & Rolling Hills

15

On this bucolic spin into the heart of the Cotswolds, you'll traverse five counties, wander time-warped, gold-washed villages, feast on local produce and pay your respects to William Shakespeare.

TRIP HIGHLIGHTS

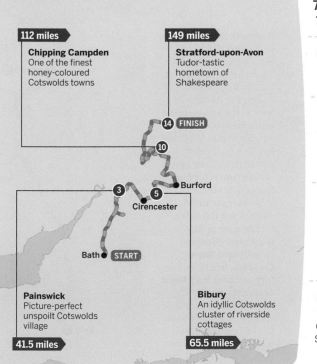

112 miles

Chipping Campden
One of the finest honey-coloured Cotswolds towns

149 miles

Stratford-upon-Avon
Tudor-tastic hometown of Shakespeare

14 FINISH

10

● Burford

3
5
Cirencester

Bath ● START

Painswick
Picture-perfect unspoilt Cotswolds village

41.5 miles

Bibury
An idyllic Cotswolds cluster of riverside cottages

65.5 miles

7–8 DAYS
149 MILES / 238KM

GREAT FOR...

BEST TIME TO GO

April, May, June and September, for better weather, minus summer crowds.

ESSENTIAL PHOTO

Broadway Tower perched spectacularly on the crest of the escarpment.

✓ BEST FOR HISTORY

Getting lost in majestic Sudeley Castle.

15 | Shakespeare & Rolling Hills

From the less-travelled, superbly pretty villages of the southwestern Cotswolds to the impossibly beautiful gold-coloured streets of the classic northern Cotswolds, this trip threads through the core of one of England's most desirable regions. Glimpse Georgian grandeur in Bath, marvel at Painswick's sleepy beauty, unearth Roman history in Cirencester, stroll Chipping Campden's honey-hued lanes and wrap up in dramatic Tudor style at Stratford-upon-Avon, home of the illustrious Bard.

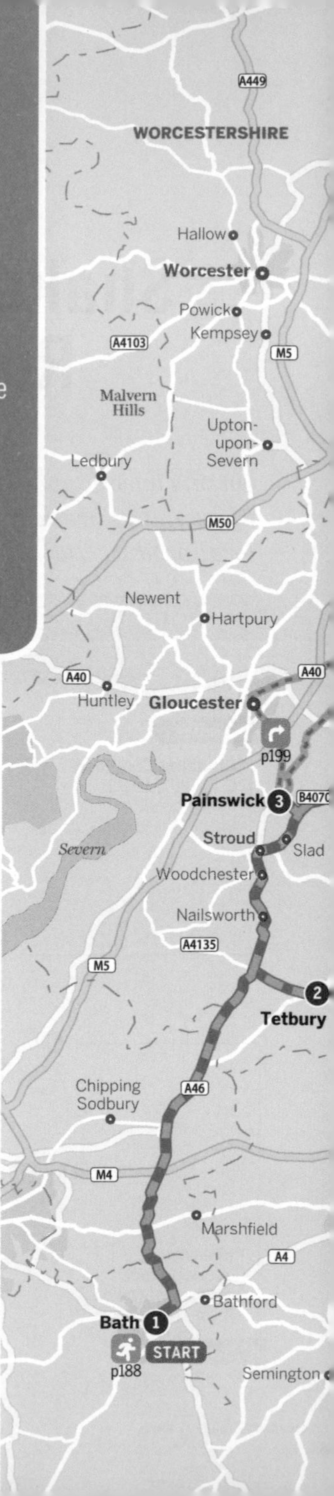

❶ Bath

A star among Britain's most beautiful cities, Bath is a sophisticated dream of splendid honey-toned Georgian buildings coupled with one of the world's most unspoilt Roman bathhouses. It's a lovely place to explore on foot (p188). Jane Austen's *Persuasion* and *Northanger Abbey* are set here.

The busy, brilliantly preserved **Roman Baths** (📞01225-477785; www.roman baths.co.uk; Abbey Church-yard; adult/child £15/9.50; ⏰9am-9pm Jul-Aug, to 5pm Sep-Jun) bubble up at 46°C, surrounded by 18th- and 19th-century buildings. Handsome **Bath Abbey** (www.bathabbey.org; Abbey Churchyard; requested donation adult/student £2.50/1.50; ⏰9.30am-5.30pm Mon, 9am-5.30pm Tue-Fri, 9am-6pm Sat, 1-2.30pm & 4.30-5.30pm Sun) emerged in its current form in the 15th century; take a **tour** (www.bathabbey.org; adult/child £6/3; ⏰10am-5pm Apr-Aug, 11am-3pm Sep-Mar, no tours Sun) up the 212-step tower for fabulous panoramas.

Nowhere is Bath's magnificent Georgian architecture as fine as on semi-circular, park-fringed **Royal Crescent**, where wonderfully restored **No 1 Royal Crescent** (📞01225-428126; www.no1royalcrescent.org.uk; 1 Royal Cres; adult/child/family £10/4/22; ⏰ noon-5.30pm Mon & 10.30am-5.30pm Tue-

Sun Feb–early Dec) **provides a peek into the glitzy period lifestyle.**

📖 p73, p151, p203

The Drive » Bath's London Rd joins the A46; follow 'Stroud' signs. Drive 24 miles north on the A46 into Gloucestershire. The countryside becomes increasingly bucolic and the road narrower as you enter the southern Cotswolds. Turn east onto the A4135; after 4 miles, you'll reach Tetbury.

- - - - - - - - - - - - - - - -

❷ Tetbury

Sitting prettily in the Cotswolds' southwestern reaches, Tetbury was once a wealthy wool town. Its easily strolled sandy-gold centre is a delightful tangle of lively streets flanked by medieval cottages, grand town houses, antique shops and a 17th-centry **Market House**

📎 **LINK YOUR TRIP**

7 Magic, Royalty & Dons

From Burford, drive 20 miles west to Oxford to explore fantastical worlds, royal hangouts and bookish colleges.

18 Battlefields, Castles & Stately Homes

Zip 9 miles northwest from Stratford-upon-Avon to Warwick to pick up this history-rich England trip.

CENTRAL ENGLAND **15** SHAKESPEARE & ROLLING HILLS

(Market Pl). The Georgian Gothic **Church of St Mary the Virgin & St Mary Magdalen** (www.tetburychurch.co.uk; Church St; ☺9am-5pm) has a towering spire (a 19th-century replica of its medieval original) and a dramatic interior of 18th-century dark-oak box pews.

If you're dropping by between April and mid-October, it's worth visiting Prince Charles' **Highgrove** (☑0303 123 7310; www.highgrovegardens.com; Doughton; tours £25; ☺Apr–mid-Oct), a mile southwest of town, for its gorgeous organic gardens. Tickets sell out months ahead, but **Highgrove Shop** (www.highgroveshop.com; 10 Long St; ☺9.30am-5pm Mon-Sat, 10.30am-4pm Sun) often offers last-minute tickets.

The Drive » Head 4 miles west from Tetbury on the A4135, then 6 miles north on the A46. Wiggle around Stroud onto the B4070, whizz 3 miles northeast through green-clad Slad Valley and follow 'Painswick' signs 1 mile northwest to Painswick. You'll pass through Slad, once the beloved home of writer Laurie Lee.

- - - - - - - - - - - -

TRIP HIGHLIGHT

❸ Painswick

Despite being one of the Cotswolds' most perfectly formed villages, hilltop Painswick basks in its own untrammelled beauty.

At its heart stands 14th-century **St Mary's Church** (www.stmaryspainswick.org.uk; New St; ☺9.30am-dusk), a

resplendent Perpendicular Gothic creation surrounded by 18th-century tabletop tombs and 99 clipped yew trees that resemble giant lollipops.

Stroll Painswick's slender, twisting streets, passing ancient honey-coloured homes, medieval inns and **Bisley St**, the original main strip. With its sprinkling of attractive accommodation, Painswick may well tempt you to stay the night.

Just north of town, the exquisite folly-dotted **Painswick Rococo Garden** (☑01452-813204; www.rococogarden.org.uk; off B4073; adult/child £7/3.30; ☺10.30am-5pm mid-Jan–Oct; [P] [♿]) is the only garden of its type in England, designed by Benjamin Hyett in the 1740s as a vast 'outdoor room'.

The Drive » Backtrack to the B4070, head 6 miles northeast and, at Birdlip, follow 'Cirencester' signs onto the A417. It's a 10-mile spin southeast past green fields to Cirencester, where signposted Brewery Car Park has central (short-term) parking.

- - - - - - - - - - - -

❹ Cirencester

Cirencester is an elegant, affluent and surprisingly down-to-earth town with a stash of fascinating sights, chic boutiques, buzzy restaurants, maze-like antique shops and striking Victorian architecture around its **Market Square**.

In Roman times, Cirencester (Corinium) was Britain's second-most-important settlement after London. Well-preserved remains of this glorious era can be found at the superb **Corinium Museum** (☑01285-655611; www.coriniummuseum.org; Park St; adult/child £5.20/2.50; ☺10am-5pm Mon-Sat, 2-5pm Sun Apr-Oct, to 4pm Nov-Mar; [♿]), where countless highlights include a beautiful set of floor mosaics and the 2nd-century 'Jupiter column'.

Cirencester's cathedral-like **St John the Baptist's Church** (☑01285-659317; www.cirenparish.co.uk; Market Sq; ☺10am-4pm), commenced in 1100, is one of England's largest parish churches. It boasts an outstanding Perpendicular Gothic tower with flying buttresses (c 1400) and a majestic three-storey, late-15th-century south porch. In the light-filled interior you'll find soaring arches, magnificent fan vaulting, a Tudor nave and the 1535 Boleyn Cup, made for Anne Boleyn.

The Drive » Wind 8 miles northeast to Bibury on the tree-lined B4425, traversing mellow, well-heeled Barnsley and peaceful countryside interspersed with sprawling Cotswolds panoramas.

- - - - - - - - - - - -

TRIP HIGHLIGHT

❺ Bibury

Once described by William Morris as England's most beautiful village, tiny Bibury embodies the

DETOUR: GLOUCESTER & CHELTENHAM

Start: ❸ Painswick

Gloucester's spectacular **cathedral** (☎01452-528095; www.gloucestercathedral.org.uk; 12 College Green; admission free, tower tours adult/child £7/1; ⊙7.30am-6pm) is among the first and most exquisite examples of the English Perpendicular Gothic style, with a 14th-century, fan-vaulted Great Cloister so enchanting and beautiful that it features in the first, second and sixth *Harry Potter* films. Throw in the fact that the cathedral contains Edward II's tomb (a magnificently elaborate work in alabaster created after the king died in suspicious circumstances at nearby Berkeley Castle), and Gloucestershire's otherwise unremarkable county town is well worth making your own little pilgrimage to. From Painswick, whizz 6 miles northwest on the B4073 to Gloucester; there's plenty of signposted parking.

A 10-mile drive east on the A40 from Gloucester brings you to the handsome Regency town of Cheltenham, a flourishing 18th-century spa resort on the western fringe of the Cotswolds. Fine accommodation and restaurants make Cheltenham an attractive overnight stop.

Cheltenham's **Promenade** is a wide, tree-lined boulevard flanked by imposing period buildings and flower-filled gardens. Also worth a look is Cheltenham's excellent museum, **The Wilson** (☎01242-237431; www.thewilson.org.uk; Clarence St; ⊙9.30am-5.15pm), which depicts local life through the ages and has wonderful displays on William Morris and the Arts and Crafts movement. Modelled on an ancient Athenian temple, the **Pittville Pump Room** (☎0844 576 2210; www.pittvillepumproom.org.uk; Pittville Park; ⊙10am-4pm Wed-Sun) is the town's outstanding Regency building.

Allow a one-night detour for these two stops. From Cheltenham, motor 10 miles southwest back to Painswick on the A46. Alternatively, rejoin the main route at Cirencester, 15 miles southeast (A417), or at Winchcombe, 8 miles northeast (B4632).

Cotswolds at its most picturesque. With a knot of narrow streets flanked by attractive stone buildings, it's popular.

The major draw is **Arlington Row**, a perfectly rustic sweep of cottages converted in the 17th century from a 14th-century wool store – and a contender for Britain's most photographed street.

🛏 p203

The Drive » We'll be sticking to gorgeous, slim, classic-Cotswolds country lanes here. Head west out of Bibury on the Ablington road, starting outside Bibury's Swan Hotel. After 1 mile, turn north, following signs for 5 miles to Northleach.

---

❻ Northleach

Little visited, under-appreciated and, therefore, well worth a stop on your Cotswolds itinerary, Northleach has been a small market town since 1227. Its centre is made up of late-medieval cottages, imposing merchants' stores and half-timbered Tudor houses.

The grand **Church of St Peter & St Paul** (www.northleach.org; Church Walk; ⊙9am-5pm), a masterpiece of the Cotswold Perpendicular style, is testimony to Northleach's wool-era wealth; its chancel, 30m tower and unusual font date to the 14th century.

On the west edge of town, pop into the **Cotswolds Discovery Centre** (Escape to the Cotswolds; www.cotswoldsaonb.org.uk; A429; ⊙9.30am-4.30pm; ℗), housed in Northleach's Old Prison. This is the official visitor centre for the Cotswolds Area of Outstanding Natural Beauty (AONB), with displays outlining local history, ecology, traditions and attractions.

The Drive » It's a quick 10-mile drive east along the (admittedly unexciting) A40, crossing into Oxfordshire, to Burford. Parking here can be tricky, but there are often spots hidden down side streets.

---

❼ Burford

Tumbling steeply down-hill to the River Wind-rush, Burford is one of the Cotswolds' busiest villages, little changed since its high-flying wool-era days. Despite the crowds, it makes a particularly picturesque overnight stop thanks to its remarkable mix of stone cottages, gold-tinged town houses, chintzy tearooms, ancient pubs, delightful hotels, antique shops and boutique delis.

Commenced in 1175 and added to over the years, Burford's **St John the Baptist's Church** (www.burfordchurch.org;

Church Lane; ☺9am-5pm) has survived reformers and Roundheads (supporters of parliament against the king in the English Civil War) with its fan-vaulting ceiling, Norman west doorway, 15th-century spire and several grand tombs intact.

If you're craving a good stretch after all that driving, there are some good walks around Burford. The **tourist office** (☎01993-823558; www.oxfordshirecotswolds. org; 33a High St; ☺9.30am-5pm Mon-Sat, 10am-4pm Sun) stocks maps.

The Drive » It's time to tackle the wonderfully scenic, undulating northern Cotswolds. Hop on the A424 northwest; after 6 miles, follow 'Little Rissington' signs east. Drive 900m, turn right, then immediately left, continuing 3 miles through Little Rissington and picturesque Bourton-on-the-Water onto the A429. Skip a mile northwest, take the signposted 'The Slaughters' turn-off and 650m west is Lower Slaughter.

---

❽ The Slaughters

Blissfully charming, the tranquil chocolate-box villages of Upper and Lower Slaughter are the perfect introduction to the golden-stone delights of the northern Cotswolds (despite pulling in plenty of visitors). Their names are derived from the Old English *sloughtre* ('slough' or 'muddy place').

The River Eye meanders peacefully through the villages, flanking classic honey-washed houses and manors and Lower Slaughter's **Old Mill** (☎01451-820052; www.oldmill-lowerslaughter.com; Lower Slaughter; adult/child £2.50/1; ☺10am-6pm Mar-Oct, to dusk Nov-Feb) museum.

✗ p203

The Drive » Back on the A429, Stow-on-the-Wold is 2.5 miles northwest past rippling fields, along what was once the Roman Fosse Way.

---

❾ Stow-on-the-Wold

Welcome to the Cotswolds' highest town, strategically positioned at 244m on the junction of six roads. Stow has long been an important market town, with thin alleyways (originally for funnelling sheep) feeding into a sprawling market square lined with graceful stone buildings, cute tearooms, a medieval-era church and old-world pubs wrapped in greenery.

THE COTSWOLD WAY

As you travel through the Cotswolds, you'll undoubtedly spot happy hikers meandering along. One of the region's most popular long-distance walks (followed at times by this drive) is the 102-mile **Cotswold Way** (www.nationaltrail.co.uk/cotswold-way). The route rambles from Chipping Campden to Bath via the northwestern and southwestern Cotswolds, passing through some lovely countryside and tiny villages, with no major climbs or difficult stretches. It's easily accessible from many points en route, such as Broadway, Chipping Campden or Winchcombe, if you fancy tackling a shorter section.

The Drive » Rejoin the A429 and zip 4.5 miles north to busy Moreton-in-Marsh, known for its local food shops and Tuesday farmers market. From Moreton, take the A44 6 miles northwest, climbing through tiny Bourton-on-the-Hill. Exit onto the B4081, following signs to Chipping Campden, 2.5 miles north of the A44.

Bath Kennet and Avon Canal

TRIP HIGHLIGHT

⑩ Chipping Campden

From the first glimpse of its honey-hued streets, Chipping Campden is undoubtedly one of the Cotswolds' most exquisite towns. It's an excellent overnight stop.

Elegant High St is flanked by a perfectly picturesque array of stone cottages, fine terraced houses, ancient inns, historic homes and the 14th-century **Grevel House** (High St; ⊘ closed to the public), with a marvellous Perpendicular Gothic–style gabled window. The premier attraction is the highly photogenic 17th-century **Market Hall** (NT; www.nationaltrust.org.uk; High St; admission free; ⊘24hr), an open-sided, timber-roofed pillared building that looks like a cross between a barn and a chapel.

Imposing **St James' Church** (☎01386-841927; www.stjameschurchcampden. co.uk; Church St; admission by donation; ⊘10am-4.30pm Mon-Sat, noon-4pm Sun Apr-Oct, 11am-3pm Mon-Sat, 2-4pm Sun Nov-Mar), built

in the late 15th century in Perpendicular Gothic style, on wool-trade riches, has an impressive tower and some graceful 17th-century monuments. Just outside, the **Court Barn Museum** (☎01386-841951; www.courtbarn.org. uk; Church St; adult/child £5/ free; ⊘10am-5pm Tue-Sun Apr-Sep, to 4pm Oct-Mar) gives a detailed insight into Chipping Campden's important connection with the Arts and Crafts movement: architect and designer Charles Robert Ashbee moved his Guild of Handicraft from East London to here in 1902.

🛏 p203

The Drive » Drive 1 mile northwest on the A44, crossing into the Cotswolds' Worcestershire pocket. Follow 'Broadway Tower' signs 1 mile southwest to the top of the escarpment.

⑪ Broadway Tower

A crenulated 18th-century Gothic folly, **Broadway Tower** (☎01386-852390; www.broadwaytower.co.uk; Middle Hill; adult/child £5/3; ⊘10am-5pm; P) stands on the windswept crest of the escarpment, offering all-encompassing views from the top. William Morris once summered here. It's also on the Cotswold Way: a 2-mile path links it to St Eadburgha's Church, a mile south of Broadway.

The Drive » Continue 1 mile south from Broadway Tower and turn right (southwest). Signs soon lead the 1-mile way to pretty little Snowshill, famed for featuring in *Bridget Jones's Diary*. If you're visiting in June or July, you'll whizz past gorgeously purple fields carpeted with blooming lavender. From Snowshill, it's 2.5 miles north to Broadway.

⑫ Broadway

Huddling beautifully at the foot of a sloping escarpment, Broadway is said to have one of the lengthiest high streets in England. A quintessentially Costwolds village, it reels in visitors with its golden cottages, art galleries, antique stores, fashionable delis and plush hotels.

Set in a grand converted coaching inn, the **Ashmolean Museum Broadway** (📞01386-859047; www.ashmoleanbroadway. org; Tudor House, 65 High St; adult/child £5/2; ⊘10am-5pm Tue-Sun) has fascinating displays of local crafts, antiques and history spanning the 17th century to today. Collections include Winchcombe pottery, vintage furniture, tapestries and paintings by Reynolds and Gainsborough.

The Drive » The fastest Broadway-to-Winchcombe route is the B4632 southwest; we're turning off 3 miles southwest of Broadway to detour through picture-perfect Stanton (signposted). Next, track 1 mile south on the road that parallels the Cotswold Way to stunning little Stanway, famous for its fabulous Jacobean mansion. Turn west onto the B4077, then southwest onto the B4632; it's 3.5 miles to Winchcombe.

⑬ Winchcombe

Once capital of the Anglo-Saxon kingdom of Mercia and a prominent Cotswolds town until the Middle Ages, Winchcombe retains its workaday bustle amid half-timbered houses, gold-stone buildings and ancient inns. With its comparatively affordable lodgings and handy location, it's a popular walkers' hangout.

Winchcombe's main attraction, spectacular **Sudeley Castle** (www. sudeleycastle.co.uk; adult/child £14.50/5.50; ⊘10am-5pm mid-Mar–Oct; 🅿🚻) has welcomed many a monarch over its thousand-year history, including Richard III, Henry VIII and Charles I. It's most famous as the home and final resting place of Catherine Parr (Henry VIII's widow), who lived here with her fourth husband, Thomas Seymour. You'll find Catherine's tomb in the castle's Perpendicular Gothic St Mary's Church, making this the only private house in England where a queen is buried. Outside lie 10 splendid gardens.

🛏 p203

The Drive » Take the B4078 north for 7 miles, then zip along the A46 for 21 miles to Stratford-upon-Avon. Stratford has plenty of central parking, though town car parks charge high fees.

TRIP HIGHLIGHT

⑭ Stratford-upon-Avon

A distinctly Tudor town with a fanatical following, Stratford-upon-Avon is a fascinating place to wander (p236), and a fittingly famous final stop on your itinerary: the birth and burial place of the greatest of English literary giants, William Shakespeare (1564–1616).

Kick off your Shakespeare story at **Shakespeare's Birthplace** (📞01789-204016; www. shakespeare.org.uk; Henley St; incl Shakespeare's New Place & Halls Croft adult/child £17.50/11.50; ⊘9am-5.30pm Jul & Aug, to 5pm Sep-Jun), where the world's most popular playwright supposedly spent his childhood. In Stratford's medieval **Holy Trinity Church** (📞01789-266316; www.stratford-upon-avon.org; Old Town; Shakespeare's grave adult/child £2/1; ⊘8.30am-6pm Mon-Sat, 12.30-5pm Sun Apr-Sep, shorter hours Oct-Mar), you can see the unexpectedly modest, much-visited grave of William Shakespeare, with its menacing epitaph: 'cvrst be he yt moves my bones'.

Book ahead to join the world-renowned **Royal Shakespeare Company** (RSC; 📞box office 01789-403493; www.rsc.org.uk; Waterside; tours adult £6.50-8.50, child £3-4.50, tower adult/child £2.50/1.25; ⊘tour times vary, tower 10am-6.15pm Sun-Fri 10am-12.15pm & 2-6.15pm Sat Apr-Sep, 10am-4.30pm Sun-Fri, 10am-12.15pm & 2-4.30pm Sat Oct-Mar) at one of its legendary productions. From here on, you're in the hands of the Bard.

🛏 p203

Eating & Sleeping

Bath ❶

🛏 Grays Bath   B&B ££££

(📞01225-403020; www.graysbath.co.uk; Upper Oldfield Park; d £90-205; 📶) Boutique treat Grays is a beautiful blend of modern, pared-down design and family treasures, many picked up from the owners' travels. All the rooms are individual: choose from floral, polka dot or maritime stripes. Perhaps the pick is the six-sided, curling room 12 in the attic, with partial city views.

Bibury ❺

🛏 New Inn   Pub ££

(📞01285-750651; www.new-inn.co.uk; Main St, Coln St Aldwyns; r incl breakfast £79-169; 🅿📶🐾) The popular jasmine-clad New Inn offers quirky contemporary comfort in 16th-century surroundings, both in the main pub building and a neighbouring cottage. The 15 bedrooms are spacious and atmospheric, with bold colours, fluffy throws, smart furnishings, the odd free-standing bathtub and a few wood beams. It's 2 miles southeast of Bibury.

The Slaughters ❽

🍴 Lords of the Manor   Modern British ££££

(📞01451-820243; www.lordsofthemanor.com; Upper Slaughter; 3-course dinner £72.50; 🕐noon-1.30pm Sat & Sun, 6.45-9pm daily; 🅿) Set inside a dazzling countryside manor, this romantic Michelin-starred restaurant concocts imaginative, beautifully presented dishes with French touches and plenty of quality local produce. It also serves popular afternoon teas and has 26 plush, comfy **rooms** (📞01451-820243; www.lordsofthemanor.com; Upper Slaughter; r incl breakfast £150-465; 🅿📶🐾). Book ahead.

Chipping Campden ❿

🛏 Eight Bells Inn   Pub ££

(📞01386-840371; www.eightbellsinn.co.uk; Church St; s £60-95, d £95-140, all incl breakfast; 📶) This refurbished 14th-century inn is a particularly friendly and atmospheric place to stay, featuring six bright, modern rooms with iron bedsteads, soothing neutral decor, flowery wallpaper and warm accents. Room 7, with its chunky old-world beams, is especially striking. The cosy **pub** (mains £13-16; 🕐 noon-2pm & 6.30-9pm Mon-Thu, noon-2.30pm & 6.30-9.30pm Fri & Sat, 12.15-9pm Sun; 🚼🐾) downstairs serves good modern British country cooking.

Winchcombe ❸

🛏 Wesley House   B&B ££

(📞01242-602366; www.wesleyhouse.co.uk; High St; s £70-95, d £85-110; 🕐 restaurant noon-2pm & 7-9pm Tue-Sat, noon-2pm Sun; 📶🐾) Methodist founder John Wesley once stayed in this wonderful 15th-century half-timbered town house with five pleasantly styled rooms and a warm welcome. 'Mumble Meadow', splashed with reds, overlooks the street, while 'Almsbury' has its own terrace gazing out across the countryside. Downstairs is split between a relaxed bar and grill, and a more formal restaurant serving fabulous modern-British cuisine (mains £16 to £24).

Stratford-upon-Avon ❹

🛏 Church Street Townhouse   Boutique Hotel £££

(📞01789-262222; www.churchstreet-th.co.uk; 16 Church St; d from £110; 📶) Some of the dozen rooms at this exquisite hotel have free-standing claw-foot bathtubs, and all have iPod docks, flatscreen TVs and luxurious furnishings. Light sleepers should avoid room 1, nearest the bar. The building itself is a centrally located 400-year-old gem with a first-rate restaurant and bar. There's a minimum two-night stay on weekends.

Industrial Powerhouse

16

As you drive from the vibrant northern city of Manchester to bucolic, hilly Great Malvern, you'll encounter Britain's industrial heritage at every turn, from former mines to factory-housed museums.

TRIP HIGHLIGHTS

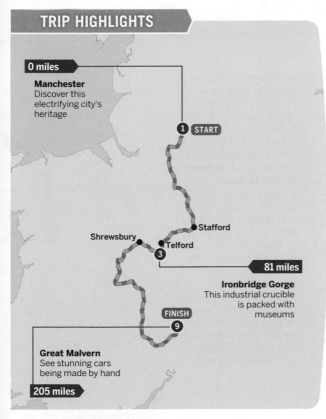

0 miles

Manchester
Discover this electrifying city's heritage

1 START

Stafford

Shrewsbury
Telford
3

81 miles

Ironbridge Gorge
This industrial crucible is packed with museums

FINISH
9

Great Malvern
See stunning cars being made by hand

205 miles

4 DAYS
205 MILES / 330KM

GREAT FOR...

BEST TIME TO GO

May to September are the most pleasant months.

ESSENTIAL PHOTO

The arched Iron Bridge that first showcased cast-iron technology.

BEST FOR HISTORY

Steam engines, locomotives and original factory machinery at Manchester's Museum of Science and Industry.

Ironbridge Gorge The world's first iron bridge

16 Industrial Powerhouse

The Industrial Revolution's humble beginnings took place deep in the English countryside: the wooded riverbanks of Ironbridge Gorge are where cast iron was first mass produced, and today the gorge teems with the factories' legacies, including its namesake bridge. Other industries you'll encounter along this attraction-packed route include pottery, cars, aircraft and cider producers (including one that supplies the Houses of Parliament).

- - - - - - - - - - - - - -

TRIP HIGHLIGHT

❶ Manchester

Manchester has a rich blend of history and culture along with a hedonistic swirl of epicurean and entertainment venues.

This northern powerhouse's industrial legacy is explored at the excellent **Museum of Science & Industry** (MOSI; ☎0161-832 2244; www.msimanchester. org.uk; Liverpool Rd; special exhibits £2.50-4; ☉10am-5pm), set within the enormous grounds of the old Liverpool St Station, the oldest rail terminus in the world. The large collection of steam engines, locomotives and original factory machinery tell the story of the city from the sewers up, while new technology (flight simulator, 4D cinema) looks to the future.

Housed in a refurbished Edwardian pumping station, the **People's History Museum** (☎0161-838 9190; www.phm.org.uk; Left Bank, Bridge St; ☉10am-5pm) tells the story of Britain's 200-year march to democracy. You clock in on the 1st floor (literally: punch your card in an old mill clock, which managers would infamously fiddle with so as to make employees work longer) and plunge into the heart of Britain's struggle for basic

democratic rights, labour reform and fair pay.

✕ ⊫ p47, p85, p211

The Drive » It's 45 miles south to Stoke-on-Trent. Take Princess Rd to Manchester Airport, where it becomes the M56 and connect to the southbound M6.

- - - - - - - - - - - - - -

❷ Stoke-on-Trent

Situated at the heart of the Potteries – the famous pottery-producing region of Staffordshire – Stoke-on-Trent is famed for its ceramics. Don't expect cute little artisanal producers: this was where pottery shifted to mass production during the Industrial Revolution, and Stoke today is a sprawl of industrial townships tied together by flyovers and bypasses.

For a good overview, visit the **Potteries Museum & Art Gallery** (🕿01782-236000; www.stoke

LINK YOUR TRIP

17 **Peak District**
Head 23 miles east of Stoke-on-Trent via the A52 to pick up the Peak District trip in Ashbourne.

4 **Urban & Art Odyssey**
The end point of this trip, Great Malvern, intersects with the epic Urban & Art Odyssey.

207

museums.org.uk; Bethesda St, Hanley; ☺10am-5pm Mon-Sat, 11am-4pm Sun), which houses an extensive ceramics display, from Toby jugs and jasperware to outrageous ornamental pieces. Other highlights include displays on the WWII Spitfire, created by the Stoke-born aviator Reginald Mitchell.

Active potteries that you can visit in the greater area include the **Wedgwood factory** (☎01782-282986; www.world ofwedgwood.com; Wedgwood Dr, Barlaston; factory tour & museum adult/child £15/7.50, factory tour only £10/5, museum only £7.50/3.75; ☺10am-5pm Mon-Fri, to 4pm Sat & Sun). The modern production centre for Josiah Wedgwood's porcelain empire displays historic pieces, including plenty of Wedgwood's delicate, neoclassical blue-and-white jasperware. A film on Josiah's life and work details his involve-

ment in canal-building and opposition to slavery.

The Drive » Drive 36 miles southwest, via the late-20th-century town of Telford (named for civil engineer Thomas Telford), to Ironbridge Gorge.

- - - - - - - - - - - -

TRIP HIGHLIGHT

❸ Ironbridge Gorge

It's hard to believe this peaceful, wooded river gorge could really have been the birthplace of the Industrial Revolution. But it was here that Abraham Darby perfected the art of smelting iron ore with coke in 1709, making it possible to mass-produce cast iron for the first time.

Abraham Darby's son, Abraham Darby II, invented a new forging process for producing single beams of iron, allowing Abraham Darby III to astound the world with the first-ever **iron bridge**, constructed in 1779. The bridge remains the focal point of this World

Heritage site, and 10 very different museums tell the story of the Industrial Revolution in the buildings where it took place. All are administered by the **Ironbridge Gorge Museum Trust** (☎01952-433424; www.ironbridge.org. uk). You'll save considerably by buying a passport ticket (adult/child £25/15) at any of the museums or the tourist office. Valid for 12 months, it allows unlimited entry to all of Ironbridge Gorge's sites.

Start at the Gothic riverside warehouse-housed **Museum of the Gorge** (The Wharfage; adult/child £4.50/3.15; ☺10am-5pm), which offers an outstanding overview using film, photos and exhibits including a 12m-long 3D model of the town in 1796. Other gorge highlights include **Museum of Iron** (Wellington Rd; adult/child, £8.85/5.65, incl Darby Houses £9.25/6.35; ☺10am-5pm), set in Abraham Darby's original iron foundry. As ironmaking fell into decline, Ironbridge diversified into manufacturing china pots, using the fine clay mined around Blists Hill. Learn more at the **Coalport China Museum & Tar Tunnel** (Coalport High St; museum adult/child £8.85/5.65, Tar Tunnel £3.40/2.50; ☺10am-5pm early Mar–early Nov), dominated by a pair of towering bottle kilns.

✕ 🛏 p211

DETOUR: COSFORD ROYAL AIR FORCE MUSEUM

Start: ❸ Ironbridge Gorge

The famous **Cosford Royal Air Force Museum** (☎01902-376200; www.rafmuseum.org.uk; Shifnal; ☺10am-5pm) is run by the Royal Air Force, whose pilots steered many of these winged wonders across the skies. Among the 70 aircraft on display are the Vulcan bomber (which carried Britain's nuclear deterrent) and the tiny helicopter-like FA330 Bachstelze glider that was towed behind German U-boats to warn them of enemy ships. You can also try out a Black Hawk simulator. It's 13 miles east of Ironbridge via the A4169.

The Drive » Head west out of Ironbridge on the B4380 along the River Severn; Attingham Park is 11 miles away.

Manchester Steam locomotive at the Museum of Science and Industry

❹ Attingham Park

Built in imposing neoclassical style in 1785, **Attingham Park** (NT; ☎01743-708123; www.nationaltrust.org.uk; Atcham; house & grounds adult/child £11.25/5.60, grounds only £6.75/3.35; ☺house 10.30am-5.30pm mid-Mar–early Nov, grounds 8am-7pm May-Sep, 9am-6pm Mar-Apr & Oct, 9am-5pm Nov-Feb) **looks like something straight out of a period drama with its grand columned facade and stagecoach turning-circle in the courtyard. The landscaped grounds swirl around an ornamental lake and are home to some 300 fallow deer. The restored walled garden is a picture.

The Drive » Cross to the southern bank of the River Severn; it's a quick 5-mile drive northwest to Shrewsbury.

❺ Shrewsbury

A delightful jumble of winding medieval streets and timbered Tudor houses leaning at precarious angles around its 16th-century **Old Market Hall** (www.oldmarkethall.co.uk; The Square), **Shrewsbury** was a crucial front in the conflict between English and Welsh in medieval days, and is famed as the birthplace of Charles Darwin (1809–82). He's commemorated by a **statue** (Castle Gates) outside the town library, formerly the Shrewsbury School, where he was educated.

Hewn from flaking red Shropshire sandstone, **Shrewsbury Castle** (☎01743-358516; www.shropshireregimentalmuseum.co.uk; Castle St; adult/child £4/1; ☺10.30am-5pm Mon-Wed, Fri & Sat, to 4pm Sun Jun–mid-Sep, to 4pm Mon-Wed, Fri & Sat mid-Feb–May & mid-Sep–mid-Dec) contains the Shropshire Regimental Museum. There are fine views from Laura's Tower and the battlements.

The Drive » Follow the A488 southwest from Shrewsbury through rolling green countryside, and take the first left after the town of Minsterley to Snailbeach (which, despite its name, is not a beach), on the edge of the Shropshire Hills – an 11-mile journey all up.

❻ Snailbeach

You'll see the relics of rusting machinery at the former lead- and silver-mining village of **Snailbeach** (☎01952-405105; www.shropshiremines.org.uk). Self-guided trails let you explore the site, or you can join one of two guided tours. The 30-minute **Day Level & Surface Tour** (every 30 minutes 11am to 4pm Sunday June to September; adult/child £7.50/3) covers the mine's exterior and entrance. The 2½-hour **Roberts/Perkins Level Tour** (by reservation Sunday June to September; £5/3) takes you deep into the mine.

The Drive » Drive southwest through the village of Stiperstones to the hilly town of Bishop's Castle (home to the 1642-founded Three Tuns Brewery). Continue south on the A488 to the black-and-white village of Clun. From here, it's 18 miles east via the B4368 to the castle-crowned market town of Ludlow, then 23 miles south via the A49 to Hereford (70 miles all up).

❼ Hereford

Surrounded by apple orchards and rolling pastures at the heart of the Marches, straddling the River Wye, Hereford is famed for its prime steaks and its cider – you can learn about the local tipple at the **Cider Museum & King Offa Distillery** (☎01432-354207; www.cidermuseum.co.uk; Pomona Pl; adult/child £5.50/3; ⏱10am-5pm Mon-Sat Apr-Oct, 11am-3pm Mon-Sat Nov-Mar). Displays cover cidermaking history and you can sample the delicious modern brews. Look for the fine costrels (minibarrels) used by agricultural workers to carry their wages, which were partially paid in cider.

Soaring **Hereford Cathedral** (☎01432-374202; www.herefordcathedral.org; 5 College Cloisters; cathedral entry by £5 donation, Mappa Mundi £6; ⏱cathedral 9.15am-5.30pm Mon-Sat, to 3.30pm Sun, Mappa Mundi 10am-5pm Mon-Sat mid-Mar–Oct, to 4pm Nov–mid-Mar) is home to the extraordinary Mappa Mundi, a single piece of calfskin vellum intricately painted with some rather fantastical assumptions about the layout of the globe in around 1290. The same wing contains the world's largest surviving chained library of rare manuscripts manacled to the shelves.

🛏 p211

The Drive » It's 13 miles southeast along the B4224 through undulating countryside and small farming villages, to Westons Cider Mills, just under a mile west of the tiny, quaintly named village of Much Marcle. Much of the journey shadows the River Wye.

- - - - - - - - - - - - - - -

❽ Westons Cider Mills

Cider producers are scattered throughout the Herefordshire countryside but one of the most prestigious is **Westons Cider Mills** (☎01531-660108; www.westons-cider.co.uk; The Bounds, Much Marcle; tours adult/child £10/4; ⏱9am-5pm Mon-Fri, 10am-5pm Sat & Sun), whose house brew is even served in the Houses of Parliament. Informative tours (1½ hours) start at 11am, 12.30pm, 2pm and 3.30pm, with free cider and perry tastings. There's also a fascinating bottle museum.

The Drive » The final stretch of this trip is also the prettiest. Take the A449 northeast, via the postcard-perfect black-and-white Tudor town of Ledbury, up into the wooded hills to Great Malvern (13 miles in total).

- - - - - - - - - - - - - - -

TRIP HIGHLIGHT

❾ Great Malvern

Tumbling down the side of a forested ridge about 7 miles southwest of Worcester is the picturesque spa town of Great Malvern.

The 11th-century **Great Malvern Priory** (☎01684-561020; www.greatmalvernpriory.org.uk; Church St; ⏱9am-5pm) is packed with remarkable features, from original Norman pillars to surreal modernist stained glass. The choir is enclosed by a screen of 15th-century tiles and the monks' stalls are decorated with delightfully irreverent 14th-century misericords, depicting everything from three rats hanging a cat to the mythological basilisk. Charles Darwin's daughter Annie is buried here.

For road-trippers, though, the real treat is the **Morgan Motor Company** (☎01684-584580; www.morgan-motor.co.uk; Pickersleigh Rd; museum free, tours adult/child £20/10; ⏱museum 8.30am-5pm Mon-Thu, to 3pm Fri, tours 10am, 12.30pm & 2.30pm Mon-Fri), which has been handcrafting elegant sports cars since 1909. You can still see the mechanics at work on two-hour guided tours (book ahead), and view vintage classics adjacent to the museum. If you want to swap your wheels for one of these beautiful machines (at least for a while), it's possible to rent one (per day from £200, including insurance).

🍴 🛏 p211

Eating & Sleeping

Manchester ❶

✕ The Kitchens International £
(http://thekitchensleftbank.com; Irwell Sq; mains £4-12; ☺noon-3pm Mon-Wed, noon-9pm Thu-Sun; Bangers & Bacon 7am-midnight Mon-Fri, from 9.30am Sat-Sun) Gathered under one roof are a number of 'street food' producers including Bangers and Bacon (@bangersandbacon), Chaat Cart (Indian street food; @chaatcart), the Hip Hop Chip Shop (@thehiphopchippy), Dim Sum Su (@dimsumsu) and Well Hung (@wellhungkitchen), which serves 28-day aged steaks. They're all terrific: check the Twitter handles for updates.

🛏 Midland Hotel Hotel ££
(☎0161-236 3333; www.qhotels.co.uk; 16 Peter St; r from £100; ❄@🐾) This refurbished Grade II–listed Edwardian hotel is back to its elegant best. Its 312 rooms are elegantly appointed: the junior suites have a separate lounge while the seven Midland suites once entertained royalty, both actual and secular. Downstairs, Simon Rogan's The French (☎0161-932 4198; www.the-french.co.uk; 6-/10-course menu £65/85; ☺noon-1.30pm & 6.30-9.30pm) and Mr Cooper's House & Garden (www.mrcoopershouseandgarden.co.uk; mains £15-25; ☺noon-2pm & 5-10pm Mon-Thu, noon-2.30pm & 5-10pm Fri-Sat, 1-8pm Sun) restaurants are among the best in the city.

Ironbridge Gorge ❸

✕ D'arcys at the Station Mediterranean ££
(☎01952-884499; www.darcysironbridge.co.uk; Ladywood; mains £11.50-15; ☺6-9.30pm Tue-Sat) Just over the bridge by the river, the handsome old station building is the backdrop for flavoursome Mediterranean dishes, from Moroccan chicken to Cypriot kebabs.

🛏 Library House B&B ££
(☎01952-432299; www.libraryhouse.com; 11 Severn Bank; s/d from £75/95; P🐾) Up an alley off the main street, this lovingly restored Georgian library building is hugged by vines, backed by a beautiful garden and decked out with stacks of vintage books, curios, prints and lithographs. There are four charmingly well-preserved, individually decorated rooms, named Milton, Chaucer, Eliot and Hardy. The affable dog whipping around is Millie.

Hereford ❼

🛏 Castle House Boutique Hotel £££
(☎01432-356321; www.castlehse.co.uk; Castle St; s/d/ste from £130/150/190; P🐾) Set in a regal Georgian town house that was once the luxurious digs of the Bishop of Hereford, this tranquil 16-room hotel has a sophisticated restaurant, sunny garden spilling down to the river, and magnificent rooms and suites. Another eight newer rooms (some wheelchair accessible) are a short walk away at 25 Castle St.

Great Malvern ❾

✕ Fig Tree Modern British ££
(☎01684-569909; www.thefigtreemalvern.co.uk; 99b Church St; mains £8-17.50; ☺noon-2pm & 5.30-9.30pm Tue-Sat) Tucked down an alleyway off Church St, this 19th-century former stable serves Mediterranean-inspired fare such as marinated pork chops with caramelised apple, red onion and rosemary potatoes, and chargrilled chicken with minted yoghurt and saffron rice.

🛏 Como House B&B ££
(☎01684-561486; www.comohouse.co.uk; Como Rd; s/d £45/70; P❄🐾) This handsome stone house benefits from a quiet location away from the central bustle. Rooms are snug, the garden is a delight and the mood is restoratively calm. Vegetarian and gluten-free breakfasts are available on request from the friendly owners, who will pick you up from the station and drop you off by the walking trails.

Peak District

17

This adventure-packed trip plunges you into the heart of the Peak District National Park and offers boundless opportunities to get out of your car and into the invigorating landscapes.

TRIP HIGHLIGHTS

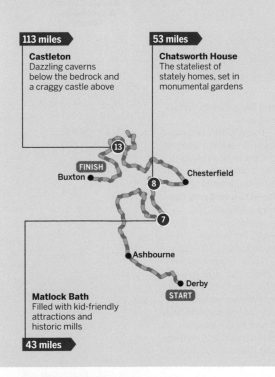

113 miles

Castleton
Dazzling caverns below the bedrock and a craggy castle above

53 miles

Chatsworth House
The stateliest of stately homes, set in monumental gardens

FINISH
Buxton

Chesterfield

Ashbourne

Derby
START

Matlock Bath
Filled with kid-friendly attractions and historic mills

43 miles

5 DAYS
123 MILES / 197KM

GREAT FOR...

BEST TIME TO GO
Easter to September lets you enjoy the best weather.

ESSENTIAL PHOTO
The dramatic view up through steep-sided Winnats Pass.

BEST FOR OUTDOORS
Spectacular walking trails fan out around Edale.

17 Peak District

On this drive you'll wind through the glorious Peak District – founded in 1951 as England's first national park – as it rolls across the Pennines' southernmost hills. The White Peak is made up of the limestone dales, while to the north, the Dark Peak is dominated by exposed moorland and gritstone 'edges'. Ancient stone villages are folded into creases in the landscape, and the rocky hillsides are strewn with stately homes.

❶ Derby

Gloriously sited at the southeastern edge of the Derbyshire hills that roll toward the Peak District, Derby is one of the Midlands' most energetic, creative cities. This was one of the crucibles of the Industrial Revolution: almost overnight, a sleepy market town was transformed into a major manufacturing centre, producing everything from silk to bone china, and later locomotives and Rolls-Royce aircraft engines.

Derby's historic potteries still turn out some of the finest bone china in England. Book ahead for 90-minute tours of the **Royal Crown Derby Factory** (📞01332-712800; www.royalcrownderby.co.uk; Osmaston Rd; museum & factory tour adult/child £5/2.50, museum only £2/1; ⏰ museum 10am-4pm Mon-Sat, factory tours 1.30pm Tue-Thu, shop 10am-5pm Mon-Sat, tearoom 10am-4pm Tue-Fri), which include a visit to the museum. Its china (including seconds and discontinued items)

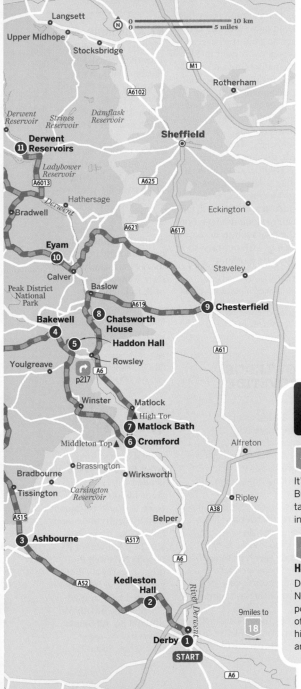

Langsett

Upper Midhope

Stocksbridge

0 — 10 km
0 — 5 miles

M1

A6102

Rotherham

Derwent Reservoir *Strines Reservoir* *Damflask Reservoir*

Sheffield

11 Derwent Reservoirs

Ladybower Reservoir

A6013

Hathersage

Bradwell

A625

Eckington

A621

A617

Derwent

Eyam 10

Calver

Staveley

Baslow

Peak District National Park

A619

9 Chesterfield

Bakewell 4

8 Chatsworth House

5

Haddon Hall

Rowsley

A61

Youlgreave

A6

p217

Winster

Matlock

High Tor

7 Matlock Bath

Middleton Top ▲ **6 Cromford**

Alfreton

Brassington

Bradbourne

Wirksworth

Tissington

Carsington Reservoir

Ripley

A38

Belper

A515

3 Ashbourne

A517

A52

Kedleston Hall

2

River Derwent

A6

9 miles to

Derby 1

START

A6

---

is sold at its on-site shop, and is used as tableware at its elegant tearoom.

The **Derby Museum & Art Gallery** (www.derby museums.org; The Strand; ⏱10am-5pm Tue-Sat, noon-4pm Sun) also has ceramics produced by Royal Crown Derby, along with an archaeology gallery.

One of Derby's biggest draws is its independent designer bars and wonderful selection of historic real-ale pubs such as the **Old Bell Hotel** (www. bellhotelderby.co.uk; 51 Sadler Gate; ⏱11.30am-11.30pm Sun-Thu, to 1.30am Fri & Sat).

🛏 p225

The Drive » Drive through Derby's outskirts along Kedleston Rd, which gives way to farmland just before the turn-off to Kedleston Hall (5 miles in total).

LINK YOUR TRIP

16 Industrial Powerhouse

It's a 23-mile drive from Buxton to Manchester to take a spin through British industrial history.

18 Battlefields, Castles & Stately Homes

Derby is a 15-mile hop from Nottingham, the starting point for discovering some of the country's most historic battlefields, castles and stately homes.

Classic Trip

❷ Kedleston Hall

Sitting pretty in vast landscaped grounds, the neoclassical mansion **Kedleston Hall** (NT; Kedleston; house & gardens adult/child £12/6, garden only £5/2.50; ⏱ house noon-5pm Sat-Thu Feb-Oct, garden 10am-6pm Feb-Oct, to 4pm Nov-Jan) is a must for fans of stately homes. Entering the house through a grand portico, you'll reach the breathtaking Marble Hall with massive alabaster columns and statues of Greek deities.

The Curzon family has lived here since the 12th century but the current wonder was built by Sir Nathaniel Curzon in 1758. Meanwhile, the poor old peasants in Kedleston village had their humble dwellings moved a mile down the road, as they interfered with the view. Ah, the good old days...

Highlights include Indian treasures amassed by Viceroy George Curzon and a domed, circular saloon modelled on the Pantheon in Rome, as well as 18th-century-style pleasure gardens.

The Drive » Head west along Buckhazels Lane and join Ashbourne Rd (aka the A52) to drive northwest into Ashbourne (10 miles all up).

LOCAL KNOWLEDGE: ROYAL SHROVETIDE FOOTBALL

Some people celebrate Mardi Gras (aka Shrove Tuesday; the last day before Lent) by eating pancakes or dressing up in carnival finery. But Ashbourne marks the occasion with a riotous game of football, where the ball is wrestled as much as kicked from one end of town to the other by crowds of revellers.

Following 12th-century rules, villagers are split into two teams – those from north of the river and those from south – and the 'goals' are two millstones, set 3 miles apart. Participants are free to kick, carry or throw the ball, though it's usually squeezed through the crowds like a rugby scrum. Sooner or later, players and the ball end up in the river. Local shops board up their windows and the whole town comes out to watch or play.

Fearless visitors are welcome to participate in the melee but, under a quirk of the rules, only locals are allowed to score goals.

❸ Ashbourne

Perched at the southern edge of the Peak District National Park, Ashbourne is a pretty patchwork of steeply slanting stone streets lined with cafes, pubs and antique shops.

The main attraction is the chance to walk or cycle along the **Tissington Trail**, part of NCN Route 68, which runs north for 13 miles to Parsley Hay. The track climbs gently along the tunnels, viaducts and cuttings of the disused railway line that once transported local milk to London.

The Drive » It's 17 miles from Ashbourne to Bakewell. Drive north into the rolling countryside (carpeted with daffodils in spring) along Buxton Rd as it winds up through the hills and valleys of the White Peak region.

---

❹ Bakewell

The Peak District's second-largest town (after Buxton), Bakewell is filled with storybook stone buildings. The town is ringed by famous walking trails and stately homes, but it's probably best known for its famous Bakewell Pudding, a pastry shell filled with jam and frangipane invented here in 1820.

Up on the hill above Rutland Sq, **All Saints Church** (www.bakewell church.co.uk; South Church

St; £2 donation requested; ◷9am-5pm Apr-Oct, to 4pm Nov-Mar) is packed with ancient features, including a 14th-century font, a pair of Norman arches, heraldic tombs, and a collection of crude stone gravestones and crosses dating from the 12th century.

Nearby, the **Old House Museum** (www.oldhouse museum.org.uk; Cunningham Pl; adult/child £4/2; ◷11am-4pm) explores local history. Check out the Tudor loo and the displays on wattle and daub, a traditional technique for building walls using woven twigs and cow dung.

Half a mile from the centre on the northwestern edge of town, the riverside **Thornbridge Brewery** (☑01629-815999; www.thornbridgebrewery. com; Buxton Rd; tours adult/child £7.50/3; ◷tours 3pm Wed & Fri, shop 9am-4.30pm Mon-Fri, 10am-2pm last Sun of month) runs tours lasting 1½ hours that take you behind the scenes and include tastings in Thornbridge glasses, which you get to keep afterwards.

✕ ⊨ p225

The Drive ≫ From Bakewell it's just 2 miles southeast along Haddon Rd, following the River Wye, to Haddon Hall.

- - - - - - - - - - - - - - -

❺ Haddon Hall

With stone turrets, time-worn timbers and walled gardens, **Haddon Hall** (www.haddonhall.co.uk; Had-

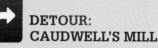

DETOUR: CAUDWELL'S MILL

Start: ❺ Haddon Hall

In the village of Rowsley, the chugging, grinding, water-powered **Caudwell's Mill** (☑01629-734374; www. caudwellsmill.co.uk; Rowsley; mill tours adult/child £4.50/2; ◷mill tours 9.30am-4.30pm, shop 9am-5pm) still produces flour the old-fashioned way (25 different types are for sale, along with eight different oat products as well as yeast and biscuits). There are various craft workshops here and a tearoom.

Rowsley is the terminus for the **Peak Rail** (☑01629-580381; www.peakrail.co.uk; adult/child £8.50/4.50; ◷Mar-Nov, hours vary) steam train, which trundles along a 4-mile length of track to the outskirts of the town of Matlock (not Matlock Bath). Tickets include unlimited travel on the day of purchase. Services run five times a day Saturday and Sunday (and some weekdays) from May to October, and some weekends at other times of the year – check timetables online. From March to November, would-be engineers can also do a one-hour train-driving course (9.45am; £115) or two-hour course (8.45am; £200); you must be aged between 18 and 70.

From Haddon Hall, Caudwell's Mill is 1.5 miles east via the A6 along the river.

don Rd; adult/child £13.50/7; ◷10.30am-5pm daily May-Sep, Sat-Mon Apr & Oct, to 4pm early–mid Dec) looks exactly like a medieval manor house should. Founded in the 12th century, it was expanded and remodelled throughout medieval times. The 'modernisation' stopped when the house was abandoned in the 18th century. Spared from the more florid excesses of the Victorian period, Haddon Hall has been used as the location for numerous period blockbusters (such as *Elizabeth*).

The Drive ≫ From Haddon Hall's car park, take your first right (south) onto the B5056 to Grange Mill, then take the A5012 southeast down along a deep gully to Cromford Mill (10.5 miles in total).

- - - - - - - - - - - - - - -

❻ Cromford Mill

Founded in the 1770s by Richard Arkwright, the **Cromford Mill** (☑01629-823256; www.cromfordmills. org.uk; Mill Lane, Cromford; tour adult/child £3/2.50; ◷9am-5pm, tours 11am, 1pm & 2.30pm Sat-Thu, by reservation 11am Fri) was the first modern factory, producing cotton on automated

Classic Trip

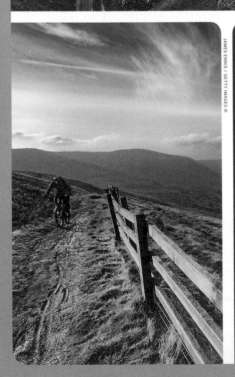

WHY THIS IS A CLASSIC TRIP
CATHERINE LE NEVEZ, WRITER

What makes this trip a true classic is its diversity. England's first national park isn't simply an outdoors playground (though there's plenty to do, including incredible walking, so pack your hiking boots!). History lessons here span grand manors to Industrial Revolution–era mills and the site of the Dambusters testing ground. And when you've finished exploring for the day, you can unwind in cosy open-fire-warmed country pubs.

Above: View from Winnats Pass
Left: Mountain biking on Mam Tor
Right: Explore the many caves near Buxton, Castleton and Matlock Bath

MAT ROBINSON / 500PX ©

JAMES ENNIS / GETTY IMAGES ©

machines, powered by a series of waterwheels along the River Derwent. This prototype inspired a succession of mills, ushering in the industrial age. The Arkwright Society runs fascinating tours.

The Drive » It's a half-mile drive north along the River Derwent to Matlock Bath (not to be confused with the larger, workaday town of Matlock 2 miles to Matlock Bath's north).

TRIP HIGHLIGHT

❼ Matlock Bath

Unashamedly tacky, Matlock Bath looks like a seaside resort that somehow lost its way and ended up at the foot of the Peak District. Following the River Derwent through a sheer-walled gorge, the main promenade is lined with amusement arcades, tearooms, fish-and-chip shops and pubs. Family-friendly attractions here include **Heights of Abraham** (📞01629-582365; www.heightsofabraham.com; Dale Rd; adult/child £15/10.50; 🕙10am-4.30pm daily mid-Mar–Oct, Sat & Sun mid-Feb–mid-Mar, closed Nov–mid-Feb). A spectacular cable-car ride (accessible with admission ticket only) from the bottom of the gorge brings you to this hilltop leisure park, which has cave and mine tours and fossil exhibitions. Old-fashioned amusement park **Gulliver's Kingdom** (📞01925-444888; www.gulliversfun.co.uk; Temple Walk;

£18; ⊙Mar-Oct, hours vary) offers plenty of splashing, churning, looping attractions.

The enthusiast-run **Peak District Lead Mining Museum** (☎01629-583834; www.peakdistrictlead miningmuseum.co.uk; The Grand Pavilion, South Pde; museum adult/child £4/3, mine £4.50/3.50, combined ticket £7/5; ⊙10am-5pm Apr-Oct, 11am-3pm Wed-Fri, to 4pm Sat & Sun Nov-Mar) provides an educational introduction to Matlock Bath's mining history. Kids can wriggle through its maze of tunnels and shafts while adults browse historical displays. At noon and 2pm daily from April to October (at weekends only from November to March) you can go into the workings

of the Temple Mine and pan for 'gold' (well, shiny minerals).

✗ 🛏 p225

The Drive » Continue north through the valley along the River Derwent and follow the road northeast up into the hills to Chatsworth House, a 9.5-mile journey.

- - - - - - - - - -

`TRIP HIGHLIGHT`

❽ Chatsworth House

Known as the 'Palace of the Peak', vast **Chatsworth House** (☎01246-565300; www.chatsworth.org; house & gardens adult/child £20/12, gardens only £12/7, playground £6, park admission free; ⊙10.30am-5pm late May–early Sep, shorter hours mid-Mar–late May & early Sep–early Jan) has been occupied by the earls and dukes of Devonshire for centuries. Inside, the lavish apartments and mural-painted state-rooms are packed with priceless paintings and

period furniture. The house sits in 25 sq miles of grounds and ornamental gardens, some landscaped by Lancelot 'Capability' Brown. Kids will love the farmyard adventure playground.

The manor was founded in 1552 by the formidable Bess of Hardwick and her second husband, William Cavendish, who earned grace and favour by helping Henry VIII dissolve the English monasteries. Mary, Queen of Scots was imprisoned at Chatsworth on the orders of Elizabeth I in 1569.

Look out for the portraits of the current generation of Devonshires by Lucian Freud.

Also on the estate is an exceptional **farm shop** (www.chatsworth.org; Pilsley; dishes £4.50-10; ⊙cafe & shop 9am-5pm Mon-Sat, 10am-5pm Sun; ⓟ) – one of the best in the UK – and an attached cafe, as well as a handful of other eateries and shops.

The Drive » From Chatsworth House it's 11 miles to Chesterfield. Head north along Bakewell Rd to Baslow, then east along the A619 and descend through the forested valley.

- - - - - - - - - -

❾ Chesterfield

Busy Chesterfield is worth a stop to see the astonishing crooked spire rising atop **St Mary & All Saints Church** (☎01246-206506; www.chesterfield parishchurch.org.uk; Church Walk; spire tours adult/child

---

✓ **TOP TIP: CYCLING IN THE PEAK DISTRIC**

Plunging dales and soaring scarps provide a perfect testing ground for cyclists.

Peak Tours (☎01457-851462; www.peak-tours.com; mountain-bike rental per day £20) Delivers rental bikes anywhere in the Peak District, and offers guided cycling tours.

Peak District National Park Authority (☎01629-816200; www.peakdistrict.gov.uk; bicycle hire per half-day/day adult £14/17, child £10/12) Operates several cycle-hire centres renting road, mountain, tandem and electric bikes as well as kids' bikes.

£5/3; ⏱ church 9am-5pm Mon-Sat, 8am-6.30pm Sun, spire tours Mon-Sat). **Dating from 1360, the 68m-high spire is twisted in a right-handed corkscrew and leans several metres southwest. It's the result of the lead casing on the south-facing side having buckled in the sun. Learn more at the engaging Chesterfield Museum & Art Gallery** (☎01246-345727; www.chesterfield.gov.uk/museum; St Mary's Gate; ⏱10am-4pm Mon & Thu-Sat), **which documents Chesterfield's history as a Roman fort through to the present today.**

The Drive ›› Take the B6051 northwest through open farmland to Owler Bar. Head west on the B6054 through the Dark Peak region and along the side of the sheer gritstone escarpment Froggatt Edge to Calver, from where Eyam is 2 miles northwest (a 16-mile journey in total).

-----

⑩ Eyam

Quaint little Eyam (ee-em), a former lead-mining village of sloping streets and old cottages backed by rows of green hills, has a poignant history. In 1665 the town was infected by the dreaded Black Death plague, carried here by fleas on a consignment of cloth from London, and the village rector, William Mompesson, convinced villagers to quarantine themselves. Some 270 of the village's 800 inhabitants suc-

Chatsworth House The 'Palace of the Peak'

cumbed, while surrounding villages remained relatively unscathed. Vivid displays on the Eyam plague are the centrepiece of the engaging **Eyam Museum** (www.eyam.museum.org.uk; Hawkhill Rd; adult/child £2.50/2; ⏱10am-4.30pm Tue-Sun Easter-Oct), alongside exhibits on the village's history of lead-mining and silk-weaving. Many victims of the village's 1665 Black Death plague outbreak were buried at **Eyam Parish Church** (www.eyam-church.org; Church St; ⏱9am-6pm Easter-Sep, to 4pm Oct-Easter). Stained-glass panels and moving displays tell the story of the outbreak.

Scenic walking trails surround the village. An interesting short walk leads to **Mompesson's Well**, where supplies were left during the Black Death plague time by friends from other villag-

es (paid for using coins sterilised in vinegar).

🍴 🛏 p225

The Drive ›› Drive west along Main Rd and turn north on the B6049, passing through the small villages of Bradwell and Thornhill, to Snake Rd. Cross the two bridges spanning Ladybower Reservoir and head northwest along the western bank to Derwent Reservoir (14.5 miles in total).

-----

⑪ Derwent Reservoirs

The upper reaches of the Derwent Valley were flooded between 1916 and 1935 to create three huge reservoirs – the Ladybower, Derwent and Howden Reservoirs – to supply Sheffield, Leicester, Nottingham and Derby with water. These constructed lakes soon proved their worth – the Dambusters squadron carried out practice runs

Classic Trip

over Derwent Reservoir before unleashing their 'bouncing bombs' on the Ruhr Valley in Germany in WWII. Their exploits are detailed in the **Derwent Dam Museum** (www.dambusters.org.uk; Fairholmes; ◷10am-4pm Sun) in the western tower atop the dam.

These days, the reservoirs are popular destinations for walkers, cyclists and mountain bikers – and lots of ducks, so drive slowly!

The Drive » Return to Thornhill and take Hope Rd west to the village of Hope, then turn north on Edale Rd through a wide valley dominated by Dark Peak slopes until you reach Edale (14 miles altogether).

⑫ Edale

Surrounded by majestic Peak District countryside, this cluster of stone houses is an enchanting place to pass the time. Walking is the number one drawcard, with plenty of diverting strolls for less-committed hill walkers.

As well as trips to Hollins Cross and Mam Tor, on the ridge dividing Edale from Castleton, you can walk north onto the Kinder Plateau, dark and brooding in the mist, gloriously high and open when the sun's out. This was the setting for a famous act of civil disobedience by ramblers in 1932 that paved the way for the legal 'right to roam' and the creation of England's national parks.

A fine circular walk starts by following the Pennine Way through fields to Upper Booth, then up a path called Jacobs Ladder and along the southern edge of Kinder, before dropping down to Edale via the steep rocky valley of Grindsbrook Clough, or the ridge of Ringing Roger.

🛏 p225

LOCAL KNOWLEDGE: THE PEAK DISTRICT – WHAT'S IN A NAME?

No one knows how the Peak District got its name – certainly not from the landscape, which has hills and valleys, gorges and lakes, wild moorland and gritstone escarpments, but no peaks. The most popular theory is that the region was named for the Pecsaetan, the Anglo-Saxon tribe who once populated this part of England.

The Drive » Leave Edale to the southwest and climb the steep hill of Mam Tor, before descending precipitous Winnats Pass to Castleton (4.7 miles in total).

TRIP HIGHLIGHT

⑬ Castleton

Castleton's village streets are lined with leaning stone houses, with walking trails criss-crossing the surrounding hills. Topping the ridge to the south, a 350m walk from the town centre, evocative **Peveril Castle** (EH; www.english-heritage.org.uk; adult/child £5.10/3; ◷10am-6pm Easter-Sep, to 5pm Oct, to 4pm Sat & Sun Nov-Easter) has been so ravaged by the centuries that it almost looks like a crag itself. Constructed by William Peveril, son of William the Conqueror, the castle was used as a hunting lodge by Henry II, King John and Henry III, and the crumbling ruins offer swooping views over the Hope Valley.

The bedrock below is riddled with fascinating caves. The most convenient, **Peak Cavern** (☎01433-620285; www.peakcavern.co.uk; Peak Cavern Rd; adult/child £10.25/8.25, incl Speedwell Cavern £17/13.50; ◷10am-5pm daily Apr-Oct, Sat & Sun Nov-Mar), is easily reached by a pretty streamside 250m walk south of the village centre. Dramatic limestone

Kinder Scout Birthplace of the national park

formations are lit with fibre-optic cables.

Just over half a mile west of Castleton, claustrophobe's nightmare **Speedwell Cavern** (☎01433-620512; www. speedwellcavern.co.uk; Winnats Pass; adult/child £11/9, incl Peak Cavern £17/13.50; ☺10am-5pm daily Apr-Oct, Sat & Sun Nov-Mar) is reached via an eerie boat ride through flooded tunnels, emerging by a huge subterranean lake. New chambers are constantly discovered here by potholing expeditions.

Captivating **Treak Cliff Cavern** (☎01433-620571; www.bluejohnstone. com; adult/child £9.50/5.20; ☺10am-4.15pm Mar-Oct, to 3.15pm Nov-Feb), just under a mile west of Castleton's village centre, has a forest of stalactites and exposed seams of colourful Blue John Stone, which is

still mined to supply the jewellery trade.

Up the southeastern side of Mam Tor, 2 miles west of Castleton, **Blue John Cavern** (☎01433-620638; www.bluejohn-cavern. co.uk; adult/child £11/6; ☺9.30am-5.30pm Apr-Oct, to dusk Nov-Mar) is a maze of natural caverns with rich seams of Blue John Stone that are mined every winter. You can get here on foot up the closed section of the Mam Tor road.

The Drive » Retrace your route up spectacular Winnats Pass and head southwest to Sparrowpit. Turn southeast onto the A623 and follow it to Tideswell (a total of 9.5 miles).

- - - - - - - - - - - -

⑭ Tideswell

Dominating the former lead-mining village of Tideswell, the massive parish church of St John the Baptist – aka

the **Cathedral of the Peak** (☎01298-871317; www.tideswellchurch.org; Commercial Rd, Tideswell; ☺9am-6pm) – has stood here virtually unchanged since the 14th century. Look out for the wooden panels inscribed with the Ten Commandments and grand 14th-century tomb of local landowner Thurston de Bower, depicted in full medieval armour.

The Drive » Take the B6049 south to join the forested A6 (you'll see clouds of snowdrops and bluebells in early spring), which shadows the River Wye to Poole's Cavern (8 miles all up).

- - - - - - - - - - - -

⑮ Poole's Cavern

The magnificent natural limestone **Poole's Cavern** (☎01298-26978; www. poolescavern.co.uk; adult/child £9.75/5.25; ☺9.30am-5pm Mar-Oct, 10am-4pm Sat & Sun Nov-Feb) is reached by

descending 28 steps; the temperature is a cool 7°C. Tours lasting 50 minutes run every 20 minutes from March to October and at 10.30am, 12.30pm and 2.30pm from November to February.

From the cavern's car park, a 20-minute walk leads up through Grin Low Wood to Solomon's Temple, a ruined tower with fine views over the town.

The Drive ≫ The last stretch is also the shortest: from Poole's Cavern it's just 1 mile northeast along the A515 to Buxton.

⑯ Buxton

The 'capital' of the Peak District National Park, albeit just outside the park boundary in the rolling hills of the Derbyshire dales, Buxton is a confection of Georgian terraces, Victorian amusements and parks. The town built its fortunes on its natural warm-water springs, which attracted health tourists in Buxton's turn-of-the-century heyday. Today, the **Devonshire Dome** (Devonshire Rd) is home to **Devonshire Spa** (☏01298-330334; www. devonshiredome.co.uk; 1 Devonshire Rd; 2hr body spa £20, ocean or frangipani wrap £50, day package from £95;

⊙9am-6pm Tue, Wed, Sat & Sun, to 9pm Thu & Fri), which offers a full range of pampering treatments.

Buxton's historic centre overflows with Victorian pavilions, concert halls and glasshouse domes. Its most famous building is the turreted **Opera House** (☏0845 127 2190; www.buxtonoperahouse. org.uk; Water St; tours £2.50; ⊙tours usually 11am Sat). Adjoining it is the equally flamboyant **Pavilion Gardens** (www.pavilion gardens.co.uk; ⊙9.30am-5pm). These 23 acres are dotted with domed pavilions; concerts take place in the bandstand throughout the year.

From the Pavilion Gardens, vintage milk float the **Buxton Tram** (☏01298-79648; adult/child £6/4; ⊙hourly 10am-5pm Easter-Oct, 11am-4pm Nov-Easter) takes you on a 12mph, hour-or-so circuit of the centre on its entertaining Wonder of the Peak tour.

In a handsome Victorian building, the **Buxton Museum & Art Gallery** (www.derbyshire.gov. uk/leisure/buxton_museum; Terrace Rd; ⊙9.30am-5.30pm Tue-Fri, to 5pm Sat year-round, plus 10.30am-5pm Sun Easter-Sep) displays local historical bric-a-brac and curiosities.

🛏 p225

🛏 p225

CAVING & CLIMBING

The limestone sections of the Peak District are riddled with caves and caverns, including the series of 'showcaves' in Castleton, Buxton and Matlock Bath. For serious caving (or potholing) trips, your first port of call should be the website www. peakdistrictcaving.info, run by the caving store **Hitch n Hike** (☏01433-651013; www.hitchnhike.co.uk; Hope Rd, Bamford; ⊙9am-5.30pm), near Castleton, which has gear and advice for climbing.

England's top mountaineers train in this area, which offers rigorous technical climbing on a series of limestone gorges, exposed tors (crags) and gritstone 'edges' that extend south into the Staffordshire Moorlands. Gritstone climbing in the Peak District is predominantly on old-school trad routes, requiring a decent rack of friends, nuts and hexes. Bolted sport routes are found on several limestone crags in the Peak District, but many use ancient pieces of gear and most require additional protection. Tourist offices throughout the Peak District can supply information.

Eating & Sleeping

Derby ❶

🛏 Farmhouse at Mackworth   Inn ££

(📞01332-824324; www.thefarmhouseat
mackworth.com; 60 Ashbourne Rd; d/f incl
breakfast from £70/90; 🅿 🛜) Overhauled
by pub conglomerate Marston's, designer inn
the Farmhouse at Mackworth is just 2.5 miles
northwest of Derby in undulating countryside,
with the bonus of plentiful free parking. Its
10 boutique rooms have checked fabrics,
rustic timber cladding and chrome fittings,
plus amenities including Nespresso machines
and fluffy robes. There's a fabulous bar and
restaurant with a Josper charcoal oven.

Bakewell ❹

🍴 Old Original Bakewell
Pudding Shop   Bakery, Tearoom £

(www.bakewellpuddingshop.co.uk; The Square;
dishes £7-12; 🕙8.30am-6pm Mon-Sat, 9am-
6pm Sun) One of those who claims to have
invented the Bakewell Pudding, this place has
a lovely 1st-floor tearoom with exposed beams
that serves light meals and afternoon teas on
tiered trays.

🛏 Rutland Arms Hotel   Hotel £££

(📞01629-812812; www.rutlandarmsbakewell.
co.uk; The Square; s £64-76, d £92-165; 🅿 🛜🐾)
Jane Austen is said to have stayed in room
2 of this aristocratic, recently refurbished
stone coaching inn while working on *Pride and
Prejudice*. The more expensive of its 33 rooms
have lots of Victorian flourishes.

Matlock Bath ❼

🛏 Hodgkinson's
Hotel & Restaurant   Hotel ££

(📞01629-582170; www.hodgkinsons-hotel.
co.uk; 150 South Pde; d/f incl breakfast from
£95/145; 🅿 🛜) The eight rooms at this central
Grade II–listed Victorian beauty conjure up
Matlock's golden age with antique furnishings,
flowery wallpaper and cast-iron fireplaces.
Arrive early to nab one of its five parking spaces.
The restaurant (two-/three-course menus
£26/29) has just 18 seats so bookings are
advised. Service is superb.

Eyam ❿

🛏 Miner's Arms   Pub ££

(📞01433-630853; www.theminersarmseyam.
co.uk; Water Lane; s/d £45/70; 🛜) Although its
age isn't immediately obvious, this traditional
village inn was built shortly before the Black
Death hit Eyam in 1665. Inside you'll find
beamed ceilings, affable staff, a blazing open
fireplace, comfy en suite rooms and good-value
pub food (mains £8 to £12.50).

Edale ⓬

🛏 Stonecroft   B&B ££

(📞01433-670262; www.stonecroftguesthouse.
co.uk; Grindsbrook; s/d from £55/99; 🅿 🛜)
This handsomely fitted-out stone house, built
in the 1900s, has two comfortable bedrooms.
Vegetarians and vegans are well catered for –
host Julia is an award-winning chef and the
organic breakfast (with gluten-free options) is
excellent. Packed lunches (£7.50) are available
by request when booking. Bike rental costs £30
per day. Free pick-up from the train station can
be arranged.

Buxton ⓰

🛏 Old Hall Hotel   Historic Hotel ££

(📞01298-22841; www.oldhallhotelbuxton.
co.uk; The Square; s/d incl breakfast from
£69/79; 🛜🐾) There's a tale to go with every
creak of the floorboards at this history-soaked
establishment, supposedly the oldest hotel in
England. Among other esteemed residents,
Mary, Queen of Scots, stayed here from 1576 to
1578, albeit against her will. The rooms are still
the grandest in town, and there are several bars,
lounges and dining options.

Battlefields, Castles & Stately Homes

18

English history unfolds in all its pomp and ceremony along this journey through the country's heart where royal battles were fought, castles were besieged and the aristocracy built palatial manors.

TRIP HIGHLIGHTS

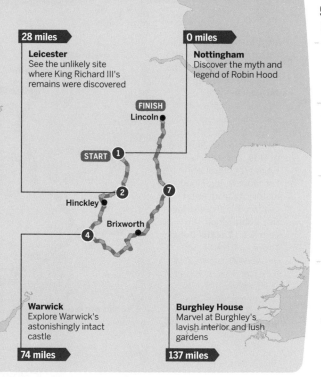

28 miles

Leicester
See the unlikely site where King Richard III's remains were discovered

0 miles

Nottingham
Discover the myth and legend of Robin Hood

FINISH
Lincoln

START ①

② ⑦

Hinckley

Brixworth

④

Warwick
Explore Warwick's astonishingly intact castle

74 miles

Burghley House
Marvel at Burghley's lavish interior and lush gardens

137 miles

---

5 DAYS
214 MILES / 344KM

GREAT FOR...

BEST TIME TO GO
June to September sees the best weather and fewest closures.

ESSENTIAL PHOTO

Newton's apple tree that inspired his theory of gravity.

BEST FOR FAMILIES

Relive medieval times at Warwick Castle.

Bosworth Battlefield Re-enactment of the Battle of Bosworth

18 Battlefields, Castles & Stately Homes

This grand tour begins and ends with a famed castle, and stops at a third mighty fortress en route. In between, you'll see the field where Richard III became the last English king to die in battle, learn the extraordinary story of the recent discovery of his long-lost remains in a city car park, and wander the opulent corridors of stately homes and their magnificently landscaped gardens and deer-roamed grounds.

TRIP HIGHLIGHT

❶ Nottingham

Nottingham is synonymous with mythologised outlaw Robin Hood. A bronze **statue** (Castle Rd) of the woodsman stands in the former moat of **Nottingham Castle** (📞0115-876 1400; www.nottinghamcastle.org.uk; Lenton Rd; adult/child £6/5, cave tours £5/free; ⏰10am-5pm daily mid-Feb–Oct, to 4pm Wed-Sun Nov–mid-Feb, cave tours hourly noon-3pm). Founded by William the Conqueror, the original castle was held by a succession of English kings before falling in the English Civil War. Its 17th-century manor-house-like replacement contains a local-history museum and art gallery. Carved into the cliff beneath the castle, **Ye Olde Trip to Jerusalem** (📞0115-947 3171; www.triptojerusalem.com; Brewhouse Yard, Castle Rd; ⏰11am-11pm Sun-Thu, to midnight Fri & Sat), founded in 1189, claims to be England's oldest pub. For more Robin Hood history, take an entertaining, highly informative Robin Hood Town Tour with **Ezekial Bone Tours** (📞07941 210986; www.ezekialbone.com; Robin Hood Town Tours adult/child £12/7; ⏰Robin Hood Town Tours by reservation 2pm Sat Mar-Oct). Tours of nearby Sherwood Forest can also be arranged.

The city's bedrock is riddled with caves, which you can delve into on **City of Caves** (☎0115-988 1955; www.cityofcaves.com; Drury Walk, Upper Level, Broadmarsh Shopping Centre; adult/child £7.95/5.95, incl Galleries of Justice £15/11.75; ⏰10.30am-4pm) tours. Audiotours (Monday to Friday) and performance tours (weekends and school holidays) lead you through a WWII air-raid shelter, a medieval underground tannery, several pub cellars and a mock-up of a Victorian slum dwelling. Book ahead for both.

✕ 🛏 p235

The Drive » It's an easy 28 miles' drive south to Leicester. The A46, which travels through a dark-green patchwork of dairy and crop fields, makes a more scenic alternative to the speedier but busier M1.

LINK YOUR TRIP

15 **Shakespeare & Rolling Hills**

From Warwick, it's 9 miles southwest to Stratford-upon-Avon for a spin through quintessentially English rolling countryside.

17 **Peak District**

It's a 15-mile hop west from Nottingham to Derby, from where you can strike out into the glorious Peak District National Park.

❷ Leicester

Built over the buried ruins of two millennia of history, Leicester (*les*-ter) suffered at the hands of the Luftwaffe and postwar planners, but a massive influx of textile workers from India and Pakistan since the 1960s has transformed the city into a bustling global melting pot.

The astonishing 2012 discovery and 2013 identification of the remains of King Richard III in a Leicester car park sparked a flurry of developments, including a spiffing visitor centre on the site, **King Richard III: Dynasty, Death & Discovery** (www.kriii.com;

4a St Martin's Pl; adult/child £7.95/4.75; ☺10am-4pm Sun-Fri, to 5pm Sat), which details the University of Leicester's archaeological dig and identification, and lets you view the site of the grave in which he was found. The discovery also led to the restoration of the **Leicester Cathedral** (www.leicestercathedral. org; Peacock Lane; ☺10am-5pm Mon-Sat, 12.30-2.30pm Sun), where the king was reburied in 2015; you can visit his grave, which is topped by a contemporary limestone tomb.

🍴 🛏 p235

The Drive 》 Travel through open farmland for 14 miles west, via the A47, to Sutton Cheney, where you'll see the turn-off to the site of the Battle of Bosworth.

↱ **DETOUR: CHARLECOTE PARK**

Start: ❹ Warwick

From Warwick, you can take a short 6.5-mile side trip southwest, via Stratford Rd and the southbound A429, to **Charlecote Park** (NT; ☎01789-470277; www. nationaltrust.org.uk; Loxley Lane, Charlecote; house & garden adult/child £10.45/5.75, garden only £7.05/3.50; ☺house 11am-4.30pm Thu-Tue mid-Mar–Oct, noon-3.30pm Thu-Tue mid-Feb–mid-Mar, noon-3.30pm Sat & Sun Nov & Dec, garden 10.30am-5.30pm Mar-Oct, to 4.30pm Nov-Feb). A youthful Shakespeare allegedly poached deer in the grounds of this lavish Elizabethan pile on the River Avon, and fallow deer still roam the grounds today. The interiors were restored from Georgian chintz to Tudor splendour in 1823. Highlights include Victorian kitchens, filled with culinary-moulds, and an original 1551 Tudor gatehouse.

---

❸ Bosworth Battlefield

Given a few hundred years, every battlefield ends up simply a field, but the site of the Battle of Bosworth – where Richard III met his maker in 1485 – is enlivened by the entertaining **Bosworth Battlefield Heritage Centre** (☎01455-290429; www.bosworthbattlefield. org.uk; Ambion Lane, Sutton Cheney; adult/child £7.95/4.75; ☺heritage centre 10am-5pm, last admission 4pm, grounds 7am-dusk), full of skeletons and musket balls. Although it lasted just a few hours, the Battle of Bosworth marked the end of the Plantagenet dynasty and the start of the Tudor era. This was where the mortally wounded Richard III famously proclaimed: 'A horse, a horse, my kingdom for a horse.' (Actually, he didn't: the quote was invented by that great Tudor propagandist William Shakespeare.) Enthusiasts in period costume re-enact the battle each August.

The Drive 》 It's 32 miles southwest from Bosworth, via the M69 (skirting the southeastern edge of Coventry) and the A46, to Warwick.

---

❹ Warwick

Regularly name-checked by Shakespeare, Warwick was the ancestral seat of the Earls of Warwick,

Warwick Warwick Castle

who played a pivotal role in the Wars of the Roses. Despite a devastating fire in 1694, Warwick remains a treasure house of medieval architecture with rich veins of history and charming streets, dominated by the soaring turrets of Warwick Castle (p235). Founded in 1068 by William the Conqueror, the ancestral home of the Earls of Warwick remains impressively intact, and the Tussauds Group has filled the interior with flamboyant, family-friendly attractions that bring the castle's rich history to life. Waxworks populate the private apartments; there are also jousting tournaments, daily trebuchet-firings, themed evenings and a dungeon. Discounted online tickets provide fast-track entry. You can even stay here – atmospheric accommodation options range from tower suites to lodges at its riverside Knight's Village and themed tents in its 'glamping' ground.

✖ ⊨ p235

231

The Drive » Take Gallows Hill Rd southeast out of Warwick and continue southeast through farmland of potato and cabbage crops along with golden fields of flowering canola. It's 27 miles in total to Sulgrave Manor.

---

⑤ Sulgrave Manor

The impressively pre-served Tudor mansion **Sulgrave Manor** (☎01295-760205; www.sulgravemanor. org.uk; Manor Rd, Sulgrave; adult/child £7.90/3.60, garden only £3.60/free; ☺10am-5pm Sat-Thu Aug, Sat & Sun late Mar–Jul, Sep & Oct) was built by Lawrence Washington in 1539. The Washington family

lived here for almost 120 years before Colonel John Washington, the great-grandfather of America's first president George Washington, sailed to Virginia in 1656.

The Drive » From Sulgrave Manor it's a 21-mile drive northeast via Northampton Rd and the A5 to another famous family home, Althorp House.

---

⑥ Althorp House

The ancestral home of the Spencer family, **Althorp House** (☎01604-770107; www.spencerofalthorp. com; adult/child £18.50/11; ☺11am-3pm early Jul–early Sep, hours vary May–early Jul

& early–late Sep, closed late Sep–Apr) – pronounced 'altrup' – is the final resting place of Diana, Princess of Wales, com-memorated by a memo-rial. The outstanding art collection features works by Rubens, Gainsborough and Van Dyck. Hours are seasonal and tickets are limited; pre-book by phone or online.

The Drive » Leaving Althorp House, head northeast, passing through the charming ivy-clad stone villages of Church Brampton and Chapel Brampton. You'll skirt the larger towns of Kettering and Corby, as well as the southern edge of Stamford, before reaching Burghley House (42 miles all up).

Charlecote Park A stately historic property

TRIP HIGHLIGHT

❼ Burghley House

Set in more than 810 hectares of grounds, landscaped by Lancelot 'Capability' Brown, resplendent **Burghley House** (www.burghley.co.uk; house & garden adult/child £14/7, garden only £8.50/5.50; ⏰ house 11am-5pm Sat-Thu mid-Mar–Oct, park & garden 8am-6pm Jun-Sep, to 5pm mid-Mar–May & Oct) – pronounced 'bur-lee' – was built by Queen Elizabeth's chief adviser William Cecil, whose descendants still live here. It bristles with cupolas, pavilions, belvederes and chimneys; the lavish staterooms are a particular highlight. In early September, the renowned Burghley Horse Trials take place here.

The estate is 1.3 miles southeast of Stamford, one of England's prettiest towns, with elegant streets lined with honey-coloured limestone buildings and hidden alleyways dotted with alehouses, interesting eateries and small independent boutiques. A forest of historic church spires rises overhead and the gently gurgling River Welland meanders through the town centre. It's a favourite with filmmakers seeking the postcard vision of England, and appears in everything from *Pride and Prejudice* to *The Da Vinci Code*.

The Drive » It's a 17-mile trip from Burghley House via the A1 to Woolsthorpe Manor.

❽ Woolsthorpe Manor

Sir Isaac Newton fans may feel the gravitational pull of the great man's birthplace, **Woolsthorpe Manor** (NT; www.nationaltrust.org.uk; Water Lane;

house & grounds adult/child £6.45/3.27, grounds only £3.50/2.27; ⏰11am-5pm Wed-Mon Mar-Oct, Fri-Sun Nov-Feb). The humble 17th-century house contains reconstructions of Newton's rooms; the apple that inspired his theory of gravity allegedly fell from the tree in the garden. There's a nifty kids' science room and a cafe.

The Drive » The final 33-mile stretch of this trip, via the High Dike road, takes you past cauliflower, corn and wheat fields. At Waddington, look out to your right to see fighter jets landing at its famous RAF air base. As you approach Lincoln, you'll see its cathedral spires and castle crenulations rising up on the ridge line to the north.

- - - - - - - - - - - -

❾ Lincoln

Ringed by historic city gates – including the **Newport Arch** on Bailgate, a relic from the original Roman settlement – Lincoln's historic centre is a tangle of cobbled medieval streets surrounding a colossal 12th-century

cathedral (📞01522-561600; www.lincolncathedral.com; Minster Yard; adult/child joint ticket with castle £16/10, cathedral £8/4.80 Mon-Sat, by donation Sun; ⏰7.15am-8pm Mon-Fri, to 6pm Sat & Sun Jul & Aug, 7.15am-6pm Mon-Sat, to 5pm Sun Sep-Jun, evensong 5.30pm Mon-Sat, 3.45pm Sun). Towering over the city like a medieval skyscraper, it's a breathtaking representation of divine power on earth. The great tower rising above the crossing is the third-highest in England at 83m, but in medieval times, a lead-encased wooden spire added a further 79m, topping even the great pyramids of Giza. One-hour guided tours (included in admission) take place at least twice daily; there are also tours of the roof and tower (£4, book ahead).

Nearby **Lincoln Castle** (📞01522-554559; www.lincoln castle.com; Castle Hill; adult/child joint ticket with cathedral £16/10, castle, Magna Carta exhibition & walls £12/7.20, walls only £5/3; ⏰10am-5pm Apr-Sep, to 4pm Oct-Mar) was one of the first castles erected by the victorious William the Conqueror to keep his new kingdom in line, and offers awesome views over the city and miles of surrounding countryside. A major restoration program has opened up the entire castle walls and given the 1215 Magna Carta (one of only four copies) a swanky, subterranean new home. One-hour guided tours, included in castle admission, depart from the eastern gate – check the blackboard for times.

The lanes that topple over the edge of Lincoln Cliff are lined with Tudor town houses, ancient pubs and quirky independent stores. Flanking the River Witham at the base of the hill, the new town is less absorbing but the revitalised Brayford Waterfront development is a popular spot to watch the boats go by.

🛏 p235

Eating & Sleeping

Nottingham ❶

✕ Delilah Fine Foods — Deli, Cafe £

(www.delilahfinefoods.co.uk; 12 Victoria St; dishes £4-16, platters £15-35; ⏰8am-7pm Mon-Fri, 9am-7pm Sat, 11am-5pm Sun; ✏) Impeccably selected cheeses (more than 150 varieties), pâtés, meats and more from artisan producers are available to take away or eat on-site at this gourmand's dream, housed in a grand former bank with mezzanine seating.

🛏 Lace Market Hotel — Boutique Hotel ££

(✆0115-948 4414; www.lacemarkethotel. co.uk; 29-31 High Pavement; s/d incl breakfast from £85/135; P ❄ 🛜) In the heart of the trendy Lace Market, this elegant Georgian town house's sleek rooms have state-of-the-art furnishings and amenities; some come with air-conditioning. Its fine-dining restaurant, **Merchants** (mains £19-30, 2-/3-course lunch menus £14.50/18.50, 3-course dinner menu £45; ⏰7-10am, noon-2pm & 5-10pm Mon-Sat, 7-10.30am & noon-2pm Sun), and adjoining genteel pub, the **Cock & Hoop** (25 High Pavement; ⏰11am-11pm Mon-Thu, to midnight Fri, to 1am Sat, to 10.30pm Sun), are both superb.

Leicester ❷

✕ Boot Room — Bistro ££

(✆0116-262 2555; www.thebootroomeaterie. co.uk; 29 Millstone Lane; mains £13-19.50; ⏰noon-2pm & 5.30-9.30pm Tue-Fri, noon-2.30pm & 5.30-10pm Sat; 🛜) A former shoe factory now houses this contemporary independent bistro. Premium ingredients are used in dishes from roast Cornish cod with smoked tomato risotto to duck leg with Clonakilty black pudding. Save room for the soufflé of the day for dessert.

🛏 Hotel Maiyango — Boutique Hotel ££

(✆0116-251 8898; www.maiyango.com; 13-21 St Nicholas Pl; d from £79; ❄ 🛜) At the end of the pedestrian High St, this sophisticated pad has 14 spacious rooms, decorated with handmade Asian furniture, contemporary art and massive plasma TVs. In addition to its candlelit **Maiyango Restaurant & Bar**, serving the city's best cocktails, it also has a fabulous **Kitchen Deli** gourmet cafe and store.

Warwick ❹

✕ Merchants — Brasserie ££

(✆01926-403833; www.merchantswarwick. co.uk; Swan St; mains £10.50-22; ⏰noon-9pm Mon-Thu, to 9.30pm Fri & Sat) Behind a black-fronted facade, this restaurant and wine bar has stylish leather furniture and chalkboard menus. Steaks and seafood are specialities; meat comes from local farms, fish is from sustainable UK fisheries where possible and all eggs are free-range.

🛏 Warwick Castle Accommodation — Resort £££

(✆01926-406660; www.warwick-castle.com; Warwick Castle; tower ste/lodge/glamping tent per night from £550/203/149; P 🛜) Accommodation offerings at Warwick Castle cater for all budgets, and include two days' castle admission. The castle itself now contains two four-poster-bed tower suites (including a private tour, champagne and breakfast). The riverside Knight's Village has woodland and knight-themed lodges (all with terraces and some with kitchenettes) and medieval entertainment. Themed tents (with shared bathrooms) make up the Glamping ground.

Lincoln ❾

🛏 Bail House — B&B ££

(✆01522-541000; www.bailhouse.co.uk; 34 Bailgate; d/f from £69/179; P @ 🛜 ♿) Stone walls, worn flagstones, secluded gardens and one room with an extraordinary timber-vaulted ceiling are just some of the charms of this lovingly restored Georgian town house in central Lincoln. There's limited on-site parking, a garden and children's playground, and even a seasonal heated outdoor swimming pool. Family rooms sleep four.

STRETCH YOUR LEGS
STRATFORD-UPON-AVON

Start/Finish Gower Memorial

Distance 1.7 miles

Duration Two hours

A willow-lined river and wonky black-and-white Tudor architecture set the stage for retracing the footsteps of the Bard at his birthplace, school room, home and final resting place, as well as the world-renowned theatres where his works come to life.

Take this walk on Trips

Gower Memorial

Designed by aristocratic sculptor Lord Ronald Gower, the multi-sculpture **Gower Memorial** in the beautiful Bancroft Gardens features the characters of Hamlet, Prince Hal, Lady Macbeth and Falstaff, as well as the Bard himself.

The Walk » Follow Bridge St northwest and continue on Henley St (500m in total).

Shakespeare's Birthplace

The jury is still out on whether Shakespeare's Birthplace (p79) is really where the Bard was born but devotees have been scratching their signatures onto the windows since at least the 19th century. Behind a modern facade are restored Tudor rooms, live presentations from famous Shakespearean characters, and an engaging Shakespeare exhibition.

The Walk » Continue northwest along Henley St. Turn southwest onto Windsor St; the American Fountain is just across the intersection on your left (260m all up).

American Fountain

Created by George W Childs in 1887 to mark Queen Victoria's Golden Jubilee, the ornate Victorian Gothic **American Fountain** (Market Sq, Rother St) was unveiled by the great Shakespearean actor Henry Irving. Although the fountain no longer runs, the clocks and bell work and the former horse troughs bloom with flowers.

The Walk » Take Rother St southwest and turn east onto Ely St. At Chapel St, turn southwest; New Place is on your left (450m in total).

Shakespeare's New Place

When Shakespeare retired, he swapped London's bright lights for a comfortable town house at New Place (p79), where he died of unknown causes in April 1616. The house was demolished in 1759, but a major restoration project has uncovered Shakespeare's kitchen and incorporated new exhibits in a reimagining of the original house. His granddaughter, Elizabeth, lived in the adjacent Nash's House.

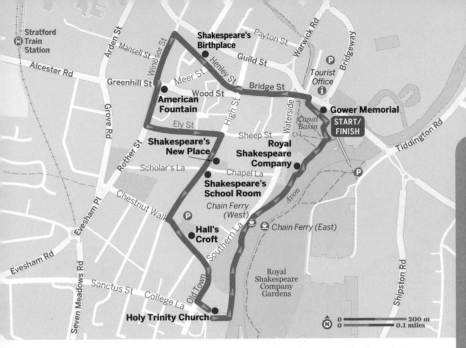

The Walk » It's a 50m stroll southwest along Chapel St, which becomes Church St, to Shakespeare's School Room.

Shakespeare's School Room

Shakespeare's alma mater, King Edward VI School, incorporates a vast black-and-white timbered building, dating from 1420, that was once the town's guildhall. Upstairs in **Shakespeare's School Room** (www.shakespearesschoolroom. org; King Edward VI School, Church St; adult/child £8.90/5.50; ⊘11am-5pm Mon-Fri during school term, 10am-5pm Sat, Sun & school holidays) you can sit in on mock-Tudor lessons and test yourself on Tudor-style homework.

The Walk » Head southwest along Church St, then turn onto Old Town (400m in total).

Hall's Croft

Shakespeare's daughter Susanna and her husband, respected doctor John Hall, lived in the handsome Jacobean town house **Hall's Croft** (☏01789-204016; www. shakespeare.org.uk; Old Town; incl Shakespeare's Birthplace & Shakespeare's New Place adult/

child £17.50/11.50; ⊘10am-5pm mid-Mar–Oct). Exhibits offer fascinating insights into medicine in the 16th and 17th centuries, and herbs employed in medicinal preparations flourish in the aromatic garden.

The Walk » Continue southeast for 220m on Old Town; you'll see Holy Trinity Church on your left.

Holy Trinity Church

The final resting place of the Bard, Holy Trinity Church (p79), is home to handsome 16th- and 17th-century tombs (particularly in the Clopton Chapel) and, of course, Shakespeare's grave.

The Walk » Take the riverside path north to the Royal Shakespeare Theatre (500m all up).

Royal Shakespeare Theatre

One of three stages belonging to the Royal Shakespeare Company (p43), the Royal Shakespeare Theatre has witnessed legendary thespians' performances. Zipping up the lift (elevator) rewards with views over the town and river.

The Walk » It's 200m to the Gower Memorial.

237

Lake District & Northern England

INSPIRATIONAL LANDSCAPES DELIVER INSPIRATIONAL DRIVES. And this swathe of northern England has long been a muse to many. Wordsworth, the Brontës and Beatrix Potter all drew on its natural splendour, and every bend in the road still reveals extraordinary views. In the west, the Lake District National Park gifts you the classic Lakes experience: craggy hilltops, glittering water and mountain tarns. Point the car east to discover the pretty villages and wilderness moors of Yorkshire's Dales. Head still further east to encounter historic York and a coast full of charm. To the north lie thriving Newcastle-upon-Tyne, Northumberland's otherworldly beaches and the Roman remains of Hadrian's Wall.

Scafell Pike Views across Wastwater
JUSTIN FOULKES / LONELY PLANET ©

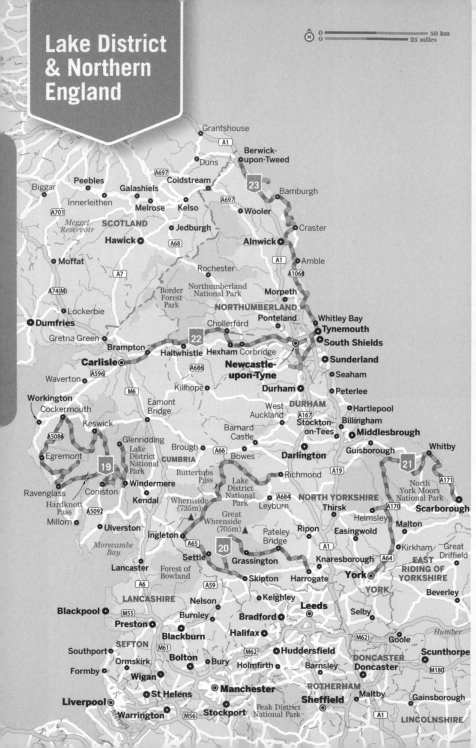

Lake District & Northern England

Langdale Pikes Hiking the multi-peak circuit

 Classic Lakes 5 Days
Literary links a-plenty, England's highest hill and utterly unforgettable views. (p243)

20 **Yorkshire Dales 3–4 Days**
A classy spa town and thrilling climbs up England's most spectacular roads. (p257)

21 **North York Moors & Coast 4–5 Days**
Combines medieval York, wild moorlands, stately Castle Howard and salty fishing ports. (p265)

22 **Hadrian's Wall 3–4 Days**
An evocative, fort-studded route tracing the length of these unique Roman remains. (p273)

23 **Northumbria 3–4 Days**
Fishing ports, castles, a sacred island and breath-taking stretches of sand. (p281)

✓ **DON'T MISS**

Tynemouth
Hanging ten at one of the best surf spots in England – this vast, Blue Flag, golden beach – on Trip 23

North Yorkshire Moors Railway
Hopping on a train at the station immortalised as Hogsmeade in the Harry Potter films on Trip 21

Hardknott Pass & Wrynose Pass
Driving England's two steepest road routes – where gradients reach 30% – on Trip 19

Chesters Roman Fort & Museum
Roaming the superbly preserved living quarters of a cavalry unit, based at Hadrian's Wall on Trip 22

Tan Hill Inn
Sipping a drink (and getting a warm welcome) at Britain's highest pub – at an elevation of 328m on Trip 20

Classic Lakes

19

Beloved of poets and painters, this road trip takes in the scenic wonders of the UK's largest and loveliest national park.

TRIP HIGHLIGHTS

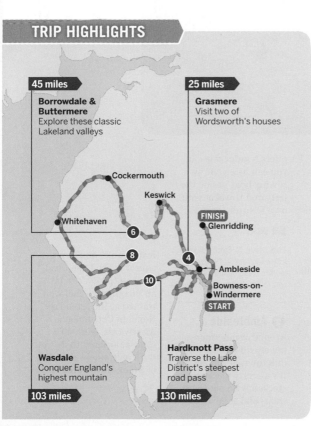

45 miles
Borrowdale & Buttermere
Explore these classic Lakeland valleys

25 miles
Grasmere
Visit two of Wordsworth's houses

Cockermouth
Keswick
Whitehaven
6
FINISH Glenridding
8
4
Ambleside
10
Bowness-on-Windermere
START

Wasdale
Conquer England's highest mountain
103 miles

Hardknott Pass
Traverse the Lake District's steepest road pass
130 miles

5 DAYS
162 MILES / 260KM

GREAT FOR...

BEST TIME TO GO
Summer and Easter can be hectic in the Lakes; spring and autumn are best.

ESSENTIAL PHOTO

Striking a pose in Wasdale, surrounded by England's highest hills.

BEST FOR FAMILIES

Bike trails, sculptures and ziplines at Grizedale Forest.

GRAHAM NORTON/500PX ©

Lake District National Park Blea Tarn

243

19 Classic Lakes

William Wordsworth, Samuel Taylor Coleridge and Beatrix Potter are just a few of the literary luminaries who have fallen in love with the Lake District. It's been a national park since 1951, and is studded by England's highest hills (fells), including the highest of all, Scafell Pike (978m). This drive takes in lakes, forest, hills and valleys, with country houses, hill walks and cosy pubs thrown in for good measure.

1 Bowness-on-Windermere

England's largest lake, at nearly 9 miles long, Windermere makes an obvious starting point for a Lakeland road trip. The town is actually split into two: Windermere, a mile or so uphill from the lake, and waterfront Bowness-on-Windermere. Cruising the lake is the classic pastime here: **Windermere Lake Cruises** (☎015394-43360; www.windermere-lakecruises. co.uk; tickets from £2.70)

offers regular trips, or you can hire your own rowing boat beside the jetty and travel at your own leisurely pace.

🛏 p255

The Drive » From Bowness, follow Rayrigg Rd north until it joins the A591 which rolls all the way to Ambleside, 6 miles north.

2 Ambleside

Around Windermere's upper end lies the old mill town of Ambleside. It's a pretty place, well stocked with outdoors shops and some excellent

restaurants: don't miss a meal at the Lake Road Kitchen (p255), run by an imaginative chef who trained at the legendary Noma in Copenhagen. Afterwards, work off some calories with a walk up to the waterfall of **Stock Ghyll Force**.

🍴 p255

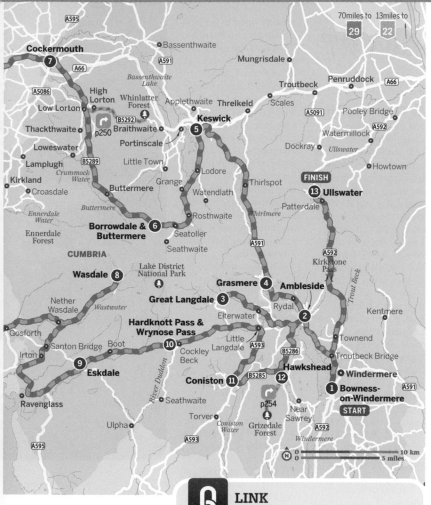

70miles to 29
13miles to 22

The Drive » Take the A593 west towards Skelwith Bridge, and follow signs to Elterwater and Great Langdale. It's a wonderful 8-mile drive that gets wilder and wilder the deeper you head into the valley. There's a large car park beside the Old Dungeon Ghyll Hotel, but it gets busy in summer; there's usually overflow parking available in a nearby field.

LINK YOUR TRIP

22 Hadrian's Wall
From Windermere, head north to Carlisle to explore Roman England's most ambitious structure.

29 The Borders
The Lake District is an obvious launchpad for travels north of the Scottish border; Glasgow is 130 miles from Ullswater.

❸ Great Langdale

The Lake District has some truly stunning valleys, but Great Langdale definitely ranks near the top. As you pass through the pretty village of **Elterwater** and its village green, the scenery gets really wild and empty. Fells stack up like dominoes along the horizon, looming over a patchwork of barns and fields. If you're up for a hike, then tackle the multipeak circuit around the **Langdale Pikes**. Alternatively, the more sedentary option is to just admire the view over a pint of ale from the cosy bar of the **Old Dungeon Ghyll** (☎015394-37272; www.odg. co.uk; Great Langdale; s £58, d £116-132; P 🛜 🐾), a classic hikers' haunt.

The Drive » Retrace the road to Ambleside and head north to Grasmere on the A591 for 5 miles.

TRIP HIGHLIGHT

❹ Grasmere

The lovely little village of Grasmere is inextricably linked with the poet William Wordsworth, who made it his home in the late 18th century and never left unless he really had to. Two of his houses

are now open to the public. The most famous is **Dove Cottage** (☎015394-35544; www.wordsworth.org. uk; adult/child £7.50/4.50; 🕙9.30am-5.30pm), a tiny house where he lived with his sister Dorothy, wife Mary and three children between 1798 and 1807. Guided tours explore the house, and next door the Wordsworth Museum has lots of memorabilia relating to the Romantic poets (including haunting life masks of John Keats and Wordsworth).

A little way south of Grasmere is the house where Wordsworth spent most of his adult life, **Rydal Mount** (☎015394-33002; www.rydalmount. co.uk; adult/child £7.50/3.50, grounds only £4.50; 🕙9.30am-5pm Mar-Oct, 11am-4pm Wed-Mon Nov, Dec & Feb). It's still owned by the poet's descendants, and is a much grander affair than Dove Cottage: you can have a look around the library, visit the poet's attic study and wander around the gardens he designed. Below the house, **Dora's Field** is filled with daffodils in springtime; it was planted in memory of Wordsworth's daughter, who died of tuberculosis.

If you have a sweet tooth, you'll also want to pick up a souvenir at **Sarah Nelson's Gingerbread Shop** (☎015394-35428; www.grasmereginger

bread.co.uk; Church Cottage; 🕙9.15am-5.30pm Mon-Sat, 12.30-5pm Sun), which still makes its gingerbread to a recipe formulated in 1854.

🛏 p255

The Drive » From Grasmere, continue north on the A591. You'll pass through the dramatic pass known as Dunmail Raise, where a great battle is said to have taken place between

Grizedale Forest Woodland stream

the Saxons and the Celtic king Dunmail, who was slain near the pass. Stay on the road past the lake of Thirlmere all the way to Keswick (13 miles).

----

❺ Keswick

Another of the Lake District's classic market towns, Keswick is a place that revolves around the great outdoors. Several big fells lie on its

TOP TIP: NATIONAL TRUST MEMBERSHIP

Being a National Trust (www.nationaltrust.org.uk) member comes in very handy in the Lake District. The Trust owns several key attractions, including Hill Top and the Beatrix Potter Gallery near Hawkshead, Wordsworth House in Cockermouth and Fell Foot and Wray Castle near Windermere. Best of all, you get to park for free at all the NT's car parks – handy in celebrated beauty spots like Buttermere, Borrowdale, Wasdale, Gowbarrow Park and Tarn Hows.

Classic Trip

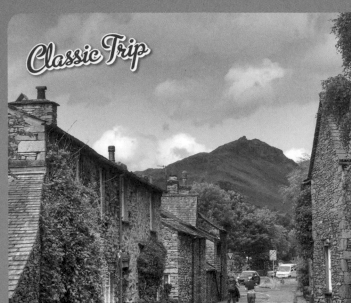

ANDREW ROLAND / SHUTTERSTOCK ©

JUSTIN FOULKES / LONELY PLANET ©

WHY THIS IS A CLASSIC TRIP
OLIVER BERRY, WRITER

For classic English scenery, nowhere quite compares to the Lake District. With its fells and waterfalls, valleys and villages, lakes and meadows, it's like a postcard that's come to life. It's visited by some 13 million people every year, but it's still easy to find peace and serenity – whether it's rowing across a lake, cycling through the countryside or standing atop a fell. Pack spare memory cards – you'll need them.

Above: Historic village Grasmere, home to poet William Wordsworth
Left: A classic ploughman's lunch at the Drunken Duck
Right: Hiking around Tarn Hows

doorstep, including the imposing lump of **Skiddaw** and the dramatic ridge of **Blencathra**, but it's the lake of **Derwentwater** that really draws the eye: it was said to be Beatrix Potter's favourite, and she supposedly got the idea for Squirrel Nutkin while watching red squirrels frolicking on its shores. The **Keswick Launch** (☎017687-72263; www.keswick-launch.co.uk; round-the-lake adult/child/family £10.25/5.15/24) travels out around the lake year-round.

Back in town, don't miss a visit to **George Fisher** (☎017687-72178; www.georgefisher.co.uk; 2 Borrowdale Rd; ⊕9am-5.30pm Mon-Sat, 10am-4pm Sun), the most famous outdoors shop in the Lake District: if you need a new pair of hiking boots, this is definitely the place to come.

🛏 p255

The Drive » The drive into Borrowdale on the B5289 is a beauty, passing several pretty villages as it travels through the valley. You can't get lost en route to Honister Pass (10 miles from Keswick) – there's only one road to take; Buttermere lies on the other side of the pass. You'll want to stop for numerous photos on the way.

- - - - - - - - - - - - - -

TRIP HIGHLIGHT

❻ Borrowdale & Buttermere

South of Keswick, the B5289 tracks along the eastern side of Derwentwater and enters

 — Classic Trip

the bucolic valley of Borrowdale, a classic Lakeland canvas of fields, fells, streams and endless drystone walls. It's worth stopping off to see the geological oddity of the **Bowder Stone**, a huge boulder deposited by a glacier, and for a quick hike up to the top of **Castle Crag**, which has the best views of the valley.

Then it's up and over the perilously steep **Honister Pass**, where the Lake District's last working **slate mine** (☎017687-77230; www.honister-slate-mine.co.uk; mine tour adult/child £12.50/7.50; ⏰tours 10.30am, 12.30pm & 3.30pm Mar-Oct) is still doing a thriving trade. You can take a guided tour down

into the mine or brave the heights along the stomach-upsetting Via Ferrata, and pick up slate souvenirs in the shop.

Nearby Buttermere has a sparkling twinset of lakes, **Buttermere** and **Crummock Water**, and is backed by a string of impressive fells. The summit of **Haystacks** is a popular route: it was the favourite fell of Alfred Wainwright, who penned the definitive seven-volume set of guidebooks of the Lake District's fells between the 1950s and '70s. It's a two- to three-hour return walk from Buttermere.

The Drive ›› From Buttermere village, bear left on the B5289 signed towards Loweswater and Crummock Water, which continues into the Lorton Valley. At Low Lorton, stay on the B5289, which continues 4 miles to Cockermouth. Total distance: 11 miles.

➤ DETOUR: WHINLATTER FOREST PARK

Start: ❻ Buttermere (p249)

Encompassing 1200 hectares of pine, larch and spruce, **Whinlatter** (www.forestry.gov.uk/whinlatter) is England's only true mountain forest, rising sharply to 790m about 5 miles from Keswick. The forest is a designated red squirrel reserve; you can check out live video feeds from squirrel cams at the visitor centre. It's also home to two exciting mountain-bike trails and a tree-top assault course. You can hire bikes next to the visitor centre.

To get to Whinlatter Forest Park from Buttermere, look out for the right turn onto the B5292 at Low Lorton, which climbs up to Whinlatter Pass.

---

❼ Cockermouth

Grasmere might be Wordsworth central, but completists will want to visit the poet's **childhood home** (NT; ☎01900-824805; Main St; adult/child £7.20/3.60; ⏰11am-5pm Sat-Thu Mar-Oct) in Cockermouth. Now owned by the National Trust, it's been redecorated in period style according to details published in Wordsworth's own father's accounts: you can wander round the drawing room, kitchen, pantry and garden, and see the rooms where little Willie and his brother John slept.

Cockermouth is also the home of local beer-maker **Jennings Brewery** (☎01900-821011; www.jenningsbrewery.co.uk; adult/child £9/4.50; ⏰guided tours 1.30pm Wed-Sat), where you can take a guided tour and learn about the brewing process, then sample a couple of ales such as Cocker Hoop and the excellently named Sneck Lifter. Just a snifter, mind – you're driving, after all.

The Drive ›› Head west on the A66 and detour onto the A595, which tracks the coast all the way to Whitehaven. To reach Wasdale (35 miles all up), turn off at Gosforth, and then follow signs to Nether Wasdale and Wasdale Head. It's quite easy to miss the turning, so keep your eyes peeled; sat-navs can be very unreliable here.

TRIP HIGHLIGHT

⑧ Wasdale

Wild Wasdale is argu-
ably the most dramatic
valley in the national
park. Carving its way for
5 miles from the coast,
it was gouged out by a
long-extinct glacier dur-
ing the last Ice Age; if
you look closely, you can
still see glacial marks on
the scree-strewn slopes
above Wastwater. Most
people come for the
chance to reach the sum-
mit of **Scafell Pike**, England's highest point; it's a
tough six- to seven-hour
slog, but the views from
the top are quite literally
as good as they get (as-
suming the weather plays
ball, of course).

Afterwards, reward
yourself with a meal at
the **Wasdale Head Inn**
(☏019467-26229; www.
wasdale.com; s £59, d
£118-130, tr £177; P ☏), a
gloriously olde-worlde
hostelry with lashings
of mountain heritage: it
was here that the sport
of rock climbing was pio-
neered in the mid-19th
century.

The Drive » Retrace your
route to Gosforth, and take the
coast road (A595) south to
Ravenglass and follow signs to
Eskdale (22 miles). Alternatively,
there's a shortcut into Eskdale
via Nether Wasdale and Santon
Bridge, but it's easy to get lost,
especially if you're relying on
sat-nav; a good road map is
really handy here.

DETOUR:
ST BEES HEAD

Start: ⑦ Cockermouth

Cumbria's coastline might not have the white
sandy beaches of Wales or the epic grandeur of the
Scottish coast, but it has a bleak beauty all of its
own – not to mention a renowned seabird reserve at
St Bees Head (RSPB; stbees.head@rspb.org.uk), where
you can spot species including fulmars, herring
gulls, kittiwakes and razorbills. You can also look for
England's only nesting black guillemots at nearby
Fleswick Bay. Just try and forget the fact that one of
the UK's largest nuclear reactors, Sellafield, is round
the corner.

The village of St Bees is 5 miles south of Whitehaven, and the headland is signposted from there.

⑨ Eskdale

The valley of Eskdale was
once a centre for mineral-
mining, and a miniature
steam train was built
to carry ore down from
the hillsides to the
coast. Now known as the
**Ravenglass & Eskdale
Railway** (☏01229-717171;
www.ravenglass-railway.co.uk;
adult/child/family return
£13.50/6.75/38; 🚗), its
miniature choo-choos
are a beloved Lakeland
attraction. They chuff
for 7 miles along the
valley from the station at
Ravenglass to the final
terminus at Dalegarth.
Nearby, the **Boot Inn**
(☏019467-23224; www.
thebooteskdale.co.uk; Boot;
mains £10-18; P) makes a
pleasant stop for lunch.

The Drive » Since you're
driving, the most sensible idea is
to park near Dalegarth Station,
ride the train to Ravenglass

and back, and then set off for
Hardknott Pass. There's only
one road east. Take it and get
ready for a hair-raising, white-
knuckle drive. It's 6 (very steep!)
miles from Eskdale to Hardknott
Pass.

TRIP HIGHLIGHT

⑩ Hardknott Pass &
Wrynose Pass

At the eastern end of
Eskdale lie England's
two steepest road passes,
Hardknott and Wrynose.
Reaching 30% gradient
in some places, and with
precious few passing
places on the narrow,
single-file road, they're
absolutely not for the
faint-hearted or for
nervous drivers – but the
views are amazing, and
they're doable if you take
things slow (although it's
probably best to leave the
caravan or motor home
in the garage). Make sure
your car has plenty of

Classic Trip

oil and water, as you'll do much of the road in 1st gear, and the strain on the engine can be taxing. Take it slow, and take breaks – you need to keep your focus on the road ahead.

From Eskdale, the road ascends via a series of very sharp, steep switchbacks to the remains of **Hardknott Fort**, a Roman outpost where you can still see the remains of some of the walls. Soon after you reach **Hardknott Pass** at 393m (1289ft). The vistas here are magnificent: you'll be able to see all the way to the coast on a clear day. Next you'll drop down into Cockley Beck before continuing the climb up to **Wrynose Pass** (393m/1289ft). Near the summit is a small car park containing the **Three Shire Stone**, where the counties of Cumberland, Westmorland and Lancashire historically met. Then it's a slow descent down through hairpins and corners to the packhorse Slaters Bridge and on into the valley of **Little Langdale**. Phew! You made it.

The Drive » Once you reach Little Langdale, follow the road east until you reach the A593, the main road between Skelwith Bridge and Coniston. Turn right and follow it for 5 miles.

- - - - - - - - - -

⓫ Coniston

South of Ambleside, the old mining village of Coniston is dominated by its hulking fell, the **Old Man of Coniston**, an ever-popular objective for hikers, but it's perhaps best known for the world speed record attempts made here by father and son Malcolm and Donald Campbell between the 1930s and 1960s. Though they jointly broke many records, in 1967 Donald was tragically killed during an attempt in his jet-boat *Bluebird*; the little **Ruskin Museum** (www.ruskinmuseum.com; adult/child £6/3; ⊙10am-5.30pm Easter–mid-Nov, 10.30am-3.30pm Wed-Sun mid-Nov–Easter) has the full story.

Coniston Water is also said to have been the inspiration for Arthur Ransome's classic children's tale, *Swallows and Amazons*. The best way to explore is aboard the **Steam Yacht Gondola** (NT; ☎015394-63850; www.nationaltrust.org.uk/steam-yacht-gondola; Coniston Jetty; half lake adult/child return £11/5.50, full lake adult/child/family £21.50/10/51), a beautifully restored steam yacht built in 1859. It travels over the lake to the stately home of **Brantwood** (☎015394-41396; www.brantwood.org.uk; adult/child £7.50/free, gardens

HILL TOP

Two miles from Hawkshead in the tiny village of Near Sawrey, the idyllic cottage at **Hill Top** (NT; ☎015394-36269; www.nationaltrust.org.uk/hill-top; adult/child £10/5, admission to garden & shop free; ⊙house 10am-5.30pm Mon-Thu, 10am-4.30pm Fri-Sun, garden 10am-5.45pm Mon-Thu, 10am-5pm Fri-Sun) is the most famous house in the whole of the Lake District. It belonged to Beatrix Potter, and was used as inspiration for many of her tales: the house features directly in *Samuel Whiskers*, *Tom Kitten*, *Pigling Bland* and *Jemima Puddleduck*, and you will doubtless recognise the kitchen garden from *Peter Rabbit*.

Following her death in 1943, Beatrix bequeathed Hill Top (along with more than 4000 acres of land) to the National Trust, with the proviso that the house be left with her belongings and decor untouched. The house formed the centrepiece for celebrations to mark the author's 150th birthday in 2016.

Entry is by timed ticket; it's very, very popular, so try visiting in late afternoon or on weekdays to avoid the worst crowds.

Drunken Duck One of the Lake District's premier dining destinations

only £4.95/free; ⊙10.30am-5pm mid-Mar–mid-Nov, to 4pm Wed-Sun mid-Nov–mid-Mar), owned by the Victorian polymath, critic, painter and inveterate collector John Ruskin. The house is packed with furniture and crafts, and the gardens are glorious.

📄 p255

The Drive ⟫ Heading north from Coniston, turn right onto the B5285 up Hawkshead Hill. You'll pass Tarn Hows and the Drunken Duck en route to Hawkshead, about 4 miles east.

- - - - - - - - - - -

⑫ Hawkshead

If you're searching for the perfect chocolate-box lakeland village, look no further – you've found it in Hawkshead, an improbably pretty confection of whitewashed cottages, winding lanes and slate roofs. It's car-free, so you can wander at will: don't miss the **Beatrix Potter Gallery** (NT; www.national trust.org.uk/beatrix-potter-gallery; Red Lion Sq; adult/child £6/3; ⊙10.30am-5pm Sat-Thu mid-Mar–Oct), which has a collection of the artist's original watercolours and botanical paintings (she had a particular fascination with fungi).

Nearby, make a detour via the manmade lake of **Tarn Hows** before stopping for lunch at the Lake District's finest dining pub, the wonderfully named Drunken Duck.

✕ p255

The Drive » Head back to Ambleside and then follow the A591 back towards Windermere. Just before you reach it, take the turn-off onto the A592 to Troutbeck Bridge, which climbs up to the lofty Kirkstone Pass – at 454m this is the highest mountain pass in Cumbria that's open to road traffic. It's steep, but it's a main A-road so it's well maintained.

⑬ Ullswater

From the windlashed heights of Kirkstone Pass, the A592 loops down towards the last stop on this jaunt around the Lake District: stately Ullswater, the national park's second-largest lake (after Windermere). It's an impressive sight, its

↱ DETOUR: GRIZEDALE FOREST

Start: ⑫ Hawkshead (p253)

Stretching for 6000 acres across the hilltops between Coniston Water and Esthwaite Water, **Grizedale Forest** (www.forestry.gov.uk/grizedale) is a wonderful place for a wander. It's criss-crossed by cycling trails, and is also home to more than 40 outdoor sculptures created by artists over the last 30 years, including a xylophone and a man of the forest. There's an online guide at www.grizedalesculpture.org.

As you leave the Hawkshead car park, you'll immediately see a brown sign for Grizedale, heading right onto North Lonsdale Rd. Just follow the brown signs from here – it's 3 miles' drive from the village.

silvery surface framed by jagged fells and plied by the puttering **Ullswater 'Steamers'** (📞017684-82229; www.ullswater-steamers.co.uk; round-the-lake adult/child £13.90/6.95); you can also hire your own vessels from the Glenridding Sailing Centre.

As you skirt up the lake's western edge, it's worth stopping for a walk around **Gowbarrow Park**, where there's a clattering waterfall to admire called **Aira Force**, and impressive displays of daffodils in springtime (Wordsworth dreamt up

his most famous poem while walking nearby, the one which starts 'I wandered lonely as a cloud...')

For an epic end to the trip, strap on your hiking boots and tackle the famous ridge climb via Striding Edge to the summit of **Helvellyn**, the Lake District's third-highest mountain at 950m. You'll need a head for heights, but you'll feel a real sense of achievement: you've just conquered perhaps the finest hill walk in all of England.

Eating & Sleeping

Bowness-on-Windermere ❶

🛏 Cranleigh   Hotel £££

(📞015394-43293; www.thecranleigh.com; Kendal Rd, Bowness-on-Windermere; d £119-189, ste £305-515; [P] [📶]) This guesthouse has gone all out on the decor, but strip away the snazziness and it's still just a B&B. It's worth bumping up to the superior for the spacious bathrooms or maybe blowing the budget on one of the two over-the-top suites (check out the Sanctuary, complete with Bose stereo, glass bath and picture-fireplace).

Ambleside ❷

🍴 Lake Road Kitchen   Bistro £££

(📞015394-22012; www.lakeroadkitchen.co.uk; Lake Rd; 5-/8-course tasting menu £50/80; 🕘6-9.30pm Wed-Sun) This much-lauded new bistro has brought some dazzle to Ambleside's dining scene. Its Noma-trained head chef James Cross explores the 'food of the north', and his multicourse tasting menus are chock full of locally sourced, seasonal and foraged ingredients, from shore-sourced seaweed to forest-picked mushrooms. Presentation is impeccable, flavours are experimental, and the Scandi-inspired decor is just so. A meal not to miss.

Grasmere ❹

🛏 How Foot Lodge   B&B ££

(📞015394-35366; www.howfootlodge.co.uk; Town End; d £76-85; [P]) Just a stroll from Dove Cottage, this stone house has six rooms finished in fawns and beiges; the nicest are the deluxe doubles, one with a sun terrace and the other with a private sitting room. Rates are an absolute bargain considering the location.

Keswick ❺

🛏 Howe Keld   B&B ££

(📞017687-72417; www.howekeld.co.uk; 5-7 The Heads; s £60-85, d £112-130; [P] [📶]) This gold-standard B&B pulls out all the stops: goose-down duvets, slate-floored bathrooms, chic colours and locally made furniture. The best rooms have views across Crow Park and the golf course, and the breakfast is a pick-and-mix delight. Free parking is available on The Heads if there's space.

Coniston ⓫

🛏 Bank Ground Farm   B&B ££

(📞015394-41264; www.bankground.com; East of the Lake; d from £90; [P]) This lakeside farmhouse has literary cachet: Arthur Ransome used it as the model for Holly Howe Farm in *Swallows and Amazons*. Parts of the house date back to the 15th century, so the rooms are snug. Some have sleigh beds, others exposed beams. The tearoom is a beauty too, and there are cottages for longer stays. Two-night minimum.

Hawkshead ⓬

🍴 Drunken Duck   Pub Food £££

(📞015394-36347; www.drunkenduckinn.co.uk; Barngates; lunch mains £7-12, dinner mains £22; 🕘noon-2pm & 6-10pm; [P] [📶]) Long one of the Lake District's premier dining destinations, the Drunken Duck blends historic pub and fine-dining restaurant. On a wooded crossroads on the top of Hawkshead Hill, it's renowned for its luxurious food and home-brewed ales, and the flagstones and sporting prints conjure a convincing country atmosphere. Book well ahead for dinner or take your chances at lunchtime.

If you fancy staying, you'll find the rooms (£105 to £325) are just as fancy as the food. The pub's tricky to find: drive along the B5286 from Hawkshead towards Ambleside and look out for the brown signs.

Yorkshire Dales

20

This rollercoaster of a route leads you through the finest scenery in the Yorkshire Dales, from pretty villages and country pubs to limestone crags and windswept moors.

TRIP HIGHLIGHTS

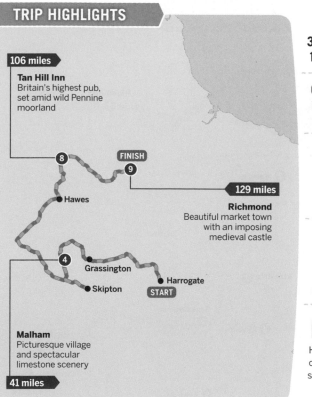

106 miles

Tan Hill Inn
Britain's highest pub, set amid wild Pennine moorland

8

FINISH
9

129 miles

Richmond
Beautiful market town with an imposing medieval castle

● Hawes

4

● Grassington

● Skipton

● Harrogate

START

Malham
Picturesque village and spectacular limestone scenery

41 miles

Swaledale Sheep outside Tan Hill Inn

3–4 DAYS
129 MILES / 206KM

GREAT FOR...

BEST TIME TO GO

May and June see wildflowers add a splash of colour to the scenery.

 ESSENTIAL PHOTO

The view north from the summit of Buttertubs Pass.

 BEST FOR OUTDOORS

Hiking to the top of Malham Cove's spectacular cliff.

20 Yorkshire Dales

The winding road over the Buttertubs Pass – a favourite of TV motoring programmes and a highlight of the Yorkshire *grand départ* of 2014's Tour de France cycling race – is regularly voted the most spectacular road in England. This trip adds a second thrilling road climb, from Arncliffe to Malham, to link six of the national park's most beautiful dales in a tour de force of scenic splendour.

❶ Harrogate

The quintessential Victorian spa town, prim and pretty Harrogate has long been associated with a certain kind of old-fashioned Englishness – it is fitting that the town's most famous visitor was crime novelist Agatha Christie, who fled here incognito in 1926 to escape her broken marriage.

Wander around the **Montpellier Quarter** (www.montpellierharro gate.com), an area of pedestrianised streets

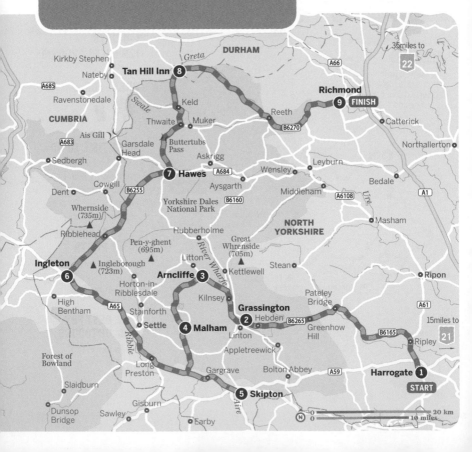

lined with restored 19th-century buildings that are now home to art galleries, antique shops, fashion boutiques, cafes and restaurants, and learn all about the town's history in the ornate **Royal Pump Room** (www.harrogate.gov.uk; Crown Pl; adult/child £4/2.35; ⊙10.30am-5pm Mon-Sat, 2-5pm Sun Apr-Oct, to 4pm Nov-Mar), built in 1842 over the most famous of the town's sulphurous springs.

 p263

The Drive » Head north out of Harrogate on the A61. After 4 miles turn left at Ripley onto the B6165 to the pretty town of Pately Bridge, then continue on the B6265 as it climbs high over Craven Moor before entering the Yorkshire Dales National Park and descending to Grassington (total 24 miles).

LINK YOUR TRIP

21 North York Moors & Coast

From Richmond it's a quick 47-mile blast down the M1 to link with our tour of Yorkshire's other national park.

22 Hadrian's Wall

One hour's drive north from Richmond (47 miles) is Newcastle, where you can begin a tour of Britain's most famous Roman legacy.

② Grassington

The perfect base for hiking the south Dales, Grassington's handsome Georgian centre teems with walkers and visitors throughout the summer months, soaking up an atmosphere that – despite the odd touch of faux rusticity – is as attractive and traditional as you'll find in these parts.

✕ p263

The Drive » Head north out of Grassington and follow the B6160 along Wharfedale for a few miles. Soon after passing the massive limestone overhang of Kilnsey Crag on your left, take the minor road on the left to Arncliffe, just 8 miles from Grassington. As you enter the village turn left to find the village green.

③ Arncliffe

The tiny village of Arncliffe sits in the heart of scenic Littondale, its neat stone houses ranged around the village green. On the north side of the green is the **Falcon Inn** (www.thefalconinn.com; Arncliffe; ⊙noon-3pm & 7-11pm Mon-Thu, noon-11pm Fri & Sat, noon-10.30pm Sun), the original for the Woolpack pub in the popular UK TV series *Emmerdale*. It's a lovely rustic inn where beer is still served from a jug on the counter.

The Drive » Exit the far end of the village green, cross the bridge and turn sharp left to

follow the steep, twisting, single-track road that climbs up the valley of Cowside Beck (beware of wandering sheep). At a fork near Malham Tarn bear left and after 400m, at another junction, continue straight across and descend steeply into Malham (9 miles).

TRIP HIGHLIGHT

④ Malham

A short walk from the picturesque village of Malham is **Malham Cove**, a huge rock amphitheatre ringed with 80m-high vertical cliffs – in the wake of the last Ice Age, this was a waterfall to rival Niagara; today it is a playground for rock climbers. Peregrine falcons nest here in spring, when the Royal Society for the Protection of Birds (RSPB) sets up a birdwatching lookout. You can hike up the steep steps on the left-hand side of the cove to see the impressive limestone scenery above the cliffs.

 p263

The Drive » Continue south on the minor road from Malham (which can be very busy on summer weekends) to the A65, and turn left to reach Skipton in 11 miles.

⑤ Skipton

This busy market town on the southern edge of the Dales takes its name from the Anglo-Saxon *sceape ton* (sheep town) – no prizes for guessing how it made its money.

Skipton's pride and joy is the broad and bustling **High Street**, one of the most attractive shopping streets in Yorkshire. Monday, Wednesday, Friday and Saturday are market days, bringing crowds from all over and giving the town something of a festive atmosphere.

No visit to Skipton is complete without a cruise along the Leeds–Liverpool Canal, which runs through the middle of town. **Pennine Cruisers** (www.penninecruisers.com; The Wharf, Coach St; per person £4; ⊙10.30am-dusk Mar-Oct) runs half-hour trips to Skipton Castle and back.

🛏 p263

The Drive » Head northwest from Skipton on the busy A65, and continue as far as Ingleton, 24 miles away. Turn off the main road and follow signs for Village Centre, and then Waterfalls Walk.

- - - - - - - - - - - - -

❻ Ingleton

The village of Ingleton, perched precariously above a river gorge, is the caving capital of England. It sits at the foot of one of the country's most extensive areas of limestone, crowned by the dominating peak of Ingleborough and riddled with countless potholes and cave systems.

The town is the starting point for a famous Dales hike, the circular, 4.5-mile **Waterfalls Trail** (www.ingletonwaterfallstrail.co.uk), which passes through native oak woodland on its way past a series of spectacular waterfalls on the Rivers Twiss and Doe (allow three to four hours).

The Drive » Follow the B6255 northeast from Ingleton. Beyond Chapel-le-Dale you'll see the spectacular 30m-high, 400m-long Ribblehead Viaduct on your left. The road continues

Yorkshire Dales National Park Dry stone walls and snowy foothills

over bleak Gayle Moor and down to Hawes (17 miles). Leave the car in the car park beside the national park centre at the eastern end of the village.

❼ Hawes

Hawes is the beating heart of Wensleydale, a thriving and picturesque market town (market day is Tuesday) with several antique and art-and-craft shops that has the added attraction of its own waterfall in the village centre. Beside the car park is the **Dales Countryside Museum** (☏01969-666210; www. dalescountrysidemuseum.org.

uk; Station Yard; adult/child £4.50/free; ⌚10am-5pm, closed Jan; P), a beautifully presented social history of the area that explains the forces shaping the landscape, from geology to lead mining to land enclosure.

At the other end of the town is the **Wensleydale Creamery** (www. wensleydale.co.uk; adult/child £2.50/1.50; ⌚10am-4pm; P ♿), devoted to the production of the animated TV characters Wallace and Gromit's favourite crumbly white cheese. Here, you can visit the cheese museum, watch some cheesemakers in

action in the viewing gallery, and then try-before-you-buy in the shop.

🛏 p263

The Drive » The 13-mile route from Hawes to the Tan Hill Inn is one of the most scenic in the Dales. Turn right and right again out of the car park (signposted Muker) and follow the minor road over the Buttertubs Pass. Turn left on the B6270 to Keld, then right on the minor road signposted West Stonesdale and Tan Hill.

TRIP HIGHLIGHT

❽ Tan Hill Inn

Sitting in the middle of nowhere at an elevation of 328m (1732ft), the **Tan**

MOUNTAIN BIKING IN SWALEDALE

Swaledale – the quietest and least-visited of the Dales – stretches west from Richmond, its wild and rugged beauty in sharp contrast to the softer, greener dales to the south. It's hard to imagine that only a century ago this was a major lead-mining area. When the price of ore fell in the 19th century, many people left to find work in England's burgeoning industrial cities, while others emigrated – especially to Wisconsin in the USA – leaving the valley almost empty, with just a few lonely villages scattered along its length.

The many rough tracks that criss-cross the moors and hillsides around the pretty village of Reeth, at the junction of Swaledale and Arkengarthdale, make this part of the Dales a paradise for mountain bikers, with dozens of miles of off-road trails to explore. The **Dales Bike Centre** (☎01748-884908; www.dalesbikecentre.co.uk; Fremington; bike hire per day £35; ☺9am-5pm), just east of Reeth, can rent you a bike and provide local trail maps.

Hill Inn (☎01833-628246; www.tanhillinn.com; Tan Hill, Reeth; ☺8am-11.30pm Jul & Aug, noon-9.30pm Sep-Jun; ☎📶🐕) is Britain's highest pub. Despite its isolation it's an unexpectedly comfortable and welcoming hostelry, with an ancient fireplace in the atmospheric, stone-flagged public bar, and an assorted menagerie of dogs, cats and even sheep wandering in and out of the building. An important watering hole on the Pennine Way, the inn offers real ale on tap and decent pub grub.

The Drive » Head east from Tan Hill on a wild and lonely single-track road that cuts across the high Pennine moors then descends through Arkengarthdale to the picturesque village of Reeth. Follow the B6270 along Swaledale through classic Dales scenery patchworked with drystone dykes and little barns, then the A6108 for the final stretch to Richmond (total 23 miles).

- - - - - - - - - - - -

TRIP HIGHLIGHT

❾ Richmond

The handsome market town of Richmond is one of England's best-kept secrets, perched on a rocky outcrop overlooking the River Swale and guarded by the ruins of massive **Richmond Castle** (EH; www.english-heritage.org.uk; Tower St; adult/child £5.90/3.50; ☺10am-6pm Apr-Sep, to 5pm Oct, to 4pm Sat & Sun Nov-Mar). A maze of cobbled streets radiates from the broad, sloping market square (market day is Saturday), lined with elegant Georgian buildings and photogenic stone cottages, with glimpses of the surrounding hills and dales peeking through the gaps.

The **Richmondshire Museum** (www.richmondshiremuseum.org.uk; Ryder's Wynd; adult/child £3/free; ☺10.30am-4.30pm Easter-Oct) is a delight, with local history exhibits including an early Yorkshire cave-dweller and displays about lead mining. You can also see the original set that served as James Herriot's surgery in the TV series *All Creatures Great and Small*. Don't miss the **Castle Walk**, a short path that loops around the south side of the castle from Millgate to New Rd – the views over the river are glorious.

🛏 p263

Eating & Sleeping

Harrogate ❶

🛏 Bijou   B&B ££

(📞01423-567974; www.thebijou.co.uk; 17 Ripon Rd; s/d from £59/94; P 📶) Bijou by name and bijou by nature, this jewel of a Victorian villa sits firmly at the boutique end of the B&B spectrum – you can tell that a lot of thought and care has gone into its design. The husband-and-wife team who own the place make fantastic hosts, warm and helpful but unobtrusive.

Grassington ❷

🍴 Corner House Cafe   Cafe £

(📞01756-752414; www.cornerhousegrassington. co.uk; 1 Garr's Lane; mains £6-9; ⏱10am-4pm; 📶 ♿ 🐾) This cute little white cottage, just uphill from the village square, serves good coffee and unusual homemade cakes (citrus and lavender syrup sponge is unexpectedly delicious), as well as tasty lunch specials such as croque monsieur or chicken and chorizo gratin. Breakfast, served till 11.30am, ranges from cinnamon toast to the full English fry-up.

🛏 Devonshire Fell   Hotel £££

(📞01756-718111; www.devonshirefell.co.uk; Burnsall; r from £129; P @ 📶 🐾) This former gentleman's club for mill owners has a very contemporary feel, with beautiful modern furnishings crafted by local experts. The conservatory (used as a restaurant and breakfast room) has a stunning view over the valley. It's 3 miles southeast of Grassington on the B6160.

Malham ❹

🛏 Beck Hall   Hotel ££

(📞01729-830332; www.beckhallmalham.com; d £90-110; P 📶 🐾) Ideally located for walks to Malham Cove, this rambling 17th-century country house has a gurgling beck (stream) flowing through the garden, 18 individually decorated rooms, all chunkily rustic with old-style furnishings and some with antique four-poster beds, and a lovely oak-panelled lounge with an open fire in winter.

Skipton ❺

🛏 Park Hill   B&B ££

(📞01756-792772; www.parkhillskipton.co.uk; 17 Grassington Rd; d £85; P @ 📶) From the complimentary glass of sherry on arrival to the hearty breakfasts based on local produce, farm-fresh eggs and homegrown tomatoes, this B&B provides a real Yorkshire welcome. It enjoys an attractive rural location half a mile north of the town centre, on the B6265 road towards Grassington.

Hawes ❼

🛏 Green Dragon Inn   Inn ££

(📞01969-667392; www.greendragonhardraw. co.uk; Hardraw; B&B per person £35-50; P 📶 🐾) A fine old pub with flagstone floors, low timber beams, ancient oak furniture and Theakston's on draught. The Dragon serves up a tasty steak-and-ale pie and offers bunkhouse accommodation (per person £17.50), camping (per person £8) or B&B in plain but adequate rooms, as well as a pair of larger, more comfortable suites. One mile northwest of Hawes.

Richmond ❾

🛏 Millgate House   B&B £££

(📞01748-823571; www.millgatehouse.com; Market Pl; r £125-165; P @ 🐾) Behind an unassuming grey door lies the unexpected pleasure of one of the most attractive guesthouses in England. While the house itself is a Georgian gem crammed with period details, it is overshadowed by the multi-award-winning garden at the back, which offers superb views over the River Swale and the Cleveland Hills. If possible, book the Garden Suite.

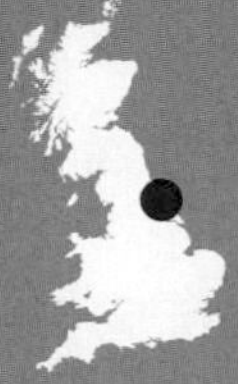

North York Moors & Coast

21

This varied tour takes in ancient architecture, wild moorland scenery, picture-postcard villages (complete with steam trains!) and two of England's most classic seaside resorts.

TRIP HIGHLIGHTS

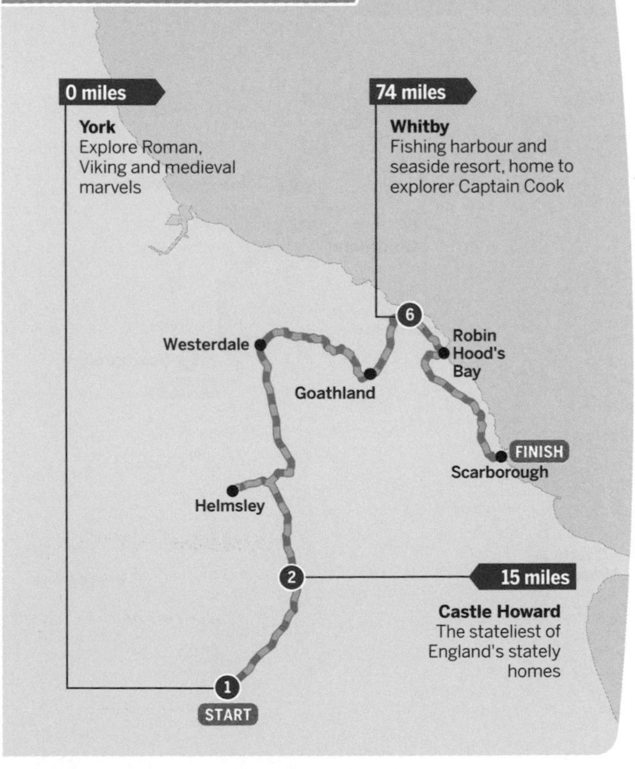

0 miles

York
Explore Roman, Viking and medieval marvels

74 miles

Whitby
Fishing harbour and seaside resort, home to explorer Captain Cook

⑥

Robin Hood's Bay

Westerdale

Goathland

FINISH

Scarborough

Helmsley

②

15 miles

Castle Howard
The stateliest of England's stately homes

①

START

4–5 DAYS
95 MILES / 152KM

GREAT FOR...

BEST TIME TO GO

The moors look their best in August when the heather is in bloom.

ESSENTIAL PHOTO

A steam train passing through Goathland station.

BEST FOR FOODIES

Browsing the market and delicatessens in Helmsley.

21 North York Moors & Coast

The Blakey Ridge road out of Hutton-le-Hole just keeps climbing and climbing, leaving behind the medieval city of York and the aristocratic spendour of Castle Howard to enter a world of windswept heather moorland, wandering sheep, lonely stone crosses and ancient footpaths. Ahead lies the bustling fishing harbour of Whitby, with its Gothic abbey and Dracula associations, and the bucket-and-spade, fish-and-chips seaside resort of Scarborough.

TRIP HIGHLIGHT

❶ York

Nowhere in northern England says 'medieval' quite like York, a city of extraordinary cultural and historical wealth that has lost little of its pre-industrial lustre. At its heart lies the immense, awe-inspiring **York Minster** (www.yorkminster.org; Deangate; adult/child £10/free, incl tower £15/5; ⊙9am-5.30pm Mon-Sat, 12.45-5pm Sun, last admission 30min before closing), **the largest medieval**

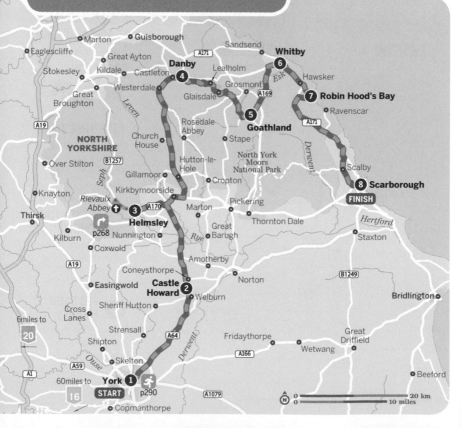

cathedral in all of Northern Europe, and one of the world's most beautiful Gothic buildings. If this is the only cathedral you visit in England, you'll still walk away satisfied.

While many railway museums are the sole preserve of lone men in anoraks comparing dog-eared notebooks and getting high on the smell of machine oil, coal smoke and nostalgia, York's **National Railway Museum** (www.nrm.org.uk; Leeman Rd; ⊙10am-6pm; **P** 🚻) is different. The biggest in the world, with more than 100 locomotives, it is so well presented and crammed with fascinating stuff that it's interesting even to folk whose eyes don't mist over at the thought of a 4-6-2 A1

Pacific class thundering into a tunnel.

Interactive multimedia exhibits aimed at bringing history to life often achieve exactly the opposite, but the much-hyped **Jorvik Viking Centre** (www.jorvik-viking-centre. co.uk; Coppergate; adult/child £10.25/7.25; ⊙10am-5pm Apr-Oct, to 4pm Nov-Mar) manages to pull it off with aplomb. Thoroughly restored and reimagined following flood damage in 2015, it's a smells-and-all reconstruction of the Viking settlement unearthed here during excavations in the late 1970s, experienced via a 'time-car' monorail that transports you through 9th-century Jorvik (the Viking name for York). You can reduce time waiting in the queue by booking your tickets online.

And don't miss the chance to walk (p290) York's magnificent circuit of 13th-century city walls.

🛏 p47, p271

The Drive » Head northeast out of York on the A64. After 11 miles, at Barton Hill, turn left on the signposted minor road to Castle Howard. After 1.5 miles of twisting and turning, the road becomes arrow-straight as it enters the castle's landscaped grounds, and passes through a monumental gate to reach the visitors' car park (total 15 miles).

TRIP HIGHLIGHT

❷ Castle Howard

Stately homes may be two-a-penny in England, but you'll have to try pretty damn hard to find one as breathtakingly stately as **Castle Howard** (www.castlehoward. co.uk; adult/child house & grounds £17.50/9, grounds only £9.95/7; ⊙ house 10.30am-4pm (last admission), grounds 10am-5pm; **P**), a work of theatrical grandeur and audacity set in the rolling Howardian Hills. Castle Howard is one of the world's most beautiful buildings, instantly recognisable from its starring role in the 1980s TV series *Brideshead Revisited* and in the 2008 film of the same name (both based on Evelyn Waugh's 1945 novel of nostalgia for the English aristocracy). You'll need to plan a visit of at least two hours to do the place justice.

The Drive » Continue north from Castle Howard on minor roads through lush farmland, following signs for Kirkbymoorside then, 5 miles north of Slingsby, turn left on a minor road signposted Harome and Helmsley. This leads through the thatched cottages of Harome, famous for its Michelin-starred gastropub, the Star Inn, and on to Helmsley (total 13 miles).

❸ Helmsley

Helmsley is a classic North Yorkshire market

LINK YOUR TRIP

20 **Yorkshire Dales**
Head west for 22 miles from York to Harrogate to discover the scenic delights of the Yorkshire Dales.

16 **Industrial Powerhouse**
A 71-mile drive southwest from York on the A64 and M62 leads to Manchester, starting point for our tour of Britain's industrial heritage.

DETOUR: RIEVAULX ABBEY

Start: ❸ Helmsley (p267)

In the secluded valley of the River Rye, amid fields and woods loud with birdsong, stand the magnificent ruins of **Rievaulx Abbey** (www.english-heritage.org. uk; adult/child £8/4.80; ⊙10am-6pm Apr-Sep, to 5pm Oct, to 4pm Sat & Sun Nov-Mar; ⓅP), pronounced 'ree-voh'. The extensive remains give a wonderful sense of the size and complexity of the community that once lived here, and their story is fleshed out in a series of fascinating exhibits in a new museum and visitor centre. On the hillside above the abbey is **Rievaulx Terrace** (www.nationaltrust.org.uk; adult/child £5.95/3; ⊙11am-5pm May-Aug, to 4pm Mar, Apr, Sep & Oct; ⓅP), built in the 18th century by Thomas Duncombe II as a place to admire views of the abbey (separate admission fee).

Rivevaulx is 3 miles west of Helmsley, signposted off the B1257.

CHRIS HUISH / 500PX ©

town, a handsome huddle of old stone houses, historic coaching inns and a cobbled market square (market day is Friday), all basking under the watchful gaze of a sturdy Norman **castle** (EH; www. english-heritage.org.uk; Castlegate; adult/child £6.40/3.80; ⊙10am-6pm Apr-Sep, to 5pm Oct, to 4pm Sat & Sun Nov-Mar; ⓅP). It's also a bit of a foodie town, sporting several good coffee shops, a couple of quality delicatessens on the main square and some renowned restaurants in the surrounding area.

South of Helmsley lies the superb ornamental landscape of **Duncombe Park** (www.duncombepark. com; adult/child £5/3;

⊙10.30am-5pm Sun-Fri Apr-Aug; ⓅP) estate, laid out in 1718 for Thomas Duncombe (whose son would later build Rievaulx Terrace). Wide grassy walkways and terraces lead through woodland to mockclassical temples, while longer walking trails are set out in the landscaped parkland, now protected as a nature reserve.

🛏 p271

The Drive » Drive east from Helmsley on the A170 and, just past Kirkbymoorside, turn left on the minor road to the picturesque village of Hutton-le-Hole. Continue on the Blakey Ridge road, which climbs high over the moors, peaking at 418m near the remote Lion Inn before swooping steeply down to Danby (total 23 miles).

❹ Danby

Danby is a compact stone-built village set deep amid the moors at the head of Eskdale. It's home to the **Moors National Park Centre** (☎01439-772737; www. northyorkmoors.org.uk; Lodge Lane, Danby; ⊙10am-5pm Apr-Oct, 10.30am-4pm Nov-

Goathland North Yorkshire Moors Railway

Mar, Sat & Sun only Jan & Feb; 📷), the national park's headquarters, which has interesting exhibits on the natural history of the moors as well as a cafe. There are several short circular walks from the village, but a more challenging objective is **Danby Beacon**, a stiff 2 miles uphill to a stunning 360-degree panorama across the moors. Or you can cheat, and just drive up.

🛏 p271

The Drive » Head east from Danby on steep and twisting minor roads winding along gorgeous Eskdale, passing through the villages of Lealholm and Glaisdale before reaching Egdon Bridge, where you turn right and follow signs to Goathland (13 miles).

- - - - - - - - - -

❺ Goathland

This picturesque halt on the **North Yorkshire Moors Railway** (NYMR; www.nymr.co.uk; Pickering-Whitby day-rover ticket adult/child £30/13.50; ☺Apr-Oct) stars as Hogsmeade train station in the Harry Potter films, and the village appears as Aidensfield in the British TV series *Heartbeat*. It's also the starting point for lots of easy and enjoyable walks, often with the chuff-chuff-chuff of passing steam engines in the background.

The Drive ≫ Continue east from Goathland then north on the A169, pausing at Blue Bank parking area to take in the sweeping view of the north Yorkshire coast, before descending into Whitby (total 9 miles).

TRIP HIGHLIGHT

❻ Whitby

Whitby is both a busy fishing port and a traditional seaside resort which has has managed to retain much of its 18th-century character. The narrow streets and alleys of the old town hug the riverside, now lined with restaurants, pubs and cute little shops. Keeping a watchful eye over the whole scene are the atmospheric ruins of **Whitby Abbey** (EH; www. english-heritage.org.uk; adult/child £7.90/4.70; ☉10am-6pm Apr-Sep, to 5pm Oct, to 4pm Tue-Sat Nov, to 4pm Sat & Sun Dec-Mar; 🅿).

James Cook, one of the best-known explorers in history, lived here – his life is celebrated in the

Captain Cook Memorial Museum (www.cookmuseum whitby.co.uk; Grape Lane; adult/child £5.40/3.50; ☉9.45am-5pm Apr-Oct, 11am-3pm Mar) – and the famous *Dracula* was written by Bram Stoker while holidaying in Whitby in 1897.

Whitby is famous for its seafood and the town is home to several award-winning fish-and-chip shops, so grab some takeaway and enjoy it while you sit on a harbourside bench.

🍴 🛏 p271

The Drive ≫ Head 5.5 miles south from Whitby on the A171 and B1447 to Robin Hood's Bay.

❼ Robin Hood's Bay

The picturesque fishing village of Robin Hood's Bay (www.robin-hoods-bay.co.uk) is one of the prettiest spots on the Yorkshire coast. Leave your car at the parking area in the upper village and walk downhill to Old Bay: a maze of narrow lanes and passages is dotted with tearooms, pubs, craft shops and artists' studios. At low tide you can go onto the beach and fossick around in the rock pools.

🍴 p271

Return to the A170 and drive 16 miles south to Scarborough.

❽ Scarborough

Scarborough is where the tradition of English seaside holidays began. It retains all the trappings of the classic seaside resort – donkey rides, fish and chips, boat trips round the bay, saucy postcards and slot-machine arcades – but is in the process of re-inventing itself as a centre for the creative arts and digital industries.

As well as seaside attractions such as **Alpamare Water Park** (www.alpamare.co.uk; 28 Burniston Rd; adult/child/family £19/15/60; ☉10am-10pm Mon-Sat, to 9pm Sun; ♿) and the **Sea Life Sanctuary** (www.sealife.co.uk; Scalby Mills; adult/child 2yr & under £18/free; ☉10am-6pm, last admission 5pm; 🅿 ♿), Scarborough offers excellent coastal walking, a **geology museum** (www.rotundamuseum.co.uk; Vernon Rd; adult/child £3/free; ☉10am-5pm Tue-Sun; ♿), one of Yorkshire's most impressively sited **castles** (EH; www.english-heritage. org.uk; Castle Rd; adult/child £6.10/3.70; ☉10am-6pm Apr-Sep, to 5pm Oct, to 4pm Sat & Sun Nov-Mar), and the renowned **Stephen Joseph Theatre** (📞01723-370541; www.sjt.uk.com; Westborough) that is the home base for popular playwright Alan Ayckbourn.

🛏 p271

Eating & Sleeping

York ❶

🛏 Middlethorpe Hall   Hotel £££

(☎01904-641241; www.middlethorpe.
com; Bishopthorpe Rd; s/d from £118/126;
🅿 📶 📧 🐾) This breathtaking 17th-century
country house is set in 8 hectares of parkland,
once the home of diarist Lady Mary Wortley
Montagu. The rooms are divided between the
main house, restored courtyard buildings
and three cottage suites. All are beautifully
decorated with original antiques and oil
paintings that have been carefully selected to
reflect the period.

Helmsley ❸

🛏 Feathers Hotel   Inn ££

(☎01439-770275; www.feathershotelhelmsley.
co.uk; Market Pl; s/d from £90/100; 🅿 📶 🐾)
One of a number of old coaching inns on the
market square that offer B&B, decent grub and
a pint of hand-pumped real ale. There are four-
poster beds in some bedrooms and historical
trimmings throughout.

Danby ❹

🛏 Duke of Wellington   Inn ££

(☎01287-660351; dukeofwellingtondanby.
co.uk/; s/d from £45/85; 🅿 📶 🐾) The Duke of
Wellington is a fine traditional pub in the middle
of the village; it serves good beer and bar meals,
and has nine guest bedrooms with appealingly
old-fashioned decor. Dating from the 18th
century, the pub was used as a recruitment
centre during the Napoleonic Wars (hence the
name).

Whitby ❻

✖ Fisherman's Wife   Seafood ££

(☎01947-603500; thefishermanswife.co.uk;
Khyber Pass; mains £8-15; ⏱ noon-8.30pm
Mon-Thu, to 8.45pm Fri & Sat, to 8pm Sun; 👶)
With a prime location overlooking the beach

and harbour entrance and smart staff dressed
in navy-blue aprons, this is the place to enjoy
local seafood in style. Whitby lobster (half/
whole around £20/36 depending on market
prices) is served as a salad, grilled with garlic,
or in Thermidor sauce, while local crab comes
with smoked salmon, avocado, apple and
fennel.

🛏 Marine Hotel   Inn £££

(☎01947-605022; www.the-marine-hotel.
co.uk; 13 Marine Pde; r £100-195; 📶) Feeling
more like mini-suites than ordinary hotel
accommodation, the four bedrooms at the
Marine are quirky, stylish and comfortable; it's
the sort of place that makes you want to stay in
rather than go out. Ask for one of the two rooms
with a balcony – they have great views across
the harbour.

The Marine offers another three top-value
rooms a few doors along at its sister restaurant,
the **Moon & Sixpence** (☎01947-604416;
www.moon-and-sixpence.co.uk; 5 Marine Pde;
mains £9-18; ⏱9am-midnight; 📶) – room 5 is
huge, with sofa, double shower and Jacuzzi.

Robin Hood's Bay ❼

✖ Swell Cafe   Cafe £

(www.swell.org.uk; Chapel St; mains £3-8;
⏱9.30am-3.30pm Mon-Fri, to 4pm Sat &
Sun; 📶 👶) Great coffee, soup, salads and
sandwiches, and a terrace with a view over the
beach.

Scarborough ❽

🛏 Windmill   B&B ££

(☎01723-372735; www.scarborough-windmill.
co.uk; Mill St; d from £85; 🅿 📶) Quirky doesn't
begin to describe this place, a beautifully
converted 18th-century windmill in the middle
of town. There are two self-catering cottages
and three four-poster doubles around a cobbled
courtyard, but try to secure the balcony suite
(from £110 a night) in the upper floors of the
windmill itself, with great views from the wrap-
around balcony.

Hadrian's Wall

22

Follow in the Romans' mighty footsteps as you trace the length of this enormous wall, built between AD 122 and 128 to separate the Romans and Scottish Picts.

TRIP HIGHLIGHTS

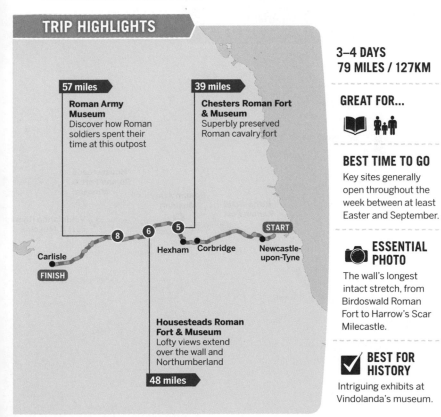

57 miles

Roman Army Museum
Discover how Roman soldiers spent their time at this outpost

39 miles

Chesters Roman Fort & Museum
Superbly preserved Roman cavalry fort

Housesteads Roman Fort & Museum
Lofty views extend over the wall and Northumberland

48 miles

3–4 DAYS
79 MILES / 127KM

GREAT FOR...

BEST TIME TO GO
Key sites generally open throughout the week between at least Easter and September.

ESSENTIAL PHOTO
The wall's longest intact stretch, from Birdoswald Roman Fort to Harrow's Scar Milecastle.

BEST FOR HISTORY
Intriguing exhibits at Vindolanda's museum.

Hadrian's Wall Sunset viewed from Walltown Crags

22 Hadrian's Wall

Traversing the island's narrow neck, you'll encounter this incredible feat of engineering firsthand. Every Roman mile (0.95 miles) had a gateway guarded by a small fort (milecastle), with two observation turrets between them. A series of southern forts (which may predate the wall) were developed as bases, and 16 lie astride it. Preserved remains and intriguing museums punctuate the route, along with remnants of the wall you can freely access.

❶ Newcastle-upon-Tyne

Against its dramatic backdrop of Victorian elegance and industrial grit, this fiercely independent city harbours a spirited mix of heritage and urban sophistication, with excellent art galleries, exceptional restaurants and, of course, interesting bars: Newcastle-upon-Tyne is renowned throughout Britain for its thumping nightlife, bolstered by an energetic, 42,000-strong student population.

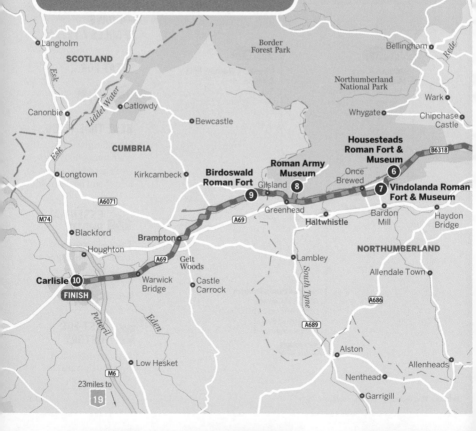

Newcastle is an ideal place for a debrief on the area's Roman legacies. The **Discovery Museum** (https://discoverymuseum.org.uk; Blandford Sq; ⊙10am-4pm), housed in the vast former Co-operative Wholesale Society building, has displays on Pons Aelius (Roman Newcastle) as well as every subsequent era throughout the city's history.

At the **Great North Museum** (☎0191-208 6765; https://greatnorthmuseum.org.uk; Barras Bridge; general admission free, planetarium adult/child £2.50/1.50;

⊙10am-5pm Mon-Fri, to 4pm Sat, 11am-4pm Sun), a fantastic interactive model of Hadrian's Wall shows every milecastle and fortress.

✕ ⊨ p85, p279, p289

The Drive » Take the A193 and A187 for 5 miles east to Segedunum.

❷ Segedunum

The last strong post of Hadrian's Wall was the fort of **Segedunum**

LINK YOUR TRIP

19 Classic Lakes
It's 43 miles south from Carlisle, via the M6 and A592, to Ullswater, where you can take the picturesque Classic Lakes drive in reverse.

23 Northumbria
Newcastle-upon-Tyne is also the starting point for a spectacular journey along the Northumberland coast to the Scottish border.

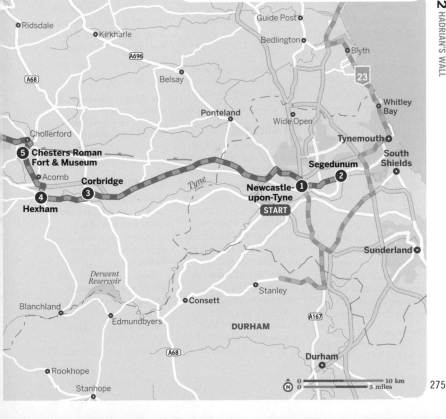

✓ TOP TIP: NEED TO KNOW

Tourist offices are located in the following places.

Hexham (📞01670-620450; www.visitnorthumberland.com/hexham; Queen's Hall, Beaumont St; ⏰10am-5pm Mon-Fri, to 4pm Sat)

Haltwhistle (📞01434-321863; www.visitnorthumberland.com; Mechanics Institute, Westgate; ⏰10am-4.30pm Mon-Fri, to 1pm Sat Apr-Oct, 10am-1pm & 1.30-4.30pm Mon-Fri, 10am-1pm Sat Nov-Mar)

Corbridge (📞01434-632815; www.visitnorthumberland.com; Hill St; ⏰10am-4.30pm Mon-Sat Easter-Oct, closed Nov-Mar)

Walltown Visitor Centre (Northumberland National Park Visitor Centre; 📞01697-747151; www.northumberlandnationalpark.org.uk; Greenhead; ⏰10am-6pm Apr-Sep, to 5pm Oct, 10am-4pm Sat & Sun Nov-Mar) Located in Greenhead.

Hadrian's Wall Country (http://hadrianswallcountry.co.uk) The official portal for the entire area.

Parking costs £4/15 per day/week; tickets are valid at all sites along the wall.

(📞0191-278 4217; http://segedunumromanfort.org.uk; Buddle St, Wallsend; adult/child £5.95/free; ⏰10am-5pm Jun–mid-Sep, 10am-4pm Easter-May & mid-Sep–early Nov, 10am-2.30pm Mon-Fri early Nov–Easter), at the 'wall's end', now the Newcastle suburb of Wallsend. Beneath the 35m-high tower, which you can climb for terrific views, is an absorbing site that includes a reconstructed Roman bathhouse (with steaming pools and frescoes) and a museum offering a fascinating insight into life during Roman times.

The Drive ≫ Hop on the A167 ring road and head west on the A69. You'll soon enter a patchwork of farmland. After 19 miles, take the B6530 into Corbridge (23 miles in total).

— — — — — — — — — —

❸ Corbridge

Above a green-banked curve in the Tyne, Corbridge's shady, cobbled streets are lined with old-fashioned shops and pubs. Inhabited since Saxon times when there was a substantial monastery, many of its charming buildings feature stones nicked from the nearby Roman garrison town of Corstopitum.

What's left of Corstopitum lies about half a mile west of Market Pl on Dere St, once the main road from York to Scotland. Now preserved as the **Corbridge Roman Site & Museum** (EH; www.english-heritage.org.uk; Corchester Lane; adult/child £6.10/3.70; ⏰10am-6pm Easter-Sep, to 5pm Oct, 10am-4pm Sat & Sun Nov-Easter), it's the oldest fortified site in the area, predating the wall itself by some 40 years. Most of what you see here though dates from around AD 200, when the fort had developed into a civilian settlement and was the main base along the wall. You get a sense of the domestic heart of the town from the visible remains. The museum displays Roman sculpture and carvings, including the amazing 3rd-century Corbridge Lion.

🗡 🛏 p279

The Drive ≫ From Corbridge, set out southwest on the B6321. Cross the River Tyne and follow the road into Hexham (4.3 miles all up).

— — — — — — — — — —

❹ Hexham

Bustling Hexham's cobbled alleyways have more shops and amenities than any other wall town between Carlisle and Newcastle.

Dominating tiny Market Pl, stately **Hexham Abbey** (www.hexhamabbey.org.uk; Beaumont St; suggested donation £3; ⏰9.30am-5pm, Saxon crypt 11am & 3.30pm) is a marvellous example of Early English architecture. It cleverly escaped the Dissolution of 1537 by rebranding as Hexham's parish church, a role it still has today. The highlight is the 7th-century Saxon crypt, the only surviving element of St Wilifrid's Church, built with inscribed stones from Corstopitum in 674.

Nearby is the **Old Gaol** (www.hexhamoldgaol. org.uk; Hallgate; adult/child £3.95/2.50; ⊙11am-4.30pm Mon-Sat Aug, 11am-4.30pm Tue-Sat Apr-Jul & Sep, 11am-4.30pm Tue & Sat Oct, Nov, Feb & Mar, closed Dec). Completed in 1333 as England's first purpose-built prison, today it presents the jail's history in all its gruesome glory. The story of the Border Reivers – a group of clans who fought, kidnapped, blackmailed and killed each other in an effort to exercise control over a lawless tract of land along the Anglo-Scottish border throughout the 16th century – is also recounted, along with tales of the punishments handed out in the prison.

🛏 p279

The Drive ›› From the River Tyne's northern bank, take the A69 west for just under a mile. Turn northwest onto the A6079 and cross the single-lane stone bridge over the North Tyne to the village of Chollerford. Turn left (west) on to the B6318; Chesters Roman Fort & Museum is half a mile ahead on your left (6.8 miles altogether).

TRIP HIGHLIGHT

❺ Chesters Roman Fort & Museum

Now the **Chesters Roman Fort & Museum** (EH; ☎01434-681379; www. english-heritage.org.uk; Chollerford; adult/child £6.20/3.70; ⊙10am-6pm Easter-Sep, to 5pm Oct, 10am-4pm Sat & Sun Nov-Easter), this Roman cavalry fort's superbly preserved remains are set among idyllic green woods and meadows. Originally constructed to house up to 500 troops from Asturias in northern Spain, they include part of a bridge (best appreciated from the eastern bank), four gatehouses, a bathhouse and an underfloor heating system. The museum has a large Roman sculpture collection.

The Drive ›› Head west on the B6318 uphill to Housesteads Roman Fort & Museum (9 miles in total). Keep a lookout for crumbling remains of the wall.

TRIP HIGHLIGHT

❻ Housesteads Roman Fort & Museum

Hadrian's Wall's most dramatic site – and the best-preserved Roman fort in the whole country – is the **Housesteads Roman Fort & Museum** (EH; www.english-heritage.org. uk; Haydon Bridge; adult/child £7/4.10; ⊙10am-6pm Easter-Sep, to 5pm Oct, to 4pm Nov-Easter), set high on a ridge and covering 5 acres.

From here you can survey the moors of Northumberland National Park, and the snaking wall, with a sense of awe at the landscape and the aura of the Roman lookouts.

Up to 800 troops were based at Housesteads at any one time. Its remains include an impressive hospital, granaries with a carefully worked out ventilation system, and barrack blocks. Most memorable are the spectacularly situated communal flushable latrines. Information boards show what the individual buildings would have looked like in their heyday. There's a scale model of the entire fort in the small museum at the ticket office.

The Drive ›› It's a short, well-signposted 2-mile hop southwest from here to Vindolanda.

❼ Vindolanda

The extensive site of **Vindolanda** (www.vindolanda.com; Bardon Mill; adult/child £6.07/3.86, with Roman Army Museum £9.55/5.50; ⊙10am-6pm Apr-Sep, to 5pm Oct, to 4pm Nov-Mar) offers a fascinating glimpse into the daily life of a Roman garrison town. The time-capsule museum is just one part of this large, extensively excavated site, which includes impressive parts of the fort and town (excavations continue) and reconstructed turrets and temple.

Highlights of the Vindolanda museum displays include leather sandals, signature Roman helmet decorations, and numerous writing tablets recently returned from the British Library. These include a student's marked work ('sloppy'), and a parent's note with a present of socks and underpants (things haven't changed – in this climate you can never have too many).

The Drive » Rejoin the B6318 at the small hamlet of Once Brewed and turn west. Below you to the south you'll see the village of Haltwhistle – one of the places that claims to be the geographic centre of the British mainland, although the jury is still out. The Roman Army Museum is ahead on your right (7 miles all up).

TRIP HIGHLIGHT

❽ Roman Army Museum

On the site of the Carvoran Roman Fort, the revamped **Roman Army Museum** (www.vindolanda. com; Greenhead; adult/child £5/2.95, with Vindolanda £9.55/5.50; ☺10am-6pm Apr-Sep, to 5pm Oct, 10am-4pm Sat & Sun Nov-Mar) has three galleries covering the Roman army and expanding and contracting empire; the wall; and colourful background detail to Hadrian's Wall life (such as how the soldiers spent their R&R time in this lonely outpost of the empire).

The Drive » It's 4.7 miles to the Birdoswald Roman

Fort. Continue along the B6318 through the hamlets of Greenhead and Gilsland, crossing the River Irthing; Birdoswald is on your left.

❾ Birdoswald Roman Fort

The remains of the once-formidable **Birdoswald Roman Fort** (EH; ☎01697-747602; www.english-heritage.org.uk; Gilsland, Greenhead; adult/child £6.10/3.70; ☺10am-6pm Apr-Sep, to 5pm Oct, 10am-4pm Sat & Sun Nov-Mar) are set on an escarpment overlooking the beautiful Irthing Gorge. The longest intact stretch of wall extends from here to Harrow's Scar Milecastle.

The Drive » Head southwest to the small village of Lanercost, where you'll see the raspberry-coloured ruins of the Lanercost Priory, before crossing the River Irthing and entering the town of Brampton. Continue west on the A689 to Carlisle (17 miles all up).

❿ Carlisle

Carlisle has history and heritage aplenty. Precariously perched on the frontier between England and Scotland, in the area once ominously dubbed the 'Debatable Lands', it's a city with a notoriously stormy past: sacked by the Vikings, pillaged by the Scots, and plundered by the Border Reivers, the city has been on the frontline of England's defences for more than 1000 years.

Reminders of the past are evident in the great crimson **Carlisle Castle** (EH; ☎01228-591922; http://www.english-heritage.org.uk/visit/places/carlisle-castle/; Castle Way; adult/child £6.40/3.80, joint ticket with Cumbria's Museum of Military Life £9.20/5.15; ☺10am-5pm Apr-Sep, 10am-4pm Oct-Mar) and **Carlisle Cathedral** (☎01228-548151; www.carlislecathedral.org.uk; 7 The Abbey; suggested donation £5, photography £1; ☺7.30am-6.15pm Mon-Sat, to 5pm Sun), built from the same rosy-red sandstone as most of the city's houses. On English St are two massive circular towers that once flanked the city's gateway.

Carlisle's **Tullie House Museum** (☎01228-618718; www.tulliehouse.co.uk; Castle St; adult/child £7.70/free; ☺10am-5pm Mon-Sat, 11am-5pm Sun) covers the city's past, from its Roman foundations onwards. The highlight is the Roman Frontier Gallery, which uses a mix of archaeological exhibits and interactive displays to tell the story of the Roman occupation of Carlisle. The Border Galleries cover the rest of the city's history, from the Bronze Age through to the Border Reivers, the Jacobite Rebellion and the Industrial Revolution. There's an awesome view of the castle from the rooftop lookout.

✕ ⌂ p279

Eating & Sleeping

Newcastle-upon-Tyne ❶

✗ Hop & Cleaver — Gastropub ££

(☎0191-261 1037; www.hopandcleaver.com; 44 Sandhill; mains £9-18; ☺kitchen noon-9pm Sun-Thu, to 10pm Fri & Sat, bar 11am-1am) Inside the magnificent Jacobean **Bessie Surtees House**, this hip spot is great for a drink (it brews its own small-batch craft beers) but the food (including house-smoked meats) is equally brilliant: smoky brisket with apple-and-onion fritters; 12-hour cooked pulled pork with homemade slaw and BBQ sauce; charred, Bourbon-marinated ribs; beer-steamed and roasted chicken. Veggie options exist but are limited.

⊨ Jesmond Dene House — Hotel £££

(☎0191-212 3000; http://jesmonddenehouse. co.uk; Jesmond Dene Rd; s/d/ste from £109/119/169; P❋@🖰) Large, gorgeous bedrooms at this exquisite property are furnished in a modern interpretation of the Arts and Crafts style and have stunning bathrooms complete with underfloor heating, as well as the latest tech. The fine-dining **restaurant** (mains £16-36, 2-/3-course lunch menus £19.50/22; ☺7-10am, noon-5pm & 7-9pm Mon-Thu, 7-10am, noon-5pm & 7-9.30pm Fri, 7.30-10.30am, noon-5pm & 7-9.30pm Sat, 7.30-10.30am & 7-9pm Sun) is sublime.

Corbridge ❸

✗ Corbridge Larder — Deli, Cafe £

(☎01434-632 948; www.corbridgelarder. co.uk; 18 Hill St; dishes £4-7, dinner mains £10; ☺9am-5pm Mon-Fri, 9am-5pm & 6.30-10.30pm Sat, 10am-4pm Sun) Gourmet picnic fare at this fabulous deli includes bread, over 100 varieties of cheese, chutneys, cakes, chocolates and wine (you can get hampers made up) as well as made-to-order sandwiches, pies, quiches, tarts, and antipasti and meze delicacies. Upstairs from the wonderland of provisions there's a small sit-down cafe. On Saturday evenings it hosts dinners accompanied by live music.

⊨ 2 The Crofts — B&B ££

(☎01434-633046; www.2thecrofts.co.uk; Newcastle Rd; s/d from £55/75; P🖰) By far the best place in town to drop your pack, this secluded B&B occupies a beautiful period home half-a-mile east of the town centre. The two high-ceilinged, spacious rooms are en suite and the energetic owner cooks a mean breakfast (packed lunches can also be organised). Guests are welcome to play the piano.

Hexham ❹

⊨ Hallbank Guest House — B&B ££

(☎01434-605567; www.hallbankguesthouse. com; Hallgate; d/f from £120/130; P🖰) Behind the Old Gaol, this fine Edwardian house combines period elegance with stylishly furnished rooms with patterned wallpaper, autumnal colours and huge beds. Evening meals can be arranged on request. It's very popular so book ahead.

Carlisle ❿

✗ Hell Below & Co — Fusion £

(☎01228-548481; www.hellbelowandco.co.uk; 14 Devonshire St; mains £8-9.50; ☺11am-midnight Mon-Sat) A new menu has given this trendy brick-walled, bare-wood bar-bistro a fresh lease of life: it spans the gamut from cheese and charcuterie sharing boards to steaks, fajitas and flat-iron chicken. If you're not hungry, inventive cocktails like bubblegum sours and starburst cosmos are served.

⊨ Willowbeck Lodge — B&B ££

(☎01228-513607; www.willowbeck-lodge.com; Lambley Bank, Scotby; d £100-130; P🖰) If staying in the city centre isn't important, then this palatial B&B is the top choice in the city. The four rooms are huge, contemporary and plush, with luxuries like underfloor heating, Egyptian cotton bedding and tasteful shades of beige and taupe. Some rooms have balconies overlooking the gardens and pond. There's also a restaurant, **Fini's Kitchen** (mains £14 to £22).

Northumbria

23

This drive along northeast England's unspoilt coastline runs through the historic medieval kingdom of Northumbria, taking in long, desolate beaches, wind-worn castles and magical islands.

TRIP HIGHLIGHTS

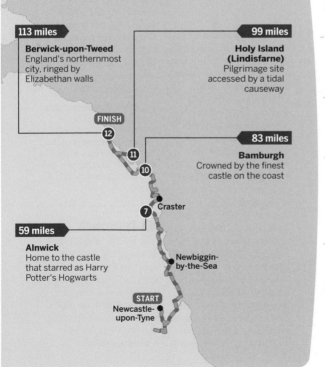

113 miles

Berwick-upon-Tweed
England's northernmost city, ringed by Elizabethan walls

99 miles

Holy Island (Lindisfarne)
Pilgrimage site accessed by a tidal causeway

FINISH
⑫
⑪
⑩

83 miles

Bamburgh
Crowned by the finest castle on the coast

⑦ Craster

59 miles

Alnwick
Home to the castle that starred as Harry Potter's Hogwarts

Newbiggin-by-the-Sea

START
Newcastle-upon-Tyne

3–4 DAYS
113 MILES / 182KM

GREAT FOR...

BEST TIME TO GO
Birdwatching is best from March to July.

 ESSENTIAL PHOTO

Ethereal priory ruins on Holy Island (Lindisfarne).

☑ BEST FOR HISTORY

Warkworth's castle and boat-accessed hermitage.

23 | Northumbria

Newcastle is renowned for its cultural and hedonistic pursuits, but once you hit the open road the pace drops down several gears. Wild and remote, this area is sparsely populated: charming, castle-crowned villages are strung along miles of wide, sandy beaches that you might just have to yourself. Along the route you'll encounter incredible birdlife and fresh-as-it-gets seafood hauled in at traditional fishing ports.

① Newcastle

The vibrant city of Newcastle is famed for its nightlife, but there's plenty to see by day too, including museums showcasing its Roman heritage.

Newcastle Castle
(☏0191-230 6300; www. newcastlecastle.co.uk; Castle Garth; adult/child £6.50/3.90; ⊙10am-5pm) – the stronghold that put both the 'new' and 'castle' into Newcastle – has been largely swallowed up by the train station, leaving only a few remaining fragments including the square Norman keep and the Black Gate. Exhibits cover the history of the city, its castle and its residents from Roman times onwards. The 360-degree city views from the keep's rooftop are superb.

Walking Newcastle's streets, you'd never know the extraordinary **Victoria Tunnel** (☏0191-261 6596; www.ouseburntrust. org.uk; Arch 6, Stepney Bank; tours adult/child £6/4; ⊙by reservation) runs for 2.5 miles beneath your feet. Built between 1839 and 1842 as a coal-wagon thoroughfare, it was used as an air-raid shelter during WWII. Volunteer-led, two-hour tours take you through an atmospheric 700m-long level section. Book ahead as numbers are limited, and wear good shoes and a washable jacket for the limewashed walls.

✕ ⊨ p85, p279, p289

The Drive ›› Cross the Tyne Bridge (which closely resembles the Sydney Harbour Bridge – both were built by the same company around the same time) and take the A167 south through Gateshead for 6.5 miles to the Angel of the North. There's a free car park by the base.

② Angel of the North

Nicknamed the Gateshead Flasher, the **Angel of the North** (Durham Rd, Low Eighton) – an extraordinary 200-tonne, rust-coloured, winged human frame – has loomed over the A1 (M) motorway since 1998. Sir Antony Gormley's iconic work (which saw him knighted in 2014) stands 20m high, with a wingspan wider than a Boeing 767.

The Drive ›› Head southeast on the A1 to pick up the northbound A194 and pass under the River Tyne through the Tyne Tunnel (one-way toll £1.70). After you resurface, take the A193 to Tynemouth (14 miles in total).

③ Tynemouth

The mouth of the Tyne is one of the best surf spots in England, with great all-year breaks off the immense, crescent-shaped Blue Flag beach, which occasionally hosts the National Surfing Championships.

For all your surfing needs, call into the **Tynemouth Surf Company** (☎0191-258 2496; www.tynemouthsurf.co.uk; Grand Pde; ☉10am-5.30pm), which also provides two-hour group lessons for £25 per person at 2pm daily (when the surf's up) from March to October. The adjoining chilled surf cafe morphs into a cool bar and live-music venue at night.

Built by Benedictine monks on a strategic bluff above the Tyne mouth in the 11th-century ruins, **Tynemouth Priory** (EH; www.english-heritage.org.uk; Pier Rd; adult/child £5.20/3.10; ☉10am-6pm Apr-Sep, to 5pm Oct, 10am-4pm Sat & Sun Nov-Mar) was ransacked during the Dissolution in 1539. The military took over for four centuries, only leaving in 1960, and today the skeletal

§ LINK YOUR TRIP

22 **Hadrian's Wall**
Newcastle is also the jumping-off point for an unforgettable drive through Roman history along Hadrian's Wall.

29 **The Borders**
From this trip's final stop, Berwick-upon-Tweed, it's 24 miles southwest to Kelso to drive the Scottish Borders trip in reverse.

LAKE DISTRICT & NORTHERN ENGLAND **23** NORTHUMBRIA

remains of the priory church sit alongside old military installations, their guns aimed out to sea at an enemy that never came.

Opposite the priory, village-like Front St runs inland from the ocean and is lined with restaurants, cafes and arty shops.

🛏 p289

The Drive » Drive north along the coast to the town of Blyth and join the northbound A189 to Newbiggin-by-the-Sea (16.3 miles altogether).

---

④ Newbiggin-by-the-Sea

Rising above the North Sea 300m offshore from Newbiggin's North Beach, British sculptor Sean Henry's immense 2007 bronze creation **The Couple** (North Beach, Newbiggin-by-the-Sea), measuring 12m high by 20m wide, depicts a man and woman standing on a pier-like structure looking out to sea. Its installation was part of a major regeneration of the surrounding area, which included shifting 500,000 tonnes of sand to the beach here in an effort to prevent erosion.

The Drive » Rejoin the A189 and head northwest to pick up the northbound A1068 through patchworked farmland to Amble (a 13-mile trip).

---

⑤ Amble

The fishing port of Amble has a boardwalk along the seafront and is the departure point for **Dave Gray's Puffin Cruises** (📞01665-711975; www.puffin cruises.co.uk; Amble Harbour, Amble; adult/child £8/4; 🕐by reservation May-Oct). An ex–Royal Navy lifeboat that saved over 132 lives in its years of service now takes birdwatchers on one-hour cruises sailing around Coquet Island (no landing), where you can see some of the 20,000 puffins that nest here each March, as well as other bird species including Eider ducks, kittiwakes and rare Roseate terns, and the island's grey seal colony.

For eight days from late May to early June, Amble celebrates the hatching of puffin chicks on Coquet Island in town during the **Amble Puffin Festival** (http://amblepuffinfest.co.uk), with events including local history talks, guided birdwatching walks, exhibitions, water sports, a craft fair, a food festival and live music as well as a daily teddy bear parachute drop.

The Drive » It's just 1.7 miles north along the River Coquet to Warkworth.

---

⑥ Warkworth

Warkworth's huddle of houses cluster around a loop in the River Coquet,
dominated by the craggy ruin of 14th-century **Warkworth Castle** (EH; www.english-heritage.org.uk; Castle Tce, Warworth; adult/child £5.80/3.40; 🕐castle 10am-6pm Easter-Aug, to 5pm Sep & Oct, 10am-4pm Sat & Sun Nov-Easter, Duke's Rooms Sun, Mon & bank holidays Apr-Sep). Looking like the ultimate sandcastle you'd see at the beach, this honey-stone edifice atop a hillock was built around 1200. From the 14th to 17th centuries, it was home to the Percy family (whose descendants still live at Alnwick Castle), and was pivotal in the War of the Roses and the English Civil War. It became a national monument in 1915 but the Duke's Rooms remained under the family's control until 1987.

Half-a-mile's walk west of Warkworth Castle (there's no car access), the tiny, magical 14th-century chapel **Warworth Hermitage** (EH; www.english-heritage.org.uk; Castle Tce, Warkworth; adult/child £4/2.30; 🕐11am-4pm Easter-Oct) is carved into the rock on the northern bank of the River Coquet. It's accessed by a short boat ride (included in admission); ring the brass bell and the ferryman will row you across. Dappled sunlight illuminates the moss-covered ruin's interior. Look for the stone-carved nativity scene in the window.

GRAHAM LAYCOCK / 500PX ©

Holy Island (Lindisfarne) Accessible only at low tide

The Drive » Continue northwest on the A1068. On your right you'll see the pastel-shaded estuary town of Alnmouth. It's a total of 7.6 miles from Warkworth to Alnwick.

`TRIP HIGHLIGHT`

❼ Alnwick

Northumberland's historic ducal town, Alnwick (pronounced 'annick') is an elegant maze of narrow cobbled streets beneath the colossal medieval **Alnwick Castle** (www.alnwickcastle. com; The Peth; adult/child £14.95/7.75, with Alnwick Garden £25.60/10.90; ☉10am-5.30pm Easter-Oct). The imposing ancestral home of the Duke of Northumberland has changed little since the 14th century. It's a favourite set for filmmakers and starred as Hogwarts for the first couple of Harry Potter films. Various free tours include several focusing on Harry Potter and other productions that have used the castle as a backdrop, including British comedy series *Blackadder*. For the best views of the castle's exterior, take The Peth to the River Aln's northern bank and follow the woodland trail east.

Nearby is spectacular **Alnwick Garden** (www. alnwickgarden.com; Denwick Lane; adult/child £12.10/4.40, with Alnwick Castle £25.60/10.90; ☉10am-6pm Easter-Oct, to 4pm Nov-Easter). This 11.8-acre walled beauty incorporates a series of magnificent green spaces surrounding the breathtaking Grand Cascade – 120 separate jets spurting some 30,000L of water down 21 weirs.

If you're familiar with the renaissance of the WWII 'Keep Calm and Carry On' slogan, it's

↱ DETOUR:
CHILLINGHAM CASTLE

Start: ❼ Alnwick (p285)

Steeped in history, warfare, torture and ghosts, 12th-century **Chillingham Castle** (☎01668-215359; www.chillingham-castle.com; Chillingham; castle adult/child £9.50/5.50, Chillingham Wild Cattle only £8/3, castle & Chillingham Wild Cattle £16/6; ⊗castle noon-5pm Sun-Fri Apr-Oct, Chillingham Wild Cattle tours 10am, 11am, noon, 2pm, 3pm & 4pm Mon-Fri, 10am, 11am & noon Sun Easter to Oct, by reservation Nov-Easter) is said to be one of the country's most haunted places, with spectres from a phantom funeral to Lady Mary Berkeley seeking her errant husband. Owner Sir Humphrey Wakefield has passionately restored the castle's extravagant medieval staterooms, stone-flagged banquet halls and grisly torture chambers. It's possible to stay at the medieval fortress in one of eight self-catering apartments where the likes of Henry III and Edward I once snoozed. Doubles start from £130.

The grounds are home to some 100 Chillingham Wild Cattle, thought to be the last descendants of the aurochs that once roamed Britain until becoming all but extinct during the Bronze Age, making them one of the world's rarest breeds of any species. Tours lasting one hour are led by a park warden; wear sturdy shoes.

From Alnwick, it's a 14-mile journey: take the B6346 northwest through forest and farmland to Chillingham.

thanks to the wonderfully atmospheric second-hand bookshop **Barter Books** (☎01665-604888; www.barterbooks.co.uk; Alnwick Station, Wagon Way Rd; ⊗9am-7pm) in Alnwick's Victorian former railway station. While converting the station, the owner came across a set of posters – the framed original is above the till – and turned it into a successful industry. Coal fires, velvet ottomans, reading rooms and a cafe make this a place you could spend days in, the silence interrupted only by the tiny rumble of the toy train that runs along the track above your head.

🛏 p289

The Drive » Head northeast through rolling farmland and hidden glens to the little seaside village of Craster (7.3 miles in total), where you'll see fishing boats moored in the harbour and the ruins of Dunstanburgh Castle beyond.

- - - - - - - - - - - - -

❽ Craster

Sandy, salty Craster is a small, sheltered fishing village that's famous for its kippers. In the early 20th century, 2500 herring were smoked here daily. The kippers still produced today by **Robson & Sons** (☎01665-576223; www.kipper.co.uk; Haven Hill; kippers per kilo from £9; ⊗9am-4.30pm Mon-Sat, 10am-4pm Sun) often grace the Queen's breakfast table. Four generations

have operated this traditional fish smokers. It's best known for its kippers, but also smokes salmon and other fish.

The dramatic 1.5-mile walk along the coast from Craster (not accessible by car) is the most scenic path to moody, weather-beaten **Dunstanburgh Castle** (EH; www.english-heritage.org. uk; Dunstanburgh Rd; adult/child £5.20/3.10; ⊗10am-6pm Easter-Sep, to 4pm Oct, 10am-4pm Sat & Sun Nov-Easter). Its construction began in 1314 and it was strengthened during the Wars of the Roses, but then left to crumble, becoming ruined by 1550. Parts of the original wall and gatehouse keep are still standing and it's a tribute to its builders that so much remains.

✄ p289

The Drive » This section of the drive skirts the edge of beautiful Embleton Bay, a pale wide arc of sand that stretches from Dunstanburgh past the endearing, sloping village of Embleton and curves in a broad vanilla-coloured strand around to end at Low Newton-by-the-Sea. En route, several side roads lead down to the water. From Craster, it's a 5.9-mile journey.

9 Low Newton-by-the-Sea

This tiny whitewashed, National Trust–preserved village centres on its village green adjoining the brewery-pub the **Ship Inn** (☎01665-576262; www.shipinnnewton.co.uk; Low Newton-by-the-Sea; mains £8.50-18; ☺kitchen noon-2.30pm & 7-8pm Wed-Sat, noon-2.30pm Sun-Tue, bar 11am-11pm Mon-Sat, 11am-10pm Sun Apr-Oct, reduced hours Nov-Mar).

Behind the bay is a path leading to the Newton Pool Nature Reserve, an important spot for breeding and migrating birds such as black-headed gulls and grasshopper warblers. There are a couple of hides where you can peer out at them. You can continue walking along the headland beyond Low Newton, where you'll find Football Hole, a delightful hidden beach between headlands.

The Drive » Bamburgh is just 11 miles north of Low Newton-by-the-Sea via the small villages of Beadnell and Seahouses (the departure point for the Farne Islands). Between Beadnell and Seahouses you'll have a sweeping view of the white-sand beach on your right; after Seahouses, the dunes rise up between the road and the shore.

TRIP HIGHLIGHT

10 Bamburgh

High up on a basalt crag, Northumberland's most dramatic castle looms over the quaint village's clutch of houses centred around a pleasant green.

Bamburgh Castle

(www.bamburghcastle.com; Links Rd; adult/child £10.75/5; ☺10am-5pm mid-Feb–Oct, 11am-4.30pm Sat & Sun Nov–mid-Feb) was built around a powerful 11th-century Norman keep by Henry II. The castle played a key role in the border wars of the 13th and 14th centuries, and in 1464 was the first English castle to fall during the Wars of the Roses. It was restored in the 19th century by the great industrialist Lord Armstrong, and is still home to the Armstrong family. Its name is a derivative

FARNE ISLANDS

The otherwise unmemorable village of Seahouses, between Low Newton-by-the-Sea and Bamburgh, is the jumping-off point for the **Farne Islands** (NT; www.nationaltrust.org.uk; adult/child excl boat transport £5.75/2.90; ☺by reservation, season & conditions permitting Apr-Oct).

During breeding season (roughly May to July) you can see feeding chicks of 20 seabird species (including puffin, kittiwake, Arctic tern, eider duck, cormorant and gull), and some 6000 grey seals, on this rocky archipelago 3 miles offshore. Four boat operators, contactable through **Seahouses' tourist office** (☎01670-625593; http://visitnorthumberland.com; Seafield car park, Seahouses; ☺10am-4.30pm Easter-Oct), depart from Seahouses' dock, including **Billy Shiel** (☎01665-720308; www.farne-islands.com; adult/child 2½hr tour £15/10, 6hr tour £35/20).

Crossings can be rough (impossible in bad weather); wear warm, waterproof clothing and an old hat to guard against the birds!

Inner Farne is the more interesting of the two islands accessible to the public (along with Staple Island); its tiny chapel (1370; restored 1848) commemorates St Cuthbert, who lived here for a spell and died here in 687.

of Bebbanburgh, after the wife of Anglo-Saxon ruler Aedelfrip, whose fortified home occupied this basalt outcrop 500 years earlier. Antique furniture, suits of armour, priceless ceramics and artworks cram the castle's rooms and chambers, but top billing goes to the neo-Gothic King's Hall with wood panelling, leaded windows and hefty beams supporting the roof.

✖ p289

The Drive » It's 16 miles to Holy Island (Lindisfarne). Check tide times at www.holy-island.info – the island is only accessible at low tide. You must park in the signposted car park (£4.60 per day). A shuttle bus (£2 return) runs from the car park to the castle every 20 minutes from Easter to September; alternatively, it's a level 300m walk to the village.

TRIP HIGHLIGHT

⓫ Holy Island (Lindisfarne)

There's something almost otherworldly about this tiny, 2-sq-mile island. Connected to the mainland by a narrow causeway that only appears at low tide, and cut off from the mainland for about five hours each day, it's fiercely desolate and isolated, scarcely different from when St Aidan arrived to found a monastery in 635.

As you cross the empty flats, it's easy to imagine the marauding Vikings who repeatedly sacked the settlement between 793 and 875, when the monks finally took the hint and left. They carried with them the illuminated Lindisfarne Gospels (now in the British Library in London) and the miraculously preserved body of St Cuthbert, who lived here for a couple of years.

The skeletal, red-and-grey ruins of **Lindisfarne Priory** (EH; www.english-heritage.org.uk; adult/child £6/3.60; ☉10am-6pm Apr-Sep, to 5pm Oct, 10am-4pm Sat & Sun Nov-Mar) are an eerie sight and give a glimpse into the isolated life of the Lindisfarne monks. The later 13th-century St Mary the Virgin Church is built on the site of the first church between the Tees and the Firth of Forth, and the adjacent museum displays the remains of the first monastery and tells the story of the monastic community before and after the Dissolution.

Built atop a rocky bluff in 1550, tiny **Lindisfarne Castle** (NT; www.nationaltrust.org.uk; adult/child £7.30/3.60; ☉10am-3pm Tue-Sun mid-Feb–Oct & some weekends Nov-mid-Feb) was extended and converted by Sir Edwin Lutyens from 1902 to 1910 for Mr

Hudson, the owner of *Country Life* magazine – you can imagine some of the decadent Gatsby-style parties to have graced its alluring rooms.

🛏 p289

The Drive » Again, check tide times before leaving the island. Every year drivers are caught midway by the incoming tide and have to abandon their cars. From the island, it's 14 miles north to beautiful Berwick-upon-Tweed.

TRIP HIGHLIGHT

⓬ Berwick-upon-Tweed

England's northernmost city is a picturesque fortress town, cleaved by the River Tweed, spanned by historic bridges. Between 1174 and 1482 this fought-over settlement changed hands 14 times between the Scots and the English.

Only a small fragment remains of the once-mighty border castle but you can walk almost the entire length of Berwick's hefty Elizabethan **walls** (EH; www.english-heritage.org.uk; ☉dawn-dusk), begun in 1558 to reinforce an earlier set built during the reign of Edward II. The mile-long walk is a must, with wonderful, wide-open views.

🛏 p289

Eating & Sleeping

Newcastle-upon-Tyne ❶

🍴 Grey Street Hotel   Boutique Hotel ££
(📞0191-230 6777; www.greystreethotel.
co.uk; 2-12 Grey St; d from £70; ❊ 🛜) On the
classiest street in the city centre, this beautiful
Grade II–listed building has been adapted for
contemporary needs, including triple-glazing on
the sash windows. Individually designed rooms
have big beds and handsome modern furnishings.

Tynemouth ❸

🍴 Grand Hotel   Heritage Hotel £££
(📞0191-293 6666; www.grandhotel-uk.
com; Grand Pde; incl breakfast d £96-199,
f £156-196) Many of the 46 rooms at this
landmark 1872-built hotel (the one-time
summer residence of the Duke and Duchess
of Northumberland) and neighbouring town
house overlook the beach, and some have four-
poster beds and spa baths, though wi-fi's only
reliable in public areas. Its Victorian-style bar,
drawing room serving high tea, and fine-dining
restaurant (mains £12 to £22) are excellent.

Alnwick ❼

🍴 White Swan Hotel   Hotel ££
(📞01665-602109; www.classiclodges.co.uk;
Bondgate Within; d/f from £115/135; P 🛜❊)
Alnwick's top address is this 300-year-old
coaching inn in the heart of town. Rooms are all
superbly appointed (including family rooms that
sleep up to four). Its architectural showpiece
is the fine-dining **restaurant** (mains £11-18,
2-/3-course lunch menus £12/15, 3-course dinner
menu £31.50; ☸ noon-3pm & 5-9pm).

Craster ❽

🍴 Jolly Fisherman   Gastopub ££
(📞016650-576461; www.thejollyfisherman
craster.co.uk; Haven Hill; mains lunch £7-10,
dinner £15-22; ☸ kitchen 11am-3pm & 5-8.30pm
Mon-Sat, noon-7pm Sun, bar 11am-11pm Mon-
Thu, to midnight Sat, to 9pm Sun; 🚸) Crab (in
sensational soup, sandwiches, fish platters and
more) is the speciality of this superb gastropub.
Great wine list, wonderful real ales, a roaring fire
in the bar and stunning beer garden overlooking
Dunstanburgh Castle, too.

Bamburgh ❿

🍴 Mizen Head   Modern British ££
(📞01668-214254; www.mizen-head.co.uk;
Lucker Rd; mains £10-32.50; ☸6-9pm Mon-
Wed, noon-1.45pm & 6-9pm Thu-Sun; P 🛜)
Bamburgh's best place to eat and/or stay is this
stunning restaurant with rooms. Local seafood
is the kitchen's speciality, along with chargrilled
steaks. Its six rooms are light, bright and
spacious. Switched-on staff know their stuff.

Holy Island (Lindisfarne) ⓫

🍴 Crown & Anchor   Inn ££
(📞01289-389215; http://holyislandcrown.
co.uk; Market Pl; s £55-80, d £70-100; 🚸) The
only locally run inn on the island is a relaxed,
down-to-earth spot with brightly coloured
guest rooms and solid pub grub, but the biggest
winner is the beer garden with a postcard
panorama of the castle, priory and harbour.

Berwick-upon-Tweed ⓬

**🍴 Marshall Meadows
Country House Hotel**   Heritage Hotel ££
(📞01289-331133; http://marshallmeadows
hotel.co.uk; Marshall Meadows; incl breakfast
s £70-90, d £89-139, f £99-149; P 🛜❊)
England's most northerly hotel, just 600m
from the Scottish border, is a treasure. Set in
15 acres of woodland and ornamental gardens,
the Georgian manor has 19 rooms (including
a ground-floor family room) with countrified
checked and floral fabrics, two cosy bars with
open fireplaces and a conservatory. Breakfast
(including kippers) is served in the oak-panelled
restaurant.

STRETCH YOUR LEGS
YORK

Start/Finish Monk Bar

Distance 2.5 miles

Duration Two to three hours

York is a city that is best explored on foot, and this walk takes in the most impressive parts of the town's medieval walls, fascinating Roman remains, a 13th-century castle and the most picturesque street in Britain.

Take this walk on Trips

Monk Bar

The 700-year-old Monk Bar is the best preserved of York's medieval city gates, with twin turrets and a dozen cross-shaped arrow slits. Inside you will find the **Richard III Experience** (www.richardiii experience.com; Monk Bar; adult/child incl Henry VII Experience £5/3; ☺10am-5pm Apr-Oct, to 4pm Nov-Mar), a museum which sets out the case of the murdered 'Princes in the Tower' and invites you to judge whether their uncle, Richard III, killed them.

The Walk ≫ Climb the steps to the top of the city wall and head northwest, enjoying grand views of York Minster. Turn the corner, and descend to the street at Bootham Bar, across from York City Art Gallery.

York City Art Gallery

York's **art gallery** (www.yorkartgallery. org.uk; Exhibition Sq; adult/child £7.50/free; ☺10am-5pm Mon-Fri, to 6pm Sat, 11am-4pm Sun) houses an exhibition dedicated to British ceramics, where the **Wall of Pots** displays more than 1000 pieces dating from Roman times to the present day. As well as an impressive collection of Old Masters, there are works by LS Lowry, Picasso, Grayson Perry and David Hockney.

The Walk ≫ Exit the gallery via its rear entrance and turn left into Museum Gardens.

Museum Gardens

In these peaceful gardens you can see the ruins of St Mary's Abbey dating from 1270 to 1294, and the **Multangular Tower**, a part of the city walls that was once the western tower of the Roman garrison's defensive ramparts. In the middle of the gardens, the **Yorkshire Museum** (www.yorkshiremuseum.org.uk; Museum St; adult/child £7.50/free; ☺10am-5pm) houses a superb exhibition on Roman York.

The Walk ≫ Leave the gardens by the main gate on Museum St, and turn right to cross Lendal Bridge, built in 1863. On the far side climb back up to the top of the city walls and follow them round to Micklegate Bar.

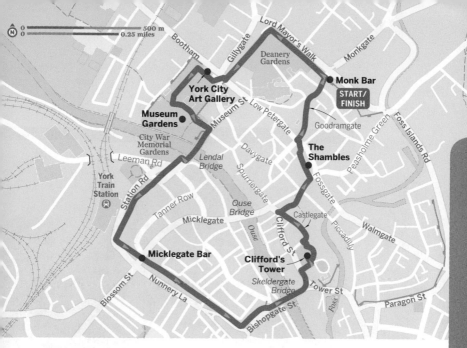

Micklegate Bar

Micklegate Bar was the most important and impressive of York's city gates, where the severed heads of traitors were once displayed on spikes. It houses the **Henry VII Experience** (www.richardiiiexperience.com; adult/child incl Richard III Experience £5/3; ⏱10am-4pm), a museum exploring the reign of Henry VII (r 1485–1509), the first Tudor king of England, who defeated Richard III at the Battle of Bosworth Field, the climax of the Wars of the Roses. Just inside the gate you'll find **Your Bike Shed** (📞01904-633777; www.yourbikeshed.co.uk; 148-150 Micklegate; mains £4-7; ⏱9am-5pm Mon-Sat, 10am-5pm Sun; 📶📷🚲); it serves great coffee and cake.

The Walk » Continue along the top of the city walls until you have to descend and cross the River Ouse again at Skeldergate Bridge. Turn left on Tower St and climb the stairs to Clifford's Tower.

Clifford's Tower

All that remains of York Castle is this evocative **stone tower** (EH; www.english-heritage.org.uk; Tower St; adult/child £5.20/3.10; ⏱10am-6pm Apr-Sep, to 5pm Oct), a highly unusual four-lobed design built into the keep after the original one was destroyed in 1190 during anti-Jewish riots. An angry mob forced 150 Jews to be locked inside the tower and the hapless victims took their own lives rather than be killed. There's not much to see inside, but the views over the city are excellent.

The Walk » Continue along Castlegate on the far side of the tower, and head right on Coppergate and Pavement to reach the south end of The Shambles.

The Shambles

The Shambles takes its name from the Saxon word *shamel,* meaning 'slaughterhouse' – in 1862 there were 26 butcher shops on this street. Today the butchers are long gone, but this narrow cobbled lane, lined with 15th-century Tudor buildings that overhang so much they seem to meet above your head, is the most picturesque in Britain.

The Walk » From the far end of The Shambles bear right across King's Sq and along Goodramgate to return to Monk Bar.

Wales

IN WALES, YOU'RE NEVER FAR FROM REMOTE, RUGGED ROADS. In this compelling corner of the country, a half hour drive leads from the thriving city of Cardiff onto the start of a meandering network of rural routes. Soon you're motoring beside the surf-dashed shores of the Gower Peninsula and into the mountainous Brecon Beacons National Park.

Further north lies an often-overlooked enclave of villages, castles and soaring hills – and delightful Hay-on-Wye, one of Britain's most literary towns.

Then comes the far north, where routes take in grand resorts and towering cliffs. Snowdonia National Park delivers a feast of adrenaline sports and magnificent mountain drives.

Parkmill Three Cliffs Bay
LEIGHTON COLLINS / 500PX ©

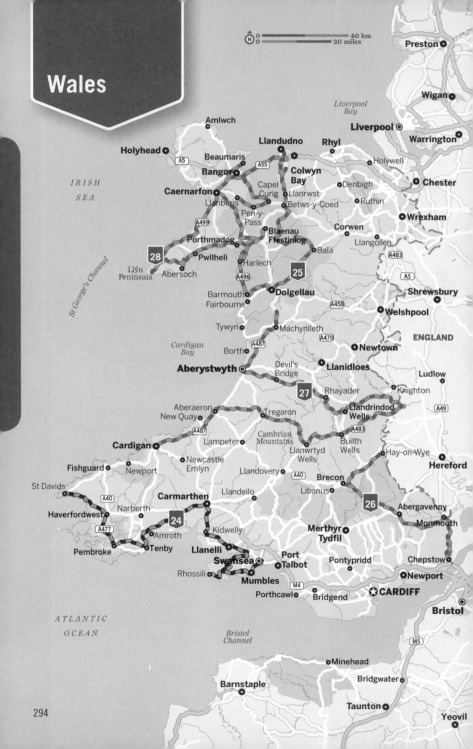

Wales

0 ─────── 40 km
0 ─────── 20 miles

Preston

Wigan

Warrington

Liverpool
Bay

Liverpool

IRISH
SEA

Amlwch

Holyhead
A5
Beaumaris
Bangor
A55
Llandudno
Rhyl
Holywell
Colwyn
Bay
Denbigh
Chester

Caernarfon
Llanberis
Pen-y-
Pass
Capel
Curig
Llanrwst
Betws-y-Coed
Ruthin

A499

Wrexham

Corwen
Llangollen
A483

Porthmadog
Blaenau
Ffestiniog
Bala
A5

28
Pwllheli
Harlech

Llŷn
Peninsula
Abersoch
A496

St George's Channel

25
Barmouth
Fairbourne
Dolgellau

Shrewsbury

A458
Welshpool

Tywyn
Machynlleth
A470

ENGLAND

Cardigan
Bay

Borth
A487

Newtown

Aberystwyth

Devil's
Bridge
Llanidloes

Ludlow

27
Rhayader
Knighton

A49

Aberaeron
New Quay
A487
Tregaron

Llandrindod
Wells

Cardigan

Lampeter
Cambrian
Mountains
Llanwrtyd
Wells
Builth
Wells
A483

Hay-on-Wye

Fishguard
Newport
Newcastle
Emlyn
Llandovery
A40
Brecon
Libanus
Hereford

St Davids
A40
Carmarthen
Llandeilo
26
Abergavenny
Monmouth

Haverfordwest
Narberth
A477
24
Kidwelly
Merthyr
Tydfil
Chepstow

Pembroke
Amroth
Tenby
Llanelli
Swansea
Port
Talbot
Pontypridd
Newport

Rhossili
Mumbles
Porthcawl
Bridgend
M4
★ CARDIFF

ATLANTIC
OCEAN

Bristol
Channel

Bristol

M5

Minehead
Bridgwater

Barnstaple

Taunton
Yeovil

Kidwelly Castle ruins

 West Wales: Swansea to St Davids 4 Days
 A glorious blast west beside sweeping beaches and vast sand dunes. (p297)

25 **Snowdonia National Park 4 Days**
Prepare for dramatic drives through Wales' spectacular mountain heartlands. (p309)

26 **Landscapes & Literature 3 Days**
Memorable touring through picturesque valleys, a bookish town and high, high hills. (p319)

27 **Wilderness Wales 4 Days**
An off-the-beaten track exploration of the wilderness at Wales' heart. (p329)

28 **Northwest Wales 4 Days**
Imposing castles and sensational coasts on some of Wales' best touring routes. (p337)

✓ **DON'T MISS**

Braich-y-Pwll
Many visitors don't get as far as this wind-buffeted headland. Shame; they miss the spectacular views to the Pilgrim's Island of Bardsey on Trip 28

Conwy Town Walls
Conwy is famous for its 13th century castle, but it also boasts Britain's most complete set of medieval town walls on Trip 25

Corris
Simply not on many visitors' radars, Corris' Victorian railway, craft shops and convivial pubs make it well worth the drive on Trip 27

The Whitebrook
Exceptional cuisine ensures gourmets are happy to track down the Whitebrook amid a maze of country lanes on Trip 26

Kidwelly Castle
The battlements of lesser-known Kidwelly prove particularly satisfying to clamber around on Trip 24

295

Classic Trip

West Wales: Swansea to St Davids

24

This route links two distinctly Welsh cities — one large and one beyond tiny — by way of Wales' two most famously beautiful stretches of coast.

TRIP HIGHLIGHTS

125 miles

St Davids
Historic micro-city set in an ancient landscape

10 St Davids **FINISH**

Haverfordwest

Carmarthen

Pembroke **7** Tenby

Llanelli **START** Swansea

Rhossili **4**

86 miles

Tenby
Postcard-perfect beach town with a medieval core

Rhossili
Miles of golden sand backed by steep-sloped downs

20 miles

4 DAYS
125 MILES / 201KM

GREAT FOR...

BEST TIME TO GO
June, July and August offer the best beach weather; although there's no assurances of sun.

ESSENTIAL PHOTO
The view of Three Cliffs Bay from Pennard Castle.

BEST FOR FAMILIES
Splashing about on the beach at Tenby.

Pembrokeshire Coast Elegug Stack Rocks

297

Classic Trip

24 West Wales: Swansea to St Davids

The broad sandy arc of Swansea Bay is only a teaser for what is to come. Once you escape the city sprawl, the wild beauty of the Welsh coast immediately begins to assert itself. Waves crash against sheer cliffs painted from a rapidly changing palate of grey, purple and inky black. In between are some of Britain's very best beaches: glorious sandy stretches and tiny remote coves alike.

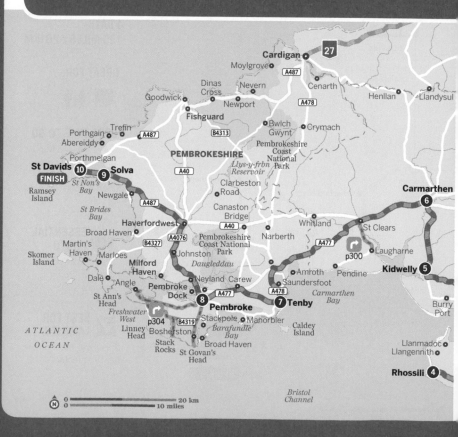

❶ Swansea

Although it's not the most immediately attractive place, Wales' second biggest city has its own workaday charm and an enviable setting on 5-mile-long, sandy, Swansea Bay. An active bar scene is enthusiastically supported by a large student population, while a new brace of affordable ethnic eateries has improved the city's once drab dining options no end.

Fuel up on Welsh cakes hot off the griddle at **Swansea Market** (www. swanseaindoormarket.co.uk; Oxford St; ⊗8am-5.30pm Mon-Sat), then dive into the whizz-bang **National Waterfront Museum** (☑0300 111 2333; www.museumwales.ac.uk; South Dock Marina, Oystermouth Rd; ⊗10am-5pm) and the charmingly old-fashioned **Swansea Museum** (☑01792-653763; www.swanseamuseum.co.uk; Victoria Rd; ⊗10am-5pm Tue-Sun). Fans of Welsh poet Dylan Thomas can tour his **birthplace** (☑01792-472555; www. dylanthomasbirthplace.com; 5 Cwmdonkin Dr, Uplands; adult/child £8/6; ⊗ tours 11am, 1pm & 3pm), explore his legacy at the **Dylan Thomas Centre** (☑01792-463980; www.dylanthomas. com; Somerset Pl; ⊗10am-4.30pm), catch a show at the **Dylan Thomas Theatre** (☑01792-473238; www.dylanthomastheatre.org. uk; Gloucester Pl), where he once trod the boards, and visit some of the many pubs he famously frequented. If you've got an interest in antiquities, seek out the fascinating **Egypt Centre** (www.egypt. swan.ac.uk; Mumbles Rd, Sketty; ⊗10am-4pm Tue-Sat) at Swansea University.

🛏 p307

The Drive ❯❯ Broad Oystermouth Rd traces the edge of Swansea Bay, changing its name to Mumbles Rd halfway along. It's only 4 miles from central Swansea to the heart of the Mumbles strip.

❷ The Mumbles

Swansea's swanky seaside suburb sprawls along the western curve of Swansea Bay and terminates in the pair of rounded hills which may have gifted the area its unusual name (from the French *Les Mamelles* – 'the breasts'). **Oystermouth Castle** (☑01792-635478; www.swansea.gov.uk/oystermouthcastle; Castle Ave; adult/child £3/1.50; ⊗11am-5pm Easter-Sep) is well worth a visit – a Norman fortress standing guard over the fashionable Newton Rd bar and shopping strip.

Pick up an ice cream at **Joe's** (☑01792-368212; www.joes-icecream.com; 526

LINK YOUR TRIP

26 **Landscapes & Literature**
It's a 90-minute (60-mile) drive from Hay-on-Wye to Swansea via a picturesque route through the Brecon Beacons.

27 **Wilderness Wales**
From St Davids it's a simple matter of continuing up a scenic stretch of the Pembrokeshire coast to Cardigan, 35 miles away.

[Map with labels:]
Lampeter
Llanybydder
Llangadog
Llandeilo
Ammanford
31 miles to 26
Pontarddulais
Llanelli
START Swansea ❶
Reynoldston
A4118 ❸ Parkmill ❷ Mumbles
Port Eynon

Mumbles Rd; ⏱10.30am-5.30pm), a Swansea institution since it was founded by an Italian immigrant in 1922, and take a stroll along the waterside promenade to the Victorian **pier** (☎01792-365225; www.mumbles-pier.co.uk; Mumbles Rd). There's a pretty little sandy beach tucked just beneath it. If you're peckish there are some good cafes and restaurants spread along the waterfront, and plenty of pubs and bars too.

🛏 p307

The Drive » From the Mumbles it's 6 miles to Parkmill on the Gower Peninsula. Head uphill on Newton Rd, following the Gower signs. Eventually the houses give way to fields and, at the village of Murton, a sharp right-hand turn leads to the B4436 and on to the A4118, the main Gower road.

- - - - - - - - - - - -

❸ Parkmill

The spectacular coastal landscape of the Gower Peninsula was recognised by officialdom when it was declared the UK's first 'Area of Outstanding Natural Beauty' in 1956.

In the village of Parkmill, historic mill buildings have been converted into the **Gower Heritage Centre** (☎01792-371206; www.gowerheritagecentre.

co.uk; Parkmill; adult/child £6.80/5.80; ⏱10am-5.30pm; 👶). Despite its worthy-sounding name, it's a great place to take kids, incorporating a petting zoo and a puppet theatre. Nearby **Parc-le-Breos** (Parkmill) contains the remains of a 5500-year-old burial chamber.

However, the real reason to stop in Parkmill is to take a stroll to **Three Cliffs Bay**. Recognised as one of Britain's most beautiful beaches, Three Cliffs has a memorable setting, with a ruined 13th-century castle above and a triple-pointed rock formation framing a natural arch at its eastern end.

DETOUR: LAUGHARNE

Start: ❻ Carmarthen (p303)

While shooting down the highway between Carmarthen and Tenby, it's worth considering taking a left at St Clears to visit the small town of Laugharne (pronounced '*larn*') on the Taf estuary. Perched picturesquely above the reed-lined shore, **Laugharne Castle** (Cadw; www.cadw.gov.wales; Wogan St; adult/child £3.80/2.85; ⏱10am-5pm Apr-Oct) is a hefty 13th-century fortress which was converted into a mansion in the 16th century.

Swansea may have been Dylan Thomas' birthplace but Laugharne is where he chose to live out his final years, providing the inspiration for his classic play for voices *Under Milk Wood*. Many fans make the pilgrimage here to visit the **boathouse** (☎01994-427420; www.dylanthomasboathouse.com; Dylan's Walk; adult/child £4.20/2; ⏱10am-5pm May-Oct, 10.30am-3pm Nov-Apr) where he lived, the shed where he wrote and his final resting place in the graveyard of St Martin's Church. Also worth a look is cosy **Brown's Hotel** (☎01994-427688; www.browns-hotel.co.uk; King St; pizza £8-10; ⏱11am-11pm), one of his favourite watering holes.

Laugharne is situated 4 miles off the highway and you're best to allocate at least a couple of hours to explore it properly. Although you can continue southwest from here on narrow roads, you're better off backtracking to the A477 to get to Tenby.

St Davids St Davids Cathedral

The Drive » From Parkmill, continue west on the A4118, following the signs to Rhossili. Eventually the road turns left towards the village of Scurlage and the Rhossili turn-off. All up it's a distance of 10 miles along good roads, but it's quite likely you'll be stuck behind a slow-moving campervan or tractor at some point along the way.

TRIP HIGHLIGHT

④ Rhossili

It can be dangerous for swimmers but the three miles of surf-battered golden sands of Rhossili Bay make it the Gower Peninsula's most dramatic and spectacular beach. Surfers tend to congregate at the village of Llangennith near the north end of the beach, but Rhossili village to the south makes for a better casual stop. There's a National Trust **visitor centre** (☎01792-390707; www.nationaltrust.org.uk/gower; Coastguard Cottages, Rhossili; ⊙10.30am-4pm) here, and the excellent Bay Bistro & Coffee House (p307), if you're after a meal or a snack.

This end of the beach is abutted by **Worms Head**, a dragon-shaped promontory which turns into an island at high tide and is home to seals and a variety of sea birds. It's safe to explore it on foot for 2½ hours either side of low tide, but keep an eye on the time and mind you don't get cut off by the incoming tide.

✗ p307

The Drive » It's only 31 miles from Rhossili to Kidwelly, but allow an hour as the narrow lanes leading out from the Gower Peninsula will slow you down. The first part of the journey zigzags along tiny lanes to the peninsula's northern edge. Before and after motoring through the scraggly outskirts of Llanelli, it's a pleasantly rural drive.

⑤ Kidwelly

Castles are a dime a dozen in this part of Wales – a legacy of a time when Norman 'Marcher' lords were given authority and a large degree of autonomy to subjugate the Welsh in the south and along the English border. The cute little Carmarthenshire town of Kidwelly has a particularly well-preserved example.

Originally erected in 1106, only 40 years after the Norman invasion of England, **Kidwelly Castle** (Cadw; www.cadw.gov.wales; Castle Rd, Kidwelly; adult/child £4/3; ⊙9.30am-5pm Mar-Oct, 10am-4pm Nov-Feb) got its current configuration of imposing stone walls in the 13th century. Wander around and explore its remaining towers and battlements, or just stop by to take a photo of the

301

Classic Trip

WHY THIS IS A CLASSIC TRIP
PETER DRAGICEVICH, WRITER

As well as traversing two of Wales' most acclaimed beauty spots – the Gower Peninsula and the Pembrokeshire Coast – this journey offers the perfect introduction to contemporary Welsh life. You'll get a taste of a large post-industrial city, visit tiny fishing villages, travel through fertile farmland and wash up in St Davids – a place as close to the Welsh soul as any could claim to be.

Top: Rhossili Bay, Gower Peninsula
Left: Colourful buildings in Solva
Right: Picturesque Tenby Harbour

BILLY STOCK / SHUTTERSTOCK ©

JOE DANIEL PRICE / GETTY IMAGES ©

BILLY STOCK / SHUTTERSTOCK ©

grey walls looming above the peaceful river far below.

The Drive » From Kidwelly, take the A484 north for 10 miles through the green fields of Carmarthenshire. Eventually you'll see Carmarthen in the distance, straddling a hill above the River Tywi.

- - - - - - - - - -

❻ Carmarthen

Although it has ancient provenance, there's not an awful lot to see in Carmarthenshire's county town. Still, it's worth stopping to stretch your legs with a stroll through its historic centre. Call into **Castle House** (Nott Sq; ⏱9.30am-4.30pm Mon-Sat) to examine the few sections that remain of a once mighty fortress. **Carmarthen Market** (www.carmarthen shiremarkets.co.uk; Market Way; ⏱9.30am-4.30pm Mon-Sat) has existed since Roman times. It's a good place to sample the local specialty, Carmarthen ham – an air-dried meat that's very similar to prosciutto. Carmarthenshire is a largely agricultural county, and the market remains an important hub for local producers.

The Drive » Twenty-six miles of verdant farmland separate Carmarthen from Tenby. Take the A40 to St Clears, where you can either detour to Laugharne (see p300) or branch off on the A477 and enter Pembrokeshire. Past Kilgetty, turn left onto the A478, which leads directly to Tenby.

WALES **24** WEST WALES: SWANSEA TO ST DAVIDS

TRIP HIGHLIGHT

❼ Tenby

Sandy, family-friendly beaches spread out in either direction from the pretty pastel-striped resort town occupying the headland. Tenby's historic core is still partly enclosed by Norman walls, although all that's left of its castle is a meagre collection of ruins gazing over the sea.

The beach is the big attraction here, but if the weather's not co-operating, pop into **Tenby Museum & Art Gallery** (☏01834-842809; www.tenbymuseum.org.uk; Castle Hill; adult/child £4.95/free; ◷10am-5pm daily Apr-Dec, Tue-Sat Jan-Mar) and the National Trust's restored **Tudor Merchant's House** (NT; ☏01834-842279; www.nationaltrust.org.uk; Quay Hill; adult/child £5/2.50; ◷11am-5pm Wed-Mon Easter-Jul, Sep & Oct, daily Aug, Sat & Sun Nov-Easter). If you've got the time, take a boat trip out to **Caldey Island** (☏01834-844453; www.caldey-island.co.uk; adult/child £12/6; ◷Mon-Sat May-Sep, Mon-Thu Apr & Oct), home to seals, seabirds, beaches and a community of Cistercian monks.

🛏 p307

DETOUR: WEST OF PEMBROKE

Start: ❽ Pembroke

The remote peninsula that forms the bottom lip of the long, deep-sea harbour of Milford Haven has some of the Pembrokeshire Coast's most dramatic geological features and blissful little beaches. The National Trust–managed **Stackpole Estate** (NT; ☏01646-661359; www.nationaltrust.org.uk; ◷dawn-dusk) covers 8 miles of coastline south and west of Pembroke. It includes the golden sands of **Barafundle Bay** and **Broad Haven South**, and a network of walking tracks around the **Bosherston Lily Ponds**.

Continue past Bosherston to the coast and a short steep path leads to the photogenic shell of **St Govan's Chapel**, wedged into a slot in the cliffs just above the pounding waves. There's a natural rock arch here, one of many along this stretch of coast. Sadly, the coast to the west of here is part of a military firing range. When the red flags are flying there's no public access to some of the Pembrokeshire Coast's most arresting natural sights – the **Elegug Stack Rocks** and the gigantic arch known as the **Green Bridge of Wales**.

After sidestepping the firing range, the road continues on to **Freshwater West** – a moody, wave-battered stretch of coast that has provided a brooding backdrop for movies such as *Harry Potter and the Deathly Hallows* and Ridley Scott's *Robin Hood*. It's widely held to be Wales' best surf beach, but also one of the most dangerous for swimmers.

From Pembroke it's 4 miles to the Stackpole Estate and 8 miles to Freshwater West. If it's beach weather, you could easily make a day of it. Take the B4319 heading south from Pembroke; Stackpole, Bosherston and the Elegug Stack Rocks are reached from narrow country lanes branching off it. The B4319 continues past Freshwater West and terminates at the B4320, where you can turn right to head back to Pembroke.

Parkmill Pennard Castle

The Drive ≫ From Tenby it's a short and sweet 10-mile hop to Pembroke. From the town centre, head west on Greenhill Rd, head under the railway bridge and turn right at the roundabout. Follow Hayward Lane (the B4318) through a patchwork of fields until you reach the Sageston roundabout. Turn left onto the A477 and then veer left on the A4075.

- - - - - - - - - - - - -

8 Pembroke

The little town of Pembroke is completely dominated by hulking **Pembroke Castle** (☏01646-684585; www.pembroke-castle.co.uk; Main St; adult/child £6/5; ☉10am-5pm; 🖼), which looms over the end of its main street. The fortress is best viewed from the Mill Pond, a pretty lake which forms a moat on three sides of the craggy headland from which the castle rises. Pembroke played a leading role in British history as the birthplace of the first Tudor king, Henry VII. Compared to many of its contemporaries, the castle is in extremely good nick, with lots of well-preserved towers, dungeons and wall-walks to explore. Needless to say, kids love it.

A strip of mainly Georgian and Victorian buildings leads down from the castle, including among them some good pubs and the excellent **Food at Williams** (☏01646-689990; www.foodatwilliams.co.uk; 18 Main St; mains £5-8.50; ☉9am-4.30pm Mon-Sat, 10am-3pm Sun; 🖃) cafe.

🛏 p307

The Drive ≫ The 24-mile journey to Solva heads through the port town of Pembroke Dock, crosses the Daugleddau estuary and then heads up through Pembrokeshire's nondescript county town of Haverfordwest. Exit Haverfordwest on the A487, which traverses farmland before reaching the coast at Newgale, a surf beach backed by a high bank of pebbles. From here the road shadows the coast.

- - - - - - - - - - - - -

9 Solva

Clustered around a hook-shaped harbour, Solva is the classic Welsh fishing village straight out of central casting. Pastel-hued cottages line the gurgling stream running through its lower reaches, while Georgian town houses cling to the cliffs above. When the tide's out, the water disappears completely from the harbour, leaving the sailing fleet striking angular poses on the sand.

There's not much to do here except to stroll about perusing the antique shops and galleries, or to settle in somewhere cosy for a meal. Our favourite for the

latter is the **Cambrian Inn** (☎01437-721210; www.thecambrianinn.co.uk; 6 Main St; mains £11-21, s/d £70/95; ☺noon-3pm & 6-9pm; 🖋), an upmarket pub known for its gourmet burgers and meat pies.

If you need to burn off some calories afterwards, a 1-mile walk will take you upstream to the **Solva Woollen Mill** (☎01437-721112; www.solvawoollenmill.co.uk; Middle Mill; ☺9.30am-5.30pm Mon-Fri Oct-Jun, 9.30am-5.30pm Mon-Sat, 2-5.30pm Sun Jul-Sep), which is the oldest working mill of its kind in Pembrokeshire.

🛏 p307

The Drive >> You really can't go wrong on the 3-mile drive to St Davids. Just continue west.

- - - - - - - - - - - - - - -

TRIP HIGHLIGHT

❿ St Davids

A city only by dint of its prestigious cathedral, pretty St Davids feels more like a small town or an oversized village. Yet this little settlement looms large in the Welsh consciousness as the hometown of its patron saint.

**LOCAL KNOWLEDGE:
ST DAVID'S DAY**

St David's Day is to the Welsh what St Patrick's Day is to the Irish – a day to celebrate one's essential Welshiness, albeit somewhat more soberly than their Celtic brethren from across the way. If you're in Wales on 1 March, there's no better place to be than the saint's own city, St Davids. All around the cathedral a host of golden daffodils explodes into flower seemingly right on cue; people pin leek, daffodil or red dragon badges to their lapels; the streets are strung with flags bearing the black and gold St David's cross; and *cawl* (a traditional soupy stew) is consumed in industrial qualities. Of course, the focus of more solemn events is the cathedral, where the saint's remains lie in a recently restored shrine, a replica of one which was destroyed during the Reformation.

Fascinating **St Davids Cathedral** (www.stdavidscathedral.org.uk; suggested donation £3, tours £4; ☺8.30am-6pm Mon-Sat, 12.45-5.30pm Sun) stands on the site of the saint's own 6th-century religious settlement. Wonderful stone and wooden carvings decorate the interior, and there's a treasury and historic library hidden within. Right next to the cathedral are the ruins of a spectacular medieval **bishop's palace** (Cadw; www.cadw.gov.wales; adult/child £3.50/2.65; ☺9.30am-5pm Mar-Oct, 10am-4pm Nov-Feb).

St David was born at **St Non's Bay**, a ruggedly

beautiful section of coast with a holy well and a cute little chapel, a short walk from the centre of town. If it's a swim or surf you're after, head to broad, beautiful **Whitesands Bay** (Porth Mawr).

Also not to be missed is **Oriel y Parc** (Landscape Gallery; ☎01437-720392; www.orielyparc.co.uk; cnr High St & Caerfai Rd; ☺10am-4pm), an architecturally interesting visitor centre and art gallery showcasing landscape paintings from the collection of the National Museum Wales.

🛏 p307

Eating & Sleeping

Swansea ❶

🛏 Christmas Pie B&B   B&B ££

(📞01792-480266; www.christmaspie.co.uk;
2 Mirador Cres, Uplands; s/d £53/82; P 📶)
The name suggests something warm and
comforting, and this suburban villa does not
disappoint. The three en-suite bedrooms are all
individually decorated. Plus there's fresh fruit
and an out-of-the-ordinary, vegetarian-friendly
breakfast selection.

The Mumbles ❷

🛏 Patricks
with Rooms   Boutique Hotel £££

(📞01792-360199; www.patrickswithrooms.
com; 638 Mumbles Rd; r £120-175; 📶) Patricks
has 16 individually styled bedrooms in bold
contemporary colours, with art on the walls,
fluffy robes and, in some of the rooms, roll-top
baths and sea views. Some are set back in
a separate annexe. Downstairs there's an
upmarket restaurant and bar.

Rhossili ❹

✗ Bay Bistro & Coffee House   Bistro £

(📞01792-390519; www.thebaybistro.co.uk;
mains £6-12; 🕐10am-5.30pm; 🅿) A buzzy
beach cafe with a sunny terrace, good surfy
vibrations and the kind of drop-your-panini
views that would make anything taste good –
although the roster of burgers, sandwiches,
cakes and coffee stands up well regardless. On
summer evenings it opens for alfresco meals.

Tenby ❼

🛏 Southside   Hotel ££

(📞01834-844355; www.southsidetenby.
co.uk; Picton Rd; s/d £45/80; 📶) Rooms are
spacious, comfortable and not at all chintzy
at this friendly little private hotel just outside

the town walls. Three of the four rooms have en
suites, while the other has a private bathroom
accessed from the corridor.

Pembroke ❽

🛏 Woodbine   B&B ££

(📞01646-686338; www.
pembrokebedandbreakfast.co.uk; 84 Main St; s/d
from £50/65; 📶) This well-kept, forest-green
Georgian townhouse presents a smart face to
Pembroke's main drag. The three pretty guest
rooms are tastefully furnished, with original
fireplaces and contemporary wallpaper. Two
have en suites, while the family room has its
bathroom out on the corridor.

Solva ❾

🛏 Haroldston House   B&B ££

(📞01437-721404; www.haroldstonhouse.co.uk;
29 High St; r £80-90; P 📶) Set in a lovely old
Georgian merchant's house, this wonderful
B&B offers chic modern style. The simple but
tastefully decorated rooms feature art by
owner Ian McDonald as well as other Welsh or
Wales-based artists. There's a free electric-car
charging point, discounts for guests arriving by
public transport, and tasty, inventive breakfast
options.

St Davids ❿

🛏 Twr y Felin   Hotel £££

(📞01437-725555; www.twryfelinhotel.com;
Caerfai Rd; r/ste from £160/240) Incorporating
an odd circular tower that was once a windmill,
this chic boutique hotel is St Davids' most
upmarket option. The entire building is lathered
with contemporary art, with dozens of pieces
in the lounge-bar and restaurant alone. The
21 bedrooms are all luxurious, but the most
spectacular is the three-level circular suite in
the tower itself.

Snowdonia National Park

25

Great fortresses of rock rising steeply from glittering lakes and ancient forests: this drive takes you deep into the Wales you've always dreamt of.

TRIP HIGHLIGHTS

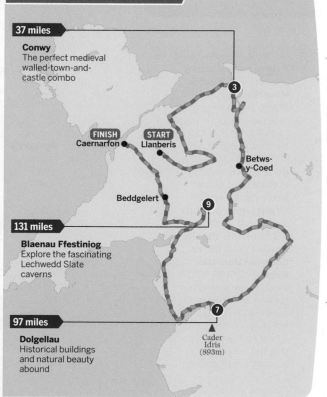

37 miles

Conwy
The perfect medieval walled-town-and-castle combo

FINISH
Caernarfon

START
Llanberis

Betws-y-Coed

Beddgelert

131 miles

Blaenau Ffestiniog
Explore the fascinating Lechwedd Slate caverns

97 miles

Dolgellau
Historical buildings and natural beauty abound

Cader Idris (893m)

4 DAYS
165 MILES/266KM

GREAT FOR...

BEST TIME TO GO

Summer is best, although trails can get crowded during the school holidays in July and August.

 ESSENTIAL PHOTO

The perfect medieval symmetry of Conwy's castle and walls.

 BEST FOR OUTDOORS

The mountain trails that radiate from Capel Curig.

25 Snowdonia NP

The treasures of the national park the Welsh call Eryri (The Highland) are laid before you, following this wild, winding route. You'll want to stop often to scramble up scree-scattered slopes, wander sober, slate-built towns, and explore some of the mightiest castles in the British Isles. Pack your hiking boots, your camera and your sense of wonder: they'll all get a thorough workout.

① Llanberis

Ground zero for rock climbers, trail traipsers and mountain lovers in general, Llanberis is an offbeat little town that also offers a fantastic introduction to Snowdonia's industrial heritage. Climbers should make a beeline for the legendary **Pete's Eats** (📞01286-870117; www.petes-eats.co.uk; 40 High St; mains £3-7; ⊙8am-8pm; 📶), where cliff-face tales have been swapped over bacon baps for decades, while the **National Slate Museum** (📞03001-112333; www.museumwales.ac.uk/en/slate; ⊙10am-5pm Easter-Oct, to 4pm Sun-Fri Nov-Easter) is a fascinating re-creation of

the area's industrial past. To get a similar sense of its present, **Electric Mountain** (📞01286-870636; www.electricmountain.co.uk; tour adult/child £8.50/4.35; ⊙10am-4.30pm Jan-May & Sep-Dec, 9.30am-5.30pm Jun-Aug) uncovers the science (and 16km of tunnels) of nearby Dinorwig, Europe's largest pumped-storage hydroelectric scheme.

Llanberis is also the starting point for the **Snowdon Mountain Railway** (📞01286-870223; www.snowdonrailway.co.uk; Llanberis; adult/child return diesel £29/20, steam £37/27; ⊙9am-5pm mid-Mar–Nov), a rack-and-pinion train that has taken the legwork out of scaling

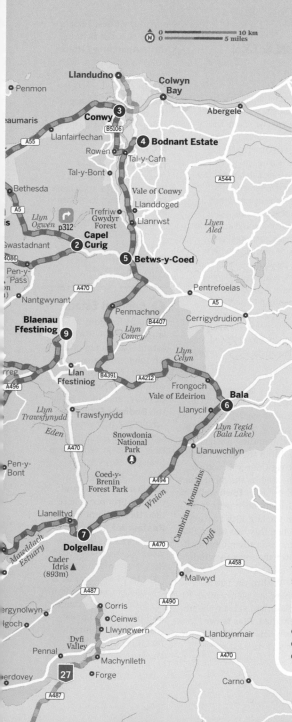

Wales's highest peak since Victorian times.

🛏 p317

The Drive » The 11-mile drive to Capel Curig offers an immediate introduction to Snowdonia's stunning heights: the scree-scattered slopes on the climb to Pen-y-Pass, and the views from the Pass itself, are awe-inspiring. Take the A4086 east out of Llanberis, then all the way to Capel Curig.

② Capel Curig

Another mecca for climbers, Capel Curig has fewer attractions than Llanberis, but is surrounded by perennially popular peaks. The Moel Siabod (6.5 miles), Crimpiau (4.5 miles) and Eastern Carneddau (8.5 miles) circuits are three that start near the town, and all could be tackled in a few hours. Those seeking to polish their Bear Grylls skills should check out the

LINK YOUR TRIP

27 Wilderness Wales
Hop off the route at Dolgellau, heading 11 miles south on the A470 and 487 to Corris, to see another side of Wales's wild heart.

28 Northwest Wales
Jump ship at Conwy or Caernarfon to see more of what the northwest corner of the Wales has to offer.

DETOUR: LLYN OGWEN & LYN IDWAL

Start: ❷ Capel Curig (p311)

If the wild calls when heading from Capel Curig to Conwy, don't resist the temptation to visit the glacial mountain lakes of Llyn Ogwen and Llyn Idwal. The Carneddau and Glyderau Mountains that border the route contain some of the most wild and ravishing landscape in Britain, and these two upland gems form the perfect focus to experience their sublime beauty. Feral goats are welcome here, but livestock isn't: the delicate balance of flora and soil demand that all intrusive species are kept out, preserving alpine species that flourish nowhere further south in Britain.

From Capel Curig, head 5 miles northwest on the A5 to the bridge at Pont Pen-y-Benglog, where both lakes, and walking trails, await (the easiest trail, circumnavigating the two lakes, is around 5.4 miles, and can be comfortably walked in around three hours). If your intention is to overnight, the **YHA Idwal** (☎08453-719744; www.yha.org.uk; Nant Ffrancon; dm/tw £22/56; ⊙daily Mar-Oct, Fri & Sat Nov-Feb) at Llyn Ogwen is the only on-site option, but a very good one. To rejoin the route, just continue up the A5 to Conwy.

excellent **Plas y Brenin National Mountain Sports Centre** (☎01690-720214; www.pyb.co.uk; A4086).

🛌 p317

The Drive >> The 26-mile drive to historic Conwy is worth it simply for the trip through the lesser-visited but breathtakingly beautiful Carneddau and Glyderau ranges. Take the A5 northwest from Capel Curig, then the North Wales Expressway northeast to Conwy.

- - - - - - - - - - - - -

TRIP HIGHLIGHT

❸ Conwy

Conwy is a banquet for medieval history buffs. Its stunning **castle** (Cadw; ☎01492-592358; www.cadw. wales.gov.uk; Castle Sq; adult/child £7.95/5.60; ⊙9.30am-5pm Mar-Jun, Sep & Oct, to 6pm Jul & Aug, to 4pm Nov-Feb; 🅿), commanding a narrow point in the mouth of the River Conwy, is complemented by the most complete set of **town walls** in Britain. Both were built in the late 13th century when this was an English garrison town lording it over the recently subdued Welsh.

Within the town, there are plenty more historical gems to be unearthed. **Plas Mawr** (Cadw; www.cadw.wales.gov.uk; High St; adult/child £6/4.20; ⊙9.30am-5pm Easter-Sep) is one of the finest Elizabethan houses in Britain, while **Aberconwy House** (NT; www.nationaltrust.org. uk; Castle St; adult/child £4/2; ⊙11am-5pm late-Feb–Oct) is a merchant's house of the same vintage as the castle and town walls.

🛌 p343

The Drive >> The short (7 mile) hop from Conwy to Bodnant Estate takes you down the bucolic Conwy Valley. Take the Llanrwst Rd (B5106) south from near the castle, turning east onto the B5279 to cross the Conwy River, then north onto the A470, from which Bodnant Estate is signposted.

- - - - - - - - - - - - -

❹ Bodnant Estate

Bodnant Estate is a stunning agricultural estate that no fan of British landscaping should miss. Its horticultural collections are internationally renowned, while the **Bodnant Farm Shop** (☎01492-651100; www.bodnant-welshfood.co.uk; Furnace Farm, Tal-y-Cafn; ⊙farm shop 10am-6pm Mon-Sat, 10am-4pm Sun; 🅿) is lavishly stocked with local and organic produce. There's also the excellent **Hayloft Restaurant** (☎01492-651102; www.bodnant-welshfood.co.uk/hayloft-restaurant; Bodnant Welsh Food, Furnace Farm, Tal-y-Cafn; mains £17-20; ⊙noon-3pm Tue-Sun, 6-9pm Tue-Sat), cultural events and plenty of courses (gardening, cooking, farming) throughout the year. And apiarists

Isle of Anglesey Lighthouse near Llanddwyn beach

swarm to the **National Beekeeping Centre** (☎01492-651106; www.beeswales.co.uk; Furnace Farm, Tal-y-Cafn; tours adult/child £7/3.50; ⏰10am-4pm Wed-Sun late Mar–early Sep), also on site.

The Drive ≫ Rejoin the A470, heading south to Llanrwst, then take the B5106 back over the Conwy and into Betws-y-Coed: about 13 miles all told.

❺ Betws-y-Coed

In many ways the outdoor-adventure capital of Snowdonia, lovely Betws is a slate-coloured village commanding the junction of the Conwy and Llugwy Rivers. Betwys is also richly stocked with excellent B&Bs, making it an ideal place to overnight. Do make sure you book ahead in peak summer periods, when walkers, climbers and nature lovers descend in droves.

Nearby **Gwydyr Forest** is ideal for an afternoon's ramble, or a few hours' riding on a mountain bike hired from the kind folks at **Beics Betws** (☎01690-710766; www.bikewales.co.uk; Vicarage Rd; ⏰9.30am-5pm Mar-Nov, call ahead at other times).

Whatever your means of exploration, make sure you call in at the fantastically informative **Snowdonia National Park Information Centre** (☎01690-710426; www.eryri-npa.gov.uk; Royal Oak Stables; ⏰9.30am-5.30pm Easter-Oct, to 4pm rest of year) for advice.

🛏 p317

The Drive ≫ The 27-mile drive to Bala is best appreciated taking winding B-roads: leave the A5 a few miles south of town, take the B4406 south through Penmachno, the B4391 east to the Tryweryn River, and the A4212 into Bala.

⑥ Bala

Bala is a haven for whitewater rafting and other forms of aquatic entertainment. The town proper isn't bursting with attractions but there's always the **Bala Lake Railway** (☎01678-540666; www.bala-lake-railway.co.uk; adult/unaccompanied child return £10.50/5.50; ☻Feb-Oct), the **Bala Watersports Centre** (☎01678-521059; www.balawatersports.com; Pensarn Rd; ☻9am-5pm, later in summer) and the **National White Water Centre** (Canolfan Dŵr Gwyn Genedlaethol;

☎01678-521083; www.ukrafting.co.uk; Frongoch; 1-/2hr trip £35/66; ☻9am-4.30pm Mon-Fri) to keep you engaged. If you're looking for somewhere for a restorative bite and pint, the **Eagles Inn** (☎01678-540278; www.yr-eagles.co.uk; mains £9-17.50; ☻11am-11pm Sun-Wed, to midnight Thu-Sat, closed lunch Mon; 🅟) in little Llanuwchllyn, at the opposite end of the lake, is the best bet.

The Drive » From Bala it's a straightforward 18-mile drive southwest on the A494 (Bala Rd) to Dolgellau.

TRIP HIGHLIGHT

⑦ Dolgellau

Dolgellau is an antiquarian's dream, with more than 200 listed buildings within its modest perimeter. With natural delights such as the climber's favourite **Cader Idris** on its doorstep, not to mention the idyllic and bird-filled **Mawddach Estuary** (www.mawddachestuary.co.uk), it's understandably well served with B&Bs (some of the finest in Snowdonia) and restaurants.

🛏 p317, p343

Barmouth A Victorian railway bridge spans the Mawddach Estuary

The Drive » The 20-mile drive to Harlech is another lovely, scenic stretch, taking in the Mawddach Estuary, the resort town of Barmouth and the Cardigan Bay coast. Heading west, take the Cader Rd out of town to the A493, head over the Mawddach to the A496 and follow it west through Barmouth, then north to Harlech.

- - - - - - - - - - -

⑧ Harlech

One of Wales's splendid 13th-century **castles** (Cadw; www.cadw.wales. gov.uk; Castle St; adult/child £6/4.20; ⏰9.30am-5pm Mar-Jun, Sep & Oct, to 6pm Jul & Aug, to 4pm Nov-Feb) – and perhaps the most

dramatically situated – commands the hill-town of Harlech. With views across Cardigan Bay to the Llŷn Peninsula in one direction, and towards Snowdonia's peaks in another, it's worth diverting up the steep road into town. Once there, you'll find top-notch B&Bs, cosy little teashops, and (incongruously) some of the best **Caribbean food** (📞01766-780416; www.soul foodcaribbeanrestaurant.co.uk; High St; mains £13-15; ⏰5.30-9pm Tue-Sat) in Wales. There's also **Theatr Ardudwy** (📞01766-780667; www.theatrardudwy.cymru;

Ffordd Newydd), a thriving local arts hub.

🛏 p317

The Drive » From Harlech, follow the Stryd Fawr (High St)/ B4573 northeast, merging with the A496 as it follows the River Dwyryd further inland. All up, this leg is 14 miles.

- - - - - - - - - - -

TRIP HIGHLIGHT

⑨ Blaenau Ffestiniog

Sometimes maligned for its grim weather and appearance, Blaenau actually has plenty to interest visitors. The northern terminus of the famed **Ffestiniog Railway** (Rheilffordd Ffestiniog; ☎01766-516024; www.festrail. co.uk; adult/child return £23/21; ⏱ daily Easter-Oct, reduced service rest of year; ♿), which winds through the hills from coastal Porthmadog, it also boasts the fascinating **Llechwedd Slate Caverns** (☎01766-830306; www.llechwedd-slate-caverns.co.uk; tours £20; ⏱9.30am-5.30pm), **zip wires** (☎01248-601444; www.zipworld.co.uk; Llechwedd Slate Caverns; ⏱ booking office 8am-6.30pm; ♿) over vast open quarries, and **Antur Stiniog's** (☎01766-832214; www. anturstiniog.com; 1 uplift £17-19, day pass £29-33; ⏱10am-4pm Thu-Mon) seriously challenging mountain-bike trails. For a more sedate cultural experience, try the converted jailhouse **Cellb** (☎01766-832001; www.cellb.org; Park Sq; ⏱ cafe/bar 10am-3pm Tue-Sat & 7-11pm Wed-Sat).

The Drive » Backtrack southwest along the A496 to where the B4410 branches off to the west. Join the A498 at Prenteg, and follow it north along the River Glaslyn to Beddgelert: all up a journey of 16 miles

⑩ Beddgelert

Beautifully preserved Beddgelert, built of dark local stones at the junction of the Colwyn and Glaslyn Rivers, is surrounded by photogenic peaks, stone-strewn farmland and whispering forests. This is prime walking territory: if you have a few hours to spare, consider dropping into the National Trust–owned **Craflwyn Farm** (NT; ☎01766-510120; www. nationaltrust.org.uk/craflwyn-and-beddgelert) and taking on the 60-minute round-trip ramble to the hilltop of Dinas Emrys, legendary site of a castle built by King Vortigern. And if you find yourself in town on an empty stomach, the charmingly-eccentric Beddgelert Bistro & Antiques serves excellent local produce in a dining room that doubles as an antique shop.

✗ p317

The Drive » Skirting the southern slopes of Snowdon, the A4085 heads 13 miles northwest to your last stop, Caernarfon.

⑪ Caernarfon

Any visit to Caernarfon inevitably focuses on its mighty **castle** (Cadw; www. cadw.wales.gov.uk; adult/child £7.95/5.60; ⏱9.30am-5pm Mar-Jun, Sep & Oct, to 6pm Jul & Aug, to 4pm Nov-Feb), whose banded, hexagonal towers were designed in the 13th century to pay aesthetic tribute to the doughty walls of Byzantium. Ironically, for somewhere that figures strongly in both the Roman and English domination of Wales, it's now a vibrant centre of Welsh language and culture. Well stocked with characterful and good-value B&Bs, it also has some excellent pubs and restaurants. **Blas** (☎01286-677707; www. blascaernarfon.co.uk; 23-25 Hole in the Wall St; mains £18-20; ⏱10.30am-3.30pm & 6-11pm Tue-Sat, 10am-3pm Sun), Welsh for 'taste', is a standout. It is the perfect base for forays across the Menai Strait to Anglesey, or along the sublime Llŷn Peninsula.

🛏 p317

Eating & Sleeping

Llanberis ❶

🛏 Beech Bank   B&B ££

(📞01286-871085; www.beech-bank.co.uk; 2 High St; s/d £60/80; 🅿 📶) First impressions of this double-gabled, wrought-iron–trimmed stone house are great, but step inside and it just gets better. A stylish renovation has left beautiful bathrooms and exuberant decor, which matches the gregarious nature of the host. Highly recommended, although not set up for children.

Capel Curig ❷

🛏 Bryn Tyrch Inn   Hotel ££

(📞01690-720223; www.bryntyrchinn.co.uk; A5, s/d from £75/90; 🅿 📶) Downstairs there's a restaurant and bar with a roaring fire – Capel Curig's liveliest spot after dark, with mains from £15 to £19. Upstairs, the rooms have all been prettied up, with feature wallpaper, exposed stonework and modern bathrooms. It also does packed lunches for walkers (£7.50 per person).

Betws-y-Coed ❺

🛏 Maes-y-Garth   B&B ££

(📞01690-710441; www.maes-y-garth.co.uk; Lon Muriau, off A470; r £75-130; 🅿 📶) Accessible from Betws by a footpath across the river and the fields (starting behind St Michael's Church), this newly built home has earned itself a legion of fans. Inside you'll find a warm welcome and five quietly stylish guest rooms with gorgeous views – perhaps the nicest is room 4, which has its own balcony and views of the valley.

Dolgellau ❼

🛏 Ffynnon   B&B £££

(📞01341-421774; www.ffynnontownhouse.com; Love Lane; s/d from £100/150; 🅿 📶) With a keen eye for contemporary design and a super-friendly welcome, this award-winning boutique B&B manages to be homey and stylish. French antiques are mixed in with modern chandeliers, claw-foot tubs and electronic gadgets, and each room has a seating area for admiring the stunning views in comfort. There's a bar, library, and even an outdoor hot tub.

Harlech ❽

🛏 Maelgwyn House   B&B ££

(📞01766-780087; www.maelgwynharlech. co.uk; Ffordd Isaf; r £70-95; 🅿 📶) A model B&B in an art-bedecked former boarding school, Maelgwyn has interesting hosts, delicious breakfasts and a small set of elegant rooms with tremendous views across the bay, stocked with DVD players and tea-making facilities. Bridget and Derek can also help arrange birdwatching trips and fungus forays. Full marks.

Beddgelert ❿

✖ Beddgelert Bistro & Antiques   Bistro ££

(📞01766-890543; www.beddgelert-bistro. co.uk; Smith St; mains £12-15; 🕙9am-5pm & 6.30-9pm; 📶 ✖) An eccentric gem, this hybrid bistro/antique store offers exceptional home cooking. By day it's more like a tearoom, but at night the tiny dining room at the heart of the 17th-century cottage fills up with happy diners enjoying specials such as goose breast in orange and Triple Sec, and Welsh black beef in creamy peppercorn sauce. Good wines, too.

There are also three en suite bedrooms above (£30 per person with breakfast).

Caernarfon ⓫

🛏 Victoria House   B&B ££

(📞01286-678263; 13 Church St; r £90-100; @ 📶) Victoria House is pretty much the perfect guesthouse – a delightful, solid Victorian building in the middle of Caernarfon's old town, run by exceptionally welcoming and attentive hosts. The four spacious, modern rooms include lovely touches – free toiletries, a DVD on the town's history, fresh milk and a welcoming drink in the bar fridge – and breakfast is a joy.

Landscapes & Literature

26

Take a magical journey through a mist-shrouded river valley before crossing verdant farmland and climbing up through Brecon Beacons National Park to Britain's most bookish town.

TRIP HIGHLIGHTS

FINISH
Hay-on-Wye ⑨ ——————— 75 miles

Hay-on-Wye
A book-lovers paradise
in a charming rural
guise

Brecon

Crickhowell

Abergavenny   Monmouth

5 miles ——————————— ② Tintern

Tintern Abbey
Ghostly ruins rising
from the most
romantic of settings

① Chepstow
START

0 miles

Chepstow Castle
Grandiose and forbidding –
in fact, everything a castle
should be

**3 DAYS
75 MILES / 121KM**

GREAT FOR...

BEST TIME TO GO
This route is enjoyable
year-round but
consider May and
June for spring
flowers and the Hay
Festival.

 **ESSENTIAL
PHOTO**
The spectral ruins of
Tintern Abbey.

 **BEST FOR
HISTORY**
Exploring the hidden
nooks of Chepstow and
Raglan castles.

26 Landscapes & Literature

The Wye Valley is the very birthplace of British tourism. From as early as 1760, English high society flocked here to view artfully ruined Tintern Abbey and the many castles along the way. The romantic vistas that inspired the likes of Turner, Coleridge and Wordsworth remain substantially intact today. The trip continues through the heart of rural Monmouthshire and enters the starkly beautiful high country of Brecon Beacons National Park.

TRIP HIGHLIGHT

❶ Chepstow

If you were in any doubt that this was a border town, check out **Chepstow Castle** (Cadw; www.cadw.gov.wales; Bridge St; adult/child £4.50/3.40; h9.30am-5pm Mar-Oct, 10am-4pm Nov-Feb), standing guard over the River Wye, which still marks the divide between the two nations. This dirty great fortress was founded by the Normans immediately after their conquest of England,

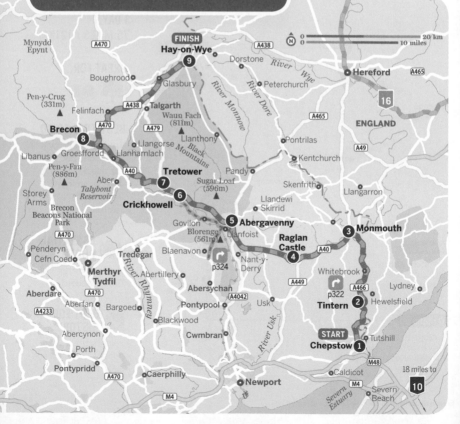

making it one of the oldest castles in Britain. It was added to over the years, its series of courts and battlements sprawling narrowly along the hillside. It's a fascinating place to poke about in, but try not to wake King Arthur, who's believed to be snoozing in a cavern underneath the castle until he's needed to save the day.

The town itself was once held in the castle's stony embrace by a surrounding wall, sections of which still remain. The old part of town is a thoroughly pleasant place to potter about in, with some good eateries, pubs and shops, and a little local **history museum** (☏01291-625981; Bridge St; ⊗11am-4pm Mon-Sat, 2-4pm Sun).

 p327

LINK YOUR TRIP

10 Winchester, Glastonbury & Bath

It's a 45-minute (30-mile) drive from Bath to Chepstow via the M4 and the Severn Bridge.

16 Industrial Powerhouse

From Great Malvern it's 45 miles to Chepstow (allow 1¼ hours); head south to Gloucester and take the A48.

The Drive ›› From Chepstow take the A466 north past famous Chepstow Racecourse and along the wooded Wye Valley. It's an enchanting 5-mile drive, made even more mysterious on a misty morning.

TRIP HIGHLIGHT

② Tintern

Immortalised by painters and poets down the ages, the enigmatic ruins of **Tintern Abbey** (Cadw; www.cadw.gov.wales; Tintern; adult/child £5.50/4.10; ⊗9am-5pm Mar-Oct, 10am-4pm Nov-Feb; **P**) are almost impossibly picturesque. Part of it is the setting, with the River Wye on one side and forested hills all around. The rest is down to the soaring grandeur of the Gothic architecture, made no less stirring by the lack of a roof or windows. Founded in 1131 by the Cistercian order, it was left to fall into elegant ruin after Henry VIII dissolved all of Britain's monasteries in the 16th century.

Tintern village sprawls along the river for about a mile. There are some good walks in the area, including some easy riverside tracks in the vicinity of the **Old Station** (☏01291-689566; www.tinternvillage.co.uk/seedo/tintern-old-station; parking per 3/5hr £1/3.50; ⊗10am-5.30pm Apr-Oct; **P**) visitor centre and cafe.

The Drive ›› Beautiful landscapes continue to unfurl as you progress up the tree-lined river valley. The road crosses the river into England and back again before reaching Monmouth, a journey of just over 12 miles.

③ Monmouth

The county town of Monmouthshire is as English a town as you'll find in Wales. In fact, the border has shifted backwards and forwards over the centuries, shunting it between the two countries.

The rivers Monnow and Wye curl around the historic town centre, creating a natural moat to what was once a walled town attached to **Monmouth Castle** (www.monmouthcastlemuseum.org.uk; Castle Hill). All that remains of this august fortress – the birthplace of Henry V – is a small section of wall and part of a tower. In a much better state of repair is **Monnow Bridge**, the UK's only remaining medieval fortified bridge, which abuts the main street.

Monmouth's other famous son was Charles Stewart Rolls, co-founder of Rolls-Royce. His statue stands outside the **Shire Hall** (☏01600-775257; www.shirehallmonmouth.org.uk; Agincourt Sq; ⊗10am-4pm) and there's a display on his life in the **Nelson Museum & Local History Centre** (☏01600-710630; Priory St; ⊗11am-4pm Mon-Sat, 2-4pm Sun). The museum has extensive displays on Admiral

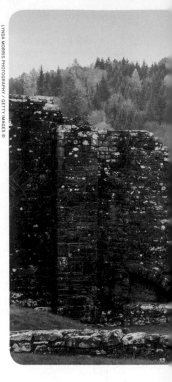

DETOUR: WHITEBROOK

Start: ➋ Tintern (p321)

The tiny hamlet of Whitebrook sits in peaceful seclusion on the Welsh side of the River Wye, reached only by extremely narrow country lanes. There's absolutely no reason to drive this way, as the main road hopped over to the easier English side of the river 2 miles earlier. Unless, of course, you're making your way to **The Whitebrook** (☎01600-860254; www.thewhitebrook.co.uk; Whitebrook; 2-/3-/7-course lunch £25/29/47, 3-/7-course dinner £54/67, r incl dinner from £214; ⊙noon-2pm Wed-Sun, 7-9pm Tue-Sun; P❓), an exceptional restaurant-with-rooms which was recently awarded a Michelin star for its inventive take on Modern British cuisine. If you feel like a little indulgence, consider booking a room upstairs and making a night of it. Plus it will save arguments over who's going to be the sober driver.

To continue on to Monmouth, you're best to backtrack along the same lane and rejoin the A466 at the bridge where it takes its English shortcut.

Horatio Nelson featuring items collected by Rolls' mother, Lady Llangattock.

✕ p327

The Drive ➤ From Monmouth take the busy A40 dual carriageway to the west for 9 miles. Raglan Castle will come into view to the right of the highway, but keep a close eye on the road signs as you'll need to overshoot the castle, continuing on to the roundabout near Raglan village, before you can double back to enter the site.

- - - - - - - - -

➍ Raglan Castle

Standing in majestic ruin at the side of a busy highway, **Raglan Castle** (Cadw; www.cadw.wales.gov. uk; adult/child £4.50/3.40;

⊙9.30am-5pm Mar-Oct, 10am-4pm Nov-Feb; P) is much more ornate than any castle needs to be. That's because defence was only part of its purpose – showing off the wealth, power and good taste of its owners was equally important. Much of the sandstone used in its construction has a pinkish hue, and elegant courtyards were backed by halls decorated with ornate windows and fireplaces.

Raglan fell into disrepair after the Civil War of the 1640s, when Oliver Cromwell's troops undermined the imposing hexagonal Great Tower, causing two of the walls

to collapse. Still, large portions of the structure are intact and you should allow at least an hour to fully explore the site.

The Drive ➤ From the castle you'll need to backtrack down the highway to the nearest roundabout before swinging back past the castle on the A40, which leads all the way to Abergavenny. The 11-mile trip passes through farmland and at times you'll catch glimpses of the River Usk on your left.

- - - - - - - - -

➎ Abergavenny

Sitting right on the doorstep of Brecon Beacons National Park, ringed by

Tintern The ruins of Tintern Abbey

oddly shaped mountains, the pleasant Monmouthshire market town of Abergavenny makes a great base for walkers and other active types. It's also garnered a reputation in recent years as a gastronomic hot spot, due to the quality of local farm produce and a handful of high-profile restaurants scattered about the surrounding countryside.

In the town itself, the main attraction is the imposing **St Mary's Priory Church** (☏01873-858787; www.stmarys-priory.org; Monk St; ⏰9am-4pm Mon-Sat), which is full of so many grand tombs that it's been dubbed the 'Westminster Abbey of Wales'. Once attached to a monastery, it survived Henry VIII's reforms by being converted into a parish church. The neighbouring 12th-century **Tithe Barn** (☏01873-858787; www.stmarys-priory.org; Monk St; ⏰9am-4pm Mon-Sat) now holds a heritage centre and food hall showcasing Welsh products.

It wouldn't be Wales if there wasn't a castle, but Abergavenny's only amounts to a few stretches of curtain wall and a local history **museum** (☏01873-854282; www.abergavennymuseum.co.uk; Castle St; ⏰11am-1pm & 2-5pm Mon-Sat, 2-5pm Sun) where the keep once stood.

🛏 p327

The Drive 》 The next leg is only a short hop of just under 6 miles. Leaving Abergavenny via the A40 you'll quickly enter Brecon Beacons National Park and, shortly afterwards, cross the county border into Powys. The highway shadows the River Usk, albeit from a distance, with the Blorenge mountain rising

323

to the left and Sugar Loaf to the right.

----

⑥ Crickhowell

Like Abergavenny, the picturesque, flower-draped village of Crickhowell is encircled by the contorted peaks of the Black Mountains, which form the eastern section of Brecon Beacons National Park. Aside from a crumbling castle, its main feature of interest is an elegant bridge over the River Usk, which has more arches on one side than the other. It's a short stroll across the bridge to the neighbouring village of Llangattock, which is every bit as pretty.

Crickhowell takes its name from **Crug Hywel** (Table Mountain), a flat-topped mountain with the remains of an Iron Age fort at its summit. It makes an excellent target for a steep 3-mile-return walk. At the top, you're

DETOUR: BLAENAVON

Start: ⑤ Abergavenny (p322)

The coalmines of the South Wales Valleys once fuelled Britain's industrial revolution and powered the might of the British Navy. That all came to a sudden halt during the mine closures of the 1980s. The close-knit communities of the valleys took a major hit, unemployment soared and whole towns faced extinction.

One such place was Blaenavon, a town that came into being in the 18th century after the construction of the world's biggest ironworks. In the year 2000, 20 years after its Big Pit coalmine was closed, Blaenavon's unique conglomeration of industrial sites was awarded World Heritage status by Unesco, igniting a rebirth of sorts.

Start your visit at the excellent **Blaenavon World Heritage Centre** (📞01495-742333; www.visitblaenavon.co.uk; Church Rd; ⏰10am-5pm Tue-Sun) to put everything into perspective. The town's main attraction is the **Big Pit National Coal Museum** (📞0300 111 2333; www.museumwales.ac.uk; car park £3; ⏰9.30am-5pm, guided tours 10am-3.30pm; 🅿), where you can head 90m down into the depths under the guidance of former miners and get a feel for what life was like working the coal seam. If that doesn't appeal, the above-ground museum is fascinating in its own right.

The historic **Blaenavon Ironworks** (Cadw; www.cadw.gov.wales; North St; ⏰10am-5pm Easter-Oct, to 4pm Tue-Thu Nov-Easter) are another must-see, the hulking ruins brought to life through audiovisual displays. A group of local enthusiasts has also resurrected a section of the **Pontypool & Blaenavon Railway** (📞01495-792263; www.pontypool-and-blaenavon.co.uk; day pass adult/child £10/5), which once hauled coal down from the mines. Check online to see when the steam trains are running to Whistle Stop, the highest station in both Wales and England.

Another byproduct of the town's reinvention is the **Blaenavon Cheddar Company** (📞01495-793123; www.chunkofcheese.co.uk; 80 Broad St; ⏰10am-5pm Mon-Sat), an enterprising crew which produces award-winning cheeses, some of which is matured in the Big Pit itself.

Blaenavon is 7 miles southwest of Abergavenny via the B4246. From here you can continue back to the Head of the Valleys Rd and on through Llangattock to Crickhowell, a distance of 10 miles.

unlikely to encounter another soul.

If you're not feeling that energetic, take a wander around the town centre. Crickhowell is known for its interesting independent shops (you won't find any chain stores here) and a clutch of terrific pubs.

🛏️ p327

The Drive » It's less than 3 miles from Crickhowell to the village of Tretower. Take the A40 out of town and then veer right onto the A479. Look for the sign to Tretower Court on your left.

- - - - - - - - - -

Hay-on-Wye Richard Booth's Bookshop

❼ Tretower

By the 15th century, the Vaughan family, like many toffs of the time, had tired of living in their drafty old castle and decided to build a more comfortable pad nearby. The result was **Tretower Court** (Cadw; www.cadw.gov.wales; Tretower; adult/child £6/4.20; ⏱10am-5pm Apr-Oct, to 4pm Wed-Fri Nov-Mar), a large fortified house, which is still standing today in the unassuming farming hamlet of Tretower.

Most of the rooms have been left bare, but the kitchens and banquetting hall have been brought to life with period-style furnishings and implements. If you feel any sense of déjà vu on your visit, it might be because the house has been used for period dramas including movies such as *Restoration* and *The Libertine*.

Don't forget to check out the medieval garden at the side of the house and to cross the fields to the Vaughan's old digs – the sturdy Norman motte-and-bailey castle, looking for all the world like a giant's abandoned chess piece.

The Drive » Continue along the lane past Tretower Court and you'll quickly rejoin the A40, which leads to Brecon. It's a good, scenic road through farmland, with the River Usk and the various peaks of the Brecon Beacons sneaking in and out of view to your left. All up, the journey is less than 12 miles; allow 20 minutes.

- - - - - - - - - -

❽ Brecon

Standing at the confluence of the rivers Usk and Honddu, the ruggedly handsome market town of Brecon presents an austere stony face to the world.

When the Normans did their spot of conquering in these parts, inevitably they built a castle and a monastery. **Brecknock Castle** (Castle Sq) has largely been consumed by a hotel, but you can still catch a glimpse of its historic form from the riverside. The monk's church has fared better, surviving the Reformation as a parish church before being converted into impressive **Brecon Cathedral** (📞01874-623857; www.breconcathedral.org.uk; Cathedral Close; ⏱8.30am-6pm). While you're visiting, make sure you call into the neighbouring tithe barn which now contains a **Heritage Centre** (📞01874-625222; www.breconcathedralshop.co.uk; Cathedral Close;

⊙11am-3pm Mon-Sat) and a cafe.

Brecon is the northern terminus of the **Monmouthshire & Brecon Canal**. Regular cruises depart from the Canal Basin, or you can hire your own boat for a self-guided trip. The canal towpath is a popular walking and cycling route.

If you're interested in military history, don't miss the **South Wales Borderers Museum** (📞01874-613310; www.royal welsh.org.uk; The Barracks, The Watton; adult/child £5/1; ⊙10am-5pm Mon-Sat Easter-Sep, Mon-Fri Oct-Easter).

🛏 p327

The Drive » The 17-mile route from Brecon to Hay-on-Wye is straightforward and pleasantly rural, and should take less than half an hour. Head east out of town along the Watton and then turn left onto the A470, which eventually becomes the A438. The road to Hay branches off at Glasbury, with views to the Black Mountains on your right.

- - - - - - - - - - -

TRIP HIGHLIGHT

❾ Hay-on-Wye

If there's anywhere more bookish than Hay-on-Wye we'd be seriously surprised. Once a pretty but nondescript agricultural centre, Hay re-invented itself in the 1970s under the instigation of local maverick Richard Booth, who opened the world's largest bookshop in a defunct cinema, bought crumbling **Hay Castle** (www. haycastletrust.org; Castle St), declared himself king and undertook a series of publicity stunts that attracted national attention and saved the town from the decline facing many rural communities at the time.

Others took note and now there are literally dozens of new, second-hand, specialist and antiquarian bookshops in this small Powys town. On top of that, Hay-on-Wye is now the setting for the **Hay Festival** (📞01497-822629; www. hayfestival.com; ⊙May-Jun), arguably the most famous literature event in the world, famously dubbed the 'Woodstock of the mind' by former US president Bill Clinton.

Spend your Hay time alternating between bookshops, antique stores and pubs, and be sure to check out some of the excellent local eateries.

🍴🛏 p327

Eating & Sleeping

Chepstow ❶

🛏 Three Tuns   Pub ££

(📞01291-645797; www.threetunschepstow.
co.uk; 32 Bridge St; s/d from £50/75) This early
17th-century pub by the castle has had an artful
makeover, with rugs and antique furniture
complimenting the more rugged features of
the ancient building. There's often live music
downstairs on weekends, but the noise winds
down at 11pm.

Monmouth ❸

🍴 Bistro Prego   Modern British ££

(📞01600-712600; www.pregomonmouth.co.uk;
7 Church St; mains £13-17, s/d from £45/65;
🕐noon-10pm; 📶) Set on a cobbled lane in the
heart of the town, this little bistro serves very
good bistro fare which, despite the name, isn't
particularly Italian. Upstairs there are eight
comfortable, clean, good-value rooms, each
with its own bathroom.

Abergavenny ❺

🛏 Angel Hotel   Hotel ££

(📞01873-857121; www.angelabergavenny.com;
15 Cross St; r/cottage from £89/177; P 📶)
Abergavenny's top hotel is a fine Georgian
building that was once a famous coaching inn.
Choose between sleek, sophisticated rooms
in the hotel itself, in an adjoining mews, in a
Victorian lodge near the castle or in the 17th-
century Castle Cottage (sleeping four). There's
also a good **restaurant** (mains restaurant
£14-18, bar £6-14; 🕐noon-11pm) and bar.

Crickhowell ❻

🛏 Gwyn Deri   B&B ££

(📞01873-812494; www.gwynderibandand
breakfast.co.uk; Mill St; s/d/f £40/70/100; P 📶
📶) The friendly couple who run this homely

B&B keep its three modern guest bedrooms
immaculately clean, and are more than happy
to share their knowledge of the area. Bonuses
include fresh fruit in the rooms and an excellent
breakfast selection. Connecting rooms are
available for family groups.

Brecon ❽

🛏 Peterstone Court   Hotel £££

(📞01874-665387; www.peterstone-court.com;
Llanhamlach; r from £150; P 📶 🏊) At this
elegant Georgian manor house, the rooms are
large and comfortable, and the views across the
valley to the Beacons are superb. The boutique
spa centre is a big drawcard, pampering guests
with organic beauty products. They also have
an excellent **restaurant** (A40, Llanhamlach;
breakfast £8-14, lunch £15-17, dinner £14-21;
🕐7.30-9.30am & noon-9.30pm). Llanhamlach is
3 miles southeast of Brecon, just off the A40.

Hay-on-Wye ❾

🍴 Tomatitos Tapas Bar   Spanish £

(📞01497-820770; www.haytomatitos.co.uk; 38
Lion St; tapas £2.25-5.95; 🕐11am-11pm Mon-Sat,
to 4pm Sun; 📶) Friendly, bustling Tomatitos
combines the atmosphere of everyone's
favourite pub with an *España*-centric menu.
Staples such as *patatas bravas* and chorizo
aside, daily specials feature guest stars such
as mushrooms stuffed with Cabrales cheese
and lamb tagine, washed down with Spanish,
Portuguese and French wine by the glass.

🛏 The Bear   B&B ££

(📞01497-821302; www.thebearhay.com; 2 Bear
St; s/d from £55/80; P 📶) This friendly and
well-run 1590 coaching inn retains its historic
ambience and combines it with interesting art,
sisal floors and bathrooms with tubs – bliss for
tired hikers. One of the three chic bedrooms has
a four-poster bed, and the excellent breakfasts
include imaginative vegetarian options. Curl up
with a book by the immense fireplace.

Wilderness Wales

27

From cetacean-rich Cardigan Bay to the great swelling upland of the Cambrian Mountains, Wales' wild heart will take your breath away.

TRIP HIGHLIGHTS

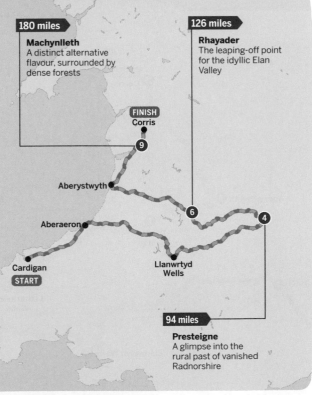

180 miles

Machynlleth
A distinct alternative flavour, surrounded by dense forests

126 miles

Rhayader
The leaping-off point for the idyllic Elan Valley

FINISH
Corris

9

Aberystwyth

6

4

Aberaeron

Cardigan
START

Llanwrtyd Wells

94 miles

Presteigne
A glimpse into the rural past of vanished Radnorshire

4 DAYS
181 MILES / 301KM

GREAT FOR ...

BEST TIME TO GO

December to February brings snow to the Cambrian uplands, but hiking, events and dolphin-spotting are best in summer.

 ESSENTIAL PHOTO

The mighty Victorian dams of the Elan Valley.

BEST FOR WILDLIFE

Red-kite feeding time outside Rhayader.

Gigrin Farm Red-Kite Feeding Station Red Kites

27 Wilderness Wales

With cities to the south and Snowdonia to the north, Mid-Wales' natural grandeur is often ignored. This drive – from the historic port of Cardigan, through spa country, pretty market towns, the great 'Green Desert' of the Cambrian Mountains to the forests and estuaries of the green northwest – shows how wrong this neglect is. We guarantee you won't forget this tour of some of Wales' loveliest, greenest places.

----

❶ Cardigan

An important port for fishing and trade in the days of Elizabeth I, Cardigan is emerging from long obscurity to stake a claim as a major centre of culture in Mid-Wales. Its riverside **castle** (Castell Aberteifi; ☎01239-615131; www.cardigancastle.com; 2 Green St) – where in the 12th century the first Eisteddfod was held – has been carefully restored, and serves once again as a bastion of Welsh culture, hosting performances, language classes

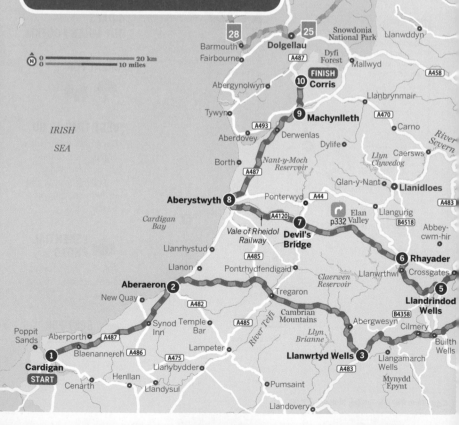

and more. Beyond the compact town, the wetlands around the River Teifi and the vast sweep of Cardigan Bay promise **encounters** (📞01239-623558; www.baytoremember.co.uk; Prince Charles Quay; 1hr trip adult/child £25/12; ☺Mar-Oct) with dolphins, seals and a stunning array of birdlife.

📖 p335

The Drive » Take the A487 out of town as it heads northeast and inland for 22 miles, before rejoining the coast just outside the pretty little harbour town of Aberaeron.

❷ Aberaeron

With its colourful quayside rows of Georgian houses and shipping offices, many now occupied by top-notch B&Bs and hotels, Aberaeron makes a great stop for a meal or sleep. Most of the appeal is to be found along Pen Cei (Quay Parade, on the waterfront), but it's well worth the 2.5-mile trek out of town to visit **Llanerchaeron** (NT; 📞01545-570200; www.nationaltrust.org.uk/llanerchaeron; Ciliau Aeron; adult/child £7.60/3.80; ☺10.30am-5.30pm, villa 11.30am-4pm), a lovely country estate that brings the genteel Welsh existence of Georgian times to life once more.

📖 p335

The Drive » It's time to leave the sea behind you, taking the A487 north to Aberarth, then the B4577/A485 inland to the market town of Tregaron. From here, the Dolecoed Rd winds through hills and pasture to Llanwrtyd Wells; all up, the journey is 36 miles.

❸ Llanwrytd Wells

Mid-Wales' capital of kooky, little Llanwrtyd and its surrounding hills are home to a variety of weird and wonderful annual events, including **bog snorkelling** (www.green-events.co.uk; adult/child £15/12; ☺bank holiday Aug), and a **fell-running competition** (www.green-events.co.uk; ☺mid-Jun) that pits man against horse. Dining, drinking and sleeping options are also rich for such a tiny town, with special mention going to the **Drovers Rest** (📞01591-610264; www.food-food-food.co.uk; Y Sgwar; 3 courses £30; ☺10.30am-3.30pm & 7-9.30pm Tue & Thu-Sat, 12.30-2.30pm Sun; 📶) and the **Neuadd Arms** (📞01591-610236; www.neuaddarmshotel.co.uk; Y Sgwar; ☺8.30am-midnight Sun-Thu, 8.30am-1am Fri & Sat) – the hub of the local community.

📖 p335

The Drive » Take the A483 northeast from Llanwrtyd, forking east at Beulah and

LINK YOUR TRIP

25 Snowdonia National Park

Corris, on the southern cusp of Snowdonia, is only 11 miles south of Dolgellau, via the A487 and A470.

28 Northwest Wales

Dolgellau is also on this itinerary, and easily reached.

continuing on to the farming and spa town of Builth Wells. From here continue east on the A481, the A44 and lastly the B4362, dipping into England then back into Wales to reach Presteigne. This leg is also 36 miles.

TRIP HIGHLIGHT

❹ Presteigne

At the far east of the former county of Radnorshire is Presteigne, its former county town. It's an appealing little place, lined with handsome old buildings and surrounded by beautiful countryside. You can eat very well here – both the **Moroccan Delicatessen** (☎01544-598351; High St; mains £5-10; ☺9am-2pm Tue-Sat) and **Duck's Nest** (☎01544-598090; www.

theducksnest.com; 10 High St; mains £14-17; ☺noon-2pm & 6-10pm Tue-Sat) are well worth saving appetite for. The **Judge's Lodging** (☎01544-260650; www.judgeslodging.org.uk; Broad St; adult/child £7.95/3.95; ☺10am-5pm Tue-Sun Mar-Oct, 10am-4pm Wed-Sun Nov, 10am-4pm Sat & Sun Dec) reanimates a Victorian rural magistrate's household in exacting detail.

The Drive ≫ Head northwest out of Presteigne on the B4356 through the hills of historical Radnorshire, through Pilleth (scene of Owain Glyndŵr's 1402 victory over Edmund Mortimer), after which the A488 and A44 take you west to the junction with the A483, at Crossgates. Then it's a short hop south to the spa town of Llandrindod Wells: all up, a 21-mile stage.

❺ Llandrindod Wells

The Victorian and Edwardian heyday of this spa town is still evident in the grand architecture of its hotels and terraces, however quiet they may be today. Hotel-spas still fly the flag of formal luxury, while the mineral fountains and rambling gardens of **Rock Park** also hint at the bygone glory days, when visitors from around Britain would arrive to take the waters. There's also the **National Cycle Museum** (☎01597-825531; www.cyclemuseum.org.uk; Temple St; adult/child £5/2; ☺10am-4pm Tue-Fri Apr-Oct) and, for real-ale and folk fans, the lovely little **Arvon Ale House**

↱ DETOUR: THE ELAN VALLEY

Start: ❻ Rhayader

If you're in Rhayader, you really should head into the man-sculpted wilderness of the Elan Valley. It feels immediately remote and wild, once you leave human habitations behind, yet its defining features are probably the four huge Victorian and Edwardian dams that were created to ensure water supplies to Birmingham. Inevitably controversial, they've nonetheless created a 70-sq-mile chain of lake, forest and bog environments in Mid-Wales in which certain plants and animals, including the totemic Red Kite, thrive. Nant-y-Gro, an early dam built here to serve the village of navvies that built the main structures, was used in 1942 as target practice by Sir Barnes Neville Wallis, the inventor of the 'dam-busting' bouncing bomb.

The **Elan Valley Visitor Centre** (☎01597-810880; www.elanvalley.org.uk; B4518; ☺10am-5pm Easter-Oct) has all the information a casual (or more determined) visitor could need, including the routes and specifics of the many walks of under three hours that can be attempted. In season, the **Penbont House** (☎01597-811515; ☺11am-5pm Fri-Mon Mar-Jul, Sep & Oct, daily Aug; 🍴) makes for a delightful lunch or tea stop, and can even provide accommodation for those organised enough to book ahead. From Rhayader, the visitor centre is less than 4 miles southwest on the B4518; just backtrack to rejoin the main route.

Elan Valley Craig Goch dam

(📞07477-627267; Temple St; 🕑4-10pm Wed-Sun).

🛏️ p335

The Drive » This very manageable 11-mile stage will probably come as something of a relief, after criss-crossing the country. Back-track north up the A483 as far as the junction with the A4081. Take this west to the River Wye, and follow it north along the A470 to Rhayader.

- - - - - - - - - - - - -
TRIP HIGHLIGHT
⑥ Rhayader

An important centre for agriculture in these parts, Rhayader has a long history, but is perhaps most appealing for its access to the surrounding wild places. It's the closest significant centre to the delightful Elan Valley, with its monumental Victorian and Edwardian dams, and is also handy for the **Wye Valley Walk** (www.wyevalleywalk.

org) and the **Gigrin Farm Red-Kite Feeding Station** (📞01597-810243; www.gigrin. co.uk; South St (A470); adult/ child £5/3; 🕑12.30-5pm daily Jan-Oct, to 4pm Sat & Sun Nov & Dec), where the dignified birds of prey can be seen tucking into their daily meat. If you're ready for refreshment, head for the diminutive but characterful **Triangle Inn** (📞01597-810537; www. triangleinn.co.uk; Cwmdauddwr; mains £8-12; 🕑6.30-11pm daily year-round, noon-3pm Tue-Sat May-Aug, noon-3pm Thu-Sat Sep-Apr; 📶).

The Drive » From Rhayader the next 18-mile stage heads northwest along the twisty B4574 to Devil's Bridge Falls.

- - - - - - - - - - - - -

⑦ Devil's Bridge

The eponymous **bridge** (www.devilsbridgefalls. co.uk; adult/child £3.75/2; 🕑9.30am-5pm) is the

main attraction at this otherwise out-of-the way corner of Mid-Wales. Spanning a cataract where the River Rheidol plunges into the gorge of the same name, it's actually a palimpsest of three overlapping bridges: the top built of iron in the early 20th century, the middle of stone in the mid-18th, and the first (also of stone) in the 11th.

So long as the weather allows, it's worth paying the few pounds to descend into the gorge and the Coed Rheidol National Nature Reserve, with its dripping oaks and glimpses of the bridge. Devil's Bridge is also the inland terminus of the **Vale of Rheidol Railway,** (Rheilffordd Cwm Rheidol; 📞01970-625819; www.rheidolrailway.co.uk; Park Ave; adult/child return £20/8; 🕑up to 5 daily late Mar–Oct,

Sat & Sun Nov, except week before Christmas closed Dec–mid-Feb) a narrow-gauge industrial train that's been preserved as a tourist attraction, and clings to the slopes as it wends its picturesque way to the coast at Aberystwyth.

The Drive » From Devil's Bridge the A4120 skirts the southern edge of the River Rheidol, through the valley for 12 miles to the coast at Aberystwyth.

- - - - - - - - - - - -

❽ Aberystwyth

A very diverting place to spend an afternoon (or evening, or night) recovering from your wild adventures, Aberystwyth is a lively student town with quite a mix of attractions. Culturally, it's hard to go past the **National Library** (☑01970-632800; www.llgc. org.uk; A487; ☺9.30am-6pm Mon-Fri, to 5pm Sat), which surmounts a hill befitting its eminence behind the town, or the **Aberystwyth Arts Centre** (Canolfan Y Celfyddydau; ☑box office 01970-623232; www.abery stwythartscentre.co.uk; Penglais Rd; ☺8am-11pm Mon-Sat, noon-8pm Sun), part of Aberystwyth University. There's also a picturesque ruined **castle**, the worthy **Ceredigion Museum** (☑01970-633088; www.ceredigion.gov. uk; Terrace Rd; ☺10.30am-4pm Tue-Sat, noon-4pm Sun Apr-Sep), and plenty of pubs to keep the students happy.

🛏 p335

The Drive » From Aberystwyth the A487 runs for 18 scenic, rural miles to Machynlleth.

- - - - - - - - - - - -

TRIP HIGHLIGHT

❾ Machynlleth

The site of the first (short-lived) Welsh Parliament, convened by the rebel Owain Glyndŵr in 1404, Machynlleth is far from a household name, yet is justifiably important in Welsh nationalist history. Today it's notable for other attractions, not least the **Centre for Alternative Technology** (CAT; Canolfan y Dechnoleg Amgen; ☑01654-705950; www.cat.org. uk; Pantperthog; adult/child £8.50/4; ☺10am-5pm; P 🚻), **MOMA Machynlleth** (☑01654-703355; www.moma. machynlleth.org.uk; Penrallt St; ☺10am-4pm Mon-Sat), and the forests, hiking paths and **mountain-biking trails** (www.dyfimoun tainbiking.org.uk) that surround it. It's a charismatic and distinctive place, with some good restaurants, pubs and inns and a quite individual charm. If you're interested in Machynlleth's history, the Parliament House and **Owain Glyndŵr Centre** (Canolfan Owain Glyndŵr; ☑01654-702932; www. canolfanglyndwr.org; Maengwyn St; ☺10am-4pm Easter-Sep) occupy the site where Glyndŵr gathered his defiant assembly (although the present structure probably dates from later

in the 15th century, and has been remodelled since).

🍽 🛏 p335

The Drive » It's a mere 6 miles to forest-swaddled Corris, taking the A487 north out of town.

- - - - - - - - - - - -

❿ Corris

A quiet and often-overlooked destination, Corris is surrounded by pine-clad slopes, walking paths and mountain-bike trails. There's also the lovingly maintained **Corris Railway** (☑01654-761303; www.corris.co.uk; Station Yard; adult/child £6/3; ☺see website for days of operation), the thoroughly convivial **Slaters Arms** (☑01654-761324; www.theslatersarms. com; Bridge St), and the best cup of coffee (or bacon sandwich) for many a mile, at **Andy & Adam's Shop** (☑01654-761391; www. andyandadam.co.uk; Bridge St; ☺9.30am-6.30pm). And, just outside of the town proper, you'll find the **Corris Craft Centre** (☑01654-761584; www.corriscraftcentre. co.uk; ☺10am-5pm), **Mine Explorers** (☑01654-761244; www.corrismineexplorers.co.uk; ☺tours by appointment) and **King Arthur's Labyrinth** (☑01654-761584; www. kingarthurslabyrinth.com; adult/child £9.95/6.65; ☺10am-5pm Easter-Oct; 🚻). All told, Corris is a lovely and very fitting place to wind up your odyssey in the Welsh wilderness.

Eating & Sleeping

Cardigan ❶

🛏 Caernant   B&B £

(📞01239-612932; www.caernant.co.uk; Gwbert Rd; s/d £40/60; 🅿 🛜) Big, bright, spacious rooms are on offer at Caernant, a delightful modern B&B just outside Cardigan. With tea and scones on arrival, incredible breakfasts (including smoked salmon and buttered kippers) and heart-felt hospitality, it's well worth the short trip from town (less than a mile from the centre of Cardigan, on the B4548).

Aberaeron ❷

🛏 Harbour Master   Boutique Hotel £££

(📞01545-570755; www.harbour-master.com; Pen Cei; s/d from £75/145; 🛜) Commanding Aberaeron's harbour entrance, this small, hip hotel offers food and accommodation worthy of any chic city bolthole. The striking Georgian buildings hold 13 quirky rooms featuring Frette linens, vintage Welsh blankets and high-tech bathrooms. Those in the newly restored grain warehouse have the same contemporary styling with excellent harbour views.

Llanwrytd Wells ❸

🛏 Lasswade Country House   B&B ££

(📞01591-610515; www.lasswadehotel.co.uk; Station Rd; s/d from £65/90; 🅿 🛜 🖊) This excellent restaurant-with-rooms makes great use of a handsome, three-storey Edwardian house looking over the Irfon Valley towards the Brecon Beacons. Committed to green tourism (it's won a slew of awards, sources hydroelectric power and even offers electric vehicle recharging), it's also big on gastronomy.

Llandrindod Wells ❺

🛏 The Cottage   B&B ££

(📞01597-825435; www.thecottagebandb. co.uk; Spa Rd; s/d £45/68) A really top-notch B&B making great use of a large, Arts-and-Crafts-style Edwardian house, the Cottage has a flower-adorned garden, and comfortable rooms decorated in period style with heavy wooden furniture and lots of original features. All rooms are either en suite or have private bathrooms, and the only TV is in the guest lounge.

Aberystwyth ❽

🛏 Gwesty Cymru   Hotel ££

(📞01970-612252; www.gwestycymru.com; 19 Marine Tce; s/d from £70/95; 🕐 restaurant noon-2.30pm & 6-9pm Tue-Sun; 🛜) A real gem, the 'Wales Hotel' is a charismatic boutique property with a strong sense of Welsh identity right on the waterfront. Local slate features throughout, paired with contemporary styling. Of the eight en-suite rooms, those on the top floor offer baths with sea views. There's an on-site restaurant.

Machynlleth ❾

🛏 Glandyfi Castle   Boutique Hotel ££

(📞01654-781238; www.glandyficastle.co.uk; A487, Glandyfi; r £90-250; 🅿 🛜) Built in 1820, this quirky Regency Gothic castle has been brought back to life as a gloriously indulgent hotel. The eight excellent-value rooms blend classical styling with modern sensibilities, while the turrets, towers, octagonal rooms and superb views over the vast grounds make it a special place to stay. A three-course set menu (£35 per head) is served in the evening, and afternoon tea can be arranged (£18 per head). The castle is 6 miles southwest of Machynlleth, off the A487.

🛏 Ynyshir Hall   Hotel £££

(📞01654-781209; www.ynyshirhall.co.uk; Eglwysfach; r from £195; 🛜) Tucked away to the south of the River Dovey (Afon Dyfi) estuary, just off the main Aberystwyth–Machynlleth road (A487), 6 miles southwest of Machynlleth, this grand manor house was once kept as a hunting lodge by Queen Victoria. It's now a quietly opulent boutique hotel and **restaurant** (5-course lunch/dinner menu £39.50/55; 🕐 noon-2pm & 7-9pm), where the friendly staff are never less than professional.

Northwest Wales

28

Shaped by pilgrims, conquerors and the unceasing sea, Northwest Wales is a stunning and historically rich corner of the British Isles that begs to be explored from behind the wheel.

TRIP HIGHLIGHTS

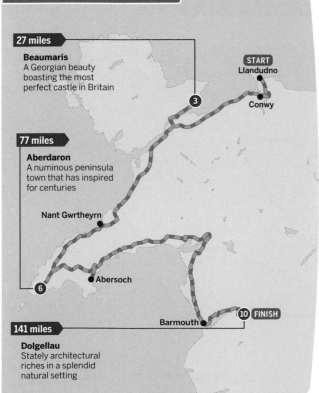

27 miles

Beaumaris
A Georgian beauty boasting the most perfect castle in Britain

77 miles

Aberdaron
A numinous peninsula town that has inspired for centuries

Nant Gwrtheyrn

Abersoch

141 miles

Dolgellau
Stately architectural riches in a splendid natural setting

START
Llandudno

Conwy

Barmouth

10 FINISH

**4 DAYS
141 MILES / 227KM**

GREAT FOR...

BEST TIME TO GO

Daffodils and spring lambs make April a particularly lovely time to visit.

 ESSENTIAL PHOTO

The Pilgrim's Island, Bardsey, from Braich-y-Pwll at the tip of the Llŷn Peninsula.

 BEST FOR HISTORY

The mock-Byzantine splendour of Caernarfon Castle.

Caernarfon Castle The castle towers over the Menai Strait

337

28 | Northwest Wales

Starting from the bustling seaside resort of Llandudno, whose Victorian heyday lingers still, this trip takes in some of the mightiest castles and most dramatic coastline in the entire country. The medieval towns of Conwy, Beaumaris and Caernarfon give way to the Llŷn Peninsula's enchanting mix of emerald fields and plunging cliffs, before the drive finishes among the heritage towns and bird-rich wetlands around the Mawddach River.

---

❶ Llandudno

Stunningly situated below the windswept prominence of Great Orme, where you can explore the most extensive **Bronze Age mine** (www. greatormemines.info; adult/child £6.75/4.75; ⏱9.30am-5.30pm mid-Mar–Oct) yet discovered, Llandudno retains many of the attractions of its Victorian heyday: a grand promenade, a rack-and-pinion **tramway** (📞01492-577877; www.greatormetramway. co.uk; Victoria Station, Church Walks; adult/child return £7/5;

🕙10am-6pm Easter-Oct), and even a **Punch and Judy show** (📞07900-555515; www.punchandjudy.com/codgal.htm; The Promenade; 🕙2pm & 4pm Sat & Sun year-round, plus daily school holidays Easter–mid-Sep) run by the same family for generations. Add a huge range of B&Bs and restaurants, the forward-looking **Mostyn Gallery** (www.mostyn.org; 12 Vaughan St; 🕙10.30am-4pm Tue-Sun) and the impressive arts centre **Venue Cymru** (📞01472-872000; www.venuecymru.co.uk; The Promenade; 🕙box office 10am-7pm Mon-Sat, plus 1hr before performances), and this amounts to one of the jewels of the North Wales seaboard.

🛏 p343

The Drive » This first leg is just 4 miles, south down the A546 to Llandudno Junction, then west onto the A456 and through the tunnel under the River Conwy.

LINK YOUR TRIP

25 Snowdonia National Park

Join this circuit of Wales' most famous uplands at Dolgellau.

27 Wilderness Wales

Follow the A487 beyond Dolgellau to start this tour of Wales' wild heart in reverse, at Corris.

---

❷ Conwy

Conwy is one of Wales' must-sees: a near-perfect medieval walled town, with a superlative example of the castle-builder's art attached. Put up in the 13th century as a key part of Edward I's 'Iron Ring', Conwy Castle (p312) has survived centuries of mixed fortunes with its dignity and walls intact. And the Old Town, studded with historical and cultural attractions nearly as impressive as the castle itself, draws the flocks of visitors that make it buzz in high summer. Excellent accommodation and pubs, and a smattering of decent eating options, round out the appeal.

🛏 p343

The Drive » The Bangor Rd/A457 heads west out of Conwy to the A55. Cross the Menai Strait on the Pont Britannia, then take the A5 east into the town of Menai Bridge, following Dale St, then High St/Cadnant Rd until it joins Beaumaris Rd. In total, it's 23 miles to your next stop.

TRIP HIGHLIGHT

❸ Beaumaris

Beaumaris' broad streets, lined with handsome Georgian buildings (many of them now B&Bs and restaurants) lead the visitor inevitably to the waterfront, and the town's unsurpassed **castle** (Cadw; www.cadw.

wales.gov.uk; Castle St; adult/child £6/4.20; 🕙9.30am-5pm Mar-Oct, to 6pm Jul & Aug, 11am-4pm Nov-Feb). While never finished, this 13th-century masterpiece is complete enough to show why it's considered the most perfectly designed fortress of its type in the British Isles. If you're not sated by history, there's also the 17th-century **Courthouse** (Llys Biwmares; www.visitanglesey.co.uk; Castle St; adult/child £3.60/2.80, incl Beaumaris Gaol £7.90/6.50; 🕙10.30am-5pm Sat-Thu Apr-Oct) and Georgian **Gaol** (www.visitanglesey.co.uk; Steeple Lane; adult/child £5/4, incl Beaumaris Courthouse £7.90/6.50; 🕙10.30am-5pm Sat-Thu Apr-Oct) to explore, before wetting your whistle at the medieval **George & Dragon** (📞01248-810491; Church St; 🕙11.30am-11pm, to midnight Sat; 🛜).

✕ 🛏 p343

The Drive » Backtrack along the roads from Beaumaris to Menai Bridge, turn south over the eponymous bridge itself to join the A487 and head southwest, 13 miles to Caernarfon.

---

❹ Caernarfon

Caernarfon's castle (p316), built during the same 13th-century push for English military consolidation as Conwy and Beaumaris, is just as impressive. The scene of Charles' investiture as the current Prince of Wales, its hexagonal Byzantine-style walls are still pretty much complete, and tower impressively over the Menai Strait and medieval town. Just outside of the town are the remains of **Segontium** (Cadw; www. cadw.wales.gov.uk; Ffordd Cwstenin; ⏱10am-4pm Tue, Wed & Sat Apr-Oct), a Roman fort from an earlier local conquest, while inside are excellent pubs, B&Bs and restaurants: among the tea shops and pub-restaurants are some of North Wales's best dining options.

🛏 p317

The Drive » The 18-mile leg to Nant Gwrtheyrn on the Llŷn Peninsula starts on the A487, south from Caernarfon. Take the A499 where it forks to the southwest, then the B4417 at Llanaelhaearn. When you hit Lithfaen, the minor road over the hill to Nant Gwrtheyrn is signposted.

----

❺ Nant Gwrtheyrn

A relic of the hard days when granite was quarried on this part of the storm-swept Irish Sea coast, Nant Gwrtheyrn has been revived as a tourist attraction and bastion of Welsh culture. The severe 19th-century buildings, once in disrepair and home to a 1970s commune, have been restored as handsome **cottages** (☎01758-750334; www.nantgwrtheyrn.org; Nant Gwrtheyrn, Llithfaen; @), a

cafe and **Welsh Language & Heritage Centre** (☎01758-750334; www.nant gwrtheyrn.org; weekend/ 3-day course incl full board £240/295; ⏱call ahead for times). The harsh beauty of the site remains, with crumbling industrial relics tended by grazing feral goats and lapped by the iron-grey sea, but it's a much more inviting and edifying destination these days.

The Drive » Backtrack over the hill, under the Iron Age hill fort of Tre'r Ceiri, to Lithfaen, then take the B4417 west through Pistyll and Nefyn, and further west once you join the B4413. All up, the trip to Aberdaron is 19 miles.

TRIP HIGHLIGHT

❻ Aberdaron

When driving down the Llŷn Peninsula, it's worth persisting to the utter end, as the best is definitely saved for last. The rocky, wildflower-strewn tip of this barren outpost of Celtic Britain is sublimely beautiful and Aberdaron, its last town, is the natural base from which to explore that beauty. The town itself boasts a **church** (www.st-hywyn.org.uk; ⏱10am-6pm Apr-Oct, to 4pm Nov-Mar) that has fare-welled pilgrims bound for Bardsey for centuries, but the real attraction is the gob-smacking coastal landscape beyond. The National Trust owned headland of **Braich-y-**

BENJAMIN ROWE / 500PX ©

Pwll (NT; www.nationaltrust. org.uk), looking across the shimmering sea to the Pilgrim's Island of Bardsey, is one of the most arresting sights Wales can offer.

The Drive » The 13-mile drive to Abersoch follows the B4413 inland, then south along a signposted minor road into town.

----

❼ Abersoch

Abersoch has a winter and a summer identity: sublimely lovely even in the colder months, with its compact harbour and views across Cardigan

Llŷn Peninsula View of the coastline

Bay to Snowdonia, it comes alive in the warmth, when hordes of visitors descend to swell its B&Bs, campsites and pubs. If you have the time to work on your sailing or surfing skills, try **Abersoch Sailing School** (☏07917-525540; www.abersochsailingschool.co.uk; ⊗Sat, Sun & school holidays Mar-Oct) or **Offaxis** (☏01758-713407; www.offaxis.co.uk; Lôn Engan; lessons incl equipment from £30; ⊗10am-5pm Mon-Fri, 9am-6pm Sat, 10.30am-4pm Sun). Abersoch's popularity sustains a number of excellent restaurants.

🛏 p343

The Drive 》 Take the A499 northeast, through Llanbedrog to Pwllheli. From there the A497 follows the coastal railway, through Criccieth to Porthmadog: all up, it's 20 miles.

- - - - - - - - - - - -

❽ Porthmadog

Porthmadog has more character than beauty, but is a natural stopping point when driving from the Llŷn Peninsula to the northwest Welsh coast. It's also the starting point for two classic Welsh heritage railways – the **Welsh Highland** (☏01766-516000; www.festrail.co.uk; adult/child return £38/34.20; ⊗Easter-Oct, limited winter service) and **Ffestiniog Railway** (Rheilffordd Ffestiniog; ☏01766-516024; www.festrail.co.uk; adult/child return £23/21; ⊗daily Easter-Oct, reduced service rest of year; ♿) lines – and a central point on the Cambrian Coast line to Pwllheli. Real ale fans will appreciate the shopfront of **Purple Moose** (Bragdy Mŵs Piws; ☏01766-512777; www.purplemoose.co.uk; 129 High St; ⊗9.30am-5.30pm Mon-Sat, plus 10.30am-4.30pm Sun in Aug), the leading craft brewer in northern Wales.

DETOUR: PORTMEIRION

Start: ❽ Porthmadog (p341)

If **Portmeirion** (http://www.portmeirion-village.com; adult/over 60/child 4–15 yr/under 4yr £11/£10/£8/free) was a 'real' town, it would be a top destination in its own right. As it is, this fantasy village, created by visionary architect Sir Clough Williams-Ellis over five decades from 1925, remains in a category of its own. Occupying a delightful peninsula with a microclimate mild enough to encourage the growth of many exotic plants, it's a homage to what Williams-Ellis saw as the ideal man-made environments of the Mediterranean. Spend an hour or two wandering its fanciful postmodern piazzas, set-piece landscapes and visually delightful follies, and you'll no doubt deem his tribute a success. The cult 1960s TV show *The Prisoner* was filmed here: every year the **PortmeiriCon** (Prisoner Convention; www.portmeiricon.com; ☺Apr) convention draws together its devotees, while the boutique mixed-arts **Festival No 6** (☎08449-670002; www.festivalnumber6.com; ☺Sep) also references the 'number' of the program's titular character.

Portmeirion is just a quick 3-mile dash along High St/Britannia Tce from central Porthmadog, heading southeast over the broad Glaslyn River Estuary. When you reach Minfford, take the signposted road to Portmeirion, where there's free parking. Just retrace your steps to recommence the itinerary.

The Drive ❯❯ The 21 miles to Barmouth takes in an attractive sweep of Cardigan Bay, on the coastal lip of Snowdonia National Park. Take Porthmadog High St north, and join the A487 heading east. Leave the A487 at Penrhyndeudraeth, take the Briwet Bridge south, join the A496 and pass through Harlech on the way to Barmouth.

❾ Barmouth

Fashionable Barmouth may not be, but charming and wonderfully situated it certainly is. Summer sees an influx of tourists, but even in peak season it's difficult to disrupt the beauty of its beach, Victorian architecture and proximity to the walks and birdlife of the **Mawddach Estuary** (www.mawddachestuary.co.uk). Its stunning trestle **railway bridge**, built in the town's Victorian heyday, spanning 700m of the Mawddach's mouth and (currently) still open to walkers, is its most distinctive feature. But eccentric pubs like the **Last Inn** (☎01341-280530; www.lastinn-barmouth.co.uk; Church St; ☺noon-11pm; 🐾) and valiant local arts centres like the **Dragon Theatre** (Theatr y Ddraig; ☎01341-281697; www.dragontheatre.co.uk; Jubilee Rd) also contribute to its charm.

✕ p343

The Drive ❯❯ The last 10-mile stretch skirts the northern edge of the lovely Mawddach Estuary. The A496 takes you to the junction with the A470, just north of the Mawddach River; from here, head south into Dolgellau.

TRIP HIGHLIGHT

❿ Dolgellau

Dolgellau is an unmistakable gem of northwest Wales: a former wool and gold town with more than its share of listed buildings, an enviable natural setting, and plenty to tempt you to stay for a night or more. Dol's proximity to Cader Idris and other highly baggable peaks makes it a natural base for hikers. And there are some exceptional B&Bs here, while wine bars and charismatic diners complete the picture. Plan to stay, if you can.

🛏 p317, p343

Eating & Sleeping

Llandudno ❶

🛏 Escape B&B   B&B ££

(📞01492-877776; www.escapebandb.co.uk; 48
Church Walks; r £95-149; P 📶) Escape brought
a style revolution to Llandudno with its boutique-
chic ambience and magazine-spread design. Its
most recent, design-led makeover then added a
host of energy-saving and trendsetting features.
Even if you're not a *Wallpaper** subscriber, you'll
love the honesty-bar lounge, Bose iPod docks,
DVD library, tasty breakfasts and atmosphere of
indulgence. Unique.

Conwy ❷

🛏 Gwynfryn   B&B ££

(📞01492-576733; www.gwynfrynbandb.
co.uk; 4 York Pl; r £65-90; 📶) Although it
seems in danger of being engulfed by butterfly
ornaments and dangling mobiles, this very
friendly five-bedroom B&B – set in a refurbished
Victorian property just off the main square – is
a great place to stay. The clean, bright rooms
are filled with thoughtful extras such as small
fridges, biscuits, chocolates and earplugs.
Guests must be 15 and over.

Beaumaris ❸

✖ Tredici Italian Kitchen   Italian ££

(📞01248-811230; www.tredicibeaumaris.com;
13 Castle St; 🕐6-9pm Sun-Thu, 5-10pm Fri &
Sat, noon-3pm Sat & Sun) Occupying an intimate
1st-floor dining room above a quality butcher
and grocer, Tredici has brought a touch of the
Mediterranean to wind-blown Anglesey. While
some Welsh produce is used (local lamb cutlets
are pan-fried with mint and redcurrant, and the
sea bass almost has the same postcode), the
swordfish, figs and the like naturally come from
sunnier climes.

🛏 Cleifiog   B&B ££

(📞01248-811507; www.cleifiogbandb.co.uk;
Townsend; s £85, d £90-110; 📶) A charming
little gem, this art-filled townhouse oozes

character and history, and boasts superb
views over the Menai Strait, particularly as the
morning sun streams in. The front bedrooms
have their original 18th-century wood panelling,
while the rear room has a 16th-century barrel
ceiling; all three are stylishly decorated.

Abersoch ❼

🛏 Venetia   Hotel ££

(📞01758-713354; www.venetiawales.com; Lôn
Sarn Bach; r £108-148; P 📶) No sinking old
Venetian palazzo, just five luxurious rooms in a
grand Victorian house decked out with designer
lighting and modern art; room Cinque has a TV
above its bathtub. The restaurant specialises
In the traditional tastes of Venice (mains £12
to £24), particularly seafood and pasta dishes,
and serves them under twinkling modern
chandeliers.

Barmouth ❾

✖ Bistro Bermo   European ££

(📞01341-281284; www.bistrobarmouth.co.uk; 6
Church St; mains £15-19; 🕐6.30-10pm Tue-Sat,
plus noon-2pm Wed-Sat Apr-Oct) Discreetly
hidden behind an aqua-green shopfront, this
intimate restaurant delivers a sophisticated
menu chock-full of Welsh farm produce and
fresh fish. Featuring dishes such as red bream
with scallops and seafood bisque, the cooking
is classical, rather than experimental, and
generally excellent. There are only half a dozen
tables, so book ahead.

Dolgellau ❿

🛏 Y Meirionnydd   Hotel ££

(📞01341-422554; www.themeirionnydd.com;
Smithfield Sq; s/d from £69/89; 📶) Slap bang
in the centre of town, this listed Georgian town
house has been thoroughly refurbished, with a hip
new look complementing the roughly hewn stone
walls and solid oak woodwork. Special touches
include bathrobes, slippers and bottled water.

STRETCH YOUR LEGS
CARDIFF

Start/Finish: The Hayes

Distance: 1.5 miles

Duration: Three hours

The historic core of Wales' buzzy little capital is easily explored on foot. This route takes you through busy shopping streets right to the doorstep of the castle and then through parkland to Cardiff's gleaming Civic Centre.

Take this walk on Trips

The Hayes

The Hayes is Cardiff's bustling car-free shopping strip, flanked by the giant **St David's** (www.stdavidscardiff.com; ⏰9.30am-8pm Mon-Sat, 11am-5pm Sun; 📶) mall on one side and a network of dainty Victorian arcades on the other. Right in the heart of it all is **Yr Hen Lyfrgell** (The Old Library; www.yrhenlyfrgell.wales), an ornate standstone library building which has been converted into a Welsh language hub. Inside there's a stylish cafe-bar, the excellent **Bodlon** (www.bodlon.com; Yr Hen Lyfrgell; ⏰9am-5pm) gift shop and the very interesting **Cardiff Story** (📞029-2034 6214; www.cardiffstory.com; Yr Hen Lyfrgell; ⏰10am-4pm Mon-Sat) local history museum.

The Walk ≫ Directly behind Yr Hen Lyfrgell is a small park, with St John the Baptist Church on the other side.

St John the Baptist Church

This elegant 15th-century **church** (📞029-2039 5231; www.cardiffstjohncityparish.org.uk; Church St; ⏰10am-3pm Mon-Sat) is one of only a few medieval buildings left in central Cardiff. The delicate stonework on its fine Gothic tower is particularly impressive, as is the grand Elizabethan tomb inside.

The Walk ≫ Exit onto Trinity St and look for the entrance to Cardiff Market opposite the park.

Cardiff Market

Old-fashioned but still vibrant, **Cardiff Market** (btwn St Mary & Trinity Sts; ⏰8.30am-5.30pm Mon-Sat) has been selling fresh produce and hardware since 1891. The cast-iron market hall still has the original market office in its centre, topped by a clock tower. The tightly packed stalls are a great place to stock up on snacks.

The Walk ≫ Exit via the opposite end of the market and turn right on to St Mary St, another blissfully car-free thoroughfare. A street market is held here most weekends. Cardiff Castle is straight ahead.

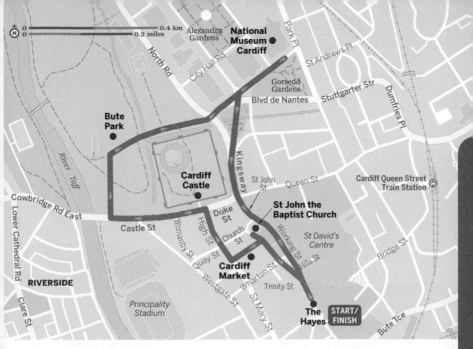

Cardiff Castle

Cardiff Castle (☎029-2087 8100; www.
cardiffcastle.com; Castle St; adult/child
£12/9, incl guided tour £15/11; ☺9am-5pm)
encompasses the entire history of the
city within its very fabric. The Normans
built their castle right on top of the
walls of an Ancient Roman fort. A
Norman keep and gatehouse survives,
flanked by a 15th-century manor
house. Most of the rest is testimony
to the wealth and flamboyance of the
Marquess of Bute, one of the families
responsible for transforming Cardiff in
the 19th century into the world's biggest
coal port.

The Walk » Exit the castle and turn right. As you
walk along, look for the stone animals decorating
the top of the walls. Keep going until you reach
the pretty West Lodge containing the excellent
Pettigrew Tea Rooms and enter Bute Park.

Bute Park

Edging the River Taff, this lovely park
incorporates lawns, mature trees and
swathes of daffodils in spring. It was

gifted to the city, along with the castle,
by the Bute family in 1947. On sunny
days, students from the nearby university drape themselves inelegantly over
the lawns, while parents push prams
and joggers endlessly circle the paths.

The Walk » Cross behind the castle and exit the
park, taking the underpass beneath busy North Rd
into the heart of Cardiff's elegant Civic Centre.

National Museum Cardiff

Standing grandly beside City Hall,
the **National Museum Cardiff** (☎0300
111 2 333; www.museumwales.ac.uk; Gorsedd
Gardens Rd; ☺10am-4pm Tue-Sun) contains a treasure trove of art, including
priceless works by the likes of Monet,
Renoir, Van Gogh and Turner, and a
significant collection of Welsh art.
There's also an excellent natural history section and a gallery devoted to
Welsh ceramics.

The Walk » Wander back past the City Hall
and look for the underpass cutting below Blvd de
Nantes. Head straight down the Kingsway, which
leads to Working St and back to The Hayes.

Scotland

SCENERY, HISTORY, ATMOSPHERE: SCOTLAND SIMPLY SPOILS YOU. To drive here is to head deep into a captivating landscape fringed by vistas that stir the soul. A sense of something special is everywhere; from the pubs alive with live music, to spectacular shores and the crisp, clear air. At the heart lie rollercoaster Highland roads, where ospreys soar above the pines. Nearby, Scotland's mighty glens deliver mountains, lochs and maybe a monster or two. A string of distilleries tempt you to motor through historic Speyside. And all around the edges, majestic coast roads offer beauty, castles, villages and life at a gentler pace.

Northwest Highlands Geopark Scotland's wild, majestic landscape

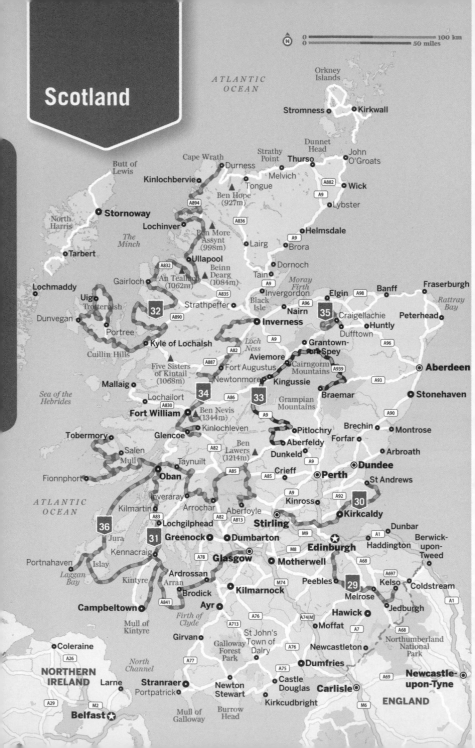

Scotland

The Borders 2–3 Days
Ruined abbeys and Knights Templar links amid a
landscape of undulating hills. (p351)

 Stirling & Fife Coast 2–3 Days
Shoreline drives taking in castles, golf links,
medieval towns and golden sands. (p359)

Lower West Coast 4–6 Days
Photogenic touring amid a coast of lochs,
mountains and thundering waterfalls. (p367)

Upper West Coast 3–5 Days
The Highlands meet the shore: imposing mountains, surging seas, and single-track roads. (p379)

  Royal Highlands & Cairngorms 4–5 Days
Where roads swerve between majestic mountains
and the Royals come to relax. (p391)

 Great Glen 2–3 Days
Bewitching lakes and mountains – plus some
monster spotting at Loch Ness. (p401)

Whisky Trails 2–3 Days
A scenic tour of historic arts and crafts, taking in
distilleries galore. (p409)

Ferry Hopping 6–8 Days
A celebration of seafood and laidback lifestyles;
enchanting island explorations. (p417)

✔ DON'T MISS

Cairngorm Sled-Dog Centre

Hanging on for dear life
as a team of huskies
careers along forest
trails (even when there's
no snow). Trip 33

Quaich Bar

Settling deep into
the armchairs at the
Craigellachie Hotel to
sample some of their
600 plus single malts.
Trip 35

Kinlochleven Via Ferrata

Tackling the ladders and
bridges of the 500m
climbing route which
weaves through the
crags of Grey Mare's Tail.
Trip 34

Holy Island

Breathing and thinking
deeply on this rocky
outcrop just off Lamlash,
now run as a Buddhist
retreat. Trip 36

Gairloch Marine Wildlife Centre

Keeping a look-out
for basking sharks,
porpoises and minke
whales on an eco-
friendly cruise. Trip 32

The Borders

29

On this drive through southeastern Scotland's enchanting Borders region, you'll take in market towns, ruins, castles and stately homes in a land of rolling hills redolent of history.

TRIP HIGHLIGHTS

0 miles

Rosslyn Chapel
Secretive Templar church hiding who knows what?

EDINBURGH ★

1 START

3

6

8 FINISH

● Jedburgh

90 miles

Kelso
Delightful market town at journey's end

Traquair House
History seeps from every pore of this ancient house

29 miles

Dryburgh Abbey
The quietest and most delightful of the ruined abbeys

55 miles

2–3 DAYS
90 MILES / 144KM

GREAT FOR...

BEST TIME TO GO
Late spring offers blooming flowers, green fields and local festivals.

ESSENTIAL PHOTO
Snapping Sir Walter's favourite vista from lovely Scott's View.

BEST FOR FAMILIES
Mountain biking and forest ziplines at Glentress.

Roslin Rosslyn Chapel

29 | The Borders

Romance and strife coincide in the Borders region, whose rough history of war and plunder is encapsulated by the magnificent ruins of four abbeys. Templar mysteries add an extra layer at atmosphere-packed Rosslyn Chapel, while a number of welcoming villages with ancient traditions pepper the countryside and grandiose mansions await exploration. Over it all is poised the benevolent ghost of Sir Walter Scott, quill in hand.

TRIP HIGHLIGHT

❶ Roslin

It's only a 7-mile journey through city suburbs from central Edinburgh to Roslin, where the success of Dan Brown's novel *The Da Vinci Code* has seen a flood of visitors descend on Scotland's most beautiful and enigmatic **church** (Collegiate Church of St Matthew; www.rosslynchapel.org.uk; Chapel Loan, Roslin; adult/child £9/free; 🕑9.30am-6pm Mon-Sat Apr-Sep, to 5.30pm Oct-Mar, noon-4.45pm Sun year-round; **P**). The chapel

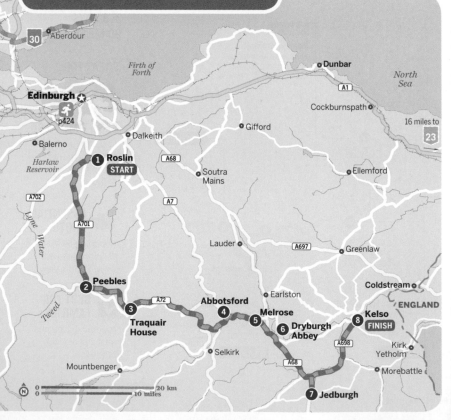

was built in the mid-15th century for William St Clair, third earl of Orkney, and the ornately carved interior – at odds with the architectural fashion of its time – is a monument to the mason's art, rich in symbolic imagery. Hourly talks by qualified guides are included in the admission price.

As well as flowers and biblical figures, the carved stones include many examples of the pagan 'Green Man'; other figures are associated with Freemasonry and the Knights Templar. Intriguingly, there are also carvings of plants from the Americas that predate Columbus' voyage of discovery. The symbolism has led some to conclude that Rosslyn could be a secret Templar reposi-

LINK YOUR TRIP

Northumbria
It's a pleasantly leisurely drive along the Tweed from Kelso to reach the coast at Berwick, where you can take on the Northumbria route in reverse.

Stirling & Fife Coast
It's 80 miles northwest from Kelso via Edinburgh's southern bypass to Stirling and this coastal route.

HISTORIC ENVIRONMENT SCOTLAND

Several of the attractions along this route are run by **Historic Environment Scotland** (Historic Scotland, HES, HS; ☎0131-668 8999; www.historicenvironment.scot), formerly known as Historic Scotland. If you'll be visiting these and other highlights such as Stirling or Edinburgh Castles, it's worth considering joining up.

tory with hidden vaults concealing anything from the Holy Grail or the head of John the Baptist to the body of Christ himself.

The Drive » The A701 is easily accessed just outside Roslin, and it's an easy drive south along it and the A703 to Peebles, 15 miles away.

❷ Peebles
With a picturesque main street set on a ridge between the River Tweed and the Eddleston Water, Peebles is one of the most handsome of the Border towns. Though it lacks a major sight, the agreeable atmosphere, fine eating and snacking choices and good walking options in the rolling, wooded hills thereabouts will entice you to linger.

Two miles east of Peebles off the A72, **Glentress forest** (www.7stanesmountainbiking.com) has one of the best of the network of mountain-biking hubs known as the 7Stanes. The shop here hires rigs and will put you on the right trail for your ability. These are some of Britain's best

biking routes. There are also marked trails, forest **ziplines** (www.goape.co.uk; Glentress Forest; adult/child £33/25; ⊙Feb-Nov) and osprey viewing available.

✗ ⊨ p357

The Drive » Cross the Tweed in Peebles and continue along the quiet country road B7062, or take the main A72 east and turn right in Innerleithen to reach Traquair House, which is well signposted. It's about a 7-mile drive whichever way you choose.

TRIP HIGHLIGHT
❸ Traquair House
One of Scotland's great country houses, **Traquair House** (☎01896-830323; www.traquair.co.uk; adult/child/family £8.70/4.40/24; ⊙11am-5pm Easter-Sep, 11am-4pm Oct, 11am-3pm Sat & Sun Nov) has a powerful, ethereal beauty. Odd, sloping floors and a musty odour bestow a genuine feel, and parts of the building are believed to have been constructed long before the first official record of its existence in 1107. The massive tower house was gradually expanded but has remained virtually unchanged since the 17th century.

Since the 15th century, Traquair has belonged to the Stuart family, and the family's unwavering Catholicism and loyalty to the Stuart cause led to famous visitors including Mary, Queen of Scots and Bonnie Prince Charlie, but also to numerous problems as life as a Jacobite became a furtive, clandestine affair.

One of Traquair's most interesting places is the concealed room where priests secretly lived and performed Mass. Other beautiful, time-worn rooms hold fascinating relics and letters.

In addition to the house, there's a garden maze, a small brewery producing the tasty Bear Ale, and a series of craft workshops.

The Drive » Head back to the A72 and head east towards Galashiels and Melrose. A couple of miles before Melrose, you'll reach Abbotsford, after a total drive of 17 miles.

- - - - - - - - - - - - -

❹ Abbotsford

Just outside Melrose, **Abbotsford** (📞01896-752043; www.scottsabbotsford.com; visitor centre free, house adult/child £8.95/4.50; ⊙10am-5pm Apr-Oct, 10am-4pm Nov-Mar,

house closed Dec-Feb) is where to discover the life and works of Sir Walter Scott, to whom we arguably owe both the modern novel and our mind's-eye view of Scotland. This whimsical, fabulous house where he lived – and which ruined him when his publishers went bust – really brings this 19th-century writer to life. The grounds on the banks of the Tweed are lovely, and Scott drew much inspiration from rambles in the surrounding countryside.

A modern visitor centre displays memorabilia

Kelso A view of the town's Georgian buildings

and gives an intriguing overview of the man, before a swish audio-guide system – with one designed for kids – shows you around the house. In the house are some gloriously over-the-top features, with elaborate carvings, enough swords and dirks to equip a small army, a Chinese drawing room and a lovely study and library. There's a cafe-restaurant atop the visitor centre.

The Drive » It's an easy couple of miles from Abbotsford to Melrose.

⑤ Melrose

Tiny, charming Melrose is a polished village running on the well-greased wheels of tourism. Sitting at the feet of the three heather-covered Eildon Hills, Melrose has a classic market square and one of the great abbey ruins.

Red-sandstone **Melrose Abbey** (HES; ☎01896-822562; www.historicenvironment.scot; adult/child £5.50/3.30; ⏰9.30am-5.30pm Apr-Sep, 10am-4pm Oct-Mar) was repeatedly destroyed by the English in the 14th century.

The remaining broken shell is pure Gothic and the ruins are famous for their decorative stonework – look out for the pig gargoyle playing the bagpipes. Though Melrose had a monastery way back in the 7th century, this abbey was founded by David I in 1136 for Cistercian monks, and later rebuilt by Robert the Bruce, whose heart is buried here.

Ask here for details of local walks.

🛏 p357

The Drive » Dryburgh Abbey is a circuitous 7-mile drive from Melrose via the B6404. Head east from Melrose on the A72, then turn north up the A68, then turn right, following signposts for the abbey. Pause to admire the vistas from the famous Scott's View outlook.

TRIP HIGHLIGHT

❻ Dryburgh Abbey

Dryburgh (HES; ☎01835-822381; www.historicenvi ronment.scot; adult/child £5.50/3.30; ☻9.30am-5.30pm Apr-Sep, 10am-4pm Oct-Mar) is the most beautiful and complete of the Border abbeys, partly because the neighbour-ing town of Dryburgh no longer exists (another victim of the wars) and partly for its lovely site by the Tweed in a sheltered birdsong-filled valley. Dating from about 1150, the abbey belonged to the Premonstratensians, a religious order founded in France, and conjures 12th-century monastic life more successfully than its nearby coun-terparts. The pink-hued stone ruins are the burial place of Sir Walter Scott.

The Drive » From Dryburgh Abbey, retrace your steps to the A68 and turn south on it. After 15 miles you'll reach Jedburgh.

❼ Jedburgh

Attractive Jedburgh, where many old buildings and wynds (narrow alleys) have been intelligently re-stored, invites exploration by foot. It's centred on the noble skeleton of its ruined **abbey** (HES; www. historicenvironment.scot; Abbey Rd; adult/child £5.50/3.30; ☻9.30am-5.30pm Apr-Sep, 10am-4pm Oct-Mar).

Dominating the town skyline, this was the first of the great Border abbeys to be passed into state care, and it shows – audio and visual presentations telling the abbey's story are scattered throughout the carefully preserved ruins (good for the kids). The red-sandstone ruins are roofless but relatively intact, and the ingenuity of the master mason can be seen in some of the rich (if somewhat faded) stone carvings in the nave.

🛏 p357

The Drive » It's 11 miles from Jedburgh to Kelso. Head north up the A68, then right on to the A698.

TRIP HIGHLIGHT

❽ Kelso

Kelso, a prosperous mar-ket town with a broad, cobbled square flanked by Georgian buildings, has a cheery feel and his-toric appeal. During the day it's a busy little place, but after 8pm you'll have the streets to yourself. The town has a lovely site at the junction of the Tweed and Teviot, and is one of the most enjoyable places in the Borders.

Once one of the richest abbeys in southern Scot-land, **Kelso Abbey** (HES; www.historicenvironment. scot; Bridge St; ☻9.30am-5.30pm Apr-Sep, 9.30am-4.30pm Sat-Wed Oct-Mar) was reduced to ruins by English raids in the 16th century, though what lit-tle remains today is some of the finest surviving Romanesque architecture in Scotland.

Grandiose **Floors Cas-tle** (☎01573-223333; www. floorscastle.com; adult/child castle & grounds £8.50/4.50, with gardens £12.50/6.50; ☻10.30am-5pm mid-Apr–mid-Oct) is Scotland's largest inhabited mansion, home to the Duke of Rox-burghe, and overlooks the Tweed about a mile west of Kelso. Built by William Adam in the 1720s, the original Georgian simplicity was 'improved' in the 1840s.

✕ 🛏 p357

Eating & Sleeping

Peebles ②

✖ Coltman's   Bistro, Deli ££
(☎01721-720405; www.coltmans.co.uk; 71
High St; mains £11-19; ⏰10am-5pm Sun-Wed,
10am-10pm Thu-Sat; 📶) This main street deli
has numerous temptations, such as excellent
cheeses and Italian smallgoods, as well as
perhaps Scotland's tastiest sausage roll – buy
two to avoid the walk back for another one.
Behind the shop, the good-looking dining area
serves up confident bistro fare and light snacks
with a variety of culinary influences, using top-
notch local ingredients.

🛏 Rowanbrae   B&B ££
(☎01721-721630; www.aboutscotland.co.uk/
peebles/rowanbrae.html; 103 Northgate; s/d
£45/68; 📶) In a quiet cul-de-sac but not far
from the main street, this hospitable spot treats
its guests like family friends. The traditional
old building has modern comforts but retains
a pleasant, comfortably old-fashioned feel;
there are three upstairs bedrooms, two of them
en suite, and a commodious guest lounge for
relaxation.

Melrose ⑤

🛏 Old Bank House   B&B ££
(☎01896-823712; www.oldbankhousemelrose.
co.uk; 27 Buccleuch St; s/d £50/75; 📶🍴)
Right in the centre, this is a superb B&B in a
charming old building. The owner's artistic
touch is evident throughout, from walls covered
with paintings, some his own, a house full
of curios and tasteful art nouveau features,
and a sumptuous breakfast room. Rooms are
spacious with comfortable furniture and top
modern bathrooms; they are complemented by
a generous can-do attitude.

Jedburgh ⑦

🛏 Willow Court   B&B ££
(☎01835-863702; www.willowcourtjedburgh.
co.uk; the Friars; s/d £75/86; 🅿📶) It seems
inadequate to call this impressive option a B&B;
it's more like a boutique hotel. Impeccable
rooms with elegant wallpaper, showroom
bathrooms and great beds are complemented
by a courteous professional welcome. Every
time we visit it's been improved in some way:
the sign of a standout establishment. The
conservatory lounge is great for admiring the
views over garden and town.

Kelso ⑧

✖ Cobbles   Bistro ££
(☎01573-223548; www.thecobbleskelso.
co.uk; 7 Bowmont St; mains £10-17; ⏰food
noon-2.30pm & 5.45-9pm Mon-Fri, noon-9pm
Sat, noon-8pm Sun; 📶) This inn off the main
square is so popular you will need to book a
table at weekends. It's cheery, very welcoming,
warm, and serves excellent upmarket pub
food in generous portions. Pick and mix from
bar menu, steaks and gourmet options. Leave
room for cheese and/or dessert. The bar's
own microbrewed ales are really excellent. A
cracking place.

🛏 Edenbank House   B&B ££
(☎01573-226734; www.edenbank.co.uk; Stichill
Rd; s/d £50/80; 🅿📶) Half-a-mile down the
Stichill road, this grand Victorian house sits in
spacious grounds where only bleating lambs in
the green fields and birds in the garden break
the silence. It's a fabulous place, with huge
opulent rooms, lovely views over the fields,
and incredibly warm, generous hospitality.
Breakfast features homemade produce, and
a laissez-faire attitude makes for an utterly
relaxing stay.

Stirling & Fife Coast

30

Travelling from Scotland's most imposing castle to the hallowed home of golf, you'll visit a perfectly preserved medieval town, Fife's best beaches and a string of pretty fishing villages.

TRIP HIGHLIGHTS

65 miles

Anstruther
A busy harbour, fascinating museum, boat trips to the Isle of May, and superb fish and chips

0 miles

Stirling Castle
Scotland's most commanding fortress, rivalling Edinburgh's in importance

FINISH
St Andrews

6

1

START

3

⭐ EDINBURGH

Culross
A favourite among film directors for its unspoilt 17th-century atmosphere

18 miles

**2–3 DAYS
82 MILES / 131KM**

GREAT FOR...

BEST TIME TO GO

July and August for summer fun on the beach at Elie.

ESSENTIAL PHOTO

Teeing off at St Andrews Old Course.

✓ BEST FOR HISTORY

Exploring the beautifully preserved medieval village of Culross.

National Wallace Monument The historic site viewed from Stirling Castle

30 Stirling & Fife Coast

Stirling and St Andrews, two of Scotland's top tourist magnets, bookend this trip along the less well known south coast of Fife, taking in the red pantiled roofs and crowstepped gables of 17th-century Culross's cobbled lanes — regularly used as a film set — the golden-sand beaches and seaside walks of Elie and Earlsferry, and the pretty-as-a-picture fishing harbours of the East Neuk, one of central Scotland's most picturesque corners.

TRIP HIGHLIGHT

❶ Stirling

With an impregnable position atop a mighty wooded crag, Stirling's beautifully preserved Old Town is a treasure trove of historic buildings and cobbled streets winding up to the ramparts of its impressive castle, which offers views for miles around. Nearby is **Bannockburn**, scene of Robert the Bruce's pivotal triumph over the English in 1314.

Many visitors find **Stirling Castle** (HS; www.stirlingcastle.gov.uk; Castle Wynd; adult/child £14.50/8.70; ⏱9.30am-6pm Apr-Sep, to 5pm Oct-Mar; P) more atmospheric than Edinburgh – the location, architecture, historical significance and commanding views combine to make it a grand and memorable sight. The undisputed highlight of a visit is the fabulous **Royal Palace**, its exterior studded with beautiful sculptures.

Sloping steeply down from Stirling Castle, the Old Town has a remarkably different feel to modern Stirling, its cobblestone streets packed with 15th- to 17th-century architectural gems, and surrounded by Scotland's best-surviving city wall.

🛏 p365

The Drive » Head north from Stirling city centre along Causewayhead Rd towards Bridge of Allan; at the junction with the A907 to Alloa, keep straight on and follow signs to the National Wallace Monument (total 2.5 miles). From the visitor centre car park, walk or shuttlebus up the hill to the monument itself.

----

❷ National Wallace Monument

Perched high on a crag above the floodplain of the River Forth, the Victorian **Wallace Monument** (📞01786-472140; www.nationalwallacemonument.com; Abbey Craig; adult/child £9.99/6.25; ⏱9.30am-5pm Apr-Jun, Sep & Oct, to 6pm Jul & Aug, 10.30am-4pm Nov-Feb, 10am-5pm Mar; P 🚻) is so Gothic it deserves circling bats and croaking ravens. In the shape of a medieval tower, it commemorates William Wallace, the hero of the bid for Scottish independence depicted in the film *Braveheart*. The view from the top over the flat, green gorgeousness of the Forth Valley, including the site of Wallace's 1297 victory over the English at Stirling Bridge, almost justifies the steep entry fee.

The climb up the narrow staircase inside leads through a series of galleries including the **Hall of Heroes**, a marble pantheon of lugubrious Scottish luminaries. Admire Wallace's 66in of broadsword and see the man himself re-created in a 3D audiovisual display.

The Drive » Return to the junction and head east on the A907 through Alloa and Clackmannan, then south on the A977 to Kincardine; at the junction with the A985 keep straight on, following signs for Fife Coastal Tourist Route until you reach Culross (16 miles).

FINISH
❽ **St Andrews**

A917

❼ **Crail**

❻ **Anstruther**
Pittenweem
❺ St Monans

Elie & Earlsferry

Dunbar

A1   Tyne

🔗 LINK YOUR TRIP

31 **Lower West Coast**
A short 20-mile hop to Callander links up with our trip around the scenic and historic highlights of the Loch Lomond, the Trossachs and Argyll.

29 **The Borders**
From St Andrews you can head south across the Forth to Rosslyn Chapel to begin our trip around the Borders' market towns, castles and stately homes.

③ Culross

Instantly familiar to fans of the TV series *Outlander,* in which it appears as the fictional village of Cranesmuir, Culross (koo-ross) is Scotland's best-preserved example of a 17th-century town. Limewashed white and yellow-ochre houses with red-tiled roofs stand amid a maze of cobbled streets; the winding Back Causeway to the abbey is lined with whimsical cottages.

Culross Palace

(NTS; www.nts.org.uk; Low Causewayside; adult/child £10.50/7.50; ⊙noon-5pm daily Jun-Aug, Wed-Sun only Apr-May & Sep, noon-4pm Wed-Sun Oct) – more large house than palace – was the 17th-century residence of local laird Sir George Bruce and features an interior largely unchanged since his time. The decorative wood panelling and painted timber ceilings are of national importance, particularly the allegorical scenes in the **Painted Chamber**, which survive from the early 1600s. Don't miss the re-creation of a 17th-century garden at the back, with gorgeous views from the top terrace.

✗ p365

The Drive » Continue east via the B9037 and A994 to Dunfermline (8 miles).

④ Dunfermline

Dunfermline is a large and unlovely town, but rich in history. The focus is evocative **Dunfermline Abbey** (HS; www.historic environment.scot; St Margaret St; adult/child £4.50/2.70; ⊙9.30am-5.30pm Apr-Sep, 9.30am-4.30pm Sat-Wed Oct-Mar), founded by David I in the 12th century as a Benedictine monastery. The abbey and its neighbouring palace was already favoured by religious royals; Malcolm III married the exiled Saxon princess Margaret here in the 11th century, and both chose to be interred here. There were many more royal burials, none more notable than Robert the Bruce, whose remains were interred here in 1329.

The Drive » Take the M90 towards the Forth Rd Bridge, but leave at Junction 1 (signposted A921 Dalgety Bay) and continue to the attractive seaside village of Aberdour. Stay on the A921 as far as Kirkcaldy, then take the faster A915 (signposted St Andrews) as far as Upper Largo, where you follow the A917 to Elie (35 miles).

⑤ Elie & Earlsferry

These two attractive villages have great sandy beaches, golf courses and good walks along the coast – seek out the **Chain Walk**, an adventurous scramble along the rocky shoreline at Kincraig Point, west of Earlsferry (allow two hours, and ask local advice about tides before setting off). On a more relaxing note, there's nothing better than a lazy summer Sunday in Elie, watching the local team play cricket on the beach.

Elie Watersports

(☑01333-330962; www.elie watersports.com; Elie Harbour; ⊙May-Sep, ring ahead at other times) hires out windsurfers (per two hours £30), sailing dinghies (per hour £25), canoes (per hour £14) and mountain bikes (per day £15), and provides instruction as well.

✗ p365

The Drive » Continue east along the Fife coast on the A917 through the pretty fishing villages of St Monans and Pittenweem to Anstruther (6 miles).

⑥ Anstruther

Once one of Scotland's busiest fishing ports, cheery Anstruther (pronounced en-ster by locals) offers a pleasant mixture of bobbing boats, historic streets and visitors ambling around the harbour grazing on fish and chips, or contemplating a boat trip to the **Isle of May**.

The excellent **Scottish Fisheries Museum** (www. scotfishmuseum.org; East Shore; adult/child £8/free; ⊙10am-5.30pm Mon-Sat

St Andrews Stroll the hallowed turf of the Old Course

& 11am-5pm Sun Apr-Sep, 10am-4.30pm Mon-Sat & noon-4.30pm Sun Oct-Mar) covers the history of the Scottish fishing industry in fascinating detail, including plenty of hands-on exhibits for kids. Displays include the Zulu Gallery, which houses the huge, partly restored hull of a traditional Zulu-class fishing boat, redolent with the scents of tar and timber. Afloat in the harbour outside the museum lies the *Reaper*, a fully restored Fifie-class fishing boat built in 1902.

🛏 p365

The Drive » It's just a short 4-mile drive east to Crail.

❼ **Crail**

Pretty and peaceful, little Crail has a much-photographed stone-built harbour surrounded by quaint cottages with red-tiled roofs. The village's history is outlined in the **Crail Museum** (www.crailmuseum.org.uk; 62 Marketgate; ⏱11am-4pm

PLAYING THE OLD COURSE

The Old Course at St Andrews is the oldest and most famous golf course in the world. Although it lies beside the exclusive Royal & Ancient Golf Club, the Old Course is a public course and is not owned by the club.

To play the Old Course, you'll need to book in advance via www.standrews.com, or by contacting the Reservations Department on ☎01334-466718. Reservations open on the last Wednesday in August the year before you wish to play. No bookings are taken for weekends or the month of September (check the latest guidelines on the website).

Unless you've booked months in advance, getting a tee-off time is literally a lottery; enter the ballot at the caddie office (or by phone) before 2pm two days before you wish to play (there's no Sunday play). Be warned that applications by ballot are normally heavily oversubscribed, and green fees are £175 in summer. A caddie for your round costs £50 plus tip.

Singles are not accepted in the ballot and should start queuing as early as possible on the day – 5am is good – in the hope of joining a group. You'll need a handicap certificate (24/36 for men/women).

If you play on a windy day, expect those scores to balloon: Nick Faldo famously stated, 'When it blows here, even the seagulls walk'.

Mon-Sat & 1-4pm Sun Jun-Sep, Sat-Sun only May & Oct), **but the main attraction is just wandering the winding streets and hanging out by the harbour.**

You can buy takeaway lobster and crab from the **Lobster Store** – the benches in the nearby grassed area are perfectly placed for enjoying your seafood al fresco while admiring the view across to the Isle of May.

🛏 p365

The Drive » The A917 continues north for 10 miles to St Andrews, passing Kingsbarns Distillery and Cambo Walled Garden.

- - - - - - - - - - - - -

❽ St Andrews

For a small town, St Andrews has made a big name for itself. Firstly as a religious centre and place of pilgrimage, then as Scotland's oldest (and Britain's third-oldest) university town. But it is its status as the home of golf that has propelled it to even greater fame, and today's pilgrims mostly arrive with a set of clubs in hand.

The **Old Course** (☎Reservations Department 01334-466718; www.standrews.com; Golf Pl), the world's most famous golf links, has a striking seaside location at the western end of town – it's a thrilling experience to stroll the hallowed turf. You are free to walk over the course on Sunday, or follow the footpaths around the edge at any time.

The ruins of **St Andrews Cathedral** (HS; www.historicenvironment.scot; The Pends; adult/child £4.50/2.70, incl castle £8/4.80; ⊙9.30am-5.30pm Apr-Sep, 10am-4pm Oct-Mar) are testimony to what was once one of Britain's most magnificent medieval buildings. There's also a museum that contains the late-8th-century **St Andrews Sarcophagus**, Europe's finest example of early medieval stone carving.

St Andrews Castle (HS; www.historicenvironment.scot; The Scores; adult/child £5.50/3.30, incl cathedral £8/4.80; ⊙9.30am-5.30pm Apr-Sep, 10am-4pm Oct-Mar) too is mainly in ruins, but the site itself is evocative and has dramatic coastline views.

✗ 🛏 p365

Eating & Sleeping

Stirling ❶

🛏 Victoria Square Guesthouse B&B ££

(☎01786-473920; www.victoriasquare
guesthouse.com; 12 Victoria Sq; s/d from
£70/105; 🅿🛜) Though close to the centre of
town, Victoria Sq is a quiet oasis with elegant
Victorian buildings surrounding a verdant park.
This luxury guesthouse's huge rooms, bay
windows and period features make it a winner –
there's a great four-poster room (from £110) for
romantic getaways, and some bedrooms have
views to the castle towering above. No children.

Culross ❸

✕ Biscuit Café Cafe £

(www.culrosspottery.com; Sandhaven; mains
£3-6; ⊙10am-5pm) Above a pottery workshop
behind the Town House, this cafe has a tranquil
little garden and sells coffee, tempting organic
cakes and scones, and tasty light meals.

Elie & Earlsferry ❺

✕ Ship Inn Pub Food ££

(☎01333-330246; www.shipinn.scot; The
Toft; mains £10-22; ⊙food served noon-3pm &
5-9pm; 👪) The Ship Inn, down by Elie harbour,
is a pleasant and popular place for a bar lunch of
local seafood. The best bit is the outside tables
overlooking the wide sweep of the bay.

Anstruther ❻

🛏 Spindrift B&B ££

(☎01333-310573; www.thespindrift.co.uk;
Pittenweem Rd; d/f £92/120; 🅿🛜👪) Arriving
from the west, there's no need to go further
than Anstruther's first house on the left, a

redoubt of Scottish cheer and warm hospitality.
The rooms are elegant, classy and extremely
comfortable – some have views across to
Edinburgh and one is a wood-panelled re-
creation of a ship's cabin, courtesy of the sea
captain who once owned the house.

Crail ❼

🛏 Selcraig House B&B ££

(☎01333-450697; www.selcraighouse.co.uk;
47 Nethergate; s/d £40/80; 🛜👪) Eighteenth-
century Selcraig House is a characterful,
well-run place with a variety of rooms. Curiously
shaped top-floor chambers will appeal to the
quirky, while the fantastic four-poster-bed
rooms will charm those with a taste for luxury
and beautiful furnishings.

St Andrews ❽

✕ Adamson Brasserie ££

(☎01334-479191; http://theadamson.com; 127
South St; mains £13-27; ⊙noon-3pm & 5-10pm
Mon-Fri, noon-10pm Sat & Sun; 🛜👪) Housed
in the former post-office building, this loud
and bustling brasserie panders to a youngish
clientele of local families, well-heeled students
and tourists with a crowd-pleasing menu of
steaks and seafood, including local lobster with
chips. Service can be over-eager or occasionally
chaotic, but it all adds to the hectic buzz.

🛏 Fairways of St Andrews B&B ££

(☎01334-479513; www.fairwaysofstandrews.
co.uk; 8a Golf Pl; d £98-130; 🛜) Just a few paces
from golf's most famous 18th green, this is
more like a boutique hotel than a B&B, despite
its small size. There are just three super-stylish
rooms; the best on the top floor is huge and has
its own balcony with views over the Old Course.

Lower West Coast

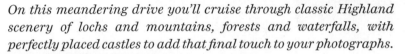

31

On this meandering drive you'll cruise through classic Highland scenery of lochs and mountains, forests and waterfalls, with perfectly placed castles to add that final touch to your photographs.

TRIP HIGHLIGHTS

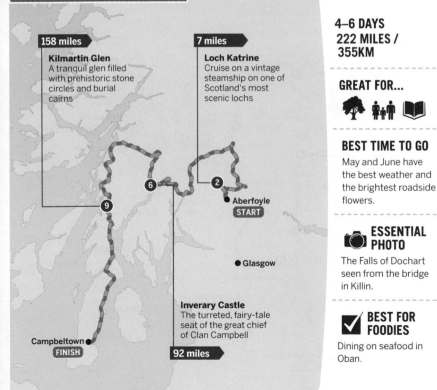

158 miles

Kilmartin Glen
A tranquil glen filled with prehistoric stone circles and burial cairns

7 miles

Loch Katrine
Cruise on a vintage steamship on one of Scotland's most scenic lochs

9

6

2

● **Aberfoyle**
START

● **Glasgow**

Inverary Castle
The turreted, fairy-tale seat of the great chief of Clan Campbell

● **Campbeltown**
FINISH

92 miles

4–6 DAYS
222 MILES /
355KM

GREAT FOR...

BEST TIME TO GO

May and June have the best weather and the brightest roadside flowers.

ESSENTIAL PHOTO

The Falls of Dochart seen from the bridge in Killin.

BEST FOR FOODIES

Dining on seafood in Oban.

Kilmartin Glen Ancient Nether Largie standing stones

31 Lower West Coast

The scenery is the star of this trip, which winds its way from the shining lakes, shady forests and foaming waterfalls of the Trossachs to the intricately fretted seaboard of Argyll, with its craggy hills and narrow, probing sea lochs. But history too is always close, and you'll explore castles both medieval and Victorian, and touch the very heart of the nation at Kilmartin's ancient glen.

❶ Aberfoyle

Aberfoyle is one of the gateways to the **Loch Lomond & the Trossachs National Park**. Picturesque waymarked trails start from the nearby Lodge visitor centre, ranging from a light 20-minute stroll to a nearby waterfall to a hilly 4-mile circuit. Also here, **Go Ape!** (☎0333-920 4859; www.goape.co.uk; Queen Elizabeth Forest Park; adult/child £33/25; ◷Sat & Sun Nov & Feb-Easter, Wed-Mon Easter-Oct) will bring out

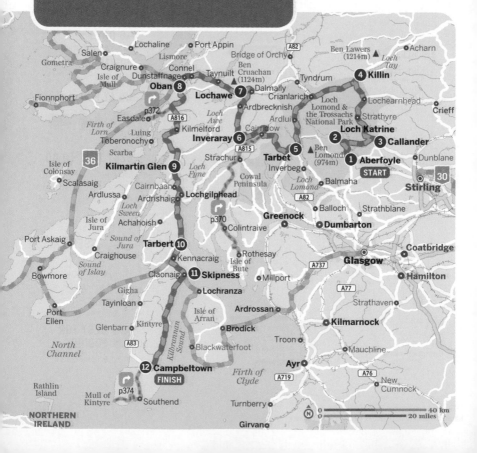

the monkey in you on its exhilarating adventure course of long zip lines, swings and rope bridges among the trees.

🛏 p377

The Drive » Head north on the A821 which leads high over the Duke's Pass, pausing for a photo opportunity at the crest of the hill, before descending to Loch Achray where a left turn leads along a narrow glen to a car park at Trossachs Pier on Loch Katrine (7 miles).

TRIP HIGHLIGHT
❷ Loch Katrine

Lovely Loch Katrine lies at the heart of the Trossachs, an area of outstanding natural beauty with thickly forested hills, romantic lochs, and excellent walking and cycling routes. Cruises depart from Trossachs Pier, including

LINK YOUR TRIP

30 Stirling & Fife Coast

From Callander, the start of this castles and coastline tour in Stirling is just 20 miles to the southeast.

36 Ferry-Hopping
This trip intersects with the Ferry-Hopping one at Oban, where you can take off on a tour of the islands.

the fabulous centenarian steamship *Sir Walter Scott*, or you can walk or cycle along the northern shore of the loch.

The Drive » Return to the A821 and drive east along the northern shores of Lochs Achray and Venachar, then turn right to arrive in the town of Callander (10 miles).

❸ Callander

Callander, the principal Trossachs town, has been pulling in tourists for over 150 years, and has a laid-back ambience that quickly lulls visitors into lazy pottering. It's home to the **Hamilton Toy Collection** (📞01877-330004; www.thehamiltontoycollection.co.uk; 111 Main St; adult/child £3/1; ☺10am-5pm Mon-Sat, noon-5pm Sun Apr-Oct), a powerhouse of 20th-century juvenile memorabilia, chock-full of dolls houses, puppets and toy soldiers. Callander is also the starting point for a woodland trail that leads up to **Callander Crags**, which offers great views over the surrounding countryside.

The Drive » The A84 leads north from Callander along Loch Lubnaig and Strathyre. Stop briefly at Balquhidder to pay respects at Rob Roy's grave; you might continue down the single-track road to Monachyle Mhor for a coffee or a posh lunch – the drive is worth it anyhow. Back on the main road, continue north to Killin (22 miles).

❹ Killin

This lovely village sits at the western end of Loch Tay and has a spread-out, relaxed feel, particularly around the scenic **Falls of Dochart**, which tumble through the centre. On a sunny day people sprawl over the rocks by the bridge, pint or picnic in hand. There is fine walking around the town, and mighty mountains and glens close at hand.

🛏 p377

The Drive » Head southwest from Killin, following the A85 along Glen Dochart to Crianlarich, then turning south on the A82. Stop and stretch your legs at the Falls of Falloch waterfall, then continue to Tarbet (total 30 miles).

❺ Tarbet

Tarbet is a tiny village at a road junction on the western shore of Loch Lomond. **Cruise Loch Lomond** (📞01301-702356; www.cruiselochlomond.co.uk; Tarbet/Luss; ☺8.30am-5.30pm early Apr-late Oct) offers boat trips from Tarbet to Arklet Falls and Rob Roy's Cave; you can also be dropped off at Rowardennan to climb Ben Lomond, getting picked up in the afternoon, or get picked up at Inversnaid after a 9-mile hike along the West Highland Way.

The Drive » Strike west from Tarbet on the A83, which soon enters mountainous territory, climbing through Glen Croe and over the high pass known as the Rest and Be Thankful (a memorial stone in the car park at the top explains the name) to reach the sea at Loch Fyne. Continue around the head of the loch to reach Inveraray (23 miles).

----

❻ Inveraray

There's no 50 shades of grey around here: this historic planned village is all black and white – even logos of high-street chain shops conform. Spectacularly set on the shores of Loch Fyne, Inveraray was built by the Duke of Argyll in Georgian style in the 18th century. **Inveraray Jail** (☏01499-302381; www.inverarayjail.co.uk; Church Sq; adult/child £10.95/6.50; ⏲9.30am-6pm Apr-Oct, 10am-5pm Nov-Mar; 🚻) has been turned into an interactive tourist attraction where you can sit in on a trial, try out a cell and discover the harsh tortures that were meted out to unfortunate prisoners.

The stunning **Inveraray Castle** (☏01499-302203; www.inveraray-castle.com; adult/child/family £10/7/29; ⏲10am-5.45pm Apr-Oct)

SCOTLAND 31 LOWER WEST COAST

DETOUR: ISLE OF BUTE

Start: ❺ Tarbet (p369)

Bute lies pinched between the thumb and forefinger of the Cowal peninsula, separated from the mainland by a narrow, scenic strait. The Highland Boundary Fault cuts through the middle of the island so that, geologically speaking, the northern half is in the Highlands and the southern half is in the central Lowlands.

Rothesay, the island's main town, was once one of Scotland's most popular holiday resorts, bustling with day-trippers disembarking from numerous steamers crowded around the pier. Cheap foreign holidays saw Rothesay's fortunes decline, but a nostalgia-fuelled resurgence of interest has seen many Victorian buildings restored. The grassy, flowery waterfront and row of noble villas is a lovely place to be once again.

Splendid ruined 13th-century **Rothesay Castle** (HES; www.historicenvironment.scot; King St; adult/child £4.50/2.70; ⏲9.30am-5.30pm Apr-Sep, 10am-4pm Sat-Wed Oct-Mar), with seagulls and jackdaws nesting in the walls, was once a favourite residence of the Stuart kings. It is unique in Scotland in having a circular plan, with four stocky round towers. The landscaped moat, with manicured turf, flower gardens and lazily cruising ducks, makes a picturesque setting.

The true jewel in Bute's crown is **Mount Stuart** (☏01700-503877; www.mountstuart.com; adult/child £11.50/6.75, grounds only £6.50/3.50; ⏲11am-2.30pm Apr, 11am-4pm May-Oct, grounds 10am-6pm Apr-Oct), 5 miles south of Rothesay. The 19th-century family seat of the Stuart Earls of Bute is one of Britain's more magnificent stately homes, the first to have a telephone, underfloor heating and heated pool. Its eclectic interior, with a magnificent central hall and chapel in Italian marble, is heavily influenced by the third Marquess's interests in Greek mythology and astrology. The drawing room has paintings by Titian and Tintoretto among other masters.

From Tarbet, follow the A83 towards Inveraray. As you descend Glen Kinglas towards Loch Fyne, the A815 forks to the left just before Cairndow; follow it 10 miles south to Strachur, then take the A886 for another 24 miles to Colintraive; a five-minute ferry crossing (departs every 30 minutes) takes you to Bute.

Loch Katrine Riding the *Sir Walter Scott* steamship

has been the seat of the Dukes of Argyll – chiefs of Clan Campbell – since the 15th century. The 18th-century building, with its fairy-tale turrets and fake battlements, houses an impressive armoury hall, its walls patterned with more than 1000 pole-arms, dirks, muskets and Lochaber axes.

Loch Fyne Oyster Bar
(☎01499-600236; www.loch fyne.com; Clachan, Cairndow; mains £11-22; ☻9am-5pm; 🛜), 9 miles north of Inveraray, is a great place to enjoy a lunch of Scottish seafood, but expect to queue if you haven't booked.

🛏 p377

The Drive ›› A ceremonial arch at the east end of town marks the beginning of the A819, which snakes north through low hills and dense forest to reach the shores of Loch Awe. When you reach the A85 junction, turn left and continue around the head of the loch to Lochawe village (16 miles).

DETOUR: ISLE OF SEIL

Start: ❽ Oban

The small island of Seil is best known for its connection to the mainland – the graceful **Bridge over the Atlantic**, designed by Thomas Telford and opened in 1793.

On the west coast of the island is the pretty conservation village of **Ellenabeich**, with whitewashed cottages and rainwater barrels backed by a wee harbour and rocky cliffs. It was built to house local slate workers, but the industry collapsed in 1881 when the sea broke into the main quarry – the flooded pit can still be seen.

Just offshore is small **Easdale Island**, which has more old slate-workers' cottages and an interesting **folk museum** (📞01852-300370; www.easdalemuseum.org; Easdale; suggested donation £3; ⏰11am-4pm Apr-Oct) with displays about the slate industry and social history. Once housing 450 people, the island's population fell to just seven old-timers by 1950 but now has a healthier 48 after a program welcoming incomers. Climb to the top of the island (a 38m peak) for great views of the surrounding area. Confusingly, Ellenabeich is also referred to as Easdale, so 'Easdale Harbour', for example, is on the Seil side.

Seafari Adventures (📞01852-300003; www.seafari.co.uk; Ellenabeich; ⏰Apr-Oct) runs a series of exciting boat trips in high-speed rigid inflatables to Corryvreckan whirlpool (call for dates of 'Whirlpool Specials', when the tide is strongest), as well as three-hour summer whale-watching trips. There are also day-long cruises to Iona and Staffa, a weekly day-trip to Colonsay, plus trips to the remote Garvellach Islands.

A ferry hop from Seil's southern end takes you to neighbouring **Isle of Luing**, a quiet backwater that has no real sights but is appealing for wildlife walks and easy-going bike rides.

To reach Seil, 10 miles south of Oban, follow the A816 to Kilninver and turn right on the B844. To rejoin the main trip, retrace your route to the A816.

- - - - - - - - - - - - -

❼ Lochawe

Loch Awe is one of Scotland's most beautiful lochs, with rolling forested hills around its southern end and spectacular mountains in the north. It is the longest loch in Scotland – about 24 miles – but is less than 1 mile wide for most of its length.

Just east of Lochawe village are the scenic ruins of the much-photographed **Kilchurn**

Castle (HES; www.historic-environment.scot; Dalmally; ⏰9am-5pm Apr-Sep). Built in 1440, it enjoys one of Scotland's finest settings. Long held by the Campbell clan, it was enlarged in 1693 to garrison government troops during the Jacobite uprising; it was then abandoned in the 1750s. You can climb to the top of the four-storey castle tower for impressive views of Loch Awe and the surrounding hills.

Three miles west of the village you can visit **Cruachan power station** (📞0141-614-9105; www.visitcruachan.co.uk; A85; adult/child £7/2.50; ⏰9.30am-4.45pm Apr-Oct, 10am-3.45pm Mon-Fri Nov-Dec & Feb-Mar), where electric buses take you more than half a mile inside Ben Cruachan to see the hydroelectric scheme which occupies a vast cavern hollowed out of the mountain.

The Drive » Continue west on the A85 to Oban (21 miles), stopping at Bridge of Connel to see the Falls of Lora, whitewater rapids under the bridge caused by the tide flowing in and out through the narrow rocky mouth of Loch Etive (depends on tide times).

- - - - - - - - - - - - -

8 Oban

Oban, the main ferry terminal for crossings to the Scottish islands, enjoys a fine setting on a broad bay with glorious views west to the hills of Mull. Some of Britain's standout places to enjoy fish and shellfish are to be found here, whether you go for no-frills crab shacks like the **Oban Seafood Hut** (www.oban seafoodhut.co.uk; Railway Pier; mains £3-13; ⏰10am-6pm

Mar-Oct), or more upmarket restaurants such as **Ee-usk** (☎01631-565666; www.eeusk.com; North Pier; mains £14-24; ⏰noon-3pm & 5.45-9.30pm; 🛜) or the **Seafood Temple** (☎01631-566000; www.facebook.com/seafoodtemple; Gallanach Rd). Sustainable sourcing is an important element that's widely practised.

In the centre of town, handsome **Oban Distillery** has been producing since 1794. The standard guided tour leaves regularly (worth booking) and includes a dram, a take-home glass and a taste straight from the cask.

🛏 p377, p423

The Drive » Head south from Oban for 29 miles on the A816 to Kilmartin Glen.

- - - - - - - - - - - - -

TRIP HIGHLIGHT

9 Kilmartin Glen

This magical glen is the focus of one of the biggest concentrations of **prehistoric sites** in Scotland. Burial cairns, standing stones, stone circles, hill forts and cup-and-ring-marked rocks litter the countryside. Within a 6-mile radius of Kilmartin village there are 25 sites with standing stones and over 100 rock carvings. In the 6th century, Irish settlers arrived in this part of Argyll and founded the

LOCH LOMOND

The 'bonnie banks' and 'bonnie braes' of Loch Lomond have long been Glasgow's rural retreat – a scenic region of hills, lochs and healthy fresh air within easy reach of Scotland's largest city. Today the loch's popularity shows no sign of decreasing.

Loch Lomond is mainland Britain's largest lake and, after Loch Ness, the most famous of Scotland's lochs. Its proximity to Glasgow (20 miles away) means that the tourist honeypots of Balloch, Loch Lomond Shores and Luss get pretty crowded in summer. The eastern shore, which is followed by the West Highland Way long-distance footpath, is quieter and offers a better chance to appreciate the loch away from the busy main road.

Loch Lomond straddles the Highland border. The southern part is broad and island-studded, fringed by woods and Lowland meadows. However, north of Luss the loch narrows, occupying a deep trench gouged out by glaciers during the Ice Age, with 900m mountains crowding either side.

There are around 60 islands, large and small, in the loch. Most are privately owned, and only two (Inchcailloch and Inchmurrin) can be reached without your own boat or canoe. **Inchcailloch** is a nature reserve reached by passenger ferry from Balmaha or Luss, while privately owned **Inchconnachan** is only accessible by boat or canoe. Unusually, it is home to a herd of wallabies, introduced by a previous owner; the rare capercaillie nests here too.

Inchmurrin is reached by passenger ferry from Arden on the loch's western shore and has walking trails, beaches, self-catering cottages and a restaurant that is open from Easter to October. See www.inchmurrin-lochlomond.com.

CORNFIELD / SHUTTERSTOCK ©

DETOUR:
MULL OF KINTYRE

Start: ⑫ Campbeltown (p376)

A narrow winding road, 15 miles long, leads south from Campbeltown to the Mull of Kintyre, passing some good sandy beaches near Southend. This remote headland was immortalised in Paul McCartney's famous song – the former Beatle owns a farmhouse in the area. From where the road ends, a 30-minute steep downhill walk leads to a clifftop lighthouse, with Northern Ireland, only 12 miles away, visible across the channel. Don't leave the road when the frequent mists roll in as it's easy to become disoriented.

kingdom of Dál Riata (Dalriada), which eventually united with the Picts in 843 to create the first Scottish kingdom. Their capital was the hill fort of **Dunadd**, on the plain to the south of Kilmartin.

Kilmartin House Museum (☎01546-510278; www.kilmartin.org; Kilmartin; adult/child £6/2; ⊙10am-5.30pm Mar-Oct, 11am-4pm Nov-23 Dec) is a fascinating interpretive centre that provides a context for the ancient monuments you can go on to explore, alongside displays of artefacts recovered from various sites. It's worth visiting here first, then heading out to explore the ancient sites around. There's also a cafe and a good shop with handcrafts and books on Scotland.

The Drive ❯❯ Continue south on the A810 and A83 through Lochgilphead and Ardrishaig to Tarbert (21 miles). If you fancy a longer and more scenic route, turn right on the B8024 south of Ardrishaig, which follows the west coast of Knapdale with views to the hills of Jura (42 miles).

- - - - - - - - - -

⑩ Tarbert

The attractive fishing village and yachting centre of Tarbert is the gateway to Kintyre, and most scenic, with buildings strung around its excellent natural harbour. A crossroads for nearby ferry routes, it's a handy stepping stone to Arran or Islay, but is well worth a stopover on any itinerary.

The picturesque harbour is overlooked by the crumbling, ivy-covered ruins of **Tarbert Castle** (⊙24hr), rebuilt by Robert the Bruce in the 14th century. You can hike up via a signposted footpath beside **Loch Fyne Gallery** (www.lochfynegallery.com; Harbour St; ⊙10am-5pm Mon-Sat, 10.30am-5pm Sun), which showcases the work of local artists.

Try to time your trip to fit in a meal at the simple but stylish **Starfish** (☎01880-820733; www.starfishtarbert.com; Castle St; mains £11-19; ⊙6-9pm Sun-Thu, noon-2pm & 6-9pm Fri & Sat; 🐟) seafood restaurant, where a great variety of specials are

Killin The Falls of Dochart during autumn

prepared with whatever's fresh off the Tarbert boats that day. Best to book.

🛏 p377

The Drive » Continue south from Tarbert on the A83 and, just past the ferry terminal at Kennacraig, turn left on the B8001 to Claonaig and another left to the road end at Skipness (13 miles).

---

⑪ Skipness

Tiny Skipness is pleasant and quiet with great views of Arran. Beyond the village rise the substantial remains of 13th-century **Skipness Castle** (HES; www.historic environment.scot; ⊙24hr, tower Apr-Sep only), a former possession of the Lords

of the Isles. It's a striking building, composed of dark-green local stone trimmed with contrasting red-brown sandstone from Arran. The tower house was added in the 16th century and was occupied until the 19th century. From the top you can see the roofless, 13th-century St Brendan's Chapel down by the

ROB ROY

Nicknamed Red ('ruadh' in Gaelic, anglicised to 'roy') for his ginger locks, Robert MacGregor (1671–1734) was the wild leader of the wildest of Scotland's clans, outlawed by powerful neighbours, hence their sobriquet, Children of the Mist. Incognito, Rob became a prosperous livestock trader, before a dodgy deal led to a warrant for his arrest.

A legendary swordsman, the fugitive from justice then became notorious for daring raids into the Lowlands to carry off cattle and sheep. Forever hiding from potential captors, he was twice imprisoned, but escaped dramatically on both occasions. He finally turned himself in and received his liberty and a pardon from the king. He lies buried – perhaps – in the churchyard at Balquhidder; his uncompromising later epitaph reads 'MacGregor despite them'. His life has been glorified over the years due to Walter Scott's novel and the 1995 film starring Liam Neeson and Jessica Lange. Many Scots see his life as a symbol of the struggle of the common folk against the inequitable ownership of vast tracts of the country by landed aristocrats.

shore. The kirkyard contains some excellent carved grave slabs.

Attached to Skipness House, near the castle, is the **Seafood Cabin** (☎01880-760207; www.skipnessseafoodcabin.co.uk; dishes £3-20; ☺11am-7pm Sun-Fri Whit Sunday-Sep), a great place for lunch on a fine summer day, serving no-frills but delicious local fish and shellfish at outdoor picnic tables with grand views over the grassy coast. It's famous for crab rolls, which are on the small side: add on a pot of mussels or plate of gravadlax.

The Drive » Return to Claonaig and turn left to follow the B842 down the eastern shore of the Kintyre peninsula to Campbeltown (30 miles), a twisting rollercoaster of a road that climbs high above the sea then swoops down to remote bays, with breathtaking views across the water to the rocky peaks of Arran

- - - - - - - - - - - - -

⑫ Campbeltown

Blue-collar Campbeltown, set around a beautiful harbour, still suffers from the decline of its fishing and whisky industries but is rebounding on the back of golf tourism and a ferry link to Ayrshire. The spruced-up seafront backed by green hills lends the town a distinctly optimistic air.

There were once no fewer than 32 distilleries around Campbeltown, but most closed in the 1920s. Today **Springbank** (☎01586-552009; www.springbankwhisky.com; 85 Longrow; tours from £7; ☺tours 10am & 1.30pm Mon-Sat) is one of only three operational. It is also one of the few around that distills, matures and bottles all its whisky on the one site, making for an interesting tour. It's a quality malt, one of Scotland's finest.

Campbeltown's most unusual sight awaits in a cave on the southern side of Davaar island, at the mouth of Campbeltown Loch. On the wall of the cave is an eerie painting of the **Crucifixion** by local artist Archibald MacKinnon, dating from 1887. You can walk to the island at low tide: check tide times with the tourist office.

🛏 p377

Eating & Sleeping

Aberfoyle ❶

🛏 Duchray Castle   B&B ££££

(📞01877-389333; www.duchraycastle.com; Aberfoyle; d £140-195; P 📶) Splendidly set in secluded rural surrounds, all forest and stream, but just three miles from Aberfoyle, this castle is a treat, with four sumptuous rooms, a noble great hall and a cosier lounge space with games, DVDs and books. It's good for a luxurious romantic break, but also for families – children will love the spiral stairs, castle atmosphere and acres to romp in.

Killin ❹

🛏 Courie Inn   Inn ££

(📞01567-831000; www.thecourieinn.com; Main St; d £90-110; P 📶) An excellent all-round choice on the Killin scene, this has quality, comfortable rooms in a variety of sizes, including a sumptuous suite with views. It artfully blends the traditional and contemporary. Downstairs, the restaurant does smart bistro food (mains £11 to £15, daily 5pm to 8.45pm, plus noon to 3pm Friday to Sunday) and there's a bar.

Inveraray ❻

🛏 George Hotel   Inn ££

(📞01499-302111; www.thegeorgehotel.co.uk; Main St E; d £85-115; P 📶🐾) The George boasts a magnificent choice of opulent, individual rooms complete with four-poster beds, period furniture, Victorian roll-top baths and private Jacuzzis (superior rooms cost £135 to £180 per double). Some are in an annexe opposite. The cosy wood-panelled bar, with rough stone walls, flagstone floor and peat fires, is a delightful place for all-day bar meals and has a beer garden.

Oban ❽

🛏 Old Manse Guest House   B&B ££

(📞01631-564886; www.obanguesthouse. co.uk; Dalriach Rd; s/d £75/88; P 📶) Set on the hillside above town, this commands magnificent views over to Kerrera and Mull. It's run with genuine enthusiasm, and the owners are constantly adding thoughtful new features to the bright, cheerful rooms – think binoculars, DVDs, poetry, corkscrews and tartan hot-water bottles. There are breakfast menus, with special diets catered for.

Tarbert ❿

🛏 Knap Guest House   B&B ££

(📞01880-820015; www.knapguesthouse.co.uk; Campbeltown Rd; d £75-99; 📶) A flight of stairs lit by Edwardian stained glass leads to this 1st-floor flat with three spacious en suite bedrooms sporting an attractive blend of Scottish and Far Eastern decor. The welcome is warm, and there are great harbour views from the lounge (leather sofas, log fire and a small library) and breakfast room.

Campbeltown ⓬

🛏 Royal Hotel   Hotel £££

(📞01586-810000; www.machrihanishdunes. com; Main St; r £142-172; 🕐food noon-9pm Sun-Thu, noon-10pm Fri & Sat; P 📶) Historically Campbeltown's best address, this reddish sandstone hotel opposite the harbour is looking swish again. It caters mostly to yachties and golfers; though rack rates feel overpriced, there are often online specials and rooms are very spacious and attractive. There are some excellent midweek specials that include golf at Machrihanish Dunes and a couple of extras.

Upper West Coast

32

Experience the most stirring of Scottish highland and island scenery, with majestic mountains looming over steely lochs and stunning coastline.

TRIP HIGHLIGHTS

182 miles

Torridon
Among many scenic exclamation marks, this valley takes the breath away

Durness
FINISH

10

263 miles

Ullapool
There's a real magic to the setting of this sweet harbour town

2

Portree
START

7

5

Trotternish Peninsula
Dramatic visuals and local history: an essence of Skye

6 miles

Plockton
The Highlands meet the Caribbean at this little bay

114 miles

**3–5 DAYS
360 MILES /
575KM**

GREAT FOR...

BEST TIME TO GO

June has long evenings and dreamy light. September is quieter, with no midges.

 ESSENTIAL PHOTO

Sunset from Applecross, with the hills of Raasay and Skye silhouetted.

 BEST FOR FOODIES

The local seafood is sublime.

Trotternish Peninsula Mealt Falls and Kilt Rock

379

Upper West Coast

Quintessential highland country such as this, marked by single-track roads, breathtaking emptiness and a wild, fragile beauty, leaves an indelible imprint on our souls. Scotland's far northwest coastline is a feast of deep inlets, forgotten beaches and surging peninsulas; looming inland are some of Scotland's most imposing and emblematic peaks. Whether it's blazing sunshine or a murky greyness, the character of the land is totally unique and constantly changing.

1 Portree

Portree is Skye's largest and liveliest town. It has a pretty harbour lined with brightly painted houses, and there are great views of the surrounding hills. Its name (from the Gaelic for King's Harbour) commemorates James V, who came here in 1540 to pacify the local clans.

MV Stardust (☑07798 743858; www.skyeboat-trips.co.uk; Portree Harbour; adult/child £25/15) offers 1½-hour boat trips around Portree Bay, with the chance to see seals, porpoises and – if you're lucky – white-tailed sea eagles. There are also two-hour cruises to the Sound of Raasay (£25/12 per adult/child). You can also arrange fishing trips, or to be dropped off for a hike on the Isle of Raasay and picked up again later.

🛏 p389

The Drive » Coming from the south, follow the road round to the right in Portree to leave town on the A855, which after about 6 miles brings you to the Trotternish Peninsula's first sights.

TRIP HIGHLIGHT

2 Trotternish Peninsula

The Trotternish Peninsula to the north of Portree has some of Skye's most spectacular – and bizarre – scenery.

Whatever the weather, it is difficult not to be blown away by the savage beauty of this place.

The 50m-high, pot-bellied pinnacle of crumbling basalt known as the **Old Man of Storr** (P) is prominent above the road 6 miles north of Portree. Walk up to its foot from the car park at the northern end of Loch Leathan (round trip 2 miles). Past the Old Man is a popular clifftop lookout over spectacular **Kilt Rock**.

At the northern end of the peninsula at Kilmuir, the peat-reek of crofting life in the 18th and 19th centuries is preserved in the thatched cottages, croft houses, barns and farm implements of the evocative **Skye Museum of Island Life** (01470-552206; www.skyemuseum.co.uk;

LINK YOUR TRIP

34 **Great Glen**
Allowing a day's journey between them, this can be tackled before or after this drive, either by heading from Fort William to the ferry at Mallaig and thence to Skye, or by dropping down from Durness to Inverness.

36 **Ferry-Hopping**
Link these trips via Oban and the Mallaig ferry to Skye.

Kilmuir; adult/child £2.50/50p; ⊙9.30am-5pm Mon-Sat Easter-late Sep; P). Behind the museum is Kilmuir Cemetery, where a tall Celtic cross marks the grave of Jacobite heroine Flora MacDonald.

🛏 p389

The Drive 》 Follow the road around the peninsula, through the ferry port of Uig and on to Borge, where you take a right on to the A850 to Dunvegan. From the Old Man of Storr it's about 54 miles via this route.

❸ Dunvegan Castle

Skye's most famous historic building, and one of its most popular tourist attractions, **Dunvegan Castle** (☎01470-521206; www.dunvegancastle.com; adult/child £12/9; ⊙10am-5.30pm Apr–mid-Oct; P) is the seat of the chief of Clan MacLeod. In addition to the usual castle stuff – swords, silver and family portraits – there are some interesting artefacts, including the

Fairy Flag, a diaphanous silk banner that dates from some time between the 4th and 7th centuries, and Bonnie Prince Charlie's waistcoat and a lock of his hair.

The oldest parts are the 14th-century keep and dungeon but most of it dates from the 17th to 19th centuries, when it played host to Samuel Johnson, Sir Walter Scott and, most famously, Flora MacDonald. Look out for Rory Mor's Drinking Horn, a beautiful 16th-century vessel of Celtic design that could hold half a gallon of claret. Upholding the family tradition in 1956, John Macleod – the 29th chief, who died in 2007 – downed the contents in one minute and 57 seconds 'without setting down or falling down'.

The Drive 》 It's 24 pretty miles across the heart of the island along the A863 to Sligachan, a crossroads and walkers' haven overwatched by the brooding Cuillins.

❹ Cuillin Hills

The Cuillin Hills are Britain's most spectacular mountain range (the name comes from the Old Norse kjöllen, meaning 'keel-shaped'). Though small in stature (Sgurr Alasdair, the highest summit, is only 993m), the peaks are near-alpine in character, with knife-edge ridges, jagged pinnacles, scree-filled gullies and hectares of naked rock. While they are a paradise for experienced mountaineers, the higher reaches of the Cuillin are off limits to the majority of walkers.

The good news is that there are also plenty of good low-level hikes within the ability of most walkers, several leaving from Sligachan.

The Drive 》 It's a 30-mile drive from Sligachan on the A87 along the Skye coast, past the Raasay ferry at Sconser, through Broadford and over the bridge onto the mainland at Kyle of Lochalsh. In town, take a left up the hill and follow this road to Plockton.

TRIP HIGHLIGHT

❺ Plockton

Idyllic little Plockton, with its perfect cottages lining a perfect bay, looks like it was designed as a film set. And it has indeed served as just that – scenes from *The Wicker Man* (1973) were filmed here, and the village became famous as the

↱ DETOUR: ELGOL

Start: ❹ Cuillin Hills

On a clear day, the 15-mile journey along the road from Broadford to Elgol is one of the most scenic on Skye. It takes in two classic postcard panoramas – the view of Bla Bheinn across Loch Slapin (near Torrin), and the superb view of the entire Cuillin range from Elgol pier. Elgol itself is a tiny settlement with a shop and cafe at the end of this long, single-track road

Assynt The romantic ruins of Ardvreck Castle

location for the 1990s TV series *Hamish Macbeth*.

With all this picture-postcard perfection, it can get busy in summer, but there's no denying its appeal, with 'palm trees' (actually hardy New Zealand cabbage palms) lining the waterfront, a thriving small-boat sailing scene and several good places to stay, eat and drink. The local langoustines (Plockton prawns) are famous.

It's fun to get out on the water here. **Calum's Seal Trips** (☎01599-544306; www.calums-sealtrips.com; adult/child £11.50/6; ⊗Apr-Oct) runs friendly seal-watching cruises – there are swarms of the slippery fellas just outside the harbour, and the trip comes with an excellent commentary. **Sea Kayak Plockton** (☎01599-544422; www.seakayakplockton.co.uk; 1-day beginner course £85), meanwhile, offers everything from beginners' lessons to multiday trips around Skye to highly challenging odysseys.

🛏 p389

The Drive » Head to the A890, running northeast along Loch Carron. Turn left along the A896 along the loch's opposite side and through likeable Lochcarron village before taking a left turn to Applecross. The magnificent Bealach na Ba (Pass of the Cattle; 626m) climbs steeply and hair-raisingly via hairpin bends, then drops dramatically to the village with views of Skye (36 miles total).

⑥ Applecross

The delightfully remote seaside village of Applecross feels like an island retreat due to its isolation and the magnificent views of Raasay and the hills of Skye that set the pulse racing, particularly at sunset. On a clear day it's an unforgettable place. Book ahead for a bed or meal at the inn.

The Drive » It's 25 winding miles north then east from Applecross along the coast of this peninsula to the pretty waterside village of Shieldaig, where you rejoin the A896 and head east for the majestic 7 miles to Torridon, along the shore of the sea loch of the same name.

`TRIP HIGHLIGHT`

⑦ Torridon

The road running through Glen Torridon is dwarfed amid some of Britain's most beautiful scenery. Carved by ice from massive layers of ancient sandstone that takes its name from the region, the mountains here are steep, shapely and imposing, whether flirting with autumn mists, draped in dazzling winter snows, or reflected in the calm blue waters of Loch Torridon on a summer day.

The road from lovely Shieldaig, which boasts an attractive main street of whitewashed houses right on the water, reaches the head of the sea loch at spectacularly sited Torridon village. It's a base for excursions to the Torridon peaks – Liathach (1054m; pronounced 'lee-agakh', Gaelic for 'the Grey One'), Beinn Eighe (1010m; 'ben ay', 'the File') and Beinn Alligin (986m;

'the Jewelled Mountain'). These are big, serious mountains for experienced hill walkers only.

The Drive » Follow the A896 northeast to Kinlochewe, then turn left along the A832, which continues to Gairloch (27 miles total). The road follows the shore of beautiful Loch Maree. From a car park 1½ miles past Beinn Eighe visitor centre, there's a great waymarked 4-mile return walk to a plateau and cairn on the side of Beinn Eighe, offering magnificent views.

⑧ Gairloch

Gairloch is a knot of villages around the inner end of a loch of the same name. It's a good base for whale- and dolphin-watching excursions and the surrounding area has beautiful sandy beaches, good trout fishing and birdwatching.

Gairloch Marine Wildlife Centre & Cruises
(☎01445-712636; www.porpoise-gairloch.co.uk; Pier Rd; cruises adult/child £20/15; ⏰10am-4pm Easter-Oct) has audiovisual and interactive displays, lots of charts, photos and knowledgeable staff. From here, cruises run three times daily (weather permitting); during the two-hour trips you may see basking sharks, porpoises and minke whales. The crew collects data on water temperature and conditions, and monitors cetacean populations, so you are subsidising important research.

✓ TOP TIP:
SINGLE TRACK ROADS

Along much of this drive you will find single-track roads that are only wide enough for one vehicle. Passing places (usually marked with a white diamond sign, or a black-and-white striped pole) are used to allow oncoming traffic to get by. Remember that passing places are also for overtaking – you must pull over to let faster vehicles pass. Be wary too of lambs dashing onto the road in springtime.

THE NORTH COAST 500

This drive up Scotland's upper western coast is part of a longer road trip that includes the northern and upper eastern coastline. Words fail to describe the sheer variety of the scenic splendour which unfolds before you as you cross this empty landscape that combines desolate moorlands, brooding mountains, fertile coastal meadows and stunning white-sand beaches.

In a clever piece of recent marketing, it's been dubbed the North Coast 500, as the round-trip from Inverness is roughly that many miles, though you'll surely clock up a few more if you follow your heart down narrow byroads and seek perfect coastal vistas at the end of dead-end tracks.

A lazy pace with plenty of photo stops makes for the best journey. It's worth taking several days over it – you could easily spend a week or more, stopping off for leisurely seafood lunches, tackling some emblematic hills, detouring down valleys to explore the legacy of the Clearances or daring a dip in the North Sea.

Though the drive hasn't actually changed, the new name has caught the imagination, so visitor numbers are well up. The villages along the way aren't overstocked with accommodation, so it's well worth reserving everything in advance if you're travelling the route in the spring or summer months.

Six miles north of Gairloch, splendid **Inverewe Garden** (NTS; www.nts.org.uk; adult/concession £10.50/7.50; ⊙9.30am-6pm Jun-Aug, 10am-5.30pm Sep, 10am-5pm Apr, May & Oct, 10am-3pm Nov-Mar) is a welcome splash of colour on this otherwise bleak coast. The climate here is warmed by the Gulf Stream, which allowed Osgood MacKenzie to create this exotic woodland garden in 1862.

The Drive ≫ It's a slow, winding, scenic 42 miles along the A832 from Gairloch north and east to the junction with the A835. Take your time and enjoy the scenic solitude.

- - - - - - - - - - - -

❾ Falls of Measach

Just west of the junction of the A835 and A832, a car park gives access to the **Falls of Measach** (Corrieshalloch Gorge), which spill 45m into spectacularly deep and narrow Corrieshalloch Gorge. You can cross the gorge on a swaying suspension bridge, and walk west for 250m to a viewing platform that juts out dizzyingly above a sheer drop. The thundering falls and misty vapours rising from the gorge are very impressive.

The Drive ≫ From the road junction, it's 12 miles northwest on the good A835 to Ullapool.

- - - - - - - - - - - -

TRIP HIGHLIGHT

❿ Ullapool

This pretty port on the shores of Loch Broom is the largest settlement in Wester Ross and one of the most alluring spots in the Highlands, a wonderful destination in itself as well as a gateway to the Western Isles. Offering a row of white-washed cottages arrayed along the harbour and special views of the loch and its flanking hills, the town has a very distinctive appeal. The harbour served as an emigration point during the Clearances, with thousands of Scots watching Ullapool recede behind them as the diaspora cast them across the world.

Housed in a converted Telford church, **Ullapool Museum** (www.ullapoolmuseum.co.uk; 7 West Argyle St; adult/child £3.50/free; ⊙10am-5pm Mon-Fri, 11am-4pm Sat Apr-Oct) relates the prehistoric, natural and social history of the town and Lochbroom area, with a particular focus on the emigration to Nova Scotia and other places. Leaving from Ullapool's

harbour, **Seascape**
(☎01854-633708; www.
sea-scape.co.uk; adult/child
£30/20; ☺May-Sep) runs
enjoyable two-hour tours
out to the Summer Isles
in an orange rigid inflat-
able boat (RIB). It also
runs shorter trips, plus
excursions to nearby Isle
Martin, with time ashore.

🛏 p389

The Drive » It's 26 miles
north along the A835 then A837
to the Skiag Bridge road junction
at the heart of the Assynt
region. Stop along the way to
appreciate the mountainscapes
and keep an eye out in the rear-
view mirror, as many of the best
perspectives unfold behind you.

---

⑪ Assynt

With its otherworldly
scenery of isolated
peaks rising above a sea
of crumpled, lochan-
spattered gneiss, Assynt
epitomises the north-
west's wild magnificence.
Glaciers have sculpted
the magnificent Tor-
ridonian sandstone
mountains of Assynt,
including Suilven's
distinctive sugarloaf and
ziggurat-like Quinag.
The area is the centre-
piece of what has been
named as the **Northwest
Highlands Geopark** (www.
nwhgeopark.com).

**DETOUR:
COIGACH**

Start: ⑩ Ullapool (p385)

The region west of the main A835 road from Ullapool
to Ledmore Junction is known as Coigach (www.
coigach.com). A lone, single-track road, off the A835
9 miles north of Ullapool, penetrates this wilderness,
leading through gloriously wild scenery to remote
settlements.

Coigach is a wonderland for walkers and wildlife
enthusiasts, with a patchwork of sinuous silver lochs
dominated by the isolated peaks of Cul Mor (849m),
Cul Beag (769m), Ben More Coigach (743m) and
Stac Pollaidh (613m). The main settlement is the
straggling township of Achiltibuie, 15 miles from the
main road, with the gorgeous Summer Isles moored
just off the coast, and silhouettes of mountains
skirting the bay.

You could head back to the main road to continue
your journey, or, at the western end of Loch Lurgainn,
a branch road leads north to Lochinver, a scenic
backroad so narrow and twisting that it's nicknamed
the Wee Mad Road.

Half a mile south of
the Skiag Bridge road
junction, perched on an
island at the edge of Loch
Assynt, are the romantic
ruins of **Ardvreck Castle**,
a 15th-century stronghold
of the MacLeods of As-
synt. There are rumoured
to be several ghosts at
Ardvreck, including the
daughter of a MacLeod
chieftain who was sold in
marriage to the devil by
her father. Thanks Dad!
Nearby are the ruins of
a barrack house built by
the MacKenzies in the
1720s. There are wonder-
ful summer sunsets over
the castle and loch.

The Drive » Head west 10
miles from Skiag Bridge along
the A837 to reach Lochinver. The
road runs along the northern
shore of wild and moody Loch
Assynt.

---

⑫ Lochinver

Lochinver is a sweet
little fishing harbour
that's a popular port of
call with its laid-back
atmosphere, good facili-
ties and striking scenery.
It's something of a gastro
hub too, with several fine
eateries.

Using local landscapes
as inspiration, **Highland
Stoneware** (☎01571-
844376; www.highlandstone
ware.com; Baddodarroch,
Lochinver; ☺9am-6pm Mon-
Fri, to 5pm Sat & 11am-3pm Sun
Easter-Oct, 9am-5.30pm Mon-
Fri Nov-Easter) ensures you
can relive the northwest's
majesty every time you

Kylesku The bridge across Loch Glencoul

have a cuppa. Even better are the mosaics outside, especially the car.

Inver Cruises (📞01571-844406; www.invercruises.uk; Lochinver; adult/child £20/10; ☺May-Oct) give a good taste of this spectacular coastline. There are four daily departures in the summer months.

Norwest Sea Kayaking (📞01571-844281; www.norwestseakayaking.com; 1-day introduction £85) offers introductory courses and trips out to the Summer Isles.

🍴 p389

The Drive » Head north from Lochinver up the narrow B869 coastal route, which rewards with spectacular views and fine beaches. From the lighthouse at Point of Stoer, a one-hour cliff walk leads to the Old Man of Stoer, a spectacular sea stack. After 23 miles, you join the A894 just south of Kylesku.

⓭ Kylesku & Around

Hidden away on the shores of Loch Glencoul, tiny Kylesku served as a ferry crossing until it was made redundant by beautiful Kylesku Bridge in 1984. It's got an excellent inn and is a good base for walks; you can hire bikes too.

Five miles southeast, in wild, remote country, lies 213m-high **Eas a'Chuil Aluinn**, Britain's highest waterfall. You can hike to the top of the falls from a parking area at a sharp bend in the main road 3 miles south of Kylesku (6 miles return). It can also be seen on **boat trips** (📞01971-502231; www.kyleskuboat-tours.com; Kylesku; adult/child £25/18; ☺Apr-Sep) from Kylesku.

The Drive » It's 10 spectacular miles up the A894 from Kylesku to Scourie. Look behind you for the best views.

⓮ Scourie & Handa Island

Scourie is a pretty crofting community with decent services, halfway between Durness and Ullapool. A few miles north lies **Handa Island** (www.scottishwildlifetrust.org.uk), a nature reserve run by the Scottish Wildlife Trust. The island's western sea cliffs provide nesting sites for important breeding populations of great skuas, arctic skuas, puffins, kittiwakes, razorbills and guillemots. Reach the island from Tarbet, 6 miles north of Scourie, via a **ferry** (📞07780-967800; www.handa-ferry.com; Tarbet Pier; adult/child

DETOUR:
CAPE WRATH

Start: ⑮ Durness

Though its name actually comes from the Norse word *hvarf* (meaning 'turning point'), there is something daunting and primal about Cape Wrath, the remote northwesternmost point of the British mainland.

The hazards involved in navigating the often stormy seas around here were long recognised and led to the building of the lighthouse at the cape by Robert and Alan Stevenson in 1828. The last keepers had left by 1997, when people were replaced by automatic equipment. Three miles to the east are the seabird colonies of Clo Mor, the British mainland's highest vertical sea cliffs (195m).

Part of the Balnakeil Estate on the moorland east of the cape is owned by the Ministry of Defence and has served for decades as a bombing range where live ammunition is used. The island of An Garbh-Eilean, 5 miles from the cape, has the misfortune to be around the same size as an aircraft carrier and is regularly ripped up by RAF bombs and missiles. (There is no public access when the range is in use – the times are displayed at Durness post office, and on the Cape Wrath Minibus website).

Getting to Cape Wrath involves a **boat ride** (☎07719-678729; www.capewrathferry. co.uk; single/return £4.50/6.50; ✪Easter-Oct) – passengers and bikes only – across the Kyle of Durness (10 minutes), connecting with a **minibus** (☎01971-511284; www. visitcapewrath.com; single/return £7/12; ✪Easter-Oct) running 11 miles to the cape (40 minutes). This combination is a friendly but eccentric, sometimes shambolic service with limited capacity, so plan on waiting in high season, and ring beforehand to make sure the ferry is running. The ferry leaves from 2 miles southwest of Durness, and runs twice or more daily from April to September. If you eschew the minibus, it's a spectacular 11-mile ride or hike from boat to cape over bleak scenery.

return £12.50/5; ✪outbound 9am-2pm Mon-Sat Apr-Aug, last ferry back 5pm).

The Drive » Continue 7 miles northeast from Scourie on the A894, then north 19 miles on the A838 to reach Scotland's north coast at Durness.

‑ ‑ ‑ ‑ ‑ ‑ ‑ ‑ ‑ ‑ ‑ ‑

⑮ Durness

Scattered Durness is wonderfully located, strung out along cliffs rising from a series of pristine beaches. When the sun shines, the effects of blinding white sand, the cry of seabirds and the spring-green-coloured seas combine in a magical way.

Walking around the sensational sandy coastline is a highlight, as is a visit to Cape Wrath. At Balnakeil, under a mile beyond Durness, a craft village occupies a one-time early-warning radar station. A walk along the beach to the north leads to Faraid Head, where you can see puffin colonies in early summer.

A mile east of the centre is a path down to **Smoo Cave** (www.smoocave. org). From the vast main chamber, you can head through to a smaller flooded cavern where a waterfall sometimes cascades from the roof. There's evidence the cave was inhabited about 6000 years ago. You can take a **boat trip** (☎01971-511704; adult/child £4/2; ✪11am-4pm Apr-May & Sep, 10am-5pm Jun-Aug) to explore a little further into the interior.

🛏 p389

Eating & Sleeping

Portree ❶

🛏 Rosedale Hotel   Hotel ££

(📞01478-613131; www.rosedalehotelskye.
co.uk; Beaumont Cres; s/d from £60/90;
🕐Easter-Oct; P 🛜) The Rosedale is a cosy,
old-fashioned hotel delightfully situated down
by the waterfront – you'll be welcomed with a
glass of whisky when you check-in. Its three
converted fishermen's cottages are linked
by a maze of narrow stairs and corridors, the
recently spruced-up bedrooms include a couple
with four-poster beds, and the dining room has a
view of the harbour.

Trotternish Peninsula ❷

🛏 Flodigarry Hotel   Hotel £££

(📞01470-552203; www.hotelintheskye.co.uk;
Flodigarry; r £160-280; P 🛜) From 1751 to 1759
Flora MacDonald lived in a cottage which is now
part of this atmospheric hotel, given a new lease
of life by adventurous new owners. You can stay
in the cottage itself (there are four bedrooms
here), or in the more spacious rooms in the main
hotel; non-guests are welcome at the stylish bar
and restaurant, with great views over the sea.

Plockton ❺

🛏 Tigh Arran   B&B ££

(📞01599-544307; www.
plocktonbedandbreakfast.com; Duirinish; s/d
£60/70; P 🛜🐾) It's hard to decide which
is better at this sweet spot 2 miles from the
Plockton shorefront – the warm personal
welcome or the absolutely stunning views
across to Skye. All three of the en suite rooms –
with appealing family options – enjoy the views,
as does the comfy lounge. A top spot, far from
stress and noise; great value too.

Ullapool ❿

🛏 The Ceilidh Place   Hotel £££

(📞01854-612103; www.theceilidhplace.com; 14
West Argyle St; s £66-92, d £140-172; 🕐Feb-Dec;
P 🛜🐾) This hotel is a celebration of Scottish
culture: we're talking literature and traditional
music, not tartan and Nessie dolls. Rooms go
for character over modernity; instead of a TV
they come with a selection of books chosen
by Scottish literati, eclectic artwork and cosy
touches. The sumptuous lounge has sofas,
chaises longues and an honesty bar. There's a
bookshop here too.

Lochinver ⓬

🍴 The Caberfeidh   Pub Food ££

(📞01571-844321; www.thecaberfeidh.co.uk;
Main St, Lochinver; tapas £6-9; 🕐 kitchen
noon-2.30pm & 6-9pm Tue-Sat, 12.30-2.30pm &
6-9pm Sun; 🛜) This convivial pub with riverside
beer garden serves a range of real ales, decent
wines and some excellent food. The menu is
based around tapas-sized portions like venison
meatballs and local langoustines. A sustainable,
low food-mile philosophy is at work and the
quality shines through.

Durness ⓯

🛏 Mackays Rooms   Hotel ££

(📞01971-511202; www.visitdurness.com;
d standard £129, deluxe £139-149; 🕐May–
mid-Oct; P 🛜🐾) You really feel you're at
the furthest corner of Scotland here, where
the road turns through 90 degrees. But
whether heading south or east, you'll go far
before you find a better place to stay than this
haven of Highland hospitality. With big beds,
contemporary colours and soft fabrics, it's a
romantic spot with top service and numerous
boutique details.

Classic Trip

Royal Highlands & Cairngorms

33

The heart of the Scottish Highlands features a feast of castles and mountains, wild rollercoaster roads, ancient Caledonian pine forest, and the chance to see Highland wildlife up close and personal.

TRIP HIGHLIGHTS

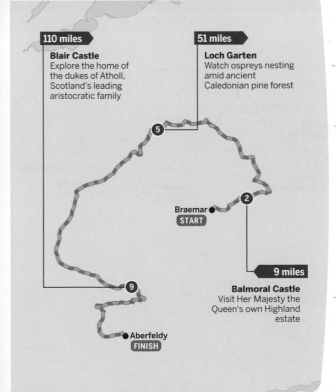

110 miles

Blair Castle
Explore the home of the dukes of Atholl, Scotland's leading aristocratic family

51 miles

Loch Garten
Watch ospreys nesting amid ancient Caledonian pine forest

5

2

Braemar ●
START

Balmoral Castle
Visit Her Majesty the Queen's own Highland estate

9 miles

9

● Aberfeldy
FINISH

**4–5 DAYS
149 MILES /
238KM**

GREAT FOR...

BEST TIME TO GO

July and August mean good weather and all attractions are open.

ESSENTIAL PHOTO

The gorgeous view of Schiehallion mountain from Queen's View on Loch Tummel.

BEST FOR WILDLIFE

Watching the nesting ospreys at Loch Garten.

Balmoral Castle One of the royal family's residences

Classic Trip

33 Royal Highlands & Cairngorms

You'll tick off the highlights of Royal Deeside and the central Highlands as you make this circuit around Cairngorms National Park. Queen Victoria kickstarted the Scottish tourism industry when she purchased Balmoral Castle in the middle of the 19th century, and her descendants still holiday here. Later, heed the call of the great outdoors with a visit to an osprey nesting site, and a funicular ride to a mountain top.

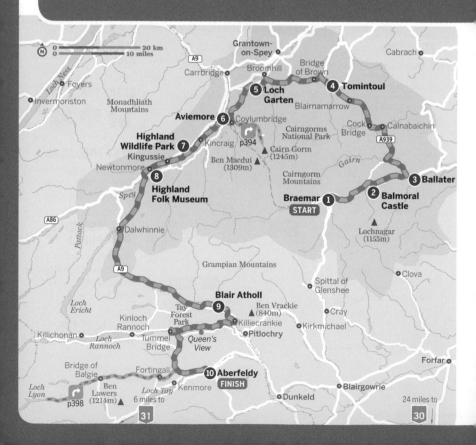

❶ Braemar

Braemar is a pretty little village with a grand location on a broad plain ringed by mountains where the Dee valley and Glen Clunie meet. In winter this is one of the coldest places in the country – temperatures as low as -29°C have been recorded.

Just north of the village, turreted **Braemar Castle** (www.braemarcastle. co.uk; adult/child £8/4; ⊙10am-4pm daily Jul & Aug, Wed-Sun Apr-Jun, Sep & Oct; P) dates from 1628 and served as a government garrison after the 1745 Jacobite rebellion. It was taken over by the local community in 2007, and now offers guided tours of the historic castle apartments.

LINK YOUR TRIP

31 **Lower West Coast**

From Aberfeldy it's a lovely 23-mile drive along Loch Tay to Killin, where you can pick up our tour of the Argyllshire coast.

30 **Stirling & Fife Coast**

A scenic 46 miles lead south from Aberfeldy to Stirling, the start of our tour of the historic and cultural jewels of Fife.

There are Highland games in many towns and villages throughout the summer, but the best known is the **Braemar Gathering** (www.brae margathering.org), which takes place on the first Saturday in September.

 p399

The Drive » The upper valley of the River Dee stretches east from Braemar to Aboyne. Made famous by its long association with the monarchy, the region is often called Royal Deeside. Head east from Braemar on the A93 for 9 miles to the car park at the entrance to Balmoral Castle.

TRIP HIGHLIGHT

❷ Balmoral Castle

Built for Queen Victoria in 1855 as a private residence for the royal family, **Balmoral Castle** (☎01339-742534; www. balmoralcastle.com; Crathie; adult/child £11.50/5; ⊙10am-5pm Apr-Jul, last admission 4.30pm; P) kicked off the revival of the Scottish Baronial style of architecture that characterises so many of Scotland's 19th-century country houses. The admission fee includes an interesting and well-thought-out audioguide, but the tour is very much an outdoor one through garden and grounds.

As for the castle itself, only the ballroom, which displays a collection of Landseer paintings and royal silver, is open to the public. Don't expect to see the Queen's private

quarters! The main attraction is learning about Highland estate management, rather than royal revelations.

You can buy a booklet that details several waymarked walks within Balmoral Estate; the best is the climb to **Prince Albert's Cairn**.

The Drive » Continue east on the A93 for another 8 miles to Ballater.

❸ Ballater

The attractive village of Ballater owes its 18th-century origins to the curative waters of nearby Pannanich Springs (now bottled commercially as Deeside Natural Mineral Water), and its prosperity to nearby Balmoral Castle.

The village recently received a double dose of misfortune when the **Old Royal Station** (its main tourist attraction) burned down in May 2015, followed by the worst flooding in living memory in January 2016. Most businesses were open again by summer 2016, but the the station may remain closed until 2018.

There are many pleasant walks in the surrounding area. The steep woodland walk up **Craigendarroch** (400m) takes just over one hour; ask at the tourist office for more info. If you'd rather cycle, you can hire bikes

Classic Trip

from **CycleHighlands**
(📞01339-755864; www.
cyclehighlands.com; The
Pavilion, Victoria Rd; bicycle
hire per half-day/day £12/18;
🕙9am-6pm) and **Bike
Station** (📞01339-754004;
www.bikestationballater.co.uk;
Station Sq; bicycle hire per 3hr/
day £12/18; 🕙9am-6pm),
which also offer guided
bike rides and advice on
local trails.

🛏 p399

The Drive » The A939 strikes
north through the mountains
from Ballater to Tomintoul (25
miles). The section beyond
Cock Bridge is a magnificent
rollercoaster of a road, much
loved by motorcyclists,
summiting at the Lecht pass
(637m) where there's a small
skiing area (it's usually the first
road in Scotland to be blocked
by snow when winter closes in).

- - - - - - - - - - - -

❹ Tomintoul

Tomintoul (tom-in-towel)
is a pretty, stone-built
village with a grassy,
tree-lined main square. It
was built by the Duke of
Gordon in 1775 on the old
military road that leads

over the Lecht pass from
Corgarff, a route now followed by the A939. The
village's recently refur-
bished and extended
museum (📞01807-580285;
The Square; 🕙10am-5pm Apr-
Oct) celebrates local history, with reconstructions
of a crofter's kitchen and
a blacksmith's forge.

There's excellent
mountain biking at the
BikeGlenlivet (www.glen
livetestate.co.uk; trails free,
parking £3) trail centre, 4.5
miles north of Tomintoul,
off the B9136 road.

🍴🛏 p399

↱ DETOUR:
CAIRNGORM MOUNTAIN

Start: ❻ Aviemore

Cairngorm Mountain (1245m), 10 miles southeast of Aviemore, is the sixth-highest
summit in the UK and home to Scotland's biggest ski area. A funicular railway ferries
skiers almost to the top of the mountain, and continues to operate throughout the
summer so that visitors can get a taste of the high mountain plateau.

The **Cairngorm Mountain Railway** (📞01479-861261; www.cairngormmountain.
org; adult/child return £11.50/7.50; 🕙every 20min 10am-4pm May-Nov, 9am-4.30pm Dec-Apr;
🅿) is the national park's most popular attraction, whisking you to the edge of the
Cairngorm plateau (altitude 1085m) in just eight minutes. The bottom station is at
the Coire Cas car park at the end of Ski Rd; at the top is an exhibition, a shop (of
course) and a restaurant. For environmental and safety reasons, you're not allowed
out of the top station in summer unless you book a guided walk or mountain-bike
descent; check the website for details.

Six miles east of Aviemore, on the road to Cairngorm Mountain, **Loch Morlich**
is surrounded by some 8 sq miles of pine and spruce forest that make up the
Glenmore Forest Park. Its attractions include a sandy beach (at the east end) and a
watersports centre.

Nearby, the **Cairngorm Reindeer Centre** (www.cairngormreindeer.co.uk; Glenmore;
adult/child £14/8; 🕙closed early Jan–mid-Feb; 👣) runs guided walks to see and feed
Britain's only herd of reindeer, who are very tame and will even eat out of your hand.
Walks take place at 11am daily (weather-dependent), plus another at 2.30pm from
May to September, and a third at 3.30pm Monday to Friday in July and August.

The Drive » Continue northwest from Tomintoul on the A939 for 8.5 miles before turning left on a minor road to the village of Nethy Bridge. In the village, turn left towards Aviemore on the B970 then, after 600m, turn left again on a minor road to Loch Garten (total 17 miles).

TRIP HIGHLIGHT

❺ Loch Garten

A car park on the shores of Loch Garten, amid beautiful open forest of Scots pine, gives access to the **RSPB Loch Garten Osprey Centre** (📞01479-831694; www.rspb. org.uk/lochgarten; Tulloch; osprey hide adult/child £5/2; ⏲osprey hide 10am-6pm Apr-Aug). Ospreys nest in a tall pine tree on the reserve – you can watch from a hide as the birds feed their young, and see live CCTV feeds from the nest. These rare and beautiful birds – the only bird of prey in the world that eats only fish – migrate here each spring from Africa, arriving in April and leaving in August (check the website to see if they're in residence).

The Drive » The minor road leads back to the B970, where you turn left along the banks of the River Spey to Coylumbridge; turn right here to reach Aviemore (11 miles).

❻ Aviemore

The gateway to the Cairngorms, Aviemore may not be the prettiest town in Scotland – the main attractions are in the surrounding area – but when bad weather puts the hills off-limits, Aviemore fills up with hikers, cyclists and climbers (plus skiers and snowboarders in winter) cruising the outdoor-equipment shops or recounting their latest adventures in the cafes and bars.

Strathspey Steam Railway (📞01479-810725; Station Sq; return adult/child £14.25/7.15; 🅿) runs steam trains on a section of restored line between Aviemore and Broomhill, 10 miles to the north-east, via Boat of Garten. There are four or five trains daily from June to August, and a more limited service in April, May, September, October and December.

The **Cairngorm Sled-Dog Centre** (📞07767-270526; www.sled-dogs.co.uk; Ski Rd; 👫) will take you on a 30-minute sled tour of local forest trails in the wake of a team of huskies, or a three-hour sled-dog safari. The sleds have wheels, so snow's not necessary.

🛏 p399

The Drive » From Aviemore drive south on the B99152, which follows the valley of the River Spey; after 8.5 miles, soon after passing through the village of Kincraig, you'll see a sign on the right for the Highland Wildlife Park.

❼ Highland Wildlife Park

The **Highland Wildlife Park** (📞01540-651270; www.highlandwildlifepark.org; Kincraig; adult/child £15.40/11.55; ⏲10am-6pm Jul & Aug, to 5pm Apr-Jun & Sep-Oct, to 4pm Nov-Mar; 🅿) features a drive-through safari park as well as animal enclosures that offer the chance to view rarely seen native wildlife, such as Scottish wildcats, capercaillies, pine martens and red squirrels, as well as species that once roamed the Scottish hills but have long since disappeared, including wolves, lynx, wild boars, beavers and European bison. Last entry is two hours before closing.

The Drive » Continue southwest on the B9152 through Kingussie to the Highland Folk Museum (6.5 miles).

❽ Highland Folk Museum

The old Speyside towns of Kingussie (kin-yew-see) and Newtonmore sit at the foot of the great heather-clad humps known as the Monadhliath Mountains. Newtonmore is best known as the home of the excellent **Highland Folk Museum** (📞01540-673551; www.highlandfolk.museum; Kingussie Rd, Newtonmore; ⏲10.30am-5.30pm Apr-Aug, 11am-4.30pm Sep & Oct; 🅿), an open-air

MIŁOSZ MAŚLANKA / SHUTTERSTOCK ©

WHY THIS IS A CLASSIC TRIP
NEIL WILSON, WRITER

Pretty much everything about this trip screams classic Scotland – romantic castles set amid forest-fringed hills (including the British royal family's own holiday home); picturesque Highland villages beside salmon-filled rivers; hiking and mountain biking amid wild mountain scenery in the heart of Britain's biggest national park; iconic Scottish wildlife experiences (think ospreys, reindeer, wildcats); there's even a whisky distillery thrown in for good measure!

Top: Wild red deer
Left: A road through Cairngorms National Park
Right: Loch Garten

CHRIS PETTY/500PX ©

collection of historical buildings and artefacts revealing many aspects of Highland culture and lifestyle. Laid out like a farming township, it has a community of traditional thatch-roofed cottages, a sawmill, a schoolhouse, a shepherd's bothy (hut) and a rural post office.

The Drive » Join the main A9 Inverness to Perth road and follow it south for 35 miles to Blair Atholl, passing through bleak mountain scenery and climbing to a high point of 460m at the Pass of Drumochter

- - - - - - - - - - - - - -

TRIP HIGHLIGHT

❾ Blair Atholl

The village of Blair Atholl dates only from the early 19th century, built by the Duke of Atholl, head of the Murray clan, whose seat – magnificent **Blair Castle** (📞01796-481207; www.blair-castle.co.uk; adult/child £10.70/6.40, family £28.90; ⏰9.30am-5.30pm Easter-Oct, 10am-4pm Sat & Sun Nov-Mar; P ♿) – is one of the most popular tourist attractions in Scotland.

Thirty rooms are open to the public and they present a wonderful picture of upper-class Highland life from the 16th century on. The original tower was built in 1269, but the castle underwent significant remodelling in the 18th and 19th centuries. Highlights include the 2nd-floor **Drawing Room**

with its ornate Georgian plasterwork and Zoffany portrait of the 4th duke's family, complete with a pet lemur (yes, you read that correctly) called Tommy; and the **Tapestry Room** draped with 17th-century wall hangings created for Charles I. The **dining room** is sumptuous – check out the 9-pint wine glasses – and the **ballroom** is a vast oak-panelled chamber hung with hundreds of stag antlers.

🛏 p399

The Drive » Follow the B8079 southeast out of Blair Atholl for a few miles, past the historic battle site of Killiecrankie, and turn right on the B8019 Strathtummel road. This gloriously scenic road leads along Loch Tummel (stop for photographs at Queen's View) to Tummel Bridge; turn left here on the B846 over the hills to Aberfeldy (29 miles).

- - - - - - - - - - - - -

⑩ Aberfeldy

Aberfeldy is the gateway to Breadalbane (the historic region surrounding Loch Tay), and a good base: adventure sports, angling, art and castles all feature on the menu here. It's a peaceful, pretty place on the banks of the Tay, but if it's moody lochs and glens that steal your heart, you

DETOUR: GLEN LYON

Start: ⑩ Aberfeldy

The 'longest, loneliest and loveliest glen in Scotland', according to Sir Walter Scott, stretches for 32 unforgettable miles of rickety stone bridges, native woodland and heather-clad hills, becoming wilder and more uninhabited as it snakes its way west. The ancients believed it to be a gateway to Faerieland, and even the most sceptical of visitors will be entranced by the valley's magic.

There are no villages in the glen – the majestic scenery is the main reason to be here – just a cluster of houses at Bridge of Balgie, where the **Bridge of Balgie Tearoom** (📞01887-866221; Bridge of Balgie; snacks £3-5; ⏰10am-5pm Apr-Oct; P 🛜 🐾), with a suntrap of a terrace overlooking the river, serves as a hub for walkers, cyclists and motorists. The owner is a fount of knowledge about the glen, and her pistachio and almond cake is legendary.

There are several waymarked woodland walks beginning from a car park a short distance beyond Bridge of Balgie, and more challenging hill walks into the surrounding mountains (see www.walkhighlands.co.uk/perthshire).

From Aberfeldy, the B846 leads to the pretty village Fortingall, famous for its ancient yew tree, where a narrow minor road strikes west up the glen; another steep and spectacular route from Loch Tay crosses the hills to meet it at Bridge of Balgie. The road continues west as far as the dam on Loch Lyon, passing a memorial to Robert Campbell (1808–94), a Canadian explorer and fur trader, who was born in the glen.

may want to push further west into **Glen Lyon**.

You arrive in the town by crossing the River Tay via the elegant **Wade's Bridge**, built in 1733 as part of the network of military roads designed to tame the Highlands. At the eastern end of town is **Aberfeldy Distillery** (www.dewars.com; tour adult/child £9.50/4.50;

⏰10am-6pm Mon-Sat, noon-4pm Sun Apr-Oct, 10am-4pm Mon-Sat Nov-Mar; P), home of the famous Dewar's whisky; tours include an entertaining interactive blending session. More expensive tours allow you to try venerable Aberfeldy single malts and others.

🛏 p399

Eating & Sleeping

Braemar ❶

🛏 St Margarets   B&B £

(📞01339-741697; soky37@hotmail.com; 13 School Rd; s/tw £34/56; 🛜) Grab this place if you can, but there's only one room: a twin with a serious sunflower theme. The genuine warmth in the welcome is delightful. It's tucked behind the church on the south side of the A93 road.

🛏 Craiglea   B&B ££

(📞01339-741641; www.craigleabraemar.com; Hillside Dr; d/f from £76/105; 🅿 🛜) Craiglea is a homely B&B set in a pretty stone cottage with three en suite bedrooms. Vegetarian breakfasts are available and the owners can rent you a bike and give advice on local walks.

Ballater ❸

🛏 Auld Kirk   Hotel ££

(📞01339-755762; www.theauldkirk.com; Braemar Rd; s/d from £80/115; 🅿 🛜 🐾) Here's something a little out of the ordinary – a seven-bedroom hotel housed in a converted 19th-century church. The interior blends original features with sleek modern decor – the pulpit now serves as the reception desk, while the breakfast room is bathed in light from leaded Gothic windows.

Tomintoul ❹

✕ Clockhouse Restaurant   Scottish ££

(The Square; mains £10-14; ⊙ noon-2pm & 6-8pm) Serves light lunches and bistro dinners made with fresh Highland lamb, venison and salmon.

🛏 Argyle Guest House   B&B ££

(📞01807-580766; www.argyletomintoul.co.uk; 7 Main St; d/f from £65/115; 🛜 🐾) Comfortable accommodation for walkers, and the best porridge in the Cairngorms!

Aviemore ❻

🛏 Cairngorm Hotel   Hotel ££

(📞01479-810233; www.cairngorm.com; Grampian Rd; s/d from £72/104; 🅿 🛜) Better known as 'the Cairn', this long-established hotel is set in the fine old granite building with the pointy turret opposite the train station. It's a welcoming place with comfortable rooms and a determinedly Scottish atmosphere, with tartan carpets and stags' antlers. There's live music on weekends, so it can get a bit noisy – not for early-to-bedders.

Blair Atholl ❾

🛏 Atholl Arms Hotel   Hotel ££

(📞01796-481205; www.athollarms.co.uk; r from £90; 🅿 🛜 🐾) This hotel, near Blair Atholl train station, is convenient for the castle, with rooms of a high standard; book ahead on weekends. The Bothy Bar here is the sibling pub of the Moulin Hotel in Pitlochry, snug with booth seating, an enormous fireplace and bucket-loads of character; there's no better place to be when the rain is lashing down outside.

Aberfeldy ❿

🛏 Tigh'n Eilean Guest House   B&B ££

(📞01887-820109; www.tighneilean.com; Taybridge Dr; s/d from £48/78; 🅿 🛜 🐾) Everything about this property screams comfort. It's a gorgeous place overlooking the Tay, with individually designed rooms – one has a Jacuzzi, while another is set on its own in a cheery yellow summer house in the garden, giving you a bit of privacy. The garden itself is fabulous, with hammocks for lazing in, and the riverbank setting is delightful.

Great Glen

34

This lake-and-mountain themed trip leads you through some of the Highlands' scenic hotspots, and along the shores of world-famous Loch Ness – here be monsters!

TRIP HIGHLIGHTS

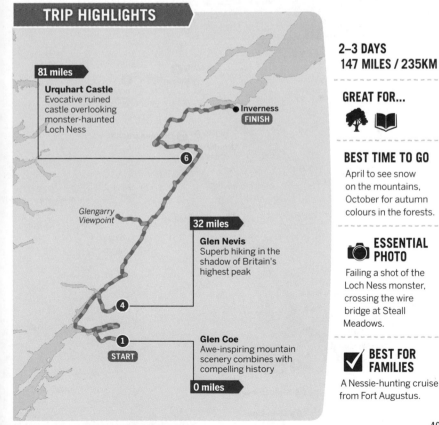

81 miles

Urquhart Castle
Evocative ruined castle overlooking monster-haunted Loch Ness

● **Inverness**
FINISH

Glengarry Viewpoint

6

32 miles

Glen Nevis
Superb hiking in the shadow of Britain's highest peak

4

1

START

Glen Coe
Awe-inspiring mountain scenery combines with compelling history

0 miles

2–3 DAYS
147 MILES / 235KM

GREAT FOR...

BEST TIME TO GO

April to see snow on the mountains, October for autumn colours in the forests.

ESSENTIAL PHOTO

Failing a shot of the Loch Ness monster, crossing the wire bridge at Steall Meadows.

BEST FOR FAMILIES

A Nessie-hunting cruise from Fort Augustus.

Glen Nevis Crossing the wire bridge through Nevis Gorge

34 Great Glen

The Great Glen is a geological fault running in an arrow-straight line across Scotland, filled by a series of lochs including Loch Ness. This trip follows the A82 road along the glen (completed in 1933 – a date that coincides with the first sightings of the Loch Ness Monster!) and links two areas of outstanding natural beauty – Glen Coe to the south, and Glen Affric to the north.

TRIP HIGHLIGHT

❶ Glen Coe

Scotland's most famous glen is also one of its grandest. The A82 road leads over the **Pass of Glencoe** and into the narrow upper glen. The southern side is dominated by three massive, brooding spurs, known as the **Three Sisters**, while the northern side is enclosed by the continuous steep wall of the knife-edged **Aonach Eagach** ridge, a classic mountaineering challenge.

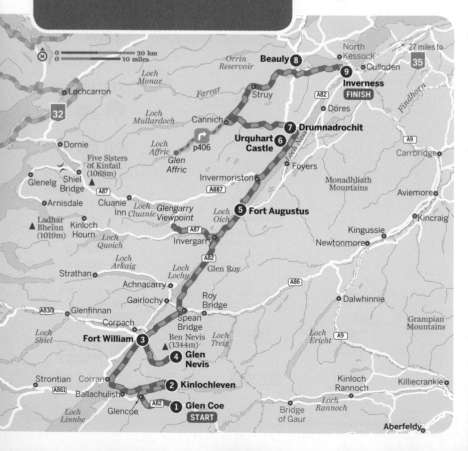

Glencoe Visitor Centre
(NTS; ☎01855-811307; www.
glencoe-nts.org.uk; adult/child
£6.50/5; ☺9.30am-5.30pm
Easter-Oct, 10am-4pm Thu-Sun
Nov-Easter; P) provides
comprehensive informa-
tion on the geological,
environmental and cul-
tural history of Glencoe,
charts the development
of mountaineering in the
glen, and tells the story
of the Glencoe Massacre
in all its gory detail.

🍴 🛏 p407

The Drive » From Glencoe
village at the foot of the glen,
head east on the B863 for 7
miles along the southern shore
of Loch Leven to Kinlochleven.

- - - - - - - - - - - - - -

❷ Kinlochleven

Kinlochleven is hemmed
in by high mountains
at the head of beauti-
ful Loch Leven, where

LINK YOUR TRIP

32 Upper West Coast

The stirring wilderness of
the northwest Highlands
awaits – Skye lies 60
miles northwest of Fort
Augustus along the A87.

35 Whisky Trails

A short drive east
from Inverness to Elgin
(39 miles) links to our
trip around the heartland
of Scotland's whisky
distilleries.

the West Highland Way
brings a steady stream
of hikers through the
village. It is also the
starting point for walks
up the glen of the River
Leven, through pleasant
woods to the **Grey Mare's
Tail** waterfall, and harder
mountain hikes into the
Mamores.

Scotland's first **Via
Ferrata** (☎01855-413200;
www.glencoeactivities.com;
per person/family £55/170) –
a 500m climbing route
equipped with steel lad-
ders, cables and bridges –
snakes through the crags
around the Grey Mare's
Tail, allowing non-climb-
ers to experience the
thrill of climbing (you'll
need a head for heights,
though!).

🍴 p407

The Drive » Return west
along the north side of Loch
Leven, perhaps stopping for
lunch at the excellent Lochleven
Seafood Cafe, then head north
on the A82 to Fort William (22
miles).

- - - - - - - - - - - - - -

❸ Fort William

Basking on the shores
of Loch Linnhe amid
magnificent mountain
scenery, Fort William has
one of the most enviable
settings in the whole of
Scotland. If it wasn't for
the busy dual carriage-
way crammed between
the less-than-attractive
town centre and the loch,
and one of the highest
rainfall records in the
country, it would be

almost idyllic. Even so,
the Fort has carved out
a reputation as 'Outdoor
Capital of the UK' (www.
outdoorcapital.co.uk).

The small but fasci-
nating **West Highland
Museum** (☎01397-702169;
www.westhighlandmuseum.
org.uk; Cameron Sq; ☺10am-
5pm Mon-Sat Apr-Oct, to 4pm
Mar & Nov-Dec, closed Jan &
Feb) is packed with all
manner of Highland
memorabilia. Look out
for the secret portrait of
Bonnie Prince Charlie –
after the Jacobite rebel-
lions, all things Highland
were banned, including
pictures of the exiled
leader, and this tiny
painting looks like noth-
ing more than a smear of
paint until viewed in a
cylindrical mirror.

🍴 🛏 p407

The Drive » At the
roundabout on the northern
edge of Fort William, take the
minor road that runs into Glen
Nevis; it leads to a car park at
the far end of the glen, 6.5 miles
away.

- - - - - - - - - - - - - -

TRIP HIGHLIGHT

❹ Glen Nevis

Scenic Glen Nevis – used
as a filming location
for *Braveheart* and the
Harry Potter movies –
wraps around the base
of Ben Nevis, Britain's
highest mountain.
The **Glen Nevis Visitor
Centre** (☎01397-705922;
www.bennevisweather.co.uk;
☺8.30am-6pm Jul & Aug,
9am-5pm Apr-Jun, Sep & Oct,

9am-3pm Nov-Mar; **P**) is situated 1.5 miles up the glen, and provides information on hiking, weather forecasts, and specific advice on climbing **Ben Nevis**.

From the car park at the end of the road, there is an excellent 1.5-mile walk through the spectacular Nevis Gorge to **Steall Meadows**, a verdant valley dominated by a 100m-high bridal-veil waterfall. You can reach the foot of the falls by crossing the river on a wobbly, three-cable wire bridge – one cable for your feet and one for each hand – a real test of balance!

The Drive » Return down Glen Nevis and head north on the A82. At Invergarry, turn left onto the A87 which climbs high above Loch Garry; stop at the famous Glengarry Viewpoint (layby on left). By a quirk of perspective, the lochs to the west appear to form the map outline of Scotland. Return to the A87 and continue to Fort Augustus (44 miles).

- - - - - - - - - - - - - -

❺ Fort Augustus

Fort Augustus, at the junction of four old military roads, was originally a government garrison and the headquarters of General George Wade's road-building operations in the early 18th century. Today it's a neat and picturesque little place bisected by the Caledonian Canal.

Boats using the canal are raised and lowered 13m by a 'ladder' of five consecutive locks. It's fun to watch, and the neatly landscaped canal banks are a great place to soak up the sun. The **Caledonian Canal Centre** (📞01320-366493; Ardchattan House, Canalside; 🕑10am-4pm), beside the lowest lock, has information on the history of the canal.

Cruise Loch Ness (📞01320-366277; www. cruiselochness.com; adult/child £14/8; 🕑hourly 10am-4pm Apr-Oct, 1 & 2pm only Nov-Mar), at the jetty beside the canal bridge, operates one-hour cruises on Loch Ness accompanied by the latest high-tech sonar equipment so you can keep an underwater eye open for the Loch Ness monster.

The Drive » It's a straightforward but scenic 17-mile drive along the shores of Loch Ness to Urquhart Castle.

- - - - - - - - - - - - - -

TRIP HIGHLIGHT

❻ Urquhart Castle

Commanding a superb location with outstanding views over Loch Ness, **Urquhart Castle** (HS; 📞01456-450551; adult/child £8.50/5.10; 🕑9.30am-6pm Apr-Sep, to 5pm Oct, to 4.30pm Nov-Mar; **P**) is a popular Nessie-hunting hot spot. A huge visitor centre (most of which is beneath ground level) includes a video theatre (with a dramatic 'reveal' of the castle at the end of the film) and displays of medieval items discovered in the castle. The five-storey tower house at the northern point is the most impressive remaining fragment and offers wonderful views across the water.

The Drive » A short hop of 2 miles leads to Drumnadrochit.

NITSAWAN KATERATTANAKUL / SHUTTERSTOCK ©

Urquhart Castle Overlooking Loch Ness

7 Drumnadrochit

Deep, dark and narrow, Loch Ness stretches for 23 miles between Inverness and Fort Augustus. Its bitterly cold waters have been extensively explored in search of Nessie, the elusive Loch Ness monster, but most visitors see her only in the form of a cardboard cut-out at Drumnadrochit's monster exhibitions.

The **Loch Ness Centre** (☎01456-450573; www. lochness.com; adult/child £7.95/4.95; ⊙9.30am-6pm Jul & Aug, to 5pm Easter-Jun, Sep & Oct, 10am-3.30pm Nov-Easter; P ♿) adopts a scientific approach that allows you to weigh the evidence for yourself. Exhibits include the original equipment – sonar survey vessels, miniature submarines, cameras and sediment coring tools – used in various monster hunts, as well as original photographs and film footage of sightings. You'll find out about hoaxes and optical

DETOUR: GLEN AFFRIC

Start: ❼ Drummadrochit (p405)

Glen Affric (www.glenaffric.org), one of the most beautiful glens in Scotland, extends deep into the hills beyond Cannich, halfway between Drummadrochit and Beauly. The upper reaches of the glen, now designated as **Glen Affric Nature Reserve**, is a scenic wonderland of shimmering lochs, rugged mountains and native Scots pine forest, home to pine martens, wildcats, otters, red squirrels and golden eagles.

A narrow, dead-end road leads southwest from Cannich; about 4 miles along is **Dog Falls**, a scenic spot where the River Affric squeezes through a narrow, rocky gorge. A circular walking trail (red waymarks) leads from Dog Falls car park to a footbridge below the falls and back on the far side of the river (2 miles, allow one hour).

The road continues beyond Dog Falls to a parking area and picnic site at the eastern end of **Loch Affric**, where there are several short walks along the river and the loch shore. The circuit of Loch Affric (10 miles, allow five hours walking, two hours by mountain bike) follows good paths right around the loch and takes you deep into the heart of some very wild scenery.

---

illusions, as well as learning a lot about the ecology of Loch Ness – is there enough food in the loch to support even one 'monster', let alone a breeding population?

The Drive ❱❱ Head west on the A831 which leads to the village of Cannich – jumping-off point for the Glen Affric detour – before turning north along lovely Strathglass to reach Beauly (30 miles).

---

❽ Beauly

Mary, Queen of Scots is said to have given this village its name in 1564 when she visited, exclaiming in French: 'Quel beau lieu!' (What a beautiful place!). Founded in 1230,

the red-sandstone **Beauly Priory** is now an impressive ruin, haunted by the cries of rooks nesting in a magnificent centuries-old sycamore tree.

Corner on the Square makes a good place to break your journey.

✘ p407

The Drive ❱❱ Drive east on the A862 for 12 miles to Inverness.

---

❾ Inverness

Inverness has a great location astride the River Ness at the northern end of the Great Glen. In summer it overflows with visitors intent on monster hunting at nearby Loch Ness, but it's worth a visit in its own

right for a stroll along the picturesque River Ness, a cruise on Loch Ness, and a meal in one of the city's excellent restaurants.

The main attraction in Inverness is a leisurely stroll along the river to the **Ness Islands**. Planted with mature Scots pine, beech and sycamore, and linked to the river banks and each other by elegant Victorian footbridges, the islands make an appealing spot. They're a 20-minute walk south of the castle – head upstream on either side of the river (the start of the Great Glen Way), and return on the opposite bank.

🛏 p407

Eating & Sleeping

Glen Coe ❶

✕ Glencoe Café   Cafe £

(☎01855-811168; www.glencoecafe.co.uk;
Glencoe village; mains £4-8; ⏰10am-4pm
daily, to 5pm May-Sep, closed Nov; ℗🛜)
This friendly cafe is the social hub of Glencoe
village, serving breakfast fry-ups till 11.30am
(including vegetarian versions), light lunches
based around local produce (think Cullen skink,
smoked salmon quiche, venison burgers), and
the best cappuccino in the glen.

🛏 Clachaig Inn   Hotel ££

(☎01855-811252; www.clachaig.com; s/d
£53/106; ℗🛜) The Clachaig, 2 miles east
of Glencoe village, has long been a favourite
haunt of hill walkers and climbers. As well as
comfortable en suite accommodation, there's a
smart, modern lounge bar with snug booths and
high refectory tables, mountaineering photos
and bric-a-brac, and climbing magazines to leaf
through.

Kinlochleven ❷

✕ Lochleven Seafood Cafe   Seafood ££

(☎01855-821048; www.lochlevenseafoodcafe.
co.uk; mains £11-23, whole lobster £40; ⏰meals
noon-3pm & 6-9pm, coffee & cake 10am-noon &
3-5pm mid-Mar–Oct; ℗👶) This outstanding
place serves superb shellfish freshly plucked
from live tanks – oysters on the half shell, razor
clams, scallops, lobster and crab – plus a daily
fish special and some non-seafood dishes. For
warm days, there's an outdoor terrace with a
view across the loch to the Pap of Glencoe, a
distinctive conical mountain.

Fort William ❸

✕ Lime Tree   Scottish ££

(☎01397-701806; www.limetreefortwilliam.
co.uk; Achintore Rd; mains £16-20; ⏰6.30-

9.30pm; ℗🛜) Fort William is not over-
endowed with great places to eat, but the
restaurant at this small hotel and art gallery
has put the UK's Outdoor Capital on the
gastronomic map. The chef turns out delicious
dishes built around fresh Scottish produce,
ranging from Loch Fyne oysters to Loch Awe
trout and Ardnamurchan venison.

🛏 Grange   B&B £££

(☎01397-705516; www.grangefortwilliam.com;
Grange Rd; d £145; ℗🛜) An exceptional 19th-
century villa set in its own landscaped grounds,
the Grange is crammed with antiques and fitted
with log fires, chaise lounges and Victorian
roll-top baths. The Turret Room, with its window
seat in the turret overlooking Loch Linnhe, is
our favourite. It's 500m southwest of the town
centre. No children.

Beauly ❽

✕ Corner on the Square   Cafe £

(☎01463-783000; www.corneronthesquare.
co.uk; 1 High St; mains £7-13; ⏰8.30am-5.30pm
Mon-Fri, 8.30am-5pm Sat, 9.30am-5pm Sun)
Beauly's best lunch spot is this superb little
delicatessen and cafe that serves breakfast
(till 11.30am), daily lunch specials (11.30am to
4.30pm) and excellent coffee.

Inverness ❾

🛏 Heathmount
Hotel   Boutique Hotel ££

(☎01463-235877; www.heathmounthotel.
com; Kingsmills Rd; s/d from £75/105; ℗🛜)
Small and friendly, the Heathmount combines
a popular local bar and restaurant with eight
designer hotel rooms, each one different,
ranging from a boldly coloured family room in
purple and gold to a slinky black velvet four-
poster double. Five minutes' walk east of the
city centre.

Whisky Trails

35

As well as visiting half a dozen famous whisky distilleries, you'll discover ancient crafts and traditions such as barrel-making, wool-spinning and hand-loom weaving on this tour of historic Speyside.

TRIP HIGHLIGHTS

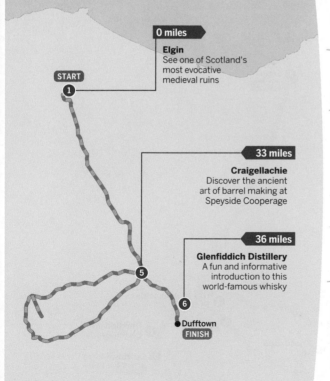

0 miles

Elgin
See one of Scotland's most evocative medieval ruins

START
1

33 miles

Craigellachie
Discover the ancient art of barrel making at Speyside Cooperage

36 miles

Glenfiddich Distillery
A fun and informative introduction to this world-famous whisky

5

6

Dufftown
FINISH

2–3 DAYS
39 MILES / 62KM

GREAT FOR...

BEST TIME TO GO

Early May or late September, when the Spirit of Speyside festivals take place.

ESSENTIAL PHOTO

A whisky-barrel maker at work in the Speyside Cooperage.

BEST FOR SHOPPING

Stocking up on gourmet goodies at Elgin's Gordon & Macphail.

Craigellachie Traditional barrel-making at the Speyside Cooperage

35 Whisky Trails

The old county of Moray, centred on the town of Elgin, lies at the heart of an ancient Celtic earldom and is famed for its mild climate and rich farmland – the barley fields here traditionally provided the raw material for Speyside's whisky distilleries. This trip leads from Elgin's historic cathedral into the heart of Speyside to experience the magic of Scotch whisky at its source.

TRIP HIGHLIGHT

❶ Elgin

Elgin, dominated by a hilltop monument to the 5th Duke of Gordon, has been the provincial capital of Moray for over eight centuries. Many people think that the ruins of **Elgin Cathedral** (HS; www.historicenviron ment.scot; King St; adult/ child £5.50/3.30; ☺9.30am-5.30pm Apr-Sep, 10am-4pm Sat-Wed Oct-Mar), known as the 'lantern of the north', are the most beautiful and evocative in Scotland; its octagonal

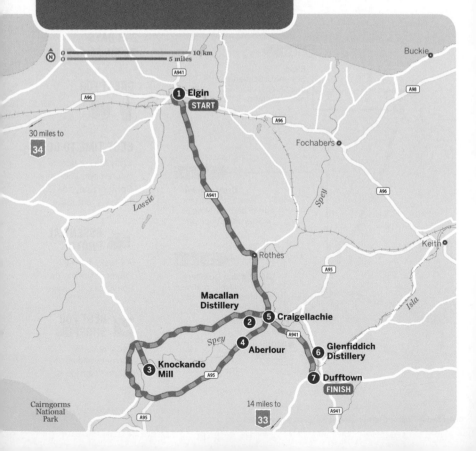

chapter house is the finest in the country.

The town is also home to Scotland's oldest independent **museum** (www.elginmuseum.org.uk; 1 High St; donations accepted; ☺10am-5pm Mon-Fri, 11am-4pm Sat Apr-Oct), a captivating collection beautifully displayed in a purpose-built Victorian building. Exhibits range from Ecuadorian shrunken heads to Peruvian mummies, and include internationally important fish and reptile fossils discovered in local rocks, and mysterious Pictish carved stones.

Look out for **Gordon & MacPhail** (☏01343-545110; www.gordonandmacphail.com; 58-60 South St; ☺8.30am-

LINK YOUR TRIP

34 **Great Glen**
Inverness, the final stop on our tour of Highland highlights, is 39 miles west of Elgin along the A96.

33 **Royal Highlands & Cairngorms**
You can extend your explorations into the Cairngorms national park by following the second half of this trip: join it at Tomintoul, 19 miles southwest of Dufftown.

5pm Mon-Sat, alcohol on sale from 10am), the world's largest specialist malt-whisky dealer. Over a century old and offering around 450 different varieties, this Elgin shop is a place of pilgrimage for whisky connoisseurs.

🍴 🛏 p415

The Drive » Follow the A941 south from Elgin to reach the River Spey at Rothes, where a welter of distillery signs announce that you have arrived in Speyside, the heart of Scotland's whisky industry. South of Rothes, turn right on the B9102, which soon leads to the Macallan Distillery (14 miles).

❷ Macallan Distillery

The Macallan – king of Speyside malts – is produced in a range of sherry and bourbon finishes. The **Macallan Distillery** (☏01340-872280; www.themacallan.com; Easter Elchies, Craigellachie; tours £15; ☺9.30am-6pm Mon-Sat Easter-Oct, to 5pm Mon-Fri Nov-Mar; P) is set amid waving fields of Golden Promise barley (used in the whisky-making process) and offers entertaining 1¾-hour guided tours (maximum group of 10 people; tours should be prebooked).

The Drive » Continue west on the B9102 for 7 miles to the Knockando Woolmill. It's down a short side road on the left – look out for the signpost.

❸ Knockando Mill

Hidden in a fold of the hills beneath Cardhu distillery, **Knockando Woolmill** (www.knockandowoolmill.org.uk; Knockando; ☺10am-4pm Easter-Nov; P) is a rare survival of an 18th-century woollen mill that has been lovingly restored to full working order. The ancient looms clank away Monday to Friday, turning out plaid and tweed textiles that can be purchased in the neighbouring shop. Guided tours cost £5.

Beyond the mill, on the banks of the Spey, lie two more distilleries, **Tamdhu** and **Knockando**.

The Drive » Return to the B9102 and turn left. After 4 miles, turn left again to cross the River Spey, and once more on the A95. You will soon pass the small, friendly and independent Glenfarclas Distillery before arriving in Aberlour (total 11 miles).

❹ Aberlour

Aberlour – or Charlestown of Aberlour, to give it its full name – is a pretty village straggling along the banks of the River Spey. **Aberlour Distillery** (☏01340-881249; www.aberlour.com; tours from £14; ☺tours 10am & 2pm daily Apr-Oct, by appointment Mon-Fri Nov-Mar; P) is right on the main street, and offers an excellent, detailed tour with a proper tasting session. Other attractions

include salmon fishing on the Spey, and some lovely walks along the Speyside Way.

As the home of Walkers shortbread as well as Aberlour single malt, the village is rightly proud of its local produce, and you can browse a huge selection of Scottish food and drink in the village's own Spey Larder (p415), or sit down to a meal and a few nips of whisky at the Mash Tun (p415).

✕ 🛏 p415

The Drive >> From Aberlour it's a short hop of just under 2 miles to Craigellachie.

- - - - - - - - - - -

TRIP HIGHLIGHT

⑤ Craigellachie

Craigellachie Hotel (p415) is famous for its wonderfully old-fashioned, hunting-lodge atmosphere, from the wood-panelled lobby to the opulent drawing room where you can sink into a sofa in front of the log fire. But the big attraction for whisky connoisseurs is the **Quaich Bar**, a cosy nook filled with green leather armchairs and lined with almost 700 varieties of single malt whisky.

Glenfiddich Distillery One of Scotland's most famous whisky brands

On the southern edge of the village is the **Speyside Cooperage** (☎01340-871108; www.spey sidecooperage.co.uk; adult/ child £3.50/2; ☺9am-5pm Mon-Fri, closed late Dec-early Jan), where you can watch the fascinating art of barrel-making during a 45-minute guided tour.

The Drive 》 Drive south along the A941 for 4 miles to Glenfiddich Distillery.

TRIP HIGHLIGHT

➏ Glenfiddich Distillery

Along with Glenmo-rangie, Glenfiddich is among the most famous of single malt whisky brands, and kept the flame of whisky apprecia-tion alive during the dark years of the 1970s and '80s, before the revival of interest in all things distilled.

Glenfiddich Distillery (☎01340-820373; www.glen fiddich.co.uk; admission free, tours from £10; ☺9.30am-4.30pm Apr-Oct, 11am-3pm Nov-Mar; **P**) is big and bustling. The standard tour (£10) starts with an overblown video, but it's fun and informative; an in-depth half-day

HOW TO BE A MALT WHISKY

'Love makes the world go round? Not at all! Whisky makes it go round twice as fast.'
Whisky Galore, Compton Mackenzie (1883–1972)

Whisky tasting today is big news: being able to tell your Ardbeg from your Edradour is de rigueur among the whisky nosing set, so here are some pointers to help you impress your friends.

What's the difference between malt and grain whiskies? Malts are distilled from malted barley – that is, barley that has been soaked in water, then allowed to germinate for around 10 days until the starch has turned into sugar – while grain whiskies are distilled from other cereals, usually wheat, corn or unmalted barley.

So what is a single malt? A single malt is a whisky that has been distilled only from malted barley and is the product of a single distillery. A pure (or vatted) malt is a mixture of single malts from several distilleries, and a blended whisky is a mixture of various grain whiskies (about 60%) and malt whiskies (about 40%) from many different distilleries.

Single malts vs blends? A single malt, like a fine wine, somehow captures the terroir or essence of the place where it was made and matured – a combination of the water, the barley, the peat smoke, the oak barrels in which it was aged and (in the case of certain coastal distilleries) the sea air and salt spray. Each distillation varies from the one before, like different vintages from the same vineyard.

How should a single malt be drunk? Either neat, or with a little water added. To appreciate the aroma and flavour to the utmost, a measure of malt whisky can be cut (diluted) with one-third to two-thirds as much spring water. Ice, tap water and (God forbid) mixers are for philistines. Or those who know what they want.

Pioneer's Tour (£50) must be prebooked.

The Drive » Continue into the centre of Dufftown, just 0.75 miles south.

❼ Dufftown

Rome may be built on seven hills, but Dufftown's built on seven stills, say the locals. Founded in 1817 by James Duff, 4th Earl of Fife, Dufftown lies at the heart of the Speyside whisky-distilling region. With seven working distilleries nearby, Duff-town has been dubbed Scotland's malt-whisky capital and is host to the biannual **Spirit of Speyside** (www.spiritofspeyside.com) whisky festival.

As well as housing a selection of distillery memorabilia (try saying that after a few drams), the town's **Whisky Museum** (☎01340-821097; www.whisky.dufftown.co.uk; 12 Conval St; ⏰1-4pm Mon-Fri May-Sep) holds 'nosing and tasting evenings' in the Commercial Hotel, where you can learn what to look for in a fine single malt (£10 per person;

8pm Wednesday in July and August). You can then test your newfound skills at the nearby Whisky Shop (p415), which stocks hundreds of single malts.

The **Keith & Dufftown Railway** (☎01340-821181; www.keith-dufftown-railway.co.uk; Dufftown Station; adult/child return £11/5; **P**) sees trains hauled by 1950s diesel motor units running on weekends from May to September, plus Fridays in July and August.

✗ ⌂ p415

Eating & Sleeping

Elgin ❶

✗ Drouthy Cobbler   Cafe, Bar ££
(☎01343-596000; thedrouthycobbler.co.uk;
48a High St; mains £11-15; ⊙food served 8am-
10pm; 🛜) This brand new cafe-bar is an all-day
venue serving everything from breakfast to
dinner, with a bistro-style menu that changes
regularly but includes dishes such as carpaccio
of beef, Caesar salad, scallops and pancetta,
and home-made burgers. It's tucked away up a
side alley, and also hosts live music and comedy
gigs in the evenings.

🛏 Moraydale   B&B ££
(☎01343-546381; www.moraydaleguesthouse.
com; 276 High St; s/d/f from £55/75/85;
P🛜) The Moraydale is a spacious Victorian
mansion filled with period features – check
out the stained glass and the cast-iron and tile
fireplaces. The bedrooms are all en suite and
equipped with modern bathrooms – the three
large family rooms are particularly good value.

🛏 Southbank Guest House   B&B ££
(☎01343-547132; www.southbankguesthouse.
co.uk; 36 Academy St; s/d/f from £55/90/140;
P🛜) The family-run, 15-room Southbank is
set in a large Georgian town house in a quiet
street south of Elgin's centre, just five minutes'
walk from the cathedral and other sights.

Aberlour ❹

✗ Spey Larder   Food & Drink
(☎01340-871243; www.speylarder.com; 96-98
High St; ⊙9.30am-5pm Mon-Sat) This deli is
the place to shop for picnic goodies to eat on
the banks of the River Spey – a great selection
of Scottish artisan cheeses, smoked salmon,
venison charcuterie, delicious home-baked
bread, and local craft beers.

🛏 Craigellachie Hotel   Hotel £££
(☎01340-881204; www.craigellachiehotel.
co.uk; Craigellachie; r from £175; P🛜) The
Craigellachie has a wonderfully old-fashioned,
hunting-lodge atmosphere, from the wood-
panelled lobby to the opulent drawing room
where you can sink into a sofa in front of the
log fire. But the big attraction for whisky
connoisseurs is the **Quaich Bar**, a cosy nook
filled with green leather armchairs and lined
with almost 700 varieties of single malt whisky.

🛏 Mash Tun   B&B ££
(☎01340-881771; www.mashtun-aberlour.com;
8 Broomfield Sq; s/d from £75/110; 🛜) Housed
in a curious stone building made for a sea
captain in the outline of a ship, this luxurious
B&B is famous for its whisky bar – a place of
pilgrimage for whisky enthusiasts – which has
a collection of old and rare single malts. There's
also an excellent restaurant (mains £10 to
£20, lunch and dinner daily) that serves posh
pub grub.

Dufftown ❼

🍾 Whisky Shop   Food & Drinks
(☎01340-821097; www.whiskyshopdufftown.
co.uk; 1 Fife St; ⊙10am-6pm Mon-Sat, to 5pm
Sun) Stocks hundreds of single malts.

🛏 Davaar B&B   B&B ££
(☎01340-820464; www.davaardufftown.co.uk;
17 Church St; d/f £65/80; 🛜) Davaar is a sturdy
Victorian villa with three smallish but comfy
rooms; the breakfast menu is superb, offering
the option of Portsoy kippers as well as the
traditional fry-up (which uses eggs from the
owners' own chickens).

Ferry Hopping

36

Jumping around the islands of the west coast on the ferry network – munching seafood and sipping whisky along the way – is one of Scotland's iconic pleasures.

TRIP HIGHLIGHTS

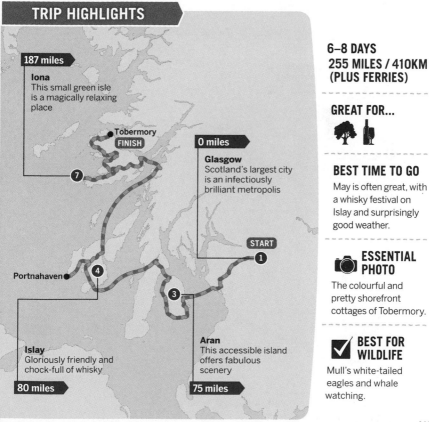

187 miles

Iona
This small green isle is a magically relaxing place

Tobermory
FINISH

7

0 miles

Glasgow
Scotland's largest city is an infectiously brilliant metropolis

START
1

Portnahaven ●

4

3

Islay
Gloriously friendly and chock-full of whisky

80 miles

Aran
This accessible island offers fabulous scenery

75 miles

6–8 DAYS
255 MILES / 410KM
(PLUS FERRIES)

GREAT FOR...

BEST TIME TO GO

May is often great, with a whisky festival on Islay and surprisingly good weather.

ESSENTIAL PHOTO

The colourful and pretty shorefront cottages of Tobermory.

BEST FOR WILDLIFE

Mull's white-tailed eagles and whale watching.

Tobermory Colourful houses line the harbour

36 Ferry Hopping

Taking in four of Scotland's most enticing islands plus the vibrant city of Glasgow, this is an in-depth exploration of southwest Scotland. The route covers stunningly scenic Arran, Islay's welcoming distilleries, Oban's seafood scene, Mull's heart-lifting landscapes and the enchanting holy isle of Iona. The ferry trips themselves – offering sensational coastal perspectives – are part of the adventure.

TRIP HIGHLIGHT

1 Glasgow

Full of excellent art, design, food and pubs, Glasgow is an intoxicatingly vibrant place with a legendary live-music scene and loads to see.

The city's **cathedral** (HES; ☎0141-552 8198; www.historicenvironment.scot; Cathedral Sq; ⊙9.30am-5.30pm Mon-Sat & 1-5pm Sun Apr-Sep, 10am-4pm Mon-Sat & 1-4pm Sun Oct-Mar) is one of Scotland's most interesting and atmospheric; don't miss a stroll in

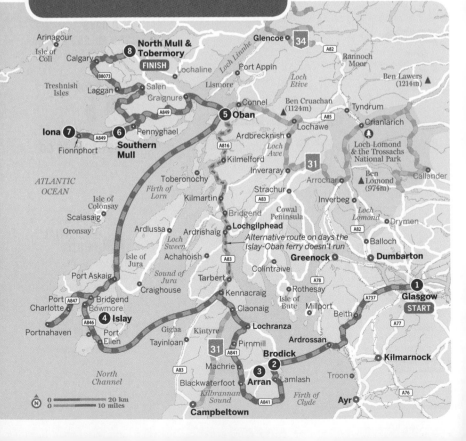

the adjacent **Necropolis** (🕐8.30am-4.30pm).

West of the centre, **Kelvingrove Art Gallery & Museum** (www.glasgowmuseums.com; Argyle St; 🕐10am-5pm Mon-Thu & Sat, 11am-5pm Fri & Sun) is a fabulous display of paintings and much more, while the **Burrell Collection** (📞0141-287 2550; www.glasgowmuseums.com; Pollok Country Park; 🕐10am-5pm Mon-Thu & Sat, 11am-5pm Fri & Sun) has a soothing parkland setting and a great art collection.

The design genius of Charles Rennie Mackintosh is best seen at the **Glasgow School of Art** (📞0141-353 4526; www.gsa.ac.uk/tours; 167 Renfrew St; tours adult/child £9.75/4.75; 🕐10am-4.30pm) and **Mackintosh House** (www.hunterian.gla.ac.uk; 82 Hillhead St; adult/child £5/3; 🕐10am-5pm Tue-Sat, 11am-4pm Sun).

LINK YOUR TRIP

31 Lower West Coast

Once you've seen Mull, head back to Oban and explore the Kintyre peninsula on this trip.

34 Great Glen

From Tobermory, you can get a ferry across to Kilchoan and approach Fort William by a lonely, scenic route.

Glasgow is a shopping paradise, with the boutiques of the central pedestrianised area counterbalanced by the vintage shops and delis of the bohemian West End.

🛏️ p423

The Drive » Take the M8 out of Glasgow to the west, then exit for the A737, which runs down to the Ayrshire coast, where you pick up the A78 northwest the last few miles to Ardrossan and the Arran ferry. The total drive is 33 miles.

----

② Brodick

The Ardrossan ferry arrives at Brodick, the beating heart of the island, backing a coastal road that follows the town's long curving bay. On a clear day it's a spectacular vista, with Goatfell looming over the forested shore.

Two miles north, elegant **Brodick Castle** (NTS; 📞01770-302202; www.nts.org.uk; castle & park adult/child £12.50/9, park only £6.50/5.50; 🕐 castle 11am-4pm May-Aug, 11am-3pm Apr & Sep, park 9.30am-sunset year-round) evolved from 13th-century origins into a stately home and hunting lodge for the Dukes of Hamilton and was used until the 1950s. The extensive grounds, now a country park with various trails among the rhododendrons, justify the steep entry fee. Nearby, **Isle of Arran Brewery** (📞01770-302353; www.arranbrewery.com; tour £5;

🕐10am-5pm Mon-Sat & 12.30-5pm Sun Apr-Sep, 10am-3.30pm Mon & Wed-Sat Oct-Mar) offers tastings and tours, while **Arran Aromatics** (📞01770-302595; www.arranaromatics.com; 🕐9.30am-5pm, to 6pm summer) has a good visitor centre plus soap- and candle-making for kids and up.

The walk up and down **Goatfell**, the island's highest point, is 8 miles return (up to eight hours).

🛏️ p423

The Drive » Take the A841 southbound to do a leisurely clockwise near-circuit of the island. It's 42 miles this way right around to Lochranza, otherwise only 14 miles away heading north.

TRIP HIGHLIGHT

③ Arran

Lamlash, just 3 miles south of Brodick, is in a dazzling setting, strung along the beachfront. Just off the coast is Buddhist-run **Holy Island**, which you can visit.

The landscape in the south of Arran is gentler than in the north; the road drops into little wooded valleys, and Kildonan has pleasant sandy beaches, basking seals and a gorgeous water outlook.

On the western side of the island is **Machrie Moor Stone Circle** (🕐24hr), a pleasant 1.3-mile stroll from the parking area on the coastal road.

The village and ferry port of Lochranza is characterised by numerous red deer and a ruined 13th-century **castle** (HES; www.historicenvironment. scot; ☺24hr). Nearby, **Isle of Arran Distillery** (☎01770-830264; www. arranwhisky.com; tours adult/child £7.50/free; ☺10am-5.30pm Mar-Oct, 10.30am-4pm Nov-Feb) produces a light, aromatic single malt and does good tours.

🛏 p423

The Drive ≫ From April to October a ferry runs from Lochranza to Claonaig on Kintyre; in winter, this goes to Tarbert. From Claonaig, the B8001 crosses the peninsula to Kennacraig (5 miles) and the ferry to Islay, which docks at either Port Askaig in the island's east, or Port Ellen in the south. From Tarbert it's 5 miles south on the A83 to Kennacraig.

TRIP HIGHLIGHT

❹ Islay

The home of some of the world's greatest and peatiest whiskies, whose names reverberate on the tongue like a pantheon of Celtic deities, Islay (eye-lah) is a wonderfully friendly place and the birdlife, fine seafood, turquoise bays and basking seals are ample non-whisky reasons to visit.

Islay has eight working distilleries, with a ninth on the way. All welcome visitors and run tours. It's worth booking by phone. Pick up the invaluable pamphlet listing tour times from the tourist office.

The island's 'capital', Bowmore, has a round church to leave the devil no corners to hide in, and the **Bowmore distillery** (☎01496-810441; www.

FERRY IMPORTANT INFO

Scotland's west-coast ferries are operated by **Caledonian MacBrayne** (CalMac; ☎0800 066 5000; www.calmac.co.uk). A comprehensive timetable booklet is available from tourist offices and on the website. There's a summer timetable and one for winter, when services are somewhat reduced. CalMac Island Hopscotch offers more than 20 tickets, giving reduced fares for various combinations of crossings. A government scheme has meant that standard ferry fares are much lower now than a few years back.

It's important to book car spaces ahead by phone; several days ahead for Islay, Mull and Arran is best. If there are no spaces, you can still turn up and wait in the standby queue; you'll often but not always squeeze on.

---

bowmore.com; School St; tours from £7; ☺9am-5pm Mon-Fri & 9am-12.30pm Sat Oct-Mar, 9am-5pm Mon-Sat & noon-4pm Sun Apr-Sep), which malts its own barley.

Three of the biggest, peatiest names in single malt are close together near Port Ellen in the south: **Laphroaig** (☎01496-302418; www.laphroaig.com; tours from £6; ☺9.45am-5pm daily Mar-Oct, 9.45am-4.30pm daily Nov & Dec, 9.45am-4.30pm Mon-Fri Jan & Feb), **Lagavulin** (☎01496-302749; www.discovering-distilleries.com; tours from £6; ☺9am-6pm Mon-Fri & 9am-5pm Sat-Sun Jun-Aug, 9am-5pm daily Apr & Sep, 9am-6pm Mon-Fri & 9am-5pm Sat-Sun May, 9am-5pm Mon-Fri & 10am-4pm Sat-Sun Oct & Mar, 10am-4pm Mon-Sat Nov-Feb) and **Ardbeg** (☎01496-302244; www.ardbeg.com; tours from £5; ☺9.30am-5pm Mon-Fri, plus Sat & Sun Apr-Oct).

On the western side of the island, two excellent distilleries are **Bruichladdich** (☎01496-850190; www.bruichladdich.com; Bruichladdich; tours £5; ☺9am-6pm Mon-Fri, 9.30am-4pm Sat & 12.30-3pm Sun Apr-Sep, 9am-5pm Mon-Fri & 9.30am-4pm Sat Oct-Mar), near Port Charlotte, and boutique-sized **Kilchoman** (☎01496-850011; www.kilchomandistillery.com; Rockfield Farm, Kilchoman; tours from £6; ☺9.45am-5pm Mar-Oct, closed Sat & Sun Nov-Feb). Head past Port Charlotte to Portnahaven to watch seals on the harbour rocks.

JOHN DOORNKAMP / GETTY IMAGES ©

Oban Ferry to the Isle of Mull

Three miles from Port Askaig, tumbledown ruins of houses and a chapel on an islet in a shallow loch mark **Finlaggan** (☎01496-840644; www.finlaggan.org; adult/child £4/2; ☺ruins 24hr, museum 10.30am-4.15pm Mon-Sat Apr-Oct), what remains of the stronghold of the Lords of the Isles. Start your exploration at the visitor centre. The island itself is open at all times.

The Drive » Try and time your exit from Islay for a Wednesday or Saturday, when there's a ferry from Port Askaig to Oban via Colonsay. Otherwise, head back to Kennacraig then north up the A83, turning left on to the A816 at Lochgilphead. It's 56 miles from Kennacraig to Oban. If going this way, stop at Kilmartin's interesting museum and prehistoric sights.

❺ Oban

Oban, main gateway to many of the Hebridean islands, is a waterfront town on a delightful bay, with sweeping views to Kerrera and Mull. In summer the town centre is crowded with holidaymakers and travellers headed for the archipelago. But the setting is still lovely, and Oban's brilliant seafood restaurants are marvellous places to be as the sun sets over the bay.

In the centre of town, handsome **Oban Distillery** (☎01631-572004; www.discovering-distilleries.com; Stafford St; tour £8; ☺noon-4.30pm Dec-Feb, 9.30am-5pm Mar-Jun, Oct & Nov, 9.30am-7.30pm Mon-Fri & 9.30am-5pm Sat & Sun Jul-Sep) has been producing since 1794. The standard guided tour leaves regularly (worth booking) and includes a dram, a take-home glass and a taste straight from the cask.

Basking Shark Scotland (☎07975-723140; www.baskingsharkscotland.co.uk; ☺Apr-Oct) runs entertaining boat trips with optional snorkelling, focused on finding and observing basking sharks – the world's second largest fish – and other notable marine species.

Sea Kayak Oban (☎01631-565310; www.seakayakoban.com; Argyll St; ☺10am-5pm Mon-Fri, 9am-5pm Sat, 10am-4pm Sun) has a well-stocked shop, rental, great route advice and sea-kayaking courses, including an all-inclusive two-day intro for beginners.

🛏 p377, p423

The Drive >> From the centre of Oban, get the ferry across to Craignure on the island of Mull. It takes about an hour.

- - - - - - - - - - - -

❻ Southern Mull

Mull can lay claim to some of the finest and most varied scenery in the Inner Hebrides. Noble birds of prey soar over mountain and coast, while the western waters provide good whale watching.

Near the Craignure ferry slip, **Duart Castle** (☎01680-812309; www.duart castle.com; adult/child £6/3; ☺10.30am-5pm daily May– mid-Oct, 11am-4pm Sun-Thu Apr), the ancestral seat of the Maclean clan, enjoys a spectacular position on a rocky outcrop overlooking the Sound of Mull.

Contact **Mull Eagle Watch** (☎01680-812556; www.mulleaglewatch.com; adult/child £8/4; ☺Apr-Sep) to observe the white-tailed eagle, Britain's largest bird of prey. Tours run in the mornings and afternoons.

Great walks in the southern part of the island include the popular climb of Ben More and the spectacular trip to Carsaig Arches.

The Drive >> From the ferry at Craignure, it's 37 miles of imposing scenery along the A849 to Mull's southwestern tip at Fionnphort. From here, a passenger ferry zips to Iona, just across the strait.

- - - - - - - - - - - -

TRIP HIGHLIGHT

❼ Iona

Like an emerald teardrop off Mull's western shore, enchanting, idyllic Iona, holy island and burial ground of kings, is a magical place that lives up to its lofty reputation.

Iona's ancient but heavily reconstructed **abbey** (HES; ☎01681-700512; www.historicenvironment. scot; adult/child £7.10/4.30; ☺9.30am-5.30pm Apr-Sep, 10am-4.30pm Oct-Mar) is the spiritual heart of the island. The spectacular nave, dominated by Romanesque and early Gothic vaults and columns, is a powerful space; a door on the left leads to the beautiful cloister, where medieval grave slabs sit alongside modern religious sculptures. Out the back, the museum displays fabulous carved high crosses and other inscribed stones, along with lots of background information. Next to the abbey is an ancient graveyard where there's an evocative Romanesque chapel as well as a mound that marks the burial place of 48 of Scotland's early kings, including Macbeth.

🛏 p423

The Drive >> Get the ferry back to Fionnphort and drive back up the A849 for 18 miles before taking a left onto the B8035. Follow this then the B8073 along the coast, a spectacular drive along the Mull coastline for a slow 50 miles to the capital, Tobermory.

- - - - - - - - - - - -

❽ Northern Mull & Tobermory

The highlights of northern Mull, apart from the spectacular drive, are the glorious beach at Calgary and the pretty capital, Tobermory, with colourful houses arrayed along a pretty harbour like a village in a picture book. It makes a great base, with a good selection of accommodation and fine seafood.

Sea Life Surveys (☎01688-302916; www. sealifesurveys.com; Ledaig) runs whale-watching trips that head out from Tobermory harbour to the waters north and west of Mull. Long day trips as well as shorter family-friendly jaunts are available.

🛏 p423

Eating & Sleeping

Glasgow ❶

🛏 15Glasgow   B&B ££

(☎0141-332 1263; www.15glasgow.com; 15 Woodside Pl; d/ste £125/155; P 🛜) Glasgow's 19th century merchants certainly knew how to build a beautiful house, and this 1840s terrace is a sumptuous example. Huge rooms with lofty ceilings have exquisite period detail complemented by attractive modern greys, striking bathrooms and well-chosen quality furniture. Your welcoming host makes everything easy for you: an in-room breakfast, overlooking the park, is a real treat. The host prefers no under-5s.

Brodick ❷

🛏 Kilmichael Country House Hotel   Hotel £££

(☎01770-302219; www.kilmichael.com; Glen Cloy; s £98, d £163-205; ☺Apr-Oct; P 🛜🍽) The island's best hotel is also the oldest building here – one section dates from 1650. Luxurious and tastefully decorated, it's a mile outside Brodick but seems a world away in deep countryside. With just eight spacious, very individual rooms and excellent four-course dinners (£45, open to nonguests), it's an ideal, utterly relaxing hideaway, that feels very classy without being overly formal.

Arran ❸

🛏 Castlekirk   B&B ££

(☎01770-830202; www.castlekirkarran.co.uk; s/d £45/75; ☺Mar-Oct; P 🛜🍽) This unusual and warmly welcoming place is a converted church chock-full of excellent artworks; there's a gallery downstairs, and paintings decorate the passageways and rooms. The breakfast area is dignified by a rose window, and there are great views of the castle opposite. Rooms are cosy under the sloping ceiling.

Oban ❺

🛏 Elderslie Guest House   B&B ££

(☎01631-570651; www.obanbandb.com; Soroba Rd; s £50-55, d £72-85; P 🛜) B&B is a difficult balancing act: making things modern without losing cosiness, being friendly and approachable without sacrificing privacy. At this spot a mile south of town the balance is absolutely right, with a big variety of commodious rooms with big showers, large towels and lovely outlooks over greenery. Breakfast is great, there's outdoor lounging space and the hosts are really excellent.

Iona ❼

🛏 Argyll Hotel   Hotel ££

(☎01681-700334; www.argyllhoteliona.co.uk; s £76, d £95-114; ☺Mar-Oct; 🛜🍽) This loveable, higgledy-piggledy warren of a hotel has great service and appealing snug rooms (a sea view costs more – £167 for a double), including good-value family options. The rooms offer simple comfort and relaxation rather than luxury. Most look out to the rear, where a huge organic garden supplies the restaurant. This is a relaxing and amiably run Iona haven.

Mull ❽

🛏 Tobermory Hotel   Inn £££

(☎01688-302091; www.thetobermoryhotel. com; 53 Main St; s £75, d £146-158; 🛜🍽) This harbourfront hotel is a conversion from fisherfolk's cottages, so thick walls and cosy, compact rooms are a given. They come in various shapes and sizes, with some looking out over the water. They feel a little overpriced in summer. The design is attractive modern Scottish, and the downstairs pub is welcoming. The restaurant is reasonable, with a bit of an uninspired menu.

STRETCH YOUR LEGS EDINBURGH

Start/Finish Castle Esplanade

Distance 1 mile

Duration Two to three hours

This walk explores the alleys and side streets around the Royal Mile, leading you away from the main tourist trail and into hidden corners and historic nooks. It involves a bit of climbing up and down steep stairs.

Take this walk on Trip

1

Castle Esplanade

Begin on the Castle Esplanade, which provides a grandstand view south over the city to the Pentland Hills.

The Walk ⟩⟩ Head towards Castlehill and the start of the Royal Mile.

Cannonball House

The 17th-century house on the right is known as Cannonball House because of the iron ball lodged in the wall. It was not fired in anger, but marks the gravitation height to which water would flow naturally from the city's first piped water supply. The building now houses an excellent **restaurant** (☎0131-225 1550; www.contini.com/contini-cannonball; 356 Castlehill, Royal Mile; mains £15-25; ⊙noon-5pm & 5.30-10pm Tue-Sat; 🛜♿; 🚌23, 27, 41, 42), a good place to sample classic Scottish cuisine.

The Walk ⟩⟩ Continue down Castlehill for barely 100m to the Camera Obscura.

Camera Obscura

Edinburgh's **Camera Obscura** (www.camera-obscura.co.uk; Castlehill; adult/child £14.50/10.50; ⊙9am-9pm Jul & Aug, 9.30am-7pm Apr-Jun, Sep & Oct, 10am-6pm Nov-Mar; 🚌23, 27, 41, 42) is a curious 19th-century device – in constant use since 1853 – that uses lenses and mirrors to throw a live image of the city onto a large horizontal screen. Stairs lead up through various displays to the **Outlook Tower**, which offers great views over the city.

The Walk ⟩⟩ Go down Ramsay Lane past Ramsay Garden – one of Edinburgh's most desirable addresses – and around to the right to the towers of New College.

New College

This neo-Gothic building is home to Edinburgh University's Faculty of Divinity. Nip into the courtyard to see the **statue of John Knox**, a firebrand preacher who led the Protestant Reformation in Scotland, and was instrumental in the creation of the Church of Scotland in 1560.

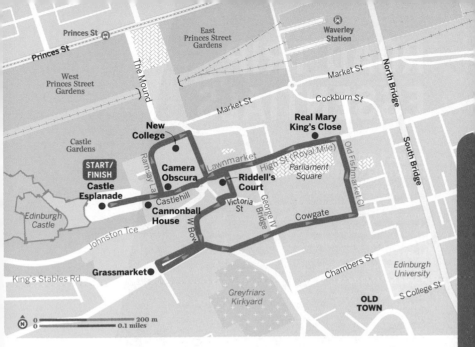

The Walk ≫ Turn right and climb the stairs into Milne's Court, a student residence belonging to Edinburgh University. Exit into Lawnmarket, cross the street (bearing slightly left) and duck into Riddell's Court at No 322–8.

Riddell's Court

Riddell's Court is a typical Old Town close. You'll find yourself in a small courtyard, but the house in front of you (built in 1590) was originally the edge of the street (the building you just walked under was added in 1726 – look for the inscription in the doorway on the right). The arch with the inscription *Vivendo discimus* (we live and learn) leads into the original 16th-century courtyard.

The Walk ≫ Turn right down Fisher's Close, which leads to Victoria Tce. Descend the stairs at the foot of Upper Bow and continue downhill.

Grassmarket

The site of a cattle market from the 15th century until the start of the 20th century, the Grassmarket was once the city's main place of execution, and over 100

martyred Covenanters are commemorated by a monument at the eastern end, where the gallows used to stand.

The Walk ≫ Head east along the Cowgate, passing under the arch of George IV Bridge. Turn left and climb up Old Fishmarket Close, a typical cobbled Old Town wynd, and emerge onto the Royal Mile; bear left across the street.

Real Mary King's Close

Edinburgh's 18th-century City Chambers were built over the sealed-off remains of **Real Mary King's Close** (☏0845 070 6244; www.realmarykingsclose.com; 2 Warriston's Close, High St; adult/child £14.50/8.75; ☺10am-9pm daily Apr-Oct, 10am-5pm Sun-Thu, 10am-9pm Fri & Sat Nov-Mar; ▯23, 27, 41, 42), and the lower levels of this medieval Old Town alley have survived almost unchanged amid the foundations for 250 years. Now open to the public, this spooky, subterranean labyrinth gives a fascinating insight into the everyday life of 17th-century Edinburgh.

The Walk ≫ Walk back up the Royal Mile to the Castle Esplanade.

ROAD TRIP ESSENTIALS

GREAT BRITAIN DRIVING GUIDE 427

Driving Licence & Documents........................ 427
Insurance 427
Hiring a Car 427
Motorhome Rental 427
Bringing Your Own Vehicle............................ 428
Maps 428
Motoring Organisations.................................. 428
Roads & Conditions 428
Road Rules 429
Parking 430
Fuel 430
Radio... 430
Great Britain Playlist....................................... 431

GREAT BRITAIN TRAVEL GUIDE........................ 432

GETTING THERE & AWAY 432
Air.. 432
Car & Motorcycle 432
Sea 432
Train.. 433
DIRECTORY A–Z 433
Accommodation 433
Electricity 435
Food 435
Internet Access 436
LGBT Travellers... 436
Money 436
Opening Hours... 437
Public Holidays 437
Safe Travel 437
Telephone 438
Tourist Information.. 438
Travellers with Disabilities............................ 438
Visas 439

Great Britain Driving Guide

Driving in Great Britain allows you to explore everything from country lanes to mountain roads. Downsides include traffic jams and high fuel and parking bills.

Driving Fast Facts

➡ **Right or left?** Left

➡ **Manual or automatic?** Manual

➡ **Legal driving age** 17

➡ **Top speed limit** 70mph (112km/h) on motorways and some (but not all) dual carriageways

➡ **Signature cars** MG, Morris Minor and Mini

DRIVING LICENCE & DOCUMENTS

At the time of writing, if you're an EU national, from the European Economic Area or from Northern Ireland you can drive any type of vehicle listed on your licence. It's not clear if or how Britain's vote to leave the EU (Brexit) will affect this (the rules are slightly different if you're from the Channel Islands or the Isle of Man).

If you're from any other country, you can drive any small vehicle (such as a car or motorcycle) listed on your licence for up to 12 months.

If asked by the police, you must be able to produce a valid driving licence and insurance documents within seven days.

INSURANCE

It's illegal to drive a car or motorbike in Britain without (at least) third-party insurance. This will be included with all rental cars. If you're bringing your own vehicle, check whether your insurance will cover you in Britain.

HIRING A CAR

Compared with many countries (especially the USA), hire rates are expensive in Britain; the smallest cars start from about £130 per week, and it's around £190 and upwards per week for a medium-sized car. All rates include insurance and unlimited mileage, and can rise at busy times (or drop at quiet times).

Some main players:

Avis (www.avis.co.uk)

Budget (www.budget.co.uk)

Europcar (www.europcar.co.uk)

Sixt (www.sixt.co.uk)

Thrifty (www.thrifty.co.uk)

Another option is to look online for small local car-hire companies in Britain that can undercut the international franchises. Generally speaking, those in cities are cheaper than in rural areas. Using a rental-broker or comparison site such as **UK Car Hire** (www.ukcarhire.net) or **Kayak** (www.kayak.com) can also help you to find bargains.

MOTORHOME RENTAL

Hiring a motorhome or campervan (£650 to £1100 a week) is more expensive than hiring a car, but saves on accommodation costs and gives almost unlimited freedom. Sites to check include:

Just Go (www.justgo.uk.com)
Wild Horizon (www.wildhorizon.co.uk)
Wicked Campers (www.wickedcampers. co.uk)

BRINGING YOUR OWN VEHICLE

You can usually use a non-GB car without registering or taxing it in the UK if all of the following rules apply:

➡ You're just visiting, and have no plans to live in the country.

➡ The vehicle is registered and taxed in your own country.

➡ You only use the car for up to six months in total (either on one visit or a number of shorter visits over a year).

For more details see www.gov.uk/ importing-vehicles-into-the-uk.

MAPS

You'll need good road maps – we recommend getting them even if you have a sat-nav system.

Road Trip Websites

➡ **Automobile Association** (AA; www.theaa.com) The UK's largest motoring organisation; also provides breakdown cover.

➡ **RAC** (www.rac.co.uk) Another key motoring organisation and breakdown cover provider.

➡ **UK Government** (www.gov.uk/ browse/driving) Official advice on driving in Great Britain.

➡ **AA Route Planner** (www.theaa. com/route-planner) Directions and maps from the AA.

➡ **BBC Travel** (www.bbc.co.uk/ travel) Traffic info from the BBC.

➡ **Traffic Report** (www.highways. gov.uk/traffic-information) A government-run, searchable database of current congestion and planned roadworks.

For country-wide cover, the AA's excellent atlas series includes the spiral-bound *AA Road Atlas Britain* (£10.99) with a scale of 1:200,000. It also produces nine indexed regional maps covering the whole of Britain (£4.99) on scales ranging from 1:200,000 to 1:300,000.

These and a broad range of other reliable maps and atlases are widely available at petrol stations and bookshops.

MOTORING ORGANISATIONS

Motoring organisations in Britain include the **Automobile Association** (www.theaa. com) and the **RAC** (www.rac.co.uk). For both, annual membership starts at around £40, including 24-hour roadside breakdown assistance. **Britannia** (www.lv.com/ breakdown-cover) offers better value at £30 a year, while a greener alternative is the **Environmental Transport Association** (www.eta.co.uk); it provides breakdown assistance but doesn't campaign for more roads.

ROADS & CONDITIONS

Motorways and main A-roads deliver you quickly from one end of the country to another. Motorways feature service stations (signed as 'Services') where you can buy fuel, food and often a meal at a fast-food eatery. Services are regularly spaced but it's still worth keeping an eye on the fuel gauge and being aware of the distance to the next one.

Lesser A-roads, B-roads and minor roads are usually more scenic and are ideal for car or motorcycle touring. You can't travel fast, but you won't care.

Toll routes are rare. The M6 (Toll) runs for a 27 mile stretch near Birmingham, and costs up to £5.50 per car; payment is either in advance or on-site, by cash or card. There are also tolls to cross bridges such as the Dartford Crossing, the Humber Bridge, the Mersey Tunnels, the Severn River Crossing, the Tamar Bridge and the Tyne Tunnel.

In winter (usually December to March), snow and ice frequently affect routes in parts of Scotland, higher ground in Wales and often to a lesser extent northern England. It can also affect the rest of the country and occur outside those months. When it does, disruption can be significant.

Driving Problem-Buster

What should I do if my car breaks down? Call the service number of your car hire company and a local garage will be contacted. If you're bringing your own car, it's a good idea to join breakdown cover providers, such as the **AA** (www. theaa.com), **Britannia** (www.lv.com/breakdown-cover) or the **RAC** (www.rac. co.uk). If you're not a member, they can still organise assistance (it'll just cost you more).

What if I have an accident? Hire cars usually have a leaflet in the glovebox about what to do in case of an accident. Exchange basic information with the other party (name, insurance details, driver's licence number, company details if the car is a rental). No discussion of liability needs to take place at the scene. It's a good idea to photograph the scene of the accident, noting key details (damage sustained, car positions on the road, any skid markings). Call the police (☎999) if required.

What should I do if I get stopped by the police? Always remain calm and polite; officers are generally courteous and helpful. They may want to see your passport or other valid form of ID, licence and proof of insurance – you're not required by law to carry these, but must be able to produce them, if asked, at a police station within seven days.

What if I can't find anywhere to stay? If you're travelling during the summer months, always book accommodation in advance. If you're stuck, call the local tourist office's accommodation hotline. If they're closed, many offices have lists of places to sleep posted in the window.

Will I be able to find ATMs? You'll find ATMs in all cities, and in most towns and at many service stations. Most are free to use, some though may be subject to a small charge – they will be labelled as such. Local shops often offer 'cash back', where in exchange for a purchase over £5 you can effectively debit cash from your account.

Will I need to pay tolls in advance? Many toll routes offer a pre-paid service but you can also usually pay on site – follow the signs ushering you into lanes specifying pre-paid, cash or card.

Rush hours can stretch from 6am to 9am and 4pm to 7pm around London and the bigger cities, but tend to be shorter in smaller cites and towns. School summer holidays bring congestion around national parks, popular cities such as Oxford, Bath Edinburgh and York, and in coastal areas – the peak-time bank holiday queues down to the West Country are notorious.

ROAD RULES

Drink driving is taken very seriously; you're allowed a maximum blood-alcohol level of 80mg/100mL (0.08%) in England and Wales, or 50mg/100mL (0.05%) in Scotland.

Some other important rules:

➡ drive on the left (!)

➡ wear fitted seat belts in cars

➡ wear helmets on motorcycles

➡ give way to your right at junctions and roundabouts

➡ always use the left lane on motorways and dual carriageways unless overtaking (although so many people ignore this rule, you'd think it didn't exist)

➡ don't use a mobile phone while driving unless it's fully hands-free (another rule frequently flouted)

Drivers often flash their hazard lights once or twice as an informal way to say 'thank you' for road courtesies extended to them.

Speed Limits

Speed limits are usually 30mph (48km/h) in built-up areas, 60mph (96km/h) on main roads and 70mph (112km/h) on motorways and most (but not all) dual carriageways.

Road Signs

See inside the back cover for some examples of Great Britain's road signs – and their meanings.

PARKING

Many cities have short-stay and long-stay car parks; the latter are cheaper though may be less convenient. 'Park & Ride' systems allow you to park on the edge of the city then ride to the centre on frequent nonstop buses for an all-in-one price. Roadside parking in villages and in city residential areas can be free – but wherever you are, it's worth checking carefully for signs indicating charges.

Yellow lines (single or double) along the edge of the road indicate restrictions. Nearby signs spell out when you can and can't park. In London and other big cities, traffic wardens operate with efficiency; if you park on the yellow lines at the wrong time, your car will be clamped or towed away, and it'll cost you £130 or more to get driving again. In some cities there are also red lines, which mean no stopping at all. Ever.

FUEL

Cities and towns have numerous petrol stations, you'll also find service stations cropping up regularly beside motorways and the more important A roads. In rural areas, petrol stations are much less plentiful; you'll also find the prices in these places tend to be higher, so it's a good idea to fill up before heading into the wild.

Prices vary but you can expect to pay around £1.10 per litre for unleaded petrol.

RADIO

Radio stations offer up-to-date traffic news, top tunes and good company. Local radio (both BBC and independent) has the most detailed travel news and weather information. National stations also include:

BBC Radio 1 (98–99.6MHz FM) Music radio, targeted at 15-29 year-olds.

BBC Radio 2 (88–92MHz FM) Hits, easy listening and chat; aimed at adults.

BBC Radio 3 (90–92.2 MHz FM) Classical, often highbrow.

Radio 4 (92–94.4MHz FM) Quality, diverse, imaginative speech radio.

BBC Radio 5 Live (909 or 693 AM) All speech, news and sports-focused.

Virgin Radio (1215Hz MW) Music, showbiz and chat.

Classic FM (100–102MHz FM) Accessible classical music.

Driving Tips

Don't rely only on your sat-nav. Although often highly reliable, they have been known to route cars across rivers where there are no bridges and down country tracks only wide enough for animals. Having a good map and being aware of your broader location is always wise.

Some parts of rural Britain have unfenced grazing. You'll be tipped off by warning signs and often cattle grids (bars set into the road to stop animals crossing). After that, watch your speed and expect to see sheep, ponies and even cows on the roads.

The real fun of driving in Britain is away from the motorways and on country, coastal and mountain routes. Here it's best to make journey time calculations bearing in mind the 'tractor factor' – how much longer it'll take if travelling behind a farm vehicle that's moving painfully slowly.

Approximate Road Distances (miles)

	Bath	Birmingham	Brighton	Cambridge	Canterbury	Cardiff	Durness	Edinburgh	Heathrow Airport	Llanberis	London	Manchester	Newcastle	Norwich	Oxford	Penzance	Portsmouthance	Stonehenge	Torquay
Birmingham	110																		
Brighton	160	170																	
Cambridge	170	100	120																
Canterbury	180	190	90	110															
Cardiff	55	110	200	200	220														
Durness	640	550	720	610	710	650													
Edinburgh	380	290	460	350	450	390	260												
Heathrow Airport	100	110	70	70	90	140	660	400											
Llanberis	250	125	330	250	330	170	560	300	260										
London	120	120	50	60	60	155	660	400	20	260									
Manchester	180	210	260	180	260	190	470	220	200	100	200								
Newcastle	310	200	340	230	330	315	380	120	280	250	280	150							
Norwich	230	160	170	60	160	270	630	370	150	310	115	185	250						
Oxford	70	70	110	85	130	105	620	360	50	200	70	160	260	150					
Penzance	210	270	280	360	340	220	810	550	270	400	310	350	480	425	260				
Portsmouth	80	150	50	135	125	155	700	440	70	280	80	240	340	205	85	240			
Stonehenge	35	130	120	140	140	90	660	400	70	260	100	220	330	200	70	200	55		
Torquay	120	190	190	250	250	130	720	460	200	330	220	260	390	310	170	110	150	110	
York	240	140	270	160	260	240	470	200	230	17	200	80	90	180	180	400	275	270	310

- - - - - - - - - - - - - - - -
GREAT BRITAIN PLAYLIST

The Bonnie Banks o' Loch Lomond
(Traditional) Catchy folk ditty about Scotland's 'low' and 'high' roads.

Road to Nowhere (Talking Heads) Oddly not prompted by Birmingham's scary Spaghetti Junction, but by fears of an apocalypse.

Road to Hell (Chris Rea) Variously attributed to being inspired by the M25, the A63 and the A19.

A13, Trunk Road to the Sea (Billy Bragg) The British version of *Route 66*.

The Combine Harvester (The Wurzels) For when you're stuck behind one.

Great Britain Travel Guide

GETTING THERE & AWAY

Flights, cars and rail tickets can be booked online at lonelyplanet.com/bookings.

AIR

Most visitors reach Britain by air, with London a global transport hub. The massive growth of budget ('no-frills') airlines has increased the number of routes – and reduced the fares – between Britain and other countries in Europe.

Airports

London's main airports:

Heathrow (www.heathrow.com) Britain's main airport for international flights; often chaotic and crowded. About 15 miles west of central London.

Gatwick (www.gatwickairport.com) Britain's number-two airport, mainly for international flights, 30 miles south of central London.

Stansted (www.stanstedairport.com) About 35 miles northeast of central London, mainly handling charter and budget European flights.

Luton (www.london-luton.co.uk) Some 35 miles north of central London, well known as a holiday-flight airport.

London City (www.londoncityairport.com; 📞) A few miles east of central London, specialising in flights to/from European and other UK airports.

Some planes on European and long-haul routes avoid London and use major regional airports including Manchester and Glasgow. Smaller regional airports such as Southampton, Cardiff and Birmingham are served by flights to and from continental Europe and Ireland.

CAR & MOTORCYCLE

If you want to drive or ride to Britain you'll have to bring your car by ferry or use the Channel Tunnel.

SEA

Ferry travel can be via port-to-port routes or combined with a long-distance bus trip, although journeys can be long and financial savings not huge compared with budget airfares. You can travel as a foot passenger or bring your car.

Ferry Fares

Most ferry operators offer flexible fares, meaning great bargains at quiet times of day or year. For example, short cross-channel routes such as Dover to Calais or Boulogne can be as low as £45 for a car plus two passengers, although around £75 to £105 is more likely. If you're a foot passenger there's less need to book ahead; fares on short crossings cost about £30 to £50 each way.

Ferry Routes

The main ferry routes between Great Britain and other European countries include:

➡ Dover–Calais (France)
➡ Dover–Boulogne (France)
➡ Newcastle–Amsterdam (Netherlands)
➡ Newhaven–Dieppe (France)
➡ Harwich–Hook of Holland (Netherlands)
➡ Hull–Zeebrugge (Belgium)
➡ Hull–Rotterdam (Netherlands)
➡ Liverpool–Dublin (Ireland)
➡ Portsmouth–Santander (Spain)
➡ Portsmouth–Bilbao (Spain)
➡ Holyhead–Dublin (Ireland)

➜ Fishguard–Rosslare (Ireland)

➜ Pembroke Dock–Rosslare (Ireland)

Ferry Bookings

Book direct with one of the operators listed below, or use the very handy www.direct ferries.co.uk – a single site covering all sea-ferry routes, plus Eurotunnel.

Brittany Ferries www.brittany-ferries.com

DFDS Seaways www.dfdsseaways.co.uk

Irish Ferries www.irishferries.com

P&O Ferries www.poferries.com

Stena Line www.stenaline.com

TRAIN

International trains are a comfortable, 'green' option; the Channel Tunnel allows direct rail services between Britain, France and Belgium, with onward connections to many other European destinations. Options include transporting your car.

Channel Tunnel Passenger Service

High-speed **Eurostar** (www.eurostar.com) passenger services shuttle at least 10 times daily between London and Paris (2½ hours) or Brussels (two hours). Buy tickets from travel agencies, major train stations or the Eurostar website.

The normal one-way fare between London and Paris/Brussels costs around £145; advance booking and off-peak travel gets cheaper fares as low as £29 one-way.

Channel Tunnel Car Service

Drivers use **Eurotunnel** (www.eurotunnel. com). At Folkestone in England or Calais in France, you drive onto a train, get carried through the tunnel and drive off at the other end.

Trains run about four times an hour from 6am to 10pm, then hourly through the night. Loading and unloading takes an hour; the journey lasts 35 minutes.

Book in advance online or pay on the spot. The standard one-way fare for a car and up to 9 passengers is between £75 and £100 depending on time of day; promotional fares often bring it down to £59 or less.

DIRECTORY A–Z

ACCOMMODATION

Accommodation in Britain is as varied as the sights you visit. From hip hotels to basic barns, the wide choice is all part of the attraction.

Hotels

There's a massive choice of hotels in Britain, from small town houses to grand country mansions, from no-frills locations to boutique hideaways. At the bargain end, single/double rooms cost from £45/60. Move up the scale and you'll pay £100/150 or beyond.

If all you want is a place to put your head down, budget chain hotels can be a good option, although most are lacking in ambience. Prices vary on demand: at quiet times twin-bed rooms start from £30; at the height of the tourist season you'll pay £60 or more. Some options:

Ibis Hotels (www.ibis.com)

Premier Inn (www.premierinn.com)

Travelodge (www.travelodge.co.uk)

Rates

There's no such thing as a 'standard' hotel rate in Britain. Many hotels, especially larger places or chains, vary prices according to demand – or have different rates for online, phone or walk-in bookings – just like airlines and train operators. So if you book early for a night when the hotel is likely to be quiet, rates are cheap. If you book late, or aim for a public holiday weekend, you'll pay a lot. But wait until the very last minute, and you can *sometimes* get a bargain as rates drop again. The end result: you can pay anything from £25 to £200 for the very same hotel room. With that in mind, the hotel rates we quote are

Book Your Stay Online

For more accommodation reviews by Lonely Planet writers, check out http://hotels.lonelyplanet.com. You'll find independent reviews, as well as recommendations on the best places to stay. Best of all, you can book online.

Sleeping Price Ranges

Reviews of places to stay use the following price ranges, all based on double room with private bathroom in high season. Hotels in London are more expensive than the rest of the country, so have different price ranges.

Category	London	Elsewhere
£	less than £100	less than £65
££	£100–£200	£65–£130
£££	more than £200	more than £130

often guide prices only. (In contrast, B&B prices tend to be much more consistent.)

B&Bs

The B&B (bed and breakfast) is a great British institution. At smaller places it's pretty much a room in somebody's house; larger places may be called a 'guesthouse' (halfway between a B&B and a full hotel). Prices start from around £30 per person for a simple bedroom and shared bathroom; for around £35 to £45 per person you get a private bathroom – either down the hall or en suite.

Prices Usually quoted per person, based on two people sharing a room. Single rooms for solo travellers are harder to find, and attract a 20% to 50% premium. Some B&Bs simply won't take single people (unless you pay the full double-room price), especially in summer.

Booking Advance reservations are preferred at B&Bs and are essential during popular periods. You can book many B&Bs via online agencies but rates may be cheaper if you book direct. If you haven't booked in advance, most towns have a main drag of B&Bs; those with spare rooms hang up a 'Vacancies' sign. Many B&Bs require a minimum two-night stay at weekends. Some places reduce rates for longer stays (two or three nights) mid-week. If a B&B is full, owners may recommend another place nearby (possibly a private house taking occasional guests, not in tourist listings).

Food Most B&Bs serve enormous breakfasts; some offer packed lunches (around £6) and evening meals (around £15 to £20).

Bed & Breakfast Nationwide (www.bedandbreakfastnationwide.com)

Pubs & Inns

As well as selling drinks, many pubs and inns offer lodging, particularly in country areas. For bed and breakfast, you'll pay around £30 per person for a basic room, around £45 for something better. An advantage for solo tourists: pubs often have single rooms.

Hostels

There are two types of hostel in Britain: those run by the **Youth Hostels Association** (www.yha.org.uk) and **Scottish Youth Hostels Association** (www.syha.org.uk); and independent hostels, most listed in the *Independent Hostel Guide* (www.independenthostelguide.co.uk).

Hostels can be found in rural areas, towns and cities, and are aimed at all types of traveller, young and old. Some hostels are converted cottages, country houses and even castles – often in wonderful locations. Sleeping is usually in dormitories; most hostels also have twin or four-bed rooms.

Camping

Campsites range from farmers' fields with a tap and basic toilet, costing from £5 per person per night, to smarter affairs with hot showers and many other facilities, charging up to £15. You usually need all your own kit.

A few campsites also offer self-catering accommodation in chalets, caravans, tepees, yurts and stylish wooden camping 'pods', often dubbed 'glamping'.

If you're touring Britain with a tent or campervan (motorhome), consider joining the **Camping & Caravanning Club** (www.campingandcaravanningclub.co.uk), which provides up to 30% discount on its sites for an annual membership fee of £37. The club owns almost 100 campsites and lists thousands more in the invaluable Big Sites Book (free to members).

Bunkhouses

A bunkhouse in Britain is a simple place to stay, usually in country areas, with a communal sleeping area and bathroom, plus stoves for self-catering. You provide a sleeping bag and possibly cooking gear. Most charge around £12 to £15 per person per night.

Some basic places are called 'camping barns' – usually converted farm buildings. Take everything you'd need to camp except the tent. Charges are from around £6 to £10 per person.

ELECTRICITY

230V/50Hz

FOOD

Britain once had a reputation for bad food, but the nation has enjoyed something of a culinary revolution over the past decade and a half. London is recognised as having one of the best restaurant scenes in the world, while all over the country stylish eateries and gourmet gastropubs are making the most of a newfound passion for quality local produce.

Where to Eat

It's wise to book ahead for midrange restaurants, especially at weekends. Top-end restaurants should be booked at least a couple of weeks in advance.

Cafes Traditional cafes are simple eateries serving simple food – sandwiches, pies, sausage and chips. Quality varies enormously: some cafes definitely earn their 'greasy spoon' handle, while others are neat and clean.

Tearooms The tearoom is a British institution, serving cakes, scones and sandwiches accompanied by pots of tea (though coffee is usually available too). Upmarket tearooms may also serve afternoon tea.

Coffee shops In most cities and towns you'll also find coffee shops – both independents and international chains – serving decent lattes, cappuccinos and espressos, and continental-style snacks such as bagels, panini or ciabattas.

Restaurants London has scores of excellent restaurants that could hold their own in major cities worldwide, while eating places in other British cities can give the capital a run for its money (often for rather less money).

Pubs Many British pubs serve a wide range of food, and are often a good-value option whether you want a toasted sandwich between museum visits in London, or a three-course meal in the evening after touring the castles of Wales.

Gastropubs The quality of food in some pubs is now so high that they have created a whole new genre of eatery – the gastropub. The finest are almost restaurants (a few have been awarded Michelin stars) but others go for a more relaxed atmosphere.

When to Eat

In parts of Britain, notably northern England and Scotland, many people use the word 'dinner' for their main midday meal, and 'tea' for a light evening meal. However, this terminology is rarely, if ever, used in restaurants.

Breakfast Served in most hotels and B&Bs between 7am and 9am, or perhaps 8am to 10am on weekends. In cafes, the breakfast menu might extend to 11am through the week.

Lunch Generally taken between noon and 2pm, and can range from a sandwich and a bag of crisps to a three course meal with wine.

Many restaurants offer a set menu two-course lunch at competitive prices on weekdays, while cafes often have a daily lunch special, or offer soup and a sandwich.

Afternoon tea A tradition inherited from the British aristocracy and eagerly adopted by the middle classes, a between-meals snack now enjoying a revival in country hotels and upmarket tearooms. It consists of dainty sandwiches, cakes and pastries plus, of course, a cup of tea, poured from a silver teapot and sipped politely from fine china cups.

Dinner The main meal of the day, usually served in restaurants between 6pm and 9pm, and consisting of two or three courses – starter, main and dessert. Upmarket restaurants might serve a five-course dinner, with an amuse-bouche to begin, and a fish course between starter and main.

Sunday lunch Another great British tradition. It is the main meal of the day, normally served between noon and 4pm. Many pubs and restaurants offer Sunday lunch, where the main course usually consists of roast beef, lamb or pork, accompanied by roast and mashed potatoes, gravy, and boiled vegetables such as carrots and peas.

What to Eat: British Classics

Fish and Chips Long-standing favourite, best sampled in coastal towns.

Haggis Scottish icon, mainly offal and oatmeal, traditionally served with 'tatties and neeps' (potatoes and turnips).

Sandwich Global snack today, but an English 'invention' from the 18th century.

Ploughman's lunch Bread and cheese – pub menu regular, perfect with a pint.

Roast beef & Yorkshire pudding Traditional lunch on Sunday for the English.

Eating Price Ranges

In reviews, the following price ranges refer to a main dish.

£ less than £10 (London less than £12)

££ £10–£20 (London £12–£25)

£££ more than £20 (London more than £25)

➡ **Cornish pasty** Savoury pastry, southwest speciality, now available country-wide.

➡ **Laverbread** Laver is a type of seaweed, mixed with oatmeal and fried to create this traditional Welsh speciality.

INTERNET ACCESS

➡ 3G and 4G mobile broadband coverage is good in large population centres, but limited or nonexistent in rural areas. However, beware high charges for data roaming – check with your mobile/cellphone provider before travelling.

➡ Most hotels, B&Bs, hostels, stations and coffee shops (even some trains and buses) have wi-fi access, charging anything from nothing to £6 per hour.

➡ Internet cafes are surprisingly rare in Britain, especially away from big cities and tourist spots. Most charge from £1 per hour, but out in the sticks you can pay £5 per hour.

➡ Public libraries often have computers with free internet access, but only for 30-minute slots, and demand is high. All the usual warnings apply about keystroke-capturing software and other security risks.

LGBT TRAVELLERS

Britain is a generally tolerant place for gays and lesbians. London, Manchester and Brighton have flourishing gay scenes, and in other sizeable cities (even some small towns) you'll find communities not entirely in the closet. That said, you'll still find pockets of homophobic hostility in some areas. Resources include the following:

Diva (www.divamag.co.uk)

Gay Times (www.gaytimes.co.uk)

Switchboard LGBT+ Helpline (www.switchboard.lgbt; 0300 330 0630)

MONEY

ATMs (usually called 'cash machines') are common in cities and towns, but watch out for tampering; a common ruse is to attach a card-reader to the slot. Visa and Master-Card are widely accepted in Britain, except at some smaller B&Bs which take cash or cheque only. Other credit cards, including AmEx, are not so widely accepted.

Practicalities

Newspapers Tabloids include the *Sun*, *Mirror* and *Daily Record* (in Scotland); quality 'broadsheets' include (from right to left, politically) the *Telegraph*, *Times*, *Independent* and *Guardian*.

TV Leading broadcasters include BBC, ITV and Channel 4. Satellite and cable TV providers include Sky and Virgin Media.

Radio National BBC stations are Radio 1 (98–99.6MHz FM), Radio 2 (88–92MHz FM), Radio 3 (90–92.2 MHz FM), Radio 4 (92–94.4MHz FM) and Radio 5 Live (909 or 693 AM). National commercial stations include Virgin Radio (1215Hz MW) and Classic FM (100–102MHz FM).

Weights & Measures Britain uses a mix of metric and imperial measures (eg petrol is sold by the litre but beer by the pint; mountain heights are in metres but road distances in miles).

Smoking Forbidden in all enclosed public places in Britain. Most pubs have a smoking area outside.

Cities and larger towns have banks and exchange bureaux for changing money into pounds, but some bureaux offer poor rates. You can change money at some post offices, which is very handy in country areas; exchange rates are fair.

OPENING HOURS

Opening hours may vary throughout the year, especially in rural areas where many places have shorter hours, or close completely, from October or November to March or April.

Banks 9.30am to 4pm or 5pm Monday to Friday; some are open 9.30am to 1pm Saturday.

Pubs & Bars 11am to 11pm Monday to Thursday, 11am to 1am Friday and Saturday, 12.30pm to 11pm Sunday.

Shops 9am to 5.30pm (or 6pm in cities) Monday to Saturday, and often 11am to 5pm Sunday. London and other cities have convenience stores open 24/7.

Restaurants Lunch is noon to 3pm, dinner 6pm to 9pm/10pm (or later in cities).

PUBLIC HOLIDAYS

Holidays for the whole of Britain:

New Year's Day 1 January (plus 2 January in Scotland)

Easter March/April (Good Friday to Easter Monday inclusive)

May Day First Monday in May

Spring Bank Holiday Last Monday in May

Summer Bank Holiday Last Monday in August

Christmas Day 25 December

Boxing Day 26 December

In England and Wales most businesses and banks close on official public holidays. In Scotland, bank holidays are just for the banks, and many businesses stay open.

On public holidays, some small museums and places of interest close, but larger attractions have their busiest times. If a place closes on Sunday, it'll probably be shut on bank holidays as well.

Virtually everything – attractions, shops, banks, offices – closes on Christmas Day, although pubs are open at lunchtime. There's usually no public transport on Christmas Day, and a very minimal service on Boxing Day.

SAFE TRAVEL

Britain is a remarkably safe country, but crime is not unknown in London and other cities.

➡ Watch out for pickpockets and hustlers in crowded areas popular with tourists such as around Westminster Bridge in London.

➡ When travelling by tube, tram or urban train services at night, choose a carriage containing other people.

➡ Many town centres can be rowdy on Friday and Saturday nights when the pubs and clubs are emptying.

➡ Unlicensed minicabs (a bloke with a car earning money on the side) are best avoided.

TELEPHONE

Mobile Phones

The UK uses the GSM 900/1800 network, which covers the rest of Europe, Australia and New Zealand, but isn't compatible with the North American GSM 1900. Most modern mobiles can function on both networks, but check before you leave home just in case.

Roaming charges within the EU are due to be entirely eliminated by June 2017 but, after the UK's vote to leave the EU (Brexit), it's not yet clear wheather this will also be the case in Britain. Other international roaming charges can be prohibitively high, and you'll probably find it cheaper to get a UK number by buying a SIM card (from £5 including calling credit) for your own phone. Or buy a cheap pay-as-you-go phone (from £10 including calling credit).

Pay-as-you-go phones can be recharged by buying vouchers from shops.

Phone Codes

Dialling into the UK Dial your country's international access code then ☎44 (the UK country code), then the area code (dropping the first 0) followed by the telephone number.

Dialling out of the UK The international access code is ☎00; dial this, then add the code of the country you wish to dial.

Making a reverse-charge (collect) international call Dial ☎155 for the operator. It's an expensive option, but not for the caller.

Area codes in the UK Do not have a standard format or length, eg Edinburgh ☎0131, London ☎020, Ambleside ☎015394.

Directory Assistance A host of agencies offer this service – numbers include ☎118 118, ☎118 500 and ☎118 811 – but fees are extortionate (around £6 for a 45-second call); search online for free at www.thephonebook.bt.com.

Mobile phones Codes usually begin with ☎07.

➡ **Free calls** Numbers starting with ☎0800 or ☎0808 are free.

➡ **National operator** ☎100

➡ **International operator** ☎155

TOURIST INFORMATION

Most British cities and towns, and some villages, have a tourist information centre or visitor information centre – for ease we've called all these places 'tourist offices'.

Such places have helpful staff, books and maps for sale, leaflets to give away, and advice on things to see or do. Some can also assist with booking accommodation. Some are run by national parks and often have small exhibits about the area.

Most tourist offices keep regular business hours; in quiet areas they tend to close from October to March.

Visit Britain (www.visitbritain.com) is the country's official tourism website.

TRAVELLERS WITH DISABILITIES

All new buildings have wheelchair access, and even hotels in grand old country houses often have lifts, ramps and other facilities. Hotel and B&Bs in historic buildings are often harder to adapt, so you'll have less choice here.

Modern city buses and trams have low floors for easy access, but few have conductors who can lend a hand when you're getting on or off. Many taxis take wheelchairs, or just have more room in the back.

Useful organisations:

Disability Rights UK (www.disability rightsuk.org) Published titles include a Holiday Guide. Other services include a key for 7000 public disabled toilets across the UK.

Good Access Guide (www.goodaccess guide.co.uk)

Tourism for All (www.tourismforall.org.uk)

Accessible Travel

Download Lonely Planet's free Accessible Travel guide from http://lptravel.to/AccessibleTravel.

VISAS

➡ At the time of writing, if you're a citizen of the EEA (European Economic Area) nations or Switzerland, you don't need a visa to enter or work in Britain – you can enter using your national identity card. It's not yet clear if or how this may be afected by the UK's Brexit vote.

➡ Visa regulations are always subject to change, and immigration restriction is currently big news in Britain, so it's essential to check with your local British embassy, high commission or consulate before leaving home.

➡ Currently, if you're a citizen of Australia, Canada, New Zealand, Japan, Israel, the USA and several other countries, you can stay for up to six months (no visa required), but are not allowed to work.

➡ Nationals of many countries, including South Africa, will need to obtain a visa: for more info, see www.gov.uk/check-uk-visa.

➡ The Youth Mobility Scheme, for Australian, Canadian, Japanese, Hong Kong, Monegasque, New Zealand, South Korean and Taiwanese citizens aged 18 to 31, allows working visits of up to two years, but must be applied for in advance.

➡ Commonwealth citizens with a UK-born parent may be eligible for a Certificate of Entitlement to the Right of Abode, which entitles them to live and work in the UK.

➡ Commonwealth citizens with a UK-born grandparent could qualify for a UK Ancestry Employment Certificate, allowing them to work full time for up to five years in the UK.

➡ British immigration authorities have always been tough; dress neatly and carry proof that you have sufficient funds with which to support yourself. A credit card and/or an onward ticket will help.

BEHIND THE SCENES

SEND US YOUR FEEDBACK

We love to hear from travellers – your comments help make our books better. We read every word, and we guarantee that your feedback goes straight to the authors. Visit **lonelyplanet. com/contact** to submit your updates and suggestions.

Note: We may edit, reproduce and incorporate your comments in Lonely Planet products such as guidebooks, websites and digital products, so let us know if you don't want your comments reproduced or your name acknowledged. For a copy of our privacy policy visit lonelyplanet.com/privacy.

ACKNOWLEDGMENTS

Climate map data adapted from Peel MC, Finlayson BL & McMahon TA (2007) 'Updated World Map of the Köppen-Geiger Climate Classification', *Hydrology and Earth System Sciences*, 11, 163344.

Front cover photographs (clockwise from top): Conwy Castle, Wales, Samot/Shutterstock ©; Scottish Highlands, Robert Birkby/AWL ©; Devon, England, Bartsch-Wohner/Alamy ©

Back cover photograph: Stonehenge, England, Justin Black/Shutterstock©

THIS BOOK

This 1st edition of Lonely Planet's *Great Britain's Best Trips* guidebook was researched and written by Belinda Dixon, Oliver Berry, Marc Di Duca, Peter Dragicevich, Catherine Le Nevez, Hugh McNaughtan, Isabella Noble, Andy Symington and Neil Wilson. This guidebook was produced by the following:

Destination Editor James Smart

Product Editors Kate Mathews, Luna Soo

Senior Cartographer Mark Griffiths

Book Designer Lauren Egan

Assisting Editors Bridget Blair, Kate Chapman, Andrea Dobbin, Carly Hall, Victoria Harrison, Christopher Pitts

Cartographers David Kemp, Gabriel Lindquist, Julie Sheridan

Assisting Book Designers Cam Ashley, Katherine Marsh

Cover Researcher Lucy Burke

Thanks to Neill Coen, Grace Dobell, Jane Grisman, Liz Heynes, Kate James, Alison Lyall, Anne Mason, Catherine Naghten, Claire Naylor, Karyn Noble, Lyahna Spencer, Tony Wheeler, Amanda Williamson

INDEX

A

Abbotsbury Swannery 166
Abbotsford 354-5
Aberaeron 331, 335
Aberdaron 340
Aberfeldy 398, 399
Aberfoyle 377, 368-9
Abergavenny 323-4, 327
Aberlour 411-12, 415
Abersoch 340-1, 343
Aberystwyth 334, 335
accommodation 433-5, see also individual places
air travel 432
Aldeburgh 126-7, 133
Alnwick 285-6, 289
Althorp House 232
Ambleside 244, 255
An Garbh-Eilean 388
Angel of the North 82, 282
Anne Hathaway's Cottage 43
Anstruther 362-3, 365
Aonach Eagach 402-3
Applecross 384
aquariums 270
architecture 21
area codes 438
Arncliffe 259
Arran 419-20, 423
art 21, see also individual art galleries & museums
Arundel 98
Ashbourne 216

Ashmolean Museum 38, 72
Assembly Rooms 189
Assynt 386
ATMs 436
Attingham Park 209
Audley End 122
Avebury 41-2, 47, 70
Aviemore 395, 399

B

Bakewell 216-17, 225
Bala 314
Ballater 393-4, 399
Balmoral Castle 393
BALTIC Centre for Contemporary Art 83
Bamburgh 287-8, 289
Banksy 76-7
Bannockburn 360
Bantham 174
Barafundle Bay 304
Barmouth 342, 343
Barnard Castle 82
Bath 12, 42, 70-1, 150, 188-9, 196-7
accommodation 73, 151, 203
Battle of Hastings 94
beaches 170, see also individual beaches
Beachy Head 67, 95, 97
Beatles Story 84
Beaulieu 69
Beauly 406, 407

Beaumaris 339, 343
Beddgelert 316, 317
Bedruthan Steps 52, 180
Ben Nevis 404
Berwick-upon-Tweed 288, 289
Betws-y-Coed 313, 317
Bibury 198-9, 203
Big Pit National Coal Museum 324
Bigbury-on-Sea 174
Birdoswald Roman Fort 278
birdwatching, see also individual species
Amble 284
Cardigan 331
Cley Marshes 129
Dolgellan 314
Farne Islands 287
Loch Garten 395
Rhayader 333
Scourie & Handa Island 387
Southern Mull 422
St Bees Head 251
Titchwell Marsh 132
Birmingham 79, 85
Blaenau Ffestiniog 315-16
Blaenavon 324
Blair Atholl 397, 399
Blakeney 129
Blandford Forum 144
Blenheim Palace 19, 71-2, 114
Blue John Cavern 223

boat trips 243-55, 417-23, 432-3
  Amble 284
  Fort Augustus 404
  Gairloch 384
  Lochinver 387
  Plockton 383
  Portree 380
  Skipton 260
Bodleian Library 38
Bodmin Moor 180
Bodnant Estate 312-13
bog snorkelling 331
book locations
  Beatrix Potter 252
  Roslin 352
border crossings 428
Borders, the 351-7
Borrowdale 249-50
Bosworth Battlefield 230
Bowder Stone 250
Bowness-on-Windermere 244, 255
Braemar 393, 399
Braich-y-Pwll 340
Brantwood 252-3
Braveheart 361, 403
Brecon 325-6, 327
Brecon Beacons National Park 53, 61
breweries 127, 217, 250, 287, 419
Bridge of Balgie 398
Brighton 66, 73, 97-8, 99
Bristol 71, 73, 76-7, 85
Brixham 171
Broadway 202
Broadway Tower 201
Brodick 419, 423
Bronze Age mine 338
Buckingham Palace 37
Bude 178, 187
budgeting 23, 434, 436
Burford 200

Burgh Island 174
Burghley House 233
Burrell Collection 419
Bury St Edmonds 120, 123
business hours 437
Bute Park 345
Buttermere 249-50, 250
Buxton 224, 225

C
Cader Idris 314
Caernarfon 316, 317, 339-40
Cairngorm Mountain 394
Cairngorms National Park 59-60, 61
Caldey Island 304
Callander 369
Cambridge 17, 46, 120-1, 134-5
  accommodation 47, 123
Camel Trail 181
Camera Obscura 424
Campbeltown 376, 377
Cannonball House 424
Canterbury 66, 73, 104, 107
Cape Wrath 388
Capel Curig 311-12, 317
car hire 427
car insurance 427
Cardiff 26, 42, 47, 77-8, 344-5
Cardigan 330-1, 335
Carlisle 278, 279
Carmarthen 303
cars, see driving
Castle Howard 83, 267
castles 15
Castleton 222-3
Caudwell's Mill 217
caverns 149, 180, 222-4, 316
caves 223, 229, 388
caving 224
cell phones 438
Cerne Giant 148
chalk figures 38-9, 78, 148

Charlecote Park 230
Chatham 106
Chatsworth House 220
Cheddar Gorge 149
Cheltenham 78, 199
Chepstow 42-3, 320-1, 327
Chesil Beach 166, 167
Chesterfield 220-1
Chesters Roman Fort & Museum 277
Chichester 98, 99
Chillingham Castle 286
Chipping Campden 201, 203
cider distilleries 210
Cirencester 198
cities 21
Cley Marshes 129
Cley-next-the-Sea 129, 133
Clifford's Tower 291
climate 22
climbing 224
Clouds Hill 164
Clovelly 158, 159
coastlines 20
Cockermouth 250
Coigach 386
Coleton Fishacre 171-2
Coniston 252-3, 255
Conwy 312, 339, 343
Corbridge 276, 279
Corfe Castle 163, 167
Cornish pasties 184
Cornwall 177-87
Corris Railway 334
Cosford Royal Air Force Museum 208
costs 23, 38, 434, 436
Cotswolds 13, 199-200
Craigellachie 412-13
Crail 363-4, 365
Crantock 181
Craster 286-7, 289
Crickhowell 324-5, 327
Cromer 128, 133

Cromford Mill 217, 219
Croyde 158, 159
Crug Hywel 324
Cuillin Hills 382
Culross 362, 365
currency 22
cycling 181, 220, 394

D

Da Vinci Code, the 352
Danby 268-9, 271
Dartmoor National Park 52, 61
Dartmouth 172, 175
Derby 79, 81, 214-15, 225
Derwent Reservoirs 221-2
Devil's Bridge 333-4
disabilities, travellers with 438
distilleries 210, 373, 376, 398, 409-15, 420, 421
Doctor Who Experience 42, 78
Dolgellau 314-15, 317, 342, 343
dolphins 331
Dover 93-4, 99
drinks 21, 46
driving 427-31, 432
    car hire 427
    congestion charge 38
    documents 428
    driving license 427
    fuel 430
    highlights 13
    insurance 427
    maps 428
    motoring organisations 428
    parking 430
    road distances 431
    road rules 428, 429-30
    roads 13
    safety 428-9
    single-track roads 384
    websites 428

Drumnadrochit 405-6
Dryburgh Abbey 356
Dufftown 414, 415
Dulverton 155, 159
Dunfermline 362
Dunster 154-5, 159
Dunvegan Castle 382
Durdle Door 164
Durness 388, 389

E

eagles 422
Earlsferry 362, 365
Easdale Island 372
Eastbourne 95
Edale 222, 225
Eden Project 186
Edinburgh 12, 28-9, 44-6, 424-5
Elan Valley 332
electricity 435
Elgin 410-11, 415
Elgol 382
Elie 362, 365
Elterwater 246
Ely 120, 123
emergencies 22
Emmerdale 259
Eskdale 251
Exford 156, 159
Exmoor National Park 53
Eyam 221, 225

F

Falls of Measach 385
Falmouth 185-6, 187
Farne Islands 287
Faversham 106
fell races 331
ferry travel 171, 432-3
Ffestiniog railway 316, 341
Fife Coast 359-65

film & TV locations, see also book locations
    Arncliffe 259
    Glen Nevis 403
    Leavesden 113
    National Wallace Monument 361
    Plockton 382-3
    Portmeirion 342
fishing 412
Flatford 119-20
Folkestone 94
food 21, 435-6
    cheese 261
    Cornish pasties 184
    gingerbread 246
    kippers 286
    picnics 129
    seafood 19
football 216
Fort Augustus 404
Fort William 403, 407
Fowey 186, 187
Freshwater West 304
fuel 430

G

Gairloch 384-5
gas 430
gay travellers 436
gin 46
Glasgow 418-19, 423
Glastonbury 148, 149, 151
Glen Affric Nature Reserve 406
Glen Coe 407
Glen Lyon 398
Glen Nevis 403-4
Glen Torridon 384
Glencoe 402-3
Glenfiddich Distillery 413-14
Gloucester 199
Goathland 269-70
Godrevy 182

golf 364
Gower Memorial 236
Grantchester 121-2
Grasmere 246, 255
Grassington 259, 263
Grassmarket 425
Great Glen 401-7
Great Langdale 246
Great Malvern 78-9, 210, 211
Great St Mary's Church 134
Grizedale Forest 254
Gwithian 182
Gwydyr Forest 313

H

Haddon Hall 217
Hadrian's Wall 57-8, 273-9
Hall's Croft 237
Hamish Macbeth 383
Handa Island 387
Hardknott Pass 251-2
Harlech 315, 317
Harrogate 258-9, 263
Harry Potter 113, 403
Hartland Abbey 158
Hastings 95, 99
Hawes 261, 263
Hawkshead 253-4, 255
Haworth 83
Hayes, the 344
Hay-on-Wye 326, 327
Helmsley 267, 271
Henley-on-Thames 111-12
Hereford 210, 211
Herne Bay 103-4
Hexam 276-7, 279
Highgrove 198
Highland Folk Museum 395, 397
Highland games 393
Highland Wildlife Park 395
Highlands 391-9
highlights 10-19, 33

Hill Top 252
Hirst, Damien 158
Historic Environment Scotland 353
historic sites 20, *see also individual sites*
holidays 437
Holkham Hall 130-1
Holkham National Nature Reserve 131
Holy Island (Lindisfarne) 288, 289, 419
Holy Trinity Church 202, 237
Housesteads Roman Fort & Museum 277

I

Ilfracombe 158, 159
Imperial War Museum 122
Inchcailloch 373
Inchconnachan 373
Inchmurrin 373
Ingleton 260
insurance 427
internet access 436
internet resources 23, 25, 26, 27, 29
Inveraray 370-1, 377
Inverness 406, 407
Iona 422, 423
Ironbridge Gorge 208, 211
Islay 420-1
Isle of Anglesey 55-6, 61
Isle of Bute 370
Isle of Luing 372
Isle of May 362
Isle of Seil 372
Isle of Skye 60

J

Jane Austen Centre 42, 150
Jedburgh 356, 357
Jorvik Viking Centre 267

K

kayaking 383, 387, 421
Kedleston Hall 216
Keith & Dufftown Railway 414
Kelso 356, 357
Kelvingrove Art Gallery & Museum 419
Kentwell Hall 119
Keswick 247, 249, 255
Kidwelly 301-3
Kielder Water & Forest Park 58
Kilchoman 420
Kilt Rock 381
Kingussie 395-7
Kinlochleven 403, 407
Knightshayes Court 156
Knockando Mill 411
Kylesku 387

L

Lacock 72
Lake District National Park 57, 61
lakes 10, *see also individual lakes*
Land's End 182
languages 22
Laugharne 300
Lavenham 118-19, 123
Leeds 82, 85
Leeds Castle 65-6
Leicester 230, 235
lesbian travellers 436
Lincoln 234, 235
Lindisfarne 288, 289
Liverpool 84, 85
Lizard, the 185
Llanberis 310-11, 317
Llandrindod Wells 332-3, 335
Llandudno 338-9, 343
Llanwrytd Wells 331, 335

Llyn Idwal 312
Llyn Ogwen 312
Loch Affric 406
Loch Awe 372
Loch Garten 395
Loch Katrine 369
Loch Lomond 58-9, 368, 373
Loch Lomond & the Trossachs National Park 368
Loch Morlich 394
Loch Ness 404-6
Lochinver 386-7, 389
lochs, see individual lochs
London 24-5, 36-8, 47, 65
Long Melford 119
Longleat 145
Low Newton-by-the-Sea 287
Lulworth Castle 163-4
Lulworth Cove 164, 167
Lyme Regis 51-2, 166, 167
Lynmouth 156-7, 159

M

Macallan Distillery 411
Machynlleth 334, 335
Magna Carta 39, 143
Malham 259, 263
Manchester 27, 44, 47, 83-5, 206-7, 211
maps 428
Margate 102-3, 107
markets 299, 303, 344
Mary Arden's Farm 43
Matlock Bath 219-20, 225
measures 437
Melrose 355, 357
Micklegate Bar 291
mobile phones 438
money 23, 436-7
Monk Bar 290
Monmouth 321, 327
moors 20

Moors National Park Centre 268-9
Morgan Motor Company 79, 210
motorcycles, see driving
motorhomes 427-8
mountain-biking 262, 316, 334
mountains 10, 17, 20, see also individual mountains
Mull 422, 423
Mull of Kintyre 374
Mumbles, the 299-300, 307
music 430-1

N

Nant Gwrtheyrn 340
National Football Museum 44, 83-4
National Library 334
National Maritime Museum 186
National Museum Cardiff 77-8, 345
National Railway Museum 267
National Trust membership 247
National Wallace Monument 361
National Waterfront Museum 299
New College 424
New Forest 50-1, 61
Newbiggin-by-the-Sea 284
Newcastle 282
Newcastle-upon-Tyne 82-3, 85, 274-5, 279, 289
Newquay 180-1
newspapers 437
Norfolk Broads 129
North Coast 500 385
North Yorkshire 265-71
northern England 18
Northleach 199-200

Northumbria 281-9
Norwich 127, 133
Nottingham 228-9, 235

O

Oban 373, 377, 421, 423
Old Man of Coniston 252
Old Sarum 144
opening hours 437
ospreys 395
Outer Hebrides 60
Oxford 17, 38, 72, 73, 113-15

P

Padstow 180, 187
Painswick 198
palaces 19, see also individual palaces
parking 430
Parkmill 300-1
Peak Cavern 222-3
Peak District National Park 56, 61, 213-25
Peebles 353, 357
Pembroke 305, 307
Penzance 184, 187
petrol 430
plague 221
Plockton 382-3, 389
plugs 435
Plymouth 174, 175
Pontypool & Blaenavon Railway 324
Poole 162-3, 167
Poole's Cavern 223-4
Porlock View Point 156
Porlock Weir 156
Porthcurno 183
Porthmadog 341
Portmeirion 342
Portree 380, 389
Portsmouth 67
Potter, Beatrix 249, 252, 253

Presteigne 332
Prior Park 149-50
Prisoner, The 342
public holidays 437
puffins 284
Pump Room 189
Punch & Judy 339

R

radio 430, 437
Raglan Castle 322
Ravenglass & Eskdale
 Railway 251
Real Mary King's
 Close 425
Reculver 103
red kites 333
reindeers 394
Rhayader 333
Rhossili 301, 307
Richmond 262, 263
Riddell's Court 425
Rievaulx Abbey 268
road distances 431
road rules 428, 429-30
Rob Roy 376
Robin Hood's Bay 270,
 271
Rock 180
Rock Park 332
Roman Army Museum 278
Roman Baths 188
Roman sites 57-8, 196,
 234, 276-8, 340, *see also*
 individual sites
Roslin 352-3
Round Church 135
Royal Crescent 196-7
Royal Shakespeare
 Company 43, 202, 237
Royal Shrovetide
 Football 216
Rye 66, 94, 99

S

safety 384, 428-9, 437-8
Saffrom Walden 122, 123
sailing 341
Salcombe 174
Salisbury 39, 70, 73, 143, 151
Sandringham 132
Scafell Pike 251
Scarborough 270, 271
scenic driving routes 382
scenic railways
 Aviemore 395
 Bala 314
 Blaenau 316
 Cairngorm Mountain 394
 Corris Railway 334
 Goathland 269-70
 Llanberis 310
 Peak Rail 217
 Porthmadog 341
 Ravenglass & Eskdale
  Railway 251
 Vale of Rheidol
  Railway 333-4
 Scourie 387-8
sea kayaking, *see* kayaking
seafood 19
seals 284, 331, 383, 419
Seasalter 105-6
Segedunum 275-6
Sennen 182-3
Seven Sisters 97
Shaftesbury 147, 151
Shakespeare, William 38, 79,
 195-203, 236, 237
Shambles, the 291
Sherborne 148, 151
Sherborne New Castle 147-8
Sherwood Forest 228
Shrewsbury 209
Shrove Tuesday 216
single-track roads 384

Skipness 375-6
Skipton 259-60, 263
Skye 380-2
Slaughters, the 200, 203
sled dogs 395
smoking 437
Snailbeach 209
Snowdonia National Park 53,
 55, 309-17
Solva 305-6, 307
South Downs National Park
 95
Southwold 127, 133
Speedwell Cavern 223
Spirit of Speyside 414
St Agnes 181
St Andrews 364, 365
St Bees Head 251
St Davids 306, 307
St Ives 181-2, 187
St John the Baptist Church
 344
St John's College 120-1
St Michael's Mount 184-5
St Paul's Cathedral 65
Start Bay 172-3
stately homes 15
Stirling 360-1, 365
Stoke-on-Trent 207-8
stone circles 419, *see also*
 Avebury, Stonehenge
Stonehenge 15, 39, 41, 70,
 143, 144-5
Stourhead 145, 147
Stowe House & Gardens 112
Stow-on-the-Wold 200
Stratford-upon-Avon 18,
 43-4, 79, 202, 203, 236-7
street art 76-7
Sudbury 119
Sulgrave Manor 232
surfing 158, 283, 301, 341
Sutton Hoo 128

Swallows and Amazons 252
Swansea 299, 307

T

Tan Hill Inn 261-2
Tarbert 374-5, 377
Tarbet 369
Tarr Steps 155-6
Tate Liverpool 84
Tate St Ives 182
telephone services 438
television 437
Tenby 304, 307
Tetbury 197-8
Thomas, Dylan 299, 300
Three Cliffs Bay 300
Tideswell 223
Tintagel 178-80
Tintern 321
tipping 23
Tissington Trail 216
Titchwell Marsh 132
Tobermory 422
Tomintoul 394, 399
Torquay 170-1, 175
Torridon 384
Totnes 172, 175
tourist information 276, 438
Tout Quarry 165-6
train travel 433, *see also* scenic railways
transport 23, 432-3, *see also* driving
Traquair House 353-4
travel seasons 22
Treak Cliff Cavern 223
Tretower 325
Trinity College 134-5
Trinity Hall College 121
Trotternish Peninsula 380-2, 389

Turner Contemporary 102-3
TV locations, *see* film & TV locations
Tynemouth 282-4, 289

U

Uffington White Horse 38-9, 78
Ullapool 385-6, 389
Ullswater 254
urban sights 21
Urquhart Castle 404

V

Valley of the Rocks 157
Verity 158
via ferratas 403
visas 439

W

Wade's Bridge 398
Wallace Monument 361
Wareham 163
Warkworth 284-5
Warner Bros Studio Tour: the Making of Harry Potter 113
Warwick 230-1, 235
Wasdale 251
water parks 270
waterfalls 244, 260, 387, 403
websites 428
Wedgwood factory 208
Wedgwood Visitor Centre 84
weights 437
Wells 149, 151
Wells Beach 129
Wells-next-the-Sea 130, 133
Welsh Highland railway 341
Welsh language 340
Wensleydale Creamery 261

West Country 12
Westons Cider Mills 210
Weymouth 165, 167
whale-watching 384, 422
Whinlatter Forest Park 250
whisky 398, 409-15
Whitby 270, 271
Whitebrook 322
white-water rafting 314
Whitstable 104-5, 107
Wicker Man, The 382
wildlife watching 384, *see also* bird-watching, individual species
Wilton House 144
Winchcombe 202, 203
Winchester 39, 73, 67-8, 143, 151
Windermere 244
Windsor 110, 115
Woodstock 114
Wookey Hole 149
Woolsthorpe Manor 233-4
Wordsworth, William 246, 250
Worms Head 301
Wroxham 128
Wrynose Pass 251-2

Y

York 46, 47, 266-7, 271, 290-1
Yorkshire Dales 56-7, 257-63
Yorkshire Museum 290
Yorkshire Sculpture Park 81-2

Z

ziplining 353
zoos 145

OUR WRITERS

OUR STORY

A beat-up old car, a few dollars in the pocket and a sense of adventure. In 1972 that's all Tony and Maureen Wheeler needed for the trip of a lifetime – across Europe and Asia overland to Australia. It took several months, and at the end – broke but inspired – they sat at their kitchen table writing and stapling together their first travel guide, *Across Asia on the Cheap*. Within a week they'd sold 1500 copies. Lonely Planet was born.

Today, Lonely Planet has offices in Franklin, London, Melbourne, Oakland, Dublin, Beijing, and Delhi, with more than 600 staff and writers. We share Tony's belief that 'a great guidebook should do three things: inform, educate and amuse'.

BELINDA DIXON

Only happy when her feet are suitably sandy, Belinda has been (gleefully) travelling, researching and writing for Lonely Planet since 2006. See her VideoBlog posts at https://belindadixon.com

OLIVER BERRY

Oliver is a writer and photographer based in Cornwall. His first trip abroad was to the south of France, aged two. Since then he's travelled to Corsica, New Zealand, the South Pacific and the midwestern USA.

MARC DI DUCA

A travel author for the past decade, Marc has worked for Lonely Planet in Siberia, Slovakia, Bavaria, England, Ukraine, Austria, Poland, Croatia, Portugal, Madeira and on the Trans-Siberian Railway,

PETER DRAGICEVICH

Peter has explored much of Europe and calls Auckland, New Zealand, his home – although his nomadic existence means he's hardly ever there.

CATHERINE LE NEVEZ

Catherine's wanderlust kicked in when she roadtripped across Europe from her Parisian base aged four, and she's been hitting the road at every opportunity since, travelling to around 60 countries. She recommends travelling without any expectations.

HUGH MCNAUGHTAN

A long-time castle tragic with an abiding love of Britain's Celtic extremities, Hugh jumped at the chance to explore Wales, from the Cambrian Mountains to the tip of Anglesey.

ISABELLA NOBLE

Isabella's travels have taken her across India, Southeast Asia, Australia, North America and Europe. She has lived in southern Spain and Melbourne, though she's now (loosely) based in London.

ANDY SYMINGTON

Hailing from Australia, Andy now lives in Northern Spain. When he's not off with a backpack in some far-flung corner of the world, he can be found watching the tragically poor local football side or tasting local wines after a long walk in the nearby mountains.

NEIL WILSON

An outdoors enthusiast since childhood, Neil is an active hill-walker, mountain-biker, sailor, snowboarder, fly-fisher and rock-climber, and has climbed and tramped in four continents,

Published by Lonely Planet Global Limited
CRN 554153
1st edition – March 2017
ISBN 978 1 7865 7327 8
© Lonely Planet 2017
Photographs © as indicated 2017
10 9 8 7 6 5 4 3 2 1
Printed in China

MIX
Paper from responsible sources
FSC™ C021741

Paper in this book is certified against the Forest Stewardship Council™ standards. FSC™ promotes environmentally responsible, socially beneficial and economically viable management of the world's forests.